The Thais have a most amazing attentiveness to detail, best demonstrated in their superb jewelry, embroidery, and carving. Give a Thai chef a carrot, and out of it he will create a fire-breathing dragon. Ask Thais to embellish a temple, and artisans will take millions of broken crockery shards and build a twinkling mural, adorned by celestial dancers, as at Bangkok's **WAT ARUN (left)**. I haven't got the patience to knit a sock.

I am constantly drawn to the wondrously varied temple styles found throughout Thailand. The stupas, or dome-shaped shrines, such as those at **LAMPHUN (above)** borrow from the bell-shaped temples of Sri Lanka. A few are gilded but most are simply whitewashed. Ziggurat-shaped temples reflect Isaan's Khmer connections, and gorgeous maroon and white frescoes adorn the low-built temples of the Lanna period around Chiang Mai.

First page: top, © Yoshio Tomii/SuperStock; bottom, © Christophe Boisvieux/Corbis

Frommer's®
Thailand

My Thailand

by Charlotte Shalgosky

STANDING ON MY BALCONY LOOKING OUT ACROSS THE SPARKLING Bangkok skyline, I feel so lucky that I actually *live* in Thailand. So much makes it worthwhile: a leisurely boat home along the twinkling Chao Phraya River, a turquoise sea churning with tropical fish, or just the surprise of an unexpected encounter with a hornbill one October morning, on an island off Phuket.

Bangkok, my home, pulses with designer malls overshadowing glittering temples, open-air bars teetering on top of 60-story skyscrapers, and superstar chef-cooked menus with New York prices. All this can be found in a city where I can also spend a dollar on seafood noodles, $10 bucks on a Thai foot massage, or find a meticulous manicurist offering to replicate Burberry plaid onto my nails. Yet even in the face of the capital's ardent move to modernity, outside the city the serene stone-hewn Buddhas of Sukhothai or the low, sweeping roofs of the Northern Lanna temples evoke a placid timelessness. While drifting in a hot-air balloon one dawn over endless rice paddies, I was reminded that rural Thailand is as seductive as its heaving cities and beaches.

As I discovered many years ago, Thailand's captivating charm lures patient explorers back, again and again, and—as in my case—some of us never leave. The photos here capture some of my favorite Thailand images and experiences—I'm sure you'll have many more of your own.

© Bruno Morandi/AGE Fotostock

The Southern Thais are a laid-back lot with a zest for explosive cuisine and a lazy life, and who can blame them? A trip to the **SIMILAN ISLANDS** (left) or Krabi is enough for me to start spouting about imminent retirement. These days there are few beach shacks going for a dollar but plenty of upscale sybaritic hideaways, pristine dive sites, and tropical fish to keep beach bunnies like me happy.

Southern Thailand's unique geomorphology has generated some of the most spectacular scenery in the world. Great rust-colored cliffs rise suddenly from turquoise waters over which sea eagles circle. Doughnut-shaped limestone formations, called *HONGS* (above) in Thai, can be entered by **LONGTAILS** (above) or small boat; they offer complete privacy, secluded white sand beaches, or hidden caves.

The full moon in November brings to life the **LOY KRATHONG FESTIVAL** (above) a highly revered Buddhist celebration. It's most spectacular in Chiang Mai, where giant 2-meter-tall paper lanterns float across the sky like a galaxy of moving stars. Fantastic!

Inside Thailand's numerous national parks, few visitors know it is possible to spot a clouded leopard or lar gibbon as it makes a rare jungle appearance. If you're accompanied by a good naturalist, or just have keen eyes, delights such as a **FLEETING HORNBILL** (right), sea eagle or the shy sambar deer may add intense excitement to your holiday.

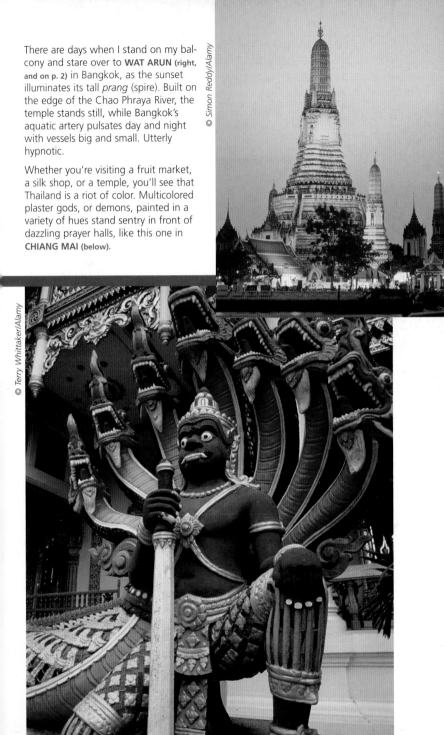

There are days when I stand on my balcony and stare over to **WAT ARUN (right, and on p. 2)** in Bangkok, as the sunset illuminates its tall *prang* (spire). Built on the edge of the Chao Phraya River, the temple stands still, while Bangkok's aquatic artery pulsates day and night with vessels big and small. Utterly hypnotic.

Whether you're visiting a fruit market, a silk shop, or a temple, you'll see that Thailand is a riot of color. Multicolored plaster gods, or demons, painted in a variety of hues stand sentry in front of dazzling prayer halls, like this one in **CHIANG MAI (below)**.

© Simon Reddy/Alamy

© Terry Whittaker/Alamy

Thailand's ancient capitals feel like a set from *Indiana Jones*, with their crumbling ruins set among wide boulevards, overlooking the river. Both **SUKHOTHAI** and Ayutthaya, feature serene Buddha statues amid immense brick ruins, like this one. Though many sites are heavily restored, a ramble around these historic complexes is nothing short of magical. © *Angelo Cavalli/AGE Fotostock*

Frommer's®

Thailand

8th Edition

by Charlotte Shalgosky

Here's what the critics say about Frommer's:

"Amazingly easy to use. Very portable, very complete."

—*Booklist*

"Detailed, accurate, and easy-to-read information for all price ranges."
—*Glamour Magazine*

"Hotel information is close to encyclopedic."

—*Des Moines Sunday Register*

"Frommer's Guides have a way of giving you a real feel for a place."
—*Knight Ridder Newspapers*

WILEY
Wiley Publishing, Inc.

About the Author

Blighted with wanderlust from a young age, **Charlotte Shalgosky** grew up in rural England where, by chance, she took up Chinese at high school and went on to specialize in Mandarin and French at university. Her early travels led to a deep love for Asian cultures and, after a stint as a documentary filmmaker in China, she left the U.K. definitively in 1990. After 8 years working in the heady corporate world in China and Hong Kong, she relocated to Bangkok to focus on her first love, travel writing. As a writer and photographer, she has since worked in over 56 countries. She currently lives on the Chao Phraya river overlooking the Temple of Dawn.

Published by:

Wiley Publishing, Inc.

111 River St.
Hoboken, NJ 07030-5774

ISBN 978-0-470-22631-5

Editor: Jennifer Reilly
Production Editor: Michael Brumitt
Cartographer: Roberta Stockwell
Photo Editor: Richard Fox
Production by Wiley Indianapolis Composition Services

Front cover photo: Koh Phi Phi (Phi Phi Don)
Back cover photo: Chiang Mai, Golden Triangle: Hill Tribe People, Meo Tribe.

For information on our other products and services or to obtain technical support, please contact our Customer Care Department within the U.S. at 800/762-2974, outside the U.S. at 317/572-3993 or fax 317/572-4002.

Wiley also publishes its books in a variety of electronic formats. Some content that appears in print may not be available in electronic formats.

Manufactured in the United States of America

5 4 3 2 1

Contents

(14) Exploring Isan: Thailand's Frontier 364

Appendix A: Thailand in Depth 372

Appendix B: A Little Bit of Thai to Help You Get By 388

Index 391

List of Maps

Acknowledgments

This guidebook is the grueling work of writers and editors spanning some 15,000 miles. In New Jersey, both Jennifer Reilly and William Travis were integral in the shaping of this rewrite and their support. In Thailand, I owe my gratitude to David Henley, whose unfailing respect for tight deadlines reflected his consummate professionalism. I must thank, too, the collaborative efforts of Kerrie Hall, Anne Powell, and Linda McKee, who went through rain and wind (and in Anne's case, a serious bike accident) in order to complete the chapter on the South. In Bangkok, Alan Cooper and Graham Lees were kind enough to update info on the Eastern coastal towns; Saifon "Joy" Daipriab lent us an administrative hand; and Richard Hermes deftly penned the Central Plains chapter. Lastly, I must thank Peter Myers, in London, who worked tirelessly on corrections (while he knew I was enjoying much better food and fabulous weather). And I am of course indebted to my sister Sarah, who—while I spent the last 25 years traveling— gallantly stayed in England.

An Invitation to the Reader

In researching this book, we discovered many wonderful places—hotels, restaurants, shops, and more. We're sure you'll find others. Please tell us about them, so we can share the information with your fellow travelers in upcoming editions. If you were disappointed with a recommendation, we'd love to know that, too. Please write to:

Frommer's Thailand, 8th Edition
Wiley Publishing, Inc. • 111 River St. • Hoboken, NJ 07030-5774

An Additional Note

Please be advised that travel information is subject to change at any time—and this is especially true of prices. We therefore suggest that you write or call ahead for confirmation when making your travel plans. The authors, editors, and publisher cannot be held responsible for the experiences of readers while traveling. Your safety is important to us, however, so we encourage you to stay alert and be aware of your surroundings. Keep a close eye on cameras, purses, and wallets, all favorite targets of thieves and pickpockets.

Other Great Guides for Your Trip:

Frommer's Singapore & Malaysia
Frommer's Southeast Asia
Frommer's Vietnam

Frommer's Star Ratings, Icons & Abbreviations

Every hotel, restaurant, and attraction listing in this guide has been ranked for quality, value, service, amenities, and special features using a **star-rating system.** In country, state, and regional guides, we also rate towns and regions to help you narrow down your choices and budget your time accordingly. Hotels and restaurants are rated on a scale of zero (recommended) to three stars (exceptional). Attractions, shopping, nightlife, towns, and regions are rated according to the following scale: zero stars (recommended), one star (highly recommended), two stars (very highly recommended), and three stars (must-see).

In addition to the star-rating system, we also use **eight feature icons** that point you to the great deals, in-the-know advice, and unique experiences that separate travelers from tourists. Throughout the book, look for:

Finds	Special finds—those places only insiders know about
Fun Fact	Fun facts—details that make travelers more informed and their trips more fun
Kids	Best bets for kids and advice for the whole family
Moments	Special moments—those experiences that memories are made of
Overrated	Places or experiences not worth your time or money
Tips	Insider tips—great ways to save time and money
Value	Great values—where to get the best deals
Warning	Warning—traveler's advisories are usually in effect

The following **abbreviations** are used for credit cards:

AE	American Express	DISC	Discover	V	Visa
DC	Diners Club	MC	MasterCard		

Frommers.com

Now that you have this guidebook to help you plan a great trip, visit our website at **www.frommers.com** for additional travel information on more than 3,600 destinations. We update features regularly to give you instant access to the most current trip-planning information available. At Frommers.com, you'll find scoops on the best airfares, lodging rates, and car rental bargains. You can even book your travel online through our reliable travel booking partners. Other popular features include:

- Online updates of our most popular guidebooks
- Vacation sweepstakes and contest giveaways
- Newsletters highlighting the hottest travel trends
- Online travel message boards with featured travel discussions

What's New in Thailand

Even with rising prices and the volatile baht, Thailand still provides great value; its diverse destinations make it perfect for young people, honeymooners, or those in search of family fun. A decade after the Asian economic crisis and a few years since the tsunami of December 2004, the country has bounced back with sparkling malls, modern high-rises, and ongoing improvements to its metropolitan infrastructure. Bangkok, in particular, is fast losing its crusty, 1970s neo-shophouses in favor of glistening glass towers. New malls boast vast designer stores, plush cinemas, and a sophisticated array of eateries. Though the average Thai cannot hope to afford these luxuries, they point to the emergence of a new, educated, middle class in the country.

It's now a lot easier to travel around Thailand as well. Since 2005, regional budget airlines such as Air Asia and Jet Star, together with Thailand's One-Two-GO and Nok Air, have made low-cost, inter-regional travel in the country a reality. Smaller companies like SGA, PB Air, and Destination Air now operate short-hop air links using light aircraft, and Thailand's Bangkok Airways is rapidly expanding its presence across Asia.

Unfortunately, rampant development here is often accompanied by environmental devastation. In Thailand, ecological ignorance, along with rabid commercial gain, poor or little-enforced regulation, and corruption, has seriously impacted hitherto unspoiled places. The once charming city center of Chiang Mai suffers from not just acute pollution, but also seasonal flooding and deadly smoke haze in dry season. On the southern coast and on resort islands, luxury villa and condominium developments are devouring the last of the prime beachfront land. As a result, places like Koh Samui are facing problems with water shortages, trash disposal, and wastewater. Thankfully, some authorities are taking eco-friendly measures—Krabi province has banned noisy jet skis, for instance, and Pattaya is taking small steps to overcome unregulated construction.

The kingdom still offers plenty of rural charm as well as glamorous, urban sophistication, though. Bangkok's five-star international hotels are now busy opening new properties in the northern cities and eastern coastal resort towns, and they offer a growing range of activities. Hotel renovations have brought the installation of broadband or Wi-Fi to a few remote outposts; spa facilities are being added even in low-end resorts.

The country is also emerging from the peaceful political coup that took place in September 2006, when a military junta wrested power from then President Thaksin Shinawatra. Elections held in late 2007 surprisingly saw a revival of support for the deposed Shinawatra camp, with the election of Samak Sundaravej—regarded as a Thaksin proxy—as prime minister.

Today, travelers can really get to know Thailand in a number of different ways. It's possible for guests to try their hand at elephant handling or hot-air ballooning in the north, or help out with turtle conservation in the south. Thai cooking classes and dive centers continue to grow in popularity, and a few luxurious hotels now provide their own schools.

BANGKOK Older shopping centers in the city have been revamped to keep pace with the latest mega-malls, such as **Siam Paragon.** Moves are also underway by **Central,** the nation's biggest department store chain, to create an architectural "icon" at its second site at Chidlom.

The capital's most glamorous (and priciest) restaurants, such as **Sirocco, Breeze,** and **Pier 56,** each exemplify the new trend in chic, skyscraping diners, while stunning remodeling has totally transformed stellar favorites such as **The Oriental's Sala Rim Nam** and **China House,** as well as **The Banyan Tree**'s famous spa.

The city has a number of stylish new hotels as well. **Dream Bangkok** (✆ 02254-8500) is a 100-room hotel that pays homage to '70s glitz and glam. Cigar bars, Apple Macs, and a pervasive cool blue light (which infuses the rooms) give it a 007 flavor. Expect the extraordinary. The young and modern **Millennium Hilton Bangkok** (✆ 02625-3333) boasts chic and sharp interiors punctuated by stylish lighting. Hip riverfront dining, funky bars, and a novel spa accentuate its high-design concept. At the summit, guests can enjoy a jazz-vibe and panoramic views from the smoky indoor rooftop bar—not to mention the splendors of sunset over the Chao Phraya River. **The Eugenia** (✆ 02259-9017) is a neocolonial-style house in the depths of Klong Toey. This new boutique trendsetter percolates with endless charm. A library, lounge, lap pool, and tropical garden make it a great hideaway.

Suvarnabhumi International Airport, opened in 2006, has generally improved air travel, despite being dogged with scandal, and suffering from innumerable design faults. However, increased air traffic forced the former Don Muang Airport—now bizarrely renamed **Don Mueang Airport**—to re-open in mid-2007 to serve domestic air routes. (Don Mueang flights are differentiated by their 4-digit codes.)

An overhead **railway link** to Suvarnabhumi is still some years off from completion, but extensions to the BTS over to Thonburi should open soon.

EAST & WEST COAST MALAY PENINSULA The situation remains unstable along the southern border with Malaysia due to Muslim insurgents; sadly, a political solution seems far from sight. In contrast, the recovery from the 2004 **tsunami** is progressing. At resort centers such as **Patong,** some tsunami damage is still visible but by September 2007, Phuket's tourism revenues were reported to have surpassed pre-tsunami levels. Construction of new hotels is still continuing unabated and prices are skyrocketing. A **tsunami early warning system** is now in place, as well as marked escape routes to high ground. The fatal crash of the budget carrier One-Two-GO in September 2007 dealt a minor blow to this region, however.

EASTERN GULF Ironically, the south's tsunami brought renewed popularity to Thailand's overlooked eastern seaboard. (In the north, stranded travelers in Chiang Mai discovered the charming rural towns of Lampang and Lamphun—tourism there has increased.)

CHIANG MAI & THE FAR NORTH The Thai government's support of cottage industries (collectively known as the "otop" brand) has brought bright, innovative designers together with the region's ample craftsmen to produce upscale housewares, textiles, furniture, glassware, and fashion items from the northern part of the country. Foreign designers such as **Franco-Scot, Jennifer Dyson,** and Danish-born **Hans Christensen** are just a few names who are working with local talent to spearhead a new wave of export-quality products made in Thailand's north.

The Best of Thailand

Beaches, bargains, palaces, and stunning temples. Thailand has much to offer anyone, from the burned-out corporate executive in search of ultraluxurious respite to the intrepid backpacker hoping to explore beyond the beaten track. What brings visitors back here time and time again is undoubtedly the warmth of the Thai people, their laidback attitude, the kingdom's at-times incomprehensible yet beguiling customs, feverish festivals, and amazing culinary adventures. For many, Thailand's most notable draws are its opulent royal palaces, ancient ruins, and ornate temples housing skillfully crafted figures of Buddha, a revered symbol that underscores a fervent and widespread devotion by the (less Westernized) traditionalists. In madcap Bangkok, you'll find an ultramodern cityscape muscling in on quiet canal and riverside communities. Mercantile hubs such as historic Chinatown consist of scores of labyrinthine alleys crammed with narrow "shophouses," markets, and diners, all evoking a heady mix of sights, sounds, and smells. Beyond Bangkok, rice paddies carpet endless flat plains in a landscape dotted by tiny villages and mountains. White sandy beaches and acres of coconut palms and rubber plantations lace the southern and eastern gulf provinces. Wherever you go, expect contradictions and oxymorons: Witness all-permeating Buddhist pacifism co-existing with popular pugilism in Muay Thai boxing. Inscrutable Thailand will incessantly intrigue and confound the curious traveler.

There is also adventure of all kinds here: Extreme sports on land and sea, trekking to hill-tribe villages, and abseiling down sheer limestone cliffs. The country's infrastructure allows travel by bus, train, car, boat, or even hot-air balloon, as well as via a network of new budget airlines serving many regional cities. Gorgeous tropical islands play host to low-end guesthouses or stylish and contemporary five-star resorts. Regional cuisines differ greatly and offer a breadth of flavors in varying blends of sweet, sour, and salty variations—not always ignited by fiery spice. In this chapter, I list the best restaurants and hotels, as well as hints on where to find what you're looking for in this dazzling kingdom.

1 The Best Cultural Experiences

- **Celebrate Loy Krathong:** Late October or early November (depending on the moon) marks this delightful festival when Thais congregate along the rivers to release handmade floats or *krathongs,* symbolically casting away troubles. The small lotus-shaped *krathong* is made of folded banana leaves and decorated with garlands topped by a candle. In Bangkok, over the Royal Palaces and the Chao Phraya River (near Saphan Taksin BTS), there are magnificent pyrotechnics. In the north in Chiang Mai, hundreds gather by the Ping River and open spaces to launch *khom* (meter-high paper lanterns) into the heavens. As the night goes on, the sky above the city is filled with thousands of orange stars as these giant lanterns drift ever upward.

- **Take a Ride along the River:** Whether it's just for an hour, or for a few days to Ayutthaya, traveling by boat along Thailand's Chao Phraya River is truly memorable. In Bangkok, you can choose from a cacophonous long-tail boat, small motor launch, or a restored rice barge to float upstream. Some hotels offer dinner shows on restored vessels or sunset cruises on a huge floating discotheque. At several points along the Chao Phraya River, you'll see the concrete jungle of urban Bangkok meet verdant mango and lychee orchards, and you'll see the city's historic quality truly reveal itself. You'll also pass by multicultural communities boasting 200-year-old Portuguese and French churches, Islamic mosques, and elaborate Chinese temples. The city's canals *(klongs)* are worth exploring at any time of day, but, at sunset, the gilded spires of the palaces and tall *prangs* of the city's temples are reminiscent of mythical castles. See chapter 6.

- **Visit a Market:** Upcountry or downtown, Thailand's markets are a colorful affair and, depending on the prevailing heat or your levels of curiosity, are worthy of an early morning meander. Visiting one is a great chance to see authentic Thai life firsthand. Everything is on sale from fragrant flower garlands to tropical fruits to the fresh ocean catch of the day—all piled upon simple trestle tables. Meat or live poultry is also available straight from local farms, as are endless varieties of exotic spices, chilies, cooking oils, and freshly prepared treats. It's a serious, sensory experience, best undertaken as early as possible, and on a light stomach.

- **Observe Elephants:** The elephant is the symbol of the monarchy in Thailand and is highly respected for its intelligence, grace, and majesty. All elephants deemed "white" belong to the king; only after strict inspections—to check for albino pigmentation in the animal's ears, toenails, tongue, genitals, and tail–will an elephant be declared as such. A number of tourism-focused elephant camps have been created in and around Chiang Mai, Lampang, and Chiang Rai. Listed below are some camps respected for their humane environments. Near Lampang at Tung Kwian, the **Thai Elephant Conservation Center** (© 05424-7876 or 05422-7051) educates and entertains visitors as well as rehabilitates sick or injured elephants. Luxury resorts such as the **Four Seasons' Tented Camp** (© 05391-0200) and the **Anantara Golden Triangle** (© 05378-4084), both near Chiang Rai, have put together pachyderm-friendly activities for guests, including *mahout* (elephant handling) skills. See p. 339, 330, and 362.

- **Discover Lanna Architecture:** The country's northern towns and cities embrace not just a different pace of life, but also a unique culture, language, and cuisine. Known as the Lanna kingdom, this area was home to five consecutive Lanna periods that bloomed and ebbed from the 12th to the 16th centuries. Lanna influence can be seen among Chiang Mai's 121 temples, the most stunning of which are **Wat Phra Singh** and **Wat Jed Yod** (the latter is partially inspired by an Indian temple). In tranquil Lampang, a wander around the sandy enclaves of **Wat Phra That Lampang Luang** will transport you centuries back in time. At Lamphun, the rare and delightful Buddhist pyramids of **Wat Chamadevi** (also known as Wat Kukut) show off the nation's earliest achievements—dating from 1218 and highlighting relics of the Haripunchai (Mon) era. But these are just a brief introduction to the spectacular ancient temples of this area. See chapters 12 and 13 for more recommendations.

- **A Night at the Patravadi Theatre:** In the quiet Bangkok suburb of Thonburi, the doyenne of Bangkok's art and theater scene holds court in a funky little arts center by the river. Patravadi Mejudhon is the woman behind some of the most creative dance performances in Thailand. Her passion for perfection and her unremitting support for classical Thai and contemporary dance have brought this former film and theater star much praise. Her latest venture is **Studio 9** (p. 107) a newly remodeled riverside venue offering dinner-dance evenings, just opposite Patravadi Theater. Studio 9 provides a platform for emerging talent and gives diners a heart-stopping display of undiscovered Thai talent of all ages and artistic genres. Call ahead for information and reservations (© 02412-7287) or consult the useful site www.patravaditheatre.com.

2 The Best Luxury Resorts & Spas

- **The Mandarin Oriental Dhara Dhevi** (Chiang Mai; © 05388-8888): This mega-resort was designed to echo a sumptuous Lanna-era palace with gardens, rice paddies, lawns, and a restored *viharn* (shrine). Many of the freestanding villas boast unique luxuries such as a piano, sauna, sun deck with Jacuzzi, and a private massage table. A number of the suites have plunge pools and the spa is modeled after a stunning teak Burmese palace. There's mouthwatering cuisine on hand, too; but deep pockets are required for that, as well as the rooms. See p. 311.

- **The Banyan Tree** (Phuket; © 07632-4374): It's chic, it's private, and it's (supposed to be) paparazzi proof. Maybe that's why the likes of pop singer Kylie Minogue and British sports star David Beckham book the Banyan Tree. This self-contained resort boasts luxurious Thai-style villas and possibly the island's best spa treatments; expect pools, palms, and lots of panache. Plus, this prestigious hotel chain prides itself on its environmental awareness schemes that benefit different communities all over the region. It appeals to celebs and jet-setters with a conscience. See p. 242.

- **The Racha** (Phuket; © 07635-5455): Escape to your own secluded island at the southernmost tip of Phuket. Cerulean seas, white-powder beaches, and a cluster of villas dot the hillside crowned with The Lighthouse—this property's self-contained suite. The Racha is an unpretentious refuge for those in search of intimacy. See p. 233.

- **JW Marriott Resort & Spa Phuket** (Phuket; © 07633-8000): This distinctive haven is set amid acres of spectacular gardens featuring ponds, flowerbeds, and landscaped lawns leading to a glistening beach; though the strong riptides make ocean swimming unsafe, two stylish pools make up for this. Balconies offer expansive sea views and guests have endless dining options, from Mediterranean to traditional Thai—all top quality. The Mandara Spa, hidden behind giant ochre walls and copper doors, is reminiscent of a Marrakech palace. The hotel's environmental efforts mean that staff and keen guests are actively involved in turtle conservation groups such as Naucrates. See p. 244.

- **Rayavadee Resort** (Krabi; ② 07562-0740): Two-story cottages are scattered over this expansive coconut grove, facing two of Thailand's best white sand beaches. Many villas have Jacuzzis or hammocks, with breezy views of some of the most magnificent cliffs in the country. A newly refurbished spa and the addition of private villas make it a dream hideaway. A trip to the nearby limestone *hongs* (caves) here is unforgettable. See p. 263.
- **Chiva-Som** (Hua Hin; ② 03253-6536): Unashamedly sleek and swanky Thai-style accommodations enhanced by personalized healthcare make this wellness retreat a popular choice for visiting celebrities in need of a body-and-soul detox. Prices are some of the highest, but the trade-offs are tangible. After experiencing any of Chiva-Som's

careful healing therapies or invigorating health regimes, nowhere else will seem quite the same. See p. 175.
- **Anantara Resort and Spa Golden Triangle** (Chiang Saen; ② 05378-4084): On the edge of the Burmese jungle, just meters from the Laos border, and overlooking the swirling Mekong River, this resort's spectacular spa and fine restaurants are just some of this two-wing property's many pleasures. The landscape is artfully punctuated with a glassy infinity pool overlooking a towering bamboo grove. An amazing museum dedicated to the history of opium is just a short walk or bike ride away, as is the hotel's Elephant Camp, where you can sharpen your pachyderm-handling skills with a 2-ton inmate. See p. 362.

3 The Best Mid- & High-End Resorts

- **The Evason Hua Hin** (Koh Samui; ② 07632-4333): Private villas hidden behind whitewashed adobe walls, gorgeous sunken poolside *salas,* and bright, modern living spaces make this resort a delight. Close enough to the beach for walks, but far enough for tranquillity, gourmets and gluttons will revel in the culinary experiences to be had here. The organically inspired mud-built spa has beehive-shaped treatment rooms, which appear to float in a lily pad pond. It's run by the sultans of spa, Six Senses; renowned for their eco-sensitivity as much as restorative treatments. See p. 198.
- **Hilton Hua Hin Resort and Spa** (Hua Hin; ② 03253-8999): This huge hotel towers over the main beach at Hua Hin and offers spacious rooms with teak floors and balconies overlooking the ocean. No less than seven restaurants are on hand to whet appetites, all of which are outlets for Hilton's impeccable service. Expect

high-speed Internet and all the other amenities of a large-scale, midrange, family-oriented hotel. See p. 176.
- **The Sarojin** (Khao Lak; ② 07642-7901): The Sarojin is a great escape from nearby Phuket. The superbly styled beach resort is scattered over 10 acres, with delightfully designed pool villas and outstanding suites, all minutes from a pristine beach. Guests can indulge in the outdoor spa and Thai cooking classes. See p. 258.
- **Twin Palms Phuket** (Phuket; ② 800/525-4800 or 07631-6500): A stunning Sirin Beach property, the Twin Palms adheres to a clean, contemporary style. Bright guest rooms overlook a leafy garden and expansive lagoon pool; a local golf course is nearby. New residences open in 2008, including a huge penthouse for the truly indulgent. Opportunities abound for culinary indulgences and there's a wine list to write home about. The health conscious can sign up for a breadth

of treatments at the Palm Spa. See p. 241.

- **Pimalai Resort and Spa** (Koh Lanta; ☏ 07560-7999): On a remote stretch of beach on the quiet island of Koh Lanta Yai, this delightfully designed hillside resort blends easily with the island's unspoiled nature. Its

sympathetic Thai architect has thoughtfully built the shady walkways around old trees. An immaculate indigo infinity pool, excellent spa, and sumptuous villas put it on top of this island's A-list. Direct speedboat connections in dry season make it a perfect upmarket escape. See p. 269.

4 The Best Luxury Hotels

- **The Oriental** (Bangkok; ☏ 800/526-6566 or 02236-0400): The Oriental houses more celebrities per square inch than a tabloid magazine. The hotel's elegant colonial style has made it the paragon of luxury for over 130 years. Today, two new resort-style swimming pools with private *salas,* the refurbished Sala Rim Nam and Verandah restaurants, the newly remodeled China House, plus a new stylish Ayurvedic Penthouse, put the final touches on this Thai hallmark of impeccable hospitality. See p. 87.
- **The Peninsula** (Bangkok; ☏ 800/262-9467 or 02861-2888): This is a shining example of modern high-rise luxury. Expect all the courtesy and efficiency of a Thai five-star hotel with no pretentiousness. Great dining in a

delightfully relaxed atmosphere is accompanied by dazzling riverside views of Bangkok, made memorable by flawless service. Built in a 1900s-style colonial villa, the new spa tops off the facilities of this impeccable hotel. See p. 90.

- **The Chedi** (Chiang Mai; ☏ 05325-3333): The rare combination of colonial and minimalism works exceptionally well for this cool newcomer to the north. Stark, contemporary rooms complement the historic two-story colonial villa that now houses the hotel's colorful restaurants and terrace, the latter of which offers a terrific high tea. Expect charming service and fantastic views of the river. See p. 311.

5 The Best Hotels with Character

- **Ibrik Resort** (Bangkok; ☏ 02254-8500): Tucked away in the arty quarter of Thonburi district near the historic Wat Rakhang, Ibrik's three airy rooms are decorated in a charming and vivid Thai palette. The vibe is intimate and homely, and the riverlife views evoke peaceful contemplation. It's both beautiful and boutique. See p. 92.
- **The Tivoli** (Bangkok; ☏ 02249-5858): This fresh new hotel oozes style from the word go. Slick, cutting-edge minimalism joins Thai coquettish charm from the rooftop

pool, to the spa, to the colorful dining room. Be sure to check the website for great deals. See p. 96.

- **Sofitel Centara Grand Resort & Villas** (Hua Hin; ☏ 800/221-4542 or 03251-2021): This historic hotel's vibrant heritage comes alive through spacious rooms, long, cool corridors, and verdant, lush grounds. High tea in the Museum Tea Corner is a definite highlight. See p. 177.
- **The Rachamankha** (Chiang Mai; ☏ 05390-4111): Quite possibly the most delicious bolt-hole in town, this monastic-style complex is a place

where Lanna minimalism meets Thai sophistication. Showcasing the region's Lanna art and culture, the quirky property has wowed everyone with its monastic courtyards, velvet lawns, beautiful decor, and exceptionally well-stocked library. See p. 316.

• **Birds and Bees** (Pattaya; ℂ **03825-0556**): An affordable resort on a hill-crest just out of town, this rustic, country-style hotel admirably supports HIV/AIDS education. Its restaurant is as good as its sister branch in Bangkok and families just love it. See p. 158.

• **Fern Resort** (Mae Hong Son; ℂ **05368-0001**): You're well off the beaten path at Fern, amid a collection of petite midrange bungalows, but the setting is lovely and self-guided hikes are made all the more enjoyable by the resort's resident pets. See p. 350.

6 The Best Fine Dining

• **Breeze** (Bangkok; ℂ **02651-3537**): The skyscraping seafood experience on offer at Breeze will amaze anyone who braves the giddy heights of this new alfresco restaurant in State Tower. The fusion-inspired menu is guaranteed to blow you (and your wallet) away, while the views of Bangkok below are irresistible. Advance reservations are obligatory. See p. 311.

• **Mei Jiang** (Bangkok; ℂ **02253-4683**): Authentic Cantonese cuisine served in elegant surroundings makes this a gastronomic must for dim sum lunch or supper. The chefs have created fabulous fare without the usual overwrought frills or overpowering sauces—whatever you eat here will be a meal to remember. See p. 106.

• **Pier 59** (Bangkok; ℂ **02679-1200**): High above the glistening city, this new supper-only venue houses vast aquariums and low blue lighting, creating an ambient glow. Seafood is the focus, but carnivores should fear not; the exceptionally long menu includes meat as well as delectable crustaceans. The miniature selection of bite-size desserts is sure to delight all. See p. 115.

• **Biscotti** (Bangkok; ℂ **02250-1000**): Few Italian restaurants impress like this Four Seasons favorite. A wonderful open-concept kitchen is surrounded by a fusion of East and West designer decor by New York–style guru Tony Chi. Expect a twist on the traditional, accompanied by an excellent wine list. See p. 114.

• **Sirocco** (Bangkok; ℂ **02624-9555**): The city's long-standing, culinary sex symbol is found at the top of State Tower. Complemented by charming service and a fantastic Mediterranean menu, this supper-only alfresco venue offers the night sky, stars, and sights for miles around. Sip a cocktail at the vertiginous Sky Bar before laying back and drinking in the superb live jazz. See p. 112.

• **Shintaro** (Bangkok; ℂ **02250-1000**): Some of the city's most innovative Japanese cuisine is served up in this designer diner in the Four Seasons. Showcasing fantastic flavors and stylishly crafted grilled items, as well as succulent sushi and sashimi, the superlative menu carries both classic and contemporary cuisine and a great selection of sake. See p. 116.

• **Fujian** (Mandarin Oriental Dhara Dhevi, Chiang Mai; ℂ **05388-8888**): It's hard to choose a more upmarket eatery in Chiang Mai. Just before the main gate to this fanciful Lanna-era styled resort is the hotel's Chinese restaurant, set in a pseudo-colonial mansion at the end of a pretty cobbled lane. Succulent dim sum lunches, or mouthwatering marinated meats, filets of waxy steamed fish, and fresh seafood complemented by devilish desserts (**Warning:** the black sesame ice cream is addictive) make for a rather pricey, but exquisite dining experience. See p. 311.

7 The Best Small Restaurants

- **Le Bouchon** (Bangkok; ✆ 02234-9109): A truly precious gem amongst the rabble, this authentic French bistro is embedded in the thick of seamy Patpong. Fine French food and endless top-notch vintages are worth the intrepid voyage into the depths of this saucy *soi*. See p. 113.
- **Taling Pling** (Bangkok; ✆ 02234-4872): This rustic-styled lunch and supper spot gets filled to bursting at lunchtime with locals craving both its authentic Thai dishes and carb-packed Western desserts. Foreigners are mercifully provided with a photographic catalog of the Thai menu; just point and eat. See p. 114.
- **Mrs. Balbir's** (Bangkok; ✆ 02651-0498): A long-time expat, TV chef, and wholly affable and approachable superstar, Vinder, aka Mrs. Balbir, cooks up a mean *biryani* as well as a finger-licking *tikka masala*. Divine desserts such as her homemade *kulfi* (a frozen dairy treat) cost next to nothing. Ask about her cooking lessons. See p. 118.
- **Crystal Jade** (Bangkok; ✆ 02250-7988): Don't be put off by its clean and sparkly department store location; this tiny Chinese eatery is part of a chain with a huge and loyal fan base. A hearty meal of *xiao long bao,* fragrant wonton soup, or authentic steamy noodles costs a few dollars and is absolutely authentic. See p. 116.
- **Itsara** (Hua Hin; ✆ 03253-0574): Set in a 1920s-inspired seaside villa, this Thai and seafood restaurant is a local favorite that incessantly pulls in crowds who come to savor its simple but elegant locale and cuisine. See p. 179.

- **Dream Café** (Sukhothai; ✆ 05561-2081): With a quiet courtyard out back and cool indoor seating, the Dream Café is reminiscent of an old temple. It's also a fun find and a great place to relax after a day of temple touring. See p. 288.
- **Khaomao-Khaofang Restaurant** (Mae Sot; ✆ 05553-2483): This saucy spot boasts an organically inspired decor that's almost as much a reason to visit as the food. True, since the restaurant is out in the boonies on the Burmese border, the pseudo-posh design is out of sync with its surroundings. But the food is plain great and the atmosphere laid-back, if a bit surreal. See p. 292.
- **The Whole Earth** (Chiang Mai; ✆ 05328-2463): At the Whole Earth, you'll get outstanding Thai and Indian vegetarian food served in a quiet *sala* in the city center. It's become so well known it's almost an institution among backpackers—mostly due to its mellow, Greenwich Village vibe. Their branch in Bangkok is equally cool. See p. 322.
- **Le Grand Lanna** (Chiang Mai; ✆ 05388-8888): Le Grand Lanna is definitely the most romantic northern Thai restaurant in Chiang Mai. You'll feast in an old wooden stilt house amid ginger blooms and orchids, and dine on fare like Burmese *khao sawy* (noodle curry) and pomelo salad. Lunch and supper come with awesome views of the resort's lily pond and, at sunset, you'll get the chance to see a delightful Lanna dance show. See p. 321.

- **The House** (Chiang Mai; ℡ 05341-9011): Supper-only is served at this vintage villa at the edge of the Old City of Chiang Mai. In cool, candlelit surrounds, Danish expat Hans Christensen's carefully trained kitchen staff serves up dynamic Pacific Rim cuisine. See p. 321.
- **Golden Triangle Café** (Chiang Rai; ℡ 05371-1339): The Thai menu here tops the list; it's a veritable guided tour of true Thai cuisine. Outside of Chiang Rai's busy market, this is the best dining going in town. See p. 358.
- **Baan Benjarong** (Pai; ℡ 05369-8010): It's hard to miss this place if you venture into northern Pai. You'll be rewarded with a great feast of authentic local cuisine, for very little. See p. 346.

8 The Best Party Beaches

- **Patong Beach** (Phuket): This busy beachside strip is not sophisticated by any means, but for many young, first-timers in Asia looking to party, it is seen as *the* place for shopping, dining, and naughty nightlife. If you want to avoid the sordid stuff, the most upmarket area is the new JungCeylon mall, with great late-night dining and famous fast food and coffee outlets. Beyond this, there's a shantytown of small bars and concrete bunker clubs, where it's a lot seedier but where the younger frat-crowd will get their kicks. See chapter 9.
- **Chaweng Beach** (Koh Samui): If you like the beach, and love to be social, Chaweng has all the action you want. With countless dining and nightlife choices, plus endless vendors and beach boutiques, you'll never walk alone here. See chapter 8.
- **Had Rin** (Koh Phangan): The now infamous Full Moon Parties on Koh Phangan's Had Rin have been attracting crowds of raving revelers for years, but they are not the hippy-trippy events of yore, since parties are taking on a more "packaged" experience. Drug busts are on the rise and, despite the warnings, plenty of over-chilled partygoers continue to come undone with serious consequences. See chapter 8.
- **Pattaya** (Pattaya, Eastern Seaboard): The once infamous red-light capital of Thailand, promiscuous Pattaya invites adulation as much as disdain with the dubious flavor of some of its late-night shenanigans. However, it's cleaning up slowly, and outwardly obscene "attractions" are making way for cleverer, cleaner entertainment. The clubs and bars attract a range of motley characters, giving it an air of a human zoo. Go to watch, and to be watched. See chapter 7.

9 The Best Outdoor Adventures

- **Rock Climbing at Railay Beach** (Krabi): The imposing cliffs above Krabi's beaches make for some of the best rock climbing in the world. And you don't have to be an expert; beginners are welcome to sign up for an intro course and enjoy both the challenge and breathtaking views. See chapter 9.
- **Scuba Diving:** Thailand is a great place to do a PADI course, whether you're a total beginner or in need of a refresher course. Most courses are affordable and staffed by experienced expatriate dive pros. Always check first that the vessels used by these outfits have valid marine safety documentation such as IMO, SOLAS,

ISM, and the more recent ISPS certificates. The most popular centers—Phuket, Koh Samui, and Koh Tao—have a large concentration of beautiful coral with an abundance of marine life. The best time of year for visibility is between December and February. See chapters 7, 8, and 9.

- **Ballooning:** From November to March, Thailand's cool north offers one of the few places in Asia to try hot-air ballooning. The tour operator Earth, Wind and Fire has been based in Chiang Mai for some years now and is the only certified ballooning outfit in Thailand. They offer pre-dawn flights over the emerald rice paddies; as the sun rises, the beauty of the land will open up below you. See chapter 12.

- **White-Water Rafting** (Pai): On a white-water rafting tour, you can paddle through conservation areas and pass by canyon walls encrusted with fossils. Check locally for outfits that organize exciting yet safe tours from the laidback center of Pai. See chapter 13.

- **Trekking** (Northern Thailand): Trekking is a perfect way to explore the country's great outdoors; it's definitely one of the best ways to get out and up into lush jungle terrain. Many worthy not-for-profit organizations are now involved in helping hill-tribe villagers build sustainable tourism initiatives and it is well worth your time to visit and support these commendable causes. See chapters 11 through 14.

10 The Best of Natural Thailand

- **Koh Hong** (near Krabi): Few can remain unmoved when they enter this seemingly unassailable limestone rock midocean. At its center is a vivid green pool completely surrounded by what seems like a limestone donut. Majestic sea eagles hover above while tropical fish flounder about in the clear waters below. See chapter 9.

- **Sea Kayaking:** John Grey is a much lauded, Phuket-based eco-warrior who has long fought to protect the marine life in the Andaman Sea (especially from the tremendous pollution emitted by trash-strewing tour groups and diesel-oozing speedboats). This highly respected guide offers day or night kayak trips, promising to reveal some rarely seen ocean sights (such as phosphorescence) as well as its unforgettable wildlife. See chapter 9.

- **Khao Yai National Park** (Northeast): Thailand's oldest and most visited World Heritage Site supports an abundance of wildlife, from elephants and tigers to more than 300 species of birds. Hike along nature trails or camp out and hold a vigil in high watchtowers at night, (the best time to see the nocturnal creatures in action). See chapter 6.

- **Cycle Rides:** It's hard to imagine, but just a few miles from Bangkok's inner city, you'll find lush greenery that can be visited by organized bike tours. A number of websites offer cycling treks nationwide; some explore cool jungle tracks, while others visit vineyards. See www.bangkok.com/cycling-tours/index.html.

11 The Best Offbeat Vacation Activities

- **Fasting and Wellness Programs:** While on holiday in Thailand, it is now possible to address the damage that years of overindulgence have caused. Wellness centers, often close to beach resorts, have made a name for themselves by offering an alternative to the fast lane. Health programs may include yoga, tai chi, monitored fasting, and even colonic irrigation, but best of all they serve carefully prepared fresh food. A wide variety of options ensures there is something to satisfy everyone's search for his or her soul. Try a course in meditation, which comes with great veggie cooking at The Spa, Samui, or its more isolated sister resort on peaceful Koh Chang. See chapters 12 and 13.

- **Novice Monk and Meditation Programs:** Almost every Thai man enters the *sangha,* or monkhood, for some period of time, usually for just a few weeks as a young man and again later during marriage. Since the first Western spiritual seekers started coming in droves to Thailand in the 1970s and 1980s, many temples opened their doors to resident foreigners interested in practicing meditation. Courses in varying lengths and intensity exist; most follow the Theravada Buddhist tradition of Vipassana, or "Insight" meditation. In the south, try Wat Suan Mokkh (near Surat Thani; p. 188). In the north, there's Wat Rampoeng (p. 328). Courses are held in Bangkok at Wat Mahathat, or The House of Dhamma; p. 131.

- **Learn Thai Massage** (nationwide): It is now easy to find massage schools all over Thailand. However, big-name spa **Chiva Som** in Hua Hin has set up an academy in Bangkok's Sukhumvit Soi 63 where, unlike most places, a huge range of wellness techniques are at last being taught *in English* by bona fide therapists. See www.chivasom academy.com, as well as p. 135.

12 The Best Shopping

- **Chatuchak Weekend Market** (Bangkok): This never-ending labyrinthine warren of stalls sells everything from commercial art to imitation designer label gear. Whole sections are devoted to pets (including the selling of live reptiles), and there's a huge swath reserved for home furnishing stalls. Get there by 10am for an authentic northern Thai breakfast, before the hoards descend. This is a great place to see Thailand's rising designer scene. See chapter 6.

- **Siam Paragon** (Bangkok): Hailed as *the* newest retail experience around, nothing in Asia quite beats Siam Paragon for its ostentatious glitz, designer brands, plush cinemas, and endless eateries—and I haven't even mentioned the vast underground oceanarium, Siam Ocean World. It outshines the city's former malls of fame (Emporium, Gaysorn, and Erawan) and there's even easy access via Siam BTS. See chapter 6.

- **Thong Lor** (Bangkok): Head up to Sukhumvit Soi 55 for the latest in designer chic, upscale spas and cafes, and superb home furnishing stores. Big boutiques like Playground— which sell clothes and designer decor—as well as the yummy Greyhound Café attract Thailand's yuppies on weekends. See chapter 6.

- **Pak Klong Talad** (Bangkok): This old riverside flower market is open

24/7, and though its narrow lanes are sometimes hard to get down, it showcases the best of Thailand's botanical offerings. Go late at night when the blossoms are fresh, or if your home-country's customs regulations allow, pop in before heading home and purchase bouquets of orchids, perfumed ginger flowers, Strelitzia, or unscented roses, all for just a few dollars. See chapter 6.

- **JungCeylon** (Phuket): This is the latest shopping magnet to draw the hordes away from the older, tout-riddled beach strips. Swanky and bright (and air-conditioned), it's got not just fast food diners and coffee shops, but also young brand fashion and sports stores, plus a whole basement crammed with some great Thai handicraft stalls. See chapter 9.

- **Nimmanheimin Road** (Chiang Mai): This long stretch of road starting at Amari Rincome Hotel is now chock-full of designer boutiques, bespoke tailors, and chic art galleries. Here you can check out some of the nation's best traditional and new-age handicrafts, jewelry, lacquer, ceramics, wood, art, candles, and luxury items. I particularly like the funky furniture at **Wit's Collection.** See chapter 12.

13 The Most Intriguing Archaeological Sights

- **Ayutthaya:** The former capital of Siam was one of the world's largest and most sophisticated cities before it was ransacked by the Burmese in 1756. Today it remains one of Thailand's greatest historical treasures, with abundant evidence of its former majesty. It is easily reached in a day from Bangkok. See chapter 10.

- **Sukhothai:** Founded in 1238, Sukhothai (The Dawn of Happiness) was a capital of an early Thai kingdom. Many of the ruins of this religious and cultural center are skillfully preserved and well maintained in an idyllic setting. See chapter 10.

14 The Best Museums

- **The National Museum** (Bangkok): Simply the biggest and best repository of the nation's treasures. Objects from Thailand's long and varied history include beautiful stone carvings of Hindu deities, exquisite Buddha images, gold jewelry, ceramics, royal costumes, wood carvings, musical instruments, and more. See p. 126.

- **The Hall of Opium** (Near Chiang Saen at the Golden Triangle): This gargantuan edifice, entered by a subterranean tunnel, is a pleasure for visitors of all ages. Its exhibits explain the cultivation process and history of opium growth in the Golden Triangle region. Supported by the royal family, the modern complex is a stone's throw from the Mekong and displays are highly informative, if shocking. See p. 361.

15 The Best Small Towns

- **Pai:** Not your typical tiny mountain-valley farming village, Pai is a favorite for budget travelers who want to put their feet up and relax. The scenery is gorgeous, the many bungalows are cheap, and the restaurants are good. You'll want to stay longer than you planned. See chapter 13.

- **Lamphun:** This charming town close to Chiang Mai is on the Kuang River in a part of the country where few travelers visit. Its quiet temples echo times past; trishaws still meander through the sleepy town center. Just outside are the relics of the early Hariphunchai era that preceded the 12th-century Lanna kingdom. See chapter 12.

- **Chiang Rai:** Blessed with some lovely attractions, such as the Mae Kok River, and some delightful *wats,* this much-overlooked town also offers local crafts, such as silver, cotton, and hill-tribe crafts. See chapter 13.

16 The Most Fascinating Temples

- **Wat Phra Kaew** (Bangkok): With its flamboyant colors and rich details, this shrine is a magnificent setting for Thailand's most revered image, the Emerald Buddha. Inside the main temple building, a profusion of offerings surround the pedestal that supports the tiny image. See p. 129.

- **Wat Arun** (Bangkok): The golden Temple of Dawn shimmers in the sunrise across the Chao Phraya River from Bangkok, but viewing it at sunset is better still. As you climb its steep central Khmer-style *prang* (tower), you'll get a close view of the porcelain pieces that make up its floral design. See p. 131.

- **The Erawan Shrine** (Bangkok): Not a site notable for its size or superstructure, the Erawan Shrine is famed for the veracity of its devotees. Not long ago, a deranged Thai took an ax to the central figure; incensed by the desecration of the site, the crowds beat him to death. The statue has since been replaced. Located between Chit Lom and Ploen Chit BTS stations in the center of town, few Thai people pass without offering a bow, or *wai,* in reverence. See p. 130.

- **Wat Yai** (Phitsanulok): One of the holiest temples in Thailand, Wat Yai is home to the Phra Buddha Chinarat image, cast in bronze. One of the few remaining Sukhothai images, the Buddha here is the prototype for many replicas throughout the country. Outside, the temple complex hums with activity, since many Thais make the pilgrimage here. See p. 277.

- **Wat Phra That Lampang Luang** (Lampang): This city is the center of southern Buddhism in Thailand, the first Thai capital to convert to Theravada Buddhism and a major influence on the kingdoms to follow. The main *chedi* (stupa) contains a relic of the Buddha brought from Sri Lanka over a millennia ago and the Lanna styled architecture is evident all around town. See p. 339.

- **Wat Phra Singh** (Chiang Mai): While most Thais head here to see the revered Lion Buddha image, it's the delightful Lanna murals in the *viharn* next door that always amaze. Dating to around 1870, these faded illustrations include images of elephants, armies, and even fanciful impressions of early Western travelers. See p. 326.

2

Planning Your Trip to Thailand

Here you'll find all of the nuts and bolts on how to get to Thailand, where and when to visit, and what documents you'll need, as well as pointers to other sources of information that can make the difference between a smooth ride and turbulent times.

1 The Regions in Brief

The Thais compare their land to the shape of an elephant's head, seen in profile, facing the West. Thailand is roughly equidistant from China and India, and centuries of migration from southern China and trade with India brought tremendous influences from each of these Asian nations. Thailand borders Myanmar (Burma) to the northwest, Laos to the northeast, Cambodia to the east, and Malaysia to the south. Its southwestern coast stretches along the Andaman Sea, its southern and southeastern coastlines perimeter the Gulf of Thailand, and every coast boasts a myriad of islands. Thailand covers roughly 466,200 square km (180,000 sq. miles) and is divided into six major geographic zones.

WESTERN THAILAND West of Bangkok are the cities of Ratchanaburi and Kanchanaburi. The latter, lying along the River Kwai (pronounced *gway*), is the site of the infamous World War II "Death Railway," where 12,000 prisoners of war died in Japanese labor camps during its construction. The Hollywood movie, *The Bridge on the River Kwai* was inspired by the historic rail bridge in Kanchanaburi, but the film was shot in Sri Lanka. Many relatives of those who died come to pay their respects at the nearby Commonwealth Cemetery. To the north of

Bangkok are the glorious ruins of Ayutthaya, Thailand's capital after it moved from Sukhothai.

THE SOUTHEAST COAST The coastline east of Bangkok—viewed as the nation's eastern seaboard—is home to Pattaya, Rayong, and Trat. These are popular weekend destinations among Thai families and expats alike. Offshore, you will find the developed resort islands of Koh Samet, Koh Chang, and Koh Kood, all of which offer luxury resorts and superb scuba diving. The region is also home to the country's greatest concentration of sapphire and ruby mines at Chantaburi (known as Mueang Chan). Chantaburi has been a gem trading center for centuries and its so-called weekend "gem" market is fun, but certainly not for treasure seekers; the standards of the precious stones sold here are infamously low.

THE SOUTHERN PENINSULA A long, narrow peninsula protrudes south to the Malaysian border with the Andaman Sea on the west and the Gulf of Thailand to the east. This eastern coastline extends more than 1,811km (1,125 miles), while the western shoreline runs 716km (445 miles). The region's primary industries are rubber, coconut and palm oil, fishing, and tourism.

This region has the most typically tropical clime in the country: heavy rainfall during the monsoon season from May to October and high winds with choppy seas. From November to April, expect clear weather and calm waters, great for diving. This weather pattern works exactly in reverse for the east coast: It's best enjoyed from May to October.

With the advent of global warming will come unpredictable weather similar to that which caused the crash of a local budget airline at Phuket in September 2007 and a Thai Airways jet in Surat Thani in 1998. Always check weather conditions if you plan to take a flight or ferry, or go diving in monsoon season.

Southern beach resorts abound. To the west are the islands of Phuket and Koh Phi Phi, the peninsula of Krabi, and Koh Tarutao. Off the east coast, Koh Samui has gone from sleepy hideaway to heaving tourist magnet. Farther down, the three southernmost provinces of Yala, Narathiwat, and Pattani are home to a considerable Muslim population. Take extreme care in this region: Violent attacks by insurgents are increasingly targeting public markets as well as transport and Buddhist centers.

THE CENTRAL PLAINS   Thailand's central plains are an extremely fertile region: Its abundant jasmine rice crops are exported worldwide. The main city of the central plains is Phitsanulok, northeast of which are the impressive remains of Sukhothai: Thailand's first capital and the ancient city of Si Satchanalai. To the south is Lopburi, an ancient Mon/Khmer settlement famous for its giant, yellow votive candles.

ISAN   The broad and relatively infertile northeast plateau that is Isan is the least developed region in Thailand. Bordered by the Mekong River, it separates the country from neighboring Laos. The people of Isan share cultural similarities with the Laotians. Many young people from

Isan work in Bangkok, many of the men as taxi drivers, and the girls in bars. Isan is dusty in the cool winter and muddy during the summer's rainy season. The region contains the remains of a Bronze Age village at Ban Chiang. There are also major Khmer ruins at Phimai, outside Surin and Buriram, and in Nakhorn Ratchisima, also known as Khorat. Other than potash mining and subsistence farming, the region has enjoyed little economic development.

NORTHERN THAILAND   In the past, this region came under the control of the Lanna kings, during which craftsmen created some of Thailand's most exquisite architecture and religious art, some of which can still be seen today. The north is largely populated by Tai Yai people today, the original Thais who migrated from southern China in the early part of the first millennium, but it's more famous for the colorful hill-tribes who dwell in the mountainous jungles here.

The north is a mountainous region and coolest from November to January. Until logging was banned, elephants provided the heavy labor needed to harvest teak and other hardwoods here. Many have now found new homes in elephant camps. The cool hills in the north are well suited for farming, particularly for strawberries, asparagus, peaches, and lychees (litchis). Today, agricultural programs and charities such as Sop Moei Arts and Mae Fah Luang do much to reskill hill-tribe villages. Those around Doi Tung have gallantly implemented crop replacement schemes propagating coffee and macadamia nuts.

This region's cooler temperatures also make the north a favorite holiday destination for Thais from November to April, when the rest of the country is comparatively warm. The major cities in the north are Chiang Mai, Chiang Rai, Lamphun, Lampang, and Mae Hong Son.

Thailand

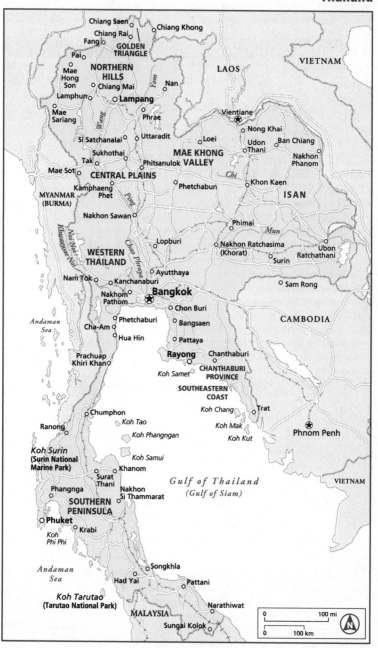

In the past, at higher elevations, some hill-tribe farmers cultivated opium poppies. Despite the erstwhile reputation of the area known as the Golden Triangle, drugs are no longer an economic mainstay—or welcome—in these parts.

2 Visitor Information & Maps

Tourism Authority of Thailand (TAT; www.tat.org.) is an extensive site with information on locations throughout Thailand. However, its listings are often incorrect or out of date. See the box "Online Traveler's Toolbox" on p. 44 for other options.

TRAVEL BLOGS & TRAVELOGS

More and more travelers are using travel Web logs, or **blogs,** to chronicle their journeys online. To read a few blogs about Thailand, try **Thingsasian.com,** a comprehensive site with some spirited contributors, many travel journalists among them.

You can search for other blogs about Thailand at **Travelblog.com** or post your own travelog at **Travelblog.org.** For blogs that cover general travel news and highlight various destinations, try **Written road.com** or Gawker Media's snarky **Gridskipper.com.** For more literary travel essays, try Salon.com's travel section (**www. Salon.com/Wanderlust**), and **Worldhum. com,** which also has an extensive list of other travel-related journals, blogs, online communities, newspaper coverage, and bookstores.

MAPS

There are a number of excellent Bangkok maps. Nancy Chandler's *Map of Bangkok* is the by far the best; it's fun, colorful, and great for finding places to eat and shop (it even comes with a short handbook). It costs just 160B (US$4.60/£2.45). At hotels and airports, you'll find the free *Thaiways Map of Bangkok* and *Groovy Map;* both offer detailed plans of the city, transportation, and, in the latter, information on Suvarnabhumi International Airport; however, these maps are notoriously outdated when it comes to phone numbers.

3 Entry Requirements

ENTRY REQUIREMENTS

PASSPORTS & VISAS   All visitors to Thailand must carry a valid **passport** with **proof of onward passage** (either a return or through ticket). Visa applications are not required if you are staying less than 30 days and are a national of 1 of 41 designated countries including Australia, Canada, Ireland, New Zealand, the United Kingdom, and the United States (New Zealanders may stay up to 3 months).

The **Immigration Division of the Royal Thai Police Department** is found at 507 Soi Suan Plu (off Sathorn Road, and a short taxi ride from Chong Nongsi BTS; ℂ **02287-3101**). Many foreigners have made use of the limitless 1-month free entry visas that many travelers used to be granted on arrival. However, since November 1, 2006, this free visa privilege only extends to an accumulated total stay of 90 days, in a 6-month period.

Visitors planning to stay for longer than a month can arrange for 60-day tourist visas at embassies overseas for a cost of 1050B ($30/£16); this is renewable in Thailand for an additional 30 days for another 1,900B (US$54/£29). If you overstay your visa, you will be charged between 500B and 1,000B (US$14–US$29/£7–£15) per day, which is payable when exiting the kingdom. Longer overstays are punishable by anything upwards of a 20,000B (US$571/£308) fine or a stay in jail. For more

(Tips Passport Savvy

Allow plenty of time before your trip to apply for a passport; processing normally takes 3 weeks but can take longer during busy periods (especially in the spring). Keep in mind that if you need a passport in a hurry, you'll pay a higher processing fee. When traveling, safeguard your passport in an inconspicuous, inaccessible place, such as a money belt, and keep a copy of the pages with your visa and passport number in a separate place. If you lose your passport, visit the nearest consulate or embassy of your native country as soon as possible for a replacement or temporary travel pass.

information, check www.thaivisa.com, but bear in mind that it may not be updated.

Warning: Until they were outlawed in 2006, small travel agencies offered "visa services" where you paid for a courier to take your passport to a border post to get a new visa stamp. A police crackdown has put a halt to this illegal practice. Foreigners who take advantage of the free 30-day visa-on-arrival service must remember that they may only do this three times in a row (allowing them a cumulative stay of a maximum of 90 days). After that they will not be allowed to enter Thailand until they pay for a new visa issued by a Royal Thai Embassy overseas.

ROYAL THAI EMBASSIES OVER-SEAS   In the **United States,** contact the **Royal Thai Embassy,** 1024 Wisconsin Ave. NW, Suite 401, Washington, DC 20007 (© **202/944-3600;** fax 202/944-3611); **The Permanent Mission of Thailand** to the United Nations, 351 E. 52nd St., New York, NY 10022 (© **212/ 754-2230;** fax 212/754-2535); the **Royal Thai Consulate-General,** 801 N. La Brea Ave., Los Angeles, CA 90038 (© **213/ 937-1894;** fax 213/937-5987); or the **Royal Thai Consulate-General,** 35 E. Wacker Dr., Suite 1834, Chicago, IL 60601 (© **312/236-2447;** fax 312/236-1906). In **Canada,** contact the **Royal Thai Embassy,** 180 Island Park Dr., Ottawa, Ontario K1Y OA2 (© **613/722-4444;** fax 613/722-6624); or the **Royal**

Thai Embassy, 106-736 Granville St., Vancouver, BC V6Z 1G4 (© **604/687-1143;** fax 604/687-4434). In **Australia,** contact the **Royal Thai Embassy,** 111 Empire Circuit Yarralumla, Canberra ACT 2600 (© **02/6273-1149;** fax 02/ 6273-1518); or the **Royal Thai Consulate-General,** 2nd floor, 75-77 Pitt St., Sydney, NSW 2000 (© **02/9241-2120;** fax 02/9247-8312). In **New Zealand,** contact the **Royal Thai Embassy,** 2 Cook St., Karori, P.O. Box 17226, Wellington (© **644/476-8618;** fax 644/476-3677). In the **United Kingdom,** contact the **Royal Thai Embassy,** 29-30 Queen's Gate, London (© **171/589-0173;** fax 171/823-9695; enquiries@thaiconsul-uk. com).

MEDICAL REQUIREMENTS   No inoculations or vaccinations are required unless you are coming from, or passing through, areas infected with Yellow Fever, but do verify what may be recommended. Yellow Fever certificates are required for those coming from 14 African and South American countries. Check at the appropriate consulate or embassy for up-to-date information about health certificates that may be required for entry. Also see your doctor before leaving your home country.

A NOTE ON PASSPORTS   For information on how to get a passport, go to "Passports" in the "Fast Facts" section of this chapter—the websites listed there provide downloadable passport applications as well as the current fees for processing passport applications. For an up-to-date, country-by-country listing of passport requirements around the world, go to the "Foreign Entry Requirement" Web page of the U.S. State Department at **www. travel.state.gov**.

4 When to Go

Study the weather information below, as an ill-timed trip can mean pouring rain, debilitating humidity, or seas too rough for diving or beach activity. The high season for tourism throughout the kingdom is the North American/European winter period, mid-October through late February. Prices skyrocket and hotels fill up then, so be sure to make advance reservations. Off-season weather, however, is not intolerable, and some travelers report joyfully trading the crowded beaches and high prices of high-season for a bit of off-peak discomfort. Low-season is generally comprised of the odd rainy afternoon, significant savings, and a lot more elbow room.

Thailand has two distinct climate zones: **tropical** in the south and **tropical savanna** in the north. The northern and central areas of the country (including Bangkok) experience three distinct seasons. The **hot season** lasts from March to May, with temperatures averaging in the upper nineties Fahrenheit (mid-30s Celsius), and with April being the hottest month. Normally, this period sees sporadic rain.

In recent years, however, the **rainy season** has begun in April and has lasted, on and off, until late November, or even December. The average temperature is 84°F (29°C) with 90% humidity. While the rainy season brings heavy downpours, it is rare to see an all-day episode. From June, daily showers will usually come in the late afternoon or evening for 3 to 4 hours; often bringing floods and forcing traffic to a standstill. Trekking in the north is not recommended during this time. In Bangkok, expect smog from April to August.

The **cool season,** from November to February, has temperatures from the high 70°F to low 80°F (26°C–30°C), with infrequent showers. In the north, the cool season coincides with the peak season for tourism. Daily temperatures can drop as low as 60°F (16°C) in Chiang Mai and 41°F (5°C) in the hills; 1 or 2 nights may even see frost.

The **Southern Thai Peninsula** has intermittent showers year-round and daily downpours during the rainy season (temperatures average in the low 80s Fahrenheit/30s Celsius). If you're traveling to Phuket or Koh Samui, it would be helpful to note that the two islands alternate peak seasons. Optimal weather on Phuket occurs between November and April, when the island welcomes the highest numbers of travelers. Conversely, Koh Samui's great weather lasts from about February to October. Refer to each destination's section for more information about peak seasons and changing weather patterns.

HOLIDAYS

Many holidays are based on the Thai lunar calendar, falling on the full moon of each month; check with the Tourism Authority of Thailand (TAT; www.tat. or.th) for the current year's schedule. Chapter 11, "Exploring Northern Thailand," includes a list of festivals and events specific to the north.

On National and Buddhist holidays, as well as polling days, government offices, banks, small shops, and offices—as well as some restaurants and bars—usually close. By law, bars cannot serve alcohol on HM Queen Sirikit's birthday in

August, nor on HM King Bhumibol's birthday in December. *Note:* In most cases there will be little advance warning given to shop, restaurant, or bar customers. Public transport still runs on holidays, though.

January to March

Thailand celebrates New Year's Day the same as the rest of the world. In **late February** or **early March** (depending on the lunar cycle) is **Makha Bucha Day,** when temples celebrate Buddha preaching to his disciples.

April

Chakri Memorial Day (April 6) commemorates the founding of the current Chakri dynasty.

Songkran is the New Year according to the Thai calendar, and it's an event that begins on April 13 and lasts from 3 to 10 days. After honoring local monks and family elders, folks hit the streets for massive water fights. Be warned—foreigners are the Thais' favorite target and areas like Khao San Road become messy war zones where everyone gets soaked (police included) and then covered in flour or colored powder. Truck-mounted power hoses can cause damage, and cellphones, cameras, and valuables should be kept in Ziploc bags. Wear your oldest clothes—anyone expecting to stay dry will be sorely disappointed!

May

National Labor Day falls on the 1st, **Coronation Day** (celebrating the coronation of HM King Bhumibol in 1946) is on the 5th, while the 14th is **Royal Ploughing Day,** the first day of the rice-planting cycle, which is celebrated with a traditional Brahman parade. **Visakha Bucha Day,** marking the birth, enlightenment, and death of the Buddha, falls around **mid-May,** depending on the lunar calendar.

July

Thais celebrate the **Buddhist Lent** immediately following Asarnha Bucha Day in mid-July (depending on the lunar calendar) signaling the beginning of the rains' retreat and the 3-month period of meditation for all Buddhist monks—this was the day that the Buddha delivered his first sermon to his first five disciples.

August

August 12 honors the birthday of HM Queen Sirikit and is also **Mother's Day.**

October

On **October 23, Chulalongkorn Day,** the country's favorite king, Rama V, is remembered.

November

Loy Krathong, in early November, is Thailand's most romantic festival, although it's not usually a public holiday. At dusk, handmade banana leaf vessels are launched down rivers and lanterns are hoisted into the sky in order to symbolize the release of sins. The most spectacular celebrations are in Ayutthaya, Sukhothai, and Chiang Mai.

December

December 5 marks HM King Bhumibol's birthday and is also **Father's Day.** December 10 is **Constitution Day** and recognizes Thailand's first constitution in 1932.

Check with the **Tourist Authority of Thailand** (© **1672;** www.tat.org, and listings in each chapter) for more information on the events listed below as well as for other holidays celebrated throughout the country. Also see specific chapters for local information and schedules.

THAILAND CALENDAR OF EVENTS

January/February

Chinese New Year, nationwide. Head for any Chinatown to see the vivid parades, firecrackers, and Lion Dances associated with this holiday. Things get most raucous in Bangkok's Yawarat district (Chinatown). It falls anytime from mid-January to mid-February, during which many businesses close for the week.

February

Flower Festival, Chiang Mai. When all of the north is in bloom, Chiang Mai springs to life with parades, floats decorated with flowers, and beauty contests. First weekend in the month.

March

King's Cup Annual Elephant Polo Tournament, used to be held in Hua Hin but now takes place near Chiang Rai in the Golden Triangle. Mahouts and madcap international polo players meet to battle it out in the mud in a hilarious but worthy week-long tournament that raises money for Thailand's main elephant charities. Entrance is free, and the cup happens during the last week of the month.

April

Pattaya Festival, Pattaya. Parades and fireworks accompany a food festival and lots of partying, during the first week of the month.

July

Koh Samui Regatta, Koh Samui. Late July brings yachtsmen and partygoers from all over to enjoy a week of fiercely competitive ocean races.

October

Vegetarian Festival, Phuket. In this bizarre religious ritual, devotees spear, pierce, and percolate themselves while in a trance. It's not for the fainthearted! It takes place the second week, and lasts for 9 days.

Naga Fireballs, Nong Khai, Isan. During this event, crowds gather along the river to witness red glowing balls rise from the waters; they're thought to be methane bubbles released from the riverbed. The second or third week of the month.

November

Elephant Roundup, Surin. Elephant parades and cultural performances take place during the third weekend of November.

December

King's Cup Regatta, Phuket. Global competitors race yachts in this exciting international event, which takes place the second week of December.

5 Getting There

BY PLANE

When you plan your trip, consider that Thailand has more than one international airport. While most international flights arrive in Bangkok's **Suvarnabhumi International Airport** (airport code BKK), you can also fly directly to Phuket, Koh Samui, and Chiang Mai from certain regional destinations like Singapore or Hong Kong. Check destination chapters for details.

FLIGHTS FROM NORTH AMERICA

Thai Airways International (© 800/426-5204; www.thaiair.com) flies daily to Bangkok from Los Angeles; also check their new direct flight from New York. **United Airlines** (© 800/241-6522; www.ual.com) and **Northwest Airlines** (© 800/447-4747; www.nwa.com) can connect pretty much any airport in North America to Bangkok via daily flights. **Canadian Airlines International**

(© 800/661-2227; www.cdnair.ca) flies to Bangkok from Vancouver via Hong Kong daily. Also check for connecting flights with **EVA Air, Japan Airlines (JAL),** and **Korean Air.**

FLIGHTS FROM AUSTRALIA Thai Airways (© 300/651-960 toll-free within Australia, 7/3215-4700 in Brisbane, or 8/9322-7522 in Perth) services Bangkok from Sydney daily and from Brisbane, Melbourne, and Perth three times a week. **Qantas** (© 13-12-11 toll-free within Australia; www.qantas.com), in addition to two dailies from Sydney and a daily flight from Melbourne (both direct), can also connect with Adelaide, Brisbane, and Canberra daily. For budget fares, Qantas' subsidiary **Jetstar** (www.jetstar.com) is now flying direct to a few points in Asia. **British Airways** (© 2/8904-8800 in Sydney, 7/3223-3123 in Brisbane, 8/9425-7711 in Perth; www.ba.com) flies twice daily from Sydney.

FLIGHTS FROM THE UNITED KINGDOM Two or three daily, non-stop flights from London to Bangkok are offered by **British Airways** (© 0870/850-9850 from anywhere within the United Kingdom; www.ba.com).

FLYING FOR LESS: TIPS FOR GETTING THE BEST AIRFARE

- Passengers who can book their ticket either **long in advance** or **at the last minute,** or who **fly midweek** or **at less-trafficked hours,** may pay a fraction of the full fare. If your schedule is flexible, say so, and ask if you can secure a cheaper fare by changing your flight plans.

- Search **the Internet** for cheap fares. The most popular online travel agencies are **Travelocity.com** (www.travelocity.co.uk), **Expedia.com** (www.expedia.co.uk and www.expedia.ca), and **Orbitz.com.** In the U.K., go to **Travelsupermarket** (© 0845/345-5708; www.travelsupermarket.com),

a flight search engine that offers flight comparisons for the budget airlines whose seats often end up in bucket-shop sales. Other websites for booking airline tickets online include **Cheap flights.com, SmarterTravel.com, Priceline.com,** and **Opodo** (www.opodo.co.uk). Meta search sites (which find and then direct you to airline and hotel websites for booking) include **Sidestep.com** and **Kayak.com**—the latter includes fares for budget carriers like JetBlue and Spirit as well as the major airlines. **LastMinute.com** is a great source for last-minute flights and getaways. In addition, most **airlines** offer online-only fares that even their phone agents know nothing about. British travelers should check **Flights International** (© 0800/018-7050; www.flights-international.com) for deals on flights all over the world.

- Keep an eye on local newspapers for **promotional specials** or **fare wars,** when airlines lower prices on their most popular routes.

- Try to book a ticket **in its country of origin.** If you're planning a one-way flight from Johannesburg to New York, a South Africa–based travel agent will probably have the lowest fares. For foreign travelers on multileg trips, book in the country of the first leg; for example, book New York–Chicago–Montréal–New York in the U.S.

- **Consolidators,** also known as bucket shops, are wholesale brokers in the airline-ticket game. Consolidators buy deeply discounted tickets ("distressed" inventories of unsold seats) from airlines and sell them to online ticket agencies, travel agents, tour operators, corporations, and, to a lesser degree, the general public. Consolidators advertise in Sunday newspaper travel sections (often in small ads with tiny type), both in the

U.S. and the U.K. They can be great sources for cheap international tickets. On the downside, bucket shop tickets are often rigged with restrictions, such as stiff cancellation penalties (as high as 50% to 75% of the ticket price). And keep in mind that most of what you see advertised is of limited availability. Several reliable consolidators are worldwide and available online. **STA Travel** (© **800/ 781-4040;** www.statravel.com) has been the world's leading consolidator for students since purchasing Council Travel, but their fares to Thailand are competitive for travelers of all ages. **Flights.com** (© **800/TRAV-800;** www.flights.com) has excellent fares worldwide, including to Thailand.

- Join **frequent-flier clubs.** Frequent-flier membership doesn't cost a cent, but it does entitle you to free tickets or upgrades when you amass the airline's required number of frequent-flier points. You don't even have to fly to earn points; **frequent-flier credit cards** can earn you thousands of miles for doing your everyday shopping. But keep in mind that award seats are limited, seats on popular routes are hard to snag, and more and more major airlines are cutting their expiration periods for mileage points—so check your airline's frequent-flier program so you don't lose your miles before you use them. *Inside tip:* Award seats are offered almost a year in advance, but seats also open up at the last minute, so if your travel plans are flexible, you may strike gold. To play the frequent-flier game to your best advantage, consult the community bulletin boards on **FlyerTalk** (www.flyertalk.com) or go to Randy Petersen's **Inside Flyer** (www.insideflyer.com). Petersen and friends review all the programs in detail and post regular updates on changes in policies and trends.

LONG-HAUL FLIGHTS: HOW TO STAY COMFORTABLE

Long flights can be trying; stuffy air and cramped seats can make you feel as if you're being sent parcel post in a small box. But with a little advance planning, you can make an otherwise unpleasant experience almost bearable.

- Your choice of airline and airplane will definitely affect your leg room. Find more details at **www.seatguru. com**, which has extensive details about almost every seat on six major U.S. airlines. For international airlines, research firm Skytrax has posted a list of average seat pitches at **www. airlinequality.com**.
- Emergency exit seats and bulkhead seats typically have the most legroom. Emergency exit seats are usually left unassigned until the day of a flight (to ensure that someone able-bodied fills the seats); it is worth getting to the ticket counter early to snag one of these spots for a long flight. Many passengers find that bulkhead seating (the row facing the wall at the front of the cabin) offers more legroom, but keep in mind that bulkheads are where airlines often put baby bassinets, so you may be sitting next to an infant.
- To have two seats for yourself in a three-seat row, try for an aisle seat in a center section toward the back of coach. If you're traveling with a companion, book an aisle and a window seat. Middle seats are usually booked last, so chances are good you'll end up with three seats to yourselves. And in the event that a third passenger is assigned the middle seat, he or she will probably be more than happy to trade for a window or an aisle.
- Ask about entertainment options. Many airlines offer seatback video systems where you get to choose your movies or play video games—but

only on some of their planes. (Boeing 777s are your best bet.)

- To sleep, avoid the last row of any section or the row in front of an emergency exit, as these seats are the least likely to recline. Avoid seats near highly trafficked toilet areas. Avoid seats in the back of many jets; these can be narrower than those in the rest of coach. You also may want to reserve a window seat so you can rest your head and avoid being bumped in the aisle.

- Get up, walk around, and stretch every 60 to 90 minutes to keep your blood flowing. This helps avoid **Deep Vein Thrombosis (DVT),** or "economy-class syndrome," a potentially deadly condition caused by sitting in cramped conditions for too long. Other preventative measures include drinking lots of water and avoiding alcohol (see next bullet).

- Drink water before, during, and after your flight to combat the lack of humidity in airplane cabins–which can be drier than the Sahara. Bring a bottle of water on board. Avoid alcohol, which will dehydrate you.

- If you're flying with kids, don't forget to carry on toys, books, pacifiers, and chewing gum to help them relieve ear pressure buildup during ascent and descent. Let each child pack his or her own backpack with favorite toys.

BY BUS

Private buses link Singapore and Malaysia with Had Yai in southern Thailand, but be aware that violent insurgencies in south Thailand are becoming a real cause for concern. In Singapore, call the **Singapore Tourism Board** at © **800/334-1335,** and in Malaysia, contact the **Malaysia Tourism Promotion Board** (© **603/293-5188**) for more information. Thai buses stop at the Thai border at Nong Khai from where pedestrians pass through to Laos. Tuk-tuks (three-wheeled,

motorized, open vehicles, also called Jumbos) connect travelers to Vientiane. Call **Laos Tourist Information** in Vientiane at © **856-21/212-248.**

BY TRAIN

Thailand is accessible via train from Singapore and peninsular Malaysia. **Malaysia's Keretapi Tanah Melayu Berhad (KTM)** begins in Singapore (© **65/222-5165**), stopping in Kuala Lumpur (© **603/273-8000**) and Butterworth (Penang; © **604/323-7962**), before heading for Thailand, where it joins service with the State Railway of Thailand. Bangkok's Hua Lampong Station is centrally located on Krung Kasem Road (© **02223-7010** or 1690). Taxis, tuk-tuks, and public buses wait outside the station and access to the MRT (subway) is a few steps away.

The **Eastern & Oriental Express** (www. orient-express.com) operates a 2-night/3-day journey between Singapore and Bangkok that makes *getting* there almost better than *being* there. The romance of 1930s colonial travel is joined with modern luxury in six Pullman cars, seven State cars, a Presidential car, plus two restaurant cars, a bar car, a saloon car, and an observation car. Along the way, stops are made in Penang (Georgetown) and Kanchanaburi (River Kwai) for light sightseeing. Current fares are per person one-way $1,860 (65,100B/£1,001) for a Pullman superior double. At certain times of the year, promotions will include overnights at the Oriental Bangkok and its sister property, the Mandarin Oriental, Singapore. Call © **800/524-2420** in the U.S., or **65/392-3500** in Singapore.

BY SHIP

Sun Cruises and Crystal Cruises are the two main cruise ships that visit the region. They call by Pattaya or Phuket before steaming on to Singapore or Malacca. These floating resorts have endless restaurants, Jacuzzis, pools, fitness centers, spas, deck games, and all manner of bars and lounges. Contact **888/722-0021** for information on Crystal Cruises or check the website, www.crystalcruises.com. Sun Cruises can be contacted through **Pacific Leisure** (156/13 Phang Nga Rd., Phuket, 83000; © **07623-2511,** fax 07623-2510; www.pacific-leisure.com).

BY CAR

Currently, it is almost impossible to pass from Thailand to any of its neighbors by rental car unless you have a vehicle import license, tax registration form, and other documentation. I don't recommend it. See p. 81 under "Getting Around Thailand: By Car" for tips on renting a car in Thailand.

6 Money

Travel in Thailand is very affordable and therefore attracts many budget travelers. While Thais love bargaining, they do not appreciate haggling over a few cents. Sometimes such tourists will be impolitely referred to as *kee neow* (meaning "stingy" or "cheapskates" in Thai). As long as you behave well, you will be afforded a warm welcome.

Before bargaining, remember that average Thai incomes are a fraction of those in developed countries. In 2005, the World Bank estimated average incomes to be around $220 (£110) per person, per month, and therefore standards of living and corresponding prices reflect this. Compared to home, many excellent hotels and restaurants cost a fraction of the price in Thailand, and because of this Thais consider any foreigner to be extremely well off.

Always bear in mind that throughout Thailand, the baht will be the only acceptable currency, and foreign currency is rarely, if ever, accepted for everyday transactions or taxis.

CURRENCY

The Thai unit of currency is the **Baht** (written B, Bt, or Bht) and is divided into 100 **satang.** Tiny copper coins represent 25 and 50 satang; silver coins are 1B, 2B (rare), and 5B. The larger 10B coin is silver with a copper inset. Bank notes come in denominations of 20B (green), 50B (blue), 100B (red), 500B (purple), and 1,000B (brown).

There are no restrictions on the import of foreign currencies or traveler's checks, but you cannot export foreign currency in excess of 50,000B (US$1,428/£769) per person.

CURRENCY EXCHANGE RATES

Before the currency crisis in July 1997, one U.S. dollar could buy you 25 Thai baht. During the worst of the crisis, the value was 55B to the dollar. Recent months have seen the Thai baht fluctuate from 40B per dollar to as little as 32B for a greenback. Amounts listed throughout this book are calculated at **$1 = 35B** and **£1=65B.** For the most up-to-date figures, see **www.xe.com.** Below are rough cross-values with major currencies.

Some travelers like to change a little money before leaving home. You can sometimes buy Thai baht at your local American Express or Thomas Cook office or order baht at your bank; however, it is much easier to visit an airport exchange booth in Thailand. There are also exchange kiosks at most international airport arrival halls in Thailand—but don't rely on them being open 24 hours.

ATMs

Alternatively, if you have an ATM or credit card, these can be used in 24-hour cash machines that dispense money in 100, 500, and 1,000 baht bills. Thai ATMs accept most international bank card systems. **Cirrus** (© **800/424-7787;**

What Things Cost in Bangkok	Thai Baht	US$	UK£
Taxi: Suvarnabhumi Airport/city incl. airport fee and expressway tolls	250-300	$7.50	£3.75
Local call (pay phone) per minute	1	3¢	5p
Double at the Oriental (very expensive)	14,000	$400	£210
Double at the Eugenia (moderate)	3,080	$88	£46
Double at Bossotel (budget)	450	$13	£7
Dinner for one, without wine, at Sirocco (expensive)	1,000	$28	£15
Dinner for one, without wine, at Taling Pling (inexpensive)	350	$10	£5
Dinner for one, without wine, at a city food court (inexpensive)	120	$3.40	£1.80
Bottle of beer at a hotel bar	150	$4.30	£2.30
Bottle of beer at a local bar	80	$2.30	£1.20
Coca-Cola	25	70¢	35p
Regular coffee at a mall cafe	100	$2.90	£1.50
Roll of ASA 100 film, 36 exposures	170	$4.90	£2.60
Admission to the National Museum	40	$1.10	60p
Movie ticket	120	$3.40	£1.80

www.mastercard.com) and **PLUS** (© **800/ 843-7587;** www.visa.com) networks span the kingdom. Look at the back of your bank card to see which network you're on, and then call or check online for ATM locations in Thailand. Be sure you know your personal identification number (PIN) and daily withdrawal limit before you depart. *Note:* Remember that many banks impose a fee *every time* you use a card and that fee can be higher for international transactions (up to $5/£2.50 or more) than for domestic ones (where they're rarely more than $2/£1). In addition, the bank from which you withdraw cash may charge its own fee. To compare banks' ATM fees within the U.S., use **www.bankrate.com**. For international withdrawal fees, ask your bank.

The best banks to visit are **Bangkok Bank, Thai Farmer's Bank, Siam Commercial Bank,** and **Bank of Ayudhya,** since each has major branches in every city and many small towns. For specific locations of ATMs, see each town's "Fast Facts" listing.

You can also get cash advances on your credit card at an ATM. To avoid your bank suspecting you are an overseas fraudster and freezing access, call your credit card company *before you leave* home to let them know you'll be traveling abroad. Keep in mind that you'll pay interest from the moment of your withdrawal, even if you pay your monthly bills on time.

TRAVELER'S CHECKS

In Thailand, traveler's checks are less seen nowadays, having been replaced by ATMs. Given the fees you'll pay for using an ATM overseas, though, you might be better off with traveler's checks if you're withdrawing money often, or traveling out of Thailand to Myanmar (Burma)

The Baht, the U.S. Dollar, the Euro, the Australian Dollar & the British Pound

Thai B	US$	Euro€	AU$	UK£
1	0.03	0.02	0.03	0.01
5	0.14	0.11	0.16	0.07
10	0.28	0.22	0.33	0.14
20	0.57	0.44	0.66	0.28
50	1.42	1.10	1.65	0.73
100	2.85	2.20	3.00	1.47
500	14.28	11.00	15.00	7.35
1,000	28.57	22.00	30.00	14.70
5,000	142.85	110.00	150.00	73.50
10,000	285.40	220.00	300.00	147.00

where credit cards are currently banned and ATMs do not yet exist.

The most popular traveler's checks are offered by **American Express** (✆ 800/807-6233 or ✆ 800/221-7282 for cardholders—this number accepts collect calls, offers service in several foreign languages, and exempts Amex gold and platinum cardholders from the 1% fee); **Visa** (✆ 800/732-1322; AAA members can obtain Visa checks for a $9.95 fee for checks up to $1,500 at most AAA offices or by calling ✆ 866/339-3378); and **MasterCard** (✆ 800/223-9920).

Be sure to keep a record of the traveler's checks' serial numbers separate from your checks in the event that they are stolen or lost. You'll get a refund faster if you know the numbers.

American Express, Thomas Cook, Visa, and **MasterCard** also offer **foreign currency traveler's checks;** they're accepted at locations where dollar checks may not be.

In Thailand, traveler's checks are best exchanged in a main branch of city-center banks or in a five-star international hotel. They may be accepted in Bangkok at the small exchange counters, but not always. (The best rates are at banks.)

CREDIT CARDS

Credit cards are another good way to carry money. They also provide a convenient record of all your expenses and generally offer relatively good exchange rates. You can withdraw cash advances from your credit cards at banks or ATMs, provided you know your PIN. If you don't know it, call the number on the back of your credit card and ask the bank to send it to you at least a month before you leave home. It usually takes 5 to 7 business days. These days banks will refuse to give this information over the phone.

Keep in mind that many banks now assess a 1% to 3% "transaction fee" on **all** charges you incur abroad (whether you're using the local currency or U.S. dollars). It's best to sit down and work out beforehand which system is better for you and your shopping needs.

International hotels and larger businesses in urban centers accept major credit cards. Despite protest from credit card companies, many smaller establishments add a 3% to 5% surcharge for payment by credit card (this is above and beyond any fees levied by your credit card company). Be sure to ask before handing over your card, and keep all receipts. When using your card in Thai department stores, also

Frommers.com: The Complete Travel Resource

Planning a trip or just returned? Head to **Frommers.com,** voted Best Travel Site by *PC Magazine.* We think you'll find our site indispensable—with expert tips; independent reviews of hotels, restaurants, and attractions; and an online booking tool. We publish the complete contents of over 135 travel guides in our **Destinations** section and have also added **podcasts, interactive maps,** and hundreds of new images across the site.

be aware that each section must ring up its receipt *separately*—so don't be alarmed when a clerk walks off with your card to process the transaction.

Never leave your cards with others for safekeeping (such as during a trek). If you don't want to carry them, put them in a hotel safe. There have been numerous reports of charges made while cards were left at guesthouses, or small shops running extra slips against a card. For tips and telephone numbers to call if your wallet is stolen or lost, go to "Lost & Found" in the "Fast Facts" section of this chapter.

7 Travel Insurance

Check your existing insurance policies and credit card coverage before you buy travel insurance. You may already be covered for lost luggage, cancelled tickets, or medical expenses.

The cost of travel insurance varies widely, depending on the cost and length of your trip, your age and health, and the type of trip you're taking; but expect to pay between 5% and 8% of the vacation itself. You can get estimates from various providers through **InsureMyTrip.com**. Enter your trip cost and dates, your age, and other information for prices from more than a dozen companies.

TRIP-CANCELLATION INSURANCE
Trip-cancellation insurance will help retrieve your money if you have to back out of a trip or depart early, or if your travel supplier goes bankrupt. Permissible reasons for trip cancellation can range from sickness to natural disasters to the State Department declaring a destination unsafe for travel. (Insurers usually won't cover vague fears, though, as many travelers discovered when they tried to cancel their trips in October 2001.) In this unstable world, trip-cancellation insurance is a good buy if you're purchasing tickets well in advance—who knows what the state of the world, or of your airline, will be in 9 months? Insurance policy details vary, so read the fine print and make sure that your airline or cruise line is on the list of carriers covered in case of bankruptcy. A good resource is **Travel Guard Alerts,** a list of companies considered high-risk by Travel Guard International (see website below). Protect yourself further by paying for the insurance with a credit card—by law, consumers can get their money back on goods and services not received if they report the loss within 60 days after the charge is listed on their credit card statement.

Note: Many tour operators, particularly those offering trips to remote or high-risk areas, include insurance in the total trip cost or can arrange insurance policies through a partnering provider, which is a convenient and often cost-effective way for the traveler to obtain insurance. Make sure the tour company is a reputable one, however, and be aware that some experts suggest you avoid buying insurance from the tour or cruise company you're traveling with. They contend it is more secure to buy from a "third party" than to put all your money in one place.

For more information, contact one of the following recommended insurers: **Access America** (© 866/807-3982; www.accessamerica.com); **Travel Guard International** (© 800/826-4919; www.travelguard.com); **Travel Insured International** (© 800/243-3174; www.travelinsured.com); and **Travelex Insurance Services** (© 888/457-4602; www.travelexinsurance.com).

MEDICAL INSURANCE For travel overseas, most health plans (including Medicare and Medicaid) do not provide coverage, and the ones that do often require you to pay for services upfront and reimburse you only after you return home. As a safety net, you may want to buy travel medical insurance, particularly if you're traveling to a remote or high-risk area where emergency evacuation is a possible scenario. If you require additional medical insurance, try **MEDEX Assistance** (© **410/453-6300;** www.medexassist.com) or **Travel Assistance International** (© **800/821-2828;** www.travelassistance.com—for general information on services, call the company's Worldwide Assistance Services, Inc., at © **800/777-8710**). For a budget option, get affordable travel insurance from **Student Travel Agency (STA; © 800/781-4040** in North America; www.sta.com or www.statravel.com). It's not just for students.

LOST-LUGGAGE INSURANCE On international flights (including U.S. portions of international trips), baggage coverage is limited to approximately $9.07 per pound, up to approximately $635 per checked bag. If you plan to check items more valuable than what's covered by the standard liability, see if your homeowner's policy covers your valuables or get baggage insurance as part of your comprehensive travel-insurance package. Some online budget-airlines will offer a low-cost travel insurance option, but don't expect it to cover much. Nowadays, with so many airlines restricting cabin luggage weight, it's best to travel with *only your most essential valuables;* besides, many items lost on board aren't covered by airline policies.

If your luggage is lost, immediately file a lost-luggage claim at the airport, detailing the luggage brand and contents. Most airlines require that you report delayed, damaged, or lost baggage within 4 hours of arrival. Scheduled airlines are expected to return found luggage directly to your hotel or destination, free of charge, but do not expect this service from budget airlines.

8 Health

STAYING HEALTHY

Thailand, like all Third World countries, poses a small risk to travelers. The same precautions for visiting tropical climes apply to the more remote areas of the Thai kingdom. Many health risks such as malaria, dengue fever, or SARS are seasonal. Ask healthcare professionals to supply you with the *latest* information about health risks specific to the region.

It is recommended that travelers have current immunizations for Hepatitis A, polio, and Tetanus. Rubella is normally given to youths to protect against the increasingly widespread TB virus; check that you are protected. Wounds heal slowly in heat and humidity, so watch out for infections; wash cuts promptly with iodine or saline solution, and keep them dry.

If you suffer from a chronic illness, consult your doctor before your departure. Anyone with epilepsy, diabetes, heart problems, or allergies should consider wearing a **Medic Alert Identification Tag** (© **800/825-3785;** www.medicalert.org), which will immediately alert doctors to your condition and give them access to your records through Medic Alert's 24-hour hotline.

Pack **prescription medications** in your carry-on luggage (bearing in mind if these are liquid, they need to be declared to airport security under new carry-on laws) and carry prescription medications in their original containers, with pharmacy labels. Also bring along copies of your prescriptions in case you lose your pills or run out. Don't forget an extra pair of contact lenses or prescription glasses. Carry the generic name of prescription medicines, in case a local pharmacist is unfamiliar with the brand name.

GENERAL AVAILABILITY OF HEALTHCARE

Dispensaries and hospital facilities in Thailand, especially in urban centers, are generally good. In Phuket, hospitals are able to deal with holidaymakers, especially victims of the islands' many car and motorbike crashes. Smaller towns will usually have a basic clinic, but Bangkok is always the best bet. (See "Fast Facts" in individual destination chapters for info.)

Contact the **International Association for Medical Assistance to Travelers** (IAMAT; © **716/754-4883** or, in Canada, 416/652-0137; www.iamat.org) for tips on travel and health concerns in the countries you are visiting and for lists of English-speaking doctors. The United States **Centers for Disease Control and Prevention** (© **800/311-3435;** www. cdc.gov) provides up-to-date information on health hazards by region or country and offers tips on food safety. The website **www.tripprep.com**, sponsored by a consortium of travel medicine practitioners, may also offer helpful advice on traveling abroad. You can find listings of reliable clinics overseas at the **International Society of Travel Medicine** (www.istm.org).

COMMON AILMENTS

STOMACH TROUBLE Often the change in climate and diet will provoke **diarrhea** in travelers to Thailand. Upset stomachs are best avoided by sticking to bottled water at all times (Thai homes and hotels often don't have potable water), and drinking lots of it. Also be sure canned or bottled drinks are unopened, and wash your hands regularly, especially before eating.

It's useful to keep good anti-diarrhea medicine such as Imodium handy in your travel bag, plus a fruit-flavored electrolyte powder such as Dechamp to mix with water to prevent dehydration. *Note:* A roll of toilet paper or packet of tissues is mandatory, too; Thai toilets do not usually provide this. Pharmacies here such as Boots or Watson's have a wide range of Western brand drugs including Imodium. 7-Eleven stores sell single toilet rolls, ready-to-go electrolyte drinks such as Gatorade, as well as the familiar items and brands like aspirin, Tylenol, and Eno antacids.

While restaurant hygiene throughout the country is fairly good, be wary of street food and check ingredients for freshness and cleanliness. Watch that the cooks prepare food before you, and never eat anything that looks like it has been sitting around, including "fresh" fruit sitting on melting ice. Avoid *anything* raw from vendors. If you develop a condition that includes cramps and lasts more than 24 hours, find a doctor for possible antibiotic treatment.

TROPICAL ILLNESSES   Hepatitis A can be avoided using the same precautions as for diarrhea. Most Asians are immune through exposure, but people from the West are very susceptible. Consider starting a course of vaccines at least 3 months before your trip.

Major tourist areas such as Bangkok, Phuket, Koh Samui, and Chiang Mai are generally **malaria free.** However, malaria is still a problem in rural parts, particularly territories in the mountains to the north and near borders with Cambodia,

Koh Samet, and Koh Chang. When you're traveling to remote areas, start taking a malarial prophylaxis well in advance (most dosages start 4 weeks before travel) such as **Malarone** (a combo of Atovaquone and Proguanil) or **Doxycycline**—but see a travel med specialist to confer and have him or her advise you on the potentially harmful **side effects.** Note that **Mefloquine** (sold under the name Larium) is no longer recommended for Thailand.

The best way to prevent malarial transmission or catching any other diseases listed here is to cover up with light-colored clothing, and wear long pants and sleeves after dark. Sleep with **Permethrin**-treated mosquito netting well tucked in and use repellents. And make sure your repellent contains a high percentage of DEET. If you develop a fever within 2 weeks of entering a high-risk area, be sure to consult a physician.

Dengue fever is now a major problem throughout Southeast Asia. Recent years have seen epidemics in the region. Similar to malaria, the virus is spread by a mosquito, but this one can bite during the day as well as at night. Symptoms are similar to flu, with high fever, severe aches, fatigue, and possible skin rashes or headaches, lasting about a week. Drink plenty of water and seek medical attention immediately if you experience these symptoms.

Japanese Encephalitis is a deadly viral infection that attacks the brain and is spread by a mosquito bite. Outbreaks have been known to occur in the region, so stay abreast of the most up-to-date CDC information. Like malaria and dengue, the best protection is to avoid being bitten, but seek medical attention if you develop symptoms like fever, severe aches, and skin rashes.

BUGS & OTHER WILDLIFE CONCERNS   On jungle hikes in particular, wear long sleeves and trousers instead of shorts, which will protect not just against

mosquito bites, but the ubiquitous ticks, leeches, nasty biting giant centipedes, and (rarely seen) snakes. In order to survive the heat and humidity, arm yourself with loose cotton pants, socks, and sturdy boots—natural fibers are perfect for this terrain. Always try to minimize the chance of getting cuts and scrapes (they can get infected 10 times faster than back home). When venturing into thick jungle terrain, do so with a qualified guide and follow his or her example. Don't pick or touch plants unless the guide says it's safe.

Rabies is a concern in Thailand, as are bites from any stray animals—infected or not. Temples house many mangy dogs because Buddhists believe their duty is to feed them. Most dogs are members of a pack and can get aggressive toward strangers of any kind. Occasionally, a **rabid** animal makes its way into the mix. Stay clear of all stray animals and seek medical attention immediately if you've been bitten. If you find yourself cornered, look for a stick to keep these mutts at bay. Bangkok has a rabies and snakebite help desk at © 02256-4214.

Avoid **freshwater streams** or **lagoons,** as they can be contaminated by chemicals or parasites. Sadly, lack of environmental regulations means sewage outlet pipes often pour into the sea or freshwater streams. **Coral reefs** pose minor risks from things like poisonous sea snakes, jellyfish, and sea urchins. Jellyfish burns can be alleviated simply by applying vinegar. In the case of any cuts or stings, try to clean with bottled water and apply an antimicrobial ointment or antihistamine if you have an allergic response. If you catch an ear infection, ear drops are sold in pharmacies, or mild boric acid or vinegar solutions can help.

RESPIRATORY ILLNESS   The air in Bangkok at certain times of the year can be smog-laden and is especially bad on sidewalks, next to busy roads, or under the BTS. Anyone with respiratory issues such as asthma should carry both regular and emergency inhalers, though brands such as **Seretide, Bricanyl,** and **Ventolin** are available without prescription. **SARS** has been a problem here in the past, but more importantly, **avian influenza,** or bird flu, is a growing problem here and globally. The risk is greater in rural Thailand, where poultry is left to roam freely and in live markets—which is most risky. To prevent getting the illness, avoid all contact with feces and never handle a bird of any species, dead or alive.

COPING WITH THE HEAT The symptoms for **sunstroke** or **heat exhaustion** are unbearable headaches, nausea, vomiting, dizziness, and extreme fatigue. Avoid it by drinking mineral (*not* purified) water, electrolyte drinks, or soda water regularly, *but in small amounts,* to replace minerals and increase hydration. An aspirin or Tylenol can help lower body temperatures. Expose yourself gradually to the heat; wearing a high SPF sunscreen and wearing a hat will prevent **sunburn** but not heatstroke. Low alcohol consumption, light meals, and eating food with minimal spiciness will help you to acclimatize much faster.

Use talcum powder after showering to avoid incapacitating **heat rash,** and only use clean, dry towels to avoid pervasive fungal growths like **tinea** or **candida.** Fast acting anti-fungal powders, creams, or suppositories such as **Canesten** (for tinea) and **Diflucan** (for yeast infections) are available in pharmacies without a prescription.

WHAT TO DO IF YOU GET SICK IN THAILAND

Medical services in Thailand are good in cities, and high street dispensaries— though unregulated—sell most drugs, even those normally available only on prescription overseas. The pharmacist may have an almanac on the counter in English where you can check the different brand names of generic pharmaceutical products in your country, but always seek professional advice.

In most cases, your existing health plan should provide the coverage you need. But double-check; you may want to buy **travel medical insurance** instead. (See the section on insurance, earlier.) Bring your insurance ID card (for hospital visits only) with you when you travel.

If you don't feel well, consider asking any hotel concierge to recommend a local doctor or clinic. Typically doctors see patients on a first-come, first-served basis unless there is an emergency. You may have to fill in a form telling of allergies or existing conditions before you see a physician. In only very grave cases will you be sent to the emergency room.

I list **emergency numbers** under "Fast Facts," p. 84.

You'll need to get a taxi to the hospital (*rohng pha yaa baan* in Thai), since Thailand does not normally offer ambulance services. In an emergency, some embassies or consulates can offer basic advice.

9 Safety

Though many here follow pacifist Buddhist teachings, violent crime does exist and is especially common after drinking. Travelers can follow some basic precautions to stay safe, though.

Since pickpockets and scam artists work the tourist areas and pounce on friendly or naïve travelers, keep an eye on valuables in crowded places and be wary of anyone who approaches you in the street to solicit your friendship. However genuine the entreaty sounds, you will end up wasting precious time on "shopping tours" where your "guide" will collect a commission and keep you from getting where you'd like to go (or worse).

In general, even in big cities, single men and women are fairly safe as long as

Sex for Sale

Prostitution in Thailand is illegal and yet every day you will see foreigners picking up Thai hookers of both sexes. Selling sex is not so much tolerated, but politely ignored. However, some travelers regard it as a tourist draw, especially when underage boys or girls are involved. These days the international police are hard on their tail; high-profile arrests are now not just common, but actively sought.

It is hard to get exact numbers for Commercial Sex Workers (CSW) in Thailand; the number fluctuates from 80,000 to 800,000, depending on the source. Due to the huge numbers involved and the dangers therein, Thailand has made significant steps to counter the spread of HIV/AIDS. Through education and the introduction of condoms, it has made efforts to stem the tide of new cases (though statistics are unreliable). A leading force in this effort is the Population & Community Development Association (PCDA), led by the courageous and innovative public health crusader, Senator Meechai Viravaidya.

The PCDA has enlarged the scope of its rural development programs from family planning and networks of distributing condoms to running seminars for CSW. In poor, uneducated, rural families, where sons provide farm labor, the sex trade has become an income-earning occupation for parents who sell their daughters to urban criminal gangs, often saying they will "go to a good job." They don't. They end up as sex slaves. Under international statutes, many are still minors; having sexual relations with them is equivalent to rape. It is a sorely misplaced myth to believe that CSW live a good

they stick to walking in brightly lit areas where there is plenty of life. Avoid public conflict, and you'll also do just fine. Making a Thai look weak or ridiculous means losing face, and that can mean very serious trouble; there were cases in 2007 of retribution meted by a gang of thugs, or the whole village. If, for whatever reason, you find tempers fraying, walk away. The tourist police hotline, © 1155, may not bring much joy if the police are friendly with your adversaries. Know you cannot win in any altercation: Every year a handful of gung-ho tourists injure themselves trying.

Thai police are some of the lowest-paid civil servants in the country, so it's not surprising that they have a reputation for harassment, intimidation, and bribery.

Involving yourself in any way whatsoever (especially amorously) with a Thai cop is dangerous. There are many cases of lovelorn officers gunning down Thai and foreign girls (and/or their new boyfriends) who had previously flirted with their affections.

Driving is another all-too-obvious danger here. Many drivers in the country have bought their licenses and hence there is no attention given to speed limits or wearing seat belts. Driving a rental car here is not for the fainthearted; extreme caution should be taken and defensive driving skills are key. Every year Thai hospitals are full of banged, bruised, and mummy-wrapped travelers recovering from road accidents. For years, Thailand's annual road death statistics have defied life of fun and freedom. Addiction to drugs, alcohol, or physical abuse is commonplace. Rape is even more frequent. Girls contract STDs or fall pregnant, and scores of unwanted children—many with HIV—are dumped on orphanages.

Poor regulations and scheming between gangs and police do nothing to stop this. Though legislation coyly prohibits full nudity in most go-go bars, it just means the illegal backroom deals, kidnappings, rape, and the enslavement of children carry on behind closed doors, funded by the profits paid by the brothels' ignorant clientele.

If you choose to support prostitution, you are not only breaking the law, but you are also supporting the trafficking and abuse of women and men, including minors. You are putting your own life at risk from STDs and perpetuating a trade that ruins lives. It's not all fair play either: Numerous cases are known where tourists have been drugged in their hotel rooms by their sleeping partner. If they are lucky, they awake 2 days later to find all their valuables gone. There are a shocking number of stories about Western travelers found dead after a liaison with a CSW, but rarely will the newspapers report the full details.

Exercise caution in your dealings with any stranger. If, in spite of all these warnings, you decide to use the services of Thailand's CSWs, take proper precautions; carry condoms at all times, and check the person's ID. If you are in any doubt, walk away—it could save your life.

belief, especially on the hilly islands of Phuket, Koh Samui, and Koh Chang, where even *improved* roads tempt drivers to their fates.

If you do get in an accident, keep in mind that Thais don't normally have insurance. If they don't flee the scene, they might try to negotiate a settlement. Local officials may actually hinder the situation, especially if the culpable faction can persuade them you are to blame. If you find yourself in this situation, take photographs of the scene and ask to get a copy of the IDs of those involved.

Since the military coup d'état in September 2006, the political situation in Thailand has become quite unstable and there are rumors of further unrest as supporters of the ousted ex-prime minister

Thaksin rally against the military powers. Most scenes of recent clashes have occurred around Bangkok's Sanam Luang district directly in front of Parliament.

At the time of writing, new elections had taken place on December 23, 2007, and despite a good turn out by former Thaksin supporters, the government will ultimately be obliged to form a coalition, working in tandem with the PPP (the pro-Thaksin party). Check up on new developments before traveling.

If there is a hint of trouble, many shops will close; in extreme cases (like the 2006 coup) local TV stations shut down. Stay off the streets and watch overseas satellite news for the latest developments, but do not be tempted to be part of history by joining the protests. If you remain indoors, it's unlikely you'll be caught up in any violence.

The far southern provinces of Yala, Narathiwat, and Pattani near the Malaysian border have seen increased sectarian violence between Thai Muslims and Thai military police. Thai institutions, schools, banks, and Buddhist temples have been targeted with small-scale bombs. The Thai government has come under international scrutiny for the brutal force used to quell uprisings. Avoid this area, or travel through it with care.

Thailand can offer illicit temptations that may seem harmless to naïve travelers. Yet the Thai government has zero tolerance of drug trafficking and use. Many people who think they are being offered a casual puff on a joint don't realize they are being set up; every year a few will end up never leaving the kingdom, serving a life sentence in a Thai jail cell. Prostitution is also illegal; read on for info on that.

DEALING WITH DISCRIMINATION

There is still a certain amount of institutionalized racism in old Siam and much pride is taken from the fact that no foreign power colonized the kingdom. Thai people are, superficially at least, tolerant,

but not always accepting of Western ways. Foreign men with young Thai girlfriends can be viewed with deep distrust, and even distaste.

Thais follow a codified hierarchy, with wealth and status going hand-in-hand. Therefore, the richer Thai-Chinese who own and operate big businesses top the scale and people from Isan, the impoverished northeast of the kingdom, come way down in the ratings. Associating yourself with any Thai will, very often, put you at their level.

Caucasians are sometimes branded *farang* (a word that originally meant French, referring to the nation's earliest Western visitors). *Farang* is not necessarily a racist term, but yes, foreign tourists are ritually overcharged and some take this personally as a form of discrimination. Look at this from a Thai, not Western, perspective. Thais believe if you have more, you are expected to give more; the rule applies to Thais as well, regardless of your budget. As a *farang* you are *automatically* seen as wealthy in Thailand. Skills in bargaining will come in time, if you practice. Just remember that Thais really appreciate generosity, rather than someone who makes a big deal about haggling over a baht or two.

10 Specialized Travel Resources

TRAVELERS WITH DISABILITIES

Disabilities shouldn't stop anyone from traveling, but sadly Thailand does not make it easy on the severely physically challenged. Visitors to Thailand will find that, short of the better hotels in the larger towns, amenities for travelers with disabilities are nonexistent, even in public places.

Things are slowly improving, however. Many travel agencies offer customized tours and itineraries for travelers with disabilities. **Flying Wheels Travel** (℃ 507/451-5005;** www.flyingwheelstravel.com)

offers escorted tours and cruises that emphasize sports and private tours in minivans with lifts. **Access-Able Travel Source** (℃ 303/232-2979; www.accessable.com) offers extensive access information and advice for traveling around the world with disabilities. **Accessible Journeys** (℃ 800/846-4537 or 610/521-0339; www.disabilitytravel.com) caters specifically to slow walkers and wheelchair travelers and their families and friends.

Avis Rent a Car has an "Avis Access" program that offers such services as a dedicated 24-hour toll-free number (© 888/879-4273) for customers with special travel needs; special car features such as swivel seats, spinner knobs, and hand controls; and accessible bus service.

Organizations that offer assistance to travelers with disabilities include **Moss-Rehab** (www.mossresourcenet.org), which provides a library of accessible-travel resources online; the **American Foundation for the Blind** (AFB; © 800/232-5463; www.afb.org), a referral resource for the blind or visually impaired that includes information on traveling with Seeing Eye dogs; and SATH (**Society for Accessible Travel & Hospitality;** © 212/447-7284; www.sath.org; annual membership fees: $45 adults, $30 seniors and students), which offers a wealth of travel resources for all types of disabilities and informed recommendations on destinations, access guides, travel agents, tour operators, vehicle rentals, and companion services. **AirAmbulanceCard.com** is now partnered with SATH and allows you to pre-select top-notch hospitals in case of an emergency for $195 a year ($295 per family), among other benefits.

For more information specifically targeted to travelers with disabilities, the community website **iCan** (www.icanonline.net/channels/travel) has destination guides and several regular columns on accessible travel. Also check out the quarterly magazine *Emerging Horizons* (www.emerginghorizons.com; $15 per year, $20 outside the U.S.); and *Open World* magazine, published by SATH (see above; subscription: $13 per year, $21 outside the U.S.).

GAY & LESBIAN TRAVELERS

Thailand is famous for its seemingly gay-friendly attitudes, but homophobia certainly does exist. Lesbians are known as *tom dee;* they have their own hangouts and are usually less vocal and ostentatious than their male counterparts, or the theatrically inclined lady-boys *(katoeys).*

There are occasional Gay Pride–style events, as well as dazzling cabaret shows and beauty competitions for lady-boys, throughout the country. The same kind of nightlife that caters to heterosexual males is offered in Bangkok, Pattaya, and Phuket's Patong Beach. Venues range from gay bars and dance clubs, men-only saunas (bathhouses), and "pay at the door" parties. In Bangkok, the most popular male-only joint is the opulent Babylon men's club, off Sathorn Road.

The International Gay and Lesbian Travel Association (IGLTA; © 800/448-8550 or 954/776-2626; www.iglta.org) is the trade association for the gay and lesbian travel industry, and offers an online directory of gay- and lesbian-friendly travel businesses; go to their website and click on "Members"—many agencies offer tours and travel itineraries specifically for gay and lesbian travelers. **Above and Beyond Tours** (© 800/397-2681; www.abovebeyondtours.com) is the exclusive gay and lesbian tour operator for United Airlines. **Now, Voyager** (© 800/255-6951; www.nowvoyager.com) is a well-known San Francisco–based, gay-owned and -operated travel service with tours to Thailand.

Gay.com Travel (© 800/929-2268, or 415/644-8044; www.gay.com/travel or www.outandabout.com) is an excellent online successor to the popular *Out & About* print magazine. It provides regularly updated information about gay-owned, gay-oriented, and gay-friendly lodging, dining, sightseeing, nightlife, and shopping establishments in every important destination worldwide. It also offers trip-planning information for gay and lesbian travelers for more than 50 destinations along various themes, ranging from Sex & Travel to Vacations for Couples.

The following travel guides are available at many bookstores, or you can order them from any online bookseller: *Spartacus International Gay Guide* (Bruno

Gmünder Verlag; www.spartacusworld. com/gayguide) and *Odysseus: The International Gay Travel Planner* (Odysseus Enterprises Ltd.), both good annual English-language guidebooks focused on gay men; and the *Damron* guides (www. damron.com), with separate annual books for gay men and lesbians.

Also check **www.utopia-asia.com** for gay-friendly information and plenty of travel tips for Thailand.

SENIOR TRAVEL

Mention the fact that you're a senior citizen when you make your travel reservations; you may be able to secure special discounts on tours and airline reservations. Senior citizens, though highly revered in Thai society, will not, however, receive any special discounts at Thai attractions.

Members of **AARP** (formerly known as the American Association of Retired Persons), 601 E St. NW, Washington, DC 20049 (© **888/687-2277;** www.aarp. org), get discounts on hotels, airfares, and car rentals. AARP offers members a wide range of benefits, including *AARP: The Magazine* and a monthly newsletter. Anyone over 50 can join.

Many reliable agencies and organizations target the 50-plus market. **Elderhostel** (© **877/426-8056;** www.elder hostel.org) arranges study programs for those aged 55 and over (and a spouse or companion of any age) in the U.S. and in more than 80 countries around the world. **ElderTreks** (© **800/741-7956;** www.eldertreks.com) offers small-group tours to off-the-beaten-path or adventure-travel locations, restricted to travelers age 50 and older. **INTRAV** (© **800/ 456-8100;** www.intrav.com) is a high-end tour operator that caters to the mature, discerning traveler (not specifically seniors), with trips around the world that include guided safaris, polar expeditions, private-jet adventures, and small-boat cruises down jungle rivers.

Recommended publications offering travel resources and discounts for seniors include the quarterly magazine *Travel 50 & Beyond* (www.travel50andbeyond. com); *Travel Unlimited: Uncommon Adventures for the Mature Traveler* (Avalon); *101 Tips for Mature Travelers,* available from Grand Circle Travel (© **800/221-2610** or 617/350-7500; www.gct.com); and *Unbelievably Good Deals and Great Adventures That You Absolutely Can't Get Unless You're Over 50* (McGraw-Hill), by Joann Rattner Heilman.

FAMILY TRAVEL

If you have enough trouble getting your kids out of the house in the morning, dragging them thousands of miles away may seem like an insurmountable challenge. But family travel can be immensely rewarding, giving you new ways of seeing the world through smaller pairs of eyes.

A visit to Thailand will certainly broaden the horizons of young visitors, and families report great experiences in the kingdom. Most of the larger resorts have kid-friendly programs, kids' clubs, connecting rooms, sports equipment rental, and kid-oriented group activities. Many of the larger hotels may offer special deals for families or young children.

Familyhostel (© **800/733-9753;** www. learn.unh.edu/familyhostel) takes the whole family, including kids ages 8 to 15, on moderately priced domestic and international learning vacations. Lectures, field trips, and sightseeing are guided by a team of academics.

Recommended family travel Internet sites include **Family Travel Forum** (www. familytravelforum.com), a comprehensive site that offers customized trip planning; **Family Travel Network** (www.family travelnetwork.com), an award-winning site that offers travel features, deals, and tips; **Traveling Internationally with Your Kids** (www.travelwithyourkids. com), a comprehensive site offering sound advice for long-distance and international travel with children; and **Family Travel Files** (www.thefamilytravelfiles. com), which offers an online magazine and a directory of off-the-beaten-path tours and tour operators for families.

WOMEN TRAVELERS

Women travelers face no particular discrimination or dangers in Thailand. Women should, however, be very careful when dealing with monks: Never touch a monk, never hand anything directly to them (it should be set on the floor in front of the monk or given to a man who will hand it to them directly), and don't sit next to monks on public transport or in the monk-only designated areas in waiting rooms. Some parts of temples do not allow women to enter; look for signs indicating this.

Thais are extremely modest, almost prudish, and though Thai bar girls dress in scanty fashions, that's not recommended if you want respect. Women should avoid tank tops and short-shorts (the equivalent of wearing nightwear outdoors). Going topless on beaches is illegal in many areas and considered a public obscenity. At all temples and mosques, be sure to wear a long skirt or trousers and have your shoulders covered. Your head should be covered in mosques, but headwear (caps, sun visors) must be removed in Buddhist temples.

Thais love asking foreign visitors, "Are you married?" Thais also commonly marry quite young and start families early, so many assume unmarried travelers to be sad or lonely. Don't take it personally. Say you are married with children, and the questioning should stop.

Check out **Journeywoman** (www. journeywoman.com), an award-winning, "real-life" women's travel-information network where you can sign up for a free e-mail newsletter and get advice on everything from etiquette and dress to safety; or the travel guide *Safety and Security for Women Who Travel* by Sheila Swan and Peter Laufer (Travelers' Tales, Inc.), offering common-sense tips on safe travel.

STUDENT TRAVEL

Discounts for students in Thailand and the rest of Southeast Asia are better earned by the tenacity of the individual traveler's bargaining skills and tolerance for substandard accommodation rather than flashing a student ID—though showing one does help when buying mass transit tickets in Bangkok. The **International Student Identity Card (ISIC),** however, offers substantial savings on plane tickets and some entrance fees. It also provides you with basic health and life insurance and a 24-hour help line. The card is available for $22 (£12) from **STA Travel** (© **800/781-4040** in North America; www.sta.com or www.statravel. com), the biggest student travel agency in the world.

If you're no longer a student but are still under 26, you can get an **International Youth Travel Card (IYTC)** for the same price from the same people, entitling you to some discounts (but not on museum admissions). (*Note:* In 2002, STA Travel bought competitors **Council Travel** and **USIT Campus** after they went bankrupt. They are still operating some offices under the Council name, but they are owned by STA.) **Travel CUTS** (© **800/667-2887** or 416/614-2887; www.travelcuts.com) offers similar services for both Canadians and U.S. residents. Irish students may prefer to turn to **USIT** (© **01/602-1600;** www. usitnow.ie), an Ireland-based specialist in student, youth, and independent travel.

SINGLE TRAVELERS

Many people prefer traveling alone, but in Thailand this is seen as rather strange and anti-social. Solo journeys offer infinite opportunities to make friends and meet locals. If you are a female of any age, be very careful that you do not give the wrong message to Thai men. Wearing clothes that Thais would deem immodest (short skirts, low-cut T-shirts exposing cleavage, or bra tops) is regarded as a come-on.

Some hotels offer single rates; if, however, you like resorts, tours, or cruises, you're likely to get hit with paying a per-room rate regardless. Single travelers can avoid these supplements, of course, by agreeing to room with other single travelers on the trip. An even better idea is to find a compatible roommate before you go from one of the many roommate locator agencies.

Many reputable tour companies offer singles-only trips. **Backroads** (© **800/462-2848;** www.backroads.com) offers more than 160 active-travel trips to 30 destinations worldwide.

For more information, check out Eleanor Berman's latest edition of *Traveling Solo: Advice and Ideas for More Than 250 Great Vacations* (Globe Pequot), a guide with advice on traveling alone, either solo or as part of a group tour. It has been updated for 2008.

11 Sustainable Tourism/Ecotourism

Each time you take a flight or drive a car CO_2 is released into the atmosphere. You can help neutralize this danger to our planet through "carbon offsetting"—paying someone to reduce your CO_2 emissions by the same amount you've added. Carbon offsets can be purchased in the U.S. from companies such as **Carbonfund.org** (www.carbonfund.org) and **TerraPass** (www.terrapass.org), and from **Climate Care** (www.climatecare.org) in the U.K.

Although one could argue that any vacation that includes an airplane flight can't be truly "green," you can go on holiday and still contribute positively to the environment. You can offset carbon emissions from your flight in other ways. Choose forward-looking companies that embrace responsible development practices, helping preserve destinations for the future by working alongside local people. An increasing number of sustainable tourism initiatives can help you plan a family trip and leave as small a "footprint" as possible on the places you visit.

Responsible Travel (www.responsible travel.com) contains a great source of sustainable travel ideas run by a spokesperson for responsible tourism in the travel industry. **Sustainable Travel International** (www.sustainabletravelinternational.org) promotes responsible tourism practices and issues an annual Green Gear & Gift Guide.

You can find ecofriendly travel tips, statistics, and touring companies and associations—listed by destination under "Travel Choice"—at the TIES website, **www.ecotourism.org**. Also check out **Ecotravel.com,** which is part online magazine and part ecodirectory that lets you search for touring companies in several categories (water-based, land-based, spiritually oriented, and so on).

In the U.K., **Tourism Concern** (www.tourismconcern.org.uk) works to reduce social and environmental problems connected to tourism and find ways of improving tourism so that local benefits are increased. The **Association of Independent Tour Operators** (AITO; www.aito.co.uk) is a group of interesting specialist operators leading the field in making holidays sustainable.

Thailand, being an extremely poor nation, is way behind the rest of the world in general eco-awareness. That said, Thai authorities are finally taking tiny steps to preserve the nature and wildlife of its many different ecological zones, from swamp jungles in the south, to mountain forests in the north, to the many marine parks in the Gulf of Thailand and the

> **Tips** **It's Easy Being Green**
>
> We can all help conserve fuel and energy when we travel. Here are a few simple ways you can help preserve your favorite destinations:
>
> - Whenever possible, choose nonstop flights; they generally require less fuel than those that must stop and take-off again.
> - If renting a car is necessary on your vacation, ask the rental agent for the most fuel-efficient one available. Not only will you use less gas, you'll also save money at the tank.
> - At hotels, request that your sheets and towels not be changed daily. You'll save water and energy by not washing them as often, and you'll prolong the life of the towels, too. (Many hotels already have programs like this in place.)
> - Turn off the lights and air-conditioner (or heater) when you leave your hotel room.

Andaman Sea. In more than 80 national parks, visitors are told about not only the local wildlife species in residence, but also the delicate balance of each habitat. Some parks have clearly displayed interpretation facilities at their visitor centers, as well as trails with bridges and catwalks, and markers explaining the important elements of the environment and its inhabitants. Others provide rudimentary bungalow accommodations or tents and supplies for campers. For more complete information, get in touch with the **Royal Forestry Department** at ℰ **02561-4292** or visit the useful English website www.forest.go.th.

Hotel groups, such as the Banyan Tree resorts in Bangkok and Phuket, have also made huge efforts over the last decade to implement sustainable projects including a pledge to reduce their carbon footprint and cut water usage in all their resorts by 10% in 2008.

12 Staying Connected

TELEPHONE TIPS

Major hotels in Thailand feature convenient but pricey international direct-dial (IDD), long-distance service, and fax services. Hotels charge a hefty surcharge on local and long-distance calls, though, which can add up to 50% in some cases. 800 numbers, credit card numbers, or collect calls may not be readily available from your hotel phone; or if they're are, a big fat service fee may be added to your bill. Check first.

Most major post offices have special offices or booths for **overseas calls,** as well as **fax** and **telex service;** they're usually open Monday to Friday 7am to 11pm. There are also **overseas telegraph and telephone offices** (also called OCO or overseas call office) open daily 24 hours throughout the country for long-distance international calls and telex and fax service. In addition, many Internet cafes, guesthouses, and travel agents offer long-distance calls using very affordable net-to-phone connections of varying quality.

Local calls can be made from any red or blue public pay telephone. Local calls cost 1B (3¢/5p) for 3 minutes; add more coins when the beeps sound. Blue public phones are for local and long-distance calls within Thailand.

Yellow TOT cards are sold in denominations of 300B and 500B (US$9–US$14/£5–£8) and are specific for domestic or international phones that are clearly marked as such. **Hatari PhoneNet** offers a variety of phone cards that are a great value and are available at convenience stores everywhere. All cards can also be purchased at **Telephone Organization of Thailand** (TOT) offices

To call Thailand: If you're calling Thailand from the United States:

1. Dial the international access code: 011.
2. Dial the country code: 66.
3. Dial the number. So the whole number you'd dial for Bangkok would be 011-66-2-000-0000.

Important Note: When making domestic calls to Thailand, be sure to omit the "0" that appears before all phone numbers in this guide (thus you will only dial eight digits after the "66" country code).

To make international calls: To make international calls from Thailand, first dial 00 and then the country code (U.S. or Canada 1, U.K. 44, Ireland 353, Australia 61, New Zealand 64). Next you dial the area code and number. For example, if you wanted to call the British Embassy in Washington, D.C., you would dial 00-1-202-588-7800.

For directory assistance: Dial ✆ 1133 or dial any hotel concierge or operator (even if you are not a guest, they can help).

Note: In smaller towns throughout this guide, I've left out phone numbers for bars/clubs that don't have permanent phone lines.

CELLPHONES

The three letters that define much of the world's **wireless capabilities** are GSM (Global System for Mobiles), a big, seamless network that makes for easy cross-border cellphone use throughout Europe and dozens of other countries worldwide. In the U.S., T-Mobile, AT&T Wireless, and Cingular use this quasi-universal system; in Canada, Microcell and some

Rogers customers are GSM compatible, and all Europeans and most Australians use GSM.

If your cellphone is on a GSM system and you have a world-capable, multiband phone, such as many Sony-Ericsson, Motorola, or Samsung models, you can make and receive calls across most First World nations and many developing countries, from Andorra to Uganda. Just call your wireless operator and ask for "international roaming" to be activated on your account. Unfortunately, per-minute charges can be high—usually $1 to $1.50 in Western Europe and up to $5 in places such as Russia and Indonesia.

That's why it is important to buy an "unlocked" world phone from the get-go. Many cellphone operators sell "locked" phones that restrict them from using any other removable computer memory phone chip (called a **SIM card**) than the ones available locally. Having an unlocked phone allows you to install a local, pre-paid SIM card (sold at Telewiz, True, or DTAC stores in Thailand). Show your phone to the salesperson; not all phones work on all networks. You'll get a local phone number—and much, much lower calling rates. Unlocking an already locked phone can be complicated, but it can be done; just call your cellular operator and say you'll be going abroad for several months and want to use the phone with a local provider. In Thailand, head to **Mah Boon Krong** (MBK; ✆ 02217-9111), near the National Stadium BTS in central Bangkok, for assistance with unlocking cellphones at any cellphone vendor.

For trips of more than a few weeks spent in one country, buying a local **SIM card** becomes economically attractive, as Thailand has a number of cheap, pre-paid phone systems such as **1-2-Call** by AIS. For less than 800B (US$23/£12), you will be given a Starter Pack, which includes a SIM card and virtually instant Thai mobile phone number, plus some free calls. Call costs depend on the package you opt for; some systems offer free off-peak messaging (SMS). With most plans, though, incoming calls are free.

Wilderness adventurers, or those heading to less-developed parts of Thailand, might consider renting a **satellite phone (satphone),** which is different from a cellphone in that it connects to satellites and works where there's no cellular signal or ground-based tower. You can rent satellite phones from **RoadPost** (© **888/290-1606** or 905/272-5665; www.roadpost.com). Satphones are still outrageously expensive to buy, so unless you're a Rockefeller, don't even think about it.

VOICE OVER INTERNET PROTOCOL (VOIP)

If you have Web access while traveling, you might consider a broadband-based telephone service (in technical terms, **Voice over Internet protocol,** or **VoIP**) such as Skype (www.skype.com) or Vonage (www.vonage.com), which allows you to make free international calls if you use their services from your laptop or in a cybercafe. Check the sites for details.

INTERNET ACCESS AWAY FROM HOME

Travelers have any number of ways to check their e-mail and access the Internet on the road in Thailand. These days, the latest appliances like e-mail–capable mobile phones, Wi-Fi–enabled laptops, PDAs (Personal Digital Assistants), or electronic organizers allow travelers to stay in touch almost anywhere. But bear in mind there's a very real risk while traveling in poor countries that any luxury electronic items, including the trendier mobile phone models (unaffordable to poorer Thais), may get stolen. If staying wired isn't a major part of your holiday, it's better to leave the hardware at home and check e-mail at cybercafes.

WITHOUT YOUR OWN COMPUTER

Thailand's Internet cafes stay open late, they're affordable, and you'll pretty much find them everywhere. Bangkok's Sukhumvit, Surawong, or Khao San roads and the country's main beach destinations are all chock-a-bloc with Internet cafes. Many hotels have business centers that also offer Internet access, but they are much pricier. However, hotels do normally offer broadband, which is much faster for downloading big files; work out what's better for you, speed or frequency of access.

Cybercafes charge upwards of around 60B (US$1.71/92p) per hour and most city connections now use high-speed lines (ADSL) and offer cheap overseas Internet calls on systems such as www.skype.com. Outside of the cities, look out for local cybercafes (usually full of schoolkids playing online shoot 'em up games); most offer acceptable, albeit slower, dial-up service.

The departure terminal of Suvarnabhumi International Airport has an **Internet access booth** close to check-in counter W, to the far right side of the departures terminal. Once inside the terminal, state-of-the-art, touch-screen Internet and telephony lecterns are available that use Thai coins and credit cards.

WITH YOUR OWN COMPUTER

More and more hotels, cafes, and retailers in Thailand offer free high-speed Wi-Fi access (or charge a small fee for usage). Most laptops sold today have built-in wireless capability. To find public Wi-Fi hotspots in the country, go to **www.jiwire.com**; its Hotspot Finder holds the world's largest directory of public wireless hotspots. You'll also find wireless services at many **Starbucks** branches—or look out for signs marked with the Thai brand "True" in malls such as Siam Paragon and Central World. Most luxury hotels here do not offer Wi-Fi service free of charge; even

Online Traveler's Toolbox

Veteran travelers usually carry some essential items to make their trips easier. Following is a selection of handy online tools to bookmark and use.

- The official **Thai government** website (www.thaigov.go.th/index-eng. htm) has info in English on current happenings in the kingdom.
- For **transportation information,** try the following sites: **Thai Airways International** (www.thaiair.com), **Bangkok Airways** (www.bangkokair.com), **Nok Air** (www.nokair.com), **SGA** (www.sga.co.th), **One-Two-GO** (www. fly12go.com), and Phuket's new amphibious plane service, **Destination Air** (www.destinationair.com). Out of the Southeast Asian hubs, there's the extensive **Air Asia** (www.airasia.com) and the smaller **Tiger Airways** (www. tigerairways.com); with newcomer **Jetstar** (www.jetstar.com) linking Asian cities with Australia. For train info, contact the **Thai State Railway** at www. srt.or.th. *Note:* The official Suvarnabhumi or Don Meuang Airport websites are not updated regularly and could be misleading to travelers. Cross-check these sites with more reliable international travel sites or blogs.
- **Thai publications** in English are numerous. *Bangkok Post* (www.bangkok post.com) and *The Nation* (www.nationmultimedia.com) are the only English-language dailies. The free *Where Magazine* lists lots of events and happenings, as does *BK Magazine,* which has a younger target audience.
- There are a few **blogs** and info sites in Thailand with (not always updated) tips about life in the Big Mango. Check the likes of **www.bangkokrecorder.com** and **www.angloinfo.com**. New Zealand writer

if you are a guest, you will have to buy a pre-paid access card from around B400 (US$11.40/£6) per hour. Some hotel executive lounges may include this service in the room rate.

For dial-up access, most business-class hotels offer a special plug, or dataport, to fit most laptop modems. **Contact your hotel in advance** to see what your options are.

Major Internet Service Providers (ISPs) have **local access numbers** around the world, allowing you to go online by placing a local call. Check your ISP's website or call its toll-free number to find out more. Thailand has its own popular ISPs, called **SAMART** or **CS Loxinfo,** which use dial-up. You can buy handy pre-paid cards at 7-Elevens.

Wherever you go, bring a suitable travel adapter, phone or digital camera chargers, and a spare Ethernet network cable—or find out whether your hotel supplies them to guests.

13 Packages for the Independent Traveler

Package tours are simply a way to buy the airfare, accommodations, and other elements of your trip (such as car rentals, airport transfers, and sometimes even activities) at the same time and often at discounted prices.

Stickman (**www.stickmanbangkok.com**) posts a useful, but cautionary "warts and all" guide to Thailand, though some info is way out of date.

- To find a **room for rent** for long stays, try www.mrroomfinder.com.
- Find out which seats to reserve and which to avoid (and more) on all major domestic airlines at **www.seatguru.com**. And check out the type of meal (with photos) you'll likely be served on airlines around the world at **www.airlinemeals.net**.
- At **Foreign Languages for Travelers** (**www.travlang.com**), learn basic terms in more than 70 languages; just click on a word to hear what it sounds like.
- **Intellicast** (www.intellicast.com) and **Weather.com** (www.weather.com) give weather forecasts for all states and for cities around the world.
- See what time (and day) it is anywhere in the world at **www.timeand date.com**.
- For **travel warnings**, visit **travel.state.gov**, **www.fco.gov.uk/travel**, **www. voyage.gc.ca**, and **www.dfat.gov.au/consular/advice**. These sites report on places where health concerns or unrest might threaten American, British, Canadian, and Australian travelers.
- See what your dollar or pound is worth in more than 100 other countries via **Universal Currency Converter** (www.xe.com).
- Check **Visa ATM Locator** (www.visa.com) for locations of PLUS ATMs worldwide, or **MasterCard ATM Locator** (www.mastercard.com) for locations of Cirrus ATMs worldwide.

One good source of package deals is the airlines themselves. Most major airlines offer air/land packages, including **American Airlines Vacations** (© 800/321-2121; www.aavacations.com), **Delta Vacations** (© 800/221-6666; www.delta vacations.com), **Continental Airlines Vacations** (© 800/301-3800; www.co vacations.com) and **United Vacations** (© 888/854-3899; www.unitedvacations. com). Several big **online travel agencies**—Expedia, Travelocity, Orbitz, and Lastminute.com—also do a brisk business in packages. If you're unsure about the pedigree of a smaller packager, check with the Better Business Bureau in the city where the company is based, or go online at www.bbb.org. If a packager won't tell you where it's based, don't fly with it.

Travel packages are also listed in the travel section of your local Sunday newspaper. Or check ads in the national travel magazines such as *Arthur Frommer's Budget Travel Magazine, Travel + Leisure, National Geographic Traveler,* and *Condé Nast Traveler.*

> ## Tips   Ask Before You Go
>
> Before you invest in a package deal or an escorted tour:
>
> • Always ask about the **cancellation policy.** Can you get your money back? Is there a deposit required?
> • Ask about the **accommodations choices and prices** for each. Then look up the hotels' reviews in a Frommer's guide and check their rates online for your specific dates of travel. Also find out what types of rooms are offered.
> • Request a complete **schedule.**
> • Ask about the **size** and demographics of the group (escorted tours only).
> • Discuss what is included in the **price** (transportation, meals, tips, airport transfers, and so on).
> • Finally, look for **hidden expenses.** Ask whether airport departure fees and taxes, for example, are included in the total cost—they rarely are.

14 Escorted General-Interest Tours

Escorted tours are structured group tours with a group leader. The price usually includes everything from airfare to hotels, meals, tours, admission costs, and local transportation.

Despite the fact that escorted tours require big deposits and predetermined hotels, restaurants, and itineraries, many people derive security and peace of mind from the structure they offer. Escorted tours—whether they're navigated by bus, motor coach, train, or boat—let travelers sit back and enjoy the trip without having to drive or worry about details. They take you to the maximum number of sights in the minimum amount of time with the least amount of hassle. They're particularly convenient for people with limited mobility and they can be a great way to make new friends.

On the downside, you'll have little opportunity for serendipitous interactions with locals. The tours can be jam-packed with activities, leaving little room for individual sightseeing, whim, or adventure—plus they often focus on the heavily touristed sites, so you miss out on many a lesser-known gem.

Here are some of the best operators for Thailand:

• **Absolute Asia** Founded in 1989, Absolute Asia offers an array of innovative itineraries, specializing in individual or small group tours customized to your interests, with experienced local guides and excellent accommodations. Talk to them about tours that feature art, cuisine, religion, antiques, photography, wildlife study, archaeology, and soft adventure—they can plan a specialized trip to see just about anything you can dream up for any length of time. 180 Varick St., 16th Floor, New York, NY 10014; ℂ **800/736-818;** fax 212/627-4090; www.absoluteasia. com.

• **Asia Transpacific Journeys** Coordinating tours to every corner of South and Southeast Asia and the Pacific, Asia Transpacific Journeys deals with small groups and custom programs that include luxury hotel accommodations. They have specific tours for Thailand and their flagship package, the 23-day Passage to Indochina tour, takes you through all of the countries in Indochina. Asia Transpacific tours are fun, promote cultural understanding and sustainable tourism, and are highly recommended. 2995 Center Green Court, Boulder, CO 80301; ℂ **800/642-2742** or 303/443-6789; fax 303/443-7078; www.southeastasia. com or www.asiatranspacific.com.

- **Diethelm** The folks at this Swiss-based tour company, with offices throughout the region (and a popular choice for European tour groups), are friendly and helpful. Diethelm has full tour programs and can provide details for travelers in-country, arrange car rental or vans for small groups, and offer discount options to all destinations. Kian Gwan Building II, 140/1 Wireless Rd., Bangkok 10330,

Thailand; ℂ **02660-7000;** fax 02660-7020; www.diethelmtravel.com.

- **Intrepid** This popular Australian operator is probably the best choice to get off the beaten path on a tour of Asia. Intrepid caters tours for the culturally discerning, those with humanitarian goals, and adventure travelers on a budget looking for a group-oriented tour of off-the-map locations. Their motto lives up to their name, and with some of the best guides in Asia, these folks will take you to the back of beyond safely, and in style. Box 2781, Fitzroy, DC VIC 3065, 12 Spring St., Fitzroy, Victoria, Australia; ℂ **613/9473-2626,** 877/488-1616 in the U.S., fax 613/9419-4426; www. intrepidtravel.com.

15 Special Interest Trips

ADVENTURE & WELLNESS TRAVEL

While for some, the ideal holiday is days spent rolling around on a beach sipping juicy cocktails, others want to push themselves to the limit, seeking thrills and adventure. Fortunately, Thailand's well-developed tourism industry offers lots of upcountry options for the more intrepid traveler. Routes have opened up nature's wild side to those who would dare, and many operators have jockeyed into place, providing adventure-travel options that are well planned and safe for everyone, from beginners to experts. The following section will give you an overview of the many options, but for planning details refer to the specific destination chapters throughout this book.

The first thing many people consider for an active vacation is **scuba diving** or **snorkeling.** Living coral reefs grace the waters of the Andaman Sea, off Thailand's southwest coast and the Gulf of Thailand. More than 80 species of coral

have been discovered in the Gulf, while the deeper and more saline Andaman has more than 210. Marine life includes hundreds of species of fish, plus numerous varieties of crustaceans and sea turtles. With the aid of scuba gear, divers can get an up-close-and-personal view of this undersea universe. For those without certification, many reefs close to the surface are still vibrant.

From Phuket (see chapter 9), you can take a day trip that includes two or three dives. **Long-term scuba trips** on live-aboard boats run seasonally; Fantasea's Ocean-Rover has just inaugurated the region's first golf-dive trips. For more information on diving, see chapter 8, "Southern Peninsula: The East Coast & Islands," and chapter 9, "Southern Peninsula: The West Coast & Islands," where many operators schedule frequent trips. Always check that an operator has PADI-certified dive masters, and that their boats are carrying the full bevy of certificates of approval issued by **international marine**

safety organizations. Scuba training and certification packages are common and can have you ready to dive in 5 days. Pretty much every beach has independent operators or guesthouses that rent snorkels, masks, and fins for the day. A few boat operators take snorkelers to reefs off neighboring islands—especially from Koh Lanta, Koh Phi Phi, Krabi, Koh Samui, and Pattaya.

Thailand's mountainous jungle terrain in the north has become a haven for **trekkers.** At the same time, human rights organizations have highlighted the damage this does to sustainability in remote villages inhabited by poor hill-tribes—where the places visited have become no more than paying human zoos.

Choose your operator carefully and look out for NGO-led projects where the local people reap real benefits from your visit. Treks can last 3 to 10 nights but usually involve no more than 3 to 4 hours of walking on jungle paths. All tours provide local guides to accompany groups, and the guides will keep the pace steady but comfortable for all trekkers involved. Some trips break up the monotonous walking with treks on elephant-back, in four-wheel-drive jeeps, or light rafting on flat bamboo rafts. Chiang Mai (see chapter 12) has the most trekking firms, while Chiang Rai, Pai, and Mae Hong Son (see chapter 13, "Touring the Northern Hills") also have their share of trekking companies. Recommended trekking operators are **North By Northeast** (© 04251-3572; www.north-by-north-east.com) and **Active Travel** (© 05327-7178; www.active thailand.com).

River rafting in rubber dinghies and kayaks is becoming increasingly popular in Thailand, with operators taking off in places like Pai (see chapter 13). Winding through dense jungles, past rock formations and local villages, these trips include camping and sometimes trekking. Rapids are rarely extreme but are big enough to be loads of fun, and safety measures are taken seriously.

A few lucky folks know that Thailand is home to one of the top 10 climbing walls in the world. **Rock climbing** at Railay Beach in Krabi (see chapter 9) is attracting lovers of the sport, who come to have a go at these challenging cliffs. Views are breathtaking—you'll get to take in truly amazing scenery out into the Andaman and surrounding islands. A few small outfits accept beginners for training or will organize climbs for more specialized experts, providing all the necessary equipment.

If the wild isn't calling you, know that Thailand also has a number of wellness programs, varying from posh beach resorts like the **Chiva-Som** (p. 175) in Hua to low-key centers, such as the chain of colonic centers known as **The Spa** (p. 170). Health programs at these centers may include yoga, tai chi, massage, fasting, and alternative therapies. Some of these centers also offer meditation, but those who'd prefer a deeper immersion can look at some of the short-stay or longer residential courses that teach the Theravada Buddhist tradition of meditation and developing insight, known as Vipassana. The most well promoted residencies are those at **Wat Suan Mokkh** (p. 188) or **Wat Khoa Tham** (p. 213). In the north, there's **Wat Rampoeng** (p. 328). Courses are held in Bangkok at **Wat Mahathat,** or The House of Dhamma (p. 131).

You might also consider a course in Thai massage. It's now easy to find massage schools all over Thailand, but most teach in Thai. However, big-name spa **Chiva-Som** in Hua Hin (p. 175) has set up an academy in Bangkok's Sukhumvit Soi 63 where, unlike most places, a huge range of wellness techniques are at last being taught in English by trained therapists. See **www.chivasomacademy.com** for info.

VOLUNTEER TRAVEL

If you've always wanted to get close to elephants, Thailand is the place for you—you can volunteer or work with elephants at a number of places here. The best are the courses at the **Thai Elephant Conservation Center** at Lampang (© **05422-9042**), where you can train to be an elephant "mahout" and learn how to hop on and steer your very own 2-ton elephant. You'll get to know the language of the elephants (a mix of Thai and Karen words) and you'll also be called upon to feed and wash them. See p. 339 for more info.

Those seriously interested in marine conservation can join the volunteer team at Koh Phra Thong near Phuket, where an Italian-led nonprofit organization called **Naucrates** (www.naucrates.org) has spent almost a decade educating local communities on ecological issues and monitoring the decline of local turtles. They also run a mangrove revitalization scheme.

Also read *Vagabonding* (Villard, 2002), travel writer Rolf Potts's own personal guide to escaping the routine and finding ways to work around the globe. It's an intriguing read for those wanting to break free and discover volunteer and work opportunities during their travels.

16 Getting Around Thailand

Thailand's domestic transport is accessible, efficient, and inexpensive. If your time is short, fly. But if you have the time to take in the countryside, travel by bus, train, or private car. Read on for details about all your transport options.

BY PLANE

Bangkok's newly reopened and now the country's largest domestic airport, **Don Mueang Airport** (airport code DMK), may not be as glitzy as the newer **Suvarnabhumi International Airport** (airport code BKK), but it still works fairly well. Airports in other cities usually tend to be more basic but will have money-changing facilities, information counters, and waiting ground transportation. In very small towns, you'll have to arrange airport pickup either through your hotel or the airline.

Most domestic flights are on **Thai Airways,** part of Thai Airways International, 89 Vibhavadi Rangsit Road, Bangkok 10900 (© **02545-1000;** www.thaiair.com), with Bangkok as its hub. Flights connect Bangkok with 11 domestic destinations, including Chiang Mai, Chiang Rai, Mae Hong Son, Phitsanulok, Krabi, and Phuket. There are also some connecting flights between these cities.

The budget subsidiary of Thai Airways, **Nok Air** (© **1318;** www.nokair.com) has a head office in the Sathorn district. It operates on lesser used routes, as does the no-frills carrier **One-Two-GO** (© **02229-4260;** www.fly12go.com) based at Asoke, in the Klong Toey district. *Note:* A flight from Bangkok to Phuket on One-Two-GO Airlines crashed in September 2007, and investigations into its cause were still ongoing at the time this book went to press.

The rapidly expanding fleet at **Bangkok Airways,** 99 Moo 14, Vibhavadirangsit Rd., Chom Phon, Chatuchak, Bangkok 10900 (© **02265-5678** or -5555 for reservations; www.bangkokair.com), now covers 19 destinations across Asia and is the sole operator of the Phuket to Koh Samui, and Bangkok to Trat routes. It also has international flights from Singapore, Vietnam, Japan, Myanmar, Laos, China, and Cambodia, as well as a new route to The Maldives.

Serving northeastern cities, and Danang in Vietnam, **PB Air** (© **02261-0220;** www.pbair.com) is a less well known carrier. **SGA Airways,** 19/18-19 Royal City Ave., Block A, Rama IX Road,

Kwang Bangkapi Huay Kwang, Bangkok (© **02641-4190;** www.sga.co.th) is a professional outfit using 12-seater Cessna Grand Caravan aircraft for short domestic hops from Chiang Mai up to Pai, Chiang Mai to Chiang Rai, and the useful Bangkok to Hua Hin route. Flying out of Suvarnabhumi International Airport, they can be chartered for private use. A small fleet of amphibious light aircraft owned by newcomer **Destination Air** (© **07632-8637;** www.destinationair.com) fly out of Phuket to most of the major resorts like Krabi, Koh Phi Phi, and Koh Lanta.

Also check what's on offer from Malaysian budget carrier **Air Asia** (© **02515-9999** in Bangkok; www.airasia.com). They now fly between Bangkok and 11 Thai cities, as well as offering good value fares internationally.

Note that as of 2007, the 700B (US$20/£11) airport tax is now included in the price of all international air tickets, as are the domestic airport taxes.

BY CAR

Renting a car may be easy in Thailand, but driving it is another matter. Driving a rental car in Bangkok is particularly hard; the one-way streets, poor and even incorrect road signage, and constant traffic jams prove frustrating. Outside the city, it is a better option, although Thai drivers are unashamedly reckless—many never learned to drive, ignore basic rules, and have a total disregard for road safety. Foreign drivers must reorient themselves fast and Americans need to readjust to driving on the left.

Among the many car-rental agencies, both **Avis** (© **02255-5300**) and **Budget** (© **02566-5067**) each have convenient offices around the country. You can rent a car with or without a driver. All drivers are required to have an international driver's license. Self-drive rates start around 1,500B (US$43/£23) per day for a family-sized sedan, much more for luxury vehicles or SUVs.

Local tour operators in larger destinations such as Chiang Mai, Phuket, or Koh Samui will rent cars for considerably less money than the larger, more well-known agencies. Sometimes the savings are up to 50%. All companies will need to see your international driver's license and a valid credit card, in case of damage. Check insurance coverage—if you are taken to court for an accident, you may be found guilty for not being properly covered. Don't sign unless it's included.

Gas stations are conveniently located along highways and in towns and cities throughout the country. Esso, Shell, Caltex, and PTT all have competitive rates.

See p. 33 under "Safety" for tips on driving in Thailand.

SURFING FOR RENTAL CARS

For booking rental cars online, the best deals are usually found at rental-car company websites, although all the major online travel agencies also offer rental-car reservations services. Priceline and Hotwire work well for rental cars, too; the only "mystery" is which major rental company you get, and for most travelers the difference between Hertz, Avis, and Budget is negligible.

BY TRAIN

Bangkok's **Hua Lampong Railway Station** is a convenient, user-friendly facility. Clear signs point the way to public toilets, coin phones, the food court, and baggage check area. A Post & Telegraph Office, Information Counter, police box, ATMs, and money-changing facilities are dotted around the main area. You'll find plenty of small convenience shops and a baggage check.

From this hub, the State Railway of Thailand provides regular service to destinations as far north as Chiang Mai, northeast to Nong Khai, east to Pattaya, and south to Thailand's southern border, where it connects with Malaysia's *Keretapi Tanah Melayu Berhad* (KTM) with service to Penang (Butterworth), Kuala Lumpur, and Singapore. Complete schedules and fare information can be obtained at any railway station or by calling **Hua Lampong Railway Station** directly at ✆ **02223-7010,** or call their information hotline at ✆ **1690.**

The State Railway runs a number of different trains, each at a different speed, and priced accordingly. First-class sleepers usually accord an air-conditioned, two-bunk compartment with wash basin; second-class sleepers are bunks with curtains and either ceiling fans or air-conditioning, depending on the ticket price. The fastest is the Special Express, which is the best choice for long-haul, overnight travel. These trains cut travel time by as much as 60% and have sleeper cars—which are a must for really long trips. Rapid trains are the next best option. Prices vary for class, from air-conditioned sleeper cars in first class to air-conditioned and fan sleepers or seats in second, on down to the straight-backed, hard seats in third class.

Warning: On trains, pay close attention to your possessions. Thievery is common on overnight trips. Also make sure if you are traveling solo that you state your sex when booking. The ticket agents won't put two strangers of opposite sexes together in first class, so don't be baffled if you are told the class is "full" when in fact there are bunks. In that case, you may have to downgrade.

BY BUS

Thailand has a very efficient and inexpensive bus system, which is highly recommended for budget travelers and short-haul trips. Buses are the cheapest transportation to the farthest and most remote destinations in the country. Options abound, but the major choices are public or private and air-conditioned or non-air-conditioned. Longer bus trips usually depart in the evenings to arrive at their destination early in the morning.

Whenever you can, opt for the VIP buses, especially for overnight trips. Some have 36 seats; better ones have 24 seats. The extra cost is well worth the legroom. Also, stick to government buses operated from each city's proper bus terminal. Many private companies sell VIP tickets for major routes, but put you on a standard bus. Ideally, buses are best for short excursions; expect to pay a minimum of 50B (US$1.25/77p) for a one-way ticket. Longer-haul buses are an excellent value (usually less than $1 per hour of travel), but can be very slow.

Warning: When traveling by long-distance bus, do not accept drinks or snacks from fellow Thai travelers; they can be spiked. And watch your possessions closely: Thievery is common, particularly on overnight buses when valuables are left in overhead racks.

BY TAXI, TUK-TUK & SONGTAEW

By law, **taxis** must charge by the meter. If you look outwardly like a tourist, a driver may try to scam you into paying a hefty fare by refusing to use the meter. Get out and find a new taxi if that happens; and avoid stationary taxis (usually parked next to expensive hotels), as these tend to be the scam artists. Note that if you're journeying to an unsavory part of town, a taxi driver may refuse you, especially when it's coming up to shift change (3–4pm) or if the weather or traffic is bad.

If you have a foreign face and don't speak any Thai, you'll be lucky to find a **tuk-tuk** ride for less than 50B (US$1.25/77p), even for the shortest hops. Be sure to bargain hard with these guys, and don't let 'em take you for a ride (in other words, to shopping trips or to massage parlors). In most provincial areas and resort islands, small pickup trucks called *songtaews* cruise the main streets offering communal taxi service at cheap, set fees. As with tuk-tuks, always remember to agree on your fare before engaging a driver.

Note: Few taxi, tuk-tuk, or *songtaew* drivers speak even basic English, so have a copy of your hotel's name, street address, and district written in Thai with you at all times.

Tipping is always expected, though it's up to you if you want to round up the figure. Since taxi or tuk-tuk drivers often don't carry change, don't leave your hotel without some small bills.

17 Tips on Accommodations

The most visited parts of Bangkok, Phuket, Chiang Mai, Pattaya, and Koh Samui offer the widest assortment of accommodations in the country. International chains such as the Mandarin Oriental group, The Peninsula, Hilton, Accor, Sheraton, and Marriott have some of their finest hotels and resorts in these areas, while Dusit and Amari chains have numerous resort and city properties that can compete with the best.

These days, smaller, independent boutique places are very much in vogue, but in Asia it's common to find that most of the best restaurants are operated by the big chain hotels. Five-star hotels and resorts spare no detail for the business or leisure traveler, providing designer toiletries, plush robes, in-room DVD or CD players, Jacuzzis and Wi-Fi, plus many other creature comforts.

Because they have more facilities, better activity options and services, and well-trained staff, luxury category hotels and resorts can charge more than 28,000B (US$800/£431) a night for a double room (see the "Very Expensive" category in any destination chapter). Many hotels in this category have started quoting prices in U.S. dollars.

Most hotels that fall into the "Expensive" category also have lots of bells and whistles, but feature less deluxe amenities; yet they may still offer perks like silk bathrobes, CD players, and DVD players. Room design and furnishings will not extend to the glamour of the higher categories, but all rooms will be well maintained and facilities tend to be of excellent quality. Expect to pay around 15,000B (US$428/£231) per night.

"Moderate" hotels and resorts start at about 8,000B (US$228/£123) and are often quite modern and a good value for your money. Most have swimming pools, good restaurants, toiletries, satellite television, in-room safes, and international direct dialing from your room. In smaller cities and towns, this category is about the best you can do, but some of these moderately priced options can have facilities and rooms of surprising quality. Prices are also discounted greatly; they may fall to as little as 1,800B (US$51/£26), depending on the season.

Thailand offers a good range of places for the budget traveler and the many mom-and-pop guesthouses and cut-price hostels here often allow for more authentic experiences. If you go really inexpensive, expect to rough it. Cold-water showers, fan-cooled rooms, and dormitories are the norm. But sometimes you'll find inexpensive accommodations that stand out from the pack—quaint beachside bungalow villages, city hotels with good locations, or small guesthouses with knowledgeable and helpful staff.

Expensive and moderately priced hotels add a 10% service charge plus 7% government tax, also called value-added tax (VAT).

Thailand has its own star rating system based on the number of amenities in any given hotel, but the system is arbitrary and takes little account of quality. Often the smaller boutique resorts of the highest quality have lower star ratings because they lack the "business center and meeting facilities for 250 or more" required. It's best to go by reputation rather than the Thai ratings system.

SURFING FOR HOTELS

Bidding for hotels online is not a bad option for the larger properties in big cities or resort areas. Lots of sites offer booking options in Thai hotels, many offering significant discounts from usual services of the big international hotel-booking sites. Try **www.asiarooms.com**, among the many local online booking agents. Most regional online booking and ticket consolidators in Thailand work through the long-established **Diethelm Travel** (www.diethelmtravel.com).

In addition to the online travel booking sites **Travelocity, Expedia, Orbitz, Priceline,** and **Hotwire,** you can book hotels through **Hotels.com, Quikbook** (www.quikbook.com), and **Travelaxe** (www.travelaxe.net).

It's a good idea to **get a confirmation number** and **make a printout** of any online booking transaction.

Important Note: If you book a budget room online, you'll likely be given a "run of the house" room, which means you'll get the least desirable one (without view, near the elevator, and so on).

SAVING ON YOUR HOTEL ROOM

The **rack rate** is the maximum rate that a hotel charges for a room. Hardly anybody pays this price, however, except in high season or on holidays. To lower the cost of your room:

- **Ask about special rates or other discounts.** You may qualify for corporate, student, military, senior, frequent flier, trade union, or other discounts.
- **Dial direct.** When booking a room in a chain hotel, you'll often get a better deal by calling the individual hotel's reservation desk rather than the chain's main number.
- **Book online.** Many hotels offer Internet-only discounts or supply rooms to Priceline, Hotwire, or Expedia at rates much lower than the ones you can get through the hotel itself.
- **Remember the law of supply and demand.** You can save big on hotel rooms by traveling in a destination's off-season or shoulder seasons, when rates typically drop, even at luxury properties.
- **Look into group or long-stay discounts.** If you come as part of a large group, you should be able to negotiate a bargain rate. Likewise, if you're planning a long stay (at least 5 days), you might qualify for a discount. As a general rule, expect 1 night free after a 7-night stay.
- **Avoid excess charges and hidden costs.** Many hotels have adopted the unpleasant practice of nickel-and-diming their guests with opaque surcharges. When you book a room, ask what is included in the room rate and what is extra. Avoid dialing direct from hotel phones, which can have exorbitant rates. And don't be tempted by the room's minibar offerings: Most hotels charge through the nose for water, soda, and snacks. Finally, ask about local taxes and service charges, which can increase the cost of a room by 15% or more.
- **Self-catering.** A room with a kitchenette allows you to shop for groceries and cook your own meals. This is a big money saver, especially for families on long stays.

Note: Private villas and timeshare properties are booming in places like Koh Samui and Phuket. While many travelers fall for the sweet talk and buy right away, it pays to consult a reputable foreign law firm first. Many foreigners have lost their life savings in Thai real estate scams.

18 Tips on Dining

One of the greatest joys of visiting Thailand is the plethora of dining options in any area. From high-class hotel restaurants with elegant buffet luncheons to simple, friendly diners, you'll find it all, and in this volume I list the whole range. (Also see Appendix A, p. 385, for tips on types of Thai food and drink.)

Storefront restaurants and street vendors, apart from those in a specified night market area, are open early morning to late at night. To ease congested streets, food vendors are now banned in Bangkok on Mondays. Restaurants catering to tourists also open from morning until late. You're not expected to tip at most Thai restaurants, but rounding up the bill or leaving 20B (57¢/30p) on top of most checks is acceptable. (A 15% to 20% tip will shock and awe in smaller restaurants, but will be readily expected at fine-dining outlets.)

Thais are very practical about table manners. If something is best eaten with the hands, then feel free. If there are seeds or bones, you can spit them out onto the table or into a tissue. Single-serve noodle soups are usually eaten with chopsticks and a Chinese spoon. Rice dishes are eaten with a spoon and fork; the spoon is commonly held in the right hand, and the fork in the left is used only to load the spoon for delivery. Follow local customs if you wish, but do whatever you're comfortable with.

Note: In small towns featured throughout this guide, many dining (and nightlife) spots don't have working land lines; in those cases, mobile numbers are provided wherever possible.

19 Tips on Shopping

Customs officers in many countries are now actively searching bags of tourists returning from Thailand and confiscating any pirated CDs and DVDs, designer knock-offs, and copy watches. In places like the U.S., U.K., and Australia, the import of counterfeit merchandise is a crime and you, as the buyer, will have your holiday purchases confiscated. A purchase may be "low dollar" to you, but when thousands of copies are sold, it damages the businesses that create and pay for the copyright of these models. Every year, media reports also confirm that earnings from these underground counterfeit industries go toward money laundering, drug production, prostitution, and child trafficking. By not buying fake brands, you are not just abiding by the law, but helping stamp out racketeering that ruins lives.

20 Recommended Books, Films & Music

BOOKS

Tiziano Terzani's book, *A Fortune-Teller Told Me* may not be about Thailand exclusively, but the late Italian journalist offers a well-crafted portrait of the interlocking cultures of Asia. The book tells of the superstitions and rituals affecting all aspects of Southeast Asian culture in an autobiography detailing a year of overland travels in a bid to outdo a fortune-teller's premonition of his death.

Carol Hollinger's *Mai Pen Rai Means Nevermind* is a personal history of time spent in the kingdom some 30 years ago, but the cultural insights are quite current.

For help in understanding what the heck is going on around you in Thailand, pick up Philip Cornwel-Smith's *Very Thai;* it's a bit obvious in parts but does make for colorful and fun entertainment (don't expect any deep intellectual insights). It will, however, explain some

Warning Shopping Scams

Gems, fake goods, illegal betting: Every year naïve tourists take the bait and get caught in a scam. To beat the cheats, follow these simple rules:
- If anyone approaches you on the street and offers to take you to a shop (or anywhere for that matter), refuse.
- If a tuk-tuk or taxi driver wants to take you shopping say, "No thanks" (or "*Mai ao, khop khun*").
- Be suspicious of strangers who flash TAT, Tourist Police, or any other "badge," in order to get something from you.
- Know that there is no such thing as a government auction, government clearinghouse, or anything "government"-related to the gems industry.
- There is no such thing as a tax-free day for gemstones purchases.
- Do not agree to let any gem purchases be shipped to your home address.
- As with any purchase you make, if you use a credit card, keep the card in your sight at all times and watch the store assistant make one print of it.
- If anyone tells you that your purchase can be resold back home for more than you paid for it in Thailand, walk away.

---

peculiar habits of the host country. Or there's the more practical *Culture Shock! Thailand* by Robert and Nanthapa Cooper.

The hilariously funny 2004 book, *Bangkok Inside Out* by Daniel Ziv and Guy Sharrett, has now been banned in Thailand (due to its containing an image of a smiling, topless bar girl in the arms of a foreign man). That fact alone says a lot. If you do get hold of a copy overseas, you'll find a raw, no-holes-barred, tell-it-how-it-is book.

Phrase-books and Thai/English dictionaries are sold everywhere; for a comprehensive study of Thai, pick up a copy of *Thailand for Beginners* by Benjawan Becker.

Books on Buddhism and Thai Theravada traditions are endless: Look for works by Ajahn Buddhadasa, founder of an international meditation center in the south of Thailand, and author of the *Handbook for Mankind* and *The ABCs of Buddhism*. Also look for writing by Jack Kornfield, an American who writes about meditation practices in works like *A Path With Heart*. Phra Peter Parrapadipo's

Phra Farang, literally "the foreign monk," tells the story of an Englishman who chose to go into the Buddhist monkhood: It makes for an unusual read.

These days there are plenty of big glossy tomes covering all aspects of Thai design, old and new. *Modern Thai Living* by Devahastin na Ayudhaya is a great example of today's stylish mix of how modern interiors can combine rustic and contemporary elements. In the book, the author collaborates with Thai floral designer Sakul Intakul, who is celebrated in Bangkok for bringing a radical postmodernist approach to Thai floral arrangements. For a great insight into Thailand's northern Lanna history, pore over a copy of Ping Amranand and William Warren's exemplary *Lanna Style*, or the more academic guide to temple design in the north, the sumptuously illustrated *Lanna, Thailand's Northern Kingdom* by long-time resident author Michael Freeman.

FILMS

Since 1974, when a debonair Roger Moore—playing the irrepressible secret agent James Bond—was seen speeding across a turquoise Phang Nga Bay in *The Man with The Golden Gun,* Thailand has attracted moviemakers. Alex Garland's novel *The Beach* (and the much maligned film of the same name featuring Leonardo DiCaprio) tells the seedy story of young backpackers in search of the perfect hideaway. They swim to a remote island (the filmmakers shot at Maya Bay on Koh Phi Phi Le), where they join a community of marijuana-stoked dropouts living in supposed bliss. Surprise surprise, things go awry. Environmentalists might suggest that there are some pretty stark parallels in reality. After filming finished in 1998, locals accused the moviemakers and ensuing tourists of ruining the site. True enough, to this day, dozens of long-tails oozing oil into the turquoise seas rock up on what is now called "The Beach" and heaps of litter are left in their wake. Is it a case of "art reflecting real life," or perhaps vice versa?

MUSIC

Thais love music, and the country has a long musical tradition dating back to at least the 7th century, especially in the rural hinterland. Most smart hotel lobbies are the stage for a Thai couple in gorgeous silks who play slow, rhythmic tunes on classical stringed instruments such as a *saw sam sai* (a vertically held, 3-string fiddle) or on a circular set of gongs called a *khong wong.* Country music is a more lively and raucous alternative; like in the U.S., it's become popularized in the last decade.

Jazz is increasingly popular among old and young as well. Thailand's king (who is an accomplished composer and musician) has been especially helpful in exposing Thais to jazz. Thailand has a number of homegrown pop stars who pump out Thai-language hits and have a huge teen following, too.

FAST FACTS: Thailand

American Express There is an office at S.P. Building, 388, Pahonyothin Rd. in Bangkok. You can reach the office at ⓒ 02273-0033; it's open Monday to Friday 8.30am to 5pm. More Thai hotlines can be found on **www.americanexpress. com,** but these will be geared to help Thai card members, so check on the back of your card for your own country's relevant help lines.

ATM Networks Most major banks throughout the country have ATMs. In general, you can get cash with your debit card at any Bangkok Bank, Thai Farmers' Bank, or Siam Commercial Bank—provided your card is hooked into the MasterCard/Cirrus or Visa/PLUS network. See the "Money" section, earlier in this chapter.

Business Hours Government offices (including branch post offices) are open Monday to Friday 8:30am to 4:30pm, with a lunch break between noon and 1pm. Businesses are generally open 8am to 5pm. Shops often stay open from 8am until 7pm or later, 7 days a week. Department stores are generally open 10am to 8pm. Most TAT visitor centers are open daily from 8:30am to 4pm.

Car Rentals See "Getting Around Thailand," earlier in this chapter.

Currency See "Money," earlier in this chapter.

Customs **What You Can Bring Into Thailand:** It is prohibited by law to bring the following items into Thailand without a license: narcotics, pornography, firearms and ammunition, blood, live animals, and agricultural products. Tourists are allowed to enter the country with 1 liter of alcohol and 200 cigarettes (or 250g of cigars or smoking tobacco) per adult, duty free, and there is no official limit on perfume. Customs no longer deem photographic film, PCs, or cameras as restricted items, as long as they are taken out of the country upon departure.

What You Can Take Home From Thailand: Pay more attention to what you can actually import to your home country, as Thai export customs are rather lax. However, one exception is cultural treasures: It is forbidden to take antique or authentic Buddha images or Bodhisattva images or fragments out of the kingdom. Special permission is required for removing antique artifacts from the country. You will be required to submit the object along with two 5×7–inch photographs showing a frontal view of the object, your passport, and a photocopy of your passport notarized by your home embassy. The authorization process takes 8 days. For further details, contact the **Department of Fine Arts,** Na Phra That Road, next to Thammasat University (© **02221-7811** or 02225-2652), open weekdays 9am to 4pm.

Please note: This is only an issue if the object in question is an antique, especially one that has been removed from a temple or palace, or a piece that has particular historic value to the kingdom. If you purchase a small Buddha image or reproduction, whether an amulet or a statue, you can ship it home or pack it in your bag. Any antique dealer will be able to notify you about which images require special permission.

U.S. Citizens: For specifics on what you can bring back and the corresponding fees, download the invaluable free pamphlet *Know Before You Go* online at **www.cbp.gov.** (Click on "Travel," and then click on "Know Before You Go! Online Brochure.") Or contact the **U.S. Customs & Border Protection (CBP),** 1300 Pennsylvania Ave., NW, Washington, DC 20229 (© **877/287-8667**) and request the pamphlet.

Canadian Citizens: For a clear summary of Canadian rules, write for the booklet *I Declare,* issued by the **Canada Border Services Agency** (© **800/ 461-9999** in Canada, or 204/983-3500; **www.cbsa-asfc.gc.ca**).

U.K. Citizens: For information, contact **HM Customs & Excise** at © **0845/ 010-9000** (from outside the U.K., 020/8929-0152), or consult their website at **www.hmce.gov.uk**.

Australian Citizens: A helpful brochure available from Australian consulates or Customs offices is *Know Before You Go.* For more information, call the **Australian Customs Service** at © **1300/363-263,** or log on to **www.customs.gov.au**.

New Zealand Citizens: Most questions are answered in a free pamphlet available at New Zealand consulates and Customs offices: *New Zealand Customs Guide for Travellers, Notice no. 4.* For more information, contact **New Zealand Customs,** The Customhouse, 17–21 Whitmore St., Box 2218, Wellington (© **04/473-6099** or 0800/428-786; **www.customs.govt.nz**).

Driving Rules See "Getting Around Thailand," earlier in this chapter.

Drugstores Throughout the country, there are many drugstores stocked with many brand-name medications and toiletries, plus less expensive local brands.

Pharmacists often speak some English, and a number of drugs that require a prescription elsewhere can be dispensed over the counter.

Electricity All outlets—except in some luxury hotels—are 220 volts AC (50 cycles). Outlets have two flat-pronged or round-pronged holes, so you may need an adapter. If you use a 110-volt hair dryer, electric shaver, or battery charger for a computer, bring a transformer and adapter.

Embassies & Consulates While most countries have consular representation in Bangkok, the United States, Australia, Canada, and the United Kingdom also have consulates in Chiang Mai. See chapters 4 and 12 for details. Most embassies have 24-hour emergency services. If you are seriously injured or ill, call your embassy for assistance.

Emergencies Throughout the country, the emergency number you should use is ⓒ **1699** or ⓒ 1155 for the Tourist Police. Don't expect many English speakers at police posts outside the major tourist areas. Ambulances must be summoned from hospitals rather than through a central service (see hospital listings in each city). You can also contact your embassy or consulate.

Holidays See "Thailand Calendar of Events," earlier in this chapter.

Information See "Visitor Information & Maps," earlier in this chapter.

Internet Access You'll find Internet cafes everywhere in Thailand. See the "Fast Facts" sections in specific destination chapters for details.

Language Central (often called Bangkok) Thai is the official language. English is spoken in the major cities at hotels, some restaurants, and a few smart shops, and is the second language of the professional class. (For more information on the Thai language, see Appendices A and B.)

Liquor Laws The official drinking age in Thailand is 18. You can readily buy and drink alcohol, even in supermarkets, but licensing laws apply, and legally, drinks can only be served after 5pm. On some public holidays and election days, no liquor can be sold at all. Most restaurants, bars, and nightclubs sell booze, and you can pick up bottles of imported and local liquor from convenience stores. Night spots must now close at 1am (and the rule is being policed vigorously). Alcohol, hitherto readily sold over the counter anywhere, anytime, is now subject to strict licensing hours.

Lost & Found Be sure to tell your credit card companies the minute you discover your wallet has been lost or stolen and file a report at the nearest police precinct. Your credit card company or insurer will require a police report, or formal record of the loss. Most credit card companies have an emergency toll-free number to call if your card is lost or stolen; they may be able to wire you a cash advance immediately or deliver an emergency credit card in a day or two. Visa's U.S. emergency number is ⓒ **800/847-2911** or 410/581-9994. American Express cardholders and traveler's check holders should call ⓒ **800/221-7282**. Master-Card holders should call ⓒ **800/307-7309** or 636/722-7111. For other credit cards, call the toll-free number directory at ⓒ **800/555-1212**.

To report a lost or stolen credit card in Thailand, the following companies' services are available: **American Express** (ⓒ **02273-5544**); **Diners Club** (ⓒ **02238-3660**).

If you need emergency cash over the weekend when all banks are closed, you can have money wired to you via **Western Union** (✆ 800/325-6000; www.westernunion.com).

Identity theft or fraud can result from losing your wallet, especially if you've lost your driver's license along with your cash and credit cards. Notify the major credit-reporting bureaus immediately; placing a fraud alert on your records may protect you against liability for criminal activity. The three major U.S. credit-reporting agencies are **Equifax** (✆ 800/766-0008; www.equifax.com), **Experian** (✆ 888/397-3742; www.experian.com), and **TransUnion** (✆ 800/680-7289; www.transunion.com). You must always report any loss of valuables to the Thai police station *nearest to the district where the loss took place.* If you think the loss took place in a taxi, find a friendly Thai-speaker who can place an alert with the local taxi radio stations. Finally, if you've lost all forms of photo ID, call your embassy for an emergency passport; while this will allow you to board a plane, you will need to get a replacement entry visa too. To be safe, always carry a copy of your passport (and visa) when you travel and make copies of the Thai police report; you will need them for replacement documents and cards.

Mail You can pick up mail while you travel by using a *poste restante,* which is simply a counter at a post office where your mail is kept for you until you pick it up; normally, 2 months is the maximum hold time. For those unfamiliar with this service, it is comparable to General Delivery in the United States. Mail is addressed to you, care of Poste Restante, GPO, Name of City. You'll need proof of ID and must sign a receipt and pay1B (3¢/5p) per letter received. Hours of operation are the same as the post office. (See individual chapters for local post offices and their hours.)

Airmail postcards to the United States usually cost 15B (42¢/75p), but rates depend on the size of the card; airmail letters cost 19B (45¢/95p) per 5 grams (rates to Europe are the same). Airmail delivery usually takes 7 to 20 days.

Air parcel post costs 610B (US$15/£9) per kilogram. Surface or sea parcel post costs 215B (US$5.25/£3) for 1 kilogram (3 or 4 months for delivery). International Express Mail (EMS) costs 440B (US$11/£7) from 1 to 250 grams, with delivery guaranteed within 7 days.

Shipping by air freight is quite costly, but most major international delivery services have offices in Bangkok and a network that extends to the provinces. These are **DHL Thailand,** Grand Amarin Tower Building, Phetchaburi Road (✆ 02207-0600), and **Federal Express,** at Rama IV Road (✆ 1782). **UPS Parcel Delivery Service** has a main branch in Bangkok at 16/1 Sukhumvit Soi 44/1 (✆ 02712-3300). Many businesses will also package and mail merchandise for a reasonable price.

Newspapers & Magazines The English-language dailies are *Bangkok Post* and *The Nation,* distributed in the morning in the capital and later in the day around the country. They cover the domestic political scene, as well as international news from Associated Press and Reuters wire services and cost 25B (71¢/39p). Both the *Asian Wall Street Journal* and *International Herald Tribune* are available Monday to Friday on their day of publication in Bangkok (in the provinces, it may be a day later). *Time, Newsweek,* and *The Economist* are sold in international hotels, as well as in a few of the major cities.

Passports **For Residents of the United States:** Whether you're applying in person or by mail, you can download passport applications from the U.S. State Department website at **travel.state.gov**. For general information, call the **National Passport Agency** (© 202/647-0518). To find your regional passport office, either check the U.S. State Department website or call the **National Passport Information Center** (© 900/225-5674); the fee is 55¢ per minute for automated information and $1.50 per minute for operator-assisted calls.

For Residents of Canada: Passport applications are available at travel agencies throughout Canada or from the central **Passport Office,** Department of Foreign Affairs and International Trade, Ottawa, ON K1A 0G3 (© 800/567-6868; www.ppt.gc.ca).

For Residents of the United Kingdom: To pick up an application for a standard 10-year passport (5-year passport for children 15 and under), visit your nearest passport office, major post office, or travel agency. Also contact the **United Kingdom Passport Service** at © 0870/521-0410, or search its website at www.ukpa.gov.uk, for info.

For Residents of Ireland: You can apply for a 10-year passport at the **Passport Office,** Setanta Centre, Molesworth Street, Dublin 2 (© 01/671-1633; www.irl gov.ie/iveagh). Those under age 18 and over 65 must apply for a €12, 3-year passport. You can also apply at 1A South Mall, Cork (© 021/272-525) or at most main post offices.

For Residents of Australia: You can pick up an application from your local post office or any branch of Passports Australia, but you must schedule an interview at the passport office to present your application materials. Call the **Australian Passport Information Service** at © 13 12 32, or visit the government website at www.passports.gov.au.

For Residents of New Zealand: You can pick up a passport application at any New Zealand Passports Office or download it from their website. Contact the **Passports Office** at © 0800/225-050 in New Zealand or 04/474-8100, or log on to www.passports.govt.nz.

Police The **Tourist Police** (© 1699 or 1155), with offices in every city (see specific chapters), speak English (and other foreign languages) and are open 24 hours. You should call them in an emergency rather than the regular police because there is no guarantee that police operators will speak English.

Restrooms The country's better restaurants and hotels will have Western toilets. Shops and budget hotels will have an Asian squat toilet, a ceramic platform mounted over a hole in the ground. Near the toilet is a water bucket or sink with a small ladle. The water is for flushing the toilet. Toilet paper is not provided, but some have tissue dispensers outside the restroom costing 5B (14¢/7p). Dispose of it in the wastebasket provided, as it will clog up rudimentary sewage systems.

Safety Anonymous violent crime in Thailand is rare, but it does exist; however, petty crime such as purse snatching or pickpocketing is common. Overland travelers should take care on overnight buses and trains for small-time thieves.

Beware of credit card scams; carry a minimum of cards, don't allow them out of your sight, and keep all receipts. Don't carry unnecessary valuables or cards, and keep those you do carry in your hotel's safe. Pay particular attention to your things, especially purses and wallets, on public transportation.

Also be wary of strangers who offer to guide you (particularly in Bangkok), take you shopping (especially to jewelry shops), or buy you food or drink. This is most likely to occur near a tourist sight. Be warned, these are well-known scam artists. There are rare exceptions, but most likely these new "friends" will try to swindle you in some way. If you are approached about such schemes, walk away, or call the Tourist Police immediately (see above for more information).

Smoking Over 5 years ago, Thailand banned smoking in public places, such as restaurants and airports. Some bars that don't serve food can get away with smokers, or have created smoker-friendly outdoor spaces, including upmarket private cigar bars. If in doubt, ask about nonsmoking sections. A few years ago, the former Prime Minister Thaksin prohibited the display of cigarettes anywhere. They are still sold but cannot appear on shelves—you'll have to ask.

Taxes & Service Charges Hotels charge a 7% government value-added tax (VAT) and typically add a 10% service charge; hotel restaurants add 8.25% government tax. Smaller hotels quote the price inclusive of these charges.

Time Zone Thailand is 7 hours ahead of GMT (Greenwich Mean Time). During winter months, this means that Bangkok is 7 hours ahead of London, 12 hours ahead of New York, and 15 hours ahead of Los Angeles. Daylight saving time will add 1 hour to these times.

Tipping If no service charge is added to your check in a fine-dining establishment, a 10% to 15% tip is appropriate. In local shops, tipping is not common. Airport or hotel porters expect tips; 50B (US$1.42/77p) is acceptable. Feel free to reward good service wherever you find it. Tipping taxi drivers is appreciated. Carry small bills, as many cab drivers either don't have change or won't admit to having any in the hope of getting a tip.

Useful Phone Numbers The U.S. Dept. of State Travel Advisory can be called at ⓒ 202/647-5225 (manned 24 hr.); the U.S. Passport Agency can be contacted at ⓒ 202/647-0518; and the U.S. Centers for Disease Control International Traveler's hotline is ⓒ 404/332-4559.

Water Don't drink the tap water here, even in the major hotels. Most hotels provide bottled water; use it for brushing your teeth as well as drinking. Most restaurants serve bottled or boiled water and ice made from boiled water, but always ask to be sure. Purified water may not have the minerals you need to replace those lost in the heat and humidity, so check the label.

3

Suggested Itineraries in Thailand

Thailand has something for everyone; it's a great place to explore, learn, or connect with a decidedly rewarding local culture. In this laid-back country, though, planned itineraries do well to give way to spontaneity. Most trips begin in **Bangkok**—the country's capital and commercial center—and travelers' itineraries tend to include some beach time mixed in with a bit of history and adventure.

Whatever you do, plan your trip around a passion. Like Thai food. Start at the **Blue Elephant** cooking school in Bangkok, or try the rural-based **Chiang Mai Kitchen Cooking School** in the north, to learn how to prepare food the Thai way. Or simply discover local specialties by exploring the country's markets and many upmarket Thai restaurants.

Interested in massage? Upscale **Chiva-Som Academy** in Bangkok teaches the art of this fascinating ancient tradition. If adventure is more your thing, head to Chiang Mai for some **hot-air ballooning,** or visit **Khao Yai National Park** north of Bangkok or **Khao Sok** in the south.

Curious about Thailand's long history and architecture? Bangkok's many temples and museums will enchant. Want to get enlightened or learn about Buddhism? Consider taking a meditation course; the "Buddhist Way" is not as easy as you may think. Try the **House of Dhamma** in Bangkok, **Wat Phra That Si Chom Thong** in Chiang Mai, **Wat Suan Mokkh** in Surat Thani, or **Wat Khao Tham** on beautiful Koh Pha Ngan. These

are just a few of the many special activities possible in Thailand. Find what suits you and go for it.

When flying directly to Thailand from the U.S. or Europe, be aware of **jetlag;** it takes some time to adjust to the abrupt climate and culinary changes. It is best to go easy at the start. Arrival in frenetic Bangkok, with its intense traffic, heat, and humidity, can be a bit overwhelming—it all takes some time to get used to, and if you're doing a 1-week tour, you might just be settling in and enjoying things by the time you leave. So do yourself a favor and factor in some rest days at the beginning and end of your trip.

Multiple-week stays allow for more opportunities to both explore the great beyond by bus and train as well as a chance to lie on a white sandy beach somewhere along the way. With shorter itineraries, you might want to limit yourself to Bangkok, a short plane ride to rural northern reaches near Chiang Mai, and then a flight to one of the beaches in the south. Be sure to factor in a few days for shopping in Bangkok or Chiang Mai at the end of your trip.

Weather plays an important part in planning, too. The winter months—November to March—are the best time to go, but this period spans the high season (Dec to Feb), which pushes up prices and makes bookings difficult. Winter in the north, around Chiang Mai, is cooler, while summer months bring heavy rain and floods. The best time to visit Phuket and areas on the western coast is from November to April. For Koh Samui and other beach destinations on the eastern coast, the optimal time to visit is from February to October (the result of opposing monsoonal systems). Check destination chapters for more weather specifics.

You also might want to plan your trip around a Thai holiday, such as **Songkran,** the Thai New Year. The celebration ranges from 2 days to a week, depending on the region, but always starts from April 13. **Loy Krathong,** celebrated in early November, is another magical holiday throughout Thailand (though the best celebrations are in the north at Sukhothai or Chiang Mai); during this holiday, small bamboo floats or paper lanterns are released to absolve the previous year's sins.

Thailand is also a great base for exploring the rest of Southeast Asia. With the emergence of budget airlines, Bangkok's many connections make it a hub for trips to hot destinations such as Hanoi in Vietnam, Yangon in Myanmar (Burma), sleepy Luang Prabang in Laos, and the temples around Angkor Wat in Cambodia.

1 Begin (or End) in Bangkok: 1 to 3 Days

The Thai capital has a lot to offer but can be rather daunting at first, what with its chaotic traffic and hectic pace. Visitors who remain calm and curious will experience the exoticism of the East without too much discomfort, though.

Tack this short itinerary onto the beginning—or the end—of any trip to Thailand. You can also split it up: Spend time touring the city sites at the start of the journey and then use a day at the end to fill your suitcase with gorgeous handicrafts, silk fashions, or souvenirs.

Day 1: Bangkok's Riverside Sites

Start your tour of Bangkok by **Central Pier** (confusingly, also known as Sathorn Pier; p. 80), where you can hop on a fast river taxi or the more comfortable wide-berth Chao Phraya Tourist Boat. Alternatively, take a long-tail boat tour of Thonburi's *klongs* (canals), which makes for a fascinating 1- to 3-hour trip. You can arrange these trips at the booths at Central Pier next to Saphan Taksin BTS, at River City, or through your hotel (riverside hotels like Ibrik and Arun Residence are good places to base yourself, because they offer shuttle boats). Also see p. 78 for tips on getting around Bangkok.

Heading north by taxi or boat along the S-curve of the river, you will pass most of the city's historical sites. Good stops along the way are **Si Phya,** which is next to River City, for pricey souvenir shopping; and **Chinatown** (known as Yaowarat; p. 78), to amble along its bustling alleyways. You should also get off at Tha Tien for **Wat Po** (p. 131) and the Giant Reclining Buddha. From there, it's a short walk to the **Grand Palace** (p. 125) and the famed **Wat Phra Kaew** (p. 129), the temple of the celebrated Emerald Buddha.

From Tha Tien, take the ferry across the river to **Wat Arun** (p. 131), the Temple of Dawn. Then you can carry on upstream to visit the **National Museum** (p. 126). After visiting the museum, you can stop at Banglampoo for **Khao San Road,** the vibrant backpacker strip.

This is a lot to see in a day—you may even want to take 2 days to see it all. But if you've got surplus energy afterwards, see the nightlife suggestions listed under Day 2 (see below). Also check out the dining options listed there for ideas on where to take breaks to eat during your river journey.

Day 2: Bangkok Shopping & Eating

One good place to start your second day in Bangkok is the **Jim Thompson House** (p. 126), home of the American who rejuvenated the Thai silk industry. It's right in the city center (near the National Stadium BTS).

Afterwards, ready yourself for a full frontal attack on the city's shops: About a 10-minute walk away from the Jim Thompson House is **Mah Boon Krang** (**MBK;** p. 141), a giant mall catering to Thai teenagers and bargain-hunters alike. Nearby **Siam Center** and **Siam Discovery Center** (p. 141) offer more upscale brand names, while adjacent to the Siam BTS is **Siam Paragon** (p. 140), a center filled with super-luxury boutiques.

Grab a coffee or snack at the Paragon's bright new food court if you need a break, and then continue on to the funky, trendy clothing stores and restaurants found across the way in **Siam Square** (p. 77). Farther down the road are two snazzy malls: **Central World** (p. 140), with some amazing restaurants that'll serve well for lunch, and the newly refurbished **Zen** store next door. Finally, on the other side of the road, check out the chic shops at the **Erawan** (p. 140) mall.

If you want to keep up the high-end shopping, hop on the subway to Phrom Phong to the designer warehouse **The Emporium** and then hop a cab to **Panthip Plaza** (p. 140), the city's biggest electronics bazaar. If it's a weekend day, try to visit the gigantic and labyrinthine **Chatuchak Market** (p. 142) by the Saphan Khwai BTS.

Once you're shopped out, other cultural sites to see in town include **Wat Suthat** (p. 133) and its giant swing (near Chinatown), stunning **Vimarnmek Palace** (p. 128) in Dusit Park, and **Wat Saket** (p. 132), better known as the Golden Mount, which is just north of Klong Banglampoo.

Or you might consider taking a half-day of **classes.** Both **The Peninsula** (p. 90) and **The Oriental** (p. 134) hotels have cooking schools, while the affable restaurateur and TV chef **Mrs. Balbir** (p. 134) teaches from her home off Sukhumvit. Meditation can be studied at **The House of Dhamma** (p. 135) or **Wat Mahathat** (p. 135), and Thai massage at the **Chiva-Som Academy** (p. 135).

If you'd rather get a massage instead of learning how to give one, indulge in one of Bangkok's many affordable massage parlors such as **Healthland** (p. 135) or **Ruen-Nuad** (p. 135), both off Sathorn Road, or in a hotel spa. The more rigorous Thai massages should help circulation and aid sleep for the jet-lagged.

Dining choices in this city run the gamut from street food to gourmet restaurants, to **dinner cruises** offered by five-star hotels like **The Oriental** (p. 90), **Banyan Tree** (p. 93), and **Shangri-la** (p. 91). For a totally mind-blowing dining experience, try the 64-story, open-air **Sirocco** (p. 112), or for ground-level authenticity, the local jazz scene at **Diplomat Bar** (p. 97).

When it comes to nightlife, **Nana Plaza** (p. 146) and **Soi Cowboy,** off Sukhumvit Road, form the hub of the go-go scene here. The area around **Silom Soi 4** (p. 145) houses the city's best gay bars and good gay/mixed clubs. And **Patpong** (p. 142) hums with a bustling night market—it's Bangkok's busiest red-light district. Bars here are as famous for their exotic shows as they are for truly extortionate prices, (enforced by hired muscle). Since the rise of HIV/AIDS in Thailand, the area has been somewhat sanitized, though.

Other nightlife options include checking out a classical Thai dinner-dance at The Oriental's **Sala Rim Nam** (p. 119), at **Studio 9** restaurant, which is part of the city's famous **Patravadi Theater** (p. 109), or at adjacent **Supatra River House**

(p. 119). Or **Muay Thai (Thai Boxing)** can be watched at **Rachadamnoen** or **Lumphini** stadiums (p. 135).

Day 3: Day Trips from Bangkok

If you've already covered all the attractions listed above, take a day trip on your third day in Bangkok. Options include a wonderful boat and bus trip to the former capital of **Ayutthaya** (p. 149), a journey to **Kanchanaburi** (p. 148), home of the "Death Railway," or a trip to **Khao Yai National Park** (p. 149), which offers welcome greenery.

2 Ancient Capitals Tour: 1 Week in Thailand

You'll start your 1-week capitals tour in Bangkok in order to take in some of the country's main historic sites, and then head elsewhere to trace the nation's legacy back to the ancient seats of power. First, you'll head north to Ayutthaya—the capital until the late 18th century—then carry on via tiny Lopburi (it's best to do so by train), to Phitsanulok. Meander onwards to Sukhothai and Si Satchanalai, the very origins of the Kingdom of Thailand, before finally ending up in the ancient Lanna capital of Chiang Mai. If you want to extend your trip, you can visit some of the archaeological sites that exist in Isan in the northeast; temples towns such as Phimai there reflect the influence of the Khmers who built Angkor Wat in Cambodia.

Pack light for this journey, as you'll be carrying your own luggage all the way (unless you arrange a private car or tour for the whole itinerary).

Day 1: Bangkok to Ayutthaya

Arrive in Bangkok and then depart for Ayutthaya, just a short trip away. You can arrange to go by boat (see "Side Trips from Bangkok" in chapter 6), as a one-way journey. It's more fun and adventurous, though, to go by local train from Bangkok's Hua Lampong train station (easily accessed by subway).

In Ayutthaya, check into **Krungsri River Hotel** (p. 277), one of the best accommodations options; though it's basic, it's convenient to the train station. From there, cross by rickety local ferry to the center of the old city and see the highlights. The city museums include the **Ayutthaya Historical Study Center** (p. 275) and the **Chao Sam Phraya National Museum** (p. 275); both contain good historical info and artifacts. Don't miss **Wat Phra Mahathat** (p. 276) in the city center, the most striking of the Ayutthaya ruins, and **Viharn Phra Mongkol Bopit** (p. 276), which is home to Thailand's largest seated bronze Buddha. Then take a late afternoon tour by long-tail boat around the city island.

In the evening, catch a meal at the colorful **Chao Phrom Night Market** (p. 278) or at one of the city's little floating restaurants. The ruins are illuminated in the evening, so a night tour is another option.

Day 2: Ayutthaya to Phitsanulok (via Lopburi)

Get an early start and hop on the first train to the small town of Lopburi—about an hour north of Ayutthaya. Leave your bags at the train station and find the TAT office just down the well-marked alley for a map. Visit **King Narai's Palace** (p. 279) and the museum on the grounds. Catch the afternoon train to Phitsanulok. Overnight at **Topland Hotel** (p. 284) in the center of Phitsanulok—then enjoy a meal at the riverside night market there or at one of the city's floating restaurants.

Day 3: Phitsanulok to Sukhothai

Wake up early to visit Phitsanulok's **Wat Phra Si Ratana Mahathat ("Wat Yai";**

Thailand Itineraries

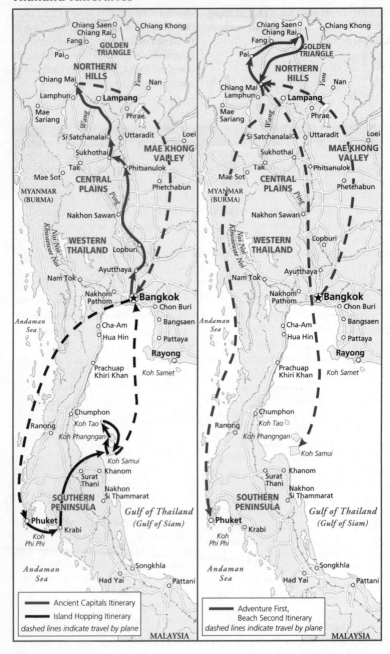

p. 285) or the intriguing **Sgt. Maj. Thavee Folk Museum** (p. 285) before heading by road to Sukhothai. You can get there by local bus, but it's best to go by rented vehicle with a driver as this gives you freedom to explore rural sites along the way. There are a number of small tour and rental agencies in Phitsanulok that'll arrange the tour for you; see p. 283 for options.

Once in Sukhothai, check in for the night at the cozy **Ruean Thai Hotel** (p. 287) or the exceptional **Tharaburi Resort** (p. 287). Wherever you stay, be sure to dine at the uniquely eccentric **Dream Café** (p. 288).

Day 4: Sukhothai to Chiang Mai (with stops in Lampang or Mae Sot)

This is a long-haul day and there are a few options for going about it. You can backtrack to Phitsanulok, unload your rented vehicle and go to Lampang (or on to Chiang Mai) by local transport (bus or train), or keep the rented vehicle and carry on straight from Sukhothai to Lampang or Chiang Mai.

Along the way north, skirt in to see the temples of **Si Satchanalai** (p. 290) just north of Sukhothai. Afterwards, you can make an extended stop in Lampang and, time permitting, visit the **Thai Elephant Conservation Center** (p. 339), where guests can train to become a *mahout* (elephant handler). Then you can head straight up to Chiang Mai.

From Sukhothai, you could also take a more intrepid route; head west for an overnight stay at the Burmese border town of **Mae Sot** (p. 290), and then travel along the rugged border of Myanmar to little **Mae Sariang** (a stop on the Mae Hong Son loop; p. 347) before going to Chiang Mai.

Day 5: Chiang Mai

During the day, explore the Old City walls and visit any of the 121 temple sites located along small alleys in the heart of Chiang Mai. In the evening, head to **The House** (p. 321) for some wine, tapas, and a fantastic dinner, or take a tuk-tuk to Charoenraj Road and the hip stores of **Vila Cini** (for the north's best silk; p. 335) or **La Luna** gallery (p. 332). Spend a little time checking out the **Night Bazaar** (p. 333), which is a street-long clutter of cheap souvenir stalls; then head to **Nimmanheimin Road**'s boutiques (p. 334), which are classier.

Day 6: Chiang Mai to Bangkok

Do some last-minute shopping in Chiang Mai before returning to Bangkok either by car, bus, or regional airline. Once there, follow the Day 1 options under the Bangkok itinerary above.

Day 7: Bangkok

Spend some time seeing more of the sites of Bangkok, listed under Day 2 of the Bangkok itinerary above. Then prepare for your flight home.

3 Island-Hopping & Adventure in the Southern Peninsula: From 2 Weeks to Eternity in Thailand

This itinerary can be lengthened at any stage. Found a great spot? Stay for awhile—but don't overstay your visa! Seasonal weather can impact both the choice of coast (east/west) and prevailing air and boat schedules.

Day 1: Bangkok

Arrive into Bangkok and follow the Day 1 itinerary listed under "Begin (or End) in Bangkok" above.

Day 2: Bangkok to Phuket

A short flight and transfer will bring you to Phuket (p. 224), which has resorts that range from luxurious to simple motels;

try for a room at Burasari (p. 239) if you like boutique properties, go for JW Marriott (p. 244) if you want a resort close to the airport, or stay at the sprawling Banyan Tree Phuket (p. 242) if you crave the sort of spa villas and double pool villas that appeal to jetsetters.

In high season, expect restaurant prices, taxis, and tuk-tuks to be double that of Bangkok prices. Be prepared to pay for everything from beach loungers to umbrellas.

Days 3 & 4: Phuket

These 2 days could turn into many more as Phuket's lure takes hold. Dine in roadside joints or sample pricey eateries such as **Oriental Spoon** at **Twin Palms** (p. 241), which has a great wine list, or the cacophonous **Ratri Jazztaurant** (p. 247), situated upon a cliff top. The island's heaving nightlife and red-light activity center around **Patong,** where Brit Super Chef Keith Floyd has opened **Floyd's Brasserie** (p. 248). Families still flock to giggle at **Phuket Fantasea**'s (p. 256) kitschy ladyboy show. But many opt for a quiet candlelit dinner at a resort like the **JW Marriott** (p. 244).

Eco-tourists will appreciate a paddle with Hawaiian John Grey of **John Grey's Sea Canoe** (p. 251), or enjoy a few days in **Khao Sok National Park** (p. 182). In season, advanced divers can visit the pristine and uninhabited **Similan Islands** (p. 257), accessible only by sea.

Days 5 & 6: Phuket to Krabi

Get geared up for extreme hot weather as you head inland: bring sunglasses, water, a hat, and waterproof sunscreen, and perhaps a sarong. Depart by boat from Phuket town pier. Stop for part of the day at **Koh Phi Phi** (p. 266), a much-promoted dumbbell-shaped isle. Climb Phi Phi Don to get great ocean views, or snorkel in warm waters, before taking an afternoon boat to **Krabi** (p. 260). You can also do part of this as a quick hop on

Destination Air's amphibious planes (www.destinationair.com) or as a coastal road trip, with stops in **Phang Nga Bay** (p. 251).

Rather than staying in Krabi town, head to Ao Nang, which has many budget places. Jetsetters love super-luxury resorts such as the remodeled **Rayavadee** (p. 263) or the new **Sofitel Phokeethra** (p. 265). From here, speed out to the wondrous islets of **Koh Poda** (p. 262) and **Koh Hong** (p. 261). Serious rock climbers can try scaling Railay's high karst cliffs.

Take an extra day here, consider a side trip to **Trang** (where you can stay at the luxury **Amari Trang;** p. 271), or hang out on sleepy **Koh Lanta** (p. 268). Return to Phuket by sea or land.

Day 7: Phuket to Koh Samui

In high season, you can hop on a **Bangkok Airways** flight from Phuket to **Koh Samui** (p. 189). The road, boat, and train routes from Phuket to Koh Samui appeal to hardier, budget travelers.

In Koh Samui, **Bophut Beach** (p. 192) offers midrange and luxury options, while **Chaweng Beach** (p. 193) offers every sort of hotel, plus it buzzes with nightlife action. The standout place to stay is **Coral Bay** (p. 200), though, which is in a relatively quiet area and boasts luxury choices. Try **The Tongsai Bay, Baan Taling Ngam Resort,** or the **Evason Hua Hin,** as these feature great spas.

Koh Samui has loads going on: You can enroll in a cooking course at **SITCA** (p. 209), sign up to do scuba diving on a day trip to **Ang Thong Marine National Park** (p. 211), play a round of golf in conjunction with a dive trip aboard **Ocean Rover** (p. 208), or get healthy with a fasting program offered at **Tamarind Springs** or **Spa Samui** (p. 209). Nightlife in Chaweng will keep you busy till late, too; see chapter 8 for info.

Day 8: Samui

Use the day to check out Samui's weird rock formations or simply chill on the beach. Book an appointment for later in the day at the delightful **Anantara Resort** (p. 176) near Bophut, which offers amazing spa treatments. Afterwards, hit the nightlife on Chaweng Beach or head down to **Laem Set** (p. 193) to take in a wonderful sunset.

Day 9: Samui to Koh Pha Ngan

Koh Pha Ngan (see chapter 8) offers a seriously alternative holiday, with revelry centered on **Had Rin** (p. 214). Party animals perennially seek out the Full Moon and Half Moon Parties, as well as regular beach raves known as "Black Moon Parties," here. If you are not into raves or dance parties, fear not; wellness-oriented **The Sanctuary** (p. 215) is a world away from the full-moon madness.

Days 10 & 11: Koh Pha Ngan to Koh Tao

If diving is your passion, check out sites around **Koh Tao** ("Turtle Island," p. 218); it's a boat ride from Koh Samui or Koh Pha Ngan. (There's still plenty to do on Koh Pha Ngan for non-aquanauts.)

Day 12: Rest Day

Wherever you are, relax. Stretch out and reflect on the trip's highlights.

Day 13 & 14: Koh Samui to Bangkok

Return by air to Bangkok (allow 1–2 days extra for boat connections from the islands during June–Oct, or Nov–Jan). Squeeze in some shopping or a farewell Thai dinner in the city before leaving.

4 Adventure First, Beach Second Tour: 2 Weeks in Thailand

Here's a good way to combine serious relaxation and great shopping with adventure: Starting from Bangkok, take an overnight train or fly to your starting point—Chiang Mai. Try your hand at river rafting, elephant handling, or experience hot-air ballooning. Then catch a flight to one of the beach destinations in the south, Krabi, Trang, Koh Lanta, Phuket, or Koh Samui. Put your feet up and chill out on some of the Andaman's loveliest beaches before finally heading back to Bangkok.

Day 1: Bangkok

Follow the Day 1 options under the Bangkok itinerary listed earlier.

Day 2: Bangkok to Chiang Mai

After a flight or car ride, arrive into Chiang Mai. Reasonable, centrally located guesthouses dot the **Old City** (p. 308) here. Alternatively, try upscale old world gems such as **The Rachamankha** (p. 316) or modern boutique properties like **The Chedi** (p. 311).

After checking into your hotel, savor the many sites inside the **Old City** (p. 308). Shop for fabulous homewares and fashions in the chi-chi **Nimmanheimin Road.** Then get ready for dinner;

riverside dining options abound, but I like the fantastic modern Thai-fusion at **The House** (p. 321) or Burmese *khao sawy* in the market.

Days 3 & 4: Chiang Mai to Pai

Consider splurging on a **hot-air balloon** ride at dawn over Doi Suthep run by the highly professional **Earth, Wind and Fire** (Nov–Mar only; p. 330). Then arrange an affordable tour with a guide and drive out to the hilly countryside. (Rental cars and motorcycles are only for the adventurous.) Explore the hills around lovely **Pai** (p. 342) and stay at the gorgeous **Belle Villa** (p. 345) outside of town. From Pai, arrange a 1- or 2-day trek or rafting adventure (see p. 344 for options).

Days 5 & 6: Adventures Outside of Pai

If you are rafting from Pai to Mae Hong Son, take a night's stay in the laid-back **Fern Resort** (p. 350) or the comfortable in-town **Imperial Tara** (p. 350). If going by road between Pai and Mae Hong Son (a scenic drive), be sure to stop at the cool **Spirit Caves** (p. 347) about halfway there.

Days 7 & 8: From Mae Hong Son (or Pai) to Chiang Rai

Journey to Chiang Rai via the sleepy towns of **Chiang Dao** (p. 340). In **Chiang Rai** (p. 353), relax at the rustic resort **The Legend Chiang Rai** (p. 356); trekking arrangements can be made though most hotels.

Head 50 minutes north to **The Golden Triangle,** an old opium-smuggling region bordering Laos and Myanmar (Burma). The lavish **Hall of Opium** (p. 361) or crumbling temple sites at **Chiang Saen** (p. 359) are worth a look. An hour away is **Mae Sai** (p. 359), a featureless town where tourists can cross into Myanmar.

Book one of the luxury riverside resorts here, such as the **Four Seasons' Tented Camp** (p. 330), or the **Anantara Golden Triangle** (p. 362), famous for hosting the annual King's Cup Elephant Polo Tournament each year, as well as its Mahout Camp.

Note: Looking for more adventure? Thailand's rugged Northeast, **Isan,** is ripe for exploration: You can fly to **Udon Thani** from Bangkok, Chiang Rai, or Chiang Mai, rent a vehicle, or join a tour (see chapter 14, "Exploring Isan: Thailand's Frontier" for details). When river conditions allow, you can travel from Chiang Rai to the Laos border (you will first need to get a Laos Visa), and then travel 2 days downriver to **Luang Prabang.** Due to high demand, you'll need to book your Laos accommodations well ahead.

Days 9 to 12: From Chiang Rai to the Beach

Leave the lush north and head south to warm, sandy beaches for a chance to rest. Choose your destination according to what's left of your budget. Popular getaways **Koh Samui** (p. 189) and **Phuket** (p. 224) are more expensive than smaller resort towns like **Trang** (p. 270). Enjoy the downtime to mull over your fascinating adventures.

Days 13 & 14: From the Beach to Bangkok

Head by flight or car back to Bangkok, and follow the options listed under Days 2 and 3 of the Bangkok itinerary earlier before heading home.

4

Introducing Bangkok

With a population of over 10 million in a country of only 64 million, Thailand's capital teems with humanity. As the cultural heart of the kingdom, the city keeps many traditions still visibly intact—yet Bangkok is also a rapidly changing city. If you go beyond the city's new transport systems (the above-road Bangkok Transit System [BTS] and the Mass Rapid Transit [MRT] subway), it can be a challenge. Heavy traffic, excessive heat and humidity, and at certain times of the year, smog, can make Bangkok truly overwhelming. Nevertheless, to find the charm of the city, all you need to do is to be adventurous and explore areas outside the central business district, packed full of skyscrapers and shopping malls.

Founded when King Rama I moved the city across the river from Thonburi in 1782, Bangkok is not a particularly ancient capital, but rather a cool mix of modernity and tradition. Saffron-robed monks mingle in the *sois* with Starbucks-drinking, cellphone-wielding yuppies or bouffant-wigged socialites known by the abbreviation *hi-so*. Luxurious, glass-clad condos brazenly penetrate the skyscape, juxtaposed by tin-roofed slums teetering along putrid canals. Amongst the concrete, glittering *wats* and ramshackle colonial edifices pepper this ancient and vibrant city.

What strikes many upon arrival in the Big Mango, as it's lovingly known, is the highly developed infrastructure, high-end shopping, world-class accommodations, and welcoming people; compared to Hong Kong and Singapore, though, the country is way behind in development, and locals aren't as fluent in English as in these wealthy former colonies. The modernity is often merely a beguiling façade—underneath there's grit and grime.

The culture here is so gloriously rich, though, that exploring Bangkok should be seen as a highlight of any trip to Thailand. And there are rooms to suit any budget. Bangkok's luxury hotels offer unrivaled rates and visitors can find anything from a basic 300B (US$8.60/£4.60) hostel to a ritzy high-rise suite. The cuisine is itself a worthy adventure; you can choose from fine dining in hip hangouts to simple market stalls.

The city is relatively safe, but unsuspecting tourists can be victims of thievery from time to time—mostly involving petty theft such as pickpocketing. For the most part, you can wander freely around the shopping districts or giddy markets unhindered. At some point, be sure to escape the frenetic pulse of the concrete jungle by ducking into a serene temple compound.

Rivaled only by Chiang Mai in the north, Bangkok is above all a great place to shop, for anything from name-brand luxury items (and, of course, knock-offs that won't last a week) to fine local handicrafts, antiques, silk, and jewels. And when it comes to nightlife, the endless array of great value night markets, bars, clubs, and eateries makes for a (potentially) sleepless night.

The Real Bangkok

Referred to as "Krung Thep" by Thais, meaning "The City of Angels," the official name of Bangkok is a proud description of Bangkok's royal legacy—and the world's longest: Krungthepmahanakhon Amonrattanakosin Mahintharayutthaya Mahadilokphop Noppharatratchathaniburirom Udomratchaniwetmahasathan Amonphimanawatansthit Sakkathattiyawitsanukamprasit.

1 Orientation

ARRIVING

BY PLANE

Bangkok's **Suvarnabhumi International Airport** (airport code BKK), opened in September 2006, is now the main hub for all international travelers arriving to Thailand; it also handles domestic flights (with three-digit codes) in and out of the capital. It's 30km (over 18 miles) east of the city. Suvarnabhumi offers a wide range of services, including luggage storage, currency exchange, banks, a branch of the British pharmacy Boots, ATMs, a post office, medical centers (two are 24-hr. clinics), Internet service, and telephones. All of Suvarnabhumi's restaurant and shopping outlets are infamously overpriced (up to 10 times city prices), though; budget travelers would do well to stop by a downtown convenience store to stock up on snacks and drinks. Five minutes away is **Novotel Suvarnabhumi Airport** (www.novotel.com), a five-star hotel. For more detailed information on Suvarnabhumi, see **www.airportthai.co.th**.

Old **Don Mueang Airport** (airline code DMG) is 24km (15 miles) north of the heart of the city and was closed for a period in 2006. It has recently reopened, serving some domestic flights (with four-digit codes) and all flights on One-Two-GO and Nok Air. It no longer offers the range of services it used to but still has cafes and diners as well as ATMs. **Amari Don Mueang Airport Hotel** (www.amari.com) is opposite the airport and accessed via a skybridge or a shuttle bus (book in advance). For more details on Don Mueang, see **www.bangkok-city.com/airport/airport_don-muang.htm**.

Note: As of 2007, passengers no longer pay any departure taxes. But there are no ATMs beyond Immigration (airside) at Suvarnabhumi, so all those leaving Thailand—or those in transit—must ensure they have enough cash for their onward destination before they enter passport control, especially those paying for visas on arrival in countries such as Myanmar and Indochina, where airside airport ATMs may not exist or may have run out of cash.

GETTING TO & FROM THE AIRPORTS   From both Suvarnabhumi and Don Mueang, it takes about 40 to 60 minutes to drive to the city, depending on traffic, and over 90 minutes in heavy rain or at rush hour (or both). The city's larger hotels offer **pickup services** for a fee, but both airports have **public taxi, limousine,** and **bus services** to Bangkok; Suvarnabhumi also has buses to Pattaya. Taking a taxi into town is your easiest and fastest option for both airports.

At the Arrival Halls at either airport, don't be tempted by the many taxi touts. In both airports, simply follow signs to the public taxi or bus stands. Get some small change, *torn satang* in Thai, in the Arrivals Hall before you leave the airport, as you'll need this for the tollbooths. Without tolls, expect to pay between 250B and 300B (US$7.10–US$8.60/£3.85–£4.60) from either airport to reach most hotels downtown.

Private limousine services such as AOT offer air-conditioned sedans and drivers from both airports. Look for the booth in Arrivals. Trips from Suvarnabhumi start at 1,200B (US$34/£18). Advanced booking is not necessary.

Airport Express buses (*©* **02995-1252**), located on Suvarnabhumi Level 1 at Gate 8, are a convenient and inexpensive alternative into the city and cost 150B (US$4.20/£2.30). Buses run every 30 minutes from 5am to midnight and cover four routes and most major hotels. For local and intercity buses, you will need to get on a free shuttle located at Level 2 or 4, going to the **Public Transportation Center.** From there, buses costing around 35B (US$1/55p) cover 11 city routes, including major BTS stops and the Southern Bus Terminal. For intercity services, go to the relevant ticket counter (daily 6am–9pm) at the Public Transportation Center; three routes serve nearby Pattaya, Jomtien, and Chonburi.

BY TRAIN

While a few southern-bound locomotives still use Thonburi's Bangkok Noi Station, most intercity trains to and from the capital stop at **Hua Lampong Station** (*©* **02223-7010** or the hotline at 1690), east of Yaowarat (Chinatown). Lying at a major intersection of Rama IV and Krung Kasem roads, it's notoriously gridlocked at morning and evening rush hours, so allow 40 minutes extra for traffic delays. Inside the station, clear signs point the way to the public toilets, pay phones, food court, and baggage check area. One bag costs 20B (50¢/30p) per day.

"Officials" may approach you in the station offering help. Be careful—not all may actually be officials; proceed to the ticketing counter or information booth directly.

Metered taxis from the station cost about 50B to 100B (US$1.40–US$2.85/ 75p–£1.55) to nearby Sala Daeng BTS on Silom Road, depending on the time of day; there is an **MRT** (subway) station at **Hua Lamphong** for connections to the BTS. For Sukhumvit Road, take the MRT to the Sukhumvit stop and then transfer to the Asok BTS.

BY BUS

Bangkok has three major bus stations, each serving a different part of the country. All air-conditioned public buses to the West and the Southern Peninsula arrive and depart from the **Southern Bus Terminal** (*©* **02434-7192**) on Nakhon Chaisi and Phra Pin-klao Road (near Bangkok Noi Station in Thonburi; west of the river over the Phra Pinklao Bridge from the Democracy Monument). Service to the East Coast (including Pattaya) arrives and departs from the **Eastern Bus Terminal,** also known as **Ekka-mai** (*©* **02391-2504**), on Sukhumvit Road opposite Soi 63 (Ekkamai BTS). Buses to the north arrive and leave from the **Northern Bus Terminal,** aka Mo Chit (*©* **02936-2841**), Kampaengphet 2 Road, near the **Chatuchak Weekend Market,** and a short taxi or bus ride from Mo Chit BTS or MRT stations. Affordable, long-distance VIP buses leave from various locations in town and can be booked by any of the agents along Sukhumvit or Khao San roads.

VISITOR INFORMATION

The **Bangkok Tourist Bureau** has offices at major junctions throughout the city. Call them with any questions at *©* **02225-7612;** or visit www.bangkoktourist.com. They provide basic information services, maps, brochures, and recommendations. Their main office is at 17/1 Phra Arthit Rd., just under the Phra Pinklao bridge near Khao San, but they also operate out of the airports and in various kiosks around the city:

Bangkok at a Glance

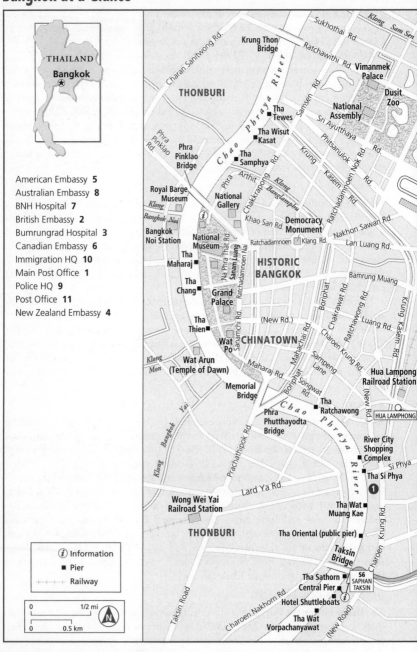

American Embassy **5**
Australian Embassy **8**
BNH Hospital **7**
British Embassy **2**
Bumrungrad Hospital **3**
Canadian Embassy **6**
Immigration HQ **10**
Main Post Office **1**
Police HQ **9**
Post Office **11**
New Zealand Embassy **4**

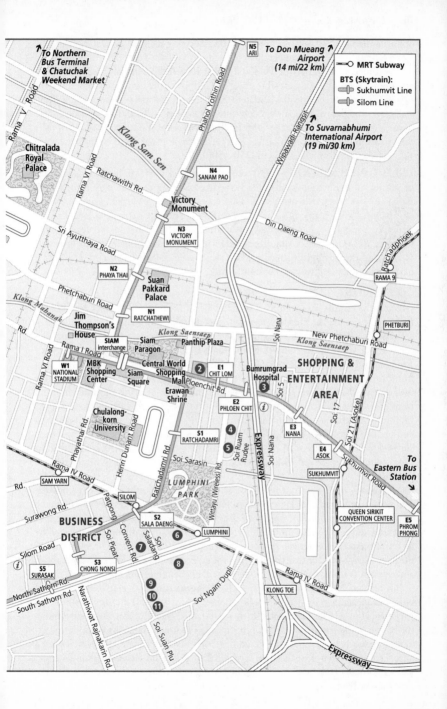

opposite the Grand Palace, in front of MBK shopping mall, at River City mall, and along Sukhumvit. All offices are open Monday to Saturday from 9am to 4:30pm.

The **Tourism Authority of Thailand** (TAT; www.tourismthailand.org) offers general information regarding travel in Bangkok and upcountry, and has a useful hotline (© **1672**) reachable from anywhere in the kingdom; it's open daily 8am to 8pm. Ironically, TAT's offices are not always conveniently located for foreigners who don't read Thai. It has a kiosk at Suvarnabhumi International Airport's arrival floor, open daily 8am to 10pm, but their main office is off the beaten track at 1600 New Phetchaburi Rd., Makkasan, Ratchathewi (© **02250-5500**).

USEFUL PUBLICATIONS   TAT produces an enormous number of glossy tourist brochures on destinations, including Bangkok; but beware, many may be outdated. Bangkok's free magazines, available in hotel lobbies, are more current. Look for *Where* or *Thaiways,* with maps, tips, and facts covering Pattaya, Chiang Mai, and Phuket. *Bangkok Dining & Entertainment* specializes mostly in restaurant reviews and nightlife. *BK Magazine* is a fun, free weekly with info on the capital's events (available at any Starbucks). English-language daily newspapers *Bangkok Post* and *The Nation* have sections devoted to Bangkok must-sees.

CITY LAYOUT

Nineteenth-century photographs of Bangkok tell of the busy life on the **Chao Phraya River,** where a ragtag range of vessels—from humble rowboats to sailing ships—crowded the busy port. This was the original gateway for early foreign visitors who traveled upriver from the Gulf of Siam. Rama I, upon moving the capital city from Thonburi on the west bank to Bangkok on the east, dug a series of canals fanning out from the S-shaped river. For strategic reasons, the canals replicated the moat system used at Ayutthaya, Siam's previous capital, in the hopes of protecting the city from invasion. The city waterways represented the primordial oceans that surrounded the Buddhist heavens. A small artificial island was cut into the land along the riverbank and became the site for the Grand Palace, Wat Phra Kaew (the Temple of the Emerald Buddha), and Wat Po. To this day, this quarter is referred to as **Koh** (island) **Rattanakosin.** This is the historical center of the city and the main tourist destination for day trips.

The canals, or *klongs,* continued eastward from Rattanakosin as the city's population grew. Chinese and Indian merchants formed settlements alongside the river to the southeast of the island. The mercantile district of **Yaowarat** (Chinatown) is a maze of busy back alleys. Its main thoroughfare, Charoen Krung Road (sometimes called by its former name, New Road), snakes southward, following the shape of the river. On the eastern edge of Chinatown, you'll find the arched **Hua Lampong railway station,** a marvelous example of fanciful, fin-de-siècle Italian engineering.

Just beyond Yaowarat, along the river, lies **Bangrak** district, where foreign interests built European-style residences, trading houses, churches, and a crumbling colonial Customs House. **The Oriental Hotel,** the Grande Dame of Bangkok, sits among them, one of the few great heritage properties left in town. Bangrak's main thoroughfares, Surawong Road, Silom Road, and Sathorn Road, originate at Charoen Krung (also known as New Road), running parallel to Rama IV Road. Within Bangrak, you'll find many embassies, hotels and high-rises, restaurants, and pubs, as well as the sleazy nightlife at Patpong or glitzy gay clubs in Silom Soi 4.

Back to Rattanakosin, as you head upriver, you'll hit **Banglampoo,** home to Bangkok's National Museum, Wat Suthat, The Giant Swing, and Klong Phu Khao Thong (Golden Mount). Its central point is Democracy Monument, a roundabout where the wide Ratchadamnoen Klong Road intersects Dinso Road. Around the corner is Khao San Road, which was once solely a backpacker hangout. It still has budget accommodations, inexpensive restaurants, lots of tour agents, good nightlife, and it's hanging onto its 1970s hippy flavor—but is also heading into the mainstream. Starbucks, Burger King, and Boots are all muscling in on the once funk-filled, alternative vibe here.

Farther north of Banglampoo is leafy **Dusit,** home to Wat Benchamabophit, Vimanmek Palace, the Dusit Zoo, and parks.

As Bangkok spread on the east shore of the river, **Thonburi,** the former site of the capital across the river, remained in relative isolation. While Bangkok was quick to fill in canals ushering in the age of the automobile, residential Thonburi's canals remained, and a long-tail boat ride through the area is a high point of any trip here. Thai riverside homes, both traditional and new, and neighborhood businesses (some housed in floating barges) reveal glimpses of life as it might have been 200 years ago. Access to Thonburi's **Bangkok's Southern Bus Terminal** is via the Phra Pinklao Bridge from Banglampoo.

Back on the other side of the river, Bangkok grew and fanned eastward. From Koh Rattanakosin, beyond Bangrak, lies **Pathumwan,** known for its huge market. This is where the famous American journalist and silk connoisseur **Jim Thompson** once lived. His stunning Thai-style house is now open to visitors. Nearby is busy **Siam Square,** with its myriad boutiques and huge shopping malls. This area's hotels, cafes, and nightclubs attract scores of local teenagers and students. Beyond Pathumwan, **Wireless (Witthayu) Road** runs north to south between **Rama IV Road** (at the edge of Bangrak) and **Rama I Road** (at the edge of Pathumwan). Here, the huge U.S. Embassy complex stands just meters from a clutch of five-star hotels and chic shopping centers like **All Seasons Place** and **Central Chidlom.**

From Siam Square, **Sukhumvit Road** extends due east, its length traced by the BTS. Many expatriates live along the small side streets, or *sois,* that branch out from Sukhumvit. This area is lined with tourist restaurants and entertainment spots, shops, and big malls—you'll find luxury hotels alongside inexpensive accommodations, fine dining and cheap local eats, as well as clothing stores and street-side bazaars. (Be aware that there are also lots of schemers in this area.) Easterly situated Sukhumvit is mostly a major commercial center and much of it is connected by the overhead BTS. **Bangkok's Eastern Bus Terminal** is at Ekkamai BTS, on Sukhumvit Soi 63.

FINDING AN ADDRESS   Note that even-numbered addresses are on one side of the street and odd-numbered ones the opposite, but they are not always close to each other. So 123 and 124 Silom Rd. will be on opposite sides of the street, but possibly 300m or even farther apart! Most addresses are subdivided by a slash, as in 123/4 Silom Rd., which simply accounts for new construction. You'll find the term *thanon* frequently in addresses; it means "street" in Thai. *Soi* is a lane off a major street and is either numbered or named. If you are looking for "45 Soi 23 Sukhumvit," it means, plot 45, on Soi 23, off Sukhumvit Road. On Sukhumvit Road, even-numbered *sois* will be on the south side (look for landmarks such as **JW Marriott, Sheraton Grande Sukhumvit,** or **Emporium Shopping Mall**), and odd-numbered *sois* on the north side (same as **Robinson's** and **Thong Lor**).

NEIGHBORHOODS IN BRIEF

Hotels, restaurants, and attractions have been subdivided into smaller regions within the city.

On the River Bangkok's grandest riverside hotels are all clustered near Saphan Taksin. You'll find wholesale silver, jewelry, and antique stores along Charoen Krung (New) Road and Soi Oriental. Farther upstream, colonial buildings and churches give these old run-down districts a certain charm. Across the river in Thonburi, you can discover Thai dance shows and theater, as well as low-cost riverside diners and luxury spas.

Yaowarat or Chinatown Also along the riverside and just west of the Grand Palace area and Banglampoo, Chinatown is a frenetic maze of stores, old trading warehouses, and great places to eat.

Banglampoo, Historic Bangkok Home to the Grand Palace, this area lies within the area known as Koh Rattanakosin. It contains the city's most important historical sites including Wat Po, the Grand Palace, and Wat Phra Kaew, as well as the Dusit Zoo and Vimanmek Palace Museum. Within the area are numerous historic *wats* (temples), the National Museum, and the National Theater and Library. Khao San Road is the city's former backpacker district, and moderate accommodations are located among the many budget guesthouses. The only drawback here is that it's a real trek to get to the BTS or MRT.

Bangrak This area likes to think of itself as the Central Business District, though its "downtown" label is debatable. It is bound by Rama IV Road on the north, Yaowarat (Chinatown) on the northwest, and Charoen Krung (New) Road due west, while Silom and Surawong roads run through its center. Many banks, businesses, and embassies have offices in this area, but it is also a good choice for travelers, with malls—such as the Silom Complex—reasonably priced restaurants, tourist hotels, and the seamier Patpong red-light area.

Sukhumvit Road, Ploenchit Road, and Chidlom Known as Rama I Road at its western end, this main east-west thoroughfare is straddled overhead by the BTS. After crossing Ratchadamri Road (at the Erawan Shrine), it then becomes Ploenchit Road and runs directly east crossing Wittayu (Wireless) Road at Chit Lom BTS (Central's flagship department store) until it finally becomes Sukhumvit Road at the mouth of the airport freeway. Hotels, shopping complexes, office buildings, and some smaller embassies serve a thriving expat community here. Though rather far from the historic sites, it's convenient for shopping and nightlife.

2 Getting Around

The city has three bus stations (p. 73) and the main train station is Hua Lampong (p. 73), with another station called Bangkok Noi, from where trains head south and to Kanchanaburi. Within the city, taxis and *tuk-tuks* (three-wheeled motorized open vehicles) cruise the small streets. (*Note:* The latter often turn out to be more expensive than the former.) Motorcycle taxis cost little but are unsafe: They're useful only for short hops down *sois* and helpful only if you know your destination in Thai. The BTS (or Skytrain) is the city's efficient elevated rail line, while the subway is known as the MRT. Both connect with the main Hua Lampong train station, but neither reaches the city's two airports.

Bangkok's taxis are quite affordable and the best choice for door-to-door transportation—if you've got the time. It can take more than 2 hours by taxi to get from one side of town to the other during rush hour. The good news is that, with the convenient BTS and MRT lines (as well as the Chao Phraya River's many boats, which act as daytime river taxis), you can avoid the standstill in the city center. Access to the town's modern and effective public transport is often a key factor in visitors' choice of accommodations and dining, and areas like Khao San Road, detached from the better modes of transport, are decreasing in popularity when compared to places like Sukhumvit and Silom.

See the inside front cover of this book for a map of the Bangkok metro lines.

BY BTS   The **Bangkok Transit System (BTS)** gets called "Skytrain" by foreigners (though calling it thus will just confuse local taxi drivers). It opened in 1999 and is the best way for the able-bodied to get around Bangkok. Sadly, its lack of elevators makes it unsuitable for the physically challenged or those who can't cope with stairs. While coverage is still limited (extensions to Thonburi are planned for 2008), the train system provides good access to Bangkok's commercial centers. The Silom Line runs from the Chao Phraya River's Central Pier at Saphan Taksin (Taksin Bridge) through the Silom area to Siam Square. The interchange point for the Sukhumvit Line is at Siam BTS and goes north to Chatuchak Weekend Market (at Mo Chit BTS), or east, along the length of Sukhumvit road to On Nut BTS.

Single-journey tickets cost from 15B to 40B (28¢–US$1.10/14p–60p). For single trips, it's fairly straightforward to buy tickets at the vending machines that have place names spelled phonetically in English; you can get small change at the information booth as needed. All ticket types let you through the turnstile and are required for exit, so be sure to hang on to them. You can also buy the new, stored-value Sky Smart Pass that can be topped up (you simply sweep them over sensors at the turnstile) for 100B (US$5.10/£1.55) plus a 30B (85¢/44p) nonrefundable deposit. It's used up as you travel and lasts 5 years. Or, there's a 1-day unlimited travel ticket for 120B (US$3.40/£1.85), as well as 30-day Smart Passes (check student and adult fares) which, though they also require a deposit, save you from fumbling for change at the vending machines every trip. These multitrip cards give you discounted rates, thus counter-balancing the small deposit.

Hours of operation are daily between 6am and midnight. For route details, see **www.bangkok-city.com/skytrain.htm**. For the latest mass transit maps and ticket info, check **www.bts.co.th/en/btstrain.asp**.

BY SUBWAY   Bangkok's **Mass Rapid Transit (MRT)** was completed in 2004. The 18-stop system will be extended over the next decade. Beginning at Hua Lamphong Train Station, the MRT heads southeast past Lumphini Park before turning north, up to Lad Phrao, and then makes a wiggle westward to Bang Sue. It has a messy and confusing interchange outside the Dusit Thani Hotel, 100m from Sala Daeng BTS (on Silom Road) and also at Asok BTS (on Sukhumvit Road) before its terminus near Mo Chit Bus Station in the north and the Chatuchak Weekend Market. Trains run from 5am to midnight and the system uses small plastic discs or stored-value Smart Passes, which, like the BTS Sky Smart Pass, are swept over sensors. Unlimited-travel Day Passes cost 120B (US$3.40/£1.85). The official website, www.bangkokmetro.co.th, is mostly in Thai and not half as useful as **www.bangkok-city.com/mrta.htm**.

BY PUBLIC RIVERBOATS Efficient and scenic, but not so comfortable, the public riverboats on the Chao Phraya are a great way to get around the sites in the city center and are a remarkable window into local life.

The boats of the **Chao Phraya Express Boat Ltd.** (© 02222-5330) travel the river's length and stop at most public piers (*tha* in Thai); the cost is 120B ($US3/£1.80) for an all-day pass. They tend to be full at rush hour and the last boats leave Central Pier around 7pm Monday to Friday. Downstream, boats tend to stop on the Thonburi side (west) and head upstream on the eastern side (Grand Palace side). The popular commuter service continues out to Nonthaburi, north of the city.

Good river maps are contained in Nancy Chandler's *Map of Bangkok* (p. 18), but river pier maps are posted at each stop. Most sightseers will board at Central Pier, down the steps from Saphan Taksin (Taksin Bridge) BTS. The major stops going upstream from Saphan Taksin are Tha Ratchawong (for Chinatown), Tha Thien (near Wat Po), and Tha Chang (near the Temple of the Emerald Buddha). Check the colored flags on the boats' sterns to know if they offer stopping service or are express (nonstop) boats. Also see **www.bangkok-city.com/expressboat.htm** for details of each route, prices, schedules, and flag codes.

Chao Phraya Tourist Boats are the most relaxed way to travel throughout the city by boat. These steady, wide-bodied vessels are huge and have plenty of seats and make regular stops along the river. Guides explain over a microphone in English about the sites you pass. The last boat leaving Taksin Bridge is at 3pm. Short trips start at 15B (35¢/18p), but you can also buy an all-day pass, good for all riverboats, for 100B (US$2.45/£1.55). Boats take about 30 minutes to go from Taksin Bridge to Banglampoo.

Cross-river ferries are small ferries that only run from the east bank to the west, so they're useful for getting to places like Wat Arun, Klong San Market, or Patravadi Theater. They cost 3B (10¢/5p) each way.

BY CHARTERED LONG-TAIL BOAT Private boats are a great way to see the busy riverside area and to tour the narrow canals of neighboring Thonburi. Boat charters are available at any pier. You can wave one down and, within seconds, you'll be greeted by the shouts of operators. But it's more convenient and probably safer to arrange trips at the riverfront kiosk at **River City** or at the **Grand Palace** (© 02225-6179). If you want a guide, check for one with a TAT license, as you're less likely to be overcharged. Trips

---

⌒Finds **Surfing the Canals**

Here's a fun but somewhat odorous way to beat rush-hour traffic, allowing you to cross Bangkok from a starting point close to the Grand Palace and trek back to Sukhumvit through the commercial heart of the city. A narrow, dirty canal, Klong Saen Saep, runs the length of New Phetchaburi Road with stops in central Bangkok (and all the way to Thong Lor after a change at Krung Kasem Road). These long, low boats are designed to fit under bridges and are fitted with tarps that are raised and lowered by pulleys to protect passengers from any toxic splashes. Rides start at just 8B (20¢/10p). Board the boats just north of Wat Mahathat. These canal buses really zip along and churn up a stink, but they offer a unique perspective on the last vestiges of what was once called the "Venice of The East," and taking one gets you back to central Bangkok without having to inhale noxious bus fumes in motionless traffic.

of varying length cost up to 1,000B (US$29/£15) per hour, per boat—though drivers will want to negotiate this. Be specific about destinations and times before you agree to one.

BY PUBLIC BUS   Bangkok buses are very cheap, frequent, and fairly fast, but a little bit confusing and not user-friendly in terms of helpful ticket-takers, or simply marked routes and stops. There are big blue buses with air-conditioned routes and also cheaper red or small green ones (non-air-conditioned). Anyone with asthma or respiratory conditions would do well to avoid these fume-filled tin cans. You'll need to be especially careful of pickpockets on buses, too.

The most practical air-conditioned routes are A1 (looping from the Grand Palace area to Rama IV Road, Siam Square, and then east down Ploenchit and Sukhumvit roads), A2 (running a loop through the Business District [Bangrak] area along Silom and Surawong roads), A3 (connecting the Dusit area near the zoo and Khao San Road before crossing the Chao Phraya), and A8 (running the length of Rama I, Ploenchit, and Sukhumvit roads). Fares are collected onboard, even for air-conditioned routes—try to have exact change. Fares are cheap, between 8B and 20B (15¢–50¢/15p–30p).

BY TAXI   Taxis are everywhere in this city—except, of course, during a change of shift (from 3 to 4:30pm) and in heavy rain. But when they do appear, they are very affordable. Few drivers speak any English, so learn a few useful Thai words. Just flag them down (you can hail taxis along any road at any time, or join queues in front of hotels and shopping malls) and always insist that drivers use the meter. At night, especially around Patpong and The Oriental Hotel, stationary taxis will try to fleece passengers with demands for an extortionately high flat fare. Let these sharks be, and opt for flagging one down that's already traveling along the main road.

Taxis charge a 35B (US$1.95/55p) flat rate for the first 3km (2 miles); thereafter it is about 5B (14¢/10p) per kilometer. Most drivers are from Isan, Thailand's rural northeast, and do not read maps, so it's good to have your hotel concierge write out any destination in Thai.

Drivers rarely carry change. The best you will get is change from 100B (US$2.85/ £1.55) notes, but drivers habitually claim that they have no change in the hope of getting a bit extra. Tipping is not necessary, but appreciated.

BY CAR & DRIVER   You'd have to be a certified lunatic to drive yourself around Bangkok: Generally anarchic traffic, seas of cavalier motor bikes recklessly breaking every rule, and aggressive tactics by (sometimes amphetamine-fueled) cabbies and truck drivers are the norm. If you're in search of your own wheels, it is best to hire a car with a driver. Reputable companies provide sedans or minivans with drivers who know the city well, some of whom speak English. They also offer the option of an accompanying tour guide—professionals or students who can take you around each sight. The best hotels provide luxury vehicles with an English-speaking driver for at least 3,000B (US$86/£46) a day; it works out far more costly per hour (check with your concierge).

World Travel (② 02233-5900) and **Sea Tour** (② 02216-5783) both arrange English-speaking drivers/guides to lead you on customized tours but expect to pay top rates for top service, about 3,000B (US$86/£46) per person. Companies like **Avis** (2/12 Wireless Rd.; ② 02255-5300) offer chauffeured cars; specify that you want a car with a driver when you call for rates.

BY TUK-TUK   As much a national symbol as the elephant, the *tuk-tuk* (named for the sound) is a small three-wheeled, open-sided vehicle powered by a motorcycle engine. It is noisy, smelly, and incredibly cramped for long legs but definitely provides good photo opportunities. They're not recommended for long hauls or during rush hour—if you get stuck behind a bus or truck you'll be dealing with unpleasant exhaust fumes and the resulting migraines. Tuk-tuks are also death traps in the event of an accident (and the drivers tend to be a bit kamikaze), so avoid using them on highways. For short trips off highways, during off-peak hours, though, they're convenient and an adventure, especially for first-time visitors to Thailand. All tuk-tuk fares are negotiated, usually beginning at 50B (US$1.40/75p) for foreigners on short trips. Bargain very hard, but know that you'll always pay 100% more than locals.

A warning: Tuk-tuk drivers are notorious for trying to talk travelers into shopping trips, and massage parlors masquerading as brothels, places where they get a commission or gas voucher. They will offer you a very low fare, but then dump you at small, out-of-the-way gem and silk emporiums, and overpriced tourist restaurants or brothels. Insist on being taken where you want to go directly or mention the word: *poleet;* it's how Thais pronounce "police."

BY MOTORCYCLE TAXI   On every street corner, packs of drivers in orange vests stand by to shuttle passengers around the city. Though they get you around fast when you're in a hurry (weaving through traffic jams and speeding down one-way streets the wrong way), they're also incredibly unsafe. These guys don't bother with safety, or insurance, and stay awake on long shifts with energy drinks such as Red Bull. Use them strictly for short distances (they're popular for short hops to the end of a long *soi,* or side street). They charge from 20B (57¢/30p) for a few blocks to 60B (US$1.70/90p) for greater distances. Hold on tight and keep your knees tucked in. Crash helmets are mandatory these days—so insist on one, but know the flimsy headwear on offer will be almost useless in the event of a crash.

ON FOOT   In general, Bangkok is not a pedestrian-friendly city, though improvements have been made in the city center with the construction of skywalks. Bangkok sidewalks are a gauntlet of buckled tiles, loose manhole coverings, and tangled (live) wires. The city also suffers greatly from flooding; be on guard and don't wear fancy open shoes in monsoon season. In addition, Bangkok's pedestrian traffic—particularly in the overcrowded BTS and at rush hour—moves at a painfully slow amble at best, infuriating folks in a hurry. It's best to go with the flow; otherwise you'll only aggravate yourself. In commercial areas, street vendors take up precious sidewalk space (except on Mon). When crossing busier streets, look for pedestrian flyovers, or, if you have to cross at street level, find others who are crossing and follow them when they head out into traffic. Unlike Western countries, crossing lights only serve as suggestions here—drivers rarely stop to allow pedestrians to cross.

FAST FACTS: Bangkok

Airports See "Arriving" earlier in this chapter.

American Express There is no specific agent that handles American Express services in Thailand anymore, but there is an **American Express** office at 388 Pahonyothin Rd. in Bangkok. You can reach the office at © **02273-5296** during business hours (Mon–Fri 8:30am–5pm) or call their customer service hotline (℡ 02273-5544) with any problems or questions.

ATMs See "Fast Facts: Thailand" in chapter 2, "Planning Your Trip to Thailand."

Banks Many international banks have offices in Bangkok, including **Bank of America,** next door to the Nai Lert Park Hotel at 2/2 Wireless Rd. (℡ 02251-6333); **Chase Manhattan Bank,** Bubhajit Building, Sathorn Nua Road (℡ 02234-5992); **Citibank,** 82 Sathorn Nua Road (℡ 02232-2484); **National Australia Bank,** 90 Sathorn Rd. (℡ 02236-6016); and **Standard Chartered Bank,** 90 Sathorn Nua Rd. (℡ 02724-6326). However, even if your bank has a branch in Thailand, your home account is considered foreign here; conducting personal banking will require special arrangements before leaving home.

Bookstores You'll find a number of bookstores offering a wide variety of English-language books. The two chains with the best choice are **Asia Books** and **Kinokuniya. Asia Books** is a local chain that specializes in regional titles and some overseas publishers—depending on the outlet. Its main branch is at 221 Sukhumvit Rd. between Sois 15 and 17 (℡ 02252-7277). Outlets with large inventory are at the following locations: **The Emporium** on Sukhumvit at Soi 22, **Silom Discovery Center,** on the 4th floor, **Siam Paragon,** on level 2, and **Thaniya Plaza,** off Silom Road.

The eclectic **Kinokuniya** has three stores in Bangkok, at **The Emporium** on Sukhumvit Road Soi 22, at **Siam Paragon,** and on the 6th floor of the **Isetan department** store at **Central World Plaza** (℡ 02255-9834). You'll also find a good selection of English language paperbacks at **Bookazine,** located in a variety of places, including Patpong on the 1st floor at CP Tower, 313 Silom Rd. (℡ 02231-0016); in Ploenchit on the 3rd floor at Amarin Plaza 494–502 Ploenchit Rd. (℡ 02256-9304); and Siam Square, 286 Siam Square opposite **Siam Center,** Rama I Road (℡ 02619-1015).

Dasa Books, 710/4 Sukhumvit (near **The Emporium** between sois 26 and 28; ℡ 02661-2993), is a great place to grab a coffee and browse for long-lost titles, or exchange old novels free of charge.

For secondhand books, visit **Elite Used Books,** 593-5 Sukhumvit Rd. (℡ 02258-0221). Almost every international hotel has a newsstand with papers, magazines, and a few books.

Business Hours Government offices (including branch post offices) are open Monday to Friday 8:30am to 4:30pm, with a lunch break between noon and 1pm. Businesses are generally open 8am to 5pm. Small shops often stay open from 8am until 7pm or later, 7 days a week. Department stores are generally open 10:30am to 9pm. **TOPS** and **Villa** supermarkets close at 10pm, but there is a 24-hour **Villa Supermarket** on Sukhumvit Road, almost opposite **The Emporium.**

Car Rentals See "Getting Around: By Car & Driver" above.

Climate See "When to Go" in chapter 2.

Currency Exchange Most banks will exchange foreign currency (at some banks you may need proof of ID) Monday to Friday 8:30am to 3:30pm. Exchange booths affiliated with the major banks are found in all tourist areas, open daily from 10am to 7pm.

Embassies & Consulates Your embassy in Thailand can (to an extent) assist you with medical and legal matters. Contact them immediately if there is a medical emergency or imminent death, if you've lost your travel documents, or if you need urgent legal advice. The following is a list of major foreign representatives in Bangkok: **Embassy of the United States of America,** 120-22 Wireless Rd. (📞 02205-4000); **Canada Embassy,** 15th floor, Abdulrahim Place, 990 Rama IV Rd. (📞 02636-0540); **Australian Embassy,** 37 South Sathorn Rd. (📞 02344-6300); **New Zealand Embassy,** 93 Wireless Rd. (📞 02254-2530); and the **British Embassy,** 14 Wireless Rd. (📞 02305-8333). Listen carefully to the phone prompts for afterhours help lines.

Emergencies In any emergency, first call **Bangkok's Tourist Police**—which is a direct-dial four-digit number 📞 **1155**, or call 02678-6800. Someone at both numbers will speak English. In case of **fire,** call either 📞 **199** or 191, both of which are direct-dial numbers. **Ambulance service** is handled by individual, private hospitals; see "Hospitals" below, or call your hotel's front desk. For operator-assisted **overseas calls,** dial 📞 **100.**

Eyeglass Repair Charoen Optical shops are on Surawong and Silom roads, and in many shopping areas; most can provide replacement glasses at reasonable prices. Always travel with a copy of your prescription. For eye problems, try the **Rutnin Eye Hospital** at 80/1 Sukhumvit Soi 21 (Soi Asok; 📞 **02639-3399**) or private hospitals (see below).

Hospitals All hospitals listed here offer 24-hour emergency service. Be advised that you may need your passport and a deposit of up to 20,000B (US$571/£308) before you are admitted. Make sure you have adequate travel insurance before you leave. Major credit cards are accepted. **Bumrungrad Hospital,** 33 Soi 3, Sukhumvit Rd. (📞 02667-1000), has respected—but costly—health practitioners and is the destination of choice in Bangkok for cosmetic surgery and (comparatively) affordable procedures. **BNH Hospital** (Bangkok Nursing Home) at 9 Convent Rd., between Silom and Sathorn roads, (📞 02686-2700) is extremely central; **Samitivej Hospital** at 133 Sukhumvit Soi 49, (📞 02711-8000) is recommended for dentistry, young children, and for its maternity and infant wards.

Hotlines There are regular meetings of **Alcoholics Anonymous (AA)** in Bangkok and around Thailand. Check their regional website at www.aathailand.org, or call the AA hotline at 📞 02231-8300.

Information See "Visitor Information" earlier in this chapter.

Internet & Wi-Fi Internet cafes abound these days, especially along Sukhumvit and Khao San roads. There's a small Internet, fax, and international phone office next to the General Post Office on Charoen Krung (New) Road that sells 3-hour pre-paid Internet cards for 100B (US$2.85/£1.55) and is open from 7am to 8pm Monday to Friday and 8am to 1pm on weekends. Generally, Internet prices range from 10B to 50B per minute (that's about 2¢ or a pence per hr.). Big hotels charge much higher rates, of course, plus a service charge, but many hotels now offer a pre-paid Wi-Fi access card to guests. Wi-Fi is also free at Starbucks coffee shops throughout the city. On Silom, near Patpong, you'll find the city's most expensive connections.

At **Suvarnabhumi International Airport,** there are cash and credit card touch-screen phones (close to Concourse G), and **Internet facilities** on Level 4 Departures (in the far corner beyond check-in row W).

Lost Property If you have lost anything or have had your valuables stolen, call the national police hotline at © **1155.** If you lose something in a taxi, try to recall the color of the cab, the time and place where you picked it up, and the time and place it dropped you off. Most hotel front desk staff will know which cab company to call to report the loss and make an appeal based on those details. You will need to make a police report at the closest station to the place of loss.

Luggage Storage **Suvarnabhumi International Airport** offers luggage storage for 150B (US$4.30/£2.30) a day, 7am to 10pm, 24 hours a day on the Arrivals level. Most hotels will allow you to store luggage while away on short trips.

Mail See "Fast Facts: Thailand" in chapter 2 for rates and info on the Thailand mail system. Head to the General Post Office (opposite Soi 45) on Charoen Krung Rd., for all mail, telegraph, and parcel services, including Western Union money transfers. If you want to send valuables home, use courier services such as **DHL** (© **02345-5000**). On Silom Road, DHL has a handy drop-off point (Mon–Sat 10am–9pm). Or call **Federal Express** (© **1782**; press 2 for English). If this proves too costly, take advantage of your hotel concierge or the postal service offered on the 4th floor of Silom Complex, Silom Rd., (adjoining Sala Daeng BTS); it's open from 10am to 8pm Monday to Friday and until 1pm on weekends.

Maps See "Visitor Information" earlier in this chapter.

Newspapers & Magazines *Bangkok Post* and *The Nation,* both English-language dailies, cover local, national, and international news as well as happenings around town, TV listings, and other useful information for just 25B (71¢/40p). Also check out *Where,* a free listings monthly, and *BK Magazine,* a free weekly publication, which publish lighthearted commentaries and event listings for Bangkok.

Pharmacies Bangkok has many local pharmacies. Drugs dispensed here differ widely in quality and authenticity; if in any doubt, visit a doctor and get drugs prescribed at a hospital or pick them up at an international store such as Watson's or Boots.

Police Call the **Tourist Police** on © **1155** or 02678-6801, open 24 hours, for assistance. English is spoken.

Post Office The main General Post Office (GPO) is a huge post and telegraph office on Charoen Krung Road (© **02233-1050**), opposite Soi 45. It's open Monday to Friday 8am to 8pm, and weekends 8am to 1pm. For international phone, fax, and Internet services, go to the small **Public Telecom Service Center** to the far side of the main building that's open 7am to 8pm daily. Other post offices may not have any English speakers.

Radio & TV In Bangkok, **Smooth 105FM** and **Easy FM 105.5** play back-to-back pop with little English. Every day at 8am and 6pm, every radio station plays the national anthem; news is broadcast in Thai.

Most TV channels broadcast local Thai programs or English-language programs either dubbed or with subtitles. Some free cable services, such as CNN, Australia Network, NHK, BBC World, or France's TV5 are readily available in serviced apartments. Most hotels receive satellite and cable channels such as CNN, CNBC, Star Movies, HBO, MTV, and Star Sports plus other foreign language channels.

Safety In general, Bangkok is a relatively safe city, but be aware at night of drug-spiked drinks and in daytime—especially on transport—of pickpockets. Do not incite trouble; avoid public disagreements and hostility (especially with locals), and steer clear of gambling-related activities. If traveling alone at night, be alert, as you would in any city, and rely on your gut instincts—if you get a bad feeling about a place or situation, remove yourself from the scene. A Thai temper is virtually unheard of, but on rare occasions, it erupts, seemingly out of nowhere, and makes for (potentially lethal) confrontations.

Taxes See "Fast Facts: Thailand" in chapter 2.

Taxis See "Getting Around" earlier in this chapter.

Telephone, Internet Telephony & Fax If you want to make international calls, head to the service center next to the **General Post Office** on Charoen Krung (New) Road; see **"Mail"** above. All post offices and 7-Elevens sell **pre-paid phone cards** for use with domestic (orange) or international calls (pink or yellow). **Public phones** can be found near 7-Elevens. These phones may also charge calls to credit cards and AT&T calling cards. **Hatari Phonenet** cards are available at 7-Eleven stores in 300B (US$8.60/£4.60), 500B (US$14/£7.70), or 1,000B (US$29/£15) denominations).

Most **Internet cafes** offer cheap international call rates via Internet or Skype.

For **information on a number** within the Bangkok metropolitan area, dial ⒞ **1133,** or ask your hotel concierge or operator.

These days, **fax services** are offered by most small Internet cafes and hotels. A single A4 page of typewritten English faxed to the United States costs up to 100B (US$2.85/£1.55).

See "Fast Facts: Thailand" in chapter 2 for additional information.

5

Where to Stay & Dine in Bangkok

Food is possibly Bangkok's greatest draw; newly launched, cutting-edge restaurants compete with traditional Thai diners here, and almost all are excellent. I've listed some of the best below. The city also boasts some of the world's most lauded hotels. But it's not just about five-star properties; lodgings in the Big Mango come in all prices and offer charming service—all at a fraction of what you'd pay in Europe or the U.S.

1 Accommodations

Bangkok offers fantastic value for money, but remember that the hotel prices listed here are, on the whole, the highest *published* rates. Wherever hotels don't have published rates, I've used those from the Internet and, when there are numerous room types and rates, only a selection may be given. Many hotels offer promotional packages that include extras such as breakfast or airport transfers; some airlines also offer great deals on hotels. Unless otherwise noted, hotel rates are subject to a 7% government value-added tax and 10% service charge. In the high season (mid-Oct to mid-April), make reservations well in advance. Check chapter 2 for more information on discounts nationwide.

Note: Hotel websites and Internet sites such as **www.asiahotels.com** often offer special rates for four- and five-star hotels in Bangkok.

AT THE AIRPORTS

Hotels at the renamed **Don Mueang** and new **Suvarnabhumi International airports** are useful if you have a very early morning flight and don't want to allow the 45 to 90 minutes' traveling time from the city. **Amari Don Mueang Airport Hotel** (© 02566-1020; www.amari.com) is linked by a bridge to the terminal and comes with a pool. Expect standard rooms from 2,975B (US$85/£46). **Novotel Suvarnabhumi Airport** is a few minutes' drive away and offers four restaurants, plus a business center, Wi-Fi, and fitness facilities. Rates run from 5,000B (US$143/£77) per room (© 02131-1111; www.novotel.com).

ON THE RIVER

During the dry season, the riverside is one of the most picturesque parts of the city. A whole range of riverside hotels exists, and all boast great views and most operate free shuttle boats along the teeming Chao Phraya River, which makes them handy for shoppers, diners, spa-goers, and anyone needing the BTS. The finest don't come cheap, but since 2006 plenty of new and reasonable midrange choices have opened.

Where to Stay in Bangkok

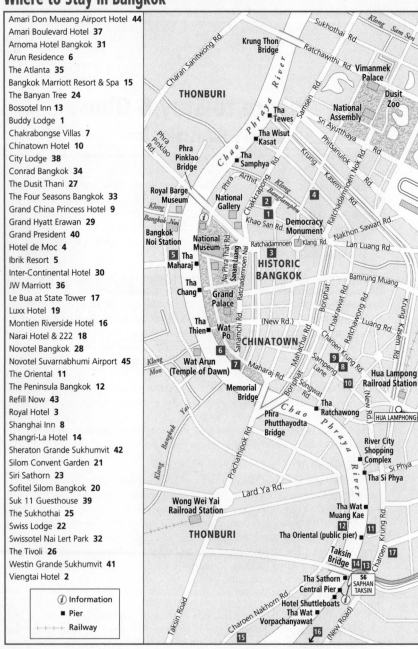

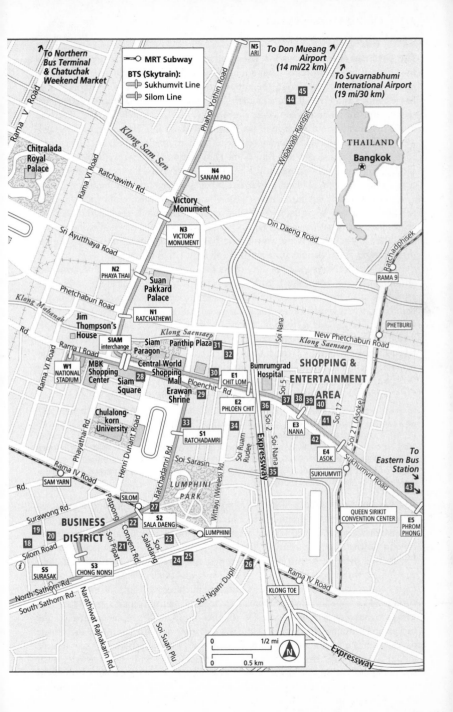

To Northern
Bus Terminal
& Chatuchak
Weekend Market

N5 ARI
To Don Mueang
Airport
(14 mi/22 km)

To Suvarnabhumi
International Airport
(19 mi/30 km)

○—○ MRT Subway
BTS (Skytrain):
☐◐ Sukhumvit Line
☐◐ Silom Line

THAILAND
Bangkok ★

44   45

Rama V Road

Klong Sam Sen

Phahol Yothin Road

Wipawadi-Rangsit

Ratchadphisek

Chitralada
Royal
Palace

Ratchawithi Rd.

Rama VI Road

N4 SANAM PAO

Din Daeng Road

RAMA 9

Sri Ayutthaya Road

Victory
Monument

N3
VICTORY
MONUMENT

Phetchaburi Road

N2
PHAYA THAI

Suan
Pakkard
Palace

Klong Mahanak

Soi Nana

New Phetchaburi Rd

PHETBURI

Jim
Thompson's
House

N1
RATCHATHEWI

Klong Saensep

Klong Saensep

Rama I Road

SIAM
interchange

Siam
Paragon

Panthip Plaza 31

32

Bumrumgrad
Hospital

SHOPPING &
ENTERTAINMENT
AREA

W1
NATIONAL
STADIUM

MBK
Shopping
Center

Central World
Shopping
Mall

30

E1
CHIT LOM

Soi 5

Soi Nana

37 38 39
40

Siam
Square

28

Erawan
Shrine

Ploenchit
Rd.

29

E2
PHLOEN CHIT

Soi 2

36

Soi 17

41   Soi 21 (Asoke)

Chulalong-
korn
University

33

34

E3
NANA

42

To
Eastern Bus
Station

Phayathai Rd.

Henri Dunant Road

Ratchadamri Rd.

S1
RATCHADAMRI

Soi Ruam
Rudee

Wittayu (Wireless) Rd.

E4
ASOK

Sukhumvit Rd

43

Rama IV Road

Soi Sarasin

Expressway

SAM YARN

SILOM

LUMPHINI
PARK

35

SUKHUMVIT

QUEEN SIRIKIT
CONVENTION CENTER

E5
PHROM
PHONG

Rd.

Surawong Rd.

BUSINESS
DISTRICT

Patpong

Convent Rd.

Soi Pipat

Soi Saladang

27

S2
SALA DAENG

23

LUMPHINI

19

18   20

21

Silom Road

24 25

S3
CHONG NONSI

26

Rama IV Road

ℹ

S5
SURASAK

North Sathorn Rd.

Soi Ngam Dupli

KLONG TOE

KLONG TOE

South Sathorn Rd.

Narathiwat Rajnakarin Rd.

Soi Suan Plu

Expressway

0   1/2 mi
0   0.5 km

N

89

VERY EXPENSIVE

The Oriental ★★★ Bangkok's oldest and most elegant hotel has been frequented by Thai royalty and glitterati, and a long roster of sports and film stars have stayed here. Established in the 1860s, the hotel's original building (today's Authors' Wing) has expanded and evolved into a modern, functional venue known for its exceptional service. But this Grande Dame does not rest easily on her laurels. During 2006 and 2007, the hotel saw the creation of two delightful new pools, both with private pavilions; a newly remodeled Verandah restaurant with an open kitchen; and the entirely revamped Thai restaurant, Sala Rim Nam. The addition of an Ayurvedic Penthouse at the Oriental Spa and a dramatic new black and red interior for its stand-alone Chinese restaurant, China House, proves it is at pains to keep up with the times.

Rooms and suites are furnished in Thai silks using soft earthy tones or vivid hues; the newer Garden Wing faces southwest onto the river and, though the two-level rooms here get rather warm, the wing offers truly picturesque views. West-facing corner suites in the River Wing, which have balconies overlooking the water, are the biggest treat. The Oriental's restaurants are all regarded as top notch.

Restaurant Le Normandie (p. 106) offers the city's finest French dining, while the glittering seafood restaurant, Lord Jim's, is perennially popular. The Oriental's cookery school and Oriental Spa sit on the other side of the river, next to the new-look Sala Rim Nam, where classical Thai dancers mesmerize diners. Private riverboats provide a shuttle service to River City mall, Saphan Taksin BTS, and Sala Rim Nam (behind which lie the hotel's gym and squash and tennis courts). Sunset dinner cruises are taken aboard a delightfully restored rice barge, the *Maeyanang*. Dress up for this; backpacks, rubber sandals, and singlets are not deemed suitable. Even if you are not a guest here, you will be treated like royalty. You might want to visit to sip a cocktail beside the river at The Verandah, just as Noël Coward did in the 1930s.

48 Oriental Ave., Bangkok 10500 (Soi 41, Charoen Krung Rd.). ℂ 800/526-6566 or 02236-0400. Fax 02236-1937. www.mandarin-oriental.com. 393 units. From 12,950B (US$370/£199) superior; 31,500B (US$900/£485) suite. AE, DC, MC, V. Saphan Taksin BTS. **Amenities:** 7 restaurants; lounge; bar (smoking permitted) w/live jazz; 2 outdoor pools; 2 lit outdoor tennis courts; fitness center; squash court; spa w/Ayurvedic treatments; complimentary ferry service; tour desk; airport transfer; business center; shopping arcade; salon; 24-hr. room service; babysitting; same-day laundry service/dry cleaning; nonsmoking rooms; cooking school. *In room:* A/C, satellite TV, dataport, minibar, fridge, coffee-making facilities, hair dryer, CD/DVD player, safe.

The Peninsula, Bangkok ★★★ From its exclusive top-floor lounge, right down to its velveteen lawns at ground level, The Peninsula proves it is as classy as the rest. Located on the western banks of the river in Thonburi, it benefits from high-rise views up and downstream. Its oversized rooms are luxurious, with all the amenities one expects of a five-star. Rooms reflect the perfect marriage of Thai tradition and high-tech luxury, with wooden paneling, silk wallpaper, and thick carpets. Each bedside features a control panel that operates everything: temperature control, TV, even the room curtains. The large marble bathrooms have separate vanity counters and a large tub with a hands-free telephone and TV monitor built in. Whether supping on the succulent Cantonese dim sum at Mei Jiang, feasting on Thai cuisine in the private pavilions at Thipthara, or enjoying the river views from Jester's or their upscale indoor-outdoor cafe, elegance is omnipresent. State-of-the-art business services, great shopping, and a new spa in a restored colonial-style house attract both leisure and business guests. Guests can sign up to be part of the Peninsula Academy, where aspects of local culture are taught, such as Thai cuisine through cooking classes.

333 Charoen Nakhorn Rd., Klongsan, Bangkok 10600. ☎ **800/262-9467** or 02861-2888. www.peninsula.com. 370 units. 8,400B (US$240/£129) superior double; 10,500B (US$300/£162) deluxe; from 38,500B (US$1,100/£592) suite. AE, DC, MC, V. Saphan Taksin BTS. **Amenities:** 4 restaurants; 2 bars; pool; tennis court; fitness center; spa; airport transfer; business center; shopping arcade; 24-hr. room service; babysitting; laundry service; dry cleaning; executive floor. *In room:* A/C, satellite TV, minibar, hair dryer, CD player, safe.

EXPENSIVE

Bangkok Marriott Resort & Spa ★★★ *Kids* Choose the Bangkok Marriott if you want to explore Bangkok, and at the same time, escape it. On the western banks of the Chao Phraya River and a few miles downstream from the heart of old Bangkok, this sprawling resort is accessed by shuttle boat or taxi. Some don't like to be so far removed, but most find the short departure from crazy Bangkok a real relief; once at the resort, the big city seems a distant memory. The three wings of the hotel surround a large landscaped pool area with lily ponds and fountains, and there is a Mandara Spa to soothe one's spirits. Recreation, dining, and drinking choices are many, including familiar restaurants like Trader Vic's and Benihana, as well as their popular Riverside Terrace restaurant with a nightly buffet and culture show (see the "Dinner with Thai Dance" section, after "Dining").

257/1–3 Charoen Nakhon Rd., Bangkok 10600. ☎ **800/228-9290** or 02476-0022. Fax 02476-1120. www.marriott hotels.com. 413 units. 4,900B (US$140/£75) deluxe; 7,175B (US$205/£110) junior suite; 9,800B (US$280/£151) deluxe suite. AE, DC, MC, V. Ferry to Central Pier. **Amenities:** 5 restaurants; bar and lounge; dinner cruise; pool; 2 outdoor lit tennis courts; fitness center; spa; salon; kids' club and programs; tour desk; airport transfer; business center; shopping arcade; salon; 24-hr. room service; babysitting; same-day laundry service/dry cleaning; nonsmoking rooms. *In room:* A/C, satellite TV, dataport, minibar, fridge, safe.

Shangri-La Hotel ★★★ The big, brassy Shangri-La, on the banks of the Chao Phraya, boasts acres of polished marble and a jungle of tropical plants and flowers surrounding the resort-style pool. Rooms are in two connecting wings, both with river views; the newer Krung Thep Wing has slightly smarter rooms and suites and offers butler service. All rooms have elegant teak furniture and marble bathrooms. The views are better from the higher-floor deluxe rooms; some have either a balcony or a small sitting room, making them closer to junior suites—and a good value. The level of service and facilities is good and the stylishly contemporary Chi spa is superb. Underneath the Krung Thep Wing is the riverside swimming pool, and beyond, a large indoor-outdoor breakfast lounge. The hotel offers sunset river cruises on the *Horizon,* a large motor cruiser equipped with live bands and broad outdoor decks

89 Soi Wat Suan Plu, Charoen Krung Rd. (New Rd.), Bangkok 10500 (adjacent to Sathorn Bridge). ☎ **800/942-5050** or 02236-7777. Fax 02236-8579. www.shangri-la.com. 799 units. 5075B–6,825B (US$145–US$195/£78–£105) double; from 10,150B (US$290/£156) executive suite. AE, DC, MC, V. Saphan Taksin BTS. **Amenities:** 6 restaurants; lounge; bar; dinner cruise; 2 outdoor pools w/outdoor Jacuzzi; 2 outdoor lit tennis courts; 2 squash courts; fitness center w/aerobics classes; spa; tour desk; car-rental desk; airport transfer; city shuttle service; business center; shopping arcade; salon; 24-hr. room service; same-day laundry service/dry cleaning; nonsmoking rooms; executive floors. *In room:* A/C, satellite TV, dataport, minibar, fridge, coffee-making facilities, hair dryer, safe.

MODERATE

Arun Residence ★★ *Value* This cool little arty hideaway comes with split-level suites, decorated in a colorful, unfussy, Thai-retro style, all with great views across to its eponymous *wat*. It's suited to those who want to feel at home in the thick of old Bangkok, since it's close to major sites. Though public transport isn't on your doorstep, the twinkling river is right there in front of you, and the property's lush plants and sun-filled lounge offer a uniquely Thai experience.

36-38 Soi Phratu Nokyung (Tha Maharaj), Maharaj Rd., Rattankosin Island, Bangkok 10200. ⟨⟩ 02221-9158. Fax 02221-9159. www.arunresidence.com. 5 units. From 2,950B (US$84/£45) standard; 4,700B (US$134/£72) suite with roof garden. AE, MC, V. BTS and MRT over 10 minutes away. **Amenities:** Restaurant; same-day laundry service. *In room:* A/C, satellite TV, minibar, fridge.

ChakrabongseVillas ⟨⟩⟨⟩   Still being (rather optimistically) touted as "Thailand's best kept secret," this clutch of traditional wooden Thai houses are now on every website and in every guide, so be sure to call ahead to reserve a space. The villas here are built on the river, opposite Wat Arun, on the grounds of a Belle Époque era mansion that was once home to a Thai prince. Though they can suffer from mildew in the rains, the rooms' rustic style is unique in urban Bangkok and the property will appeal to people who don't mind somewhat lackluster service or language skills (no English speakers pick up the phone on weekends or after office hours). In dry months, the garden, riverside decks, and pool are a delight. For the price, though, the venue risks being overrated despite the addition of a new Pool Villa.

396 Maharat Rd., Tha Tien, Bangkok 10200. ⟨⟩ 02224-6686. Fax 02225-3861. www.thaivillas.com. 4 units. 8,000B–25,000B (US$228–US$714/£123–£385). MC, V. Hua Lamphong MRT. **Amenities:** Restaurant; bar; tour desk; limited room service; laundry service; dry cleaning. *In room:* A/C, TV, minibar, safe.

Ibrik Resort ⟨⟩⟨⟩   Pronounced "eye-breek," this petite contemporary home situated in Thonburi, a historic district where the first royal palace stood, is billed as a "resort by the river" but is more like a private home. Hidden in a narrow *soi*, its three bright, stylish rooms are all nonsmoking, with balconies overlooking the water. Its boutique size, small café, and location a few meters from the historic Wat Rakang, make it popular with return visitors who want to explore more of the "real" Bangkok. Opposite is the Patravadi cafe and contemporary dance theater, and next door is Studio 9, a relatively new venue for weekend Thai dinner-dances.

256 Soi Wat Rakang, Arunamarin Rd., Bangkoknoi, Bangkok 10700. ⟨⟩ 02848-9220. Fax 02866-2978. www.ibrik resort.com. 3 units. 4,000B (US$114/£62). MC, V. BTS and MRT over 10 minutes away. **Amenities:** Cafe; laundry service; dry cleaning. *In room:* A/C, satellite TV, minibar, hair dryer, safe.

Montien Riverside Hotel ⟨⟩⟨⟩ (Value)   Located just off Rama III road, with easy access to highways to both airports, this towering edifice may not be a beauty but has great river views and, if you book on the Internet, it offers an excellent value. Appealing to those who want to kick back at the end of their Thailand stay, it may not be centrally located, but offers great facilities and a free hourly shuttle bus to the downtown Montien Hotel on Silom Road for shopping.

372 Rama 3 Rd., Bangkhlo, Bangkok 10120. ⟨⟩ 02292-2999. Fax 02292-2962-3. www.montien.com. 462 units. 5,000B (US$143/£77). MC, V. BTS and MRT over 10 minutes away. **Amenities:** 5 restaurants; 2 bars; dinner cruise; outdoor pool; 2 outdoor tennis courts; fitness center w/sauna, steam, massage, and dance classes; tour desk; city shuttle service; business center w/Internet access; limited room service; laundry service; dry cleaning. *In room:* A/C, satellite TV, minibar, safe.

INEXPENSIVE

Bossotel Inn ⟨⟩ (Value)   A convenient 5-minute walk to Saphan Taksin BTS, this basic, cheap, and cheerful option attracts Thailand's many budget travelers. Most rooms are large but very basic, and the furniture and decor fairly monotone. With the higher grade rooms things get a bit brighter—and there's Wi-Fi throughout. You'll find the staff helpful but some have limited English. Ask about discount rates for longer stays.

55/12–13 Soi Charoen Krung 42/1, Bangrak, Bangkok 10500 (on Soi 42, near Shangri-La Hotel). ⟨⟩ 02630-6120. Fax 02237-3225. www.bossotelinn.com. 46 units. 1,800B–2,600B (US$45–US$74/£28–£40) double; 4,500B

(US$129/£69) suite. AE, MC, V. Saphan Taksin BTS. **Amenities:** Coffee shop; tour desk; small business center; limited room service; massage; same-day laundry service; Wi-Fi. *In room:* A/C, satellite TV, minibar, fridge.

SATHORN, SILOM & SURAWONG

If Bangkok were to have one single business district (it actually has many), this would be it. The area between Surawong (also written Surawongse) and Silom roads contains the city's oldest shopping and tourist haunts—including the former G.I. haunt and today's red-light district, Patpong. Parallel to them is the busy eight-lane Sathorn Road, off which you'll find the city's bigger embassies, top hotels, police, and immigration HQs. Some hotels in *sois* off Sathorn (such as The Tivoli) even offer a shuttle to the Sala Daeng BTS. The one problem with this area is that it snarls up with static traffic from 5:45pm to 8pm daily, but the Lumphini MRT stop at the top of Sathorn Road helps avoid the gridlock.

VERY EXPENSIVE

The Banyan Tree ★★★ Just before Soi Suan Plu, midway down South Sathorn Road, this immense all-suite skyscraper hidden behind Thai Wah Tower provides the city's most exceptional panoramas, a plethora of trendy dining venues, and a chic, newly renovated spa with spacious suites (including segregated wet-rooms for thalasso treatments). While the brown, gold, and black lobby decor indicates its five-star status, Banyan Tree has a relaxed, resort ambience throughout its public areas, highlighting its claim to provide a slick, urban resort in the city. Pier 59 and Vertigo are just two of its popular, upscale dining options; both come with great views and the latter offers alfresco dining on the vertiginous roof. Feast on Chinese dim sum galore at Bai Yun or sip champagne under the stars at Moon Bar. Given its stellar reputation in Asia, the skyscraper hotel is popular with Asian families and tour groups. A new addition is the *Apsara I*, a restored rice barge that takes diners out on the river for cocktails and sunset cruises, serving fine Thai cuisine courtesy of the hotel's Saffron restaurant. Mention the Thai Wah building right out in front to ensure your taxi doesn't miss the theatrical torch-lit entrance; it's on a busy one-way highway.

21/100 South Sathorn Rd., Sathorn, Pathumwan, Bangkok 10120. © **02679-1200.** Fax 02679-1199. www. banyantree.com. 216 units. From 11,500B (US$330/£177) standard suite; 70,000B (US$2,000/£1,076) presidential suite. AE, MC, V. Lumphini MRT. **Amenities:** 6 restaurants; 2 bars; lounge; outdoor pool; fitness center; spa; tour desk; airport transfer; business center; shopping; salon; 24-hr. room service; same-day laundry service/dry cleaning; free DVD/CD players on request; Wi-Fi. *In room:* A/C, satellite TV, minibar, fridge, safe.

The Sukhothai ★★★ Inside The Sukhothai, visitors find peaceful serenity and privacy, thanks to American designer Ed Tuttle's eclectic eye. This hip hotel is a maze of low pavilions, pools, and courtyards, deftly combining crisp, contemporary lines with Thai objets d'art, Thai silks, and rich tones. Colonnaded corridors surround lotus pools adorned with serried brick *chedis;* the terracotta friezes and the celadon ceramics are all motifs borrowed from its namesake city. Expansive guest rooms carry fine silk walls, mellow teak furniture, and rustic floor tiles; all have double bathrooms with oversize bathtubs, a separate shower, and toilet. Most rooms have personal fax machines and Internet connections. The hotel's Thai restaurant, Celadon, is well established, while the modern La Scala is more relaxed (that is, until you see the bill). The small gym is a popular appendage for its delightful dark-tile pool, meters away.

13/3 South Sathorn Rd., Bangkok 10120. © **02344-8888.** Fax 02344-8822. www.sukhothai.com. 210 units. 10,500B (US$300/£162) double; 14,700B (US$420/£226) executive suite; 23,450B (US$670/£361) garden suite; 73,500B (US$2,100/£1,131) Sukhothai suite. AE, DC, MC, V. Lumphini MRT. **Amenities:** 3 restaurants; bar; lobby lounge; outdoor pool; outdoor lit tennis court; squash court; fitness center w/aerobics classes; spa; airport transfer; 24-hr. business center; 24-hr. room service; babysitting. *In room:* A/C, satellite TV, fax, dataport, hair dryer, safe.

EXPENSIVE

The Dusit Thani ★★   Once upon a time this was Bangkok's grandest address (and tallest building). Now this old girl just across from Lumphini Park—close to the BTS and the Rama IV flyover—lies overshadowed by her neighbors. Despite the traffic jams in the area, the hotel still has one of the best locations in the city. Its architecture offers some retro quirkiness, too: The extensive lobby is grandiose, with splashing fountains and exotic flowers. The large outdoor pool is surrounded by foliage, providing a great escape after a day of sightseeing. Rooms, though smaller than most in this category, come with balconies, built-in blonde wood paneling and low lighting, plus views over the teeming intersection and park. The hotel chain's Devarana Spa, tucked upstairs behind the hotel's restaurants, has wowed spa aficionados with its superbly Thai-style double suites and stellar treatments.

946 Rama IV Rd., Bangkok 10500. © **02236-0450.** Fax 02236-6400. www.bangkok.dusit.com. 517 units. 5,530B (US$158/£85) double; 14,000B (US$400/£215) suite. AE, DC, MC, V. Sala Daeng BTS. **Amenities:** 8 restaurants; lounge; bar; pool; driving range and chipping green; fitness center; spa; airport transfer; business center; shopping arcade; salon; 24-hr. room service; babysitting; same-day laundry service/dry cleaning. *In room:* A/C, satellite TV, minibar, fridge, hair dryer, safe.

Le Bua at State Tower ★★★   Some may know this swish all-suite hotel as the former Meritus Suites, but it has been reborn into something far grander. Occupying the 64-story State Tower (easily spotted from afar by its gilded dome), the new-look hotel has been re-launched and renamed (Bua means lotus) by the same company responsible for The Dome's plethora of super-stylish dining joints upstairs in the same building. Stunningly spacious 1-, 2-, and 3-bedroom suites are wholly contemporary, decked out in icy white, deep brown, and steel hues. The larger suites come with fully equipped kitchenettes, washing machines, and large sitting areas. The tempting balconies sadly cannot be accessed, but the in-house seafood restaurant, Breeze, with a spectacular outdoor setting and views, makes up for it. The Ocean 52 restaurant serves dim sum to die for, but be prepared for prices as high as the building; Café Mozu is a more reasonable bet. There's an outdoor pool and decent gym, plus lots more great dining or drinking options, literally right up to the roof at The Dome.

1055 Silom Rd., Bangrak, Bangkok 10500 (on the corner of Silom and Charoen Krung rds.). © **02624-9999.** Fax 02624-9998. www.lebua.com. 350 units. 9,800B–28,000B (US$280–US$800/£150–£430) 1- to 3-bed suite. AE, DC, MC, V. Saphan Taksin BTS. **Amenities:** 3 restaurants; bar; lounge; outdoor pool; fitness center; sauna; steam; airport transfer; business center; 24-hr. room service. *In room:* A/C, satellite TV, DVD/CD, free in-room broadband, minibar, fridge, coffee-making facilities, hair dryer, safe.

Sofitel Silom Bangkok ★★   As with most hotels that mix business and leisure guests, this swish venue is pleasantly modern and relatively efficient, though it perhaps offers more functional luxury than the opulence of the city's other well-known brands. The location is not bad, equidistant to the river and Sala Daeng BTS, 10 minutes' stroll away. It has some good (if pricey) wine bars and restaurants, all with fabulous views. Its location avoids the heady chaos of upper Silom Road and the Patpong area, but is not too far if you don't mind what can be a fume-filled walk. Chic, contemporary Thai-style rooms are fitted with dark wood; rich, striped textiles; and clean, minimalist lines. Bathrooms are large, with a separate shower and bath and slick granite counters. The 35th floor recently opened in October 2007 with flashier rooms, executive amenities, and, of course, great views. Executive services are fairly good, and it is one of very few hotels with a foreign-run (French) hair salon on the fifth floor. The adjoining gym and pool are limited in both size and amenities. The small Anne

Semonin spa is a bonus for women who love luxury facials. Downstairs is the French bakery chain, Le Nôtre, which tends to tag Paris prices on its all-too-tempting, but nonetheless Bangkok-made, buns.

188 Silom Rd., Bangrak, Bangkok 10500 (50m from the Silom and Narathiwat Rd. intersection). © **02238-1991.** Fax 02238-1999. www.sofitel.com. 469 units. 7,200B (US$205/£111) deluxe; from 8,800B (US$251/£137) suite. Seasonal discounts offered. AE, MC, V. Chong Nonsi BTS. **Amenities:** 3 restaurants; 2 bars; pool; fitness center; spa; tour desk; airport transfer; business center; salon; 24-hr. room service; same-day laundry service/dry cleaning. In room: A/C, satellite TV, minibar, fridge, hair dryer, safe.

MODERATE

Luxx 🏵🏵 Just around the corner from Sofitel Silom is a tiny boutique property that has completely remodeled itself within a narrow, 1970s façade. This contemporary hideaway is the new face of Bangkok; its fashionably minimalist size and prime location appeal to the young and style-conscious. Within walking distance of Silom's shops and night market, but off the busy main drag of Silom, Luxx provides large airy rooms, flat-screen TVs, wooden barrel tubs, rain showers, and pebble gardens in an eclectic mix of Thai-Zen minimalism. Perks like Wi-Fi, iPod docks, and breakfast in bed confidently affirm its claims to evoke a "home-away-from-home" feel.

6-11 Soi Decho, off Silom Rd., Bangkok 10500 (30m from Silom). © **02635-8800.** Fax 02635-8088. www. bangkok.com/luxxbangkok. 13 units. 2,800B–5,000B (US$80–US$142/£43–£77). AE, DC, MC, V. Chong Nonsi BTS. **Amenities:** Room service; laundry service; dry cleaning; Wi-Fi. In room: A/C, satellite TV, iPod dock, minibar, fridge.

Narai Hotel and 222 (Triple Two) 🏵🏵 This hotel duo is found 15 minutes' walk from Chong Nonsi BTS. The larger, much-older Narai Hotel is a clean, comfortable standard hotel, popular with tour groups. There is nothing particularly stylish about the lobby, but rooms are adequate, everything works, and service is amenable. Downstairs is the swish new Italian restaurant and just next door is their sister venture, the newer and much smaller Triple Two (referring to its Silom Rd. address), which shares its pool and fitness facilities. Rooms here come with a sleek, contemporary look with silk furnishings and traditional Thai fixtures that provide a gentle contrast with the ultra-modern lines. Triple Two's indoor-outdoor downstairs dining venue is sadly overshadowed by constant traffic noise and fumes, but Silom Road offers lots of alternative shopping and dining options.

Narai Hotel: 222 Silom Rd., Bangrak, Bangkok 10500. © **02237-0100.** Fax 02236-7161. www.naraihotel.co.th. 473 units. 4,000B (US$114/£62) single; 19,000B (US$543/£292) suite. AE, MC, V. Chong Nonsi BTS. **Amenities:** 4 restaurants; bar; lounge; outdoor pool; fitness center; business center; shopping arcade; 24-hr. room service; same-day laundry service/dry cleaning; Wi-Fi. In room: A/C, satellite TV, minibar, fridge. **Triple Two Silom:** 222 Silom Rd., Bangrak, Bangkok 10500. © **02627-2222.** Fax 02627-2300. www.tripletwosilom.com. 75 units. 5,500B (US$157/£85) double; from 6,900B (US$197/£106) suite. AE, MC, V. Chong Nonsi BTS. **Amenities:** Restaurant; bar; 24-hr. room service; same-day laundry service/dry cleaning; Wi-Fi. In room: A/C, satellite TV, DVD player, minibar, fridge, safe.

Siri Sathorn 🏵🏵 (Finds) Officially, this gorgeously contemporary apartment hotel is for long-stay guests, but those in the know can get day rates. It's managed by the same folks who own The Sukhothai Hotel and it boasts a similar spacious, pared-down designer chic that mimics New York loft-style living. All suites have fully equipped kitchens, smooth wood, and stone floors; some come with superb terraces and most have tubs—check when you make a booking. There's Wi-Fi throughout the building and a very cool bar and small diner downstairs, next to a private dining room. There are a few meeting rooms, too, for busy executives. The small pool is shady and the gym and yoga room is bright and clean. The friendly staff outweighs the sometimes iffy service. Considering the quality and size of accommodations, rates are a bargain, and the location, in the quiet, tree-lined *soi* Sala Daeng 1, means you're just a short walk to Silom Road and the Sala Daeng BTS.

27 Soi Sala Daeng 1, Silom Rd., Bangrak, Bangkok, 10500 (between Sathorn and Silom rds.). ℭ **02266-2345**. Fax 02267-5555. www.sirisathorn.com. 111 units. 5,000B (US$143/£77) 1-bed suite; 10,000B (US$286/£154) 2-bed suite; 12,000B (US$343/£185) 2-bed terrace suite; 14,000B (US$400/£215) 2-bed deluxe suite. AE, DC, MC, V. Sala Daeng BTS. **Amenities:** Restaurant; bar; pool; fitness center; spa; business center; limited room service; laundry service; dry cleaning; high-speed Internet. *In room:* A/C, satellite TV, CD player, full kitchen, minibar, fridge, hair dryer, safe.

Swiss Lodge ★★ Just a short skip down Convent Road (off Silom Rd.), near the Sala Daeng BTS, is this cozy, convenient hotel. Swiss Lodge started out as a small guesthouse and is now a popular choice for business folks (many Europeans on long-stay) and travelers. Though near the red-light district of Patpong, there's no sleazy vibe to the place, and front desk staff is friendly. Rooms are large and quite plain, with simple furnishings, but everything is clean and there are lots of good amenities (including in-room Wi-Fi). They have a good restaurant with daily buffet, and the swimming pool is but a postage stamp, but not a bad escape.

3 Convent Rd., Silom, Bangkok 10500. ℭ **02233-5345**. Fax 02236-9425. www.swisslodge.com. 46 units. 5,200B (US$148/£80) superior; 5,600B (US$160/£86) deluxe; 8,250B (US$236/£127) suite. AE, MC, V. Sala Daeng BTS. **Amenities:** Restaurant; bar; pool; business center; 24-hr. room service; same-day laundry service/dry cleaning; Wi-Fi. *In room:* A/C, satellite TV, dataport, minibar, fridge, safe.

INEXPENSIVE

Silom Convent Garden ★★ *Value* Brand new and unbelievably central, this apartment-cum-hotel is suited for longer stays or short stints (day, weekly, monthly, or yearly rates are offered accordingly); check if the (unexciting) breakfast is included. Rooms are clean, bright, and contemporary, and come with the added bonus of being equipped with kitchenettes and communal laundry facilities, while being just a few paces from Soi Convent and busy Sathorn Road. The petite building is decked out in bright colors and good taste. Long-stays warrant a bit of haggling, but prices remain incredibly affordable (as long as you ensure the electricity charges do not come with a hefty surcharge). Check the website for deals.

35/1 Soi Piphat 2, Sathorn Soi Convent, Bangkok 10500. ℭ **02667-0130**. Fax 02667-0144. www.silomconventgarden. com. 44 units. Daily rates 1,650B–3,650B (US$47–US$104/£25–£56). AE, DC, MC, V. Sala Daeng BTS. **Amenities:** Restaurant; communal laundry; Wi-Fi. *In room:* A/C, satellite TV, kitchenette.

The Tivoli ★★ *Finds* The tiny Tivoli outdoes the competition. This new and wonderfully friendly, midsize hotel is set some way back from the fumes and traffic of Sathorn Road (and also accessible via Rama IV). Unusually, The Tivoli offers different rates for both single and double rooms, but all are superbly decorated in a contemporary Thai style and offer exceptional value for money. The hotel helpfully provides a free tuk-tuk to those guests heading to the shops, renewing a visa at immigration HQ, or seeing a doctor at nearby BNH hospital. It's a 5-minute ride to the Lumphini MRT station and an 8-minute ride to Silom in good traffic. Few Bangkok hotels of this range offer this luxury and service standard, plus the bonus of a rooftop swimming pool and spa.

71/2-3 Soi Sri Bumphen, Yen-Arkart Rd., Thungmahamek, Sathorn, Bangkok 10120. ℭ **02249-5858**. Fax 02249-5818. www.thetivolihotelbangkok.com. 133 units. 2,200B–3,100B (US$63–US$88/£34–£48). AE, DC, MC, V. Sala Daeng BTS. **Amenities:** Restaurant; bar; pool; spa; Wi-Fi. *In room:* A/C, satellite TV, DVD player, hair dryer, safe.

SUKHUMVIT ROAD AREA

Accessed along its entire length by the convenient BTS, Sukhumvit Road is the heart of commercial Bangkok. Here you'll find many of the town's finest large shopping complexes and restaurants, as well as busy street-side shopping and dining stalls. Many businesses line this endless thoroughfare, and the small lanes or *sois* are crammed with bars and clubs—not all of them tacky hooker joints. Tourists as well as business travelers will find this the most convenient location to stay in town, with many comfortable hotel options. There are a few good budget choices (which are much better than busy and inconvenient Khao San Rd.), and direct access to the BTS means you can get anywhere you need to go in town at any time of day—which is a bonus when gridlock strikes.

Note: Siam (pronounced *see-yam*) BTS lies at the heart of the Rajadaprasong shopping area. Covered walkways link it to a number of Bangkok's larger and swankier malls, but sadly there are few elevators for wheelchairs or baby strollers.

VERY EXPENSIVE

Conrad Bangkok ✦✦✦   On Wittayu (Wireless) Road, just a few doors down from the U.S. Embassy's Consular section, this fashionable high-rise springs out of the smart All Seasons Place complex, cluttered with expensive shops and fast food outlets. When it opened, Conrad was Bangkok's hippest house of style with then unheard-of luxuries, such as Wi-Fi Internet throughout. It still boasts an elegant medley of contemporary styles and confidently chic decor (though now most other hotels in the area can say the same). Interiors are decked out in rich, earthy colors. Rooms are furnished with pretty artwork and faux antiques, and offer every modern convenience; some even have welcome little extras, such as coffeemakers. Baths have freestanding tubs with flatscreen TVs, and some have large sliding doors so the tubs can open up to sleeping areas. Service is sleek and professional. The lobby is often full of well-heeled partiers from its jazz-filled, cigar-smoke-drenched Diplomat Bar, as well as 87, the hotel's nightclub, where local DJs bring lonely business execs and swinging party girls together. A spa and beautiful pool terrace give a sense of serenity and the Chinese, Japanese, and Italian restaurants are all top class.

87 Wireless Rd., Bangkok 10330. © **02690-9999.** Fax 02690-9000. www.conradhotels1hilton.com. 391 units. 7,840B (US$224/£121) single; 8,365B (US$239/£129) double; from 15,190B (US$434/£234) executive suite. AE, DC, MC, V. Chit Lom BTS. **Amenities:** 5 restaurants; bar; nightclub; pool; 2 outdoor lit tennis courts; outdoor running track; fitness center; spa; tour desk; car-rental desk; business center; shopping arcade; 24-hr. room service; same-day laundry service/dry cleaning; nonsmoking floors; executive floor; free Wi-Fi. *In room:* A/C, satellite TV, fax, minibar, fridge, coffeemaker, hair dryer, safe.

The Four Seasons, Bangkok ✦✦✦   The Four Seasons, Bangkok (formerly The Regent) is a smart, well-appointed low-rise property. The entrance and lobby are overwhelming, with a sweeping staircase adorned with giant Thai murals and detailed gold paintwork on the high ceilings. The impeccable service begins at the threshold, and an air of luxury pervades the urban resort. Rooms are spacious and feature handsome color schemes and plush carpeted dressing areas next to the large bathroom area. The more expensive rooms have a view of the Royal Bangkok Sports Club racetrack or pool. Newly renovated Cabana Rooms face the large pool and terrace area, which is filled with palms, lotus ponds, and tropical greenery. Wi-Fi is available at the pool and in a few public areas such as the lobby. The Four Seasons' dining is exemplary. Designed by New York's style guru Tony Chi over a decade ago, Shintaro and Biscotti restaurants merit a visit even if you don't stay here (see "Dining," later in this chapter). There's also a cool outdoor cafe, Aqua, and a busy deli. Plus, the concierge service is second to none in Asia. Close to the center of town and the Ratchadamri BTS, it's a real hideaway (despite the constant construction in the area).

155 Ratchadamri Rd., Bangkok 10330. © 02251-6127. Fax 02253-9195. www.fourseasons.com. 353 units. From 10,000B (US$286/£154) superior; 10,700B (US$306/£165) deluxe; 11,400B (US$326/£175) deluxe view; 15,200B (US$434/£234) cabana; from 16,200B (US$463/£249) premier suite. AE, DC, MC, V. Ratchadamri BTS. **Amenities:** 4 restaurants; lounge w/live music; pool; fitness center; spa; airport transfer; 24-hr. business center; shopping and art gallery; salon; 24-hr. room service; babysitting; same-day laundry service/dry cleaning; nonsmoking rooms; executive floor; Wi-Fi. *In room:* A/C, satellite TV, minibar, hair dryer, safe.

Grand Hyatt Erawan 🌟🌟🌟 Where in the 1970s the former Erawan Hotel famously stood, the hulking white Grand Hyatt was built a decade or so ago. For a time, this was *the* hotel for hosting visiting dignitaries. Today it still exudes comfort, convenience, and style, though perhaps not such exclusive status. It also enjoys a great central (if smog-bound) location: pool loungers and residents of the new, delightful spa cottages are regularly looked over by commuters on the BTS. The hotel's design epitomizes the glamour and exuberance of the 1980s, with giant columns and staircases reminiscent of the TV show *Dynasty*. The lobby (which has Wi-Fi) and its lush indoor landscaping is a cool contrast to the throbbing noise outside on the city's busiest intersection. Spacious rooms are decked out in delightful silks, celadon ceramics, pseudo-antique furnishings, and parquet floors. The bathrooms are equally generous, and city views abound. Isawan, the exclusive spa floor, comes with an excellent New York–style nail salon and superbly crafted surroundings, a mix of modernity and cool Zen simplicity. Rooms have Internet access and compact control panels. In the basement, there are good dining options including fine Italian, a more casual noodle cafe, and a luxury patisserie. Next door is the opulent Erawan shopping center, with high-end outlets such as Mulberry and Burberry, as well as a top-floor colonics center and Urban Kitchen, a basement food hall for cheap eats. Just a few meters away is the glittering Erawan shrine (built to ward off the bad luck that seemed to plague the new hotel during its construction).

494 Ratchadamri Rd., Bangkok 10330 (corner of Rama I Rd.). © **800/233-1234** or 02254-1234. Fax 02254-6308. www.bangkok.grand.hyatt.com. 380 units. 9,800B–10,500B (US$280–US$300/£151–£162) double; from 16,450B (US$470/£253) suite. AE, DC, MC, V. Phloen Chit BTS. **Amenities:** 8 restaurants; lounge; night club; pool; tennis court; fitness center; spa; nail salon; tour desk; airport transfer; 24-hr. business center; shopping arcade; salon; 24-hr. room service; babysitting; same-day laundry service/dry cleaning; nonsmoking rooms; executive floor. *In room:* A/C, satellite TV, dataport, minibar, hair dryer, safe.

JW Marriott 🌟🌟🌟 Right in the heart of the busy Sukhumvit Road area, the JW Marriott is a huge, black marble hive of action, with great eats, a fine spa, and unparalleled convenience. Business travelers love it, for its extensive executive services and efficient staff, but it tends to be emptier over the year-end holidays—giving vacationers an opportunity to enjoy its luxuries without paying a premium. Perfect as it is for shopping along Sukhumvit Road, and close to Nana BTS, Marriott's only drawback (for single women especially) is that it's slap bang in the heart of the go-go club zone, which attracts drunk or unsavory characters late at night. The hotel's dining choices include a casual—but top quality—delicatessen and cafe, renowned steakhouse, and downstairs an amazing contemporary Japanese dining duo, Tsu and Nami. The 16th floor health club is popular, with a pleasant outdoor pool that lends an urban oasis feel in this rather gritty part of town. Upper floors of the hotel overlook the busy Nana

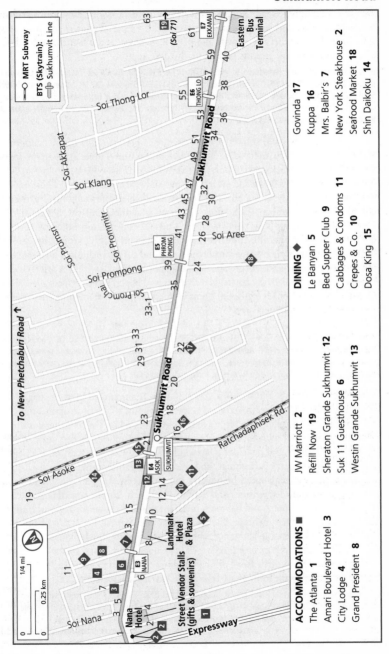

To New Phetchaburi Road ↑

Expressway

ACCOMMODATIONS ■

The Atlanta **1**
Amari Boulevard Hotel **3**
City Lodge **4**
Grand President **8**

JW Marriott **2**
Refill Now **19**
Sheraton Grande Sukhumvit **12**
Suk 11 Guesthouse **6**
Westin Grande Sukhumvit **13**

Govinda **17**
Kuppa **16**
Mrs. Balbir's **7**
New York Steakhouse **2**
Seafood Market **18**
Shin Daikoku **14**

DINING ◆

Le Banyan **5**
Bed Supper Club **9**
Cabbages & Condoms **11**
Crepes & Co. **10**
Dosa King **15**

MRT Subway
BTS (Skytrain):
Sukhumvit Line

area and Sukhumvit Road. Rooms are tastefully upmarket with famously soft beds, handy desk space, and large marble bathrooms with a separate shower and large bathtub. Suites are vast. Service is swift and helpful. A bonus is the fact that the tollway serving both Bangkok airports is right on the doorstep.

62 Langsuan Rd., Lumphini, Pathumwan, Bangkok 10330. © 02656-7700. Fax 02656-7711. www.bangkok.com/jw marriott. 442 units. 10,000B (US$286/£154) deluxe; 12,000B (US$345/£185) suite. AE, DC, MC, V. Nana BTS. **Amenities:** 5 restaurants; 3 bars; health club; spa; car-rental desk; business center; shopping; 24-hr. room service; babysitting; laundry service; dry cleaning; nonsmoking rooms; executive floor; Wi-Fi. *In room:* A/C, satellite TV, dataport, minibar, fridge, coffeemaker, hair dryer, iron/ironing board, safe.

Sheraton Grande Sukhumvit ★★★
Be sure to get the name of this Sukhumvit Road behemoth exactly right. (The Royal Orchid Sheraton is miles away on the river). This is one of two Starwood properties (see the Westin below), both close to Asok BTS. However, this is by far the most luxurious and efficient of the lot. There is a certain formulaic quality to the Sheraton, but it is a high-end formula that's extremely comfortable and familiar. Each room has great amenities, and the height gives it superb views. There is a renowned spa downstairs with top-notch wraps and hydrotherapy. The beautiful 10th-floor lagoon pool looks as if it's set in a jungle. The Sheraton Grande's style places it firmly upmarket and comes with some high-end dining choices that suit business people—but may not always fall within tourist budgets. Popular ground-floor BarSu has regular live acts and happily now attracts a less sleazy crowd; the third-floor Living Room hums with jazz nightly—sometimes these outlets may featuring international acts.

250 Sukhumvit Rd. (between sois 12 and 14) Bangkok 10110. © 02649-8888. Fax 02649-8000. www.starwood hotels.com/bangkok. 445 units. From 8,700B (US$248/£134) double; from 13,500B (US$386/£208) grande suite. AE, DC, MC, V. Asok BTS/Sukhumvit MRT. **Amenities:** 4 restaurants; bar; outdoor pool; fitness center; spa; tour desk; car-rental desk; business center; shopping arcade; 24-hr. room service; same-day laundry/dry cleaning service; nonsmoking floors; Wi-Fi. *In room:* A/C, satellite TV, minibar, fridge, coffeemaker, safe.

Swissôtel Nai Lert Park ★★★ *Kids*
Raffles International now manages this sprawling low-rise hotel set in luxuriant tropical grounds, which once upon a time was known as the Hilton Bangkok. Sitting in the verdant Nai Lert Park, the hotel is a great little inner-city oasis with four room types—including rooms decked out for those traveling with kids—and no less than six kinds of suites. Rooms are plush, with either classic or contemporary furnishings, and offer city or garden views from their sunny balconies. All have high-speed broadband Internet access. Its gym, pool, and tennis courts all back onto leafy forest, and Raffles' renowned Amrita Spa adds a touch of luxury. Its meeting rooms and ballroom make it a popular choice for regional business travelers and for large functions. The coolly revamped Syn bar is the talk of the town and provides an enjoyable ambience without much sign of the dubious custom that typifies most business bars near Sukhumvit. The hotel is on a busy one-way road that makes access to Sukhumvit Road difficult and time-consuming in traffic, but it's only a short, 8-minute walk from Nana BTS and Central Department Store.

2 Wittayu (Wireless) Rd., Pathumwan, Bangkok 10330. © 02253-0123. Fax 02253-6509. www.swissotel.com. 338 units. 7,700B (US$220/£118) standard; 10,850B (US$310/£167) deluxe; from 11,900B (US$340/£183) suite. Nana BTS. **Amenities:** 3 restaurants; deli; 2 bars; outdoor pool; tennis court; fitness center; spa; tour desk; business center; 24-hr. room service; laundry service; dry cleaning. *In room:* A/C, satellite TV, dataport, fridge, minibar, coffee-making facilities, hair dryer, safe.

Westin Grande Sukhumvit ★★★
Across the street from the Sheraton Grande Sukhumvit, the much-renamed and renovated Westin begins on the seventh floor,

above Robinson's department store. It's a more affordable choice, but perhaps not as posh as its sister property, with decent-size rooms and passable dining but no great views or glamour peeking through its urbane decor. The hotel's business services are of good standard, and the Club Floor rooms offer a few more benefits such as Wi-Fi. Though it has nothing superior to that offered by its glamorous neighbor, the location of the Westin, plus its prices, gives it the edge for tourists who'd rather save their dollars for shopping. BTS and MRT access at the nearby Asok intersection means that the city is at your disposal, and unlike the guests at Sheraton, you don't have to hike over a smog-filled overpass to get here.

259 Sukhumvit Rd., Bangkok 10110. © 02207-8000. Fax 02255-2441. www.starwoodhotels.com. 362 units. From 6,500B (US$186/£100) deluxe; from 8,600B (US$246/£132) suite. AE, DC, MC, V. Nana BTS. **Amenities:** 2 restaurants; 2 bars; outdoor pool; fitness center; tour desk; car-rental desk; airport transfer; business center; shopping arcade; salon; 24-hr. room service; same-day laundry service/dry cleaning; Wi-Fi. *In room:* A/C, satellite TV, minibar, fridge, safe.

EXPENSIVE

Amari Boulevard Hotel 🎇🎇 Set back from the heaving sidewalks of Sukhumvit, the Amari is an upscale option that caters well to both businessmen and tourists. This well-known triangular-shaped landmark sits like a wedge of cheese right in the heart of the busy bar and red-light district known as Nana, off Sukhumvit Road. Wide-ranging shopping and dining options are on your doorstep here, but the late-night sleaze of the surrounding *sois* may put off families—in which case, check out the posher **Amari Watergate** (© **02653-9000**), a 10-minute drive away. Inside, the Amari Boulevard is a world away from Sukhumvit Road's seedier side. Nicely furnished, its—albeit average size—rooms have sunny color schemes and pleasant touches such as elegant Thai handicrafts and touches of teak wood. Deluxe rooms afford a few more luxuries such as a separate bath and shower and DVD players. There's Wi-Fi in the lobby and friendly staff. It's a short walk to the night markets and just a 5-minute walk to the BTS, from where the whole city is within easy reach.

2 Soi 5, Sukhumvit Rd., Bangkok 10110. © 02255-2930. Fax 02255-2950. www.amari.com. 309 units. From 8,645B (US$247/£133) double; from 13,125B (US$375/£202) suite. AE, DC, MC, V. Nana BTS. **Amenities:** 2 restaurants; 2 bars; pool; fitness center; tour desk; airport transfer; business center; 24-hr. room service; babysitting; same-day laundry service/dry cleaning. *In room:* A/C, satellite TV, minibar, fridge, hair dryer, safe.

Inter-Continental Hotel 🎇🎇🎇 With an advantageous location near Chit Lom BTS and downtown shopping malls such as Gaysorn and Siam Paragon, the Inter-Con' is oft overlooked but well worth a try if you wish to be close to the key shops and don't mind fighting daily gridlock at the Rama I intersection. It's also next to its lower-end sister property, Holiday Inn. Enclosed in a glass and steel tower, rooms are decked out in swanky, high-end business hotel standards and come with unobstructed views of the seething city. If you can pay the executive floor rates, you get perks such as free broadband Internet and high tea. It's a good choice for shoppers; within 10 minutes' walk lie nine of the city's most popular malls, and if that's not enough, the gigantic, labyrinthine Pathumwan Market is 5 minutes away for truly adventurous (and non-claustrophobic) bargain hunters.

973 Ploenchit Rd., Pathumwan, Bangkok 10330. © **800/225-5843** or 02656-0444. Fax 02656-0555. www.inter continental.com. 375 units. From 6,650B (US$190/£102) deluxe; from 9,060B (US$259/£139) corner suite; 11,050B (US$316/£170) executive suite. AE, DC, MC, V. Chit Lom BTS. **Amenities:** 3 restaurants; lounge w/live music; outdoor pool; fitness center; spa; tour desk; car-rental desk; airport transfer; business center; shopping; salon; 24-hr. room service; babysitting; same-day laundry service/dry cleaning; nonsmoking rooms; executive floor. *In room:* A/C, satellite TV, dataport, minibar, fridge, coffeemaker, hair dryer, safe.

Novotel Bangkok ★★   This midrange Novotel lying in the thick of the Siam Square shopping area has been around for ages but manages to keep up appearances. The marble and glass lobby leads to an expansive lounge, complemented by soft sofas. Pastel tones carry over into relatively spacious rooms. Wi-Fi comes free for corporate guests, but others pay a small hourly or daily charge. If the more than adequate Chinese or international restaurants are beyond your budget, head outside where there are a bevy of cheaper noodle shops and a variety of Western diners from local pizza parlors to donut chains filling up Siam Square's packed backstreets. In contrast to the many five-stars close by, Novotel offers considerably lower prices but comparable extras such as nonsmoking and meeting rooms. The hotel's facilities, including its busy bars, attract a mix of midrange travelers and executives, but the popular disco (famously) tends to attract a sleazier crowd.

Siam Square Soi 6, Bangkok 10330 (off Rama I Rd.). ℂ 02209-8888. Fax 02254-1328. www.novotel.com. 429 units. From 6,400B (US$183/£98) double; 8,000B (US$228/£134) junior suite. AE, DC, MC, V. Siam BTS. **Amenities:** 2 restaurants; 4 bars; nightclub; outdoor pool; fitness center; tour desk; airport transfer; business center; shopping arcade; salon; 24-hr. room service; massage; babysitting; same-day laundry service/dry cleaning; nonsmoking rooms; Wi-Fi. *In room:* A/C, satellite TV, minibar, fridge, safe.

MODERATE

Arnoma Hotel Bangkok ★★   Arnoma is hardly a stylish option, but it's a convenient address for shoppers, though traffic (and pollution) at the busy Ratchadamri intersection is hideous at best. It's plunked right among the Rajadaprasong district's many shopping outlets; the gargantuan Zen and Central World mall are opposite, the posh Gaysorn, Erawan, and Siam Paragon malls are all within a few minutes' walk. Rooms are comfortable; the top five floors are termed business class and are slightly more modern and better appointed than the 1980s-style standard rooms below, but the rates are reasonable for this part of town. There are handicap-accessible rooms available on request, as well as nonsmoking rooms (recommended). Light sleepers would do well to ask for a room away from the road. The place is busy, but the staff does well to cope.

99 Ratchadamri Rd., Pathumwan, Bangkok 10330. ℂ 02255-3444. Fax 02655-3444. www.arnoma.com. 369 units. 5,700B (US$163/£88) double; from 8,830B (US$252/£136) suite. AE, MC, V. Phloen Chit BTS. **Amenities:** 3 restaurants; bar; pastry shop; outdoor pool; fitness center; spa; car-rental desk; business center; 24-hr. room service; laundry service; dry cleaning. *In room:* A/C, satellite TV, fridge, minibar, safe.

City Lodge ★ *Value*   Budget travelers will appreciate the two small, spiffy City Lodges that come under the Swiss-run Amari group's wing. The newer lodge on Soi 9, and its nearby cousin, the older (but better equipped and slightly pricier) 34-room City Lodge on Soi 19 (ℂ 02253-7710; fax 02255-7340), provide pleasant, modern rooms. Each has its own pasta restaurant and a few frills, such as a DVD player and broadband (at Soi 19 only). A big bonus is the shared fitness and pool facilities available at the more deluxe Amari Boulevard Hotel on Soi 5 (see above). Low-season discounts mean you can get good value for money. Both hotels are very convenient for shopping, bars, and the Nana BTS.

137/1–3 Sukhumvit Soi 9, Bangkok 10110 (corner of Sukhumvit and Soi 9). ℂ 02253-7705. Fax 02255-4667. www.amari.com. 28 units. From 3,325B (US$95/£51) double. MC, V. Nana & Asok BTS. **Amenities:** Cafe; limited room service; babysitting; same-day laundry service/dry cleaning; Wi-Fi. *In room:* A/C, satellite TV, minibar, fridge, safe.

Grand President ★★   Off the perennially popular Soi 11, close to Nana BTS, this old favorite, comprising three different wings, is a good midrange find for families, singles, or those who like to be right in the thick of things without paying premium. The Grand President's 1-, 2-, and 3-bed studios and suites are geared up for long and short stays and offer small luxuries such as an aging but fairly extensive gym, and several swimming pools. Rooms are comfortable but rather worn at times, with good closet space, modern bathrooms with tubs, and the added bonus of kitchenettes equipped with microwave ovens, sinks, and giant fridges. The Royal Suite has a full kitchen and washing machine. The service is friendly, but not overly capable. The biggest disadvantage here (or advantage, depending on your perspective) is the proximity to bars, which mean the corridors are often noisy at night with drunken revelers returning home. Ear plugs may be useful.

14-16, Soi 11, Sukhumvit Rd., Bangkok 10110. © **02651-1200**. Fax 02651-1260. www.grandpresident.com. **437 units.** 2,900B (US$83/£45) studio; 3,100B (US$88/£48) executive studio; from 28,000B (US$800/£431) regency suite; 32,000B (US$914/£492) royal suite. AE, DC, MC, V. Nana BTS. **Amenities:** 3 restaurants; 3 outdoor pools; sauna; fitness center; business center; laundry service; dry cleaning; Wi-Fi. *In room:* A/C, satellite TV, DVD/CD player, video player, kitchenette, fridge, coffee-making facilities.

INEXPENSIVE

The Atlanta   These days, the crusty old concrete bunker known as The Atlanta has little by way of comfort; however, it does have character, most of it left over from 1952 when it first opened. It claims to be the first hotel in Bangkok to have a swimming pool—and it looks very much as if it hasn't been renovated since. That said, the dining area does serve great Thai treats and features a small library and occasional film screenings of classic movies. The famous pool is still out back in an unkempt leafy garden. What the reception lacks in warmth is made up for by the more amenable travel counter. Rooms are basic, with a choice of air-conditioning or fan (only A/C rooms have hot water, and some facilities are shared). The sign: NO COMPLAINTS AT THESE PRICES is for real, and if that kind of wit appeals, you'll find it charmingly eccentric. At the far end of Sukhumvit Soi 2, it's a hot hike to Nana BTS.

78 Soi 2 Sukhumvit Rd., Bangkok 10110. © **02252-6069**. Fax 02656-8123. www.theatlantahotelbangkok.com. **49 units.** 500B (US$14/£7.35) double with fan; 800B (US$23/£12) double with A/C. Cash only. A 15-min. walk from Nana BTS. **Amenities:** Restaurant; pool; tour desk; library; laundry service; free broadband Internet. *In room:* A/C in some, safe (bring your own lock).

Refill Now ★ *Finds*   A fun and friendly budget choice, this new little upmarket backpackers joint is a cool place, way above the rest. It's a bright, breezy place with bunk beds and communal bathrooms, a cozy restaurant, and a lot more style than some of the comparable budget options elsewhere. Though it's situated at the end of town, it's within a 50B (US$1.40/75p) ride to Phra Khanong BTS on Sukhumvit Road (just one stop east of Ekkamai Bus Station). Don't be put off that its location is off most maps. It's bound to rapidly become a hip new hangout, so book online, no matter what the season.

191 Soi Predi Bhanomyong 42, yak 5, Sukhumvit Rd. Soi 71, Bangkok 10110. © **02713-2044-6**. www.refillnow. co.th. **24 bunk beds, 8 private rooms.** 525B–1,470B (US$15–US$40/£8.10–£23) double. MC, V. Phra Khanong BTS. **Amenities:** Restaurant; laundry service; Wi-Fi. *In room:* A/C.

Suk 11 Guesthouse   The rusticated Suk 11 is modeled on a primitive wooden Thai house and provides convenient access to Nana BTS. Because of its rock-bottom prices, this hostelry needs to be booked a minimum of 3 days ahead (use the website) and won't accept walk-ins. Rooms are basic and service can be surly—it's as if they've had it too good for too long. There's a range of rooms from dormitory to family rooms with en-suite bathrooms, but walls in all are thin. Single and double rooms with en suite bathroom are the best bets. There are some quiet sitting areas and even a yoga room. Credit cards can be used for Internet bookings only.

1/13 Soi Sukhumvit 11 (behind 7-Eleven), Bangkok 10110. ℂ 02253-5927. www.suk11.com. 75 units. 250B (US$7/£3.65) dorm; 480B–900B (US$14–US$26/£7–£13) single/double with shared facilities; 600B–1,500B (US$17–US$43/£8.85–£22) family room. Cash only except online. Nana BTS. **Amenities:** Restaurant; games room; laundry service; yoga room; library; Internet. *In room:* A/C.

BANGLAMPOO & KHAO SAN ROAD

This now fast-gentrifying area still caters to a core clientele of budget backpackers, aging hippies, and drug-addled dropouts—which makes for noisy nighttimes in the cheaper guesthouses. It is slowly trying to court more midrange customers, though. Cheap eats and funky fashions abound here; so do thieves: Secure your room and valuables well. Most of the major tourist sights are located a 20-minute walk away in Dusit or Sanam Luang, so sightseeing on foot is possible, if you can take the heat. It's a pleasant boat ride to Saphan Taksin BTS, though a long way to Sukhumvit's bars and shops.

INEXPENSIVE

There are budget places from as low as 250B (US$7/£3.85) in and around Khao San, including the **Viengtai Hotel** (42 Rambutri Rd., Banglampoo; ℂ **02280-5434-45;** www.viengtaikhaosan.com), a rather spartan, battered enclave, but with clean rooms, a pool, and good prices—just 1,400B to 3,000B (US$40–US$86/£22–£46) a night.

Buddy Lodge ⒻⓇ This is one of the area's best-known, smaller-size hotels providing upscale accommodations. Rates are higher than the guesthouses for sure, but this brings a modicum of comfort, with facilities such as a rooftop pool, air-conditioning, TV, and, most of all, security. It can get pretty raucous in the echoing hallways, but all rooms are clean, with a pretty 1930s Thai rustic look, wicker furnishings, and comfy beds; some rooms have balconies. You can dine in their popular restaurant or feast in the many nearby eateries. There's also a mall right next door.

265 Khao San Rd., Bangkok 10200. ℂ 02629-4477. Fax 02629-4744. www.buddylodge.com. 75 units. From 2,200B (US$63/£32) double. MC, V. Hua Lamphong MRT. **Amenities:** Restaurant; bar; outdoor pool; fitness center; tour desk; laundry service. *In room:* A/C, satellite TV, minibar, fridge, safe.

Hotel De Moc ⒻⓇ Recently renovated into a great midsize budget option, this 1960s hotel is 10 minutes by taxi east of Khao San and just north of Klong Banglampoo. Now run by Buddy Lodge (see above), it provides 100 spick and span guestrooms with air-conditioning and small balconies overlooking a mostly residential area near Democracy Monument (from where the hotel takes its name). There are simple but good-quality room amenities, doubles and triples, marble bathrooms, Wi-Fi, plus the added bonus of complimentary use of a daytime tuk-tuk shuttle to Khao San Road, as well as bikes and the gym at Buddy Lodge. Out back, there's a big concrete pool surrounded by trees. It's a world away from the swanky five-stars, but old world charm rides high here nonetheless.

78 Prachathipatai Rd., Pra-Nakorn, Bangkok 10200. ℂ **02282-2831-3** or 02629-2100-5. Fax 02280-1299. www.hoteldemoc.com. 100 units. From 1,435B (US$41/£22) double. BTS and MRT over 10 minutes away. **Amenities:** Restaurant; bar; tour desk; massage; laundry service; Wi-Fi. *In room:* A/C, TV, fridge, coffee-making facilities, safe.

Royal Hotel ⒻⓇ Located on the broad Ratchadamnoen Avenue, this three-story brick colossus is a 5-minute walk to the Royal Palace, but rather isolated from other sites. As a result, the Royal is a great choice for budget travelers who find the crazies on Khao San to be too much and who don't mind a smattering of shabbiness amongst the 1950s polished floors, chandeliers, and Corinthian columns. The clean, kitschy rooms are spacious and comfortable. A small pool and buffet breakfast are added luxuries. Regular political rallies in the nearby park (the closest to Parliament) can make it noisy, so choose a room at the back.

2 Ratchadamnoen Ave., Bangkok 10200 (2 blocks east of National Museum). © 02222-9111. Fax 02224-2083. 300 units. 1,100B (US$29/£17) double; from 4,000B (US$114/£62) suite. MC, V. Hua Lamphong MRT. **Amenities:** 2 restaurants; lobby bar; outdoor pool; fitness center; tour desk; salon; same-day laundry service/dry cleaning; Internet. *In room:* A/C, satellite TV, minibar.

CHINATOWN

Yaowarat (Chinatown) is a cramped, pungent trip back in time, riddled with traffic jams and chaotic at best. But it's also one of the most fascinating mercantile districts of Old Bangkok, with great eats, sights, and color.

MODERATE

Grand China Princess Hotel ⚘ Affordable and close to many attractions, this towering edifice peers down from 10 stories above, overshadowing the bustling shophouses and businesses of colorful Chinatown. Guest rooms are typical of a Chinese-style hotel, with all the useful amenities usually found in more expensive hotels, without sparing Thai-style touches and character. Suites are especially large. The 25th floor features Bangkok's first revolving diner, with spectacular views over the city and Chao Phraya River.

215 Yaowarat Rd., Bangkok 10100. © 02224-9977. Fax 02224-7999. www.grandchina.com. 155 units. 2,000B–7,000B (US$57–US$200/£31–£108) double. AE, MC, V. Hua Lamphong MRT. **Amenities:** 3 restaurants; pool; fitness center; Jacuzzi; sauna; tour desk; airport transfer; business center; 24-hr. room service; massage; same-day laundry service/dry cleaning; Wi-Fi. *In room:* A/C, satellite TV, minibar, fridge, coffee-making facilities, safe.

Shanghai Inn ⚘ This newish hotel is a small but superb example of some of Bangkok's more characterful boutique hotels that are springing up. The average-size rooms (and slightly larger suites) are all eclectically furnished in a 1930s style, with vivid pink, green, and red silks, and Chinese lattice frame beds, all evoking Old Shanghai. While they tend to be on the small side, rooms make up for it in color and ambience. The hotel offers only a few facilities—such as delicious Chinese teas and free Wi-Fi—but its sumptuous atmosphere far outstrips its better equipped neighbors.

479 Yaowarat Rd., Bangkok 10100. © 02221-2121. Fax 02221-2124. www.shanghai-inn.com. 55 units. From 2,250B (US$64/£35) double; from 3,800B (US$108/£58) suite. AE, MC, V. Hua Lamphong MRT. **Amenities:** Restaurant; lounge; spa; laundry service; dry cleaning; Wi-Fi. *In room:* A/C, satellite TV, minibar, fridge, coffee-making facilities, hair dryer, safe.

INEXPENSIVE

Chinatown Hotel ⚘ From the rather ugly exterior, you can tell the Chinatown Hotel is hardly going to be an architectural stunner, but behind the blue glass façade there are some decent, if diminutive rooms, decorated to a fair level. The China Room has a microwave oven and the suites are more spacious; though they lack any style, they are at least a good value. New amenities include broadband Internet (for a fee). The facilities are few, but the public areas are well kept.

562 Yaowarat Rd., Bangkok 10100. © 02225-0204-26. Fax 02226-1295. www.chinatownhotel.co.th. 60 units. From 1,350B (US$38/£21) double; from 2,600B (US$74/£40) suite. MC, V. Hua Lamphong MRT. **Amenities:** Cafe; tour desk; limited room service; massage; same-day laundry service/dry cleaning. *In room:* A/C, satellite TV, minibar, fridge, hair dryer, safe.

2 Dining

If you have tasted Thai food back home, it may not necessarily taste like the stuff you're about to try here. What you'll eat in Bangkok will (hopefully) be the real thing; be warned that many restaurants catering to foreigners in big resort towns adjust their Thai cuisine radically to cater to foreign palates. Happily, Bangkok offers many authentic choices, from simple noodle stands to sophisticated, upmarket joints. You don't have to limit your diet to Thai food either; the city is one of the best places in the world to dine out on international fare. Check the free listings magazines, such as *BK Magazine,* and you may even stumble across a visiting chef from an overseas Michelin-starred eatery making a quick visit to a five-star hotel or an annual food festival.

You will not go hungry in the Big Mango, and the truly adventurous will find interesting and more authentic fare off the beaten track in smaller roadside eateries. Prices vary from really rock-bottom-priced street food to unashamedly wallet-melting, posh new restaurants. But on the whole, menu costs are comparatively reasonable. You'll be able to eat well for around 3,000B (US$86/£46) for two, even at some of the town's better restaurants. (If you order wine, Thai taxes on good vintages mean you may double that figure, though.)

ON THE RIVER
VERY EXPENSIVE
Le Normandie ✦✦✦ FRENCH   The Le Normandie is the apex of formal dining in Thailand, both in price and quality. The ultra-elegant restaurant, atop the renowned Oriental Hotel, offers panoramic views of Thonburi and the Chao Phraya River. The dining room literally glistens, from place settings to chandeliers, and the warm tones of the butter-yellow silks impart a delicious glow. Some of the world's highest-ranked master chefs have made guest appearances here, adding their own unique touches to the various menus, a la carte, degustation, or set, all of which change regularly. Watch out for daily specials, or seasonal delicacies such as goose liver, Brittany lobster, frogs' legs, or guinea fowl. Main courses such as pan-fried Dover sole, steamed sea bass, and lamb saddle are good examples of the diversity. The summer set menu is one of the hotel's best-kept secrets—lunch can cost less than a main course. If you want to really indulge your sweet tooth, opt for the dessert tray on the a la carte menu. Wines of every caliber pepper the extensive wine list, but be prepared to splash out for the best.

The Oriental Bangkok, 48 Oriental Ave. ✆ 02236-0400. Reservations required at least 1 day in advance. Jacket required for men, no jeans or sports shoes. Main courses 2,000B (US$57/£31); special summer set lunch/supper menus from 1,000B–1,900B (US$28–US$54/£15–£29). AE, DC, MC, V. Daily noon–2:30pm and 7–10pm; closed Sun lunch. Ferry to Central Pier or Saphan Taksin BTS.

EXPENSIVE
Mei Jiang ✦✦✦ CHINESE   In the plush lower level of The Peninsula lies a Chinese restaurant that serves fresh, unfussy Cantonese dim sum and superbly authentic regional specialties from the Chinese provinces of Guangzhou, Fujian, and Sichuan, not forgetting Northern classics such as the succulent Beijing Duck, eaten with warm pancakes, sweet plum sauce, cucumber, and shallots. Elegantly simple Chinese decor that doesn't overwhelm and delightful private rooms give it an edge over the city's other—more showy—Chinese restaurants. As the dim sum selection attests, this place is all about quality. Reasonably priced set lunches (with dim sum) or set dinners make

light work of a head-spinningly broad menu that includes (more extravagantly priced) Chinese delicacies such as lobster, Australian abalone, and sharks' fin. Don't overlook desserts such as chilled sago pudding, black sesame ice cream, or the wonderfully warming sesame paste dumplings in a spicy ginger tea.

The Peninsula, Bangkok, 333 Charoen Nakhorn Rd., Thonburi (overlooking the river). *C* **02861-2888.** Main courses (average) 500B–1,600B (US$14–US$46/£7.70–£25). AE, DC, MC, V. Daily 11:30am–2:30pm and 6–10:30pm. Short ferry from Hotel Shuttle Boat Pier (next to Saphan Taksin BTS).

Thiptara *✦✦✦* THAI   This alfresco riverside venue is set amid a pretty Thai garden with lotus ponds, goldfish pools, and individual, private wooden pavilions, all next to the Chao Phraya River. Flaming torches light the passing boats, giving it a truly romantic air. The menu includes both spicy and nonspicy Thai dishes, all of which carefully encapsulate the taste of simple home cooking. Try a refreshingly zesty pomelo salad with grilled prawns (mention to the waitress if you don't like it too spicy) or dip into a Thai-style duck curry or fresh seafood dishes. If you don't want to risk street eats and are dying to try some Thai classics, Thiptara offers the well-loved Thai-style noodle, *pad thai goong sod,* or *tom yum goong* (spicy coconut and prawn soup), as well as the addictive Thai dessert, mango and sticky rice. More adventurous diners can try the more unusual *pollamai nampheung,* a two-person dessert of Thai fruits roasted in honey with splashes of chili and vanilla, served with a refreshing lemon sorbet. You can take the free hotel shuttle boat from Saphan Taksin BTS, or from the hotel's own private pier next to the Shangri-La Hotel, to get here.

The Peninsula, Bangkok, 333 Charoen Nakhorn Rd., Thonburi. *C* **02861-2888.** Main courses 360B–780B (US$10–US$22/£5.55–£12). AE, DC, MC, V. Daily 6–10:30pm. Short ferry from Hotel Shuttle Boat Pier (next to Saphan Taksin BTS).

MODERATE

Harmonique *✦✦* THAI   A popular tourist haunt, Harmonique is set in the courtyard of a century-old house and, despite the cramped space and unending clutter, it oozes character. The entrance to this ramshackle eatery is via Wat Meung Kae. There is courtyard seating, as well as small open-air dining areas, stuffed with fun bric-a-brac and ephemera. The cuisine is Thai, tailored to Western tastes—the *tom yam* is delicious, served only as spicy as you like, and with enormous chunks of fish. The sizzling grilled seafood platter is nice and garlicky (chilies on the side). They also feature good Western desserts such as brownies, which are great with a cool tea on a hot day. This is a nice stop when you're touring the riverfront or visiting the antiques stores of nearby River City.

22 Charoen Krung [New] Rd., a few meters on right down Soi 34. *C* **02630-6270.** Main courses 300B (US$8.50/£4.60). AE, MC, V. Mon–Sat 11am–10pm. Closed in summer. 20-min. walk from Saphan Taksin BTS.

Studio 9 & Patravadi Theater Café *✦✦* THAI/INTERNATIONAL   Studio 9 provides the adjoining theater complex with a smart little eatery right on the water with tables overlooking the Grand Palace on the opposite bank. Come over the weekend for the contemporary dance-dinner evening shows, or just pop in after a performance at the Patravadi Theater for a quick bite and glass of wine. The very reasonably priced menu leans towards Thai-fusion fare but is aptly amended for foreign palates. Since there's no charge for the weekend dance performances, it makes for a fantastic cultural evening without breaking the bank. The Theater Cafe across the road is a relaxed open air eatery for enjoying coffee, cakes, snacks, and cold drinks. You can try

Where to Dine in Bangkok

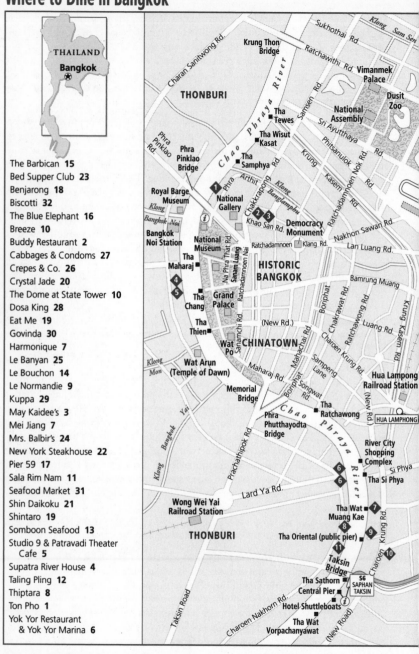

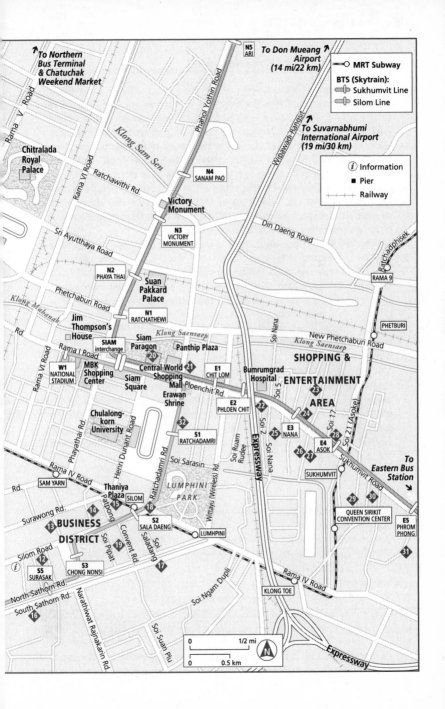

Tips on Dining: Bangkok Cheap Eats

As in most areas of the country, the city's many night bazaars and hawker stalls are where you'll find the best eats, but those who are nervous of tummy bugs or who are not inclined toward culinary adventures would do well to stick to the many food courts usually located inside shopping malls. Here, young Thais enjoy cheap eats in the luxury of air-conditioning; they can get packed with office workers noon to 1pm. In all food courts, you should buy coupons first, and cash in any you don't use afterwards. In addition to the ones reviewed below, other notable food courts include All Seasons Place, Emporium, Siam Square, MBK, and the Central department stores' Loft concept. All are usually located on the top floor or basement of stores and resemble simple self-service cafeterias.

The city's small, open-air joints and markets are also popular for snacks and quick lunches; they open dawn until late. Food vendors are now banned on Mondays in Bangkok, in an effort to free up the already cluttered pavements. Eating right next to smoke-belching buses may not be your idea of gastronomic heaven, but surrounded by the pungent aromas of garlic, chili, and barbecued meats, as well as the cacophony of the traffic or glaring lights, make it a totally Thai experience. On the other hand, if you are missing hearty home fare or a sugar fix from Western desserts, fear not; even budget-strapped travelers can enjoy a range of clean and hearty dining spots all over town, at all hours.

Surawong and Silom Roads Every day except Mondays, the length of upper Surawong Road (the end closest to Rama IV Rd.) is a cluster of snack stalls and fruit vendors that spill into adjoining Thaniya Plaza. In places like Soi Convent off Silom Road (close to California Gym), you'll find stalls selling crab and shrimps, noodles, fried vegetarian patties, and delicious boiled chicken on rice.

to hitch a free ride here on the Supatra River House steamer (see the "Dinner with Thai Dance" section later).

Arunamarin Rd., 69/1 Soi Wat Rakhang. Siriraj, Thonburi. ☏ **02412-7287-8.** Main courses 200B (US$6/£3.10). AE, MC, V. Mon–Thurs 2–10pm; Fri–Sun noon–midnight (performances start at 7:30pm). Tha Thien Pier and 5-min. shuttle boat ride.

INEXPENSIVE

Yok Yor Restaurant 21 and Yok Yor Marina THAI   These two riverside hangouts, which sit practically side by side, are both popular with Thais and Chinese tour groups thanks to their seafood served outdoors or inside. Both restaurants offer no frills whatsoever, but the views, fresh air, and seafood make them good culinary escapes after sightseeing. In the evenings, expect painfully tuneless karaoke sessions to unfold on their stages. Lunch is a more tranquil bet. Evening diners can catch the free Yok Yor ferry from River City shopping mall.

Suan Lum Night Bazaar Just next to Lumphini Park, this sprawling shopping compound was slated to be torn down in 2007. But things move slowly in Thailand, so it may yet live on another year. The open-air food court is hardly Thai haute cuisine, but it's open from 6pm and costs little. Because it boasts a large central stage, you'll be serenaded by Thai rock bands who belt out deafening (and pretty tuneless) renditions of Western hits during your meal. Pre-purchase food coupons (about 100B/US$2.85/£1.55 is enough) and choose from the many stalls.

Siam Paragon Food Court Right at Siam BTS, this glitzy mega-mall doesn't just cater to big-brand boutique shoppers; downstairs, it has a host of low-cost diners, pastry shops, and ice-cream parlors, as well as classy restaurants. The cheaper food stalls have just about every type of fare including Thai, Indian, Japanese, and Vietnamese.

Khao San Road Area Starting from Phra Arthit Road, cutting through Soi Rambutri and heading toward Khao San Road will lead you past heaps of low-budget diners that serve Thai and Western food. Look out for great BBQ fish, served hot off the coals or sizzling satays. These small-time diners extend to the busy Rambutri Road (parallel to Khao San Rd.) and many cater to late-night nibblers. Apart from Burger King and McDonald's, there are also plenty of stalls selling cheap pad thai, Chinese congee *(johk),* or fried rice.

Note: Many are put off by the seemingly unhygienic conditions of street stalls, and for good reason. Even if you are an adventurous eater, take some precautions: Check all ingredients for freshness, and be sure that anything you eat is prepared fresh and hasn't been languishing on liquefied ice for ages.

Soi Somdej Chaowpraya, 17. ① 02860-1266-7. www.yokyor.co.th. Yok Yor Marina, Somdej Chao Phraya Soi 17. Main courses 70B–200B (US$1.70–US$4.90/£1.10–£2.10). Mon–Sun 11am–11pm. Saphan Taksin BTS and 5-minute shuttle boat ride.

SILOM & SURAWONG ROADS

This is where you'll find the country's most expensive joints, nestled a few meters from busy street vendors and more familiar fare, from McDonald's to pizzas. Head to the basements of any large shopping mall (for example, **Silom Complex**) to find excellent low-priced diners, and great value Japanese sushi chains such as Fuji, as well as small cafes serving different noodles or Chinese hotpot. This area also has many independent restaurants, but beware; the majority serve up Thai food for tourists, so look out for places patronized by locals for more authentic eats.

VERY EXPENSIVE

Breeze ★★★ ASIAN/SEAFOOD The relatively new Le Bua hotel has brought to Bangkok a unique Asian seafood experience that will amaze anyone who braves the giddy heights of this alfresco restaurant on the 51st and 52nd floors of State Tower. After crossing a long, illuminated "skybridge," descend into a cozy outdoor terrace overlooking the city. The fusion-inspired menu focuses on top-notch dim sum; fresh fish, such as steamed cod; and some contemporary pan-Asian seafood delicacies, including poached South Australian lobster and wasabi prawns and soft-shell crab (some of which can cause major collateral damage to the holiday budget). The menu also includes items such as a wide selection of barbecued meats, imported lamb rack, or prime rib-eye steak, and some decent desserts such as the Breeze On Ice, a selection of mousses with cantaloupe served on crushed ice. If you really want to splash out, there are rare Scotch whiskies or world-class wine labels (such as Chateau Petrus) priced at the equivalent of a first-class airfare back home. They're guaranteed to blow you—and, if you're not careful, your wallet—away. Advance reservations are obligatory, and a dress code applies to all fine-dining venues in State Tower.

State Tower (corner of Silom Rd. and Charoen Krung [New] Rd.), 1055 Silom Rd. ℂ 02624-9999. www.breezebkk. com. Reservations recommended. Main courses from 1,000B (US$28/£15). AE, DC, MC, V. Mon–Thurs 11:30am–2pm; Fri–Sun 6:30–11:30pm. Saphan Taksin BTS.

The Dome at State Tower ★★★ INTERNATIONAL   This award-winning dining complex is home to three of the city's most popular (and at times, most expensive) dining venues, and two of the top-rated rooftop bars. **Sirocco** is a smart and stunningly positioned, supper-only outdoor terrace serving top-class Mediterranean-inspired cuisine, with live jazz most nights. On an adjoining outdoor deck, the **Sky Bar** is a chic, illuminated bar counter (no seats), perched meters above the seething traffic below. Access to both means taking a lift to the 65th floor and then descending down a vertiginously steep staircase, worthy of a Hollywood musical. **Distil** offers a more casual, low-lit lounge scene with a fashionable bar as well as great lunch and supper menus; there's a separate oyster counter and an unending list of spirits and fine wines (check out the private cellar). Upstairs from Distil, **Mezzaluna** is a rare and refined, contemporary Italian eatery with an open kitchen, serving five-star Italian food together with panoramic views of the city. The entire complex is geared for well-heeled, well-dressed professionals or high-spending holidaymakers who are looking for an awesome Bangkok experience; indeed, the views of Bangkok below are irresistible. See the website for details on the dress code, which applies to all venues in State Tower (including Breeze, reviewed above).

State Tower (corner of Silom Rd. and Charoen Krung [New] Rd.), 1055 Silom Rd. ℂ 02624-9999. www.thedome bkk.com. Reservations recommended. Dress code and age restrictions apply to children. Main courses 400B–2,000B (US$11–US$57/£6.15–£31). AE, DC, MC, V. All outlets close at 1am. See website for all details and individual outlet opening times. Saphan Taksin BTS.

EXPENSIVE

Benjarong ★★ THAI   Named for the exquisite five-color pottery once reserved exclusively for the royal family, Benjarong's fine Thai cuisine focuses on the five basic flavors of Thai cooking (salty, bitter, hot, sweet, and sour) in traditional "royal" dishes. While the a la carte menu is extensive, the most popular dishes are the sweet red curry crab claws and the exotic grilled fish with black beans in banana leaves. The illustrated menu will help you navigate your way through the choices. For after-dinner treats, the *khong-wan* is an ornate selection of typical Thai desserts—distinctive, light, and not too sweet.

The Dusit Thani, Rama IV Rd. (corner of Silom Rd. and Rama IV Rd.). ℂ 02236-0450. Reservations recommended. Main courses 180B–900B (US$5.10–US$26/£2.75–£14). AE, DC, MC, V. Daily 11:30am–2:30pm and 6:30–10:30pm; closed for lunch Sat–Sun. Sala Daeng BTS.

The Blue Elephant ★★ ROYAL THAI Long-known and respected for its cooking school, the Blue Elephant attracts diners looking for a taste of Royal Thai and Thai fusion cuisine. Set in a gorgeously renovated colonial house, the restaurant boasts an ambience that's both elegant and unpretentious. Though the spiciness of some dishes has been tempered for foreign diners, the high standards and superb flavors of items such as the classic betel leaf appetizer, sea bass, satay, and fish cakes, still make it extremely enjoyable. Dig into the signature dishes of salmon *larb*, *foie gras* accompanied by a tart, tamarind sauce, or the Thai green curry made with black skinned chicken. There are also vegetarian dishes aplenty. The wine list contains Thai and international wines, some of which carry the restaurant's own label.

233 South Sathorn Rd. ℂ 02673-9353. Reservations recommended. Main courses 700B (US$20/£11). AE, DC, MC, V. Daily 11:30am–2pm and 6:30–10:30pm. 5-min. walk from Surasak BTS.

MODERATE
The Barbican ★ INTERNATIONAL This old favorite is still packing in expatriate punters with its casual British-pub style and a menu featuring plenty of international staples such as pasta, goulash, or "Guinness pie." It's hardly chic, but at the heart of the somewhat sleazy Thaniya Plaza, its casual atmosphere attracts foreign office workers and travelers hankering for some home cooking. It's most popular when the offices close and the happy hour starts, when it can be standing room only. Fight your way in—it's worth it.

9/4–5 Soi Thaniya, Silom Rd. (1 block east of Patpong between Silom and Surawong rds.). ℂ 02234-3590. Reservations not necessary. Main courses from 180B (US$5/£2.75). AE, DC, MC, V. Daily 11:30am–1am. Sala Daeng BTS.

Eat Me ★★ INTERNATIONAL Eat Me is all about exposed industrial beams, dark wood, and indirect lighting on walls of an ever-changing exhibition space. It tends to get billed as a supper-only art cafe (but thankfully the food is much better than the art, which is almost always purely commercial fare). The menu features a smattering of great fusion dishes (the tuna tartar and spicy lemongrass chicken are delicious), as well as fantastic desserts such as sticky date pudding or lemongrass crème brulée, brilliant culinary inspirations from the Aussie-Thai owners. The main air-conditioned room is a better bet than the mosquito-infested balcony overlooking a small courtyard. The young waiters' all-black uniforms and hands-free headsets would give them an ominous air if they weren't all so hysterically camp. There are some decent wines to boot.

1/6 Soi Pipat 2, off Soi Convent (connecting Sathorn and Silom rds.). ℂ 02238-0931. Main courses from 350B (US$10/£5.40). AE, MC, V. Daily 3pm–1am. Chong Nonsi BTS.

Le Bouchon ★★ FRENCH This hush-hush little French bistro is the kind of place that gets packed with French expats on lunch breaks and makes a great little candlelit venue in the evening. Since it's right in the thick of Patpong, you'll have to elbow your way past the hordes of sex show touts and cat-calling lady-boys to get there, but that is part of the fun. The food is delicious, though the rich sauces used can make the main courses rather heavy going—go for the goat cheese salad or poached salmon for lighter options. There are also classic French desserts such as pears poached in wine. The chalkboard features daily specials, and the wine list is quite thorough. Lunches and dinner here can linger on—the food's so good, you may not want to leave. *Bon appetit.*

37/17 Patpong Soi 2 (between Surawong and Silom Rd.). ℂ 02234-9109. Main courses from 300B (US$8.50/£4.60). AE, DC, MC, V. Daily noon–3pm and 7–11:15pm. Sala Daeng BTS.

Somboon Seafood ⊕ SEAFOOD   This place is good for anyone willing to sacrifice atmosphere for excellent food. Though it's packed nightly, you'll still be able to find a table because the place is so huge. The staff is extremely friendly—between them and the picture menu, you'll have no problem picking out the best dishes. Peruse the large aquariums outside to see all the live seafood options such as prawn, fishes, lobsters, and crabs (guaranteed freshness). The house specialty, chili crab curry, is especially good, as is the *tom yum goong* soup (spiced to individual taste).

169/7–11 Surawong Rd. (just across from the Peugeot building). ⓒ **02233-3104**. Main courses 150B–500B (US$4.20–US$14/£2.30–£7.70); seafood at market prices (about 800B/US$23/£12 for 2). No credit cards. Daily 4–11pm. Chong Nonsi BTS.

INEXPENSIVE
Taling Pling ⊕ THAI   I've just one word for this friendly low-end Thai diner. Go! Because it's packed with office workers at lunch times, it's better to try for a table after 1pm or in the evening. Rustic wooden decor and delightful old photographs adorn the walls. Menus come with photographs for foreigners, but the taste is thoroughly Thai and the low prices reflect this. Try the dry, fluffy catfish salad or the spicy green curry with beef. For those who really want to taste local dishes, the roast duck *panaeng* is recommended. Chicken in pandanus leaf and Thai fish cakes appease those whose palates prefer it less spicy. Unusually, this simple Thai restaurant has some heavy-duty Western desserts such as lemon meringue pie. It's a fabulous place to feast.

60 Soi Pan (midway down the *soi*, connecting Silom and Sathorn rds.). ⓒ **02234-4872**. Main courses 150B (US$4.30/£2.30). AE, MC, V. Daily 11:30am–10:30pm. Surasak BTS.

RATCHADAMRI, SATHORN & SUKHUMVIT AREA
EXPENSIVE
Bed Supper Club ⊕⊕ INTERNATIONAL   Love it or hate it, this place has been on all the tourist trails since it opened in 2002. Billed as one of the coolest places in Bangkok, it consists of an all-white, two-story eatery located in what can only be described as an industrially styled, white illuminated tube. The atmosphere is surreal, and it's only accentuated by the trance music that's regularly spun by DJs. Instead of sitting at tables, diners take off their shoes and lounge on long white ottomans while the music pumps. (Great, if you can eat lying down, not so fun if you can't.) A fixed, set menu is served nightly (with allowances for vegetarians), with three courses on Sunday to Thursday and four courses on Friday and Saturday. Culinary combinations of dishes such as marinated orange salad with Marsala wine and mint, seafood penne with Sicilian pesto, or lemon granite with raspberries and zabaglione set the tone. If you like this style of contemporary, Asian-meets-Mediterranean food and don't mind eating in bed, you'll think this supper club is fantastic.

26 Soi 11 (by Sukhumvit Rd.). ⓒ **02651-3537**. www.bedsupperclub.com. Reservations required. No shorts for men. Set menu 1,250B–1,600B (US$36–US$45/£19–£25). AE, DC, MC, V. Mon–Fri 7:30pm–midnight and until 1am on weekends. 8-min. walk from Nana BTS.

Biscotti ⊕⊕ ITALIAN   This must be Bangkok's most stylish and consistently praised Italian restaurant. Its open kitchen and slick, minimalist decor give it a modern sophistication that few Italian restaurants in Bangkok can match. The long tables and polished wood floors give it a welcome, homely air. Equally unmatched are its cuisine and top-class service, which don't come with too big a price tag, like so many others. Choose from the plate of miniature Italian appetizers (this can consist of anything from scallops, tuna, or beef); there's a great choice of fresh fish, a range of wood-fired pizzas, and an unending list of antipasti—not to mention homemade pastas and risottos. Save space for one of the irresistible desserts, or finish off with one of the excellent wines. It's smart, it's elegant, and it's utterly timeless.

The Four Seasons, 155 Ratchadamri Rd. © 02251-6127. Reservations recommended. Main courses 250B–450B (US$7–US$13/£3.85–£6.90). AE, DC, MC, V. Daily noon—2:30pm and 6–10:30pm. Ratchadamri BTS.

Le Banyan ✹✹ FRENCH A spreading banyan tree on the edge of the garden-like grounds inspires this restaurant's name. An upscale venue that serves suppers only, Le Banyan has for years been the domain of Michel Binaux and Bruno Bischoff. The decor is warm in tone, furnished with sisal matting and white clapboard walls adorned with Thai carvings, old photos, and prints of early Bangkok. The house special is a dish for two, a Rouennaise pressed duck with goose liver; other high-end choices include lobster bisque, chateaubriand with Armagnac, or Provençal-style rack of lamb. There are daily specials and a list of fine wines. If you come on foot, you'll run the gauntlet of all the girly bars at the entrance of the *soi*, but ignore those until you arrive at this little upscale gem and you'll enjoy an evening of fine dining and effusive service.

59 Sukhumvit Soi 8. © 02253-5556. Reservations recommended. Main courses 800B (US$23/£12). AE, DC, MC, V. Mon–Sat 6:30–9:30pm. 10-min. walk from Nana BTS.

New York Steakhouse ✹✹✹ STEAK One of the best steakhouses in the region, the JW Marriott's steakhouse offers plenty of dark wood and high, leather wing chairs, and is the best place for a juicy imported Angus steak served with a host of hearty sides (mushrooms, broccoli with cheese, mashed potatoes, and veggies). If money is no object, splash out on roast prime rib or grilled lamb chops. Seafood choices cover the whole gamut from oysters, to Alaskan crab, to tiger prawns, to Phuket lobster. The long wine list is, not surprisingly, dominated by red wines. Dress code is casual (but no shorts or sandals). Expect professional service and a business-like atmosphere.

JW Marriott (second floor), 4 Sukhumvit Rd., Soi 2. © 02656-9798 (direct) or the hotel at 02656-7700. Reservations recommended. Main courses 1,600B–6,900B (US$46–US$197/£25–£106). AE, DC, MC, V. Daily 6–11pm. Nana BTS.

Pier 59 ✹✹✹ SEAFOOD This newly opened and fashionably high-floor seafood restaurant on the 59th floor of the Banyan Tree Hotel caters to the new generation of Bangkok diners who don't mind paying handsomely for cool and contemporary decor, superb Asian-infused cuisine, and impeccable service. Guests wade into a dark, cavernous room, divided by luminous aquariums, glowing a deep, dazzling indigo. There they'll be given a menu that features treats such as oysters and caviar, and plenty of fish dishes (choose from barramundi, wild salmon, and sea bass) that are all cooked with a contemporary twist. While seafood is the focus, the menu also includes meat as well as vegetarian dishes. The chocolate brandy ice cream is a great finale or go for the miniature selection of bite-size desserts, including a cube of fragrant apple jelly, a button-sized macaroon, and teeny chocolate mosaic. The venue's beautiful views and the standards of culinary excellence are helping raise the benchmark for contemporary culinary elegance in this otherwise heavily tourist-populated part of town.

The Banyan Tree, 21/100 South Sathorn Rd. (halfway down Sathorn Rd.). © 02679-1200 Reservations recommended. Main courses 1,000B (US$28/£15). AE, DC, MC, V. Daily 6pm–12:30am. A short taxi ride from Chong Nonsi BTS or Lumphini MRT.

Shin Daikoku ✹ JAPANESE This is the most central outpost of a popular Japanese eatery (there's another branch in Sukhumvit Soi 19). It's a home away from home for many Japanese expatriates in Bangkok, so not surprisingly the food is deliciously authentic. Noodle dishes come in the form of soba and udon, and there's plenty of sushi, sashimi, and teppanyaki steaks. Female staff wear cotton robes known as *yukata* and pad around politely, hovering over every detail of the meal. Desserts include the perennially popular green tea ice cream crepe with brandy. The roaring laughter and shouts of "Kampai!" tell you that they're doing it right here. A la carte dishes are small and rather expensive, but they're worth it. And they have good sushi and sashimi sets. Order some saké, take your shoes off, and enjoy.

Inter-Continental Hotel, 973 Ploenchit Rd. © **02656-0096.** Reservations preferred. Main courses from 350B (US$10/£5.40). AE, DC, MC, V. Daily 11am–2pm and 5–10:30pm. Phloen Chit and Siam BTS.

Shintaro ★★ JAPANESE   A Japanese restaurant with a difference. Gone are the cliches of kimono-clad, bowing waitresses tottering along on wooden clogs yelling "Konban-wa!" This small but snazzy diner is decked out in contemporary decor and offers not just classic Japanese but some cutting-edge culinary offerings too. Packed as it is with young, well-heeled locals and businessmen, this must be the city's most fashionable Japanese restaurant. (Check out what look like noodle-clad walls by designer Tony Chi.) Whether dining along a long bench, facing the busy chefs, or at the side tables, expect the unexpected; the finest quality slabs of sashimi, artfully hand-rolled sushi, succulent *foie gras* rolls, or tasty soba noodles. Hot dishes include grilled salmon, done to perfection. Don't pass up the desserts such as sago with fresh melon; they're the perfect ending to a superb lunch or supper.

The Four Seasons, 155 Rachadamri Rd. © **02251-6127.** Reservations recommended. Main courses 250B–450B (US$7–US$13/£3.85–£6.90). AE, DC, MC, V. Daily 11:30am–2:30pm and 6–11pm. Ratchadamri BTS.

MODERATE

Crystal Jade ★★ CHINESE   Located in the heart of the shopping area in the Siam Paragon Mall, this popular two-story Chinese restaurant has many branches across Asia. At Siam Paragon, the decor is elegant and enclosed—it's a nice escape from the seething food court. The Chinese fare is fast and fresh, with northern-style dumplings, noodles, and wonton soup. You'll also find Cantonese favorites such as suckling pig, deep-fried prawns, and barbeque pork, plus extravagances like abalone. At the Erawan mall branch, the decor is more like a fast food joint, and the food is cheaper and more casual.

Ground Floor, Siam Paragon Mall. 991 Rama I Rd. © **02129-4343.** Main courses from 350B (US$10/£5.40). AE, MC, V. Daily 11am–2:30pm and 5:30–10pm. Siam BTS.

Kuppa ★★ INTERNATIONAL   This laid-back Western cafe-restaurant is the brainchild of a Thai couple, who spend their time between Bangkok and Perth, Western Australia. Located off the Asok BTS in a former warehouse (reputedly a CIA hangout), it boasts a chic, minimalist interior with plenty of polished concrete and artworks. The food has a neo-Australian flair, with plenty of pan-Asian and Pacific Rim dishes, blending the best of Thai and Western cuisine, with stacks of salads, seafood, and fish. The soft-shell crab, Parma ham, and salami platter; grilled dory; and duck liver parfait are all superb. Grilled items are sometimes served with mashed potato, and the daily specials provide a diverse dining choice. Desserts are the classic Australian stuff: puddings, cakes, and hearty dollops of cream. Kuppa has good couches for kicking back and a section for smokers. If you haven't got time to grab a lunch, come for the great coffee and don't miss the hulking roaster machine, a centerpiece of the dining area where Kuppa's own blend is roasted weekly. Brunch on weekends is a fun social event.

Cricket, Anyone?

Look for the snack stands along Sukhumvit Road (also Khao San Rd.) that sell all sorts of fried insects. Grasshoppers, beetles that look like cockroaches, scorpions, ants, and grubs are a favorite snack for folks from Isan, in the northeast, where bugs are in fact cultivated for the dining table and are an important source of protein in the region. How does it taste? Crickets are a bit like popcorn, and the beetles are something like a crispy chicken. A great photo op.

39 Sukhumvit Soi 16.. (℗ **02663-0450**. Main courses 350B (US$10/£5.40). AE, DC, MC, V. Daily 10am–11:30pm. Short taxi ride from Asok BTS.

Seafood Market ⭐ SEAFOOD   This place is fun but very touristy. If you're a seafood fan, you'll love it. Few people will have had a dining experience like this before. You'll enter the giant hangar of a fish market and, before you sit down, you can wander around the seafood counters and choose your supper, either live or on ice, all priced by the kilo. Pay for it all at the cashier and then cart it back to the table. At this point, choose how you'd like it cooked and what sauces you prefer. Waiters can help with suggestions for your catch, but what comes out of the kitchen is always good. Cooking charges and corkage are paid separately at the end of the meal. The seafood is market price, and the fish, incredibly fresh.

89 Sukhumvit Soi 24 (Soi Kasami). (℗ **02261-2071**. Reservations suggested for weekend dinner. Market prices. AE, MC, V. Daily 11:30am–midnight. Phrom Phong BTS.

INEXPENSIVE

Cabbages & Condoms ⭐ THAI   Here's a restaurant with a purpose. Opened by local senator Mechai Viravaidya, founder of the Population & Community Development Association, this restaurant helps fund population control, AIDS awareness, and a host of rural development programs. Set in a large compound, the two-story restaurant has air-conditioned indoor dining—but if you sit on the garden terrace, you're in a fairyland of twinkling lights that's quite romantic. Share a whole fish or try the *kai hor bai teoy* (fried boneless chicken wrapped in pandanus leaves with a dark sweet soy sauce for dipping). There's also a large selection of vegetable and bean curd entrees. Before you leave, be sure to check out the gift shop's whimsical condom-related merchandise.

10 Sukhumvit Soi 12. (℗ **02229-4610**. Reservations recommended. Main courses 70B–200B (US$2–US$5.70/£1.10–£3.10). AE, DC, MC, V. Daily 11am–10pm. 15-min. walk from Asok BTS.

Crepes & Co. ⭐⭐ *Kids* EUROPEAN   Popular among Bangkok foreign residents (and their kids), this is a great place to satisfy your sweet tooth. Crepes here are light, fluffy, and filled with dozens of combinations, both savory and sweet—all of them delicious. They also serve good Mediterranean main courses such as mezze or couscous. Everyone is friendly—even the cat, who sometimes likes to curl up and sleep next to diners. They have great coffee and a good selection of tea.

18/1 Sukhumvit Soi 12. (℗ **02653-3990**. Reservations recommended. Main courses 100B–300B (US$3–US$8/£1.55–£4.60). AE, DC, MC, V. Daily 9am–midnight. 10-min. walk from Nana BTS.

Dosa King ⭐ INDIAN/VEGETARIAN   Newly renovated in late 2007, this corner restaurant close to Asok BTS serves the popular Punjabi dish that is a large, lentil flour pancake, filled with savory goodies such as curry. It's folded and served with delicious sauces, and is 100% vegetarian. Dosa King does have other traditional Indian dishes, but stick with the house special and you'll enjoy a quick, healthy meal while escaping the masses along Sukhumvit.

265/1 Sukhumvit Soi 19. ℂ 02651-1700. Main courses 150B (US$4.30/£2.30). MC, V. Daily 11am–11pm. Asok BTS.

Govinda ✯ ITALIAN/VEGETARIAN   No one can resist this home-styled eatery that makes some of the best Italian food in the city and yet charges very reasonable prices. Plus, it's a wholly vegetarian menu, which means that those people who have been living on tofu and eggs all holiday can finally splurge on fabulous pastas, dozens of soya-meat dishes, and even vegetarian salamis and sausages. The Italian couple who runs this low-key, two-story diner is typically welcoming and works hard to keep the food absolutely authentic. Dive into handmade gnocchi (made with pumpkin), excellent vegetarian lasagna, or egg-based pasta. Though the desserts are not as impressive, the ice cream is a great end to one of the best value meals you can find in Bangkok. If you are lucky, you may meet Govindina, the restaurant's rotund cat, who normally likes to sleep upstairs in the air conditioning.

6/5-6/6 Sukhumvit Soi 22 (7-min. walk from Sukhumvit Rd.). ℂ 02663-4970. Reservations recommended for dinner. Main courses 150B (US$4/£2.30). AE, MC, V. Wed-Mon 11:30am–3pm and 6–11:15pm. 15-min. walk from Phrom Pong BTS.

Mrs. Balbir's ✯ INDIAN   You won't be able to fault this small, hole-in-the wall diner that has existed for several decades, thanks to the affable and effervescent owner, Mrs. (Vinder) Balbir, whose jolly banter accompanies any lunch or supper. The menu covers all sorts of Punjabi goodies such as biryani, dahl, chicken tikka masala, and deliciously smooth cheese and spinach dishes. All of Mrs. Balbir's food comes with homemade pickled onions and chutneys. Dine on tables downstairs or sit on the floor cushions upstairs. As famous for being a TV chef as much as a restaurateur, Mrs. Balbir also runs highly enjoyable cooking classes from her home close by.

Sukhumvit Soi 11, in the first sub-*soi* on the right from Sukhumvit Rd. ℂ 02651-0498. Reservations recommended for dinner. Main courses 150B (US$4/£2.20). Cash only. Tues–Sun 11:30am–2:30pm and 6:30–10:30pm. 5-min. walk from Nana BTS.

BANGLAMPOO & KHAO SAN ROAD

Khao San Road used to be Bangkok's busy backpacker quarter, but it's moved rapidly upmarket in the last 3 years. It's still where you'll find every manner of food, from kosher and halal cuisine, to Italian, as well as tasty Thai food served streetside. Avoid the blander versions of Western food served at budget guesthouses, but do have a seat somewhere along the busy road, order up a fruit shake, and watch the nightly parade of young travelers. Below are a few well-known choices near Khao San.

INEXPENSIVE

Buddy Restaurant THAI   A popular bar as much as anything, Buddy Restaurant is part of the growing Buddy Lodge "compound." The second-floor restaurant serves good Thai and Western and is always full, even late into the night with clubbers.

265 Khao San Rd., Banglampoo. ℂ 02629-4477. www.buddylodge.com. Main courses 70B–350B (US$2–US$10/£1.10–£5.40). MC, V. Daily 24 hrs. Ferry to Banglampoo Pier.

May Kaidee's *Finds* VEGETARIAN/THAI   Over the years, May Kaidee's has become a bit of a pilgrimage spot for visiting foodies. This place has little more than some modest tables tucked into a little alleyway, but nevertheless it's the home of some

CLOSED due to accidental demolition

WEGEN BISSIGEN EICHHÖRNCHEN GESCHLOSSEN

CERRADO CABRAS

Κλειστό Μετεωρίτες

プール も POOL CLOSED 閉鎖中 ELECTRIC EELS

Hotel closed for facelifting

FERMÉ POUR RAISON DE GRÈVE DES BONNES

FECHADO! POR CAUSA DE ATAQUES DOS CROCODILOS

— I don't speak sign language.

A hotel can close for all kinds of reasons.

Our Guarantee ensures that if your hotel's undergoing construction, we'll let you know in advance. In fact, we cover your entire travel experience. See www.travelocity.com/guarantee for details.

travelocity
You'll never roam alone.

healthy and delicious Thai vegetarian dishes. Mrs. May (pronounced *My*) has developed a real following by cooking up dishes such as the spicy massaman or the Thai green curry, as well as soups and stir-fries. All dishes come with a choice of white or brown rice. For dessert, don't pass up the black sticky rice with mango. Her cookbook is for sale and she even offers cooking classes.

At the end of Khao San Rd., in a sub-*soi* off Soi Damnoen Klang. ℂ **02629-4839**. Main courses 60B–120B (US$1.70–US$3.40/90p–£1.85). Cash only. Daily 7am–10pm. No MRT or BTS within 10 minutes.

Ton Pho ⋇ THAI   This almost 20-year-old restaurant is popular with locals, and a good place to try real Thai food (at real Thai prices). The restaurant is riverside but overlooks the busy public boat pier that accesses Banglampoo and the popular Khao San Road area—which means that the view is of groups gathering and departing on smoke-belching river buses rather than a wide riverside landscape. Great stir-fries and classic Thai dishes like *tom yum goong* and coconut milk–infused soups and curries make up for the poor view.

43 Phra Arthit Rd., Banglampoo. ℂ **02280-0452**. Main courses 80B–200B (US$2.30–US$6/£1.25–£3.10). Cash only. Daily 11am–10pm. Ferry to Banglampoo Pier.

DINNER WITH THAI DANCE

Sala Rim Nam ⋇⋇ THAI   The Oriental Hotel re-opened this beautiful riverside Thai restaurant in late 2007 with a glittering new interior but the same impeccable standards of cuisine and commendable entertainment. The location is across the river from the main hotel, and the ferry boat ride across is quite lovely. The set menu is more like an extensive *dégustation* menu of Thai favorites. Nothing is too heavy, but do mention to the waiter before your dine if you can't take spicy food. Guests can choose between sitting Thai-style on floor pillows or the plush Western-style seating, from where they watch classical Thai dancers, in full glittering regalia, perform ancient Thai legends and rousing drum-frenzied folk dances. A free shuttle boat leaves the hotel's pier regularly; or take the BTS to Saphan Taksin and follow the signs to the Hotel Shuttle Boat pier, just next to Central Pier.

The Oriental, Bangkok (on Charoen Nakhorn Rd., on the Thonburi side of the Chao Phraya River). ℂ **02437-2918**. 1,700B (US$48/£26). AE, DC, MC, V. Daily 7–10pm, performance at 8:30pm. Saphan Taksin BTS.

Supatra River House ⋇⋇ THAI   This is another well-written-up tourist spot, yet despite its popularity, it is still a great place to relax while feasting on fresh seafood, fish cakes, spring rolls, steamed fish, or a host of great Thai favorites, including vegetarian dishes. Most of the spicy dishes have been tamed for tourists. If it's too hot to enjoy the outdoor tables overlooking the Grand Palace, reserve a seat in the indoor pavilion that has arctic air-conditioning. There are dance spectaculars in the evenings on the weekends and a little steamer that can pick up diners from the Central Pier, if you call ahead.

266 Arunamarin Rd., Soi Wat Rakhang, Siriraj, Thonburi (diagonally opposite Patravadi Theater). ℂ **02411-0305** or 02411-0874. Main courses 200B (US$5.70/£3.10). AE, MC, V. Mon–Sun 11am–10pm. 5-min. boat ride from Tha Maharat pier, 15-min. boat from the Hotel Shuttle Pier.

DINNER & LUNCH CRUISES ON THE CHAO PHRAYA RIVER

There are a number of tour operators who offer dinner cruises along the Chao Phraya River. These vary from massive, floating discotheques with all-you-can-eat buffets to plush rice barges with delightful old world decor and more intimate surrounds. Most offer special rates for children. All serve Thai set dinners or buffets; less pricey cruises may just offer cocktails at sunset. Some may come with traditional music, live rock bands, or Thai dance shows, depending on the operator; see individual websites for details. Based out of the **Bangkok Marriott Resort & Spa** (© 02476-0021), the *Manohra, Manohra Moon,* and *Manohra Star* are elegantly restored rice barges that offer various day, sunset, and evening dinner cruises on the Chao Phraya River, from 750B (US$21/£12). Numbers are limited and boats can be chartered for private functions. (See www.manohracruises.com.) The **Shangri-La Hotel** (© 02236-7777) offers a totally different experience on the gargantuan *Horizon II;* this neon-drenched vessel heads upstream with its live band belting out Elvis Presley hits from 8 to 10pm and offers fun-packed nights of feasting and dancing. Cruises start at 1,980B (US$56/£30). Similar in style to the *Horizon II* is the *Grand Pearl* cruise (rates from 1,250B/US$36/£19), while another rice barge option is offered by *Loy Nava* with two sailings daily at 6 to 8pm and 8 to 10pm; prices start from 1,295B (US$37/£19).

Most cruises start from their respective hotels, or in the case of the two latter cruises, leave from River City Shopping Mall pier, next to the Royal Orchid Sheraton Hotel. Contact the hotels (or see www.bangkok.com/dinner-&-shows-tours) for details.

What to See & Do in Bangkok

A stroll down any of Bangkok's thousands of sprawling and labyrinthine alleyways can bring untold adventures for visitors who are keen to unearth the *real* Thailand. First-time visitors are often amazed by central Bangkok's glittering modernity, and at the same time, delighted by the treasures found amid the grunginess of ramshackle back streets; it's very easy to stumble across hidden markets, museums, or spectacular temples. This chapter presents the main highlights of the city's sights plus a final section detailing a few worthy side trips from Bangkok. Each section will give you an idea of the scope of things to do. "Bangkok's Waterways" gives you the ins and outs of the city's canals; "Bangkok's Historical Treasures" covers the city's magnificent palaces, charming traditional residences, and fascinating museums. "Cultural Pursuits" lets you in on unique local experiences, and "Staying Active" is for sports people—both participants and observers.

The "Shopping" section gives you the lowdown on what to buy and where, and "Bangkok After Dark" details the city's unending entertainments, such as dance, theater, and nightclubs. Bangkok is famous for being just as vibrant after dark as in the day. Many of its largest boulevards are swathed in fairy lights, and a bevy of swish, rooftop bars all offer fantastic night views. Admittedly, things aren't as crazy as 10 years ago when the party scene ran nonstop until dawn, and alcohol flowed, day or night. Under laws imposed under ex-Prime Minister Thaksin, all bars and clubs must now close at 1am. That said, Bangkok has many markets, bars, and clubs open until at least midnight, plus the big department stores and malls don't close until around 9pm—which should sate even the hardiest shopaholic.

1 Bangkok's Waterways

The key to Bangkok's rise lies in the Chao Phraya River, which courses stealthily through its center, feeding a complex network of canals and locks that, until relatively recently, were the focus of city life. Lying just a few miles from the Gulf of Thailand, the river was a major conduit for trade, and the main reason behind its rapid growth. Today, nothing much has changed: great black barges filled with teak, coal, or sand are towed up and down the river by small yellow tugs; at any time of the day you might spot grey Royal Naval vessels, police on Port Authority jet skis, stout wooden sampans, even blue barges stacked with Pepsi-Cola bottles, all plying these waters.

In the 18th century, Thailand's first monarch, Rama I, moved the capital eastward from Thonburi (a suburb of today's Bangkok) across the river to the district that became known as Rattanakosin Island, so-called due to the man-made canals that surrounded this entire area. Like medieval moats, these canals (*klongs*) acted as a defensive barrier. Other canals were soon added, channeling the waters of the Chao Phraya

Bangkok Attractions

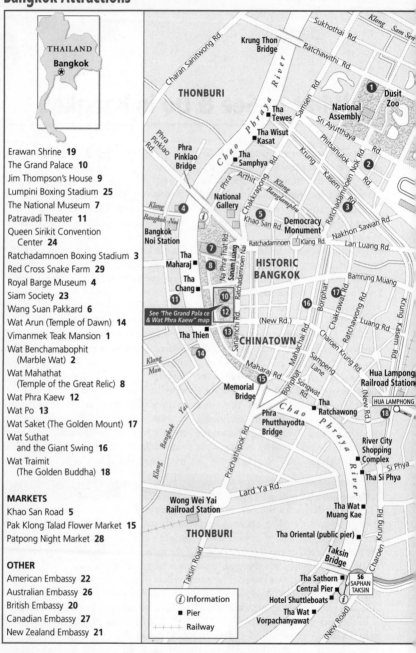

Erawan Shrine **19**
The Grand Palace **10**
Jim Thompson's House **9**
Lumpini Boxing Stadium **25**
The National Museum **7**
Patravadi Theater **11**
Queen Sirikit Convention
   Center **24**
Ratchadamnoen Boxing Stadium **3**
Red Cross Snake Farm **29**
Royal Barge Museum **4**
Siam Society **23**
Wang Suan Pakkard **6**
Wat Arun (Temple of Dawn) **14**
Vimanmek Teak Mansion **1**
Wat Benchamabophit
   (Marble Wat) **2**
Wat Mahathat
   (Temple of the Great Relic) **8**
Wat Phra Kaew **12**
Wat Po **13**
Wat Saket (The Golden Mount) **17**
Wat Suthat
   and the Giant Swing **16**
Wat Traimit
   (The Golden Buddha) **18**

MARKETS
Khao San Road **5**
Pak Klong Talad Flower Market **15**
Patpong Night Market **28**

OTHER
American Embassy **22**
Australian Embassy **26**
British Embassy **20**
Canadian Embassy **27**
New Zealand Embassy **21**

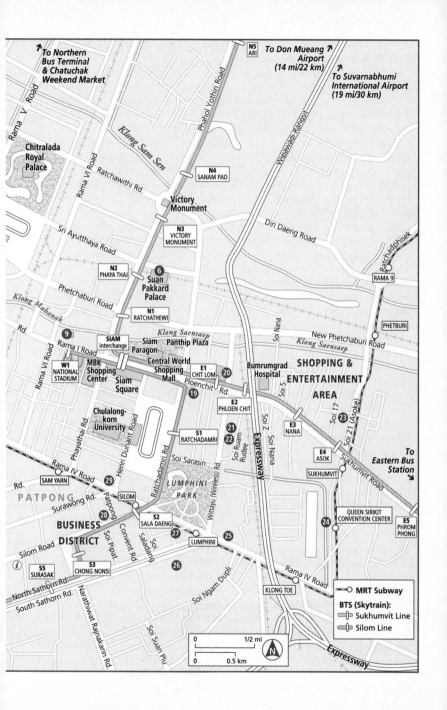

To Northern
Bus Terminal
& Chatuchak
Weekend Market

To Don Mueang
Airport
(14 mi/22 km)

To Suvarnabhumi
International Airport
(19 mi/30 km)

N5
ARI

Rama V Road

Chitralada
Royal
Palace

Klong Sam Sen

Rama VI Road

Ratchawithi Rd.

N4
SANAM PAO

Wiphawadi-Rangsit

Ratchadaphisek

Victory
Monument

Din Daeng Road

Sri Ayutthaya Road

N3
VICTORY
MONUMENT

RAMA 9

N2
PHAYA THAI

Phetchaburi Road

6
Suan
Pakkard
Palace

PHETBURI

Klong Mabanak

Rd.

N1
RATCHATHEWI

New Phetchaburi Road

Klong Saensaep

Soi Nana

Klong Saensaep

SHOPPING &

9

Rama I Road

SIAM
interchange

Siam
Paragon

Panthip Plaza

ENTERTAINMENT

W1
NATIONAL
STADIUM

MBK
Shopping
Center

Central World
Shopping
Mall

E1
CHIT LOM

20

Bumrumgrad
Hospital

AREA

Rama VI Road

Siam
Square

Ploenchit Rd.

Soi 5

Soi Nana

Soi 17

23

Soi 21 (Asoke)

Chulalong-
korn
University

19

E2
PHLOEN CHIT

E3
NANA

To
Eastern Bus
Station

Phayathai Rd.

Henri Dunant Road

S1
RATCHADAMRI

21
22

Soi Ruam
Rudee

Soi Nana

Sukhumvit Road

E4
ASOK

Rama IV Road

Soi Sarasin

Ratchadamri Rd.

SAM YARN

29

LUMPHINI
PARK

Wittayu (Wireless) Rd.

SUKHUMVIT

PATPONG

Surawong Rd.

SILOM

Patpong

QUEEN SIRIKIT
CONVENTION CENTER

E5
PHROM
PHONG

BUSINESS
DISTRICT

28

Convent Rd.

S2
SALA DAENG

Soi
Saladang

27

LUMPHINI

25

24

Rama IV Road

Silom Road

Soi Pipat

S5
SURASAK

S3
CHONG NONSI

26

KLONG TOE

North Sathorn Rd.

South Sathorn Rd.

Narathiwat Rajnakarin Rd.

Soi Ngam Dupli

Soi Suan Plu

Expressway

0   1/2 mi
0   0.5 km

N

MRT Subway
BTS (Skytrain):
Sukhumvit Line
Silom Line

Expressway

123

into peripheral communities, feeding fish ponds or rice paddies, and nurturing the city's many tropical fruit orchards. These waterways fast became the aquatic boulevards and avenues of this low-lying, swampy city. Apart from structures built for royalty, ordinary Bangkok residents lived on water, in bamboo raft homes, or on boats. As foreign diplomats, missionaries, and writers traveled to Bangkok, they drew parallels with the Italian city of Venice and renamed it the "Venice of the East." Not until the early 1800s were nonroyal houses built on dry land.

Due to the health hazards posed by these open *klongs,* and the gradual need for more stable land in the advent of vehicular transport, many of the canals were paved over in the last century. By the late 1970s, most of the city's paddy fields had disappeared. In fact, much of today's Bangkok has been reclaimed from former marshland. Fears are growing as global warming raises sea levels and the effects of seasonal flooding on the city are becoming more drastic.

For a glimpse of traditional Thai life, schedule a few hours to explore the waterways. You'll see people using the river to bathe, wash their clothes, and even brush their teeth at water's edge (not recommended). Floating kitchens occupy small motorized canoes from which the pilot-cum-chef serves rice and noodles to the occupants on other boats. Men, wrapped in nothing more than a loincloth, tiptoe across floating carpets of logs en route to the lumber mills; ramshackle huts on stilts adorned with 100-year-old fretwork, tumble down into *klongs,* while at low tide, the ribcages of sunken boats appear out of the oozing mud.

Opportunities abound for exploring Bangkok's small *klong* networks and river arteries. The most frequently seen boat on the river is the **long-tail,** a needle-shaped craft driven by a raucous outboard engine and covered in a striped awning. These act as river taxis for both tourists and locals. Private long-tails congregate at **Maharaj, Chang,** and **Si Phya** public piers and at **River City** (℡ 02235-3108). If you are confident of your haggling skills, you can try to charter a **long-tail** yourself for about 1,000B (US$29/£15) an hour—be sure to agree on the charge before you get in the boat. *Note:* Beware of independent boat operators who offer to take you to souvenir or gem shops.

Otherwise, if you head to the riverside exit of Saphan Taksin BTS, there's also an official kiosk down on the riverfront, with tour information, including tickets for the hop-on, hop-off **Chao Phraya Express** (℡ 02623-6001). This runs every half-hour, daily from 9:30am to 3:30pm, and is a more comfortable option than the (more cramped) long-tails or tatty wooden express boats that act as the city's river taxis.

You can also go on a formal tour of the *klongs.* The following operators can arrange itineraries, with 3-hour tours costing about 1,300B (US$37/£20) per person, including an English-speaking guide: **World Travel** (℡ 02233-5900), **Sea Tours** (℡ 02216-5783, with a counter at the Shangri-la Hotel), and **Diethelm Travel** (℡ 02660-7000; www. diethelmtravel.com). Any hotel concierge can also make arrangements.

However you tour the *klongs,* take the time to explore **Klong Bangkok Noi** and **Klong Bangkok Yai.** Also stop at the **Royal Barge Museum** (see "Bangkok's Historical Treasures" below), a wonderful riverside hangar crammed with long, narrow vessels covered in gilt carvings, brought out only to commemorate rare events such as a milestone in the monarch's reign, or the visit of a dignitary.

Many visitors are disappointed by the hugely commercial (some may say overrated) **floating market** at Damnoen Saduak, about 80km (48 miles) southwest of Bangkok in Ratchaburi Province. A better and more authentic experience is to head upstream to picturesque **Koh Kret,** see "Side Trips from Bangkok," later in this chapter.

2 Bangkok's Historical Treasures

Thailand is a veritable mishmash of cultures, a crossroads where Indian, Khmer, Chinese, European, and Thai histories collide. This becomes most apparent in the architectural whimsy seen in its grandest structures. No trip to Thailand is complete without a visit to the Grand Palace, Wat Phra Kaew, and Wat Po.

Note that strict dress codes apply to visiting these sites, so be sure to wear appropriate attire; remember, shoes must be removed in places of worship and you won't be allowed into any royal or religious site if you're exposing your shoulders or dressed in skirts/shorts above the calf.

The Grand Palace ⟳⟳⟳   The number-one destination in Bangkok is also one of the most imposing and visually fascinating. Though it's seen by thousands of tourists—who arrive at the gates in busloads—its immensity still dwarfs the throngs. After passing muster with the fashion police at the main gate (rules are inconsistently enforced, but many have been turned away for inappropriate dress), and queuing at the turnstiles for your ticket (keep it safe for admission to other sites), you'll be directed to the temple entrance on the left of the kiosk. There, you'll come to the **Wat Phra Kaew** (p. 129), one of the highlights of a visit here.

As you leave the temple cloisters and move into the grounds of the Grand Palace, it's easy to see that the buildings here were greatly influenced by Western architecture, including Italian, French, and British motifs. The royal family moved from this royal residence to the nearby Chitlada Palace after the death of King Ananda in 1946. As you enter the main gate, built in the 1780s, you'll see the **Pavilion for Holy Water,** where priests swore loyalty to the royal family and purified themselves with water from Thailand's four main rivers. Nearby is the **Chakri Mahaprasad,** The Grand Palace Hall; built by British architects as a royal residence for Rama IV to commemorate the centennial of the Chakri dynasty; it features an unusually florid mix of Italian and Thai influences. The Thai temple-style roof rests physically (and symbolically) on top of an otherwise European building.

The whitewashed stone building nearby now serves as the **Funeral Hall,** though it was originally the residence of Rama I and Rama II. The corpse of a deceased royal figure is kept in this building for a year before it is cremated. On each of the four corners of the roof is a *garuda* (the half-human, half-bird steed of the God Rama, an avatar of the Hindu god Vishnu). The *garuda* symbolizes the king, who is considered a reincarnation of King Rama. The Grand Palace also has an enclosure called the **Forbidden Quarters** where the wives of previous monarchs lived; no one other than the king was allowed to enter. When HM King Bhumibol Adulyadej came to the throne in 1946, this age-old tradition died out, though Thai culture has been slow to follow. Adjoining is the **Amarindra Hall** built by Rama I, which underwent subsequent restorations under later kings. Today, this splendid building is used for royal coronations, weddings, and lavish state events.

If you arrive at 8:30am when the gates first open, you may have the place virtually to yourself; also remember that it closes at 3:30pm, so don't show up any later than 2:00pm.

East of the river, on Na Phra Lan Rd., near Sanam Luang. ⓒ 02222-8181. www.palaces.thai.net. Admission 250B (US$7.10/£3.85). Price includes Grand Palace, Wat Phra Kaew, and the Coin Pavilion inside the Grand Palace grounds, as well as admission to the Vimanmek Palace (in Dusit Park). Daily 8:30am–3:30pm; most individual buildings are closed to the public except on special days proclaimed by the King. Take the Chao Phraya Express Boat to the pier called Tha Chang, then walk due east, and then south.

Jim Thompson's House 🕿🕿   American architect Jim Thompson settled in Bangkok after World War II where he worked for American Intelligence and became fascinated by Thai culture and artifacts. He dedicated himself to reviving Thailand's ebbing silk industry, bringing in new dyes to create the bright pinks, yellows, and turquoises we see sold today. It was Jim Thompson silks that were used by costumier Irene Sharaff for the Oscar-winning movie *The King & I* starring Yul Brynner. Mr. Thompson mysteriously disappeared in 1967 while vacationing in the Cameron Highlands of Malaysia. Despite extensive investigations, his disappearance has never been resolved. (Respected local writer, William Warren, a contemporary of Thompson, has suggested he may have been hit by a vehicle unintentionally.)

Thompson's legacy is substantial, both as an entrepreneur and a collector. His Thai house contains a splendid collection of Khmer sculpture, Chinese porcelain, and Burmese carvings and scroll paintings. In some rooms, the floor is made of Italian marble, but the wall panels are pegged teak. The house slopes toward the center to help stabilize the structure; the original houses were built on stilts without foundations. The residence is composed of a cluster of six teak and *theng* (a wood harder than teak) houses from central Thailand that were rebuilt—with a few Western facilities— in what must have been a lovely garden next to, what is today, an oily, polluted *klong*. No doubt it would have been magnificent 50 years ago.

Rounding out the attractions here are a gallery space with a revolving collection of local artists and of course a shop—though the silk selections at the flagship shop on Surawong Road (see "Shopping," p. 137) are better.

6 Soi Kasemsan. 🕿 02216-7368. Admission 100B (US$2.85/£1.55). Daily 9am–5:30pm. On a small *soi* off Rama I Rd., near the National Stadium BTS.

The National Museum 🕿🕿   The National Museum, just a short (15-min.) walk north of the Grand Palace and the Temple of the Emerald Buddha, is the country's central treasury of art and archaeology (32 branches are located throughout the provinces). Some of the buildings are themselves works of art.

The current museum was built as part of the Grand Palace complex when the capital of Siam was moved from Thonburi to Bangkok in 1782. Originally the palace of Rama I's brother, the deputy king and appointed successor, it was called the Wang Na ("Palace at the Front"). The position of princely successor was eventually abolished, and Rama V had the palace converted into a museum in 1884. Thammasat University, the College of Dramatic Arts, and the National Theater were also built on the royal grounds, along with additional museum buildings.

To see the entire collection, take a free map at the ticket office and give yourself a few hours; if you prefer not to wander, plan to catch a weekly guided tour. Start with the **Thai History and the Prehistoric Galleries** in the first building. If you're short of time, proceed to the **Red House** behind it, a traditional 18th-century Thai building that was originally the living quarters of Princess Sri Sudarak, sister of King Rama I. It contains many personal effects originally owned by the princess.

Another essential stop is the **Buddhaisawan Chapel,** built in 1795 to house one of Thailand's most revered Buddha images, brought here from its original home in Chiang Mai. The chapel is an exquisite example of Buddhist temple architecture.

From the chapel, work your way back through the main building of the royal palace to see the gold jewelry, some from the royal collections, and the Thai ceramics, including many pieces in the five-color *Bencharong* style. The **Old Transportation Room** contains ivory carvings, elephant chairs, and royal palanquins. There are also rooms

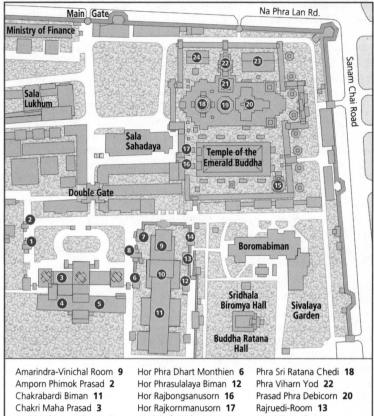

Amarindra-Vinichal Room **9**
Amporn Phimok Prasad **2**
Chakrabardi Biman **11**
Chakri Maha Prasad **3**
Dusida-Bhiromya Room **7**
Hor Kantnararasdr **15**
Hor Monthien Dharma **23**
Hor Phra Naga **24**
Hor Satrakom **14**

Hor Phra Dhart Monthien **6**
Hor Phrasulalaya Biman **12**
Hor Rajbongsanusorn **16**
Hor Rajkornmanusorn **17**
Model of Angkor Wat **21**
Moonstarn-
  Baromasna Room **5**
Paisal-Taksin Room **10**
Phra Mondop **19**

Phra Sri Ratana Chedi **18**
Phra Viharn Yod **22**
Prasad Phra Debicorn **20**
Rajruedi-Room **13**
Royal Council **1**
Snamchandr Room **8**
Somut-Devaraj-
  Ubbat Room **4**
Amarindra-Vinichal Room **9**

full of all kinds of memorabilia: royal emblems and insignia, stone and wood carvings, costumes, textiles, musical instruments, and Buddhist religious artifacts. Fine art and sculpture are found in the newer galleries at the rear of the museum compound.

Na Phra That Rd. ✆ 02224-1333. Admission 40B (US$1.15/60p). Wed–Sun 9am–3:30pm. Free English-language tours Wed and Thurs 9:30am. Ask your Thai-speaking hotel staff to call the museum to check the current schedule. About 1km/ ⅔ mile north of the Grand Palace.

Royal Barge Museum ✸✸✸   If you've hired a long-tail boat on the Chao Phraya, stop by this unique museum housing the sumptuous royal barges. These elaborately decorated sailing vessels—the largest measures over 46m (50 yd.)—are used by the royal family on state occasions or for religious ceremonies. The king's personal barge, the *Suphannahong,* has a swan-like neck and central chamber; the boat itself is decorated with scarlet and gold carvings of fearsome mythological beasts.

If you can't make it to the royal barges, there is a smaller display of barges at the National Museum (see above).

On the west bank of the river, on Klong Bangkok Noi (canal), north of the Phra Pinklao Bridge. © 02424-0004. Admission 30B (85¢/45p) adults, additional fees for cameras. Daily 9am–5pm. Take a taxi all the way or use the cross-river ferry from Tha Phra Arthit.

Siam Society   The 19th-century Kamthieng House, on the grounds of the Siam Society Headquarters, was a rice farmer's teak house transplanted from the banks of Chiang Mai's Ping River. Its collection, organized with financial help from the Asia and Rockefeller foundations, is oriented toward ethnographic objects illustrating the culture of everyday life. Many agricultural and domestic items, including woven fish baskets and terracotta pots, are on display, and there's an interesting exhibit on the Chao Vieng, or city dwellers, from the northern Lanna Thai kingdom.

Walking through the small but lush grounds, which are landscaped like a northern Thai garden, offers respite from the Asok intersection, just behind the hedge. The Siam Society also supports an excellent library and gallery, with information on nearly every aspect of Thai society, concentrating on regional culture. Check newspapers for talks and tours given by experts.

131 Soi Asok (north of Sukhumvit on Soi 21). © 02661-6470. Admission 100B (US$2.85/£1.55) adults, 50B (US$1.45/75p) children. Tues–Sat 9am–5pm. 10-min. walk from Asok BTS station.

Vimanmek Teak Mansion ☆☆   Your ticket to the Grand Palace will also get you in to visit King Chulalongkorn's stunning golden teakwood mansion, often called Vimanmek Palace, a short stroll away via delightful Dusit Palace Park. Built in 1901, this mansion once stood on the small island of Koh Si Chang and was restored in 1982 for Bangkok's bicentennial. It's now a private museum with a collection of the royal family's memorabilia. Despite the (sometimes spotty) standard of English employed by the guides, the hour-long tour here does take you through over 80 exquisite apartments and rooms. Also in Dusit Park is the original **Abhisek Dusit Throne Hall,** housing a display of Thai handicrafts and buildings displaying photographs, clocks, fabrics, royal carriages, and other regalia.

193/2 Ratchawithi Rd., Dusit Palace Park (opposite the Dusit Zoo, north of the National Assembly Building). © 02281-8166. Admission 100B (US$2.85/£1.55); free if you purchase a joint ticket. Daily 9:30am–4pm. Take a taxi from Tha Thien pier.

Wang Suan Pakkad   Wang Suan Pakkad ("Palace of the Lettuce Garden") is one of Bangkok's most delightful retreats. This peaceful oasis was the home of Princess Chumbhon of Nakhon Sawan, an avid art collector and one of the country's most dedicated archaeologists—credited with having partly financed the excavations at Ban Chiang I in 1967. In 1952, five 19th-century teak houses were moved from Chiang Mai and rebuilt in a beautifully landscaped garden on a private *klong,* separated by a high wall from the tumult of Bangkok's streets. The **Lacquer Pavilion** (moved here in 1958) came from a monastery grounds and was a birthday present from the prince to the princess.

The balance of the collection here is diverse, with Khmer sculpture, ivory boxes, and some marvelous prints by European artists depicting images of Siam before the country opened to the Western world. There is an entire room of objects from the Ban Chiang I site, including pottery and jewelry. Look out for a superb Buddha head from Ayutthaya, and an example of a royal barge outside in a shed in the garden. Be sure to ask to

Avoiding the Touts

Tourists are harangued going in and out of the major sites around the Grand Palace, and sadly this area is now famous for its scam artists. Avoid unnecessary frustration by not engaging with these characters just as you would at home. Visitors are frequently told that sites are "closed" by "helpful" types who then suggest alternate destinations. This is the start of the famous **"Bangkok shopping tour scam."** If you are approached by a stranger, whether it's someone purporting to be a "guide," or a tuk-tuk driver in this area, just say "no thanks," and walk away. If you end up riding a tuk-tuk near these main sites, make sure you've agreed to a price with the driver and insist on "NO shopping." If you have any problems, don't hesitate to use the word *poleet* (police in Thai) or call the Tourist Police on ✆ 1155.

see the pavilion housing the princess's collection of Thai and Chinese ceramics. The gift shop at Wang Suan Pakkad offers reproductions, and prices are quite reasonable.

352 Sri Ayutthaya Rd., (between Phayathai and Ratchaprarop rds.). ✆ 02245-4934. www.suanpakkad.com. Admission 100B (US$2.85/£1.55) adults, 50B (US$1.45/75p) children, including material for a self-guided tour of grounds and collections. No photographs. Daily 9am–4pm. 10-min. walk from Phaya Thai BTS.

Wat Phra Kaew ★★★   Sitting to the east of the enormous compound of palaces, lawns, and old tamarind trees at the Grand Palace (see above) is the royal chapel Wat Phra Kaew, or "Temple of the Holy Jewelled Image." The temple, more often called "Temple of the Emerald Buddha," is one of the most revered by Thai people. The temple's name refers to the petite jadeite (not emerald) statue that sits atop a huge gold altar in the temple's main hall, or *bot*. The Buddha, like many others in Thailand, is clothed in seasonal robes, changed three times a year to correspond to the summer, winter, and rainy months. The changing of the robes is an important ritual, performed by the king, who also sprinkles water over the monks and well-wishers to bring good fortune during the upcoming season. The statue is the subject of much devotion among Thais; bizarrely, it is also the religious icon to which politicians (accused of corruption) swear innocence. The magically empowered statue was rumored to have been made in North Thailand in the 15th century, before being installed at a temple in Laos, only to be taken back by the Thais and brought to the capital around 1780—a sore subject between both nations.

The central shrine, or *bot,* where the Emerald Buddha is housed is magnificent and used for important religious rituals; note the exquisite inlaid mother-of-pearl work on the door panels. The interior walls are decorated with late Ayutthaya–style murals depicting the life of the Buddha; the images flow counterclockwise and end with the most important stage: enlightenment. The surrounding portico of the *bot* is an example of masterful Thai craftsmanship. On the perimeter are 12 open pavilions, built during the reign of Rama I. The inside walls of the compound are decorated with murals depicting the entire *Ramakien,* a Thai epic, painted during the reign of Rama I and regularly restored. Its 178 scenes begin at the north gate and continue clockwise.

Among the most interesting of the other monuments and structures here are the three pagodas to the immediate north of the *ubosoth,* representing the changing centers of Buddhist influence: The first, to the west, is **Phra Si Rattana Chedi,** a 19th-century Sri Lankan–style stupa housing ashes of the Buddha; second, in the middle, is the library, or **Phra Mondop,** built in Thai style by Rama I, known for its excellently crafted Ayutthaya-style mother-of-pearl doors, bookcases containing the *Tripitaka* (sacred Buddhist manuscripts), human- and dragon-headed *nagas* (snakes), and statues of Chakri kings; and third, to the east, is the **Royal Pantheon,** built in Khmer style during the 19th century—it's open to the public in October for 1 day to commemorate the founding of the Chakri dynasty. To the immediate north of the library is a model of Angkor Wat, the most sacred of all Cambodian shrines. The model was constructed by King Mongkut as a reminder that the neighboring state was once under the dominion of Thailand. West of the *bot,* near the entry gate, is a stone statue of a hermit, considered a patron of medicine, before which, relatives of the infirm pay homage and make offerings.

In the Grand Palace complex. ℂ 02222-0094. Admission included in the Grand Palace fee, 200B (US$4.90/£2.50). Daily 8:30am–3:30pm. Take the Chao Phraya Express Boat to Tha Chang Pier; then walk east and south.

3 The *Wats*

Bangkok's many temples are each unique and inspiring. If you can only see a few, pay attention to the star ratings and hit the highlights (Wat Phra Kaew is listed in the above section due to its location within the Grand Palace compound). But while the big temples of Bangkok are highly recommended, don't pass up smaller neighborhood temples where you have a good chance of learning about Buddhism in daily practice. Early morning is a good time to visit temples: the air is cool, monks busy themselves with morning activities, and the complexes are generally less crowded.

Thai people make regular offerings to temples and monasteries as an act of merit-making. Supporting the *sangha,* or monkhood, brings one closer to Buddhist ideals and increases the likelihood of a better life beyond this one. Many shops near temples sell saffron-colored pails filled with everyday supplies such as toothbrushes, soap, and other common necessities, and Thais bring these and other gifts as offerings to Buddhist mendicants as a way of gaining good graces. You may even see an early morning alms collection by (often barefoot) monks carrying their bowls around the neighborhood.

Small monetary contributions (the amount is up to you) are welcome at any temple. Devotions at a temple involve bowing three times, placing the forehead on the ground at the foot of the Buddha, as well as lighting candles and incense and chanting. Tourists are welcome to participate, but they are asked to pay particular attention to proper dress—take off your shoes and avoid baring your shoulders, thighs, upper arms, or back.

Erawan Shrine 𝒜𝒜   The Erawan Shrine is not old, but it is an interesting testament to faith (or superstition, perhaps) in Thai society. Built in 1956 next to what is now the Grand Hyatt Erawan, it stands defiantly at the center of a busy corner plot, right next to fume-belching buses and overshadowed by the BTS. In a sumptuous pavilion at the center of this yard, a gilded statue of the four-faced Hindu god of creation, Brahma, named Phra Phrom in Thai, is enshrined. Its construction is believed to have put a stop to all the accidental deaths of workers involved in the hotel site, and due to such mystic powers, it is today one of the most revered spots in the kingdom. The area is crowded with worshippers wafting bunches of incense. It is common to see people giving a *wai* as they pass by. The shrine made news very recently when a mentally deranged Thai man decided to take an ax to the statue. As painful testament to the depth of Thais devotion to their gods (and a pitiful lesson in human rights), the onlookers turned on him and beat him to death in broad daylight.

On the corner of Rama I and Ratchadamri Rd. (next to the Grand Hyatt Erawan). No entrance fee (from 20B/50¢/30p for incense and flowers). Daily dawn–8pm. Phloen Chit BTS.

Wat Arun (Temple of Dawn) ✿✿✿

Formerly known as Wat Jaeng, the 79m-high (260-ft.), Khmer-inspired tower was renamed the "Temple of Dawn," by King Thaksin, Bangkok's founder. He was keen to signal the rise of a new kingdom after Ayutthaya was decimated, and so borrowed the name—which means dawn—from the Hindu God, Aruna. Fittingly, it's at its most wondrous as the sun rises and sets.

The original tower was only 15m (50 ft.) high but was expanded during the rule of Rama III (1824–1851) to its current height. The exterior is decorated with flower and decorative motifs made of ceramic shards donated to the monastery by local people, at the request of the King. At the base of the complex are Chinese stone statues, once used as ballast in trading ships, which were gifts from Chinese merchants.

You can climb the central *prang,* but be warned: The steps are treacherously tall, narrow, and steep—and even more precarious coming down. If you go up, notice the Hindu gods atop the three-headed elephants. The view of the river, Wat Po, and Grand Palace is well worth the climb. Be sure to walk to the back of the tower to the monks' living quarters, a tranquil world far from the bustle of Bangkok's busy streets.

West bank of the Chao Phraya, opposite Tha Thien Pier. ✆ **02465-5640.** 20B (50¢/30p) admission. Daily 9am–5:30pm. Take a water taxi from Tha Tien Pier (near Wat Po), or cross the Phra Pinklao Bridge and follow the river south on Arun Amarin Road.

Wat Benchamabophit (the Marble Wat)

Wat Benchamabophit, called the Marble Wat because of the white Carrara marble of which it is built, is an early-20th-century temple designed during the rule of Rama V. It is the most modern and one of the most beautiful of Bangkok's royal *wats*. Unlike the older complexes, there's no truly monumental *viharn* or *chedi* dominating the grounds. Many smaller buildings reflect a melding of European materials and designs with traditional Thai religious architecture. Even the courtyards are paved with polished white marble. Walk inside the compound, beyond the main *bot,* to view the many Buddha images that represent various regional styles. During early mornings, monks chant in the main chapel, sometimes so intensely that it seems as if the temple is going to lift off.

Sri Ayutthaya Rd. (south of the Assembly Building near Chitralada Palace). ✆ **02281-2501.** 20B (50¢/75p) admission. Daily 8am–5pm.

Wat Mahathat (Temple of the Great Relic) ✿

Built to house a relic of the Buddha, Wat Mahathat is one of Bangkok's oldest shrines and the headquarters for Thailand's largest monastic order. It's also the Center for Vipassana Meditation at the city's Buddhist University, which offers some programs in English. (See "Cultural Pursuits," below, for more information about courses.)

Adjacent to it, between Maharaj Road and the river, is the city's biggest **amulet market,** where a fantastic array of religious amulets, charms, talismans, and traditional medicine is sold. Each amulet brings a specific kind of luck—to get the girl, pass your exams, to keep bugs out of your rice stock, or to ward off your mother-in-law—so if you buy one, choose carefully. (The newer amulet market is part of Wat Ratchanada, off the intersection of Mahachai and Ratchadamnoen Klang roads, across from Wat Saket.)

Na Phra That Rd. (near Sanam Luang Park, between the Grand Palace and the National Museum). ✆ **02222-6011.** Donations welcome. Daily 9am–5pm.

Wat Po ✿✿✿

Wat Po is among the most photogenic of all the *wats* in Bangkok; it's also one of the most active. Also known as the Temple of the Reclining Buddha, Wat

Po was built by Rama I in the 16th century and is the oldest and largest Buddhist temple in Bangkok. The compound, divided into two sections by Chetuphon Road, is a 15-minute walk south of the Grand Palace. The northern area contains the most important monuments, and the southern portion is where monks reside.

Most people go straight to the enormous Reclining Buddha in the northern section. It is more than 43m (140 ft.) long and 15m (50 ft.) high, and was built during the mid-19th-century reign of Rama III. The statue is brick, covered with layers of plaster, and gold leaf; the feet are inlaid with mother-of-pearl illustrations of 108 auspicious *laksanas* (characteristics) of the Buddha.

Outside, the grounds contain 91 *chedis* (*stupas* or mounds), four *viharns* (halls), and a *bot* (the central shrine in a Buddhist temple). Most impressive, aside from the Reclining Buddha, are the four main *chedis* dedicated to the first four Chakri kings and, nearby, the library.

The temple is considered Thailand's first public university. Long before the advent of literacy or books, many of its murals and sculptures were used to illustrate and instruct scholars on the basic principles of religion, science, and literature. Visitors still drop 1-satang coins in 108 bronze bowls—corresponding to the 108 auspicious characteristics of the Buddha—for good fortune, and to help the monks keep up the *wat*.

Wat Po is also home to one of the earliest Thai massage schools; a 30-minute Thai massage here costs a reasonable 220B (US$6.30/£3.40). These days, you'll find dozens of more luxurious spas around town costing maybe 3 to 10 times as much, but offering far more service and comfort. (See the "Cultural Pursuits" below.) You can learn about traditional Thai massage and medicine at the **Traditional Medical Practitioners Association Center,** an open-air hall to the rear of the *wat*. True Thai massage, such as that taught here, involves chiropractic manipulation and acupressure, as well as stretching, stroking, and kneading. Massage courses are available, but many overseas therapists prefer schools with tutors who speak more proficient English. There are also a few astrologers and palm readers available for consultation. For a small donation you can receive a blessing from a monk and a bracelet of braided colored string to commemorate the occasion. Donations go toward upkeep and renovations.

Maharaj Rd., near the river (about 1km/⅔ mile south of the Grand Palace). ✆ 02222-0933. 20B (50¢/30p) admission. Daily 8am–5pm; massages offered until 6pm. A short walk or taxi from Tha Thien pier.

Wat Saket (The Golden Mount) ✦

Wat Saket is easily recognized by its golden *chedi* atop a fortress-like hill near busy Ratchadamnoen Road and Banglampoo. King Rama I restored the *wat,* and 30,000 bodies were brought here during a plague in the reign of Rama II. The hill, which is almost 80m (262 ft.) high, is an artificial construction begun during the reign of Rama III. Rama IV brought in 1,000 teak logs to shore it up because it was sinking into the swampy ground. Rama V built the golden *chedi* to house a relic of Buddha, given to him by the British. The concrete walls were added during World War II to keep the structure from collapsing.

The Golden Mount is interesting for its vistas of Rattanakosin Island and the rooftops of Bangkok and is beautifully lit at night. Every late October to mid-November (for 9 days around the full moon) Wat Sakhet hosts Bangkok's most important temple fair, when the Golden Mount is wrapped with red cloth and a carnival erupts around it, with food and trinket stalls or theatrical performances.

Ratchadamnoen Klang and Boripihat rds. Entrance to the *wat* is free; admission to the *chedi* is 10B (28¢/15p). Donations welcome. Daily 8am–5pm.

Wat Suthat and the Giant Swing   This temple is among the oldest and largest in Bangkok, and Somerset Maugham declared its roofline the most beautiful. It was begun by Rama I and finished by Rama III; Rama II carved the panels for the *viharn* doors. It houses the beautiful 14th-century Phra Buddha Shakyamuni, a Buddha image that was brought from Sukhothai. The ashes of King Rama VIII, Ananda Mahidol, brother of the current king, are contained in its base. The wall paintings for which it is known were created during Rama III's reign.

Outside the *viharn* stand many Chinese pagodas, bronze horses, and figures of Chinese soldiers. The most important religious association, however, is with the Brahman priests who officiate at important state ceremonies, and there are two Hindu shrines nearby. To the northwest across the street is the Deva Sathan, which contains images of Shiva and Ganesh, and to the east, the smaller Saan Jao Phitsanu is dedicated to Vishnu. The huge teak arch—also carved by Rama II—in front is all that remains of an original giant swing, which was used until 1932 to celebrate and thank Shiva for a bountiful rice harvest and to ask for the gods' blessing on the next. The Minister of Rice, accompanied by hundreds of Brahman holy men, would lead a parade around the city walls to the temple precinct. Teams of men would ride the swing on arcs as high as 25m (82 ft.) in the air, trying to grab a bag of silver coins with their teeth. Due to injuries and deaths, the dangerous swing ceremony has been discontinued, but the thanksgiving festival is still celebrated in mid-December after the rice harvest.

Sao Chingcha Sq. (near the intersection of Bamrung Mueang and Thi Thong rds.). ☎ 02222-0280. Donations welcome. Daily 9am–9pm.

Wat Traimit (The Golden Buddha)   Wat Traimit, thought to date from the 13th century, would hardly rate a second glance if not for its astonishing Buddha image, which is nearly 3m (10 ft.) high, weighs over 5 tons, and is believed to be cast of solid gold. It was discovered by accident in 1957 when, covered by a plaster image, it was dropped from a crane during a move. The impact shattered the outer shell, revealing the shining gold beneath. This powerful image is truly dazzling and is thought to have been cast during the Sukhothai period. It was perhaps covered with plaster to hide it from Burmese invaders. Pieces of the stucco are also on display at the site.

Traimit Rd. (west of Hua Lampong Station, just west of the intersection of Krung Kasem and Rama IV rds.). Donations welcome. Daily 9am–5pm. Walk southwest on Traimit Rd., look for a school on the right with a playground; the *wat* is up a flight of stairs overlooking the school.

4 Cultural Pursuits

Culture is all around you in Thailand—and there are ample opportunities to take part in the daily activities, festivals, ceremonies, events, and practices that weave the fabric of this society. Keep an eye on free magazines such as *BK Magazine* or local newspapers, *The Nation* and *Bangkok Post,* for major events during your stay. (A calendar of events is listed in chapter 2, "Planning Your Trip to Thailand.") You may want to check with the **TAT** (☎ 1155) or the **Bangkok Tourism Bureau** (☎ 02225-7612), though these organizations may not always be as well informed as the local press. The best part of Thai festivals is that, whether getting soaked by buckets of water at Songkran or watching candlelit floats drift downstream at Loy Krathong, foreign visitors are usually invited to join in. Thais are very proud of their cultural heritage, and opportunities abound to learn and participate.

THAI COOKING

Fancy a chance to take back some of the delicious recipes you have been feasting on? Thai cooking is fun and easy, and there are a few good hands-on courses in Bangkok. You'll learn about Thai herbs, spices, and unique local produce. You'll never look at a produce market the same again. Lectures on Thai regional cuisine, cooking techniques, and menu planning complement classroom exercises to prepare all your favorite dishes. The best part is afterwards, when you get to eat them.

- **The Oriental Cooking School** 𝒜𝒜𝒜 is located in a quaint colonial house across the river from the famed hotel. Morning courses run daily (except Sun), and end with lunch. Their chefs are excellent and you'll learn, through demonstration and practice, every aspect of Thai cooking. The course is open to anyone from beginner to expert. Different dishes are taught each day, so you can attend for a week and always learn something new. The cost is 4,500B (US$128/£69) per person, per day. Call the hotel at 𝒞 **02659-9000.**

- **The Blue Elephant** 𝒜𝒜 is part of a large, Belgian-owned Thai restaurant chain popular throughout Europe. The cookery school stands in the same locale as the restaurant, a yellow-painted mansion close to Surasak BTS. Classes begin at 8:45am, with a visit to the market to pick up fresh ingredients for the day. Back in the classroom, you'll first watch demonstrations before stepping up to your own cooking station to practice what you've learned under the watchful eye of a teacher. Afterwards, you can share your creations with the rest of the class, as part of a delicious lunch spread. Visit them at 233 South Sathorn Rd., just below Surasak BTS, or call 𝒞 **02673-9353** (www.blueelephant.com). One-day (group) courses cost 2,800B (US$80/£43) per person; private classes are available.

- The woman behind **Mrs. Balbir's** 𝒜𝒜 is hilarious, dedicated, and an indefatigable charity worker as well as a TV star. The giggles that abound in the home of this regionally acclaimed, Malaysian-born chef are all part of the fun. Cookery courses with Vinder Balbir are (unlike hotel or restaurant courses) no sedate affair; eager students gather around her giant kitchen table to chop, pare, or grind ingredients before rallying around her stove to see her reveal some of her secrets. Because Vinder is fluent in several languages (including English and Thai), these lessons are much more informative and interactive than most. She will carefully explain why a particular type of herb is required or what ingredients can be used as replacements in your home country. True to her ethnic roots, she can also teach fabulous Punjabi cuisine, as well as Thai. After a Saturday morning spent cooking with Mrs. B. you'll have paid next to nothing but leave filled with good humor and great food. Courses start around 1,200B (US$34/£18) per person and take place at her home, close to her restaurant (𝒞 **02651-0498**), in the first sub-*soi* at 155/18 Sukhumvit Rd. (Soi 11 close to Nana BTS). For all course inquiries, call her restaurant Tuesday to Sunday from 11am–2pm or 6–11pm. Or see the website, www.mrsbalbir.com.

THAI MASSAGE

A traditional Thai massage involves manipulating your limbs to stretch each muscle and then applying acupressure techniques to loosen up tense muscles and start energy flowing. Your body will be twisted, pulled, and sometimes pounded in the process.

For Thai massage to be beneficial, it should be fairly rigorous and at times it can be punishing: If the therapist is loath to use pressure from the start, you'll know you are wasting your time. If you chose a street-side spa, chose one away from tourist areas—such as Khao San, Sukhumvit, or Silom roads, where Thais are patrons. *Note:* Many massage or foot reflexology parlors on Silom and Sukhumvit roads are fronts for brothels where (male) tourists will be propositioned for a variety of sexual favors.

There are countless spas and massage parlors around Bangkok, many offer good services at very reasonable rates, such as the humongous **Healthland** (② 02637-8883; 120, Sathorn Rd.), which operates a bit like a neon-lit, spa production line, or the quieter **Ruen-Nuad** (② 02632-2662), a small, but homely spa tucked in a small *soi* opposite the BNH Hospital on Soi Convent (in between Silom and Sathorn rds.). It offers excellent foot massages as well as authentic Thai massage.

Wat Po (p. 131) has long been promoted as the only place to learn Thai massage, and though it's cheaper than some, it's still pretty overrated. These days, better options abound. Good courses are offered at the Sukhumvit Road location of the award-winning **Chiva-Som Academy** ★★ (② 02711-5270; www.chivasomacademy.com). These cover therapies such as Reiki and other alternative treatments, but Bangkok's finest spas are almost always those in the most respected hotels where time and money are invested in training and language skills. **The Banyan Tree Spa** ★★★ (② 02679-1054; www.banyantree.com) and **The Oriental Spa & Ayurvedic Penthouse** ★★★ (② 02439-7613; www.mandarin-oriental.com) are two of the finest places going but come with a hefty price. Yet you pay for expertise that leaves your muscles soothed, gets your blood flowing, and gives you a feeling of unparalleled well-being.

Budget spas that use untrained staff with no English skills make for not just an unpleasant experience, but a potentially painful one. If your masseuse doesn't understand a word of English, or there is no one to help translate your needs or aspects of your health such as varicose veins or respiratory or skin conditions, you are taking a serious risk.

THAI BOXING

Muaythai, or Thai Boxing, is Thailand's national sport, and a visit to the two venues in Bangkok, or in towns all over Thailand, displays a very different side to the usually gentle Thai culture. The mystical pre-bout rituals, live musical performances, and, of course, the frenetic gambling, appeal to fans of this raw, and often bloody, spectacle. In Bangkok, catch up to 15 bouts nightly at either of two stadiums. The **Ratchadamnoen Stadium** (Ratchadamnoen Nok Ave.; ② 02281-4205) hosts fights on Monday, Wednesday, Thursday, and Sunday, while the **Lumphini Stadium** on Rama IV Road (② 02251-4303) has bouts on Tuesday, Friday, and Saturday. Tickets cost 1,000B to 2,000B (US$29–US$57/£15–£31) at both venues; ringside seats are only bookable in advance. In the second-class seats, you may still have a good view of the action in the ring and will see close-ups of the gambling action. The guys with multiple cellphones screaming and shouting often overshadow the action in the ring.

Keen to try some kicks and punches yourself? Check out the website **www.muaythai.com**, which details training camps for rookies.

MEDITATION

The House of Dhamma (② 02511-0439; www.houseofdhamma.com) and **Wat Mahathat** (see "The *Wats*," earlier in this chapter) serve as meditation centers for overseas students of Buddhism. The latter is one of Thailand's largest Buddhist Universities and has become a popular center for meditation lessons, with English-speaking monks overseeing students of *Vipassana,* also called Insight Meditation. Instruction is held daily; call ahead (© 02222-6011) to get the schedule and to make an appointment. Both offer good introductions to basic techniques.

THAI LANGUAGE STUDY

So you've learned your "Sawadee-khrup" or "Sawadee-kha," but want to take it a little further from there? Thais are very gracious and welcoming with foreigners butchering their language (the tones make you pronounce the most mundane phrases in laughable ways), but there are a few good schools in Bangkok to help you get the pronunciations right. Among the many offered, try the superlative **American University Alumni Language Center** (179 Ratchadamri Rd.; © 02252-8170) or the **Union Language School** (7th floor, 328 CCT Office Building, Phayathai Rd.; © 02214-6033; www.unionlanguage.com).

OTHER

Lovers of all things reptilian can witness a sight rarely encountered anywhere else. The **Red Cross Snake Farm,** at 1871 Rama IV Rd. (© 02252-0161) is located in the heart of Bangkok (opposite the old Montien Hotel). Don't expect a bucolic "farm" setting; this is in fact nothing more than a cluster of pretty colonial buildings in the heart of the city, which provide a research institute for the study of venomous snakes. Established in 1923, this was the second facility of its type in the world. For a fee of 70B (US$2/£1.10), you can see slide shows and snake-handling demonstrations weekdays at 11am and 2:30pm; and on weekends and holidays at 11am. You can also watch the handlers work with deadly cobras and (equally poisonous) banded kraits with demonstrations of venom milking. The venom is later injected into horses, which produce antivenin for the treatment of snakebites in humans. The Red Cross sells medical guides and will also inoculate you against such maladies as typhoid, cholera, and smallpox in their clinic. The institute is open daily Monday to Friday 8:30am to 4:30pm, and Saturday and Sunday 8:30am to noon.

5 Staying Active

FITNESS

All the finest five-star properties in town boast quality fitness centers complete with personal trainers and top equipment. In addition, **California WOW** has an enormous club just on the corner of Silom Road and Soi Convent, at Liberty Square (© 02631-1122) and a newly opened center (© 02627-5999) at Siam Paragon mall; expect to pay 800B daily (US$23/£12) for access to both locations. Both take day visitors, but don't be intimidated into paying anything more than you can afford—the reps use famously hard-sell tactics. The upscale Ascott serviced residences down on Sathorn Road benefit from the members-only **Cascade Club** (© 02676-6969), a stunning state-of-the-art gym, which comes with two studios for pilates and aerobics, a shady outdoor pool, and spa. Day passes in 2007 cost 500B (US$14/£7.70), good value if you love long workouts. At press time, a brand new **Fitness First** (no phone) gym was about to open at Life Center, a new mall on the corner of Sathorn and Rama IV roads, next to Lumphini MRT.

If these places listed above are too expensive, check the three- to four-star hotels in your district; many offer day passes for as little as 350B (US$10/£5.40).

GOLF

Various golf courses lie close to the city, a number of which are championship quality. Due to their huge popularity, access is sometimes limited. Visitors can get around this by booking upscale packages offered by hotel concierges or agents, such as **Golf A La Cart** (www.golfalacart-thailand.com), who can arrange access during the busiest seasons. These fully inclusive deals include car transfer and all fees.

- **Thai Country Club** (© **02651-5300-6** or 03857-0234) is praised for its consistent greens and sumptuous clubhouse. This stunning 18-hole course lays just 45 minutes southwest of Bangkok. The following fees refer to low/high season rates: Greens fees are weekdays 3,600B–4,800B (US$103–US$137/£55–£74) and weekends 4,800B–6,000B (US$103–US$171/£48–£92). Note that visitors' hours on weekends are restricted.
- **Pinehurst Golf & Country Club** (© **02516-8679**), located in Pathom Thani, is a popular 9-hole, par-27 course that served as the venue for the 1992 Johnnie Walker Classic. Greens fees on weekdays before noon are 1,700B (US$48/£26); on weekdays after noon, fees are 1,200B (US$34/£18); and on weekends, fees are 2,300B (US$66/£35).
- **Bangkok Golf Club** (© **02501-2771**), a short 45-minute drive from the city center, is an 18-hole course that's always popular and regularly plays host to local and regional tournaments. Night golf is available. Greens fees on weekdays are 1,800B (US$51/£28) and, on weekends, 2,600B (US$74/£40).

HORSE RACING

The prestigious **Royal Bangkok Sports Club** (RBSC) holds horse-racing events that are open to the paying public every second Sunday of the month. The grounds occupy a prime spot on Henri Dunant Road, opposite Chulalongkorn University, north of Rama IV Road (© **02251-0181**). Nominal admission fees and minimum bets apply.

YOGA

Apart from the many hotels in town that schedule regular yoga classes, some downtown studios may offer special packages for visitors on extended stays. Expect to pay up to 3,000B (US$86/£45). One such studio is **Absolute Yoga** (© **02252-4400;** www.absoluteyogabangkok.com) with many branches including one in Amarin Plaza, close to the Grand Hyatt Erawan on Ploenchit Road. Hot yoga, sometimes called bikram yoga (where yoga is practiced in a room at sauna-like temperatures) is available at **Absolute Yoga**'s Soi Piphat 2 branch (© **02242-4500**). There are numerous daily classes and schedules are posted on the website. Wear loose workout gear, bring a big bottle of water, and be ready to sweat buckets. **Yoga Elements Studio** (© **02655-5671**) on the 23rd floor of the Vanissa Building, just behind Central Chidlom department store on Soi Chidlom (5 min. from Chit Lom BTS), is another locally run studio with a wide variety of yoga classes. The big commercial fitness clubs in town, such as **California WOW** (see above), also offer yoga and pilates.

6 Shopping

Bangkok pulls in shoppers from all over the world, clamoring to find bargains at the endless street-side stalls or in the new ultra-chic, brand name boutiques. High-quality goods at very reasonable prices are available if you look hard, but any discussion of shopping in Thailand must be prefixed by a warning about shopping scams; see p. 55

in chapter 2 for info. If you encounter problems with any merchants, take their business card and contact the **Tourist Police** (© **0694-1222,** ext. 1, or the hot line at © **1155**) or report the incident to your hotel concierge.

WHERE TO BUY

Shopping is a real adventure in Bangkok. The big markets are a visual onslaught (don't miss the Weekend Market; see below), and there are great upmarket gift and antique dealers as well as small souvenir stalls scattered about town. Nancy Chandler's *The Market Map and Much More* is available at bookstores throughout the city for 160B (US$4.60/£2.45) and has detailed insets of places such as Chinatown and the sprawling Weekend Market. Below is a breakdown according to the top shopping areas.

TOWARD THE RIVER

Charoen Krung (New) Road is full of goodies: antiques stores, jewelry wholesalers, and funky little galleries. **Lek Gallery,** at 1124-1134 Charoen Krung (New) Rd. (© **02639-5870**), has decorative items and furniture that are downright sexy. On the same road, next to Soi 42, is **Four Sisters** (© **02234-0053**), selling gorgeous beadwork, handbags, Chinese furniture, and sexy Indian-inspired fashions and shoes.

The silk shops at the low-rise mall known as **River City** (© **02237-0077**) have a great selection but are overpriced (avoid the tailoring shops here, as the low standards of craftsmanship do not warrant the big bucks). Equally overpriced are the extensive antique dealers here—rumors warn of many fakes on sale. Close to The Oriental Hotel is **OP Place** (© **02266-0186**), featuring a heap of high-end shopping venues, from stores selling expensive designer luggage to jet-setter jewelry stores and amazing antiques, carpets, and fine silver tableware (much of which is Tiffany-like quality). In the same *soi* as The Oriental Hotel are some of the city's better tailoring shops and, in **The Oriental** (p. 87) itself, look out for exquisite one-off jewelry at **Lotus Arts de Vivre** or pop into the branch of **Jim Thompson's** for great silks.

SUKHUMVIT ROAD

This area is lined with shops from one end to the other, as well as some of Bangkok's biggest shopping malls (see "Department Stores & Shopping Plazas," below). For fine silk, stop in at **Almeta** (20/3 Sukhumvit Soi 23; © **02204-1413** or 02258-4227), a rival to Jim Thompson's. **Celadon House,** on 85 Ratchadaphisek (© **02253-9237**), carries attractive celadon ceramic.

For men's tailoring, there are many shops along Sukhumvit Sois 11 and 19. Most ship your order off to have clothes made in a factory and quality is iffy, so bargain like mad. **Ambassador Fashion** (28–28 Sukhumvit Soi 19; © **02253-2993**) has been in the business for years and is near the Asok BTS. Directly opposite it is **The Cynosure** (© **02255-5800**) for fine ladies' fabrics.

At night, the whole road fills up with **night market** stalls. Down at Soi 5, you will find endless supplies of wooden toys, crafts, and suitcases. After Soi 11, the pavements get packed with clothes, weaponry, and surfwear. At Soi 15, there's the excellent **Asia Books** (© **02252-7277**); it's close to **Robinson's Department Store** (© **02651-1567**), which is the place to shop for quality brands. It has a fair range of midrange luggage, children's wear, ladies' fashions, T-shirts, and brand-name sunglasses, though clothing sizes will not normally extend to oversized European or American sizes.

SILOM & SURAWONG ROADS

This area is packed with shopping malls and vendors—you'll find any number of jewelry shops, silk retailers, and plenty of touristy tailors, but few places in this area are top notch. Check out the main store of **Jim Thompson's** (9 Surawong Rd.; ✆ **02632-8100**); a factory outlet is 5 minutes away down Surawong Road, as well as at 153 Sukhumvit Rd., Soi 93. **Silom Complex** (✆ **02632-1199**) next to Sala Daeng BTS contains **Central Department Store** (www.central.co.th), which sells well-known brands of casual clothing such as Giordano and Esprit. On the second floor of Central, there's a **Marks & Spencer's** store from the U.K., selling food and clothing—it's a great stop if you can't find any local fashions that fit or if you need things such as thermal underwear for your return trip. Right across the road from Silom Complex is the 24-hour British pharmacy **Boots** (no phone), which you should visit for things like European prescription drugs and contact lens cleaner. **Watson's** (no phone), a similar Hong Kong-based pharmacy, is just at the entrance to Silom Complex.

The **Patpong Night Market** (p. 142), which runs between Silom and Surawong roads, sells mostly counterfeit goods. Watch out for pickpockets there.

WHAT TO BUY
ANTIQUES

Buying antiques to take out of Thailand is tricky. Authentic antiques are more than 200 years old (they must date from the beginning of the Chakri dynasty in Bangkok), but these days most items are good reproductions that have been professionally "distressed"—even the Certificate of Authenticity can be a forgery. If you do find something real, remember that the Thai government has an interest in keeping authentic antiquities and sacred items in the country, and will require special permission for export.

By law, Buddha images are prohibited from export, except for religious or educational purposes, and even in these instances, you'll still have to obtain permission from the **Department of Fine Arts** to remove them from Thailand. This rule is little enforced, though, and the focus is more on antique Buddhas than those you'll find in tourist markets. (Details on how to contact the Department of Fine Arts and file for permission is provided in chapter 2, on p. 57.)

Almost all the reputable antiques stores in Bangkok are along the endless **Charoen Krung (New) Road** (centered along the section either side of the post office), but many of these are shamelessly priced for wealthier tourists. Most items are Chinese, not Thai. **River City,** just off this road, is another place where high-end shoppers go. Neither quality nor authenticity is guaranteed there, but it's certainly convenient—you can hit several stores within an hour.

DEPARTMENT STORES & SHOPPING PLAZAS

Bangkok's downtown looks more and more like urban Tokyo these days. The size and opulence of Bangkok's many malls and shopping areas are often a shock to those who imagine Bangkok to be an exotic, impoverished destination. Sipping cappuccino at a Starbucks overlooking a busy city street may not be what you've come to Asia to find, but to many it is a comfort (especially after long trips in more rugged parts of the kingdom). The truth is, malls are as much about today's consumer-obsessed Thai youth as anywhere you'll visit; these hallowed halls of materialism are (sadly) much closer to the pulse of the nation than the many temples foreign visitors are keen to experience. Malls are where most wealthy Thais hang out, meet friends, dine, and shop. I've listed some malls under "Where to Buy" above; below are some more highlights (unless otherwise stated, these places open daily at 10am):

- **Central World** (*℗* **02635-1111**), on the corner of Rama I and Rachadamri roads, has been recently revamped and is now a great place to buy slightly funkier upmarket brands and cool gadgets, as well as to visit some of the city's slickest Internet cafes. It contains Zen and Isetan stores and is crowned with a fab food hall, and, of course, a bevy of cinemas. Closes 9pm. The Chit Lom and Siam BTS are both nearby.

- **Emporium** (*℗* **02664-8000**) stands proudly on the corner of Sukhumvit Soi 24. Bangkok's first luxury shopping mall, this old-timer still offers the top designer outlets from Gucci to Prada and Sony to Walt Disney (there are cinemas on the top floor). The food court on the top floor covers just about any craving. Closes 10pm. The closest BTS is Phrom Phong.

- **Erawan** (next to Grand Hyatt Erawan, at the corner of Ratchadamri and Rama I roads; *℗* **02650-7777**) is a swanky, mercantile mecca that's truly glamorous but never crowded. Brands such as Coach rub shoulders with fashion stores such as Club 21 and the city's top watch shops. Drop in on Urban Kitchen, its basement area featuring a range of foodie shops and diners. The top floor is dedicated to an alternative health center, offering treatments such as colonic irrigation. Closes 10pm. Take the Chit Lom BTS here.

- **Mah Boon Krong,** or **MBK** (*℗* **02217-9111**), lies at the intersection of Rama 1 and Phayathai. This massive mega-mall is in fact a mass of small shops, fast food joints, and tiny vendors. The **Tokyu Department Store** is within the mall, and it attracts teeny-boppers and tourists due to its bargain-priced local fashions, accessories, and gadgets, along with its huge array of tourist souvenirs on the lower floor. Cinemas are at the top. Open daily 9am to 9pm. Take the BTS to the National Stadium.

- **Panthip Plaza,** (*℗* **02254-9797**) on Petchaburi Road, is an older, rather scruffy mall that's dedicated to all things electronic. Among the shoddy bootleg software, there are stacks of innovative gadgets, as well as shops selling secondhand or new and affordable computers, mobile phones, or components for either. Not much English is spoken, but it may not matter if you are into IT and can speak fluent Nerdish. Closes 8pm. It's a 15-minute walk from the Ploen Chit BTS.

- **Siam Paragon** *★★* (*℗* **02658-3000**) on Rama 1 Road is one of those glitzy malls that just goes on and on. Downstairs is **Siam Ocean World,** where kids can watch the sharks swim; above are floors of brand-name stores such as Hermès, MNG, Zara, and Shanghai Tang. The mall also has a whole floor of fun eateries, as well as a top-class food hall, a department store, and even a gymnasium. Closes 10pm. There's easy access via Siam BTS.

FASHION & TAILORING

Bangkok has some small, independent designers of its own creating Thai-influenced fashions that look good back home. **Nagara, Kloset, Fly Now, Grey by Greyhound,** and **Anurak** are all well-established local labels producing great ready-to-wear for men and women. It's certainly not Parisian *haute couture,* but the designs are fresh and original, and prices will be a fraction of those in designer boutiques back home. If you want really unique clothes or accessories, have a trawl around **Siam Square** for the latest Thai styles—but don't expect European sizes!

If you want to check out the more cutting-edge, contemporary Thai design scene, **Thong Lor** (Sukhumvit Soi 55; no phone) has a great array of yuppified boutiques catering for the younger, well-heeled Thais. Big boutiques such as the hip fashion and lifestyle center, **Playground,** and the yummy **Greyhound Café** also attract Thailand's yuppies on weekends.

Tailors may be widespread in popular malls such as **River City** and in **Sukhumvit Road's Soi 11** and **19.** Remember, this is not Hong Kong and—as all the concierges of major hotels repeatedly attest—Thailand's backstreet tailors aren't perfect. Men's shirts normally pose no serious problems, but ambitious ladies' wear can be a disaster when designs skills are limited and fabric quality is poor. Paying a knock-down price often leads to shoddy workmanship and cloth; don't risk the roughly 3,500B (US$100/£54) you'll have to pay when it all goes wrong. The rule of thumb is, expect to pay 60% of prices in Europe or the U.S. for something decent, and always schedule at least two fittings with an English speaker present. Only very few places, such as **World Group** (✆ 02238-3344) in Soi Oriental (off Charoen Krung Rd.), can cope with precise cutting or copying of garments. You will pay a high price for their expertise, though—around 30,000B (US$857/£451).

GIFTS, CRAFTS & SOUVENIRS
Street vendors throughout the city are a good source of affordable and fun souvenirs. The best stalls are along **Sukhumvit Road** beginning at Soi 4, and on **Khao San Road.** Little of the stuff sold there is unique, but the prices are great and many people stock up for gifts such as mango wood bowls, chopsticks, candles, incense, or small decorative lamps made of mulberry paper or coconut shells. Impressive brass, bronze, and pewter items, as well as fine celadon (green ceramic ware), are all available in many outlets on **Sukhumvit and Charoen Krung (New) Roads.** Look out too, for the **OTOP** label, designating quality crafts that have been made in rural villages for export.

Head to the OTOP crafts floor in the **Silom Galleria** (✆ 02630-0944) mall on Soi 19, next to the Holiday Inn Hotel. Up on Sukhumvit Road, the **Emporium** (see above) boasts a dazzling range of beautiful crafts and textiles on its penultimate floor. **Mah Boon Krang** (MBK) has a lower ground floor stuffed with very reasonably priced gifts and handicrafts, carvings, and castings. The North Thailand-based charity, **Mae Fah Luang,** has a boutique in **Siam Discovery** on Rama I Road (✆ 02658-1000) selling upmarket textiles, wood, and ceramic designs. If you are already on your way home, fear not—it also has duty-free boutiques located at Suvarnabhumi International Airport and a few of the larger provincial airports, such as Chiang Mai's.

JEWELRY
Sapphires, rubies, garnets, turquoise, and zircons are mined in Thailand, and nearly every other stone you can think of is imported and cut here. Thai artisans are among the most skillful in the world; work in gold and silver is generally of high quality at very good value. If you're interested in a custom setting, bring a photo or drawing of what you'd like and prepare to discuss your ideas at length.

You'll find gemstone, silver, and gold stores in every part of town. Around **Charoen Krung (New) Road,** you'll find the wholesalers of gorgeous semi-precious stones. Gold is sold in **Chinatown;** try the lower end of **Silom** and **Khao San roads** for silver in bulk. The **Asian Institute of Gemological Sciences** (11th floor, Jewelry Trade Center; 919/1 Silom Rd.; ✆ 02267-4315) is useful for verifying the quality of cut stones (although it's not an appraiser). The TAT (p. 133) and the Thai Gem and Jewelry Traders Association have created an organization called the **Jewel Fest Club.** Ask the TAT which shops are members of this reputable organization.

MARKET GOODS

Visiting Bangkok's many markets is as cultural as it is a consumer experience; goods come in from all corners of the kingdom, and bargaining is a fast and furious experience. Smaller markets with fewer tourists are great for wandering. Try these: **Bangrak Wet Market,** behind the Shangri-La Hotel, is an early morning gourmet's delight. **Pratunam Market,** at the intersection of Phetchaburi and Ratchaprarop roads, is a big wholesale center, with a vast array of inexpensive clothing. **Pak Klong Talad** 🎋🎋, near Saphan Phut (Memorial Bridge), on the fringes of Chinatown, is home to Bangkok's cut-flower market, with huge bouquets of cut flowers passing through here all day and all night.

A word of warning: Cheap goods flood many markets in Thailand and Bangkok is no exception. Most market stalls, such as those in Patpong, are filled with stalls of brand-name handbags, sneakers, and watches, all of which are fake. Though some tourists revel in getting a cheap brand-name items for a few bucks, doing so can result in dire consequences. See p. 55 in chapter 2 for info.

Khao San Road Area The nighttime stalls on Khao San Road cater to young travelers and as such, this is where you'll find the funkiest bits and bobs in town. From everything from hip-hop fashions and cool T-shirts, to silver wares or original artworks, this is your place. It's worth the trip for the atmosphere alone—bass-thumping clubs, busy bars, and Internet cafes attract crowds of tattooed, pierced, and, yes, plain ordinary travelers, going or coming from all corners of Asia. The area just north of Khao San Road is a maze of small department stores, shops, and very affordable retail goods. In Banglampoo, just north of the Grand Palace area and Ratchadamnoen Road.

Patpong Night Market The Patpong area is famous for its bars, neon lights, girls, sex shows, and massage parlors, but in recent years has spawned a bustling Night Market along the central streets (hemmed in on all sides by go-go bars and sex-show clubs). This popular Night Market has lots of faux brands: pirated CDs and tapes, designer knockoffs, copy watches (including fake "Rolexes" that we've gotten some good reports on), leather goods stamped with desirable logos (sure to hold up better than cardboard)—not especially cheap, but lively and fun, especially if you enjoy crowds and the challenge of hard bargaining. Open daily after sundown. Patpong Soi 1, between Silom and Surawong rds.

Weekend Market (Chatuchak) 🎋🎋 Adjacent to the Mo Chit BTS at the northern terminus of the BTS, this vast tract of land is filled with head-spinning numbers of stalls selling everything: souvenirs, art, antiques, fresh and dried seafood, vegetables and condiments, pottery, pets of every sort, orchids and other exotic plants, clothing, and a host of strange exotic foods. A visit here is a great way to introduce yourself to the exotic sights, flavors, and colors of Thai life; and it is the best one-stop shop for all those souvenirs you haven't bought yet. In the hot season, try to get there early in the morning before the heat and leave by early afternoon—before the downpours. *Hint:* Hop off the BTS at Saphan Khwai and walk the one stop to the main market area, staying on the left (or west) side of the train. All along here you'll find some great antique and jewelry stalls. It's open on Saturdays and Sundays from 9am to 5pm. Chatuchak Park at Mo Chit BTS.

SILK

There are numerous silk outlets throughout the city, from shopping malls to the lobbies of international hotels. Synthetics are frequently sold as silk; if you're in doubt about a particular piece, select a thread and burn it—silk should smell like singed hair. Sometimes only the warp (lengthwise threads) is synthetic, because it is more uniform and easier to work with. For some of the city's priciest silk, try outlets like **Jim Thompson's** (9 Surawong Rd., near Silom; ℂ **02632-8100**), or the Thai silk specialists **Almeta** (20/3, Sukhumvit Soi 23; ℂ **02204-1413** or 02258-4227). They can even offer "silk a la carte," whereby silk is woven to the customer's desired weight and dyed to a particular shade. Products include silk wall coverings, silk fashions, bed linen, and casual wear.

For the best cottons from all over the world, as well as chiffons and silks, head to **The Cynosure** (ℂ **02255-5800-3**) on Sukhumvit Soi 19, where you will enter an Aladdin's cave of ornate brocades, linens, and rainbow-hued satins, as well as top-class Chantilly laces, along with sequined and beaded fabrics. Expect to pay top price for what is in effect, the cream of the crop.

7 Bangkok After Dark

Bangkok's reputation for rowdy nightlife tends to precede it; however, it's not all raunchy sex shows and public debauchery. There are plenty of nighttime cultural events, such as music, theater, puppetry performances, and orchestral maneuvers. For the hippest nightlife updates, check out *BK Magazine* (free and available at bookstores and restaurants). Featuring weekly listings of events as well as up-to-date info about the club scene, it is the best entertainment source in Bangkok. Both the *Bangkok Post* and *The Nation* also offer daily listings of cultural events and performance schedules.

THE PERFORMING ARTS

Most travelers experience the Thai performing arts at a commercially staged dance show in a hotel, sometimes accompanied by a Thai banquet; see "Dinner with Thai Dance," in chapter 5. Bangkok does, however, provide much more appetizing slices of theater, whether it be the avant-garde choreography seen at the **Patravadi Theater,** traditional puppet shows by **Joe Louis,** or international music recitals as part of annual festivals.

The **National Theater,** 1 Na Phra That Rd. (ℂ **02224-1342**), presents demonstrations of Thai classical dancing and music by performers from the School of Music and Dance in Bangkok, which are generally superior to those at the tourist restaurants and hotels. There are also performances by visiting ballet and theatrical companies. Call the TAT (p. 133) or check with your hotel for the current schedule.

The **Thailand Cultural Center,** Thiem Ruammit Road off Ratchadaphisek Road, Huai Khwang (ℂ **02247-0028**), is the newest and largest performance center in town, offering a wide variety of programs. The Bangkok Symphony performs here during its short summer season. Other local and visiting companies also present theater and dance at the center.

Bangkok's unique contemporary dance theater **Patravadi Theater** at Soi Wat Rakheng, off Anamarin Road (ℂ **02412-7287**), occupies a laid-back arty corner of the Thonburi district and can be relied upon to challenge cultural conformity by putting on inspiring performances that combine all manner of Thai and international dance forms, including dazzling *likay* (similar to the style of Broadway musicals).

Overseen since its founding by Patravadi Mejudhon, a former Thai classical dancer now in her late fifties, the theater is well worth the trip for those fascinated by Thailand's performing arts.

For some years, the **Joe Louis Theater** has been holding nightly **puppet theater** performances of stories from the *Ramakien* (the Thai national epic) at the Suan Lum Night Market (adjacent to Lumphini Park). With this popular night market slated to be razed, it is unsure how long this wonderful theater group will last or where they will go. Complex puppets are manipulated by up to three masters; the theater has hitherto been a training facility for Thai kids. Shows have been running nightly at 7:30pm. Call ℂ **02252-9683** for program details, ticket prices, and the latest news on its future, or visit www.thaipuppet.com.

CINEMA

Bangkok cinemas are almost always located in malls and show a small selection of Hollywood films—with most leaning towards action films, though occasionally you may catch an art house movie at two of the city's oldest cinemas, **Siam** and **Lido.** A couple of **Film Festivals** are held annually; alas, poor publicity, movie star no-shows, and haywire scheduling have been commonplace. Below are information hot lines for the city's major cinemas. The English-language newspapers also carry timings:

EGV: ℂ **02812-9999** at Siam Discovery, Central Pinklao
Lido: ℂ **02252-6498** at Siam Square
Major Cineplex: ℂ **02512-5555** at Sukhumvit Soi Ekkamai, Central World
SF Cinema City: ℂ **02611-6444** at Mah Boon Krong (MBK) on Phayathai Rd.
SFX Cinema: ℂ **02260-9333** at Emporium on Sukhumvit Rd.
Siam: ℂ **02251-3508** at Siam Square

THE CLUB & BAR SCENE

Bangkok's steamy nightlife brings adventures in just about any *soi* in town. Bars and discos along Sukhumvit Road are the common hunting ground of sex workers—Soi Nana and Soi 11 are favorite haunts because of their many bars and clubs. If you want to avoid lurid scenes of Thai hookers openly propositioning clients, or the sight of very young women draped over paunchy pensioners, forget this patch of town.

If you'd prefer to unwind with an evening cocktail and avoid the sleaze, head to two of the coolest bars in town, both at **The Dome at State Tower** ✹✹ (1055 Silom Rd.; ℂ **02624-9555**). The low-lit, indoor-outdoor lounge bar, **Distil,** sits just above the equally vertiginous, wholly outdoor **Sky Bar.** From both venues, the views of the city are amazing. The live jazz soloist who performs outside under the stars is always fabulous. The Dome instigates strict (smart) dress codes at all its venues, but it's definitely worth dressing up for.

To take in the heavy aroma of cigars mixed with the sultry sounds of jazz, the **Bamboo Bar** at **The Oriental Hotel** (Soi Oriental, Charoen Krung [New] Rd.; ℂ **02236-0400**) is the place to go see and be seen—it's popular with visiting celebs. Just across the water is the towering silhouette of the **Millennium Hilton, Bangkok** (123 Charoennakorn Rd.; ℂ **02625-3333**), whose rooftop lounge **360°** is where night owls congregate to watch the city lights.

SILOM ROAD & PATPONG

Patpong, which covers Soi Patpong 1 and 2, between Surawong and Silom roads, gets crammed with crowds and is prime territory for pickpockets. Though the area is known for its strip bars and clubs, you don't need to visit for risqué entertainment—there's a night market area to check out, too (p. 142). If you do venture into a go-go bar or strip joint, be prepared to pay hugely inflated prices for your drinks. Web blogs recount vivid tales of how bars with sex shows sell overpriced drinks; when punters object, bouncers have been called in to "help." It can all end very nastily.

There are a number of bars just near Patpong. **The Barbican** (9/4–5 Soi Thaniya off Silom Rd.; ⓒ **02234-3590**) is a stylish hangout with good bar food and live music. **The Irish Xchange** on Convent Road (at 1/5–6 Sivadon Bldg.; ⓒ **02266-7160**) caters to Bangkok yuppies and foreign expatriates with Irish pub style and live music after hours.

Head to Silom Soi 4 (between Patpong 2 and Soi Thaniya off Silom Rd.) to find small home-grown clubs spinning great music, as well as the city's prominent gay clubs: **Telephone Bar** (114/11–13 Silom Soi 4; ⓒ **02234-3279**) and **The Balcony** (86–8 Silom Soi 4; ⓒ **02235-5891**), foremost among them.

On Sathorn Nua Road, not quite as far as Surasak BTS, you'll find the supercool **Hu'u Bar** ⓡⓡ (ground floor of Ascott serviced residences; ⓒ **02676-6677**; www. huuinasia.com), a hip bar with amazing cocktails as well as a classy art gallery-cum-diner upstairs.

KHAO SAN ROAD

Over on Rattanakosin Island in Old Bangkok, the backpackers on Khao San Road still party on at **Gulliver's,** on the corner of Khao San and Chakrabongse roads (ⓒ **02629-1988**). There are quite a few small dance clubs that come and go around here. You'll find lots of travelers in their twenties, and the atmosphere is always laid-back. In the middle of Khao San, look for **Silk Bar** (129–131 Khaosan Rd.; ⓒ **02281-9981**), a dolled-up hideaway across from the Krung Thai Bank. Also don't miss **Lava** (249 Khao San Rd.; ⓒ **02281-6565**), a popular basement dance club. For a more laid-back evening, head west of Khao San to **Phra Athit Road,** where there are any number of small cafe performances banging out folk, blues, and rock tunes. These small venues are full of Thai college students going "beat." Acts change nightly, so walk the road's length, and have a peek in each spot. Down the small *sois* surrounding the temple compound (on the river end of Khao San), look for lots of little open-air bars—they're a good place to meet fellow travelers. One to try is **Bangkok Times** (12 Soi Rongmai; ⓒ **02629-1596**).

SUKHUMVIT ROAD

As mentioned earlier, by sunset, Sukhumvit Road morphs into a giant red-light zone, so don't venture out here unless you are ready to be hassled by touts and hookers. Sukhumvit plays host to a wide range of pub-style bars as well as a couple of Bangkok's popular clubs.

Q Bar (34 Sukhumvit Soi 11; ⓒ **02252-3274**) has a sleazy reputation but is a great venue—if you don't mind being pestered by the working girls. A few meters away, **Bed Supper Club** (26 Sukhumvit Soi 11; ⓒ **02651-3537**) has a great dance club adjoining its sci-fi–inspired restaurant. Like Q Bar, it smacks of industrial chic, with polished concrete and unisex loos. The expat DJs are fantastic, but the hookers seriously detract from its cool city vibe.

The Bull's Head (Sukhumvit Soi 33/1; ⓒ **02259-4444**) is a fun local pub that draws crowds with frequent theme parties and a clubhouse vibe. **Roots Reggae Club** (6/7–8 Sukhumvit Soi 26; ⓒ **02259-7002**) is as it sounds, a cool reggae club with occasional hip-hop and tech. **Huntsman** (at The Landmark Hotel, Sukhumvit Rd., ⓒ **02254-0404**) is a popular place for cold draft beer and big screen sports.

Barsu at the Sheraton Grande Sukhumvit, 250 Sukhumvit Rd. (© **02649-8888**), offers soul, funk, rock, and plenty of '70s and '80s sounds.

In a little alleyway off Soi 11 (near Suk 11 guesthouse), there's a weird makeshift outdoor bar, known as **Cheap Charlie's,** where drinks are affordable and you'll encounter a young, after-work atmosphere.

The **Conrad Bangkok** ★ (87 Wireless Rd.; © **02690-9999**) hosts two of Bangkok's hottest spots: **87** is a contemporary bar dance club patronized by wealthy Thai yuppies, Indians, and expats, with theme nights and special events with guest DJs. Despite its name, the **Diplomat Bar** is not filled with diplomats, but young Thais or cigar-puffing corporate guests in smart suits enjoying the regular jazz performances.

THE SEX SCENE

Since the 1960s—and particularly since the Vietnam War—Bangkok has had a reputation as the sin capital of Asia. Its hundreds of saunas, sex clubs, bars, and massage parlors act as fronts for organized prostitution, drug peddling, child-trafficking rackets, pedophile rings, and people smugglers. First-time tourists are sometimes staggered by the numbers of septuagenarian gentlemen trawling these areas looking for teenage Thais of either sex. Of course, the clientele is not just foreign; Thai men frequently engage the services of hookers.

While prostitution is technically illegal in Thailand, this law is rarely enforced, making foreigners feel it is therefore "safe" to pay for sex in Thailand. It is not. Too often, the people working this industry are doing this because they have no choice; and some are underage, though they may purport to be older than they are. Reports about poor families selling their children into prostitution are true—many children are held in brothels against their will. Those adults seen making even the slightest sexual advances toward them, if caught, risk a heavy prison sentence and a subsequent, global media frenzy, as has happened numerous times in 2006 and 2007. The worst areas are concentrated in the **Patpong, Nana Plaza,** and **Soi Cowboy** districts.

A startling increase in HIV-positive cases in the last 20 years has encouraged the education of commercial sex workers about the use of condoms, but AIDS is still a major concern, as are other STDs. Recent crackdowns in Patpong means that some of the raunchier shows have closed but still, men and women in the clubs are all "for sale"—clients simply pay a "bar fine." If this is your scene, be aware of the risks and play safe.

Note that the city's smarter hotels will all stop you if you bring a hooker into the lobby. Other hotels require guests to register night visitors, and the client will have to pay the hotel for this privilege. Also know that every year in Bangkok hundreds of cases are reported of prostitutes drugging their customers and robbing them in their hotel rooms. If you believe this cannot happen to you, think again.

8 Side Trips from Bangkok

There are plenty of easy day trips from Bangkok. Favorites include various cruises along the Chao Phraya to the more distant *klongs* and to the ancient capital of Ayutthaya, north of Bangkok, with a stop at the Bang Pa-in Summer Palace. Kids will enjoy most of these listed below.

EASY 1-DAY EXCURSIONS

ROSE GARDEN

Besides its delightful rose garden, this attractive theme park and resort is known for its all-in-one show of Thai culture that includes Thai classical and folk dancing, Thai boxing, sword fighting, and cock fighting. It's hardly authentic, but it is a convenient way for visitors with limited time to digest some canned Thai culture. It is located 32km (20 miles) west of Bangkok on the way to Nakhon Pathom on Highway 4 (© 03432-2588; www.thaiculturalshow.com). Surprisingly, the resort's restaurant is very appealing and not expensive. Admission is 840B (US$24/£13) adults, 420B (US$12/£6.45) for kids. It is open daily from 8am to 6pm; the cultural show is at 2:45pm.

THE ANCIENT CITY (MUEANG BORAN)

This remarkable museum is a giant scale model of Thailand spread over 81 hectares (200 acres), with models of the country's major landmarks either life-size or in miniature. It was built over the last 30 years by a local millionaire who has played out his obsession with Thai history on a grand scale. Because it is far from the heart of Bangkok, the Ancient City is best visited by organized tour, though you can certainly go on your own. It is at kilometer 33 on the old Sukhumvit Highway in Samut Prakan Province. All travel agents offer package tours that combine the Rose Garden (see above) with other attractions in the area, such as the Crocodile Farm or the huge Buddhist *chedi* in nearby Nakhon Pathom. Admission to the Ancient City is 300B (US$8.60/£4.60). Additional fees apply for a car and guide, but it's also possible to rent bikes or hop on a tram to ride around the sites. Mueang Boran is open daily from 8am to 5pm. Contact © 02709-1644 or visit www.ancientcity.com for info.

CROCODILE FARM

Only 3km (2 miles) from the Ancient City, you'll find the **Samutprakarn Crocodile Farm and Zoo,** at kilometer 30 on the Old Sukhumvit Highway (© 02703-4891-5). Supposedly the world's largest, it has more than 40,000 crocs, both fresh and saltwater. In the hourly show, handlers wrestle the crocs in murky ponds—enough to scare the living daylights out of junior. Admission is 300B (US$8.60/£4.60). It's open daily from 7am to 6pm, and feedings take place every hour.

SAMPHRAN ELEPHANT GROUNDS & ZOO

Located 1 km (⁹⁄₁₀ mile) north of the Rose Garden in Yannowa (30km/18½ miles from the city), the **Samphran Elephant Grounds and Zoo** (© 02284-1873) is a lush 9-hectare (22-acre) garden complex offering an entertaining elephant show, plus thousands of crocodiles, including what is claimed to be the world's largest white crocodile. Admission is 350B (US$10/£5.40) for adults, 200B (US$6/£3.10) for children. The zoo is open daily from 9am to 6pm. Crocodile wrestling shows are at 12:45 and 2:20pm; elephant show times are at 1:45 and 3:30pm, with additional shows on Saturday, Sunday, and holidays at 10:30am.

ACTIVITY PARKS

If the heat and the kids have got to you, splash out (literally) with a trip to **Siam Water Park,** in Minburi (© 02919-7200-19), a large complex of water slides, enormous swimming pools with artificial surf, waterfalls, playgrounds, and a beer garden. It's 30-minute drive east of town, (or 1 hr. by bus no. 26 or 27, from Victory Monument). Admission is 200B (US$6/£3.10), including rides. Siam Park is open weekdays 10am to 6pm and weekends 9am to 7pm. Also on the bus no. 26 route is the nearby **Safari World & Marine Park,** an outdoor zoo tailormade for restless kids, with restaurants and shows.

FLOATING MARKET AT DAMNOEN *Kids*

The **Floating Market at Damnoen Saduak,** Ratchaburi, is about 40 minutes south of Nakhon Pathom. This market is still popular for photographers, though it's gotten quite touristy and crowded over the years. Some tours combine the Floating Market with a visit to the Rose Garden (see above for info). If you choose to go via organized tour, such as **World Travel Service** (𝒞 02233-5900), expect to pay about 1,500B (US$37/£22) for the 1-day trip combo with the Rose Garden.

SITES FARTHER AFIELD
KANCHANABURI
139 kilometers (86 miles) NW of Bangkok

Kanchanaburi lies on the **River Kwae** (*Mae Nam Kwae* in Thai) better known to the West as the **River Kwai.** The city became famous for a single-track rail bridge, built under the Japanese occupation in WWII by Allied prisoners of war (POWs), linking Myanmar and Thailand. Due to the thousands of servicemen and women who lost their lives in this project, and in the notoriously inhumane Japanese internment camps, it became known popularly as the Death Railway. The city, and the dark passage of time associated with it, came to fame following the hugely successful British film *The Bridge over the River Kwai* (which was shot in Sri Lanka). The original wooden bridge no longer exists, so today visitors, pilgrims, and former POWs head to a similar, but now heavily commercialized, iron bridge, built around the same time spanning a tributary.

Every year, in the last days of November, the city hosts several evenings of light shows to commemorate the town's past. Many former Allied prisoners, as well as local Thai tourists, fill the city and hotels are booked out. There are, however, lots of other good excursions in the area, including golf courses, bike trails, caves, and waterfalls in the surrounding hills. There are also a few nice hotels and riverside guesthouses, making this a popular escape from the heat of Bangkok.

Getting to Kanchanaburi

You can connect by railway from Bangkok's **Hua Lamphong Station** (𝒞 1690) on regular weekend junkets starting in the early morning, or go by slow daily trains from Thonburi's **Bangkok Noi Station** (𝒞 02411-3102) to **Kanchanaburi Station** (𝒞 03456-1052); rail trips here are quite scenic and cost next to nothing (about 25B/70¢/35p each way). They're a great experience—just be prepared for no air-conditioning for 3 long hours. There are also frequent regular buses from the **Southern Bus Terminal** (𝒞 02434-5557).

Accommodations

It's a bit stuck in the 1980s and worn in parts, but the immense **Felix River Kwai Resort** (9/1 Moo 3 Tambon, Kanchanaburi; 𝒞 03451-5061; www.felixhotels.com) is still the best place to stay in town. Expect room rates around 3,500B (US$100/£51) and know that the grounds make up for the chunky decor. Or try the **Bamboo House** (3–5 Soi Vietnam; 𝒞 03462-4470), which is basic but well located.

On Mae Nam Khwae Road, the pretty **Inchantree Resort** (𝒞 03462-4914) at number 443 and the friendly **Ploy Guesthouse** at number 79/2 (𝒞 03451-5804) are good midrange (more atmospheric) choices near the bridge. See **www.kanchanburi-info. com** for more tips on accommodations.

Attractions

The town's sites focus on the World War II history of the area. Start any tour of Kanchanaburi at the so-called **Bridge over the River Kwai,** emulating its more famous predecessor, built by World War II prisoners, and the main backdrop to the suspenseful 1957 film of the same name, directed by David Lean, which won seven Oscars. The bridge is about 5km (3 miles) north of the Kanchanaburi city center.

The **Allied War Cemetery** is where many of the 16,000 POWs who died building the railway are laid to rest; graves are organized country by country. It is a sobering thought to realize that perhaps up to 100,000 people died in the construction project, mostly conscripted laborers and prisoners. It's a 10-minute walk from the train station on Saengchto Road. It's open daily 8:30am to 6pm, and charges no entry fee.

Adjacent to the cemetery is the **Thailand–Burma Railway Center** (© 03451-0067; www.tbrconline.com), which displays a well-organized collection of photos and memorabilia with ample English descriptions, maps with detailed historical background, and good audio-visual presentations recounting the terrifying fate of the Allied POWs during World War II. Nearby (just south of the cemetery along the river) find the mustier, but no less moving **JEATH War Museum** (Wat Chaichumpol, Bantai, Kanchanaburi; © 03451-5203; daily 8:30am–6pm; 30B/86¢/45p). JEATH is an acronym for Japan, England, Australia/America, Thailand, and Holland. Here you'll see haunting photos and artifacts in a rustic bamboo museum adjacent to Wat Chaichumpol. Most poignant are the letters and faded photos of the many GIs who've returned since the end of the war.

Some 45km (28 miles) north of Kanchanaburi, you'll find **Wat Pha Luangta Bua Yannasampanno Forest Monastery,** better known as the **Tiger Temple,** (www.walking withtigers.org). Featured in dozens of TV shows and magazines, this huge nature preserve is home to deer, wild boar, and various jungle animals, as well as a famous clutch of large tigers, most rescued from poachers as cubs. As the media has shown, the monks here have a remarkable understanding with these man-eating beasts. It's easiest to grab a tour offered by a local hotel rather than attempting it without transport. The temple is open to visitors daily from 8:30am to 5pm, but it is best to go between 1:30 and 5pm to see the tigers close up. The monastery accepts volunteers and donations from visitors to help with the steep costs of feeding the animals.

Other sites farther afield from Kanchanaburi include the **Hellfire Pass,** which can be visited by train, as well as the **Erawan National Park,** north of town.

KHAO YAI NATIONAL PARK 🎯

Located 3 hours from the big smoke near Nakhon Ratchasima (known as Khorat) on the edge of Thailand's rural northeast, the park is home to some high peaks and therefore boasts cooler temperatures year-round. It's a good place to spot local wildlife, such as golden gibbon, barking deer, and any number of bird species, as well as the chance to see wild elephants congregated around roadside salt-licks.

AYUTTHAYA & 1-DAY RIVERBOAT TRIPS 🎯🎯
76km (47 miles) NW of Bangkok

The temple town of Ayutthaya and the nearby Summer Palace compound of Bang Pa-in are both popular day trips from Bangkok. Ayutthaya was the capital of Thailand from 1350 until it was sacked in 1767 by the Burmese; thereafter, the capital moved to Thonburi, close to present-day Bangkok. Ayutthaya's temples are magnificent—both Khmer and Thai-style ruins lie along the rivers here, in what was once Thailand's greatest city. It's also an excellent place to rent a bicycle (the terrain is flat) and worth an overnight, in conjunction with an enjoyable 1-day boat trip. Nearby Bang Pa-in is home to some wonderfully whimsical mid-19th century royal palaces, set amid splendid gardens with topiary elephants.

Most people get to Ayutthaya and Bang Pa-In by river cruise. Most travel agents or hotels can arrange this for you, including the early morning transfer from your hotel to the boat pier, or coach. Usually at least one leg of the journey is undertaken by luxury coach, with a guide. It's an early rise and an all-day trip: Tour buses can leave as early as 6:30am in order to pick up from a number of Bangkok hotels (which itself can take hours). Sometimes, there's an option to travel by coach both ways. Departure points are close to the River City pier, and tickets cost in the range of 1,800B (US$51/£28) per person (bus and boat) or slightly more if you choose to travel both ways by bus. Contact **River Sun Cruises** (© 02266-9125) for more details, but check websites (such as www.thairivercruise.com) for the full range of cruise options.

For an optimum river experience (without the coach travel), the **Chao Phraya Express Co.** (© 02222-5330) runs high-season tours on Sundays throughout December that go both ways by river. Tours depart Maharaj Pier at 7am (999B/US$28/£15), returning around 7pm. For a super-luxury cruise option, the Marriott Resort & Spa operates **Manohra Cruises** (© 02477-0770; www.manohracruises.com), offering a variety of day and evening cruises, including overnight trips to Ayutthaya and Bang Pa-in. Sometimes they also run trips to **Koh Kret,** a small river island just north of Bangkok, famed for its terracotta ware, crafted by descendants of the country's Mon people. These trips use fully renovated, traditional rice barges. Though they usually cost hundreds of dollars, special packages are available online or through travel agents.

For more specific information on Ayutthaya, see the first section of chapter 10, "Central Thailand."

7

The Eastern Seaboard

Tracing the coastline directly east of Bangkok along the Gulf of Thailand, there are many hot spots. One of the key advantages of destinations here is their proximity to the capital and the new Suvarnabhumi International Airport. The closest is **Pattaya,** one of the oldest resort developments in the country, which is working hard to shed its bad reputation as a place for sex tourism, not to mention the cagey underworld that goes with it. The town is repositioning itself as a family vacation spot with an array of top-quality, self-contained resorts, a wide choice of restaurants, and numerous outdoor and water activities.

The main Pattaya beach is still overcoming the effects of unregulated construction, during which heavy industrial and human pollutants leaked into the bay, but there's now a sewage treatment plant nearby. The beach is a long, thin strip of coarse sand, and offshore motorboats buzz like hornets. Nearby **Jomtien,** just south of town, is quieter and more appealing but still suffers from pollution. For those who want to swim in the sea,

it's best to rent a boat and go to the outlying islands, where the water is cleaner and a range of water-friendly sports is available.

Continuing east from Pattaya, **Koh Samet** in Rayong Province is a small island with heaps of affordable bungalows. It is a low-luxe, laid-back retreat reachable by a short ferry ride from the mainland in the town of **Ban Phe** (via Rayong). Though isolated, Samet is popular with foreigners on a budget and gets very crowded on weekends when Thai yuppies from Bangkok visit.

Koh Chang, the last holiday stop before Cambodia, has grown into a popular resort destination. It now boasts sprawling luxury resorts as well as a host of midrange and budget options. But in terms of tourist numbers and accessibility, this—Thailand's second largest island—is way behind both Phuket and Koh Samui. By road, Koh Chang is 5 hours east of Bangkok; Bangkok Airways offers 55-minute flights from the capital to nearby Trat, making it a much more manageable trip.

1 Pattaya

147km (91 miles) E of Bangkok

The slow evolution of Pattaya from a sleepy fishing town to a sprawling development of high-rise coastal resorts began in 1959 when U.S. Army GIs stationed in the northeast came here for R & R. Word spread, and with more U.S. troops arriving to fight in the Vietnam War, the town became a hot destination for weekend partying. The impression left by those early visitors accounts for its ill repute today, propagated by hundreds of go-go clubs, beer bars, and seedy massage parlors along the beachside.

Tourism boomed in the 1980s and unchecked resort development was exacerbated by a lack of infrastructure upgrades—so much so that beaches became flooded with raw sewage. Recent years have seen a few civil projects to clean up the bay area with some success, but environmental work is still needed to improve water quality.

Despite this, Pattaya now supports a collection of large, sophisticated international resorts. Smaller hotels set in sprawling, manicured seaside gardens and upscale restaurants dot the landscape. The town is also trying to create an image as a family destination, expat retirement magnet, and convention hub—and it now has the facilities to back this up. Pattaya's close-knit expatriate community is not only at the forefront in the effort to clean up the town's image, but is also very active in other local activities, particularly in charity-related events.

Neighboring Jomtien is a popular alternative to Pattaya. Less seedy surroundings complement the narrow beaches; however, government reports state that water quality is still under par. Jomtien's best accommodations are private condominiums, but it does have a few high-quality hotels.

ESSENTIALS
GETTING THERE
By Plane   The nearest airport is in U-Tapao, 45 minutes east of the city (② 03824-5595). It is served by **Bangkok Airways,** which has flights daily to Phuket (3,060B/US$87/£47 one way) and a daily flight from Koh Samui (3,710B/US$106/£57 one way). Trip time for both is approximately an hour. Make reservations through their offices in Bangkok (② 02265-5555; www.bangkokair.com). They have an office in Pattaya at Royal Garden Plaza, 218 Beach Rd., 2nd floor (② 03841-1965).

To get to and from the U-Tapao airport to Pattaya, you can arrange a private transfer through your resort. A limo can be as steep as 1,500B (US$43/£23), though. If you are arriving at Suvarnabhumi International Airport and heading to Pattaya, your only option is by car or bus (see below).

By Train   An inconvenient and slow (weekdays only) local train chugs away from Bangkok's **Hua Lampong station** at 6:55am, the homebound train departs Pattaya at 2:20pm. The 4-hour trip costs only 31B (88¢/50p). Call **Hua Lampong** in Bangkok (② 02223-7010 or 1690) or the train station in Pattaya (② 03842-9285). The Pattaya train station is east of the resort strip off Sukhumvit Road and *songtaew* (communal pickup trucks) connect with all destinations on the main beach for around 30B (85¢/50p).

By Public Bus   The most common and practical form of transportation to Pattaya is the bus. Buses depart from **Bangkok's Eastern Bus Terminal** on Sukhumvit Road (opposite Soi 63 at the Ekkamai BTS; ② 02391-2504) every 20 minutes beginning from 5am until 10pm every day. For an air-conditioned coach, the fare is 117B (US$3.35/£1.80). There are also regular buses from **Bangkok's Northern Bus Terminal** on Kampaengphet 2 Road (near Mo Chit; ② 02936-2841)—leaving from there is a good way to avoid the Bangkok rush hour.

The bus station in town is on North Pattaya Road (② 03842-9877). From there, you can catch a shared ride on a *songtaew* to your hotel for about 40B (US$1.15/60p), or a bit more for a taxi.

By Private Bus   Major hotels or travel agencies in both Bangkok and Pattaya operate private shuttles, so be sure to inquire when booking. **Rung Reung Tour** (② 03842-9877) has big air-conditioned buses for 150B (US$4.30/£2.20) departing every 2 hours from 6am to 7pm (trip time: 2 hr.) to and from Bangkok's Suvarnabhumi International

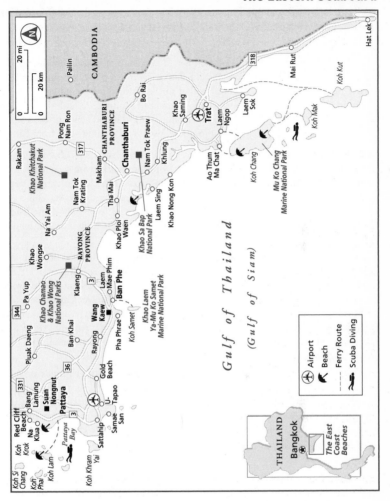

Airport, and minibuses also depart from Khao San Road in Bangkok. Check with the agent about discounts.

By Taxi Taxis from the Suvarnabhumi taxi counter go for upwards of 1,500B (US$43/£23), and any hotel concierge can negotiate with a metered taxi driver to take you to or from Pattaya resort, door to door, for about 1,200B (US$34/£18).

By Car Take Highway 3 east from Bangkok; tolls are payable on the new toll roads. See "Getting Around" below for info on car rentals.

VISITOR INFORMATION

The **Tourism Authority of Thailand (TAT) office** (609 Moo 10, Pratamnak Rd.; ℃ 03842-8750) is located south of Pattaya City, up the hill on the road between Pattaya and neighboring Jomtien. Plenty of info is available in most hotel lobbies, along with free local maps and publications, like *What's On Pattaya* and *Explore Pattaya and the East Coast. Pattaya Mail* is the local English-language paper (25B/60¢/42p).

ORIENTATION

Pattaya Beach Road is the heart of the town; a long strip of hotels, bars, restaurants, and shops overlook Pattaya Bay. Pattaya 2nd and Pattaya 3rd roads run parallel to Beach Road and form a busy central grid of small, crowded *sois* bound by North Pattaya and South Pattaya roads, bisected by Central Pattaya Road. At both the far northern (The Dusit Resort) and southern (Sheraton Pattaya Resort) ends of the strip are two bluffs. Due south is condo-lined Jomtien Beach—a 15-minute ride from Pattaya.

GETTING AROUND

By Minibus or Songtaew   *Songtaews* are red pickup trucks with wooden benches that follow regular routes up and down the main streets. Fares within Pattaya start at 20B (57¢/28p). Getting to far-flung beaches such as Jomtien costs about 40B (US$1.15/60p). Drivers will try to charge you a taxi rate (especially if the truck is empty). If you are on a shoestring budget, don't give in; bargain hard or wait for a full truck. Some hotels operate their own minibuses.

By Car   Car rental agencies offering discounts outside the high season abound. Well-known car rental companies such as **Avis** have a counter at the **Dusit Resort** (© **03836-1627**); rates start at 1,580B (US$45/£24) per day for a Suzuki Caribbean (a very low-end jeep), to 2,770B (US$79/£42) upwards for a compact sedan. **Budget Car Rental**'s office at Beach Road (© **03871-0717**) offers comparable rates. There are plenty of local agencies, but beware of the poor reputation of the older-model jeeps; read the contract and check the vehicles before renting. One such agency is **Chalee Car Rental**, 312/13 14 Moo, 9 Pattaya 3rd Rd. (© **03872-0413**; cars from 800B/US$23/£12).

By Motorcycle   Let's be honest. Pattaya is a party town and its busy roads are full of drunk and reckless drivers. But the brave (or foolish) can rent 150cc motorcycles for 250B (US$7.15/£3.85) a day. You don't technically need insurance—just your passport as collateral—but accidents are so common, you should invest in some. Big choppers and Japanese speed bikes (500cc) start at 1,000B (US$28/£15) per day. Helmets are mandatory by law—so wear one, even if the locals don't.

FAST FACTS

There are many independent **money-changing booths,** 24-hour bank exchanges (with better rates), and ATMs at every turn in town. The **post office** is on Soi Post Office near the **Royal Garden Plaza** (© **03842-9341**). **Bangkok Pattaya Hospital** (© **03825-9999**) has full services and English-speaking staff. In Pattaya, the number for the **Tourist Police** is © **03842-9371** or 1155. Internet services are easy to find. Rates are 60B per hour (that works out to about US$2/£1 per hr.). There are a number of **Internet cafes** along the waterfront (try Soi Yamato).

WHAT TO SEE & DO

Wat Khao Prayai is a small temple complex high above town to the south (go by *songtaew* toward Jomtien, and then hop off and climb the steep hill). The temple has excellent vistas and a 10m (32½-ft.) gold Buddha serenely surveying the western sea.

   Alangkarn is a high-tech entertainment complex centered on the uniqueness of being decidedly "Thai" and features a stage with laser and lighting effects. The shows include scenes from famous historical events such as an elephant battle or Thai dancing. It also has a Thai restaurant and shopping area containing local products.

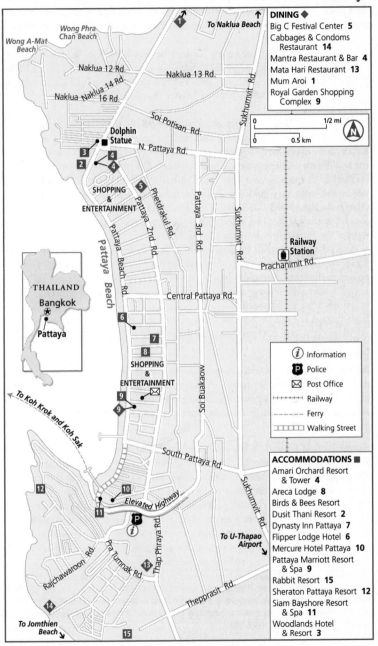

Pattaya

DINING ◆
- Big C Festival Center **5**
- Cabbages & Condoms Restaurant **14**
- Mantra Restaurant & Bar **4**
- Mata Hari Restaurant **13**
- Mum Aroi **1**
- Royal Garden Shopping Complex **9**

0		1/2 mi
0	0.5 km	

Wong Phra Chan Beach
To Naklua Beach
Wong A-Mat Beach
Naklua 12 Rd.
Naklua 13 Rd.
Naklua 14 Rd.
Naklua Naklua 16 Rd.
Soi Potisan Rd.
Sukhumvit Rd.

Dolphin Statue
N. Pattaya Rd.

SHOPPING & ENTERTAINMENT

Phetrakul Rd.
Pattaya 2nd Rd.
Pattaya 3rd Rd.
Sukhumvit Rd.
Pattaya Beach Rd.

Pattaya Beach

THAILAND
Bangkok
Pattaya

To Koh Krok and Koh Sak

Railway Station
Prachanimit Rd.

Central Pattaya Rd.

SHOPPING & ENTERTAINMENT

Soi Buakaow

ⓘ Information
🅿 Police
✉ Post Office
├┼┼┼┼┤ Railway
- - - - - Ferry
▭▭▭▭ Walking Street

South Pattaya Rd.

Sukhumvit Rd.

Elevated Highway

🅿
ⓘ

To U-Thapao Airport

Pra Tummak Rd.
Thap Phraya Rd.
Rajchawaroon Rd.

Thepprasit Rd.

To Jomthien Beach

ACCOMMODATIONS ■
- Amari Orchard Resort & Tower **4**
- Areca Lodge **8**
- Birds & Bees Resort
- Dusit Thani Resort **2**
- Dynasty Inn Pattaya **7**
- Flipper Lodge Hotel **6**
- Mercure Hotel Pattaya **10**
- Pattaya Marriott Resort & Spa **9**
- Rabbit Resort **15**
- Sheraton Pattaya Resort **12**
- Siam Bayshore Resort & Spa **11**
- Woodlands Hotel & Resort **3**

Alangkarn (© **03825-6000**) is 10km (6 miles) from Pattaya at Km. 155 on the Sukhumvit Highway. The entrance fee is 1,400B (US$40/£22), and it's open daily from 5:30 to 11pm.

For something a bit more hokey, **Ripley's Believe It or Not,** 3rd floor, Royal Garden Plaza, 218 Beach Rd. (© **03871-0294**), is open daily 10am to 11pm (admission 580B/US$17/£8.95). It's full of unusual exhibits and odd facts from around the globe. Just next door is the Ripley's Motion Master simulation ride. Both are great fun for kids of all ages.

The Pattaya Elephant Village (© 03824-9818; www.elephant-village-pattaya. com) is a not-for-profit sanctuary dedicated to saving former working elephants. To help with funding, the village offers elephant treks and a 90-minute daily show, starting at 2:30pm, on elephant-training techniques. The treks range in price from 1,000B (US$29/£15) for a 1-hour ride to 2,000B (US$57/£31) for a full-day excursion, which also includes a guided walk in the forest and a 30-minute raft trip, while the show only costs 500B (US$14/£7.70). The village is 7km (4⅓ miles) off Sukhumvit Road: Turn left at Km144.5, follow the signs to Siam Country Club, and then turn right at the intersection for 4km (2½ miles).

Another option outside Pattaya, by 18km (11½ miles), is **Nong Nooch** (© **03870-9358**), a 500-acre botanical garden and elephant park with shows that feature elephants performing alongside dancers, musicians, and other acts. Cultural performances, music, Thai boxing, audience participation and dozens of amusing photo ops make this a fun albeit touristy activity. Book directly and take advantage of a shuttle from Pattaya at either 8:30am or 1:15pm. The shows run four times a day (9:45am, 10:30am, 3pm, and 3:45pm daily). Tickets cost 420B (US$12/£6.45).

WHERE TO STAY

Busy central Pattaya features a range of accommodations, from downright seedy hotels to international upmarket resorts. Among the maze of bars, tailor shops, and eateries are some semi-isolated getaways. During the high season, reservations are recommended at least 2 weeks in advance, especially December through January.

EXPENSIVE

Amari Orchid Resort & Tower ✦✦✦ (Kids)   The Amari provides all the comforts you'd expect from a large, high-end resort. The open-air lobby is inviting and guest rooms are large and trimmed in dark wood with parquet floors and contemporary lines. The location is great, on the quieter northern end of town, just out of the bustle, but within walking distance of restaurants and shops. And since the hotel is set on 10 acres of prime beachfront, rooms have good views of the gardens or the sea. In addition, the staff is helpful, and there's a playground and lots of space in the grassy central area—which makes this a great choice for the family. They also have excellent in-house dining. (See "Where to Dine" below.)

Pattaya Beach, Pattaya 20150 (on the northernmost end of the beachfront road). © 03842-8322. Fax 03842-8165. www.amari.com/orchid. 527 units. 9,000B–9,800B (US$220–US$240/£138–£151) double; 11,000B (US$314/£169) suite. AE, DISC, MC, V. **Amenities:** 3 restaurants; 3 bars; pool; fitness center; spa; playground and kids' club; tour desk; business center; salon; 24-hr. room service; babysitting; laundry service; dry cleaning; nonsmoking rooms; Wi-Fi. In room: A/C, satellite TV, minibar, fridge, safe.

Dusit Thani Resort ✦✦   This sprawling, manicured resort straddles the bluff on the north end of the main beach and is chock-full of top-notch amenities: two lovely pools, access to two small but well-kept sandy beach coves and watersports, several dining outlets, and a small shopping arcade. Most of the balcony rooms overlook Pattaya Bay, but the garden view rooms offer the best value. Tasteful, modern rooms are trimmed with stained wood and each has fine furnishings and marble bathrooms. Larger rooms and suites have outdoor showers on breezy balconies. For those seeking extra amenities, the resort offers special Dusit Club and Dusit Grand rooms, a spa, and fitness center. Overall, the accommodations are comfortable, with an "olde worlde" feel.

240/2 Pattaya Beach Rd., Pattaya 20150, Chonburi (north end of Pattaya Beach). ℭ 03842-5611. Fax 03842-8239. www.dusit.com. 462 units. 6,000B–6,800B (US$171–US$194/£92–£105) double; from 9,300B (US$265/£143) suite. AE, DC, MC, V. **Amenities:** 3 restaurants; lobby bar w/live music; 2 pools; 3 outdoor tennis courts; fitness center; spa; watersports; game room; tour desk; car-rental desk; airport transfer; small business center; shopping arcade; 24-hr. room service; babysitting; same-day laundry service/dry cleaning; nonsmoking rooms. *In room:* A/C, satellite TV, dataport, minibar, fridge, coffeemaker, hair dryer, safe.

Pattaya Marriott Resort & Spa 🏆🏆 🄺𝑖𝑑𝑠

For those wanting to be right in the thick of it, the Marriott is the place to be. Located in the center of Pattaya, adjacent to the Royal Garden Plaza shopping complex, this five-star resort is abuzz with activity for adults and kids. Rooms have wooden floors and spacious balconies with views of gardens or the sea. Bonuses are the resort's beautiful pool area in the well-kept, spacious garden, large fitness center, and highly regarded spa. The resort contains three restaurants and two bars, including the Elephant Bar, a popular meeting place overlooking the pool.

218 Beach Rd., Pattaya 20150, Chonburi. ℭ 03841-2120. Fax 03842-9926. www.marriott.com. 293 units. 8,000B–12,540B (US$228–US$358/£123–£193) double; from 20,140B–35,720B (US$575–US$1,020/£310–£550) suite. AE, DC, MC, V. **Amenities:** 3 restaurants; 2 bars; pool; 2 lit tennis courts; fitness center; spa; watersports; game room; tour desk; airport transfer; shopping mall; salon; 24-hr. room service; babysitting; same-day laundry service/dry cleaning; nonsmoking rooms; executive floor; Wi-Fi. *In room:* A/C, satellite TV, minibar, fridge, coffeemaker, safe.

Rabbit Resort 🏆🏆 𝐹𝑖𝑛𝑑𝑠

The Rabbit Resort may be hard to find, but it's worth the search. This four-star boutique hotel on Dongtan Beach, in Jomtien, lies just south of Pattaya and is an ideal place for those needing a quiet retreat and escape from name-brand luxury resorts. Set on 4 acres of ocean-front land, it has superb gardens graced by two pools. The rooms are mostly 2-story Thai-style villas, decorated with antiques personally selected by the owners. The friendly Thai staff members are always willing to please and the proprietors are on hand to attend to special needs. The hotel serves complementary buffet breakfasts and has a grill house overlooking the sea.

318/84 Moo 13, Soi Dongtan Police Station, Jomtien 20260. ℭ 03830-3303. Fax 03825-1628. www.rabbitresort.com. 49 units. 3,900B–10,500B (US$111–US$300/£60–£162) off peak; 5,600B–13,000B (US$160–US$371/£86–£200) high season. AE, DC, MC, V. **Amenities:** Restaurant; 2 pools; babysitting services; laundry service; dry cleaning; free Internet. *In room:* A/C, satellite TV, minibar, fridge, microwave, hair dryer, safe.

Sheraton Pattaya Resort 🏆🏆🏆

This five-star facility offers perhaps the most luxurious accommodations around this part of the coast—and it's a great romantic getaway. Nestled on a headland just south of Pattaya, it offers spectacular views of the Gulf of Siam and terraced gardens, revealing large lagoon-style pools and pleasant nooks. A mixture of stunning private villas, pavilions, and standard rooms in the main building blend traditional Thai style and modern decor. Top-notch service includes an efficient and helpful activities desk. The resort has three upscale restaurants and a chic cocktail lounge, all with ocean views. There's also an alluring spa.

37 Phra Tamnak Rd., Pattaya 20150. ℭ 03825-9888. Fax 03825-9899. www.sheraton.com. 156 units. 9,800B–12,000B (US$280–US$343/£151–£185) deluxe; 13,500B–15,500B (US$385–US$443/£208–£238) pavilion; 60,000B–80,000B

(US$1,714–US$2,286/£923–£1,231) villas. **Amenities:** 3 restaurants; 2 bars; 3 outdoor pools; fitness center; Jacuzzi; bike rentals; DVD rentals; library and lounge; kids' club; tour desk; car-rental desk; airport transfer; 24-hr. room service; massage; babysitting; laundry service; dry cleaning; Wi-Fi. *In room:* A/C, satellite TV, fridge, minibar, coffeemaker, hair dryer, safe.

Siam Bayshore Resort & Spa 🦋

Under the same management as the nearby Siam Bayview Resort, this is a slightly more upmarket sibling. The resort is situated on the southern tip of Beach Road near to the heaving (some might say sleazy) Walking Street. The rooms have a bright Thai contemporary feel and its open-air lobby is very welcoming. Though it provides all the expected amenities of a top-grade hotel, it is not quite as luxurious as its competitors. Still, the totally self-contained and extensive leisure facilities make it perfect for active holidaymakers. Bring a racquet, since there are six tennis courts. It's also conveniently next to the pier and offers boat trips to some of the outlying islands.

310/2 Beach Rd., Pattaya 20150. (℃) **03842-8871.** Fax 03842-3879. www.siamhotels.com. 270 units. 3,000B–7,000B (US$86–US$200/£46–£108) double. AE, MC, V. **Amenities:** 3 restaurants; 2 bars; 2 pools; Jacuzzi; 6 lit tennis courts; fitness center; spa; 24-hr. room service; laundry service; dry cleaning. *In room:* A/C, satellite TV, dataport, minibar, fridge, safe.

MODERATE

Birds and Bees Resort 🦋🦋

This fun, inviting resort was originally known as Cabbages & Condoms. It was built by Senator Meechai Viravaidya, a Thai activist in the field of sex education and rural development projects throughout Thailand. Rooms have a rustic feel, but all the required amenities are there. Its attraction mainly lies in its two pools and the isolated hilltop location overlooking the sea in a quiet part of Pattaya. The property is very family-friendly and contains wishing wells, as well as an herb garden (with special exercise bikes designed to irrigate them). It is also home to the acclaimed Cabbages & Condoms restaurant (see below), which has a branch in Bangkok.

366/11 Moo 12 Phra Tamnak 4 Rd., Nongprue, Banglamung, Chonburi 20150 (south of town on the hilltop). (℃) **03825-0556.** Fax 03825-0034. www.cabbagesandcondoms.co.th. 50 units. 1,800B–2,400B (US$52–US$68/£28– £37) double; 3,500B–7,200B (US$100–US$205/£54–£111) 1- and 2- bedroom suites. AE, MC, V. **Amenities:** Restaurant; 2 pools; spa; tour desk; limited room service; laundry service. *In room:* A/C, satellite TV, minibar, fridge.

Mercure Hotel Pattaya

A friendly, well-run hotel, the Mercure is only a few minutes' walking distance from the city's best shopping and the beach. The rooms are business-like in style, not so huge, but with bright contemporary artwork mixed with Thai touches and gorgeous, slick bathrooms. The trio of swimming pools that fill the gardens—including a large free-form pool—is among the best features of a stay here. Family-friendly amenities include TV video games—great if the weather turns wet!

484 Moo 10 Pattaya Second Rd. Soi 15, Pattaya 20150. (℃) **03842-5050.** Fax 03842-5080. www.mercure.com. 245 units. 2,000B–3,000B (US$57–US$86/£31–£46). AE, MC, V. Private indoor parking included in rates. **Amenities:** 3 restaurants; bar; pool; Internet. *In room:* A/C, satellite TV, video games, minibar, fridge, safe.

Woodlands Hotel & Resort 🦋*Kids* 🦋*Value*

This four-star hotel in Naklua, the quieter northern area of Pattaya, offers great seasonal deals, which tend to attract families, repeat visitors, and long-term guests, mainly from Europe. The rooms, though not luxurious, are very comfortable with views overlooking the pools and lush, tropical gardens. It also has good spa facilities, a well-equipped fitness center, and Thai cooking classes to keep everyone busy.

164/1 Moo 5 Pattaya-Naklua Rd., Pattaya 20150. (℃) **03842-1707.** Fax 03842-5662. www.woodland-resort.com. 135 units. 2,500B–9,200B (US$71–US$262/£38–£142). **Amenities:** 2 restaurants; bar; 2 pools; spa; fitness center; Internet. *In room:* A/C, satellite TV, minibar, fridge.

INEXPENSIVE

Budget lodgings in Pattaya attract a rough clientele and can be pretty unpleasant, but you're sure to find cheap deals starting as low as 500B (US$14/£7.70). Many have counters for the mandatory registration of "new friends," meaning night visitors. Some of the more reputable establishments include the **Areca Lodge** (✆ **03841-0123;** www.areca lodge.com) on Soi Diana, not far from the beach and shops, with rooms starting at 875B (US$25/£13) in low season. **Dynasty Inn Pattaya,** 55 Soi 13, Pattaya Beach Rd. (✆ **03841-5941**), is centrally located and rooms start at 1,050B (US$30/£16). **Flipper Lodge Hotel** (✆ **03842-6401;** www.flippergroup.com) is located in the thick of it, so it can get a bit noisy. Nevertheless, it's a good value for the money. Rooms start at 1,050B (US$30/£16).

WHERE TO DINE

Pattaya is teeming with small storefront bars and eateries. You'll find the big fast-food chains well represented (mercifully for some, they include **Starbucks**) along the beachfront road, and **Subway Sandwich** at the **Royal Garden Shopping Complex** (south of town). The **Big C Festival Center** (on Pattaya 2 Rd., north end of town) supports a number of other familiar restaurants. But there are excellent high-end diners too. Local dining is best at open-air joints down any *soi*. Various types of cuisine are available here and the prices range immensely. You'll get good value meals at any of the fresh seafood establishments found in the various beachfront areas.

EXPENSIVE

Cabbages and Condoms Restaurant THAI   South of town on a hilltop in the Birds and Bees Resort (see above), this is Pattaya's version of the much-lauded restaurant in Bangkok. Both are known not only for their food, but also their efforts to educate Thais about HIV/AIDS. The mainly Thai cuisine is good, though, with wide choices ranging from seafood to regional specialties. (Tastes are only slightly adjusted for the foreign palate.) The open-concept restaurant is set in the resort's tropical gardens and offers delightful views of the sea.

Birds and Bees Resort, 366/11 Moo 12 Phra Tamnak 4 Road, Nongprue, Banglamung, Chonburi. ✆ 03825-0556. www.cabbagesandcondoms.co.th. Main courses 70B–200B (US$2–US$5.70/£1.10–£3.10). MC, V. Daily 11am–10pm.

Mantra Restaurant and Bar 🍴🍴 INTERNATIONAL   Offering a unique hotel dining experience in the pleasant surrounds of the Amari (p. 156), the Mantra has a menu that's based on eight types of cuisines. Everything is prepared in an open-air kitchen, enabling the guests to sample exotic food combinations in a modern setting. The sleek glass building is decorated with artifacts from all over Asia. Seating 80 over two levels, the restaurant has an extensive walk-in wine cellar. The dress code is "chic, smart, and stylish," so that means no shorts, tank tops, or sandals.

Amari Orchid Resort & Tower, Beach Rd. ✆ 0384-29591. Reservations recommended. Main courses 220B–3,500B (US$6–US$100/£3.20–£51). AE, MC, V. Mon–Sat 5pm–1am and Sun 11am–3pm.

Mata Hari Restaurant 🍴🍴 INTERNATIONAL   This highly acclaimed, dinner-only restaurant specializes in fine European cuisine. The atmosphere is casual but elegant. The innovative menu is a favorite among the expatriate community. The convivial bar area for pre-supper drinks and the extensive wine list are big bonuses. It's often very busy (even in the low season), so reservations are recommended.

482/57 Moo 12, Thappraya Rd., Nongprue (on the rd. between Pattaya and Jomtien). ✆ 03825-9799. www.pattaya city.com/matahari. Main courses 700B and up (US$20/£11). AE, MC, V. Tues–Sun 4pm–11:30pm.

Mum Aroi ✦ SEAFOOD   This upmarket seafood restaurant is popular among resident Thais and Thai visitors. In addition to premium-quality seafood, it is known for its laid-back beach ambiance. Live music adds to the atmosphere. The restaurant is just 5 minutes from Pattaya, close to the luxurious Ananya, a block of condo flats.

Beachfront Condominium. 83/4 M.2 Naklua Banglamung. ✆ 03823-4352. Main courses 180B and up (US$5/£2.60). Cash only. Daily 5–11pm.

OUTDOOR ACTIVITIES IN PATTAYA
GOLF

The hills around Pattaya are known for their great courses, with many international-class greens in a short 40km (25-mile) radius of the city. Caddy fees are reasonable, around 250B (US$7/£3.85), and golf carts are usually compulsory, but rationally priced. Among the recommended are:

- **Burapha Golf Club,** 281 Moo 4, Tambon Bung, Sri Racha (✆ 03837-2700), is the home of numerous tournaments. Greens fees are 2,000B (US$57/£31) on weekdays; weekends 2,500B (US$71/£38); 600B (US$24/£9.25) 2-person golf cart.
- **Laem Chabang International Country Club,** 106/8 Moo 4 Tambon Bung, Sri Racha (✆ 03837-2273, dial 0), has three 18-hole courses (A, B, and C) designed by Jack Nicklaus and very dramatic scenery. Greens fees are 2,500B (US$71/£38) weekdays; weekends 3,000B (US$86/£46).
- **Siam Country Club,** 50 Tambol Pong, Banglamung (✆ 03824-9381; fax 03824-9387), is a short hop from Pattaya and is said to be one of the country's most challenging courses. Greens fees are 2,500B (US$71/£38) weekdays; 3,000B (US$87/£46) weekends.

WATERSPORTS

For those who come to Pattaya to do more than party, there is plenty on offer, particularly when it comes to watersports. Pattaya's less than pristine beaches are a good excuse to head to outlying areas where the conditions are more inviting. Day trips to nearby islands such as **Koh Khrok, Koh Lan,** and **Koh Sok** start at 1,000B (US$28/£15) per head on a full boat (more for a private charter). To go to far-out Bamboo Island, it will cost you a bit more—about 2,800B (US$80/£43). **Paragliding** around the bay behind a motorboat is a popular beachfront activity and a 5-minute flight costs from 300B (US$8.50/£4.60).

Jomtien Beach hosts **windsurfing** and **sea kayaking;** boards and boats are rented along the beach for 800B (US$23/£12) per hour.

Pattaya is a good place to learn to **scuba dive.** It has a number of reputable dive companies with PADI- and NAUI-certified instructors. The underwater visibility is consistently good, so the sport can be done year-round. There are a few dive sites near the islands, just offshore in **Pattaya Bay,** as well as **Koh Si Chang** to the north—once famous as the summer playground of foreign ambassadors to Siam during the 19th century—and **Sattahip** to the south, with diving to a depth of 40m (131 ft.). **Adventure Divers,** 391/77 78 Moo 10 Tappraya Rd. (✆ 03836-4453; www.pattayadivers.com), is one of many PADI-certified companies offering daily trips and courses for all levels.

PATTAYA AFTER DARK

Central Pattaya is predominantly a sea of flashing neon and blaring music, even in the smaller *sois.* **Walking Street** becomes a pedestrian zone in the evening in South Pattaya on Beach Roach. Here you will see debauchery at its fullest, with an array of go-go bars, open-air drinking establishments, Thai boxing venues (before you place a bet, the fights are all fixed), and of course overpriced tourist restaurants. Regular bars and places with live music can also be found. The energy on the street, whether good or bad, is riotous by evening. In daylight, the passageway is bleak with bleary-eyed revelers stumbling through seedy storefronts.

Sex for money in Pattaya is an unashamedly direct business. Dubious massage parlors are numerous in northern Pattaya. Hotels insist "visitors" (a euphemism for prostitutes) register their ID with security guards, whereupon the client pays a "joiner fee." Despite its prevalence, prostitution in Thailand is illegal, so be prepared to risk a police raid, or hefty bribe to the local police or mafia, not to mention a call to your embassy. It's *not* all innocent fun. Stories of laced drinks and aggravated theft (or worse) abound. AIDS and STDs are major concerns. To prove they are cracking down, authorities are particularly happy to splash photos of any foreigners caught with young girls or boys across the international media. (See "Sex for Sale," in chapter 2, for more info.)

Happily, Pattaya is not entirely sleazy these days, as indicated by some of its finer eateries and upscale resorts. There are a number of bars where you can go to enjoy a drink and maybe listen to live music without being propositioned. Topping the list is the **Hopf Brew House** 𝕗𝕗𝕗 (219 Beach Rd.; ✆ 03871-0870). Designed like a German brewery, this spacious watering hole brews its own beer and serves Northern European bar food. It also has an in-house band that plays mostly easy-listening tunes. **Shenanigan's** is a fun Irish bar hangout at the Royal Garden Complex (near the Marriott; ✆ 03871-0641), with the front entrance on Pattaya 2nd Road. It's a good place to watch major sporting events on the big screen. Then there's **Henry J. Bean's Bar and Grill** (on the beach near the Amari Orchid Resort & Tower; ✆ 03842-8161), which is a friendly bar with live music nightly, except Sunday. It serves Tex-Mex food, complete with margaritas and a wide assortment of beers.

The town's camped-up cabaret shows are always good, lighthearted fun. Pattaya's sensational *katoeys* (transsexuals) love to don sequined gowns and feather boas and strut their stuff to packed houses nightly. Both **Tiffany's** (464 Moo 9, 2nd Rd.; ✆ 03842-1700) and **Alcazar** (78/14 Pattaya 2nd Rd., opposite Soi 5; ✆ 03841-0225) have hilarious shows, much like those in other tourist towns in Thailand.

2 Ban Phe & Koh Samet ✦

220km (136 miles) E of Bangkok on Highway 3 via Pattaya, or 185km (115 miles) on Highway 3 via the Pattaya bypass. Ban Phe is 25km (15½ miles) southeast of Rayong City.

Tiny Koh Samet, better known simply as Samet (or Samed), is well known to Thais through an epic poem by Sunthorn Phu, a venerated 18th-century author and Rayong native who set his famous work, *Phra Aphimani*, on Samet. Just 1km (⅔-mile) wide, the island is a long, triangular pennant shape, split by a rocky ridge. It's now deemed a national park, hence there's a 400B (US$11/£6.15) per-adult landing fee (children pay half that price). As with so many of Thailand's "protected" areas, though, developers have devoured so much of the long sandy coastline here that one has to wonder what is being protected with the admission fee.

Ferries from Ban Phe land at Na Dan, the island's main port on the northern coast, from where it's a 15-minute walk south to Had Sai Kaew (Diamond Beach), a popular stretch with a serious party vibe. Or it's a short 20B to 50B (57¢–US$1.40/30p–75p) hop on a shared *songtaew* to fun-filled Ao Wong Deuan, or the more isolated Ao Phutsa.

Ao Phai's beaches just south of Had Sai Kaew are said to be treacherous for swimmers, so take care; in contrast, Ao Thia is popular with divers. Right down south is the chilled-out bay of Ao Kiu Nan Nok. There are a few upmarket resorts on the west side of the island at Ao Prao where speedboats run guests over to Ban Phe. Ferries also run to east coast resort beaches in good weather.

Accommodations here get overpriced on weekends and in high season, and bookings may not always be honored. Stay cool and shop around. If you need to kick back and chill, avoid the busy weekend rush, when big groups of young Thai weekenders come over for some serious karaoke and drinking sessions. Peak season is similar to Pattaya's, with July through October bringing fewer travelers and lower rates.

ESSENTIALS
GETTING THERE

By Bus   Buses leave Bangkok every 30 minutes between 4am and 10pm for the 2½-hour journey, departing from **Ekkamai,** Bangkok's Eastern Bus Terminal on Sukhumvit Road opposite Soi 63 (© **02391-2504**). The one-way trip to Rayong costs 146B (US$4.15/£2.25), and from there it is a 20B (50¢/30p) shared *songtaew* to the ferry landing at Ban Phe. From Pattaya, either flag down a passing air-con or public bus from the corner of Sukhumvit and Pattaya Neua roads or book the 200B (US$5.70/£3.10) minibus option at any agency. **Malibu-Garden Resort** on Samet owns a Pattaya travel agency (© **03871-0676**; www.malibu-samet.com) from which they run regular day trips and minibus transfers. Day trips cost 900B (US$26/£14) round-trip. Private cars can also be arranged. From Khao San, travel agencies offer minibus seats to Ban Phe for 250B (US$7.15/£3.85).

By Car   Take the Suvarnabhumi Airport tollway from Bangkok east to Pattaya, then Highway 36 to Rayong, and then the coastal Highway 3145 to Seree Ban Phe (for about 3 hr.). See p. 81 in chapter 4, "Introducing Bangkok," for info on car rentals.

GETTING TO KOH SAMET

By Ferry   From the Saphan Nuan Tip ferry pier at Ban Phe, ferries leave for Na Dan every half-hour (trip time: 40 min.; 50B/US$1.42/73p one-way), or when full. Scheduled ferries also run at 9:30am, 1:30pm, and 5pm to Ao Wong Duean. Rates are one-way for 70B (US$2/£1.10) or 110B (US$3.15/£1.70) for a round-trip.

Speedboats to Ao Prao Resort can be booked at their dockside office in Ban Phe; prices vary. If you fancy whizzing over to Na Dan, it'll cost around 1,200B (US$34/£18).

FAST FACTS

Koh Samet now has three ATMs. The easiest to find is at the 7-Eleven at the Na Dan pier. The post office is at the Naga Bungalows (©/fax **03864-4035**) south of Had Sai Kaew, and there's a satellite phone for overseas calls found at the visitor center in the National Parks office. There are plenty of Internet places, great nightlife, and seafood eateries by the beach. A clinic is just south of the Na Dan pier before Had Sai Kaew. (Though the island is no longer supposed to be malarial, it's plagued with the mosquitoes; take plenty of repellent and an antihistamine-based cream for post-bites.)

GETTING AROUND

Island transport is limited to shared pickups, or rented motorbikes and mountain bikes, but many people simply choose to walk the hilly paths. No phone numbers for bike rental shops were available at press time, but you should be able to walk into any of the operators in town and make a reservation that day.

WHERE TO STAY

It's always risky if you haven't booked a hotel ahead, especially on busy weekends, but fear not, travel agents and "helpful" locals hover at the Ban Phe Pier touting rooms. With few exceptions, budget accommodations are very basic here. There are now some gorgeous luxury resorts and midrange bungalows, though. Samed Resorts (www.samedresorts.com) represents five of the best.

VERY EXPENSIVE

Ao Prao Resort ✻✻   One of the oldest, upscale properties in the area, Ao Prao is still one of the best. The pretty bungalows here make for quaint little holiday retreats. Rooms have delightful teak furnishings and decor, as well as four-poster beds, and some come with enormous double tubs overlooking the blissful scenery. There are plenty of watersports available and large meeting facilities, all set within a sprawling tropical garden.

60 Moo 4, Tambon Phe, Rayong 21160. ⓒ **03861-6881**. Fax 03861-6885. www.samedresorts.com. 52 units. 5,900B (US$163/£91) superior; 16,500B (US$471/£254) 2-bed family suite. MC, V. **Amenities:** Restaurant/bar; outdoor pool; watersports rentals; speedboat and ferry arrangements; tour desk; room service; babysitting; laundry service; dry cleaning; Wi-Fi. *In room:* A/C, satellite TV, minibar, fridge, coffeemaker, hair dryer, safe.

Le Vimarn Cottages & Spa ✻✻✻   Ao Prao has gone seriously upmarket with the arrival of this small, hillside hideaway for wannabe jetsetters; accommodation comes in three room types. All of the huge thatched villas come with four-poster beds and lovely balconies overlooking the beach and ocean, while the resort's pool villas have Jacuzzis sharing the same wondrous sea views.

40/11 Moo 4, Tambon Phe, Rayong 21160. ⓒ **038644-1047**, or 02438-9711 Bangkok office. Fax 03864-4109. www.samedresorts.com. 28 units. 10,700B (US$305/£153) deluxe cottage; 14,100B (US$403/£202) spa villa; 31,000B ($US886/£443) spa villa suite. MC, V. **Amenities:** Restaurant; bar; outdoor pool; spa; speedboat and ferry arrangements; tour desk; airport transfer; business center; room service; laundry service; dry cleaning; Internet. *In room:* A/C, satellite TV, minibar, fridge, coffeemaker, hair dryer, safe.

Paradee ✻✻   The third member of Samet's super-luxury trio is this fabulous villa-only resort right on the island's southernmost tip and straddling two beaches. Elegant Thai decor accompanies perks such as tranquil private pools, Jacuzzis, and personal DVD players. It's perfect for couples (in fact, children are actively discouraged from staying here). At this exclusive sanctuary for the chosen few, you even get a butler with each sumptuous villa just to ensure that your every need is met.

76 Moo 4, Tambon Phe, Rayong 21160. ⓒ **02438-9711** Bangkok office. Fax 03864-4283. www.paradeeresort.com. 30 units. 15,000B (US$428/£231) garden villa; 20,000B (US$571/£308) garden pool villa; 80,000B (US$2,285/£1,231) suite villa. MC, V. **Amenities:** Restaurant; bar; individual pools in private villas; spa; speedboat and ferry arrangements; tour desk; airport transfer service; business center; room service; laundry service; dry cleaning; butler service; Internet. *In room:* A/C, satellite TV w/DVD player, minibar, fridge, coffeemaker, hair dryer, safe.

EXPENSIVE

Club Samed   It's fun, it's young, and it's affordable. The Club Samed offers midrange luxury rooms and amenities; you get most of the frills of expensive resorts, but for far less. The decor is modern, walls are painted with bright colors, there are walk-in tiled showers, and rooms overlook the central pool, around which sun-lovers can chill out under a parasol. The more active have a wide choice of beach sports, sailing, and windsurfing activities on hand. One of the highlights is the great location off the main drag, along a quiet beach on the northern coast, but close enough to enjoy a good night out on Had Sai Kaew.

Ao Noi Na, Tambon Phe, Rayong 21160. ℂ/fax **03864-4064**. www.samedresorts.com. 30 units. 3,000B–4,000B (US$86–US$114/£46–£62) double. MC, V. **Amenities:** Restaurant; bar; outdoor pool; speedboat and ferry arrangements; tour desk; transfer service; massage; laundry service; Internet. *In room:* A/C, satellite TV, minibar, fridge, hair dryer, safe.

MODERATE

Sai Kaew Beach Resort (ℂ **03864-4195-7**) dominates Had Sai Kaew and provides the biggest concentration of restaurants and bars, with rates starting at 4,700B (US$135/£70). There is also any number of simple, basic bungalows in town, with fans, starting at 600B (US$17/£9.25). One is the **Samed Grand View** (ℂ **03864-4220**) which also has posher, pricier room at higher rates. Nearby, at Ao Phai, you'll find **Samed Villa's** (ℂ **03864-4094;** www.samedvilla.com) bungalows, set in pretty gardens and with swish interiors. **Mooban Talay** (ℂ **03864-4251**) offers an upscale feel to its 24 rustic bungalows on Noi Na Bay. Quiet **Samet Ville Resort** (ℂ **03865-1682;** www.sametville resort.com) is a romantic midrange option away from the noise, and popular with Bangkok yuppies and expats.

INEXPENSIVE

For cozy huts at good prices (and some great food in Jep's diner next door), head past heady Had Sai Khaew to Ao Hin Khok where cool dudes hang at **Jep's Bungalows** (ℂ **03864-4112**). In sleepy Ao Phai, check out **Silver Sand Resort** (ℂ **086530-2417** mobile; www.silversandresort.com). Its cute white clapboard bungalows are right on the beach and its hopping bar offers burgers, crepes, movies, and (quite literally) buckets of cocktails. At all of these places, you can get a full meal for under 300B (US$9/£4.50).

WHERE TO DINE

The standard fish and rice dishes available at the town's resorts will keep you sated, but it'd be a shame to miss out on some of the upscale dining, as well as great local seafood restaurants, that are available in town. Most bungalows on Samet have their own dining areas for inexpensive, fresh seafood (don't miss the locally caught squid and cuttlefish, which are barbecued on skewers). Every day around sunset on **Ao Hin Khok** and **Ao Phai beaches,** tables are set up under twinkling lights for big seafood barbecues brimming with the day's catch.

The somewhat inevitably named (yes, it's named after the TV show) **Baywatch Bar** (ℂ **08182-67834,** mobile) on Ao Wong Deuan does great kebabs and Thai dishes, as well as reasonable Western fare. In Ao Pai just south of Had Sai Khaew, **Naga Bar** (ℂ **03864-4035**) is a popular hangout and serves a fine menu of local eats and tasty baked items. All restaurants on the island can turn into all-night party affairs depending on the crowd—and the amounts of alcohol consumed.

3 Chanthaburi Province

250km (155 miles) E of Bangkok

Travelers heading east to rugged Koh Chang (see "Trat & Koh Chang," below) will pass through Chanthaburi province and its capital, Chanthaburi (known as Mueang Chan). This region is known for its tropical fruit and lucrative gem mines. Durian, pineapple, longan *(lamyai)*, and rambutan thrive here. Don't be startled by the roadside 7.9m-high (26-ft.) durian "sculptures" you'll see piled at food stands along the way.

ESSENTIALS

Chanthaburi straddles the Chanthaburi River. The city's main avenue is Tha Chalab Road. The taxi stand and bus station (to Trat or Bangkok) are just west of the Chanthaburi Hotel on this street.

WHAT TO SEE & DO

In Taksin Park (the center of Chanthaburi), there's a statue of King Taksin on horseback, commemorating the victory over the Burmese in 1767, and a few temples built over Khmer ruins, highlighting the city's Cambodian connections. A large Catholic church built in 1909 still stands in the center as well.

Gem Markets line the predictably named Gem Street near the main market. If you are traveling in early December, take note—the annual Gem Fair packs the town with visitors. You may find a few choice rubies on offer, but no room at any inn.

The 17,000-hectare (42,000-acre) **Namtok Philu National Park** is a popular day trip from Chanthaburi, as is **Laem Sadet,** a stunning beach and rocky cape located some 35km (22 miles) southwest of the city. Both sites can be visited by private car or taxi. Contact agents such as Thai South (www.thaisouth.com) for more details.

WHERE TO STAY

City lodging is spartan. **River Guest House** (3/5-8 Si Chan Rd.; ℂ 03932-8211) is not quite downtown but offers basic and homely rooms (starting at 350B/US$10/£5), with quieter (fan only) rooms out back. **K. P. Grand** (35/200–201 Trirat Rd.; ℂ 03932-3201) is a smarter, modern facility in town. Its comfortable rooms start at 1,200B (US$34/£18).

4 Trat & Koh Chang

310km (192 miles) E of Bangkok

The capital of Trat Province is Trat, hitherto regarded as the gateway to the Koh Chang Marine National Park. Because of the region's new, improved direct transport links, though, visitors can now head straight to any of three piers to access the park's many islands, and it's becoming less of a gateway. A single, looping, cliff road runs along 90% of both coasts but doesn't yet link the whole island.

Despite having Marine National Park status, many of the islands here have been subjected to large-scale developments. The largest, Koh Chang (Elephant Island), is no exception. For years it was purely a foreign backpacker and Thai weekend getaway, but now, with the opening of Amari Emerald Cove (p. 168) in 2005, a more upscale international clientele is visiting. A luxury marina and condominium complex at Klong Son Bay is planned, a new Dusit Princess resort (ℂ 03955-8055) opened in late 2007, and a super-deluxe Soneva Kiri will open on isolated Koh Kood in 2008. All are bound to bring more visitors, so the environmental impact on the waste disposal system and dry-season water supply is a concern. For now, adventurers will find plenty of activities, including elephant treks, waterfalls, and kayak trips through the mangroves in Koh Chang. The island also has a top-notch vegetarian detox retreat at The Spa, Koh Chang (p. 170). Plus, in dry season (late Oct–May), there's good scuba and snorkeling.

ESSENTIALS
GETTING THERE
By Plane Bangkok Airways (ℂ 02265-5555; www.bangkokair.com) has two to three flights daily depending on the season between Bangkok and Trat, each taking 55

minutes. Airport minivans serve Ao Thammarat pier from where the larger ferries serve Koh Chang, 15 minutes' drive away, and will hang around if a flight is delayed. Prices start around 250B (US$7.15/£3.85). Save time and money by asking your hotel to organize a round-trip transfer (it works out cheaper than a one-way). Some companies offer cheap limousine transfers for around 500B (US$14/£7.50), which often stop everywhere—check before you pay. On Koh Chang itself, **World Travel Service** (*©* **03955-3091,** ext. 4148) at the Amari (see "Where to Stay & Eat," below) offers a one-way (nonstop) transfer for 600B (US$17/£9.25).

By Bus   From Bangkok's **Eastern Bus Terminal** at **Ekkamai** (*©* **02391-2504**) and **Khao San Road** (no phone), there are now dozens of buses direct to the three ferry piers; the trip time is around 5 to 6 hours. Fares range from 190B to 500B (US$5.45–US$14/£2.95–£7.70); the pricier tickets include the ferry. Buses usually stop at Suvarnabhumi International Airport's **Public Bus Terminal** (p. 152).

Daily minivans operate from Pattaya, via Ban Pae (Koh Samet's ferry port). From Pattaya, allow 4 hours and from Ban Pae 2½ hours; costs are 400B (US$11/£6.15) and 300B (US$8.50/£4.60), respectively.

By Car   There are two routes out of Bangkok, the faster Bagna-Trat tollway past Suvarnabhumi International Airport, as well as a route via Highway 3 to Chonburi. From the latter route, take Highway 344 southeast to Klaeng (bypassing Pattaya and Rayong), and then pick up Highway 3 again through Chanthaburi, after which you can turn south to Trat. This route takes about 5 to 6 hours.

GETTING TO KOH CHANG & BEYOND

There are now many ways to bypass Trat and go directly to or from Koh Chang from Bangkok. From Trat airport, **minivans** link passengers to Ao Thammachat pier (for Koh Chang only) or Laem Ngop piers, where during dry season (Oct–May), weatherbeaten ferries cross to the nearby islands of Koh Chang, and much farther afield, Koh Wai, Koh Kood, Koh Maak, and Koh Kham. From Trat, *songtaews* (shared pickups) journey between all piers for around 50B (US$1.40/75p). On the island, white *songtaews* charge from 40B to 100B (US$1.15–US$2.85/60p–£1.55) to take visitors to their hotels. In low season, if you are alone you may be obliged to charter the whole *songtaew* for 500B (US$14/£7.70).

The fastest ferry service departs Ao Thammachat daily from 6:30am to 7pm (trip time is 30 min.) and lands at Koh Chang's Ao Sapparos. Ferries from here are more frequent in high season and on public holidays. One-way fares cost 100B (US$2.85/£1.55), and a return trip is 120B (US$3.40/£1.85). From the ramshackle Center Point Pier, it's 50 minutes and only 80B (US$2.30/£1.25) round-trip. Your slowest option is the cheap but infrequent fishing boat from Laem Ngob, costing 60B (US$1.70/95p) round-trip, which takes an hour to reach Dan Mai Pier on the east of Koh Chang.

VISITOR INFORMATION

The **TAT** has an office in Trat (Moo 1 Trat-Laem Ngop Rd.; *©* **03959-7259**) and provides information about the nearby islands. At Bangkok Airways' information counter in Suvarnabhumi International Airport, or at Koh Chang's hotels, you can pick up the latest *Koh Chang Trat and the Eastern Islands* quarterly with good maps and info.

The island's narrow, mountainous cliff roads are steep and perilous; road fatalities are common. For emergencies, call *©* **1719.** For serious injuries, Trat has a modern hospital at 376 Moo 2, Sukhumvit Road, Wangkhrajae (*©* **03953-2735**).

ORIENTATION

Koh Chang, Thailand's second-largest island after Phuket, is the anchor of the 52-island **Mu Koh Chang Marine National Park.** Thickly forested hills rise from its many bays, which, due to the tides, are narrow and rocky in wet season (June–Oct) and sandier in dry season (Nov–May). Coconut palms (and now billboards) dominate the west coast and roads are hair-raisingly precipitous. Ferry piers are all in the north; fishing villages, mangroves, and orchid farms exist on the flatter and more tranquil east coast. In high season, some dive and boat trips leave from **Bang Bao Bay** on the southernmost tip. The island's west coast is chock-a-block with resorts of all types and prices. At the northern end is **Had Sai Khao (White Sand Beach),** the busiest place to hang out. Its kilometer-long (⅔-mile) sands are now so crowded that it's been divided into "north" and "south" like Samui's Chaweng. More upmarket and family options abound at **Had Khlong Phrao,** and farther south is the ramshackle **Had Kai Be** and last of all, **Bang Bao,** a stilted fishing village that suffers badly from a terrifyingly rollercoaster-like road and trash-strewn mudflats.

WHERE TO STAY & EAT

Note: Currently, all luxury hotels subject credit cards to surcharges and very few places accept American Express.

Five-star resorts on Koh Chang undoubtedly offer the area's best gourmet choices, while roadside diners and seafood shacks are great budget options. **Invito** (© 03955-1326), on Had Sai Khao, serves wood-fired pizzas. Or splash out on the modern Italian fare on offer at Amari's **Sassi** (© 03955-2000) in Klong Phraew. On Had Sai Khao is **Paddy's Palms** (© 084930-3240), serving Sunday roasts and British pub grub as well as Guinness. Farther south, you'll find **Cinnamon** at Aana resort (© 03955-1539), which serves up Thai seafood favorites. **Crust** (© 03955-7157) is a delightful new bakery serving fresh breads, sandwiches, and cakes in Klong Phraew (opposite the temple). For sublime veggie food, head to **The Spa** (© 03955-3093) at Salak Kok; it's worth the hike.

TRAT

If you arrive after the last ferry and get stranded, head into Trat. The **Muang Trad Hotel,** at 4 Sukhumvit Rd. (© 03951-1091), has 144 very basic rooms: A double with a fan costs 450B (US$11/£6.95), while it's 650B (US$16/£10) for a double with air-conditioning.

KOH CHANG

Accommodations-wise, Koh Chang has everything for everyone, from cheap jungle huts to full-on luxury resorts; keep in mind that smaller places will be very much DIY. If you fancy a week of serious detox, colonics, meditation, and yoga, head to The Spa at **Koh Chang** (p. 170)—it's the sole upscale resort on the peaceful, less developed east coast.

Also, nightlife and cheap eats are available all down this coast from **Had Sai Khao** (White Sand Beach), through **Had Kai Mook** (Pearl Beach), **Laem Chaichet, Kai Bae, Had Tha Nam** (Lonely Beach), and **Bai Lan** down to **Bang Bao.** The best seafood is found at no-name shacks on the east coast, though.

AO KLONG SON TO HAD KLONG PRAOW

The buzzing northern strip of Had Sai Khao, Had Kai Mook, or Bang Bae tends to pull in budget travelers, while Had Klong Praew is more upscale. In between, Laem Chai Chet, offers a relatively quieter option.

Expensive

Amari Emerald Cove Resort ★★★ *Kids*   Affordable luxury is the watchword at Koh Chang's most glamorous resort. The Amari Emerald Cove is truly a study in contemporary comfort. Three-story guest room wings skirt a delightful courtyard with walkways and lotus ponds. A huge jade-green pool overlooks the ocean, while there's a smaller bathing pool for kids. Rooms are oversized, with slate tile and wood floors. Outstanding beige marble bathrooms and humongous tubs are an unexpected luxury. Wi-Fi is being installed throughout, and the efficient and helpful staff provides comprehensive tour info.

The resort's restaurants offer spicy Thai fare, modern Italian dishes, or international cuisine. Romantic seafood suppers can be arranged on the quiet, sandy beach, too. The Breezes bar rocks until 11pm (except Mon) with a sizzling Filipino band; meanwhile, the kids can stay home and goggle at free DVDs, or enjoy the pool or foosball in an airy game room. The Sivara Spa offers a range of professional therapies in delightful seaside bungalows.

88/8 Moo 4, Had Klong Phraow, Koh Chang 23170. ⓒ **03955-2000**. Fax 03955-2001. www.amari.com. 165 units. 5,950B–12,915B (US$170–US$396/£92–£199) superior/deluxe double; from 12,250B (US$350/£188) suite. AE, MC, V. **Amenities:** 3 restaurants; 2 bars, 1 w/live music; 2 pools; spa; fitness center; kayaks; dive desk; tour desk; airport transfer; business center; room service; babysitting; laundry service; Wi-Fi. *In room:* A/C, satellite TV, DVD/CD player, minibar, fridge, coffeemaker, hair dryer, safe.

Barali Beach Resort & Spa ★★★   Manicured lawns and central laterite path lend a designer feel to this boutique resort. The lush garden surrounds free-standing villas with unusual high, curved roofs, and two villas with plunge pools hide discreetly behind tall walls. Rooms are luxuriously furnished and have wood floors, canopy beds, plenty of light, and smart bathrooms. The deckside dining is upscale and the delightful new spa gives the resort a pleasant touch of splendor. Since the resort is set back from the busy main road, it's a long walk to the main drag; for those seeking some respite from the city, it's refreshingly far from the madding crowds. Off-season discounts make this a more affordable option.

77 Had Klong Phraow, Koh Chang 23170. ⓒ **03955-7238** or 02652-2195 in Bangkok. Fax 03955-7239. www.barali resort.com. 40 units. 7,000B–12,000B (US$200–US$342/£108–£185) villas. MC, V. **Amenities:** Restaurant; outdoor pool; spa; tour desk; laundry service. *In room:* A/C, TV, fridge, minibar.

Moderate

Koh Chang Tropicana Resort & Spa ★★   Palm-fringed bungalows scattered across gardens with ponds and tropical flora give this sprawling resort a Robinson Crusoe–like feel. A wide range of rustic 1- and 2-story bamboo and rattan rooms are on offer; the pricier ones are freestanding. For a small extra charge, opt for one with sea views. All come with new tiled bathrooms, inside and outdoor showers, and petite sun decks. The majority are surprisingly well maintained. The huge beach restaurant sits on a vast wooden deck next to the crashing surf, which competes with the Filipino band. The nearby Sunset bar is a pleasant place for sundowners. A professional yoga tutor teaches classes near the beach and there are sea kayaks for rent. More rooms will be added in 2008; reservations are best made in advance through the Bangkok office.

26/3 Moo 4, Had Klong Phraow, Koh Chang 23120. ⓒ **03955-7122** or 02642-4420 in Bangkok. Fax 03955-7123. www.kohchangtropicana.net. 77 units. 4,000B–7,375B (US$114–US$210/£62–£113) semi-detached or detached bungalows, and 2-story villas. MC, V. **Amenities:** Restaurant; 2 bars; pool; spa; yoga classes; kayak rentals; tour desk; laundry service; library; Wi-Fi. *In room:* A/C, TV, minibar, fridge, safe.

Inexpensive

There are stacks of inexpensive joints along Had Sai Khao, but some of the most popular larger hotels in the area are the concrete behemoth **Cookies Hotel** (© 03955-1056) and the more rustic **KC Grande Resort** (© 03955-1199; www.kcresortkohchang.com), which has a pool and a slightly wider range of prices.

Baan San Sabay Resort ✿ *Value*   This pocket-sized bungalow resort is on the lower end of Had Sai Khao (White Sand Beach), opposite the Koh Chang Clinic on the beach side. Rooms are clean, with rattan and wood decor, balconies, and small but adequate en-suite shower rooms. All the basics are available, including air-conditioning, making it a good value stopover in the busiest part of the island. It's a few minutes to the roadside restaurants. Since it's so small, you should book well ahead; look out for special Internet room and tour packages.

16/8 Had Sai Khao, Koh Chang 23120. © **03955-1061**. Fax 03955-1063. www.sansabaytravel.com. 6 units. 1,100B–1,800B (US$31–US$51/£17–£28) detached bungalows. No credit cards. **Amenities:** Kayak and motorbike rentals; tour desk; massage; laundry service. *In room:* A/C, satellite TV, dataport, minibar, fridge.

KAI BAE TO BANG BAO
Moderate

KB Resort ✿✿ *Kids*   Off the busy main drag but still only a short walk to shops, this simple bungalow property perches amid well-kept lawns and gardens, a few steps from the beach. Free-standing bungalows (of varying size and quality) sleep up to four—making this a good value for families. Resort accommodations run from basic to top-end beachfront villas—the latter have extra amenities such as DVD players. All rooms are decorated with simple wood furnishings and bright yellow walls. As added bonuses, the beach here is not as crowded as farther north, and there's a decent pool and Thai massage services.

10/16 Moo 4, Had Kai Bae, Koh Chang 23170. © **03955-7125**. www.kbresort.com. 46 units. 1,150B–5,000B (US$32.80–US$143/£18–£77). MC, V. **Amenities:** Restaurant; outdoor pool; Jacuzzi; watersports equipment; tour desk; laundry service; library. *In room:* A/C in some, satellite TV, dataport, fridge.

Siam Beach Resort ✿✿ *Value*   This popular resort looks older than its 2 years, but—for the moment—it is still a charming, good-value hideaway with direct beach access. Accommodations come in 2-story (upper or lower) units, built amid gardens. New, more expensive luxury accommodations (complete with extra luxuries like a DVD player, flatscreen TV, and MP3 player) and pool villas arrived in late 2007, along with a spa. The best value rooms are currently those on the upper floors, located around a lagoon-style pool. All are airy with excellent amenities, bathtubs, and showers. There's delightful in-house dining near the sea and a helpful reception staff that can advise on tours.

100/1 Moo 4, Had Tha Nam (Lonely Beach), Koh Chang 23170. © **08914-65995** (mobile) or 02277-5256. Fax 02417-1948. www.siambeachresort.in.th. 60 units. 1,500B–2,500B (US$43–US$71/£23–£38) standard rooms; 10,000B (US$286/£154) luxury suites. MC, V. **Amenities:** 2 restaurants; beach bar; outdoor pool; kayak rental; tour desk; laundry service; Internet. *In room:* A/C in some, satellite TV, fridge, minibar, hair dryer.

Inexpensive

Remark Puzi Hut ✿   About as far off the track as you can get in Koh Chang, and quite difficult to reach in wet weather, this quaint little collection of thatched huts sits on the southern tip of the island near Bang Bao pier. Choose from seaview or garden-view rooms with fans. Each hut is raised on stilts with a basic bathroom, lots of rattan decor, and is positioned in a shady coconut grove.

11/1 Moo 1 Bang Bao Bay, Koh Chang 23170. © 03955-8116. Fax 03955-8117. 20 units. 400B–700B (US$11.40–US$20/£6.15–£11) double. No credit cards. **Amenities:** Restaurant, laundry service. *In room:* A/C in some.

EAST COAST

The Spa, Koh Chang ⋆⋆ *(Finds* Far away from the busy west coast strip, this delightful health retreat is the newest branch of The Spa, Koh Samui, that has for over a decade offered very reasonably priced 4- to 7-day fasting retreats and colonic cleansing. However, the detox programs are not obligatory to stay as a guest (slightly different rates apply for nonfasters). Rooms are set in stilted 1- and 2-story houses built of rustic recycled wood, which stand almost hidden from view by a lush hillside garden. The resort's rooms are a delightful mix of modern Thai-European with sleek bathrooms of polished terrazzo, DVD players, and good-size balconies. The restaurant is open to anyone and serves superb vegetarian food, smoothies, and powerfully cleansing shots of homegrown wheat grass or the green herb, *gotakula,* but there's plenty of choices for carnivores (or nonfasters) all made of wholesome organic produce. A pool sits among sculpted rocks and tropical flora next to a vast pond, yoga and massage pavilion, and delightful sauna.

15/4 Moo 4, Salak Kok, Koh Chang 23170. © 03955-3091. Fax 03955-3093. www.thesparesorts.net. 26 units. 1,200B–3,950B (US$34–US$113/£18–£61). AE, MC, V. **Amenities:** Restaurant; outdoor pool; Jacuzzi; sauna; tour desk; laundry service; library; Internet. *In room:* A/C, satellite TV w/DVD player, fridge, coffeemaker; hair dryer.

STAYING ACTIVE
DIVING & SNORKELING

Dive and snorkeling trips operate here only in the dry season, from mid-October until May; most trips head to the islands of Koh Khlum and Koh Wai (a particularly beautiful island), or to Koh Phrao (for wreck dives). **Ploy Scuba** (© 086-155-1331; www.ployscuba.com) is just one of the island's many diving multilingual outfits.

KOH CHANG ADVENTURE: HIKING, KAYAKING & ELEPHANT CAMPS

Several well-marked hiking trails criss-cross the island's peaks, but possibly the most enjoyable leads up from Had Klong Phraew to **Klong Plu Waterfall,** which is most spectacular in July through August.

Three operators run elephant treks on Koh Chang, but the best-regarded is **Ban Kwan Chang** in the north at Ban Klong Son village (© 081-919-3995; www.bankwanchang.com). You can book tours of varying durations (starting at 8am) at most hotels, which can involve an elephant safari, a short performance and painting, and then a chance to feed the animals before a splashy bath.

During the dry season, budding bands of Indiana Joneses can explore the east coast's mangrove forests via the **Salak Kok Community Foundation** (© 084-106-7541). The foundation organizes a two-man kayak for 100B (US$2.85/£1.55) per hour, or a more interesting guided mangrove tour for 200B (US$5.70/£3.10). It also arranges sunset suppers on a small boat in Salak Kok bay for 1,400B (US$40/£22) per person (minimum of 4 persons).

More outdoor fun can be had at the new **Treetop Adventure Park** (no phone at press time) in Bai Lan, where you can teeter along walkways suspended over the jungle. Some operators are also offering **Dolphin Tours,** but the keen-eyed may be able to spot these delightful creatures without help in October—they perennially bound alongside the ferries as they cross the short channel.

Southern Peninsula:
The East Coast & Islands

Thailand's slim peninsula extends 1,250km (775 miles) south from Bangkok to the Malaysian border at Sungai Kolok. The towns of Cha-Am and the royal retreat of Hua Hin are just a short hop south of Bangkok, and the ancient temples of Phetchaburi—the last outpost of the Khmer Empire—are a good day trip from there. Passing through coastal towns like Prachuap Kiri Khan and Chumphon and heading farther south, you come to Surat Thani, the jumping-off point for islands in the east: Koh Samui, Koh Pha Ngan, and Koh Tao. If the beach resorts of Phuket dominate the tourist landscape on the west coast, Koh

Samui, a heavily developed resort island in the Gulf of Siam, dominates the east. Nearby Koh Pha Ngan, famed for its wild full-moon parties, continues to gain prominence as a rustic resort destination, as does Koh Tao for its access to some of Thailand's best dive sites.

With its fine islands and beaches, the Gulf of Siam is truly Thai paradise. Whether you come armed with little money and lots of time, or lots of money and little time, there's an adventure and a little bit of heaven for everyone among its palm-draped beaches, lacy coral reefs, small mainland towns and fishing villages, and Buddhist retreats.

1 Hua Hin/Cha-Am

Hua Hin is 265km (164 miles) S of Bangkok; 223km (138 miles) N of Chumphon

Cha-Am is 240km (149 miles) S of Bangkok; 248km (154 miles) N of Chumphon

Hua Hin and Cha-Am, neighboring towns on the Gulf of Thailand, are together the country's oldest resort area. Developed in the 1920s as getaways for Bangkok's elite, the beautiful "Thai Riviera" was a mere 3 or 4 hours' journey from the capital by train, thanks to the southern railway's completion in 1916. The Thai royal family was the first to embrace these two small fishing villages as the perfect location for both summer vacations and health retreats. In 1924, King Vajiravudh (Rama VI) built the royal Mareukatayawan Palace amid the tall evergreens that lined these stretches of golden sand. Around the same time, the Royal Hua Hin golf course opened as the first course in Thailand. As Bangkok's upper classes began building summer bungalows along the shore, the State Railways opened the Hua Hin Railway Hotel for tourists, which stands today as the Sofitel Centara Grand Resort and Villas. To this day, the King of Thailand spends much of his time at his regal residence just north of town (note the constant presence of Royal Thai Naval frigates offshore).

When Pattaya, on Thailand's eastern coast, hit the scene in the 1960s, it lured vacationers away from Hua Hin and Cha-Am with promises of a spicier nightlife. Since then, Pattaya's tourism has grown to a riotous, red-light din, and quiet Hua Hin and Cha-Am are a good, discerning alternative. These days, the younger generation of Thais are driving 45 minutes farther south to Pranburi, where a clutch of Thai-run resorts on isolated beaches are drawing well-heeled families away from Hua Hin.

Plan your trip for the months between November and May for the most sunshine and least rain, but note that from about mid-December to mid-January, Hua Hin and Cha-Am reach peak levels, and bookings should be made well in advance (at a higher rate). Low season means more rain, but rarely all day long.

ESSENTIALS
GETTING THERE
By Plane   Hua Hin's expanded airport has four daily connections to Bangkok's Suvarnabhumi International Airport, with 12-seater Cessna 208B Caravan planes operated by **Siam General Aviation (SGA;** ✆ **02664-6099;** www.sga.co.th). The journey takes 40 minutes. Round-trip fare costs 5,200B (US$148/£80). See "By Car" below for info on driving from Bangkok.

By Train   Both Hua Hin and Cha-Am are reached via the train station in Hua Hin. Ten trains make the daily trek from Bangkok's **Hua Lampong Railway Station** (✆ **02223-7010** or 1690). A second-class seat from Bangkok to Hua Hin generally costs about 262B (US$6.40/£4). The trip takes just over 4 hours.

The **Hua Hin Railway Station** (✆ **03251-1073**) is at the tip of Damnoenkasem Road, which slices through the center of town straight to the beach. Pickup trucks acting as taxis *(songtaew)* and tuk-tuks wait outside to take you to your hotel; fares start at 50B (US$1.20/75p).

By Bus/Minibus   Going by road is the best choice from Bangkok to Hua Hin and the best means of transport are the minibuses that connect with central Cha-Am and Hua Hin. You can arrange **minivan connections** from your hotel in the city, or go to the busy traffic circle at the base of the **Victory Monument** (a stop on the BTS) and look for the minivans that depart when full throughout the day, which cost just 260B (US$7.40/£4) to Hua Hin.

Regular buses depart from **Bangkok's Southern Bus Terminal** (✆ **02434-7192**) every 20 minutes from 5am to 10pm (155B/US$4.40/£2.40). There are also daily buses to Cha-Am hourly between 5am and 8pm (140B/US$4/£2.15).

Buses from Bangkok arrive in **Hua Hin** at the air-conditioned bus station (✆ **03251-1230**) on Srasong Road, 1 block north of Damnoenkasem Road. From here it is easy to find a *songtaew* or tuk-tuk to take you to your destination. The **Cha-Am bus station** (✆ **03242-5307**) is on the main beach road.

By Car   From Bangkok, take Route 35, the Thonburi–Paktho Highway, southwest and allow 2 to 4 hours, depending on traffic.

SPECIAL EVENTS
A free **jazz festival** is held annually in June over 2 or 3 days, featuring local and international bands. The main event attracts thousands of visitors to a unique beach setting, with a stage usually set up in front of the Sofitel hotel. Spectators sit on the sand or can hire chairs. Extra jazz events take place around town at the same time. The event date varies annually. See www.huahinafterdark.com/hua-hin-jazz-festival or contact the Hua Hin Tourist Information Center at ✆ **03251-1047.**

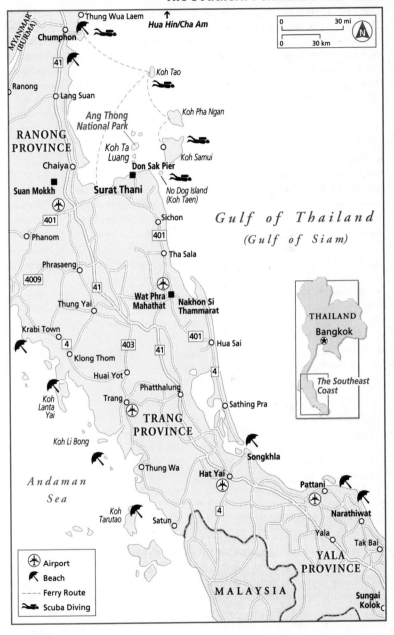

Thung Wua Laem

Hua Hin/Cha Am

Chumphon

41

Ranong

Lang Suan

Koh Tao

Koh Pha Ngan

RANONG
PROVINCE

Ang Thong
National Park

Koh Ta
Luang

Chaiya

Don Sak Pier

Koh Samui

Suan Mokkh

Surat Thani

No Dog Island
(Koh Taen)

401

Sichon

Gulf of Thailand
(Gulf of Siam)

Phanom

401

Phrasaeng

Tha Sala

4009

41

Wat Phra
Mahathat

Thung Yai

Nakhon Si
Thammarat

Krabi Town

4

401

403

41

Hua Sai

Klong Thom

4

Huai Yot

Phatthalung

THAILAND

Bangkok

Trang

Koh
Lanta
Yai

Koh Li Bong

Sathing Pra

The Southeast
Coast

TRANG
PROVINCE

Andaman
Sea

Thung Wa

Hat Yai

Songkhla

Pattani

Koh
Tarutao

Satun

4

Narathiwat

Yala

Tak Bai

YALA
PROVINCE

MALAYSIA

Sungai
Kolok

✈ Airport
⚑ Beach
--- Ferry Route
🐢 Scuba Diving

30 mi
30 km

ORIENTATION

Despite all the tourist traffic, Hua Hin is easy to navigate. The main artery, Petchkasem Road, runs parallel to the waterfront about 4 blocks inland. The wide Damnoenkasem Road cuts through Petchkasem and runs straight to the beach. On the north side of Damnoenkasem toward the waterfront, you'll find a cluster of guesthouses, restaurants, shopping, and nightspots lining the narrow lanes. Across Petchkasem to the west are the bus terminals, railway station, and night market.

Smaller Cha-Am is a 25-minute drive north of Hua Hin along Petchkasem Road. Ruamchit Road, also known as Beach Road, hugs the shore and is lined with shops, restaurants, hotels, and motels. Cha-Am's resorts line the 8km (5-mile) stretch of beach that runs south from the village toward Hua Hin.

GETTING AROUND

By _Songtaew_ Pickup trucks follow regular routes in Hua Hin, passing the railway station and bus terminals at regular intervals. Flag one down that's going in your direction. Fares range from 15B to 30B (35¢–70¢/25p–45p) within town, while stops at outlying resorts will be up to 50B (US$1.20/75p). Trips between Hua Hin and Cha-Am cost between 100B and 200B (US$2.45–US$4.90/£1.55–£3.10).

By Tuk-Tuk Tuk-tuk rides are negotiable; always agree on a price before you start, but expect to pay as little as 30B (85¢/45p) for a ride within town.

By Motorcycle Taxi Within each town, motorcycle taxi fares begin at 20B (50¢/30p). These taxis, whose drivers are identifiable by colorful numbered vests, are a good way to get to your resort if you're in Cha-Am after hours. A ride from there costs about 100B (US$2.45/£1.50).

By _Samlor_ Trishaws, or _samlors,_ can be hired for short distances in town, from 20B (50¢/30p). You can also negotiate an hourly rate.

By Car or Motorcycle **Avis** has a desk at both the Hotel Sofitel Centara Grand in Hua Hin (_©_ **03251-2021**) and the Dusit Resort and Polo Club in Cha-Am (_©_ **03252-0008**). **Budget** has an office at the Grand Hotel (_©_ **03251-4220**). Self-drive rates start at 1,500B (US$37/£23). Call ahead to reserve at least a day in advance. A cheaper alternative is to rent from one of the smalltime agents near the beach on Damnoenkasem Road. A Suzuki Caribbean goes for around 1,100B (US$34/£17) per day. Motorbikes (100cc) are available for 200B (US$4.90/£3.10) per day.

On Foot Hua Hin is a labyrinth of busy streets and narrow alleys with little guesthouses, colorful local bars, and a wide assortment of casual eating venues. Most everything in town is accessible on foot.

VISITOR INFORMATION

The **Hua Hin Tourist Information Center** (_©_ **03251-1047** or 03253-2433) is in the center of town, tucked behind the city shrine at the corner of Damnoenkasem and Petchkasem roads. Opening hours are from 8:30am to 4:30pm daily. In Cha-Am, the **Tourism Authority of Thailand (TAT) office** (_©_ **03247-1005** or 03247-1006) is on the corner of Petchkasem and Narathip roads (the main Beach Road is about 1km/ ⅔ mile away). There are lots of free local event calendars and maps.

FAST FACTS

IN HUA HIN All major banks are along Petchkasem Road to the north of Damnoenkasem, and there are many money changers throughout the town. The main post office (© 03251-1350) is on Damnoenkasem Road near the Petchkasem intersection. Both Hua Hin and Cha-Am have Internet cafes along the more-traveled shopping streets. The **Hua Hin Hospital** (© 03252-0371) is located in the north of town along Petchkasem Road. Call the **Tourist Police** for either town at © 03251-5995.

IN CHA-AM   Banks are centered along Petchkasem Road, and the post office is on Beach Road. The **Thonburi Cha-Am Hospital** (© 03243-3903) is off Narathip Road. Internet access is available in a few places along Beach Road.

WHAT TO SEE & DO

The stunning Khmer-style temples of **Phetchaburi** (see "Side Trips from Hua Hin & Cha-Am," at the end of this section) are the most significant cultural sites near Hua Hin and Cha-Am, but really what attracts so many to this area is what first attracted the Thai royal family: proximity to the capital; lovely beaches; watersports; and activities such as golf, scuba, and horseback riding. Hua Hin also supports fine resorts such as The Hilton, Hua Hin, which come with great facilities, extensive dining, and top-notch spas.

One of the oldest resorts here is the newly rechristened **Sofitel Centara Grand Resort and Villas,** originally built for Thai royalty and their guests in the 1920s. Visitors are welcome to wander around its pretty colonial buildings and gardens (don't miss the giant topiary elephant). High Tea at the Sofitel costs 450B per person (US$13/£6.90) on weekdays, and 600B (US$17/£9.25) on weekends. It offers a chance not just to sip tea and nibble scones in a lovely original wing of the hotel, but transports guests back in time to the era when Hua Hin was a getaway purely for the Thai upper crust.

Don't miss the town's **Night Market** (on Decha Nuchit Rd., on the northern end at town center), which is busy from dusk to late with small food stalls and vendors. There are also lots of shops in and around the central beachfront, and Hua Hin—not unlike most resort areas in Thailand—is a good place to get that suit made or buy your brother a Buddha ornament.

The big Buddha and viewpoint from spiky **Khao Takiap (Chopstick Peaks)**—a small cape just a bit south of Hua Hin (hop on a tuk-tuk for 100B/US$2.85/£1.55)— is a pretty area worth a visit. Also near Hua Hin is the **Mareukatayawan Palace,** or the Teakwood Mansion (no phone; daily 8:30am–4pm; free admission). Built and designed in 1924 by King Rama VI, it served for many years as the royal summer residence and is now open to the public.

Horseback riding is popular along the busy beaches at Hua Hin and Cha-Am. Frisky young fillies can be rented by the hour from 600B (US$17/£9.25). At 100B (US$2.85/£1.55) for 10-minute kids' rides, you can ride with a Thai escort leading the horse (safest idea), or on your own if you're confident. If you're interested, take a walk down to the beach and you'll be besieged by young men eager to rent out their horses.

See "Side Trips from Hua Hin & Cha-Am" at the end of this section for trips to nature sites.

WHERE TO STAY IN HUA HIN
VERY EXPENSIVE

Chiva-Som International Health Resort ✿✿✿   One of the finest high-end health resorts in the region, this ultra-peaceful campus is a sublime collection of handsome pavilions, bungalows, and central buildings dressed in fine teak and sea-colored tiles nestled in 7 acres of exotic tropical gardens beside the beach. Fine accommodations aside, what brings so many to Chiva-Som are the extensive fitness, spa, and holistic health facilities. There are more than 120 treatments and fitness programs, including tai chi, pilates, yoga, and personal training.

A stay at Chiva-Som is a chance to escape the workaday world and focus on the development of body and mind. Leave the kids at home, turn off the cellphone, and change your suit for loose-fitting cotton, because even if you just come to relax, a visit to Chiva-Som is proactive. Upon check-in, you'll fill out an extensive survey, have a brief medical check, and meet with a counselor who can tailor a program to fit your needs, goals, budget, or package you have booked (there is a wide range). From there, guests might focus on early morning yoga, stretching, and tough workouts, or go for gentle massages, aromatherapy, even isolation chambers and past-life regression workshops. The choices are many, and the staff and facilities are unmatched in the region.

The resort's spa cuisine is not all granola and oats, but simple, healthy fare, and a nice bond develops between guests and staff in weekly barbecues and frequent "mocktail" parties. The spa treatments are fantastic: Don't pass up their signature Chiva-Som Massage. Day spa visitors are welcome. It all comes with a high price tag, but it is worth it.

73/4 Petchkasem Rd., Hua Hin 77110 (5-min. drive south of Hua Hin). ℂ 03253-6536. Fax 03251-1615. www. chivasom.com. 57 units. All double rates are quoted per person. Contact the resort directly about spa and health packages. 14,350B (US$410/£221) oceanview double; 18,300B (US$525/£282) pavilion; from 32,000B (US$915/£492) suite. Nightly rate includes 3 spa cuisine meals per day, health and beauty consultations, daily massage, and participation in fitness and leisure activities. AE, DC, MC, V. **Amenities:** 2 restaurants; indoor and outdoor pools; golf course nearby; fitness center w/personal trainer and exercise classes; his-and-hers spas w/steam and hydrotherapy treatments; watersports equipment; bike rental; library; tour desk; airport transfer; salon; 24-hr. room service; same-day laundry service/dry cleaning; nonsmoking rooms. In room: A/C, satellite TV, minibar, fridge, safe.

EXPENSIVE

Anantara Resort and Spa 🏵🏵   A series of elegantly designed Thai-style pavilions are set in 16 acres of possibly the most exotic gardens you'll see in Thailand, maintained by 20 gardeners just north of Hua Hin. A lovely tapestry hangs prominently in the open-air sala-style lobby, which is tastefully decorated with ornately carved teak wooden lanterns, warm wood floors, and oversize furniture with Thai cushions. The Lagoon is an area of teak pavilions surrounded by lily ponds, and from the hotel's most luxurious rooms, you can hear chirping frogs and watch buzzing dragonflies from wide balconies. Other rooms cluster around a manicured courtyard. Consistent with the lobby, rooms are furnished Thai style with teak and rattan furniture. Superior rooms have a garden view and deluxe rooms overlook the sand and sea. Beach terrace rooms have large patios perfect for private barbecues. Junior suite rooms have enormous aggregate bathtubs that open to guest rooms by a sliding door. Fine dining includes an Italian restaurant and the resort's spa is large and luxurious.

43/1 Petchkasem Beach Rd., Hua Hin 77110. ℂ 03252-0250. Fax 03252-0259. www.anantara.com. 197 units. 6,825B–10,675B (US$195–US$305/£105–£164) double; 7,700B (US$220/£118) terrace double; suite from 22,225B (US$635/£342). AE, DC, MC, V. **Amenities:** 4 restaurants; lounge; outdoor pool w/children's pool; outdoor lit tennis courts; fitness center; spa; watersports equipment and instruction; bike and motorcycle rental; children's playground; tour desk; car-rental desk; airport transfer; shopping arcade; salon; 24-hr. room service; babysitting; same-day laundry service/dry cleaning; nonsmoking rooms. In room: A/C, satellite TV, minibar, fridge, coffee/tea-making facilities, hair dryer, safe.

Hilton Hua Hin Resort and Spa 🏵🏵🏵   Right in the heart of downtown Hua Hin, this 17-story tower block overlooks the main beach. The staff is courteous and professional and the hotel is geared for families, with many facilities for kids. The beachside pool is luxurious. The property displays a top international standard and its environs are ideal for strolling the main beach area, in-town shopping, and nightlife. The breakfast buffet is spectacularly big. One restaurant features an in-house brewery producing three beers.

33 Narsdamri Rd., Hua Hin 77110. ✆ 03251-2888. Fax 02250-0999. www.huahin.hilton.com. 296 units. 5,575B–7,875B (US$165–US$225/£86–£121) double; from 10,080B (US$288/£155) suite. AE, DC, MC, V. **Amenities:** 3 restaurants; 2 bars; outdoor pool; 2 tennis courts; health club; spa w/massage; children's playroom; tour desk; car-rental desk; shopping arcade; salon; 24-hr. room service; babysitting; laundry service; dry cleaning. In room: A/C, satellite TV w/in-house movies, minibar, fridge, coffeemaker, hair dryer, safe.

Hua Hin Marriott Resort & Spa ★★★ Kids

From the giant swinging couches in the main lobby to the large central pavilions, this hotel is done up in a grand, if exaggerated, Thai style. The Marriott attracts large groups but is a good choice for families. Ponds, pools, boats, golf, tennis, and other sport venues dot the jungle-like grounds leading to their open beach area, and there is a good kids' club. The hotel is relatively far from the busy town center and provides shuttle service. Deluxe rooms are the best choice—large, amenity-filled, and facing the sea. Terrace rooms at beachside are worth the bump up. The spa is luxurious, too.

107/1 Petchkasem Beach Rd., Hua Hin 77110. ✆ 800/228-9290 in the U.S., or 03251-1881. Fax 03251-2422. www.marriot.com. 216 units. 5,950B (US$170/£92) double; 6,650B–8,400B (US$190–US$240/£102–£129) beach terrace; from 12,950B (US$370/£199) suite. AE, DC, MC, V. **Amenities:** 3 restaurants; lounge; outdoor pool; golf course nearby; outdoor lit tennis courts; fitness center; spa; watersports equipment; bike rental; children's playground and zoo; tour desk; car-rental desk; airport transfer; shopping arcade; salon; 24-hr. room service; babysitting; same-day laundry service/dry cleaning; nonsmoking rooms. In room: A/C, satellite TV, minibar, coffee/tea-making facilities, hair dryer, safe.

Sofitel Centara Grand Resort ★★★

A stay at the Sofitel Centara is a luxurious romp into another time. Though it opened in 1922, it still offers the classiest accommodations in the area. Renovations over the years have expanded the hotel into a large and modern full-facility hotel without sacrificing a bit of its former charm. The whitewashed buildings, shaded verandas and walkways, fine wooden details, red-tile roofs, and immaculate gardens with topiaries create a cool, calm, colonial effect. There is a small hotel museum of photography and memorabilia, and the original 14 bedrooms are preserved for posterity. The original rooms have their unique appeal, but the newer rooms are larger, brighter, and more comfortable. Though they boast furnishings that reflect the hotel's old beach resort feel, they are still modern and cozy.

Sofitel's three magnificent outdoor pools are finely landscaped and have sun decks under shady trees. The new Spa Health Club, in its own beachside bungalow, provides full-service health and beauty treatments, and the fitness center is extensive. They have Wi-Fi in public spaces, and there is a can-do attitude to the service. The adjoining **Centara Hua Hin Village** (✆ 03251-2021) is now under Sofitel management and features luxurious private bungalows (41 in total) at seaside. Come for the Afternoon Tea special at least, and don't miss their popular Japanese restaurant, **Hagi,** which is street-side on Damnoenkasem Road and popular with outside guests.

1 Damnoenkasem Rd., Hua Hin 77110 (in the center of town by the beach). ✆ 800/221-4542 in the U.S., or 03251-2021. Fax 03251-1014. www.sofitel.com. 248 units (including Centara Hua Hin Village). 6,400B–7,600B (US$156–US$185/£98–£117) double; from 10,000B (US$244/£154) suite. DC, MC, V. **Amenities:** 5 restaurants; lounge; bar; 3 outdoor pools; putting green and miniature golf; golf course nearby; outdoor lit tennis courts; new fitness center; spa w/massage; watersports equipment; bike rental; kids' club; daily craft and language lessons; nature tours; billiards room; tour desk; car-rental desk; airport transfer; business center; shopping arcade; salon; 24-hr. room

service; babysitting; same-day laundry service/dry cleaning; nonsmoking rooms; executive floor. *In room:* A/C, satellite TV, minibar, fridge, hair dryer, safe.

MODERATE

There are lots of mid- and low-range choices in and around central Hua Hin. **City Beach Resort** (16 Damnoenkasem Rd.; ℂ 03251-2870; www.citybeach.co.th) abuts the Hilton and is not bad in a pinch (rooms from 1,920B/US$55/£30), and nearby **Sirin Hotel** (ℂ 03251-1150) has basic rooms from 1,600B (US$46/£25) comparable to those below, and with an outdoor pool.

Jed Pee Nong Hotel   This hotel is a clean and comfy budget choice less than 100m from the Sofitel. There is a small pool and the simple balconied rooms are carpeted and have air-conditioning. The higher-priced rooms have better decor and hug the pool, cabana-style. Its friendly staff and decent rates make it popular with Thai weekenders as well as tourists, so book well ahead.

17 Damnoenkasem Rd., Hua Hin 77110 (on the main street near the town beach). ℂ 03251-2381. Fax 03253-22036. www.jedpeenonghotel-huahin.com. 25 units. 1,400B–1,700B (US$40–$48/£22–£26) double. No credit cards. **Amenities:** Restaurant (international); pool; laundry service. *In room:* Minibar.

PP Villa   It's not the Ritz, but it is comfortable. You'll get little more than basic rooms with parquet floors and balconies here, but you'll be close to the central beach and shopping. Plus, the staff members are super-friendly and there's a pool.

11 Damnoenkasem Rd., Hua Hin 77110 (near the central beach area and shopping). ℂ 03253-3785. Fax 03251-1216. 52 units. 1,200B–1,500B (US$29–US$37/£18–£23) double. MC, V. **Amenities:** Restaurant; outdoor pool; laundry service. *In room:* A/C, TV, fridge.

WHERE TO STAY IN CHA-AM

Along the quiet stretch between Hua Hin and Cha-Am there are a number of fine resorts (and a growing number of condos). Cha-Am village itself is a bit raucous (the Ocean City, New Jersey, to Hua Hin's The Hamptons) and most stay outside of town; for in-town lodging, try the Methavalai, below.

EXPENSIVE

Dusit Resort and Polo Club ℛ   A "polo club" in theme only; the Dusit has all the amenities of a fine resort. The elegant marble lobby features bronze horses and hunting tableaux; hall doors have polo mallet handles and other equine-themed decor. Guest rooms, renovated in 2007, carry the same theme and are spacious, with big marble bathrooms. Room rates vary with the view, although every room's balcony faces the lushly landscaped pool. Ground-floor rooms are landscaped for privacy, with private verandas leading to the pool and the beach. Suites are enormous, with elegant living rooms, and a full pantry and dressing area. For all its air of formality, the resort is great for those who prefer swimsuits and T-shirts to riding jodhpurs, and a relaxed holiday air pervades. All sorts of watersports are available on the quiet beach. It is a bit far from both Hua Hin and Cha-Am, but the resort is completely self-contained.

1349 Petchkasem Rd., Cha-Am 76120. ℂ 03252-0009. Fax 03252-0296. www.dusit.com. 300 units. 6,300B–7,000B (US$180–US$200/£97–£108) double; 12,000B (US$343/£185) Landmark suite. AE, DC, MC, V. **Amenities:** 5 restaurants; lounge; huge outdoor pool; mini-golf; golf course nearby; outdoor lit tennis courts; squash courts; fitness center; equestrian center and horseback riding; watersports equipment; bike and motorcycle rental; billiards and game room; tour desk; car-rental desk; airport transfer; business center; shopping arcade; salon; 24-hr. room service; babysitting; same-day laundry service/dry cleaning; nonsmoking rooms; executive floor. *In room:* A/C, satellite TV, minibar, fridge, coffee/tea-making facilities, hair dryer, safe.

MODERATE

The Cha-Am Methavalai Hotel 🎇🎇   The Methavalai is the best of the rag-tag collection in busy Cha-Am town. Large, clean, and on the main Beach Road in Cha-Am, it is convenient for the restaurants, shopping, and small nightlife scene in town. Guest rooms are painted from a pastel palette and are peaceful, all with balconies and sun deck and clean but not luxurious bathrooms. Rooms look out over the good-size central pool (front-facing rooms can be a bit noisy, though). If you want to stay in downtown Cha-Am, this is the best choice of the lot. There's even a Japanese restaurant on site—a rarity in these parts.

220 Ruamchit Rd., Cha-Am 76120. ✆ **03247-1028.** Fax 03247-1590. www.methavalai.com. 118 units. 3,500B (US$100/£54) double; from 4,000B (US$114/£62) pavilion and suite. AE, DC, MC, V. **Amenities:** 2 restaurants; lounge; pool; golf course nearby; tour desk; salon; limited room service; massage; babysitting; same-day laundry service. *In room:* A/C, satellite TV, minibar, fridge.

Holiday Inn Regent Beach Cha-Am 🎇🎇   No relation to the Regent chain, this sprawling beachside property was taken over by the Holiday Inn group in 2006. It consists of three resorts with a total of 708 rooms, including the more luxurious Regency Wing and Regent Chalet. There are lots of services, large pools, watersports, squash, and a small fitness area. The main resort is a massive courtyard, and the Chalet is a separate, quieter bungalow facility (the best choice). Standard rooms are comfortable and affordable, done up like the average chain hotel. The resort is on the road between Hua Hin and Cha-Am and a long ride to either; there's a shuttle bus to Hua Hin and private taxis outside. This place is always busy on the weekends with Bangkok visitors.

849/21 Petchkasem Rd., Cha-Am 76120. ✆ **03245-1240.** Fax 03245-1277. www.regent-chaam.com. 708 units. 3,500B–4,800B (US$100–US$137/£54–£74) double; from 6,300B (US$180/£97) suite. AE, MC, V. **Amenities:** 3 restaurants; lounge; 3 pools; outdoor lit tennis courts; squash courts; fitness center; watersports equipment; bike and motorcycle rental desk; game room; tour desk; airport transfer; business center; salon; 24-hr. room service; massage; babysitting; same-day laundry service/dry cleaning. *In room:* A/C, satellite TV, minibar, fridge.

WHERE TO DINE IN HUA HIN

If you wake up at about 7am and walk to the piers in either Hua Hin or Cha-Am, you can watch the fishing boats return with their loads. Workers sort all varieties of creatures, packing them on ice for distribution around the country. In both Hua Hin and Cha-Am, look for the docks at the very north end of the beach; nearby open-air restaurants serve fresh seafood at a fraction of prices inland.

The Night Market on Dechanuchit Road, west of Petchkasem Road in the north end of town, is a great place for authentic local eats for very little. The resorts have more restaurants than there is room to list, and no matter where you stay, you'll have great dining options in-house. In town, there are lots of small storefront eateries and tourist cafes as well.

An old expat favorite, **Il Gelato Italiano** (✆ **03253-3753**) on Damnoenkasem Road, near Jed Pee Nong Hotel, serves the real deal: home-made Italian gelato. It's a good place to meet, greet, and people-watch.

Itsara 🎇 THAI   In a two-story seaside home built in the 1920s, this restaurant has real laid-back charm, from the noisy, open kitchen to the terrace seating and views of the beach—it's quite atmospheric and a good place to get together with friends and enjoy the good life. Specialties include a sizzling hot plate of glass noodles with prawns, squid, pork, and vegetables. A variety of fresh seafood and meats are prepared steamed or deep-fried, and can be served with salt, chili, or red curry paste.

7 Napkehard St. (seaside, a 50B/US$1.20/75p *samlor* ride north from the town center). ℭ 03251-4517. Reservations recommended for Sat dinner. Main courses 60B–290B (US$1.50–US$7.10/90p–£4.45). MC, V. Mon–Fri 10am–midnight; Sat–Sun 2pm–midnight.

Meekaruna Seafood SEAFOOD   This small family-run restaurant, on a wooden deck overlooking the main fishing pier in Hua Hin, serves fresh fish prepared as you like it. Though it's surrounded by other seafood restaurants, there's no carnival barker out front to drag you in, and such a lack of hype alone is refreshing. They have great *tom yum goong*—also try the fried crab cakes, fish served in any number of styles, and baby clams fried in chili sauce.

26/1 Naratdamri Rd. (near the fishing pier). ℭ 03251-1932. Main courses 120B–500B (US$2.95–US$12/£1.85–£7.70). AE, DC, MC, V. Daily 10am–10pm.

ACTIVITIES
GOLF
Probably the most popular activity in Hua Hin and Cha-Am is **golf,** and the town boasts some fine courses. Reservations are suggested and necessary most weekends. Many of the hotels run FOC (free of charge) shuttles, and most clubs can arrange pickup and drop-off to any hotel.

- **Palm Hills Golf Resort and Country Club,** 1444 Petchkasem Road, Cha-Am (ℭ 03252-0800), just north of Hua Hin, is a picturesque course set among rolling hills and jagged escarpments (greens fees: 2,000B/US$57/£30.75; daily 6am-6pm).
- **Royal Hua Hin Golf Course,** Damnoenkasem Road near the Hua Hin Railway Station (ℭ 03251-2475), is Thailand's first championship golf course, opened in 1924. Don't miss the many topiary figures along its fairways (greens fees: 1,700B/US$48/£26.15; daily 6am–6pm).
- **Springfield Royal Country Club,** 193 Huay-Sai Nua, Petchkasem Road, Cha-Am (ℭ 03247-1303), designed by Jack Nicklaus in 1993, is in a beautiful valley setting—the best by far (greens fees: 2,800B/US$80/£43.05; daily 6am-6pm).

WATERSPORTS
While most of the larger resorts will plan watersports activities for you upon request, you can make arrangements with small operators on the beach (for significant savings). Most resorts forbid noisy **jet skis,** but the beaches are lined with young entrepreneurs renting them out for 500B (US$12/£7.70) per hour. Windsurfers and Hobie Cats are for rent at most resorts or with small outfits along the beach (starting at 300B/US$8.60/£4.60 and 600B/US$17/£9.25 per hr., respectively).

Call **Western Tours** at ℭ 03253-3303 and ask about their **snorkeling trips** to outer islands for about 2,100B (US$60/£32) per person. Their office is at 11 Damnoenkasem Rd. in the city center.

SPAS
Hua Hin is famous for its fine spas, and each of the top resorts features excellent services (see the Marriot, Anantara, and Hilton in "Where to Stay in Hua Hin," above). There are lots of small massage storefronts in Hua Hin, but this is a great place to go upscale and get the royal treatment.

The best choice for a day of pampering is at **Chiva-Som** ᴿᴿᴿ (73/4 Petchkasem Rd., Hua Hin; 5-min. drive south of town; ℭ 03253-6536), where you pay a lot and get a lot. There's nothing like it.

Far south of town, luxury **Evason Resort and Spa** ✵✵ (9 Paknampran Beach, Pranburi 77220; 30km/19 miles south of Hua Hin; © 03263-2111) is a destination spa worth visiting in and of itself, but also a fine stop for high-end day treatments. It's comparable in quality with Chiva-Som.

SHOPPING

Hua Hin is a popular tourist town and close to the country's largest city, and the result is all of the good shopping services you would find in Bangkok—from fine tailors and jewelers to souvenir shops. The **Day Market** along Damnoenkasem Road near the beach features local crafts made from seashells, batik clothing, and other handicrafts. The 2-block-long **Night Market** on Dechanuchit Road west of Petchkasem Road is a great stop for tasty treats and fun trinkets. Beware of fake brands.

NIGHTLIFE

For nightlife, your best bet is Hua Hin. A 15-minute stroll through the labyrinth of *sois* between Damnoenkasem, Poolsuk, and Dechanuchit roads near the beach reveals all sorts of small places to stop for a cool cocktail and some fun.

SIDE TRIPS FROM HUA HIN & CHA-AM
PHETCHABURI ✵✵
Phetchaburi, one of the country's oldest towns, possibly dates from the same period as Ayutthaya and Kanchanaburi, though it is believed to have been first settled during the Dvaravati period. After the rise of the Thai nation, it served as an important royal military city and was home to several princes who were groomed for ascendance to the throne. Phetchaburi's palace and historically significant temples make it an excellent day trip. It is just 1 hour from Hua Hin.

The main attraction is **Phra Nakhon Khiri** (© 03242-8539), a summer palace in the hills overlooking the city. Built in 1858 by King Mongkut (Rama IV), it was intended as not only a summer retreat for the royal family, but for foreign dignitaries as well. Combining Thai, European, and Chinese architectural styles, the palace buildings include guesthouses and a royal Khmer-style *chedi,* or temple. The Phra Thinang Phetphum Phairot Hall is open for viewing and contains period art and antiques from the household. Once accessible only via a 4km (2½-mile) hike uphill, you'll be happy to hear there's a funicular railway (it's called a "cable car," but that's not an accurate description) to bring you to the top for 40B (US$1/60p). It's open Monday through Friday 8:15am to 5pm and Saturday and Sunday from 8:15am to 5:50pm. Admission is 45B (US$1.30/70p).

Another fascinating sight at Phetchaburi, the **Khao Luang Cave,** houses more than 170 Buddha images underground. Outside the cave, hundreds of noisy monkeys descend upon the parking lot and food stalls looking for handouts. Sometimes you'll find a guide outside who'll escort you through the caves for a small fee.

Wat Yai Suwannaram is a stunning royal temple built during the Ayutthaya period. The teak ordination hall was moved from Ayutthaya after the second Burmese invasion on the city (don't miss the axe-chop battle scar on the building's carved doors). Inside there are large religious murals featuring Brahmans, hermits, giants, and deities.

Another *wat* with impressive paintings is **Wat Ko Keo Suttharam,** also built in the 17th century. These representational murals, painted in the 1730s, even depict some Westerners: There are several panels depicting the arrival in the Ayutthaya court of European courtesans and diplomats (including a Jesuit dressed in Buddhist garb).

Another fabulous temple is **Wat Kamphaeng Laeng,** originally constructed during the reign of Khmer ruler King Jayavarman VII (1157–1207) as a Hindu shrine. Made of laterite, it was once covered in decorative stucco, some of which still remains. Each of the five *prangs* (towers) was devoted to a deity—the center *prang* to Shiva is done in a classical Khmer style. During the Ayutthaya period, it was converted to a Buddhist temple.

The temples of Phetchaburi are best visited during daylight hours, from early morning until 5pm.

Lastly, the **Phra Ram Raja Nivesana,** or **Ban Puen Palace** (© 03242-8506; daily 8am–4pm, free admission) is a nice stop. A royal palace built by Rama V, the German-designed grand summer home comes alive with colorful tile work, neoclassical marble columns, and floor motifs. Today it sits on military grounds and is a popular venue for ceremonies and large occasions.

Western Tours, 11 Damnoenkasem Rd. (© 03253-3303), has day excursions for 850B (US$24/£13) per person, though any of these sites can be seen on a day trip by rented car.

KHAO SAM ROI YOT NATIONAL PARK

Just a 40-minute drive south of Hua Hin, Khao Sam Roi Yot, or the "Mountain of Three Hundred Peaks," is comparatively small in relation to the nation's other parks, but offers great short hikes to panoramic views of the sea. There is abundant wildlife here (seen only if you're lucky). Of the park's two caves, Kaew Cave is the most interesting, housing a *sala* pavilion that was built in 1890 for King Chulalongkorn. For more information, call the park services at © 02561-2919. To arrange a tour, call **Western Tours** (© 03253-3303; 850B/US$24/£13 per person). A half-day trip to the Pala-U waterfall close to the Burmese border (63km/39 miles west of Hua Hin) is another nature trekking option. Nature trails take you through hills and valleys until you end up at the falls. Western Tours does the trip for 950B (US$27/£14.60) per person. The driver can stop at the **Dole Thailand pineapple factory** for a tour and tasting (© 03257-1177; daily 9am–4pm; 200B/US$5.70/£3.10 admission), and the Kaew Cave.

PRACHUAP KHIRI KHAN

If you've had enough of Thailand's many overdeveloped beach areas, the small town and beaches near Prachuap Khiri Khan (just a 1-hr. drive south of Hua Hin) might just be the answer. Some of the kindest people in Thailand live here, the beaches are lovely and little-used, and the town begs a wander. There is little in the way of fine dining and accommodations, but it is a good stop on the way south to Chumphon.

2 Chumphon

463km (287 miles) S of Bangkok; 193km (120 miles) N of Surat Thani

Chumphon was once known for simply being a stop on the way south; plans are now under way to transform this little town into a tourist hub. Today it's got a new pier, completed in 2007, and is a busy transit point for boats to Koh Tao and other islands. It's also got **Ang Thong Marine National Park** due south, virtually on its doorstep, an interesting (and still largely unexplored) diving area. Surrounded by its famous fruit orchards inland, and a couple of great beaches—like **Sairi Beach,** 22km (13 miles) east of town, and **Thung Wua Laen Beach,** 12km (7½ miles) northeast, it's a good place to slow down and take time out.

ESSENTIALS
GETTING THERE
By Plane Currently no flights serve Chumphon. (Air Andaman's flights are defunct, despite website info that hints to the contrary).

By Train Eleven daily trains stop in Chumphon from Bangkok. Call Bangkok **Hua Lampong Railway Station** (℅ 02223-7010 or 1690) for info. The priciest second-class sleeper fare to Bangkok is 770B (US$20/£12), but prices vary according to upper/lower berths and if the carriage is air-conditioned. **Chumphon Railway Station** (℅ 077-511103) is on Krom Luang Chumphon Road, where there are oodles of restaurants and guesthouses.

By Bus Standard air-conditioned buses depart from Bangkok's Southern Bus Terminal (℅ 02435-1199). The trip lasts 7 hours and costs 340B (US$11/£5.25). The main Chumphon bus terminal (℅ 07750-2725) is 16km (10 miles) north of the town center (a tuk-tuk will cost 100B/US$3.30/£1.55), so jump off in town if your bus stops there first.

By Ferry Songserm (℅ 07750-6205; www.songserm-expressboat.com) and **Lomprayah** (℅ 07755-8212; www.lomprayah.com) run daily express boat services connecting Chumphon with Koh Tao, Koh Pha Ngan, Koh Samui, and Surat Thani with connecting buses from the station. There's also a night boat. Expensive (but totally unecofriendly) speedboats run in dry season.

By Car From Bangkok, use Highway No. 4 or Highway No. 35 (Thon Buri-Pak Tho) and join Highway No. 4; continue past Petchaburi, Prachuap Khiri Khan to Chumphon junction, and then turn left along Highway No. 4001 to reach town.

VISITOR INFORMATION
A tourist information office is on the corner of Sala Daeng and Krom Luang Chumphon Roads. A handful of local tour operators is located on Tha Taphao Rd., such as **CS Leisure Travel** (℅ 07750-3001), **New Infinity Travel** (℅ 07750-1937), or **Suwannatee Tour** (℅ 07750-4901), a 10-minute walk southeast of the train station.

GETTING AROUND
By *Songtaew* *Songtaews,* or covered pickups, cruise the main roads and charge about 20B to 40B per trip (60¢–US$1.15/30p–60p).

By Motorcycle Taxi Look for the colored vests designating motorcycle taxi drivers, and bargain hard. Trips start from 20B (57¢/30p).

By Taxi Taxis stop behind the old market, opposite Chumphon Bus Terminal. Vehicles can be hired to Lang Suan, Ranong, and Surat Thani; inquire at your hotel for details.

ORIENTATION
Chumphon's center is small enough to negotiate on foot: Krom Luang Chumphon Road, near the railway station, is the place for dining and accommodations options, and Tha Taphao Road houses a small bus terminal and a variety of tour operators.

FAST FACTS
Numerous **banks** sit on Sala Daeng Road, which runs parallel to Tha Taphao Road. The main **post office** on Poramin Mankha Road is out of the town center; mail can generally be sent from your hotel. For **Internet service,** the guesthouses and travel agencies along Tha Taphao Road can all assist. For **police** assistance, call ℅ 07751-1505.

WHAT TO SEE & DO

Most guesthouses and tourist offices can arrange rafting trips and tours to local water-falls in the nearby rainforest. The best beaches are **Sairi Beach,** for island excursions, and **Thung Wua Laen** beach to the northeast of town, where kite-boarding is proving popular. Diving over Chumphon's offshore pinnacles reveals pristine reefs and abundant marine life—including whale sharks (in season), turtles, and a range of tropical fish.

The town of **Ranong** straddles the Myanmar/Thai border west of Chumphon and is a popular daytrip because of its **hot springs,** but inquire about visas before you book.

The **Chumphon National Museum** (Office of Archeology, Sam Kaew Hill, Na Cha Ang subdistrict; ② **07751-4105;** 30B/86¢/45p) is open 9am–4pm from Wednesday to Sunday and covers historic events such as the Japanese invasion of 1941.

WHERE TO STAY

EXPENSIVE

Tusita Resort & Spa Hotel ✦✦✦   This swish new resort of petite red-tiled villas is virtually unknown to tourists and takes Chumphon accommodations to a new level. Sitting on unspoiled Arunothai beach, Thai exteriors shield homely interiors that fuse flamboyant colors. Elegant bathrooms and an abundance of light are the main advantages, and the beach villas couldn't get closer to the sea if they tried. Service is good (though it could be exceptional, given the prices). A big plus is the high-standard restaurant.

259/9 Moo 1, Arunothai Beach, Paktako, Chumphon 86230. ② **07757-9073.** Fax 07757-9050. www.tusitaresort. com. 22 units. From 5,700B (US$163/£88) double; 18,500B (US$528/£285) beachside villas. AE, MC, V. **Amenities:** Restaurant; bar; outdoor pool; fitness center; spa; fishing; scuba diving; snorkeling; game room; business services; laundry service; free Wi-Fi. *In room:* A/C, satellite TV, coffee-making facilities, minibar, hair dryer, safe.

MODERATE

Chumphon Cabana Resort and Diving Center ✦✦ *Value*   Located 30 minutes from town on the fabulously tranquil Thung Wua Laen Beach, this low-rise, family-friendly resort of staggered concrete rooms and pretty bungalows is looking a bit worn now, but still has great views, a 30m pool, and, most importantly, an outstanding reputation for its ecological work. Part of the pull is the long list of activities and the organic rice and vegetable gardens. Produce from the latter gets served up in the superb seafood restaurant that's on site.

69 Moo 8, Thung Wua Laen Beach, Chumphon 86230. ② **07756-0245.** Fax 07756-0247. www.cabana.co.th. 128 units. 1,500B (US$50/£23) double; 1,850B (US$62/£28) bungalow. AE, MC, V. **Amenities:** Restaurant; lounge; outdoor pool; children's pool; watersports equipment and dive center; bike rental; laundry service. *In room:* A/C, satellite TV, minibar.

INEXPENSIVE

Budget hotels with decent-enough amenities include **Sri Chumphon Hotel** (② **07751-1280**) on Sala Daeng Road. On Thai Taphao Road, there's **Chumphon Gardens Hotel** (② **07750-6888**) and the perennially popular **Suda Guest House** (Soi Bangkok Bank; ② **07750-4366**). Expect to pay between 200B and 490B (US$5.70–US$14/£3.10–£7.55) at any of these properties.

WHERE TO DINE

The best bites can be had at the diners scattered around Tha Tapao and Krom Luang Chumphon roads, or the seafood eateries at the beach hotels. Try **PaPa** (Kromluang Rd.; ② **07751-1972**), a popular, affordable seafood restaurant.

3 Surat Thani

644km (399 miles) S of Bangkok

Surat Thani, or "Surat," was an important center of the Sumatra-based Srivijaya Empire during the 9th and 10th centuries. Today, it is a rich agricultural province yielding rubber and coconuts. Apart from its night market, its seedy massage parlors and pushy touts give it little appeal to the many travelers who use it merely as a gateway to farther destinations. From Surat, you can catch ferries to **Ang Thong Marine National Park,** as well as **Koh Samui, Koh Pha Ngan,** and **Koh Tao.** It's not impossibly far to the jungles of **Khao Sok National Park** or to go from here farther north to **Phuket, Krabi,** and the **Andaman coast.** Popular local produce includes the Surat oyster and the rambutan (*ngor* in Thai). Near Surat is **Suan Mokkh,** an international meditation center (see "Day Trips from Surat Than" at the end of this section).

ESSENTIALS
GETTING THERE
By Plane   From Bangkok, there are three choices. **Thai Airways** (✆ 02356-1111; www.thaiair.com) has two daily flights (trip time: 70 min.). Thai Airways' office is at 3/27–28 Karunrat Rd. (✆ 07727-2610), just south of town. Budget airlines **Air Asia** (✆ 02515-9999; www.airasia.com) and **One-Two-GO** (✆ 02229-4100, call 1126 in Bangkok, or 1141 out of Bangkok; www.fly12go.com) also have daily flights from Bangkok. **Air-conditioned vans** connecting the airport and town cost up to 80B (US$2.30/£1.25) per person.

By Train   Eleven trains leave daily from **Bangkok's Hua Lampong station** (✆ 1690; www.railway.co.th) to Surat Thani (trip time: 13 hr.). Second-class sleepers cost 848B (US$24/£13), and second-class seats run 578B (US$17/£9). Surat Thani station is some 12km (7½ miles) from town.

If you are connecting with the ferry, avoid the aggressive touts and look for representatives from the boat companies **Songserm** or **Panthip** (✆ 07727-2230), who provide buses to meet trains. Otherwise you can grab a shared minivan to town for around 80B (US$2.30/£1.25).

By Bus   VIP 24-seater buses leave daily from **Bangkok's Southern Bus Terminal** (✆ 02434-5578; trip time: 10 hr.; 590B/US$17/£9.10). *Note:* These buses are safer than the cheaper private buses, where organized theft is endemic. Air-conditioned buses leave daily from **Phuket's bus terminal** off Phang Nga Road, opposite the Royal Phuket City Hotel (✆ 07621-1977; trip time: 4 hr.; 150B/US$4.30/£2.30). The Surat Thani Bus Terminal is on Kaset II Road, a block east of the main road.

By Minivan   Privately operated air-conditioned minivans offer affordable and regular services from Surat Thani to/from Chumphon, Ranong, Nakhon Si Thammarat, Had Yai, Phuket, and beyond. The best way to arrange these trips is via your hotel's front desk. You can go door to door, usually for less than 200B (US$5.70/£3.10).

By Car   Take Highway 4 south from Bangkok to Chumphon, and then Highway 41 directly south to Surat Thani (trip time: 12 hr.).

VISITOR INFORMATION
For information about Surat Thani, Koh Samui, and Koh Pha Ngan, contact the **TAT** office, 5 Talad Mai Rd., Surat Thani (✆ 07728-8818), near the Wang Tai Hotel.

ORIENTATION

Surat Thani is built up along the south shore of the Tapi River. Talad Mai (meaning new market) Road, 2 blocks south of the river, is the city's main street. The TAT office is on this same road but to the far west of town, en route to the bus and train stations. Ferry piers are on Ban Don, Na Meuang; out of town to the east is the Tha Thong pier. (Depending on your arrival hour, you can get transfers directly to the piers from the bus and train stations without going through town.)

FAST FACTS

Major **banks, exchange kiosks,** and a branch of the **post office** lie along Na Meuang Road close to Witeetad Road in the center of town. The **Web Guesthouse** (℃ 07727-5771) on Talad Mai Road is a friendly place for advice or help, **Internet, phone access,** and good value Thai and Western food. Situated near transportation services to the station and ferries, its dormitory rooms are pretty basic but bearable for an overnighter.

WHAT TO SEE & DO

Surat is a typical small Thai city, with few sites worthy of mentioning. The day and night markets are worth a look, though. Those with some extra time may want to head to **Khao Sok** and the beautiful Ratchaprapha Dam, or visit the small town of **Chaiya** and its Suan Mokkh monastery, a renowned Buddhist retreat with meditation study programs in English (see "Day Trips from Surat Thani," below). If you are in town at the end of Buddhist Lent (around mid-Oct) it's worth seeing the **Chak Phra festival,** where Buddhist images are towed up the river and boat races take place.

WHERE TO STAY

In addition to the below options, you might try **SRHotel** ℛ (℃ 07727-5064), which is well positioned near the main junction, and comes with parking and clean, comfy rooms.

MODERATE

Diamond Plaza Hotel ℛℛ   What this concrete edifice lacks in aesthetic charm, it makes up for with a gamut of creature comforts. If you need a treat after a long bus ride, Diamond Plaza has decent rooms and bathrooms, and good facilities, including a fitness center and swimming pool. Suites are reasonably priced.

83/27 Sriwichai Rd. Moo 2, Surat Thani 84000. ℃ 07720-5333. Fax 07720-5352. 400 units. www.diamondplaza hotels.com. 1,250B (US$36/£19) deluxe; 2,800B (US$80/£43) single junior suite; 3,800B (US$108/£58) twin executive suite. MC, V. **Amenities:** Restaurant; bar; coffee shop; pool; fitness center; massage; Wi-Fi. *In room:* A/C, satellite TV, minibar, hair dryer.

Wang Tai Hotel ℛ *Value*   Though this hotel isn't centrally located, it's worth the 25B (71¢/40p) tuk-tuk ride from the bus terminal or ferry. There's a nice pool and sun deck, plus the lobby cafe sells coffee and pastries—great if you're running to catch your morning ferry. Guests can dine overlooking the Tapi River. The spacious rooms are clean and comfortable, with varying rates according to view.

1 Talad Mai Rd., Surat Thani 84000 (south side of town near TAT). ℃ 07728-3020. Fax 07728-1007. 238 units. 950B–1,000B (US$27–US$29/£15–£16) double; from 2,000B (US$57/£30) suite. AE, MC, V. **Amenities:** Restaurant; lounge; pool; limited room service; same-day laundry service. *In room:* A/C, satellite TV, minibar, fridge.

Surat Thani

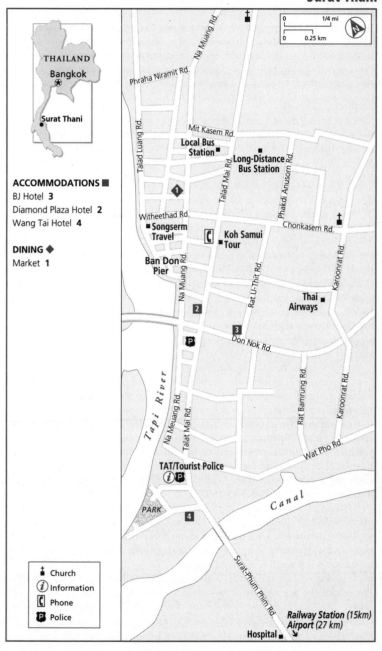

THAILAND
Bangkok
Surat Thani

ACCOMMODATIONS ■
BJ Hotel **3**
Diamond Plaza Hotel **2**
Wang Tai Hotel **4**

DINING ◆
Market **1**

Na Muang Rd.
Phraha Niramit Rd.
Talad Luang Rd.
Mit Kasem Rd.
Local Bus Station ■
Long-Distance Bus Station ■
Talad Mai Rd.
Phakdi Anusorn Rd.
Witheethad Rd.
Chonkasem Rd.
■ **Songserm Travel**
Koh Samui Tour ■
Karoonrat Rd.
Ban Don Pier
Na Muang Rd.
Rat U-Thit Rd.
Thai Airways ■
Don Nok Rd.
Tapi River
Na Meuang Rd.
Talat Mai Rd.
Rat Bamrung Rd.
Karoonrat Rd.
Wat Pho Rd.
TAT/Tourist Police
Canal
PARK
Surat-Phum Phim Rd.

0   1/4 mi
0   0.25 km

✝ Church
ⓘ Information
📞 Phone
🅿 Police

Railway Station (15km)
Airport (27 km)
Hospital ■

INEXPENSIVE

BJ Hotel This hotel is not much more than a basic, clean pit stop—but it lies just a short walk south and east of the town center. Simple but clean tile rooms come with small showers. Staff can help with travel arrangements and there's a small restaurant.

17/1 Donnok Rd,. Surat Thani 84000 (about 1km/⅔ mile south of the bus station). © **07721-7410.** Fax 07721-7414. 72 units. 500B (US$14/£7.70) double. MC, V. **Amenities:** Restaurant; laundry service. *In room:* A/C, TV, minibar, fridge.

WHERE TO DINE

When in season, Surat Thani's famous oysters are on the menu at any street-side cafe; there is a small cluster of open-air eateries along Talad Mai (New Market) near the turn to BJ Hotel.

DAY TRIPS FROM SURAT THANI

CHAIYA TOWN & SUAN MOKKHABALARAMA

The town of **Chaiya** itself is a little-visited stop on the southern railroad line, a kind of "Main Street, Thailand." There's an active central market and small stores by the dozen (look out for the old Chinese tea shops). Most people here are visitors to Suan Mokkh Forest temple, and the people of Chaiya are used to lots of wide-eyed foreigners wandering the town before and after retreats. There are a few Internet cafes along the main drag and food stalls selling low-price Thai meals.

Suan Mokkhabalarama (the Grove of the Power of Liberation; better known as Suan Mokkh) just south of Chaiya, was founded in 1932 by Bhikkhu Buddhadasa, a widely published monk who is highly respected in Thailand. His back-to-basics approach attracts Buddhist monks and students of meditation from many countries, and his knowledge of English (among other languages) brought him many Western students in the 1970s and 1980s.

After his death, Bhikkhu bequeathed a large forest monastery to Dhamma study; foreign visitors are invited to join retreats from the 1st to the 10th of each month. Retreats are open to beginners and applicants are accepted on a first-come basis from the end of each month (it's a good idea to pitch up a few days early, on the 29th/30th, in high season). The meditation schedules are rigorous but short. Despite the rule of silence, there are opportunities to pose questions to monks, nuns, and lay volunteers.

Check in at the main monastery (follow signs to "information") and then walk or ride the 1km (⅔ mile) to the retreat center. For 10 days of dorm lodging and meals, the recommended donation is 1,500B (US$43/£23). See www.suanmokkh.org or call the retreat manager at © **07743-1597.**

Day visitors are welcome at the forest monastery, where you can wander the many jungle paths and visit the **"Spiritual Theatre,"** which Buddhadasa described as a pictorial interpretation of Dhamma featuring an eclectic mixture of Thai, Egyptian, Chinese, Indian, Japanese, Tibetan, and European-style murals and sculptures. The monastery is just south of the town of Chaiya, 50km (31 miles) north of Surat Thani on Highway 41. Long-distance buses and public pickup trucks pass the entrance throughout the day and can drop you off as requested. *Songtaews* (pickups) costing 20B (57¢/30p) also connect to and from Chaiya; you have to wave them down.

A short ride north of Chaiya, the town of **Pum Riang** is a Muslim fishing village where there are many small storefront weaving factories still in operation.

KHAO SOK NATIONAL PARK

One of the largest unspoiled areas of rainforest in the south, Khao Sok is known for its stunning scenery, caves, and exotic wildlife. The park is a convenient stop between

Surat Thani and Phuket, and the main east–west road (Rte. 401) passes the park headquarters.

The park is some 646 sq. km (249 sq. miles) in area and is traced by jungle waterways; steep trails climb through underbrush, and thick vines hang from craggy limestone cliffs—imagine the jutting formations of Krabi, only inland. Rising some 1,000m (3,280 ft.), the dense jungle habitat is literally crawling with wildlife, such as tigers, leopards, and even elephants, but you may be hard-pressed to actually spot any. More commonly seen are guar, Malaysian sun bear, gibbons, magur, macaques, civets, and squirrels, along with more than 200 species of birds like hornbills, woodpeckers, and kingfishers. As for the flora, it is equally varied. This is one of the rare places where you may come across the stinking "rotting flesh" odor that typifies the Rafflesia, the largest flower in the world. (The largest blooms are up to 1m/3¼ ft. wide.)

One of the best ways to get up close with the varied fauna of the park is by kayak along the nether reaches of a large reservoir, about an hour from Surat Thani on Route 415. At **Rajaprarabha Dam,** you can go boating, rafting, and fishing among the limestone cliffs that appear as islands, or stay in beautiful floating bungalows and explore this pristine jungle on elephant back.

Farther west, the **park area** (off Highway 401 at kilometer marker 109) has several bungalow resorts in the jungle off the 1.5km-long entrance road, some set as tree houses. There are several Internet cafes, too. From here, well-marked trails lead you through the park. The park office can provide camping equipment, and guides will offer their services and help plan your itinerary.

Caution: It's important to know that waterfalls and caves pose real risks during rainy season. In 2006 and 2007, a number of Thai and foreign tourists lost their lives when flash floods inundated caves in this very park. Whether visiting the caverns and waterfalls, or considering a jungle hike or tubing down the River Sok, always book through a reputable travel agent so that help is at hand if you run into trouble.

The Park's **Natural Resources Conservation Office** (Royal Forestry Department, 61 Pahonyothin Rd., Chatuchak, Bangkok 10900; ℂ **02579-7223**), or the TAT offices in Phuket Town (p. 228) or Surat Thani (p. 185), have maps and info. Alternatively, contact **Paddle Asia** in Phuket (53/80 Moo 5, Thambon Srisoonthon, Thalang, Phuket 83110; ℂ **07631-1222;** fax 07631-3689; www.paddleasia.com) for details of their soft adventure trips. **Grand Trans Samui** (ℂ **07741-5203**) also offers various tours to Khao Sok from Samui.

4 Koh Samui

644km (399 miles) S of Bangkok to Surat Thani; 84km (52 miles) E from Surat Thani to Koh Samui

The island of Koh Samui lies 84km (52 miles) off the east coast in the Gulf of Thailand, near the mainland town of Surat Thani. Since the 1850s, Koh Samui was visited by Chinese merchants from Hainan Island in the South China Sea. The island is said to have more coconut species than any other place in the world. The harvesting of coconuts (and rubber) still takes place in the hills of the island's hinterland, but alas, many plantations have given way to wide-scale tourist developments, which is now the island's main income.

Once a hippie haven of pristine beaches, idyllic thatched bungalows, and eateries along dusty red dirt roads, Samui is now packed with upscale resorts, low-end bars, and posh spa retreats. Up to 20 flights a day land at Samui International Airport and this voracious tourist onslaught has brought severe water shortages and environmental problems such as waste water and refuse disposal.

If you leave the main tourist hubs, Koh Samui still has a few idyllic sand beaches and simple villages, but it is certainly not the sleepy island it was 10—or even 5—years ago, and prices reflect this.

Peak season is from mid-December to mid-January, but January to April has the best weather—before its gets very hot—with the occasional tropical storm bringing relief. Storms don't tend to last long, however, and as this is low season, more bargains can be found. October through mid-December are the wettest months, with November bringing some heavy rain and winds that make the east side of the island rough for swimming. July and August see a brief increase in visitors, but during those months, the island's west side is often buffeted by summer monsoons from the mainland.

ESSENTIALS
GETTING THERE
By Plane   Up to 17 flights depart daily from Bangkok on **Bangkok Airways** (© **02265-5555** in Bangkok; 07742-2512 in Samui; www.bangkokair.com). Two daily flights connect with Phuket (Bangkok Airways' Phuket office is at © **07622-5033**) and another daily connects with U-Tapao airport near Pattaya (Pattaya office © **03841-1965**); they also have a much underpromoted direct flight to Hong Kong. From Singapore, **Silk Air** (© **02236-5301** in Bangkok; www.silkair.com) flies daily. Bangkok Airways also flies this route, up to four times each week.

Koh Samui Airport (© **07742-5012**) boasts open-air pavilions with thatched roofs surrounded by gardens and palms. If you're staying at a larger resort, airport shuttles can be arranged when you book your room. There's also a convenient minivan service from the airport that will cost you less than haggling with taxi drivers. Book your ticket at the transportation counter upon arrival and you'll get door-to-door service for around 200B (US$5.70/£3.10). A trip to the farther tip of the island (Laem Set) will take around 45 minutes.

If you're unable to book a flight directly to the island, you can fly to Surat Thani on the mainland—it's cheaper and not much longer—with direct ferries to Samui (subject to delay in choppy seas).

By Ferry   **Songserm Travel** (© **07728-7124** in Surat Thani) runs a loop from Surat Thani pier to Samui in 2 hours. Rates are: Surat–Samui 150B (US$4.30/£2.30); Samui–Koh Pha Ngan 130B (US$3.70/£1.90); Koh Pha Ngan–Koh Tao 250B (US$7.10/£3.70); Koh Tao–Chumphon 400B (US$11/£6.15). Other car ferries run from Donsak pier, which is 60 km (37 miles) south of Surat Thani. **Seatran Discovery** (© **07724-6086**) offers a popular choice for comfortable interisland travel and day trips. It costs 150B (US$4.30/£2.30) from Surat to Samui, and 240B (US$6.85/£3.50) from Surat on to Koh Pha Ngan. **Raja Ferries** (© **07742-3190-1**) is another car and passenger service from Donsak to either Koh Samui or Koh Pha Ngan. **Lomprayah** (© **07742-7765**) links the islands by high-speed catamaran and runs some specialized trips. (There are still no connections for cars between the islands.) Both companies charge between 300B and 450B (US$8.50–US$12.60/£4.50–£6.70) per trip depending on the season.

You can buy ferry tickets at the port, although many book a bus ticket with ferry included from Bangkok, or other points in Thailand.

If you book ahead at a resort, most will arrange transport from the Samui ferry pier at Nathon to your hotel. Otherwise, *songtaews* make the trip to most beaches on the

Koh Samui

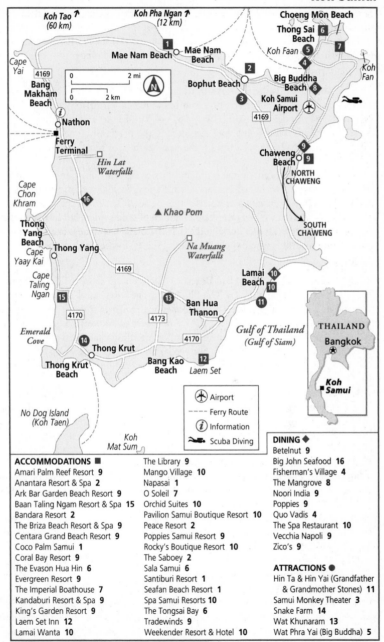

Koh Tao ↑
(60 km)

Koh Pha Ngan ↑
(12 km)

Choeng Mon Beach

Thong Sai Beach **6**

1 Mae Nam Beach · Mae Nam Beach

Koh Faan **5**

Cape Yai

7

4169

Bang Makham Beach

2

Big Buddha Beach

Koh Fan

Bophut Beach

3

Koh Samui Airport

8

i Nathon

4169

Ferry Terminal

Hin Lat Waterfalls

Chaweng Beach **9**

9

NORTH CHAWENG

Cape Chon Khram

16

▲ Khao Pom

SOUTH CHAWENG

Thong Yang Beach

Thong Yang

Cape Yaay Kai

Na Muang Waterfalls

Lamai Beach **10**

10

Cape Taling Ngan

4169

15

13

Ban Hua Thanon

11

4170

4173

THAILAND

Emerald Cove

4170

Gulf of Thailand (Gulf of Siam)

Bangkok ★

14 Thong Krut

Thong Krut Beach

Bang Kao Beach **12**

Laem Set

Koh Samui ▪

No Dog Island (Koh Taen)

Koh Mat Sum

✈ Airport
--- Ferry Route
i Information
🤿 Scuba Diving

DINING ◆

Betelnut **9**
Big John Seafood **16**
Fisherman's Village **4**
The Mangrove **8**
Noori India **9**
Poppies **9**
Quo Vadis **4**
The Spa Restaurant **10**
Vecchia Napoli **9**
Zico's **9**

ACCOMMODATIONS ■

Amari Palm Reef Resort **9**
Anantara Resort & Spa **2**
Ark Bar Garden Beach Resort **9**
Baan Taling Ngam Resort & Spa **15**
Bandara Resort **2**
The Briza Beach Resort & Spa **9**
Centara Grand Beach Resort **9**
Coco Palm Samui **1**
Coral Bay Resort **9**
The Evason Hua Hin **6**
Evergreen Resort **9**
The Imperial Boathouse **7**
Kandaburi Resort & Spa **9**
King's Garden Resort **9**
Laem Set Inn **12**
Lamai Wanta **10**

The Library **9**
Mango Village **10**
Napasai **1**
O Soleil **7**
Orchid Suites **10**
Pavilion Samui Boutique Resort **10**
Peace Resort **2**
Poppies Samui Resort **9**
Rocky's Boutique Resort **10**
The Saboey **2**
Sala Samui **6**
Santiburi Resort **1**
Seafan Beach Resort **1**
Spa Samui Resorts **10**
The Tongsai Bay **6**
Tradewinds **9**
Weekender Resort & Hotel **10**

ATTRACTIONS ●

Hin Ta & Hin Yai (Grandfather & Grandmother Stones) **11**
Samui Monkey Theater **3**
Snake Farm **14**
Wat Khunaram **13**
Wat Phra Yai (Big Buddha) **5**

east coast for as little as 50B (US$1.40/75p) if they can get a packed truckload from the boat landing (and it can be very packed). *Songtaews* make stops along the way as required, so you can jump on or off. There are also private taxis at the pier; expect to pay at least 200B (US$5.70/£3.10) from Nathon pier to Chaweng.

ORIENTATION

Though Koh Samui is the country's third-largest island, with a total area of 233 sq. km (90 sq. miles), its entire coastline can be toured by car or motorcycle in about 2½ hours. The island's main road (Hwy. 4169), also called the "ring road," circles hilly, densely forested terrain. Koh Samui airport is in the northeast corner near Bo Phut. The ferries and express boats arrive on the west coast, in or near Nathon (depending on the boat).

Samui's best beaches are on the north and east coasts. The long, sandy east coast is home to Chaweng and Lamai beaches, both frenetic in high season. It's here you'll find the heaviest concentration of hotels and bungalows. The south coast has a few little hideaways and the west coast reveals a handful of sandy strips, but few amenities.

Nathon is where the ferries dock on the west coast, and being the island's main town and community, this is where you'll find banks, the TAT office, and the post office.

THE BEACHES

Clockwise from Nathon, **Mae Nam Beach** on Samui's north shore is 12km (7½ miles) from the ferry pier, facing nearby Koh Pha Ngan. The coarse sand is shaded by palm trees and its peaceful calm bay has water deep enough for swimming; it is often spared the fierce winds that whip up during the stormy months. Although bigger, upmarket resorts are taking over here, too, there are still some affordable resorts and a number of simple, charming bungalows—it's fast becoming the budget choice on Samui. Ban Mae Nam, a small commercial hub, is just east of the Santiburi Resort and has lots of good little restaurants and shops.

Bophut Beach, the next village along the north coast, is one of the island's fastest developing areas. Bophut's long coarse-sand beach narrows considerably in the monsoon season, but the water remains fairly calm year-round. Turning off at "Big Buddha," there's a sign marking the entrance to **Fisherman's Village,** a delightful small street where you'll find restaurants and guesthouses among a beach-side clutch of small houses and shops. It's definitely worth a wander.

Big Buddha Beach (Bangrak) is just east of Bophut and has a fairly clean, coarse-sand beach and a calm bay for swimmers (shallow in the monsoon months). Many small restaurants, businesses, shops, and an increasing number of new resorts and taxis create a busier pace than is evident at other, more removed beaches. It is, however, becoming a popular choice with several new resorts that look out over Koh Faan, the island home of Koh Samui's huge seated Buddha. The Queen Ferry leaves from Big Buddha pier, taking full-moon party goers to Had Rin on Koh Pha Ngan four times a day. Speedboats also leave from a nearby pier, departing hourly during Full-Moon Party time (see "Koh Pha Ngan," later in this chapter).

Koh Samui's northeastern tip features the beautiful headland of **Choeng Mon,** with stunning views all around from west to east, but it's also attracting real estate development. Bold rock formations create private coves and protected swimming areas—though from mid-October to mid-December the monsoon can stir up the wind and waves, creating a steep drop-off from the coarse-sand beach, and a strong undertow.

Tongsai Bay is a beautiful cove dominated by one resort (reviewed later in this chapter); its privacy is a plus or a minus, depending on what you are looking for.

Southeast of Tongsai, as the road descends from the headland down towards Chaweng, is the fine sandy stretch called **Choeng Mon Beach,** a gracefully shaped crescent about 1km (⅔ mile) long, and lined with shady palm trees (and an increasing number of shops). Swimming here is excellent, with few rocks near the central shore, although the water level can become very low from May to October (low season). Across the way is **Koh Fan Fa,** a deserted island with an excellent beach. You can swim or, if the tides are right, walk there—but be careful of the rocks at low tide.

Although Chaweng is the busiest destination on Koh Samui, if you don't mind the hustle and bustle (or Starbucks or McDonald's), it can be great fun. Money changing, Internet cafes, laundry facilities, travel and rental agencies, medical facilities, shopping, restaurants, and nightlife are all on your doorstep. The two Chaweng beaches (**North Chaweng** and south **Chaweng Noi**) are the longest on the island, but in some places an offshore reef limits the water to wading depth only—an advantage if you have young kids. Still, you should at least take a wander here to see what you're missing. The more recently developed north end of the strip abuts rocky coast, but the swimming is better to the south (though a bit shallow near the shore in low season).

The long sand beach of **Lamai Bay** in the southeast is comparable to Chaweng's, and although many top-range resorts are moving in, there are a few budget options offering bungalows at the north end of the beach. The town area is less developed but does have a wide range of services, cafes, and restaurants, although nightlife tends to be centered around the small bars on the main street. Samui's waterfalls lie inland of Lamai towards Ban Thurian at Na Muang.

Laem Set Bay is a small rocky cape on Samui's southeast coast, with dramatic scenery that prompted the construction of a few resorts, some of which have been around for 25 years.

On the west coast, you'll find one of Samui's better beaches at Ao Phang Kha (Emerald Cove), south of **Ban Taling Ngam** on Route 4170. Generally, the west coast beaches are the most isolated on the island, offering few facilities and rocky waters, making the beaches barely swimmable. Many Thai families stop for picnics at Hin Lat Falls, a rather uninteresting inland site 2km (1¼ miles) southeast of Nathon. Samui used to supply enough freshwater for the whole town, but now high season droughts blight the island.

VISITOR INFORMATION

The **TAT Information Center** is on Thawi Ratchaphakti Road just north of the main ferry terminal in Nathon (© 07742-0504). This office has TAT accommodation lists and information pamphlets, published annually, but often websites may be more up-to-date. Pick up free magazines such as the *Samui Explorer, Samui Guide,* and *What's On Samui. Samui Dining Guide* (www.samuidiningguide.com) lists the best restaurants on the island. You can also pick up any number of free maps with lots of adverts and info on spas, events, or fun local happenings.

GETTING AROUND

By *Songtaew* These pickup trucks are the easiest and most efficient way to get around the island and advertise their destinations with colorful signs. They follow Route 4169, the ring road, around the island. Hail one anywhere along the highway and beach roads. To visit a site off the beaten track, ask the driver to make a detour.

Most stop after sundown, after which they tour Chaweng. Night owls face steep fares (up to 300B/US$8.60/£4.60).

By Rental Car   Renting a car is far safer than a motorcycle, though the mountainous roads here have many hairpin bends and steep gradients. Remember your defensive driving skills; they will be required to navigate around common obstacles such as motorcycles coming at you in your lane, a wandering dog, or an intoxicated truck driver with a death wish.

Budget Car Rental (② 07742-7188) has an office at Samui Airport. Contact **Avis** (② 084700-8161, mobile) at the airport or at the Santiburi Resort (② 07742-5031) and Tongsai Bay resort (② 07742-5454). **Hertz** is at the Central Samui Beach Resort (② 07723-0500). All offer a range of vehicles, starting as low as 1,500B (US$43/£23), and do pickup and delivery.

Local rental companies and travel agents have good deals for car rentals and they're generally sound. Bargains can come as low as 900B (US$26/£14) per day, but don't expect comprehensive insurance coverage. Read all the fine print, and if you don't have an international driver's license, make sure that your local license is acceptable.

By Motorcycle   The roads on Samui are busy, narrow, and poorly maintained, with plenty of novice drivers (usually gung-ho foreigners). Road accidents injure or kill an inordinate number of tourists and locals each year, mostly motorcycle riders, but two wheels and a motor is still the most popular way to get around the island, so stick to the left-hand lane and go easy. A 500B (US$14/£7.70) fine is imposed on any locals not wearing a helmet, but as a well-heeled foreigner, you may well be forced to pay a much higher fee. Bring an international license from the AAA in the U.S. (or a similar fine will be imposed). Travel agencies and small operators rent motorcycles, and most resorts can make arrangements. A 100cc Honda scooter goes for as little as 150B (US$4.30/£2.30) per day, while a 250cc chopper is around 700B to 900B (US$20–US$26/£11–£14). For the best big bikes, look for **Ohm Cycles** on the far southern end of Chaweng (on the road heading to Lamai; ② 07723-0701).

FAST FACTS

All the major **banks** now have branches in every town, with their main branches in Nathon along waterfront Thawi Ratchaphakti Road. You will find numerous money-changers and ATMs across every part of the island, many with Western Union **money transfer services;** the latter has an office in Chaweng at the Central Samui Resort. There are post offices in Chaweng, Mae Nam, and Lamai—all on the main Samui ring road. The **main post office** (② 07742-1013) is on Chonwithi Road in Nathon. Most resorts will also handle post for you, and stamps can be purchased in small shops in beach areas. For **Internet service,** there are numerous places at almost every step of the island. Try the kind folks at **Multi Travel and Tour** (164/3 Moo 2 Chaweng, ② 07741-3969).

There are excellent private hospitals and 24-hour rescue and evacuation services if required. They are expensive but will deal direct with medical insurance companies. **Bangkok Samui Hospital** (② 07742-9555) and **Samui International Hospital** (② 07723-0781-2) provide top-class medical care. **Bandon International Hospital** (② 07742-5382) is also a fine facility, with English-speaking physicians who make house calls. All are located around Chaweng.

For emergencies, dial ② **1155** or 07742-1281 for **Tourist Police.**

WHAT TO SEE & DO

Busy Samui has a host of entertainment apart from the usual beach outings. Have a look at "Exploring Koh Samui" at the end of this section for more outdoor activities and happenings.

Many of the sites below can be seen on day trips or combined with **jungle tours** in jeeps, such as **Mr Ung's Magical Safari Tour** (© 07723-0114; www.ungsafari.com) starting at a reasonable 1,400B (US$40/£22). Join in and enjoy the adventure—even lunch is taken care of. There are also several companies offering trips with multichoice activities, including **quad-biking, jungle coaster cable rides,** and even **mountain-biking**—so look around to find the best travel agent for you.

Samui has a number of important temples and Buddhist sites to visit. **Wat Phra Yai** is home to Samui's primary landmark, the **Big Buddha,** more than 12m (36 ft.) tall and the most important temple for the local islanders. It is set on Koh Faan, a small islet connected to the shore by a causeway, with shops and restaurants at the base. Admission is free, but donations are accepted.

Two temples in Samui hold bodies of **mummified monks,** which some may find ghoulishly interesting. The most popular is **Wat Khunaram,** along the main road (Rte. 4169) as it shoots inland far south of Lamai. Here, the **mummified body** of monk Loung Pordaeng is in the same meditation position, or *mudra,* as when he died 20 years ago.

Four engraved imprints of the **Lord Buddha's Footprint** are held in a shrine near the turn-off to the **Butterfly Farm** off the 4170 Road near Laem Din. At the southernmost end of Lamai Beach lie Koh Samui's two famous rocks, **Hin Ta** and **Hin Yai,** Grandfather and Grandmother Stone, respectively. They have always caused a stir due to their likeness to male and female genitalia (you can guess which is which). The rocks are seen as strong fertility symbols, and local myth has it that these rocks were where a people known as the Mui originated.

Just across Route 4169 from Wat Khunaram is the dirt track leading up to the **Na Muang Falls,** one of which reveals a large bathing pool (be careful of sharp rocks). You can walk the steamy 5km (3-mile) trek from the coast road to the falls or take the easier route on the back of an elephant (any travel agency in town can arrange this). Once you've finished your picnic, visit the newly accessible **Wang Saotong Waterfall** a little farther off-road on the other side of Route 4169. *Caution:* Due to a fatal accident at a waterfall in 2007, visitors are warned to be aware of the likelihood of sudden landslides during heavy rain.

You can escape the heat with the kids at Samui's latest attraction, **Paradise Park Farm** (© 07741-3440; daily 7am–6pm). The cool mountain air will be a welcome relief as you walk through towering natural rocks surrounded by waterfalls, small rivers, canyons, wildlife animals, and exotic birds. Here you can learn about rubber tapping and local flora and fauna. You can then dine in the restaurant, relax in the infinity pool with spectacular views down the valley, or unwind in the spa.

Also well worth a visit is the **Magic Statue Garden,** if only for the trek deep into the jungle-clad mountains. Built by local farmer, Nim Thongsuk, in 1976, when he was 77, it is now proudly maintained by his son. The road is challenging, so book with a tour company such as Jungle Safari (© 07723-0144).

The more adventurous can try being Tarzan and swing through the jungle with **Canopy Adventures** (© 07741-4150-1). Or, if you prefer a quicker adrenaline rush, the **British Jumpmasters bungee jump** (© 08788-74662, mobile) is in Chaweng Center just behind the Reggae Bar.

You won't be surprised that Koh Samui suffers from water shortages when you see the new **Samui Aquapark** (no phone at press time) that was slated to open in mid-2008. Located off the ring road near the Na Muang waterfalls, prices are expected to be around 1,000B (US$29/£15) for adults and 600B (US$17/£9.25) for children.

If you don't intend to snorkel, but would like to sample some underwater life, **Samui Aquarium and Tiger Zoo** (© 07742-4017-8) is open daily from 9am–5pm at Samui Orchid Resort, Laem Set Beach, and costs 250B (US$7.10/£3.85) entrance.

Most Thai tourist spots have a **snake show,** and Samui's snake farm is at the far southwest corner of the island on 4170 Road (© 07742-3247), with daily shows at 11am and 2pm. Tickets cost 250B (US$7.10/£3.85). **Samui Crocodile Farm** (© 07724-7262) also has **reptiles and monkeys.** It's open from 9am to 6pm daily and costs 250B (US$7.10/£3.85). At the **Samui Monkey Theater** (© 07724-5140), just south of Bophut village on 4169 Road, you can see "working" demonstrations of monkeys collecting coconuts. Showtimes are at 10:30am, 2pm, and 4pm daily; entrance is 10B (28¢/15p).

WHERE TO STAY ON KOH SAMUI

Thirty years ago there were but a few makeshift beachside bungalows along the nearly deserted coast of Samui. Today, luxury resorts stand shoulder to shoulder with upscale beach bungalows, all vying for supremacy. But whatever your budget, all enjoy virtually the same sand and views.

For more detailed information on each beach, check out "The Beaches" section above. Below is a small accommodations selection from each area, including some of the best of the many new options.

MAE NAM BAY
Very Expensive

Napasai 🌟🌟🌟   A few years ago, Orient-Express Hotels took over this prize resort that nestles on a rocky headland leading to the white-sand Baan Tai beach at the western end of Mae Nam. A selection of rustic-themed teak cottages with high ceilings come with private pools, sumptuous decor, and large bathtubs, all with balconies. Though isolated, it is gorgeously self-contained. A top spa and good in-house dining make it a plum choice for well-heeled romantics.

65/10 Moo 5, Maenam, Koh Samui 84330. © 07742-9200. Fax 07742-9201. www.napasai.com. 45 units. 7,070B–13,370B (US$202–US$382/£109–£206) sea-view/beachfront cottages; 8,540B–16,900B (US$244–US$484/£131–£260) garden pool/beachfront cottages; 29,400B–40,800B (US$841–US$1,168/£452–£628) 2–3 bed villas. **Amenities:** Restaurant; bar; outdoor pool; tennis courts; fitness center; spa; watersports rentals; tour desk; car-rental desk; limited room service; laundry service. *In room:* A/C, satellite TV, fridge, minibar, coffeemaker, safe.

Santiburi Resort 🌟   Santiburi was the first high-end property in the area. Modern state-of-the-art amenities are discreetly infused into contemporary Thai architecture. The resort's top villas—with outside Jacuzzis—front the beach, while the others are set among lush greenery around a central pool and spa. Each bungalow comes with a large sunken tub. Guests can take advantage of windsurfing and sailing (free), and there is a sailing junk to tour surrounding islands (it's also used for supper cruises). Santiburi also hosts the island's top golf course, **Santiburi Golf,** near the resort.

Santiburi has a more affordable companion in nearby Bophut called the **Bophut Resort and Spa** at a similar high standard, with 61 luxury seaside villas.

12/12 Moo 1, Tambol Mae Nam, Koh Samui 84330. © **07742-5031.** Fax 07742-5040. www.santiburi.com. 57 units. 19,000B–24,000B (US$542–US$685/£292–£369) deluxe suites; 24,000B–35,520B (US$542–US$1,000/£369–£546) villas. AE, DC, MC, V. **Amenities:** 2 restaurants; 2 bars; lounge; outdoor pool; golf course (nearby, connected by free shuttle); outdoor lit tennis courts; fitness center; spa; watersports equipment; car-rental desk; airport transfer; salon; 24-hr. room service; babysitting; same-day laundry service/dry cleaning; Wi-Fi. *In room:* A/C, satellite TV, DVD library, stereo system, minibar, fridge, hair dryer, safe.

Moderate/Inexpensive

Coco Palm Samui 🎔🎔 *Value*   Under the swaying palms of peaceful Mae Nam beach, this bargain bungalow resort provides the fast-disappearing beach ambience that Samui was once famous for. New features are the deluxe pool villas, offering superb comfort. The bungalows are spotless and furnished with simple rattan and wooden decor. Food is remarkably good, and another plus is that Wi-Fi is available, albeit for a fee (you'll need to buy a card from reception). The Lomprayah boat service to Koh Pha Ngan and Koh Tao conveniently leaves from the nearby pier.

26/4 Moo 4, Maenam Beach, Koh Samui 84330. © **07724-7288.** Fax 07742-5321. www.cocopalmsamui.com. 70 units. 1,200B–2,600B (US$34–US$74/£18–£40) garden cottages; 2,500B–3,200B (US$71–US$91/£38–£49) beachfront cottages; 6,000B–8,000B (US$171–US$228/£92–£123) pool villas. MC, V. **Amenities:** Restaurant; pool; jeep and motorcycle rental; tour desk; transfer service; laundry service; tailor; Wi-Fi. *In room:* A/C, minibar, TV.

Seafan Beach Resort   The traditional semi-deluxe Thai beach bungalows here attract returning guests, as do the friendly staff and family amenities such as a nursery. Each rustic rattan and coconut-wood house has two queen-size beds, an extra rattan daybed, built-in bamboo furnishings, and a large, all-tiled bathroom with nice robes and slippers for padding about. Bungalows are private, although some are set away from the beach in the 3 hectares (8 acres) of landscaped grounds fronting the bay. The pool is small but has a sunken pool bar and Jacuzzi overlooking the beach. The restaurant features good Thai, continental, and seafood options.

Mae Nam Beach, Koh Samui 84330 (west end of beach). © **07742-5204.** Fax 07742-5350. www.samui-hotels. com/seafan. 40 units. 2,400B (US$68/£37) single; 2,600B (US$74/£40) double, slightly more for seafront; special rates available. AE, DC, MC, V. **Amenities:** Restaurant; outdoor pool and children's pool; watersports equipment; children's playroom; tour desk; airport transfer; massage; same-day laundry/dry cleaning service. *In room:* A/C, minibar, hair dryer, safe.

BOPHUT BEACH
Expensive

Anantara Resort and Spa 🎔🎔   This has to be one of Bophut's most popular hangouts; generous-size rooms have a modern feel, plenty of wood, and make use of exquisite local textiles. The resort provides luxuries like yoga, Thai cooking, wine appreciation, and superb spa therapies—while maintaining a low-key, unpretentious approach.

101/3 Bophut Bay, Koh Samui 84320. © **07742-8300.** Fax 07742-8310. www.anantara.com. 106 units. 5,600B– 8,600B (US$160–US$246/£86–£132) deluxe double; from 10,500B–13,800B (US$300–US$394/£162–£212) suite. AE, MC, V. **Amenities:** 2 restaurants; bar; outdoor pool; tennis court; fitness center; spa; watersports rental; library; game room; limited room service; massage; laundry service. *In room:* A/C, satellite TV, dataport, minibar, fridge, coffeemaker, safe.

Bandara Resort   One of the many new resorts in Bophut, Bandara has a range of villas, standard and deluxe rooms that flank a main courtyard area, and a good-size, raised pool. Seaside villas are luxurious, but the real wow-factor is that some have private pools. A free-form pool is set at the beachside next to the restaurant. Water babies have complimentary use of watersports facilities such as the fleet of Hobie Cats. The vibe is slick and contemporary, with some nice Thai touches.

178/2 Moo 1, Bophut, Koh Samui 84320. (C) **07724-5795**. Fax 07742-7340. www.bandararesort.com. 151 units. 5,500B–6,500B (US$157–US$185/£85–£100) double superior/deluxe; 8,500B (US$242/£131) grand deluxe; from 12,000B (US$342/£185) pool villa. MC, V. **Amenities:** 2 restaurants; bar; outdoor pool; fitness center; watersports rentals; tour desk; car-rental desk; limited room service; massage; laundry service. In room: A/C, satellite TV, fridge, minibar, safe.

Moderate/Expensive

Peace Resort *(Kids)*   Living up to its name, this family-run resort offers four types of free-standing bungalows set in lush, peaceful gardens, the largest being 49 sq. m. (527 sq. ft.) All villas come with terraces and feature sunny yellow interiors and modern furnishings that have a rustic quality. Great for families, the large central pool has a separate kids' pool and a playground, but when the place is busy you'll have to rise early if you want to bag a sun bed.

Bo Phut Beach, Koh Samui 84320 (central Bophut). (C) **07742-5357**. Fax 07742-5343. www.peaceresort.com. 102 units. 4,000B–16,000B (US$114–US$457/£62–£246) double. MC, V. **Amenities:** Restaurant; bar; pool w/kids' pool; spa; kids' club; playground; tour desk; car and motorbike rental desk; babysitting; limited room service (6am–11:30pm); laundry service; Internet. In room: A/C, satellite TV, minibar, fridge, safe, no phone.

BIG BUDDHA BEACH
Moderate

The Saboey *(ji)(ji) (Finds)*   Newly revamped, this gorgeous little boutique resort oozes style with its sumptuous-hued interiors and unique Morocco-meets-Asia style. Rooms offer top-quality furnishings and useful added extras like a writing desk and free Wi-Fi. Superior amenities such as DVD and CD players mark it out from the fray. The long, glassy infinity pool has ocean views and a wonderful Jacuzzi cascading down to the beach. Dine surrounded by candles and the sounds of waves at the beachside Breeze restaurant or try the **Quo Vadis** restaurant (see "Where to Dine in Koh Samui").

51/4 Moo 4 Tambon Bophut, Koh Samui 84320. (C) **07743-0456**. www.saboey.com. 20 units. 2,900B–3,900B (US$83–US$111/£45–£60) suites; 3,900B–4,700B (US$111–US$134/£60–£72) garden villas; 4,400B–5,100B (US$125–US$145/£68–£78) pool villas; 4,900B–6,900B (US$140–US$197/£75–£106) penthouse and beach villas. **Amenities:** 2 restaurants; bar; pool; Jacuzzi; game/TV room; DVD/CD rental; tour booking; car-rental desk; laundry service; Wi-Fi. In room: A/C, satellite TV, DVD/CD player, minibar, coffee-making facilities, safe.

TONGSON BAY

On the northeastern tip of Samui (just around the promontory that shelters Tongsai Bay) is Tongson Bay, which hosts a few high-end choices and provides a good getaway.

Very Expensive

The Evason Hua Hin *(ji)(ji)(ji)*   This cluster of private villas and suites—many with private infinity pools—is scattered over the craggy hilltop overlooking Tongson Bay, with views from east to west. You're far removed from it all, and that is the point. The eco-friendly owners have created a resort that utilizes natural themes and encourages eco-awareness among its guests, staff, and the local community. Service is tops. Daily complimentary cocktail parties enable you to meet the friendly staff and fellow guests. Fine dining options, fantastic spa facilities, and private-pool villas make it an ideal choice for couples looking for romance.

9/10 Moo 5, Baan Plai Laem Bophut, Koh Samui 84320. (C) **07724-5678**. Fax 07724-5671. www.evasonresorts.com. 66 units. 15,500B–23,200B (US$442–US$663/£238–£357) villas; 21,500B–36,900B (US$615–US$1,054/£331–£568) pool villas; 92,500B (US$2,642/£1,423) presidential villa. AE, MC, V. **Amenities:** 2 restaurants; 2 bars; wine cellar;

infinity pool; health club; spa; watersports rentals; tour desk; car-rental desk; 24-hr. personal butler room service; laundry service; DVD rental. *In room:* A/C, satellite TV w/DVD player, minibar, fridge, coffeemaker, hair dryer, safe.

Expensive

Sala Samui 𝒜𝒜𝒜 Hip, slick, and cool; that's the vibe at Sala Samui. Stylish rooms, most with their own private pools, have views onto private courtyards or the sea. The place has a boutique vibe, blending traditional Thai architecture with modern facilities and amenities. Polished concrete is accented in Thai silk hangings and canopy beds. Construction in the area is ongoing here, so beware that it might be noisy.

10/9 Moo 5, Baan Plai Lam Bophut, Koh Samui 84320. ℭ **07724-5888.** Fax 07724-5889. www.salasamui.com. 69 units. 9,100B (US$260/£140) deluxe; 12,250B–22,400B (US$350–US$640/£188–£345) pool villa; 28,000B (US$800/£431) presidential villa. AE, MC, V. **Amenities:** Restaurant; bar; 2 outdoor pools; fitness center; spa; watersports rentals; tour desk; car-rental desk; limited room service; laundry service. *In room:* A/C, satellite TV, minibar, fridge, coffeemaker, safe.

TONGSAI BAY

Expensive

The Imperial Boathouse 𝒜𝒜 When it opened a long while ago, The Boathouse was lauded for its originality. Even today, the concept is pretty unique: 34 authentic teak, dry-docked rice barges converted into charming free-standing suites. The less-expensive rooms in the three-story buildings are fine but not nearly as atmospheric. Hotel facilities are extensive, and if you can't get a boat suite, you can swim in their boat-shaped swimming pool.

83 Moo 5, Tambon Bophut, Koh Samui 84320 (southern part of beach). ℭ **07742-5041.** Fax 07742-5460. www.imperialboathouse.com. 210 units. 3,675B–4,375B (US$105–US$125/£57–£67) double; 5,775B–6,825B (US$165–US$195/£89–£105) boat suite. AE, DC, MC, V. **Amenities:** 2 restaurants; bar; 2 outdoor pools; fitness center; spa; gameroom; watersports equipment; tour desk; car-rental desk; airport transfer; business center; 24-hr. room service; babysitting; same-day laundry service/dry cleaning. *In room:* A/C, satellite TV, minibar, fridge, hair dryer, safe.

The Tongsai Bay 𝒜𝒜𝒜 Built like an amphitheater, and tripping down a hillside to its own beach, this former backpacker hideaway is now an all-suite complex with some very unique touches—such as its "Bath-with-a-View"—that set it apart. You'll get plenty of outdoor terrace space to enjoy the sea views; suites have outdoor bathtubs, and the Grand Tongsai Villas have gazebos for guests who like open-air sleeping. Tongsai Pool Villas have private plunge pools. There is a beautiful half-moon-shaped pool set in the gardens half-way down, and a large pool at the beach with a separate children's pool. The end result is casual outdoors ambience. The only drawback is the many steps between the hilltop reception area, bungalows, and beach.

84 Moo 5, Ban Plailaem, Bophut, Koh Samui 84320 (northeast tip of island). ℭ **07742-5015.** Fax 07742-5462. Bangkok office 02254-0056. Fax 02254-0054. www.tongsaibay.co.th. 83 units. 11,000B–13,000B (US$314–US$371/£169–£200) beachfront or cottage suite; 18,000B–22,000B (US$514–US$628/£277–£338) family cottages; from 22,000B (US$628/£338) grand villa; from 25,000B (US$714/£385) pool villa. AE, DC, MC, V. **Amenities:** 3 restaurants; 2 bars; outdoor pool; outdoor lit tennis court; fitness center; spa; watersports equipment; snooker room; tour desk; car-rental desk; airport transfer; limited room service; same-day laundry service/dry cleaning; DVD library; Internet center. *In room:* A/C, satellite TV w/DVD player, minibar, fridge, coffeemaker, hair dryer, safe.

Choeng Mon

O Soleil *Value* The affordable spick-and-span bungalows here are well spaced for serious peace and quiet, but book early, as they are popular with Europeans. Down a small dirt road, the large, rustic bungalows with comfortable beds, tidy tile bathrooms, and broad porches are scattered across an expansive lawn. Furnishings are simple but sufficient. There's also a basic bamboo bar and dining pavilion right on the seafront.

Choeng Mon Beach (down the dirt track at the north end of beach, past White House Hotel). © **07742-5160**. 27 units. 1,000B–1,200B (US$28–US$34/£15–£18) double with A/C. MC, V. **Amenities:** Restaurant; laundry service. *In room:* A/C in some; no phone.

CHAWENG & CHAWENG NOI BAYS
Expensive

Amari Palm Reef Resort ✮✮✮ *Kids*   This fine-looking Amari hotel is both a fun family choice and a honeymooner's delight, with sea-facing suite rooms that merge slick-contemporary with traditional-Thai decor. Older accommodations in the main block are not as luxurious. A newer block of midrange units lies in a small "village" location across the road from the beach and with a separate pool. The central beach-side pool area is appealing, as is the dining terrace overlooking it. The resort is far enough from Chaweng strip to be quiet and comfortable (but close enough to party). Though it's a short walk to get to less rocky beach, the beach is beautiful. Sybarites will adore the superb spa here, and everyone should like **Prego,** which is fast becoming Samui's most talked about Italian restaurant.

Chaweng Beach, Samui 84320 (north end of the main strip). © **07742-2015**. Fax 07742-2394. www.amari.com/palmreef. 187 units. 6,125B–7,770B (US$175–US$222/£94–£120) superior double; 7,140B–13,265B (US$204–US$379/£110–£204) deluxe; 20,615B–26,950B (US$589–US$770/£317–£415) suite. AE, MC, V. **Amenities:** 3 restaurants; 2 outdoor pools; squash court; spa; Jacuzzi; bike rental; kids' club; tour desk; car-rental desk; boutique shopping arcade; babysitting; postal services; same-day laundry/dry cleaning service; nonsmoking rooms. *In room:* A/C, satellite TV, minibar, fridge, coffeemaker, hair dryer, safe.

Centara Grand Beach Resort ✮   By late December 2007, this sprawling resort (formerly **Samui Central Beach Resort**) right in the heart of Chaweng will have been totally remodeled with not just extravagant new rooms (including Deluxe Pool Villas) and a Club Lounge open to pool villa guests, but it will sport a whole spanking new luxury feel. Happily, though, for its many returning guests, Centara won't have lost any of its well-loved village ambience, and its plethora of dining options will still include Brazilian fare at **Zico's** across the road (see "Where to Dine in Koh Samui," later) and **Hagi,** for Japanese food. If anything changes, it's that Centara will offer even more peace and seclusion from the rampant development around this busy strip. Off season discounts should make the resort a very reasonable choice for this five-star establishment. More information will be available in 2008—the below rates are guidelines only.

38/2 Moo 3, Chaweng Beach, Koh Samui 84320. © **07723-0500**. Fax 07742-2385. www.centralhotelsresorts.com. 206 units. From 9,500B–18,000B (US$271–US$514/£146–£277) double. AE, MC, V. **Amenities:** 6 restaurants; 2 bars; outdoor pool; tennis courts; fitness center; spa; watersports rentals; tour desk; car-rental desk; shopping arcade; limited room service; laundry service; Internet. *In room:* A/C, TV, fridge, minibar, safe.

Coral Bay Resort ✮   North of giddy Chaweng, but close enough to commute, these upscale thatched bungalows sit atop a picturesque hill. Rooms line the hillside (you have to trudge a bit to get to some), and each has a large balcony (some are shared with adjoining rooms). Baths are set in small gardens with waterfall showers and delightful stone work. At the side of the resort is a private villa with two master bedrooms and its own pool. The central pool area is high above the rock and coral beach below (not good for swimming), but the bay offers good snorkeling and fishing. Guests can dine at The Pakarang restaurant and a small spa provides affordable treatments.

9 Moo 2, Bophut, Chaweng Beach, Koh Samui 84320 (on a hill crest at the north end of Chaweng). © **07742-2223**. Fax 07742-2392. www.coralbay.net. 53 units. 5,000B–9,750B (US$142–US$278/£77–£150) double bungalow;

7,000B–19,000B (US$200–US$543/£108–£292) family units/suites; 20,000B–32,000B (US$571–US$914/£308–£492) Baan Chomjan villa. AE, MC, V. **Amenities:** 2 restaurants; bar; pool; spa; kids' club; tour desk; car-rental desk; library; TV/video room; babysitting; laundry service; nonsmoking rooms; Internet. *In room:* A/C, satellite TV, DVD, minibar, fridge, coffee-making facilities, safe.

The Library ✹✹✹   This ravishingly minimalist resort offers a startlingly different contemporary slant. Designed by a Bangkok architect, its rooms—called pages—are on the ground floor. Those on the upper floor are called "chapters," and in keeping with the hotel's name, their main feature is an array of books and DVDs. State-of-the-art rooms (with Jacuzzis and rain showers) provide an extraordinary range of luxuries, from huge plasma TVs and iMacs, to light boxes and self-controlled colored lighting. It's cool, original, and appeals to those with a leaning toward techno-Zen. The red-tiled pool, while innovative, somehow brings to mind Agatha Christie.

14/1 Moo.2 Bophut, Koh Samui, 84320. ✆ **07742-2767-8.** Fax 07742-2344. www.thelibrary.name. 13 units. 9,000B–9,600B (US$257–US$274/£138–£148) studio; 11,250B–12,000B (US$320–US$343/£173–£185) suites. AE, MC, V. **Amenities:** Restaurant; bar; pool; fitness room; library. *In room:* A/C; satellite TV w/DVD player, iMac, data-port, safe.

Expensive/Moderate

The Briza Beach Resort & Spa ✹✹✹   One of the finer newcomers on Samui, The Briza offers a pure lifestyle experience, aiming to recapture the spirit and serenity of the Srivjaya empire, a historic Buddhism-inspired period. You'll almost feel the tranquillity as you mount the majestic entrance steps. Just steps away from north Chaweng beach, the accommodations range from pool-access villas to beachfront villas with large private pools. All villas are super-size, with a bathtub and a separate shower; fine furnishings reflect the grandeur and serenity of the resort's theme. Guests are treated to exclusive perks such as a private butler, who endeavors to satisfy guests' every whim.

173/22 Moo 2, Chaweng Beach, Tambon Bophut, Koh Samui 84320. ✆ **07723-1997.** Fax 07723-1990. www.thebriza.com. 57 units. 14,000B–18,500B (US$400–US$528/£200–£285) pool villas, 19,000B–30,000B (US$543–857/£292–£461) beachfront villas. AE, DC, MC, V. **Amenities:** Pool; spa; beach games and watersports; library; wine cellar; Thai cultural lessons. *In room:* A/C, satellite TV, DVD player, dataport, fridge, minibar, coffee-tea making facilities, hair dryer, safe.

Kandaburi Resort & Spa ✹✹✹   This upscale low-rise resort is part of the Kata Group and sits right on the north Chaweng seafront, among tropical vegetation and lotus ponds. Rooms are decorated in a pleasant modern Thai style and there's Mediterranean, Thai, and all manner of grilled goodies (as well as a fun food court) when hunger takes hold. In high season, enjoy dance shows and a live band in the evenings. An onsite Dive Academy assists those seeking pelagic pleasures by day, including fishing trips.

20 Moo 2 Chaweng, Samui 84320. ✆ **07742-8888.** Fax 07742-8899. www.katagroup.com. 183 units. 6,000B–8,000B (US$170–US$228/£92–£123) superior rooms; 7,500B–9,000B (US$214–US$257/£115–£138) deluxe rooms; 24,000B (US$685/£369) family suites; 18,000B (US$514/£277) honeymoon suite. **Amenities:** 4 restaurants; 3 bars; 2 pools; spa; fitness center; tour desk; laundry service; dive center; Internet. *In room:* A/C, satellite TV, minibar, coffee-making facilities, hair dryer, safe.

Poppies Samui Resort   At the southern end of busy Chaweng, this popular old-timer is newly revamped, and, unlike the concrete behemoths around this part of town, Poppies features just two-dozen luxury cottages nestled amongst lush foliage, with paths and wooden bridges crossing over streams and cascading waterfalls. The Balinese-style cottages have unique open-air bathrooms with sunken bathtubs and marble floors, set in private gardens. Unwind at the Body Care Spa in a *sala* by the central free-form pool, which is surrounded by natural boulders. The Ayutthaya-style wooden pavilion is home to the resort's well-loved restaurant, known for years as one of Samui's finest (see "Where to Dine in Koh Samui," below). Given its top service and amenities, this place books up quickly—reserve in advance.

P.O. Box 1, Chaweng, Koh Samui 84320 (on the south end of the Chaweng strip). ℂ 07742-2419. Fax 07742-2420. www.poppiessamui.com. 24 units. 8,900B–13,500B (US$254–US$385/£137–£208) double. AE, MC, V. **Amenities:** Restaurant; pool; spa; tour desk; shopping arcade; limited room service; laundry service. *In room:* A/C, satellite TV, minibar, fridge, coffee-making facilities, safe.

Moderate

Evergreen Resort   A dying breed of unfussy accommodations in the heart of Chaweng, Evergreen sits on a quieter spot not far from the beach. This is one of very few Chaweng pads that still offer inexpensive to midrange options in the form of smart rooms and villas; the junior suite here provides a touch of luxury with an open-air bathtub on the terrace.

167/32 Moo 2, Chaweng Beach, Koh Samui 84320. ℂ 07741-3017. Fax 07741-3018. www.evergreensamui.com. 32 units. 990B–2,090B (US$28–US$59/£15–£32) double villas; 2,200B–2,530B (US$63–US$72/£34–£39) deluxe; 3,300B–4,400B (US$94–US$125/£51–£68) junior suite. MC, V. **Amenities:** Tour desk; motorbike/car-rental desk; airport transfer; laundry service. *In room:* A/C, minibar, satellite TV, safe, no phone.

Tradewinds ★★   One of the earliest hotels in Chaweng, Tradewinds is a super midrange choice to this day. From the higher-priced bungalows, you can step right off your front porch into the powder-soft sand, while standard bungalows are in a secluded garden not far from the beach. Rooms have large beds and rattan furnishings, new large bathrooms, and terraces big enough for barbecues. A newer motel-style block is now available but a better choice might be the bungalows. The property is also home to Samui's catamaran sailing center, under the tutelage of long-time sailor and islander, John Stall.

17/14 Moo 3, Chaweng Beach, Koh Samui 84320. ℂ 07741-4294. Fax 07741-4293. www.tradewinds-samui.com. 22 units. 2,970B–3,650B (US$85–US$104/£46–£56) garden cottage; 3,500B–4,100B (US$100–US$118/£54–£63) seaview cottage/superior rooms. AE, DC, MC, V. **Amenities:** Restaurant; bar; catamaran hire; safety deposit boxes; laundry service. *In room:* A/C, satellite TV, minibar, fridge, coffee-making facilities, safe.

Inexpensive

Ark Bar Garden Beach Resort   Ark Bar is a good budget choice for party people. Its single-story hotel rooms may have been squeezed into a narrow strip of gardens leading to the beach right in the heart of Chaweng, but it's got the basics (and even a pool). The restaurant, serving western and Thai food and fresh seafood, is popular, with an indoor restaurant and beachside restaurant, featuring cozy tables with Thai cushions, both served by ultra-friendly staff. As the sun goes down, Ark Bar becomes one of the main focal areas on Chaweng beach to gather at nighttime. On Wednesdays from 2pm until 1am, bikini-clad tourists and locals alike join in the fun, when some of the island's best funk and house music DJs perform.

159/75 Moo 2, Chaweng Beach, Koh Samui 84320. ℂ/fax 07741-3798. www.ark-bar.com. 59 units.1,450B–2,400B (US$41–US$68/£22–£37) superior/garden rooms. MC, V. **Amenities:** Restaurant; pool. *In room:* A/C, satellite TV, minibar, fridge.

LAMAI BAY
Expensive
Pavilion Samui Boutique Resort ★★★   Applying the term "boutique" is apt in this instance. Boasting grand-scale style with top service, the newly renovated Pavilion

offers everything from Mediterranean-themed bungalows to luxurious honeymoon suites. Most feature private pools or huge, opulent bathrooms, plus a courtyard area where guests can enjoy a Jacuzzi and shower under the stars. They also have a fine new spa; a small pool and dining pavilion are on the beach. Proximity to Lamai's nightlife is a plus for night owls.

124/24 Moo 3, Lamai Beach, Koh Samui 84310 (north end of Lamai Beach). ℭ 07742-4030. Fax 07742-4029. www.pavilionsamui.com. 70 units. 10,000B (US$286/£154) superior spa room; 12,000B (US$345/£185) junior spa room; 18,000B (US$514/£277) hydro villa; 28,000B (US$800/£431) grand pool villa. AE, DC, MC, V. **Amenities:** Restaurant; bar; outdoor pool; spa; tour desk; car-rental desk; transfer service; limited room service; laundry service; Wi-Fi. *In room:* A/C, TV, CD/DVD player, minibar, coffee-making facilities, hair dryer, safe.

Rocky's Boutique Resort 𝕽𝕽𝕽   A relatively new resort, Rocky's pushes the boundaries of luxury with two beautiful pools and individually designed one- to four-bedroom villas, which cascade down a rocky hillside to a private sandy beach. Just 5 minutes north of Lamai, it's easily accessible—but a hard slog up steep hills for villa residents. The resort boasts a one-to-one staff/guest ratio and great views from the private villa terraces. The hotel long-tail boat can whisk you to the Marine Park or secluded beaches (for a price).

438/1 Moo 1, Lamai, Tambon Maret, Koh Samui 84310. ℭ 07741-8367. Fax 07741-8366. www.rockyresort.com. 33 units. 700B–4,200B (US$20–US$120/£11–£65) gardenview; 5,200B–8,000B (US$148–US$228/£80–£123) ocean-view; 8,500B–11,500B (US$242–US$328/£131–£177) suite; 12,000B–13,000B (US$343–US$371/£185–£200) family beachfront; 12,500B–14,000B (US$357–US$400/£192–£215) deluxe villa. AE, MC, V. **Amenities:** 2 pools; restaurant; bar; boat; fishing and snorkeling trips; bike and jeep rental desk; tour desk; massage; babysitting; laundry service; Wi-Fi. *In room:* A/C in some, satellite TV, CD player, safe.

Moderate

Mango Village 𝕽   Another of the area's newer resorts, Mango Village comprises somewhat cramped and characterless concrete cottages with blindingly bright red-tile roofs and petite front porches. The rooms are nevertheless very adequate, clean, and well-equipped for the price, but the decor lacks any charm—great if you like '70s kitsch: sunflower yellow walls and purple floral bedspreads. Your best bet here is one of the seaview garden bungalows, which are closer to the pretty palm-lined pool. All rooms are set in a tropical garden, on a slope leading to what the resort claims is a private beach, just south of the "Grandfather and Grandmother Rocks." Reception service after hours, or on weekends, can be somewhat haphazard—but hey, you're on holiday! Simple Italian fare can be found at the resort restaurant.

438/2 Moo 1, Lamai, Tambon Maret, Koh Samui 84310. ℭ 07741-8958. Fax 07723-2237. www.mangovillage samui.com. 20 units. From 2,900B (US$83/£45) bungalows. MC, V. **Amenities:** Restaurant; 2 bars; pool; Jacuzzi; tour desk; Wi-Fi. *In room:* A/C, TV, fridge, safe.

Spa Samui 𝕽𝕽 (Value   This family-operated wellness retreat has been around for years and is known for its fasting and cleansing programs as well as great vegetarian/raw food and yoga and meditation courses. There are two resorts on Samui: the original **Spa Beach,** comprising a laid-back cluster of rustic bungalows and pool just north of Lamai, and the newer **Spa Village,** a hillside retreat studded with amazing rock formations. Rooms at both locations range from simple bungalows to large private suites with large balconies. (All rooms are equipped for colonics.) Spa Village has a pool, herbal steam bath in a large stone grotto, massage, body wraps, and facial treatments—and is open to day visitors (see "Where to Dine in Koh Samui," below). A newer (franchise) sister resort opened in 2006 on Koh Chang.

Spa Village: Lamai Beach, Koh Samui 84320 (just south, in the hills over Lamai Beach). ✆ **07723-0855.** Fax 07742-4126. www.spasamui.com. 39 units. 900B–3,500B (US$29–US$61/£14–£54) double. MC, V. **Spa Beach:** Lamai Beach (on the north end of the main strip in Lamai). 32 units. 500B–2,000B (US$12–US$49/£7.70–£31). MC, V. **Amenities:** Restaurant; juice bar; pool; spa; herbal sauna; massage; laundry service. *In room:* A/C, minibar, fridge, safe.

Weekender Resort and Hotel *(Value)*

This resort offers many accommodations options at a very reasonable price, from bungalows, superior, and deluxe rooms spread across three separate buildings to Thai-style houses. Plus, there are lower rates for singles, appealing to solo travelers who don't want to pay for twin occupancy. The teak-floored rooms are spread over a large area of beautiful landscaped tropical gardens. It's right on the soft white-sand beach of southern Lamai (with great swimming), but—just as important—it's also near enough to town.

124/19 Moo 3 Lamai, Koh Samui 84310. ✆ **07742-4429.** Fax: 07742-4011. www.weekender-resort.com. 149 units. 1,200B–1,700B (US$43–US$49/£18–£26) bungalows; 1,300B–1,800B (US$37–US$51/£20–£28) standard room; 2,300B–2,900B (US$65–US$83/£35–£45) superior room; 3,100B–3,800B (US$89–US$109/£48–£58) deluxe room; 1,900B–2,400B (US$54–US$69/£29–£37) Thai house; 2,500B–3,100B (US$71–US$89/£38–£48) beachfront terrace villa. MC, V. **Amenities:** Restaurant; juice bar; pool; spa; laundry service. *In room:* A/C, minibar, fridge, safe.

Inexpensive

Lamai Wanta Located on the beach side of the north end of Lamai, this little complex of clean and contemporary cottages complements a cluster of rooms in a two-story hotel block. There is little in the way of service here, but the small seaside pool is an oasis, and you are close to town for services. Tidy rooms have balconies, terracotta tiles, and high ceilings.

124/264 Moo 3, Lamai, Samui 84310 (north end of Lamai Beach). ✆ **07742-4550.** Fax 07742-4218. www.lamai wanta.com. 50 units. 1,360B–1,600B (US$35–US$46/£21–£25) hotel wing; 2,000B–3,400B (US$57–US$97/£31–£52) bungalows. MC, V. **Amenities:** Tour desk; laundry service; Wi-Fi. *In room:* A/C, satellite TV, DVDs for rent, minibar, fridge, safe.

Orchid Suites *(Value)*

This wonderful and informal family resort is made up of very simple thatched cottages with teak floors. These are hidden in beautiful tropical gardens in the middle of Lamai beach. Simple rattan furnishings are quite adequate and the balconies are large and airy, with sea or pool views. The flat rate is an excellent value, though a high season surcharge applies like in many places. The large pool with a poolside bar looks out over Lamai bay.

Lamai Beach, Koh Samui 84310. ✆ **07723-2303-4.** Fax 07723-2305. www.orchidsuite.com. 20 units. 1,500B (US$42/£23) single/double. MC, V. **Amenities:** Restaurant; bar; pool; free shuttle bus from Chaweng and Samui Yacht Club. *In room:* A/C, satellite TV.

LAEM SET BAY

Laem Set Inn *(Kids)* Under its former British owner, this little hotel made a huge name for itself over the last 25 years in the European glossy magazines. Today, it caters less to upscale British bohemians and more to mass market travelers and families. The funfair now installed at the entrance, and rambling ponds and bridges, give it an air of whimsy. Choose from Thai thatched bungalows, studio suites, and private pool villas—many built from salvaged rural teak homes. Family suites have bunk beds, private baths for kids, and small family dining nooks. Large porches bookend all villas from which the pounding surf can be heard. Kayaks, mountain bikes, and snorkeling gear are available to explorers but very low tides and hundreds of squishy sea cucumbers make wading an experience. The elevated pool sits alongside the (once world-famous) teak restaurant.

110 Moo 2, Hua Thanon, Laem Set, Koh Samui 84310. © **07742-4393**. Fax 07742-4394. www.laemset.com. 30 units. 1,200B–2,750B (US$34–US$78/£18–£42) bungalows; 3,000B–8,800B (US$85–US$251/£46–£135) suites; 5,800B–21,000B (US$165–US$600/£89–£323) villas. MC, V. **Amenities:** 2 restaurants; bar; pool; fitness center; Jacuzzi; sauna; watersports equipment; bike and motorcycle rental; kids' program; business center; limited room service; massage; babysitting; same-day laundry service; free Wi-Fi. *In room:* A/C, minibar, fridge, coffee-making facilities, hair dryer, safe.

WEST COAST

Baan Taling Ngam Resort and Spa ✿✿✿

(Formerly Le Royal Meridien.) On the western side of the island some 40 minutes' drive from Samui Airport—and overlooking the ocean—this is one of the ritziest addresses on Samui. The deluxe guest rooms, beach villas, and deluxe suites all have outstanding Thai-style furniture, exquisite textiles, and pretty louvered doors leading to the terraces. The Cliff Villas and the Royal Villa Baan Napa offer sumptuous Thai interiors and large private patios. The hilltop lobby and restaurant, as well as the guest rooms, have fantastic views of the sea and resort gardens, and the main pool (one of seven) appears to spill over its edges into the coconut palm grove below. The beach is small, and it's quite a schlep from the action at Chaweng (a 30-min. drive away)—for some, this is the resort's real draw. However, there's a wealth of things to do on site: kayaks, catamarans, snorkeling, and windsurfing, as well as tennis courts and mountain bikes. A PADI dive school offers courses. With great dining opportunities and a spa to soothe away those blues, this is an all-round superb place to really get away.

295 Moo 3, Taling Ngam Beach, Koh Samui 84140. © **800/225-5843** in the U.S., or 07742-3019. Fax 07742-3220. www.kosamui.com/baantalingngam. 70 units. 18,000B–20,500B (US$514–US$585/£277–£315) deluxe room; 31,150B (US$890/£479) suite; 31,150B–90,600B (US$890–US$2,588/£479–£1,394) villa. AE, DC, MC, V. **Amenities:** 3 restaurants; lounge; 7 pools; outdoor lit tennis courts; fitness center; spa; watersports equipment and dive center; car and bike rental desk; tour desk; airport transfer; salon; 24-hr. room service; babysitting; same-day laundry service/dry cleaning. *In room:* A/C, satellite TV, CD/DVD player, minibar, hair dryer, safe.

WHERE TO DINE IN KOH SAMUI
CHAWENG

Chaweng is lined with eateries, with everything from McDonald's to the finest dining (the best of which are below). Increasingly, larger resorts in the area are setting up free-standing restaurants for both in-house and outside guests. **Poppies** (© 07742-2419) on South Chaweng is famous for its beachside dining, Balinese fare, and romantic atmosphere, and brings in guest chefs from around the world. Reservations are recommended. Look out also for the new and highly recommended **Padma** (part of **Karma Resort**), **Red Snapper** (from the Chaweng Regent), **Prego** (from Amari), and **Zico's** from Centara (listed below).

In addition to the places reviewed below, also try to check out the branches of **Will Wait** (© **087742-4263;** 087723-0093) in Chaweng and Lamai, where you get a hearty breakfast in town at a decent price. And don't forget the recently opened diner **Dr Frog's** (© 07741-3797), which sits on the hill between Chaweng and Lamai and is sure to become popular with its tasty Thai and Western food, free Wi-Fi, and spectacular views over the bay.

Bear in mind that if you use any credit cards on Samui, your payments are often surcharged up to 5%.

Betelnut ✿✿ INTERNATIONAL   Down a quiet *soi* off the south end of Chaweng lies one of the island's most popular restaurants. You'll most likely be greeted at the door by Jeffrey Lord, owner, proprietor, and witty raconteur. The menu is divided into

"Eats Big" and "Eats Small," and runs the gamut from the evocatively named "Buddha Jumped Over the Wall" (an ostrich steak, not the famous Chinese vegetarian taro dish of the same name), to clam chowder with green curry. Come with friends, order a spread of tapas choices, select from among their fine wines, and enjoy a great evening.

46/27 Chaweng Blvd. down Soi Colibri, Chaweng (across from Central Resort). ℂ 07741-3370. Main courses 475B–650B (US$12–US$16/£7.30–£10). MC, V. Daily 6pm–last order.

Noori India INDIAN   This long-running family business owns two restaurants in Chaweng. Noori serves a variety of true Indian dishes, offering an alternative to those for whom Thai spices may be a wee bit too piquant. Although a spot of redecorating wouldn't go amiss, the music and decor of traditional Indian artworks makes for a truly authentic experience. They also run an island-wide delivery service.

Opposite Chaweng Buri on Central Chaweng Strip, and another just before Poppies Resort. ℂ 07741-3315 for reservations at either outlet. Main courses from 200B (US$5.70/£3.10). No credit cards. Daily 11am–11:30pm.

Vecchia Napoli ✦ ITALIAN   The simple and authentic Northern Italian cuisine at this restaurant fits the bill for great pastas, grills, pizza, and the house special, shellfish soup. Follow it up with a tiramisu and espresso and you won't believe you're just a stone's throw from busy Chaweng. Also ask about their new upmarket venue, **Bellini** (46/26 Chaweng Beach, Soi Calibri; ℂ 07741-3831; www.bellini-samui.com), serving up similar Italian delights. Chow down on grilled vegetables with goat cheese or cannelloni crepe with rock lobster.

166/31 Moo 2, Chaweng Beach (central Chaweng). ℂ 07723-1229. Main courses 120B–420B (US$3.40–US$12/£1.85–£6.45). MC, V. Daily 11am–11pm.

Zico's ✦✦ BRAZILIAN   (Part of Centara Resort.) For a wild night out, this unique Brazilian-themed restaurant is a riot of music, drink, and dance, with Brazilian performers shaking their tail feathers from table to table. Roving waiters, called *passadors,* come around with massive skewers of meat and trays of delicacies (you can also choose from the extensive salad bar). For a set price, you pick what you like, and as much as you like, by laying a small coin on the table with the green side up for "More please," and the red side up for "Enough for now, thanks." Quite an experience.

38/2 Moo 3, Chaweng Beach (on the south end of Chaweng across from the Centara Resort). ℂ 07723-1560. 680B (US$19/£10) for an unlimited buffet. MC, V. Daily 7–10:30pm. Dance shows at 8, 9:30, and 10pm.

FISHERMAN'S VILLAGE

You should take time out to wander through the Fisherman's Village area, just off the busy road to Bophut's beach and piers. Now transformed into a foodie paradise, it is lined with several atmospheric pubs and small upmarket restaurants along the water's edge. You can savor good pub food in the friendly and laid-back **Frog and Gecko** (ℂ 07742-5248), or, if it's stylish dining you're after, pop into **Starfish and Coffee** (ℂ 07742-7201) in the center of the street. Vegetarians will adore the friendly, laid-back ambience at **Art Café** (ℂ 089724-9673, mobile), which dishes up healthy breakfasts, coffees, or light meals such as King Fish Pesto Sauce salad or the Special Tofu salad with curry dressing. You can also join yoga and art classes here; just ask at the counter.

BOPHUT/BIG BUDDHA

The Mangrove ✦✦ *Finds* FRENCH/INTERNATIONAL   This well-known—and well-promoted—fine French restaurant sits up near the airport. Famous not just for its food but also its romantic atmosphere, Mangrove lies on a quiet stretch of road.

The open-air dining area overlooks eponymous mangrove forests and echoes with the sounds of the jungle. The place is run by a young (but experienced) Franco–Belgian couple who go to great lengths to please all palates; the menu changes monthly to cater to the oft-returning expatriate clientele. For a starter, try the crab salad, followed by roasted salmon with lime butter sauce, or the delectable seared tuna. Do also ask for the daily specials. Don't scrimp on dessert: Try the rich chocolate mousse and follow it up with a Rum Ginger, their signature after-dinner drink. Note the 3-day, month-end holiday; plan ahead so as not to miss an utterly charming dining experience.

32/6 Moo 4, Bophut, Koh Samui 84320 (on the airport road between Bophut and Big Buddha). © 07742-7584. Main courses 280B–520B (US$8–US$15/£4.30–£8). AE, MC, V. Daily 5–10pm. Closed last 3 days of each month.

Quo Vadis ✸ MOROCCAN/ASIAN   Don't be put off if the service staff is not so fluent in English here—the cuisine created in this new "Morocc–Asian" restaurant makes a great change from the usual beach diners. And it's not just North African–influenced meals; there's a mouthwatering selection of tapas, too. The main dishes are mainly Moroccan in flavor and arrive (as one would expect) in the Arab *tajine,* a traditional clay pot, along with amazing couscous.

51/4 Moo 4 Tambon Bophut. © 07743-0456. www.saboey.com. Meals from 400B (US$11/£6.15). AE, MC, V. Daily 5–10pm.

LAMAI BEACH
The Spa Restaurant ✸✸ VEGETARIAN   It's not just for veggies (they serve a few seafood and chicken dishes as well) but for anyone who'd like to get away from Big Macs and enjoy a healthy, tasty dish made almost entirely from organic fare. Open from breakfast time for its house guests, The Spa serves yummy smoothies, Mexican snacks, steamed snapper, an amazing variety of great tofu dishes (the tofu burgers are huge), and delicious curries—along with excellent Thai fare. If you can, plan to arrive a few hours in advance to take advantage of the herbal steam and massage facilities at the Health Center here. Try either their new mountain-top retreat or the older resort just north of Lamai.

Rte. 4169, between Chaweng and Lamai beaches. © 07723-0855. Reservations recommended in peak season. Main courses 30B–250B (85¢–US$7.10/45p–£3.85). MC, V. Daily 7am–10pm.

WEST COAST BEACHES
Big John Seafood SEAFOOD   This is worth the ride across the island—to Lipa Noi—especially if you like fresh seafood. Although the atmosphere is a mix of raucous revelry and Thai families out to graze, this has become a longtime popular spot with live music most nights. Order the day's catch as you like, and accompany it with a myriad of good Thai curries and side dishes. Big John overlooks a pretty stretch of palm-lined beach.

95/4 Moo 2, Lipa Noi Beach. © 07741-5537. www.bigjohnsamui.com. Seafood by kg. No credit cards. Daily 11am–11pm.

EXPLORING KOH SAMUI
SCUBA & SNORKELING
Local aquanauts agree that the best **scuba diving** in the region is off **Koh Tao** and nearby **Koh Nang Yuan** (just off the northwest tip of Koh Tao), which benefits from deep water just offshore and great visibility. However, local dive shops will be able to offer advice on sites around Samui, and, more importantly, will know local prevailing conditions (the open water around Samui can be notoriously squally). Many shops are

attached to PADI dive schools offering trips ranging further afield to some of the 80 or so islands scattered across this archipelago. **Ang Thong Marine National Park** (with 40 islands) makes a great destination from Samui. The few shops listed below are good options among the many on the island. *Note:* There is a **decompression chamber** on Samui; call © 07742-7427 for info.

Samui International Diving School (at the Malibu Resort, Chaweng Beach; © 07742-2386; www.planet-scuba.net) is a good bet for full services. **Easy Divers,** open since 1987, has locations in Chaweng (© 07741-3373; www.easydivers-thailand. com) and other beaches, and offers good deals for beginners. Both outfits offer all sorts of PADI courses and daily dive tours, and have international safety standard boats, good equipment, and complete insurance packages. Daily dives (two dives per day) start from about 3,000B (US$86/£46) per person including land transportation, breakfast, equipment, lunch, and drinks.

Big Blue (© 07745-6179; call for prices) provides custom trips for divers of any skill level and is a good choice for small groups or those seeking private attention.

Some of the better **snorkeling** off Koh Samui is found along the rocky coast between Chaweng Noi and Lamai bays. Several shops along Chaweng Beach rent snorkeling gear for about 100B (US$2.85/£1.55) per day.

GOLF

Samui boasts the picturesque hilltop **Santiburi Golf Course,** part of the Santiburi Resort (12/12 Moo 1, Mae Nam; © 07742-5040; www.santiburi.com). It sits high in the hills on the north end of the island. Greens fees start from 3,350B (US$82/£52) for 18 holes, but additional caddy and golf buggy fees apply. Opposite the turn-off to Fisherman's Village, the newly opened **Bo Phut Hills Golf Club** (© 087267-1042, mobile) offers a more affordable option for golfers on a 9-hole course and costs 875B (US$25/£13), or 1,500B (US$43/£23) if played as 18 holes. If you feel that you haven't got the swing just yet, the new game of **football golf** needs no special skills; it's as it sounds, a matter of kicking a football into the holes. Just north of Chaweng in Choeng Mon, the course at **Samui Football Golf** (no phone) is set under swaying palms.

KAYAKING

Blue Stars Sea Kayaking at the Gallery Lafayette in Chaweng (© 07723-0497; call for prices) is easy to contact through most booking agents. The outfit takes people kayaking and snorkeling to the Marine National Park. The rubber canoes are perfect for exploring the caverns underneath limestone cliffs. If you can't get to Phang Nga (which has the most fantastic sea cave scenery), this trip is another fun option. Alternatively, try **Samui Island Tour** (© 07742-1382).

CRUISING, SAILING & KITEBOARDING

Dutch seafarer and Phuket resident, Jeroen Deknatel of Fantasea Divers' **Ocean Rover Cruises** ⚓ (© 07628-1388; www.ocean-rover.com), is one of the south's most experienced dive operators. With a reputation for rigorous safety, his outfit has just launched the first of luxurious annual **dive-golf** trips on a live-aboard, starting (or finishing) in Koh Samui. The vessel sails the length of the eastern peninsular coast, all the way to Singapore, via some of most outstanding dive sites and golf courses in Asia. In 2008, these will run in June and July, but book early because of the demand.

Shorter cruises can be taken on a stunning **Chinese junk,** *The Fortune* (© 07723-1169), which can accommodate up to eight people (or wedding parties) and offers trips from a day to a week. On-board activities include diving, snorkeling, fishing, and island trekking. **Easy Charter** (© 07724-6280; www.easycharter.com) has a beautifully renovated **wooden ketch** *Pinisi* for sunset and day (or longer) luxury cruising.

For **catamaran sailing,** check out **Tradewinds Resort** in Chaweng (© 07723-0602; www.sailingkohsamui.com). Owner and long-time resident, John Stall offers—and leads—courses. There's now a growing bunch of **kiteboarders** descending on Samui in the peak season (Dec–Feb); more information can be found on sites like **www.kiteboardingasia.com**. A center is based out of Samui Orchid Resort on Laem Set Beach (www.samuiorchid.com).

CULTURAL PURSUITS
COOKING COURSES
For daily Thai cooking and fruit-carving lessons, try **Samui Institute of Thai Culinary Arts (SITCA;** © 07741-3172; www.sitca.com), which is a professional operation with a friendly cooking school; it's a great way to have fun and meet others—especially if your beach plans get rained out. After the course you can invite a guest to dine with you at a group meal. Classes meet daily at 11am and 4pm and cost 1,850B (US$53/£28); they accept all major credit cards. Call for more details, or pop into the Institute on Chaweng Beach strip, across from the Centara Grand Beach Resort (p. 200).

SPAS
Like many places in Thailand, the spa scene has really taken off on Samui. All the big, international five-star resorts, like **Anantara** (p. 197), offer top-range (and top-priced) treatments by well-trained staff. But there are also some reasonably priced haunts too, including a number of good day spas for those wanting a serious and dedicated wellness retreat. Whether as an escape from the kids on a rainy day or as part of a larger health-focused mission, Samui has all the services you'll need.

Ban Sabai on Big Buddha Beach (© 07724-5175; www.ban-sabai.com) has a wide range of therapies that take place in one of two teak Thai houses or in a *sala* at the beachside. Personal attention is the hallmark in this little Garden of Eden. Two houses are available for booking as part of a package or simply as a relaxing location to stay. Treatments start around 1,000B (US$29/£15).

Eranda Herbal Spa 🏵 just north of Chaweng on the road to Choeng Mon (© 07742-2666; www.erandaspa.co.th), is set in tropical gardens with plunge pools, steam rooms, and Jacuzzis on a high perch above Chaweng Bay—so you get sea views while getting pampered. Choose from an open communal *sala* or luxury private pavilions with their own steam rooms and Jacuzzis.

Just expanded with new relaxation areas and a large lotus pond, the highly respected day spa **Tamarind Springs** 🏵🏵 (© 07742-4221; www.tamarindsprings.com) is set on a palm-clad hillside just above the beach at Lamai and is a rare place that truly takes you back to nature. The natural herbal steam room sandwiched between boulders is awesome; after a few minutes, you'll savor slipping into the outdoor plunge pool. Book well in advance.

Traditional massage is available at any number of storefronts in Chaweng and along the beach. Expect to pay between 200B and 400B (US$5.70–US$11/£3.10–£6.15) per hour for services; it's much the same as the average spa, but without the pomp, ceremony, or incense.

Another gem is **Natural Wing Health Spa & Resort** (© 07742-0871; www.naturalwing.com), located on Bang Por Beach (near the Four Seasons Resort), a spa resort with rooms from 1,700B (US$48/£26), villas for 3,500B (US$100/£54), and even long-stay options from 22,000B (US$628/£338) a month. Prices include daily breakfast and detox (cleansing) and slimming programs, in conjunction with acupuncture and a variety of spa treatments.

Natural Wing is home to the quizzically named restaurant **I Do You Eat** (© 07724-7855) offering Thai, Japanese, Vietnamese, and European cuisine. Two hundred seats make it good for big parties, and delivery services are available on request if you find yourself stranded without wheels.

SHOPPING

There is very little in terms of local craft production on the island—almost everything is imported from the mainland—so save the big purchases for Bangkok or Chiang Mai. New shopping areas are growing in number by the day, however, around Chaweng. **Pearls** are cultivated locally and you'll see some good examples in several shops. Ask local tour operators about trips to **Naga Pearl Farm** on **Koh Matsum.**

KOH SAMUI AFTER DARK

At any given time, the Chaweng strip is certain to be disrupted occasionally by roaming pickup trucks with crackling PA systems blaring out advertisements in Thai and English for local **Thai boxing bouts.** Grab a flyer for times and locations, which vary.

Watch out also for notices about seasonal **buffalo fights,** which also vary according to Thai festive days. Rather than being bloody affairs, the animals in these competitions don't actually gore each other—the losing steer simply runs off to fight another day. These rituals are steeped in animist traditions and superstition, with special offerings and prayers made to the buffalo before the matches, and of course a huge amount of betting and boozing accompanying the fights.

Many of Samui's hotels and resorts have cultural shows featuring Thai dance that can be magical. If you like sequins and glamour, Samui puts on some entertaining *katoey* (drag queen) shows as well. **Christy's Cabaret** (© 08167-62181) at the north end of Chaweng puts on a gala extravaganza of high camp that's free of charge. Come well before the show starts at 11pm to get a good seat, and be prepared to make up for the free admission with cocktail prices.

For bars and discos, Chaweng is the place to be. There are new classier clubs such as **Mint Bar** in Soi Green Mango, which hosts international DJs in a stylish setting, and the fashionable **Q Bar** up on the hill, a little remote from the main center. **Solo Bar,** on the beachfront road in the center of Chaweng (next to Starbucks), throws the best party Samui has to offer every Friday from 2pm to 1am, with free barbecue. Because it has DJs spinning great sounds, a pool table, and six plasma TV screens showing major sporting events, people tend to gather at Solo early before going on a walk-about, reconvening later at **Solo Club** just behind (part of the same enterprise).

A somewhat dubious legend among a certain crowd in Chaweng is the nearby **Green Mango** which bangs out cheesy house music while commercial sex workers cruise for foreign business. **Just Jonno's** (© 08578-99451) is a newly opened bardiner at the entrance of Sala Samui Resort in Choeng Mon and provides a refreshing alternative to Chaweng bars. Appealing less to grungy bar flies—more to the yuppies—it fills a much needed gap in this isolated corner. It plays cool house music in the evenings and offers a free Full Moon BBQ with English-style beef burgers cooked by Jonno himself.

For **live music** on Chaweng, go no farther than **Beatles' Bar** in Fisherman's Village, which sees gatherings of local expat musicians, or **Coco Blues Company** on Chaweng

Beach Road (www.cocobluescompany.com), a popular Blues club-cum-restaurant with New Orleans–style atmosphere. Irish-owned/managed **Tropical Murphy's** across from McDonald's in south Chaweng (© **07741-3614**) is a slice of Ireland with an authentic pub atmosphere, a full range of beers, and good tasty British grub. Live music on the second floor boosts the ambience but doesn't hinder conversation.

On Sunday afternoons, be sure to truck on over to **The Secret Garden Pub** ☞☞ on Big Buddha Beach (© **07724-5253**) for barbecue food, cheap beer, and a succession of local and guest musicians performing blues and rock songs. The crowd is more or less evenly split between tourists and expats and it's all very relaxed and family-friendly. There are also accommodations available at the attached bungalows.

Over at Lamai Beach, there's everything from beer bars of the sleazier variety to mud wrestling, Thai lady boxing, and a few decent music venues. **Fusion** breaks the mold with acid jazz, funk, soul, and drum 'n' base nights, and down at **Sub Club,** decent DJs, a good drink selection, and professional dancers (not go-go girls) whip the crowd up into a frenzy till the small hours. Sports fans may be impressed by the gigantic screen that looms over the beer garden here. **Bauhaus** has cheap drinks and holds foam parties and attracts football fans to its screens in high season.

The **Buddy Beer** folks are building a brand new huge resort here due to open in 2008, which is sure to have a bar; look out for this development.

SIDE TRIPS FROM KOH SAMUI
ANG THONG NATIONAL MARINE PARK ☞☞
Ang Thong National Marine Park comprises over 40 more islands northwest of Samui and is well known for its scenic beauty and coral reefs. Many of these islands are limestone rock towers of up to 40m (131 ft.), fringed by beaches and tropical rainforest.

Koh Wua Talab (Sleeping Cow Island) is the largest of the 40 and is home to the **National Park Headquarters** where there are some very basic 4- to 8-person accommodations (booked only through the park headquarters at © **07728-6025**), but most just visit for the day. The island has freshwater springs and a park-run restaurant. *Note:* Pack a pair of strong walking shoes for the steep hills; flip flops won't be able to take the gradient.

Koh Mae Ko (Mother Island) is known for both its beach and Thalay Noi, an **inland saltwater lake** with an undiscovered outlet to the sea (made famous by the film *The Beach*). Known to the Thais as **Ang Thong,** or "Golden Bowl," this turquoise-green lagoon gave its name to the entire archipelago. Endless companies offer day trips, by speedboat or the bigger **Seatran Discovery** boat (© **07742-6000**). Some include snorkeling and kayaking trips with a range of prices; **Blue Stars** (© **07723-0497;** www.bluestars.info) in Chaweng is a good operator to try.

5 Koh Pha Ngan

644km (399 miles) S of Bangkok to Surat Thani; 75km (46½ miles) E from Surat Thani to Koh Pha Ngan

For the time being at least, Koh Pha Ngan is a more rustic alternative to busy and developed Koh Samui, attracting many backpackers in search of that well-used cliché "island paradise." However, although Koh Pha Ngan still attracts an adventurous young crowd, it is following the same model of development as Samui and Phuket—once-basic bungalow resorts are turning into upmarket villas with air-conditioning and swimming pools. This, in turn, is forcing prices to increase.

Just say "Mai!"

When it comes to doing drugs in Thailand, remember that "Mai" means "no." Thai authorities issue harsh penalties to anyone dealing, in possession of, or using drugs. Numerous undercover drug busts are staged, not just at Full Moon Parties, but at bungalow hotels, and at pre- and post-party roadblocks. Many of these stings are setups that you'll never be able to counterprove. Dealers and police often work in cahoots and the lackadaisical Thai legal system offers you no protection or parole. Even scarier, recent reports have highlighted not just the selling of dodgy pharmaceuticals but the lethal herbal hallucinogen *ton lamphong*, a poisonous weed. Taking this is nothing short of suicide. Every month local hospitals repeatedly find themselves treating tourists suffering severe psychological damage after taking recreational drugs or hallucinogens—they are the lucky ones; some revelers simply go home in a body bag.

Easily visible from Koh Samui but about two-thirds its size, with similar terrain and flora, Koh Pha Ngan boasts beautiful beaches and some secluded upmarket resorts on the farther reaches of the island—the rugged north and west coast areas are accessible only by bumpy road, or chartered boat. The southeastern peninsula of **Had Rin** (also written Haad Rin) is home to the now infamous monthly **Full Moon Party,** a nightlong beach rave that attracts thousands of revelers who pack the island to groove to every kind of dance music—and consume (and usually later regurgitate) buckets of alcohol. These parties are no longer the hippy, trippy, love-fests of the '70s, but blatantly commercial gigs geared to squeeze as much cash out of revved-up partygoers as possible; at Full Moon, even the basic bungalows are going for double the normal rates. As a result, **Leela Beach** on the northern spur now pulls more punters than the noisier beach at Had Rin Nok (known as Sunrise Beach).

A word of warning: Party time is also a petty thief's paradise. Do yourself a favor and lock all your valuables in the hotel safe before you party—as experienced thieves take the opportunity to swoop on insecure accommodations while you have fun.

Boats from Koh Samui leave at regular intervals all day and night on Full Moon nights from either Big Buddha Beach or Bophut (running from 5pm; returning between 3am and 8am). Many revelers just make a night of it, crash on the beach, and come back to Samui in the morning. At other times the small area of Had Rin is busy with young travelers. You'll find New Age crystal, trinket and T-shirt shops, vegetarian restaurants, bars playing DVDs, masseurs, cheap beer, and even cheaper bungalows just a Frisbee throw away from perfect white-sand beaches. Be careful of the rip tides here in monsoon months, and pay attention to the attendant lifeguards now present on the beach.

Don't be too put-off by Koh Pha Ngan's party reputation. Had Rin can be avoided altogether and, even during the full moon, you can find peace and quiet in any of a number of tranquil hideaways on the island, such as **Thong Nai Pan** to the north and **Had Salad** or **Had Yao** to the west. **Koh Ma** is a small island connected to Koh Pha Ngan by a sandbar on **Had Mae Had** beach. It's a paradise surrounded by an amazingly colorful, living reef—making it an ideal location for snorkeling or learning to dive.

GETTING THERE

By Boat   Frequent boats link the mainland towns of Chumphon or Surat Thani with the islands of Koh Samui, Koh Pha Ngan, or Koh Tao. From Samui's Nathon Pier, the trip to Thong Sala in Koh Pha Ngan takes 45 minutes with the **Songserm Express Boat** and costs 130B (US$3.70/£2). Contact them in Koh Samui (© 07742-0157); the **Seatran** vehicular ferry service is once-daily, leaves from Bang Rak, takes longer, and is only slightly cheaper.

The fastest way to Koh Pha Ngan from Samui is by the twice-daily **Lomprayah Catamaran** (on Samui, © 07742-7765-6; on Koh Pha Ngan, © 07723-8412; www.lomprayah.com), which leaves from **Wat Na Phra Larn** on Maenam. The crossing takes about 30 minutes and costs 250B (US$7.10/£3.85). Lomprayah also makes daily connections on to Koh Tao and back to the mainland at Chumphon (but not to Surat Thani). The **Haad Rin Queen** also runs a service four times daily from Big Buddha beach directly to Had Rin Pier that takes 30 minutes for 150B (US$4.30/£2.50). Boats can also be chartered from **Petcharat Marina** at Samui's Big Buddha Beach (© 07742-5262) or Bophut Beach (rates are greatly inflated during Full Moon Parties). You'll also find getting back to the mainland much cheaper than getting there, but exert caution between June and December as freak storms have been known to put lives at risk.

FAST FACTS

The tourist police operate a small information kiosk on the north end of the ferry offices at Thong Sala pier; contact them at © 07742-1281 for info or © 1155 in an emergency. There are branches of all the high street banks with **ATMs** along both the main street of Thong Sala and in Had Rin. **Internet** service is chockablock around the island; prices are an inflated 120B (US$3.40/£1.85) per hour.

GETTING AROUND

Jeep and **motorbike rental** on Koh Pha Ngan is available at most tour companies and resorts across the island (basic jeeps run from 900B [US$26/£13]; regular motorbikes run from 150B [US$4.30/£2.30] per day). The island roads are steep and treacherous—especially over the hills near Had Rin—so drive carefully. Many interior roads, including the trek to secluded Thong Nai Pan in the north, are hilly, muddy tracks, requiring off-road skills. (It's not just the state of the roads, but the inexperienced riders on the road, that are problematic.) Jazzed-up **scooters** are rented out for about 300B (US$8.60/£4.60) per day, but if you are not experienced in off-road biking, it's much safer to stick to *songtaews* (communal pickups) which follow the main routes and cost from 50B (US$1.40/75p); more at night, or during party season.

WHAT TO DO & SEE

The rugged roads of Koh Pha Ngan beg to be explored, and interior routes connect bays and small towns across unspoiled countryside—a window into a laid-back island lifestyle that's now slowly disappearing. **Wat Khao Tham** (spelt differently by the retreat) is a well-known international meditation center and temple compound just north of Ban Tai; see www.watkowtahm.org for info. Since 1988, Steve and Rosemary Weissmann (from the U.S. and Australia, respectively) have been offering intensive Theravada Buddhism-based meditation retreats. Introductory 10- to 20-day courses, as well as 3-month work retreats, are open to anyone over 20 years of age and cost 4,500B–9,000B (US$128–US$257/£69–£138). As with any retreat, conditions governing behavior apply. The temple is also open to day visitors and overlooks one of the best views on the island. For more details, check the Web or write to Wat Kow Tahm, P.O. Box 18, Koh Pha Ngan, Surat Thani, 84280.

WHERE TO STAY
BAN TAI BEACH

Most visitors head east to nearby Ban Tai beach, close to the pier at Thong Sala—here they find a quiet stretch of sand away from the hubbub of Had Rin but close enough to visit the party zone and readily accessible by communal taxi *(songtaew)*. The water is unfortunately not really deep enough for swimming, but the fine sand beach is wide and most resorts now have pools set on the beachfront. There's a good number of accommodations on hand, from a few original fan bungalows to newly built complexes offering every amenity.

Mac Bay Resort Even with a new pool, it's hard for this simple little hideaway to compete with the growing array of better presented and more fashionable resorts along the beach. Rooms are basic concrete huts, but they are right on the sand. Some were being revamped in late 2007. Larger air-conditioned rooms are a better choice. The original owners are currently building a new budget resort due to open in 2008, called Mac's Bungalows; it hopes to retain the original feel and still cater for the lower-end budget traveler.

Ban Tai Beach, Koh Pha Ngan 84280 (down a small lane south of the main east–west road). ⓒ 07723-8443. 25 units. 300B–450B (US$7.30–US$11/£4.60–£6.90) double with fan; 700B (US$17/£11) double with A/C. MC, V. **Amenities:** Restaurant; pool; tour desk; motorbike rental desk; laundry service. *In room:* A/C in some.

Milky Bay Resort 🐾🐾 Friendly service and midrange luxury is on tap at this beautifully presented resort set in lush gardens with meandering paths to individual bungalows and villas. Chose from five room types, each of which is different in style and creature comforts; rates vary according to low, high, and peak seasons (the below rates just give an idea of the huge range). Next to the stunning oceanfront pool, the restaurant serves delicious BBQ, Thai, and Italian food (you'll even find a proper pizza oven) and overlooks a white-sand beach lapped by the sea. A couple of pool tables will keep some guests happy, while others can indulge in a wonderful Thai massage. The fitness room and steam room come at no extra charge. You can request a pickup from the ferry pier.

102 Moo 1 Ban Tai Beach, Koh Pha Ngan 84280 (4 miles east of Thong Sala). ⓒ 07723-8566. Fax 07737-7726. www.milkybay.com. 34 units. 1,200B–1,600B (US$34–US$46/£18–£25) standard; 3,000B–4,000B (US$86–US$114/£46–£62) studio room; 5,000B–8,000B (US$143–US$228/£77–£123) beachfront villa. MC, V. **Amenities:** 2 restaurants; bar; pool; fitness center; gameroom; tour desk; car-rental desk; salon; massage; laundry service; safety deposit boxes; Wi-Fi. *In room:* A/C, TV, DVD player.

HAD RIN

Had Rin (aka Haad Rin) is a narrow peninsula on the island's southeastern tip filled with bungalows, busy shopping streets, funky clothes shops, and an array of restaurants between east facing Had Rin Nok (Sunrise Beach) and Had Rin Nai (Sunset Beach) on the west side. Check out the popular **Rin Bay View Bungalow** (no phone) or the aptly named **Mellow Mountain Bungalows** (no phone) for low-end choices, from 300B to 600B (US$8.60–US$17/£4.60–£9.25).

If you wish to transcend it all, tucked away on the soft white-sand beach of Leela (or Had Seekantang) beach, just 5 minutes over the hilltop, is **Cocohut Village** (ⓒ 07737-5368; www.cocohut.com). Spacious bungalows of all sizes start at 1,200B (US$34/£18); budget guesthouse rooms cater to backpackers at 600B

(US$17/£9.25). Next door, Sarikantang (© **07737-5055-6;** www.sarikantang.com) has rooms that go from basic fan and cold-shower bungalows right up to the ocean-view suite; rates range from 500B to 4,200B (US$14–US$120/£8–£65). Both have beachside restaurants and pools, and are just far enough from town for a bit of peace and quiet, but are close enough to walk down and join festivities. The original **Leela Bungalows** (© **08773-75094,** mobile) at the end of the beach still offers rustic bungalows, although they could do with a bit of freshening up. **Lighthouse** (no phone) has secluded bungalows set around the rocky cape hillside, accessible by the wooden bridge. Rates for both Leela and the Lighthouse start at 500B (US$14/£8).

Sea Breeze Bungalow (94/11 Moo 6, Had Rin; © **07737-5162**) also offers a quiet, lofty perch high enough above town and is close enough to walk down and join the fun. Fan rooms are 500B (US$14/£8) and air-conditioned rooms are 1,000B (US$29/£15) except at Full Moon. Choose the fan rooms on the cliff for the best views; plus, the breeze makes air-conditioning unnecessary. There's a hilltop pool with a bar and a wooden boardwalk and rickety stairway providing access to Seekantang beach.

Drop Inn Club Resort and Spa (157/1-10 Had Rin © **07737-5444-7;** www.dropinclub.com) is a relatively new resort made up of elegant Thai-style houses clustered around a pool. The air-conditioned rooms are already a bit knocked about, and as a result, the high-end prices for the penthouse (19,000B/US$543/£292) seem overblown. Another disadvantage is its location in town, nowhere near the sea, though the Full Moon beach is a short walk away.

Pariya Haad Yuan Resort (Had Yuan; © **07723-0414;** www.pariyahaadyuan.com) claims to be the island's first boutique resort. These days it has upgraded, renamed itself, and grown more toward an exclusive little hideaway with a clutch of newly upgraded rooms and villas that cater to the better-heeled traveler. The resort lies—as it name suggests—on the increasingly popular and totally gorgeous Had Yuan (Yuan Beach) in the east. Being accessible only by boat has guarded it against the crowds, but it won't be long before it becomes a well-known spot. The style is modern-rustic and comes with the kind of modern amenities that would have been unheard of in this neck of the woods 10 years ago. Prices range from 2,500B to 12,000B (US$71–US$343/£38–£185). Reservations are best made through the Samui office.

The Sanctuary Resort and Spa ✮✮ Hidden behind trees on Had Thien beach, just a short boat ride to the north of Had Rin, The Sanctuary bills itself as alternative—and it certainly is, with a dazzling range of wellness, dance, and meditative activities and courses, as well as colonic treatments at its adjacent **Wellness & Detox Center.** As much as its yoga, massage, and cleansing programs, the main draw is its tranquillity, and there are plenty of beach activities, too. The choice of accommodations is wide, ranging from simple low-cost dorms and yogi rooms to houses tucked away in the jungle. These jungle homes are a model of outdoor living that even Tarzan would approve of; small kitchens and bathrooms have been designed with the idea that they should be fully open to the jungle. It's a stark (and perhaps much needed) contrast to the endless nights of overindulgence at Had Rin.

Note: Not all rooms can be booked in advance; some are on a first-come, first-served basis. You'll also need to arrange a taxi boat from Had Rin Sunrise Beach to Had Thien (100B–300B/US$2.85–US$8.60/£1.55–£4.60, depending on number of passengers). If coming from Koh Samui, the Thong Nai Pan ferry departs from Mae

Nam pier every day at noon and brings you directly to Had Thien on its way. If the weather prevents the boats from running—or if you are feeling energetic—you could simply walk over the hill on a marked path.

Had Thien, Koh Pha Ngan ⒸⒸ 08127-13614 (mobile). www.thesanctuarythailand.com. 30 units. 100B (US$2.85/ £1.55) dorm; 450B–1,540B (US$12.85–US$44/£6.90–£24) bungalows with en-suite bathroom; 1,500B–4,400B (US$43–US$126/£23–£68) jungle houses. No credit cards. **Amenities:** Restaurant; bar; spa; watersports rentals; laundry service; Wi-Fi. *In room:* Suites w/satellite TV, kitchenette, fridge, safe, no phone.

WEST & NORTH COAST

The west and north coasts have white-sand beaches and are far from the monthly hippy hoe-down at Had Rin, which might be a relief for many. Resorts here are quiet and affordable, and growing in number and quality of amenities. The beautifully tranquil Laem Son freshwater lake lies close to Ao Chao Phao but reports warn that it may be contaminated—don't take any risks. The resorts below follow a clockwise route starting at Had Son on the west.

Had Son

Haad Son Resort (ⒸⒸ 07734-9104; www.haadson.com) is a great find, on its own secluded sandy beach over from Had Yao, with good hilltop views of the sea. It's always expanding, and current renovations should be finished by 2008. Expect to find four luxury executive penthouse suites, each with stunning views and a private balcony, situated around a Jacuzzi. Just 10 minutes west of Thong Sala is **Phangan Cabana** (ⒸⒸ 02673-0966), a 34-room joint popular thanks to high standards of both accommodation and service. It has a swimming pool and, although prices have risen, they are not yet overblown. The majority of its rooms have air conditioning at 1,400B (US$40/£22); fan rooms are 800B (US$23/£12).

Had Yao ⒻⒻ

Had Yao or Long Beach is considered by many to be the perfect beach, a quiet but huge stretch of white sand, good for swimming, with the best sunset views and a laidback vibe that drew the first travelers here. A couple of supermarkets and Internet cafes up on the main road provide the bulk of services you'll need; good eats can also be found along the beach—it's big enough to play football on.

There are several bungalow resorts ranging from very basic choices, such as the rough-and-ready **Ibiza** (no phone), starting at 200B (US$6/£3) or the original **Had Yao** (no phone) and **Sandy Bay Bungalows** (no phone), both offering budget prices from 300B (US$8.60/£4.60).

Long Bay Resort Ⓕ ⒾⒹⒾ This great family resort sits in the middle of Had Yao beach; its free-form pool has been designed so that there's a children's area, too. The property offers a comfortable international standard of rooms and proximity to lots of good local adventure. Families should ask for an extra bed or try the VIP suite that has more space. The open-air beachfront restaurant provides a vast array of delicious Thai and international cuisine. Treat yourself to the fresh catch of the day at the sunset BBQ.

Had Yao, Koh Pha Ngan 84280 (11km/7 miles north of Thong Sala along the west coast). ⒸⒸ 07734-9057. www.long-bay.com. 32 units. 1,500B (US$42/£23) double with fan; 1,600B–4,500B (US$45–US$128/£25–£69) double with A/C. MC, V. **Amenities:** Restaurant; bar; pool; tour desk; car/motorbike rental desk; airport transfer; mini-mart; massage; laundry service; Internet. *In room:* A/C, TV, minibar, fridge.

Had Salad

This beautiful and secluded sandy beach used to be a pirates' hideout and is good for swimming (Nov to Apr), with a reef about 150m offshore that is a well-known dive site.

Green Papaya   This mellow resort of luxury rustic bungalows is set in gardens and around the beautiful beachside tear-shaped infinity pool. Okay, so it's a little remote, but it's a nature lover's paradise (there's actually solar-heated water). All rooms are well furnished and have bonuses like outdoor bathrooms with tubs; the two-bed executive suite pool villas even have outside Jacuzzis. The unique boat shaped restaurant on site is a highlight despite the service being rather slow. Some may find the rooms overpriced for what is on offer; nonetheless, resorts of this level are not yet commonplace here.

Had Salad, Koh Pha Ngan, 84280 (on the far northwest of the island, about 16km/10 miles north of the ferry). ©/fax 07734-9280. www.greenpapayaresort.com. 18 units. 4,800B–15,000B (US$137–US$428/£74–£231) double. MC, V. **Amenities:** Restaurant; bar; large pool; tour desk; laundry service; Wi-Fi. *In room:* A/C, TV, DVD, minibar, coffee-making facilities, hair dryer.

Salad Beach Resort ★   Just next to Green Papaya (see above), this is a better value choice, with nice rooms featuring stylish sleeping areas and designer baths. The small pool is lovely and the restaurant is delightful. Thankfully, the sometimes less than helpful staff does not detract from the otherwise beautiful setting.

Had Salad, Koh Pha Ngan 84280 (on the far northwest of the island, about 16km/10 miles north of the ferry). © 07734-9274. www.saladbeachphangan.com. 48 units. 2,100B (US$60/£32) double; 4,200B (US$120/£65) bungalow. MC, V. **Amenities:** Restaurant; bar; pool; tour desk; massage; beach activities. *In room:* A/C, cable TV, minibar, fridge.

Ao Chalok Lam

This has to be one of the nicest bays set around an unspoiled, but rapidly growing, fishing village popular with trawlers. The beach is not great for swimming due to its shallow waters, but trips to other northern beaches are possible in rented boats. The newly opened **Shisha Hotel** (no phone) is a wholly contemporary hotel—which travelers are quick to say looks slightly out of place in the middle of the village. There are clusters of rustic bungalows on the beaches, though, such as **Chaloklum Bay Resort** (68/1 Moo7 Ao Chalok Lam, © **07737-4147-8;** www.chaloklumbay.com), which has lots of amenities, including a mini-supermarket.

NORTHEAST/AO THONG NAI PAN

Two adjoining crescent-shaped beaches, 17km (10½ miles) north of Had Rin, are differentiated by the suffix *yai* (big) and *noi* (small). This secluded paradise is easily reached by rented boat, or less easily by bumpy dirt track. **Thong Nai Pan Yai** is quieter, while **Thong Nai Pan Noi** has a more bohemian vibe and a small village with some cool bars and restaurants.

Panviman ★★★   The Panviman has got everything you need for a good hideaway vacation. Designed for sophisticated travelers craving tranquillity and natural beauty, this sprawling resort's luxury cottages are scattered over the hillside above Thong Nai Pan Beach. Rooms are set on a hill with stunning views across the bay, surrounded by tropical plants and shaded by swaying coconut palms. Service is remarkably good and most staff members speak English well. The pool is a multi-tiered affair with gorgeous views of the bay below. You're a long hike from the hilltop to the beach, but they have convenient shuttles, and their upscale dining options mean you never have to leave home to find great food.

22/1 Moo 5, Ao Thong Nai Pan Noi Bay, Koh Pha Ngan 84280. © 07744-5101. Fax 07744-5100. www.panviman. com. 72 units. 4,500B–6,600B (US$128–US$188/£69–£102) superior and deluxe hotel rooms; 6,000B–12,000B (US$171–US$342/£92–£185) cottages; 15,000B (US$428/£231) spa villas; 17,000B (US$485/£262) presidential suite. MC, V. **Amenities:** 3 restaurants; 2 bars; pool; Jacuzzi; watersports rental; tour desk; limited room service; laundry service; library and video lounge; Wi-Fi. *In room:* A/C, satellite TV, minibar, fridge, hair dryer, Jacuzzi.

WHERE TO DINE

Cheap eats of every type abound in busy Had Rin and, increasingly, even in the smaller villages here. Note that most restaurants use mobile numbers, not landlines.

For a homely meal, check out the recently opened **L'Embuscade** (© 087061-0116), a French restaurant on the Post Office road, which has a small terrace and chunky wood chairs. The French owners produce great croissants and fresh bread, and they dish up French favorites including the classic duck breast, *magret de canard.* Near the pier, **Om Ganesh** (© 07737-5123) serves up authentic curries and all-you-can-eat Indian *thali* meals, but it's very popular—book ahead. The new Italian restaurant **Kimera** (© 084842-8718) on the beach road serves delicious pizzas. Also on the beach road in Had Rin, don't miss **Emotion of Sushi** (© 089505-6078), **Bamboozle** for Mexican delights (© 087896-4941) or **Nira's Bakery** (© 07737-5109) for breakfast.

For a special occasion, try **Menu** over near Ao Hin Kong on the coastal road north of Thong Sala (© 089289-7133 mobile; www.menu-phangan.com). In Had Yao, check out the **Hideaway Bakery** (no phone) for fresh breads and cakes. At night the two-story **Eagle Pub** (no phone), built into the rocks at the southern end of the beach, is a cool nightspot with a steakhouse and DJs playing tunes to suit every mood.

6 Koh Tao

About 55km (34 miles) NE of Koh Samui

Some 75 years ago, tiny **Koh Tao** or **Turtle Island**—so-named from its outline and resident marine life—was a penitentiary for insurgents, though few visitors these days would find any punishment in being marooned on its idyllic shores. Until lately, it has been known almost exclusively as a destination for divers. With the arrival of some chic new resorts recently, the island's appeal is far wider and, in turn, the island is rapidly going upmarket. Though dive resorts (and a social scene based around the local diving expats) do dominate, there are still lots of rustic budget choices, as well as the sort of secluded high-end hideaways that won't oblige you to book a dive.

As its popularity grows, power outages become more frequent and each high season the island suffers from a scarcity of water. Nonetheless, it is blessed with pretty offshore isles, clear turquoise waters, and pristine coral reefs. Nestled in secluded bays are numerous stunning resorts, reached by boat, or by a rollercoaster ride in a jeep or four-wheel drive. Just off the northwest corner lies a trio of islets known as **Koh Nang Yuan** or **Koh Hang Tao** (Turtle's Tail). **Had Sai Ree** and **Ban Mae Had,** both on the west coast, form the main centers where you'll find most of the budget and dive resorts. There are excellent restaurants, some fun bars, and Internet cafes along this long shore, and there are plenty of funky boutiques and trendy shops over at the **Sairee Shopping Center.**

As many properties here don't have land lines, you should instead head to the useful website www.kohtaoonline.com. It offers an Internet booking service as well as lots of updated info on island life, boat timetables, dive packages, and environmental concerns.

GETTING THERE

Songserm Express (in Koh Tao; © 07745-6274) boats leave from Surat Thani and connect nearby islands with fares around 455B (US$13/£7): from Koh Samui 300B (US$7.30/£4.60); Koh Pha Ngan 250B (US$6.10/£3.85); plus a daily morning boat from Chumphon 450B (US$12/£5.85). Boats run subject to weather conditions in monsoon season.

Lomprayah High Speed Catamarans (☏ **07742-7765;** www.lomprayah.com) also make the connection from Samui, via Koh Pha Ngan, and onto Chumphon twice daily: From Chumphon the fare is 550B (US$13/£8.45); from Koh Samui 550B (US$13/£8.45); and from Koh Pha Ngan 300B (US$7.30/£4.60). There are also night boats from Surat Thani and Chumphon with basic sleeping accommodations.

Caution: The south and western beaches can get blasted by the monsoon winds June through October when the normally transparent seas get churned up; but even during November to January (high season), there can be squalls. If you have an onward flight to catch, reserve an extra day or two, in case of delays.

ORIENTATION & GETTING AROUND

All boats arrive in **Ban Mae Had** on the west of the island. Touts from resorts and scuba operators alike line the quay. (As long as it's not high season, and you can be flexible, you can find good deals by bargaining here.) A single concrete road connects the northwestern tip from the basic CFT resort to **Ban Had Sai Ree** and heads south (with the island's longest beach running parallel) through **Ban Mae Had** to stop just short of **Ao Thian Ok** (Shark Bay), but elsewhere the roads are steep, loose dirt tracks, most of which are very challenging. It's possible to walk over headlands (just be mindful of the occasional dropping coconut). Pickups and motorbike taxis (prices vary from 20B–300B/60¢–US$8.55/30p–£4.40) can be found parked in busy areas, or can be stopped at the roadside. Taxi prices are not fixed, and fares tend to double after dark.

Scooters can be rented for upwards of 100B (US$2.85/£1.50) per day from most resorts; it's a good idea not to hire bikes from the cowboys around the pier. If you are looking at car hire, beware that some companies charge outrageously for damages.

More remote bays like the eastern bays of **Ao Leuk, Ao Ta Note,** and **Ao Hin Wong,** are reachable by four-wheel-drive or boat, but most high-end resorts can simply arrange pickup.

WHERE TO STAY
EXPENSIVE/MODERATE

Charm Churee Villa ★★   These rustic lodgings sit on a forested hill atop a secluded cove, just a 10-minute walk from Ban Mae Had. Every room is uniquely designed with magnificent sea views, and the private cove is a great spot to explore the blue waters with snorkel and mask. Chaba Seafood restaurant is known as one of the best in the area.

30/1 Moo 2, Jansom Bay (just south of the ferry landings at Ban Mae Had), Koh Tao 84280. ☏ **07745-6393.** Fax 02884-0045 (Bangkok). www.charmchureevilla.com. 30 units. 5,900B–6,990B (US$168–US$200/£91–£108) double; from 7,990B (US$228/£123) suite. MC, V. **Amenities:** 2 restaurants; spa; tour desk; car-rental desk; massage; laundry service. *In room:* A/C, TV, fridge, minibar, safe.

Jamahkiri Spa & Resort ★★★   Perhaps the island's most upmarket resort, the awesomely designed Jamahkiri is accessible by precipitous mountain track that might make you reconsider the return trip. The good news is that you might not mind being stranded at this unique boutique gem. Overlooking the bay are a clutch of grey-tile and glass pavilions and suites; some are duplex, but all have ocean-view balconies. There is a top-notch spa area and fine dining outlet; public areas are grand, with pleasant nooks but lots of steep steps. Though it's far from the action, this is undoubtedly the most extravagant option on the island.

Ao Thian Ok, on the southern end of the island. © 07745-6400. www.jamahkiri.com. 12 units. 5,900B–9,900B (US$168–US$283/£91–£152) pavilion; 8,900B–14,900B (US$254–US$426/£137–£229) suite. MC, V. **Amenities:** Restaurant; bar; pool; fitness room; spa; tour desk; salon; massage; babysitting; laundry service; wine cellar. *In room:* A/C, satellite TV, DVD, minibar, fridge, coffeemaker, hair dryer, safe.

Thipwimarn Resort 🐟🐟   Tiny, but utterly charming, this vertiginous cliffside boutique resort may not have that many bells and whistles, but is one of the most charming places in the south. Thatched cottages with lots of steps and wood walkways teeter above the azure ocean. Superbly designed rooms are furnished with canopy beds, stunning Thai silks and teak wood; only some have air-conditioning. The four suite types all offer glorious views of the Nang Yuan islets; while the sunset can be seen from either the huge balconies, or picture perfect infinity pool. A spa with ocean-view Jacuzzi tops off this elegantly rustic, but nonetheless, refined gem; book well in advance to secure a room (closes annually in Nov).

14/5 Moo 1, Had Sai Ree (northern tip of Had Sai Ree), Koh Tao 84280; ©/fax 07745-6409 or 07745-6512. www. thipwimarnresort.com. 11 units. 1,800B–4,900B (US$51–US$140/£28–£75) double. MC, V. **Amenities:** Restaurant; spa; tour desk; massage; laundry service. *In room:* A/C in some, satellite TV, DVD, minibar, fridge, safe.

INEXPENSIVE

Had Sai Ree has an enormously wide range of budget options available to walk-in guests, but many are booked through budget scuba packages—popular with long-stay guests who want to get more extensive scuba certification. On the far south end of the island, one popular all-inclusive scuba resort is **Big Bubble Dive Resort** (© 07745-6669; www.bigbubble.info); rooms range from 250B to 1,300B (US$7–37/£4–£191).

AC Bungalows (© 07745-6197) and In Touch (© 07745-6514) on Had Sai Ree are popular bungalow resorts, with rooms from 800B (US$23/£12) and good restaurants and nightlife. **Simple Life** (© 07745-6142) is a dive resort with comfy bungalows with fans or air-conditioning running from 400B (US$11/£6), and a busy bar.

WHERE TO DINE

The choices for where to dine here are endless, since most resorts have their own in-house dining facilities or fun bars. In Sai Ree Village, on the north end of Sai Ree Beach, **Papa's Tapas** (no phone) is the brainchild of a group of expat entrepreneurs who conjure up a constantly evolving menu in a casual candlelit, open-air pavilion. **Choppers Bar and Grill** (no phone) has a multilevel diner with big screen sports. Also on the north end, look for **New Heaven Home Bakery** (© 07745-6554), a popular sandwich and breakfast stop.

In Mae Had, there's **La Matta** (no phone) for delicious Italian pizzas and a shot of good Italian espresso (it's in Sai Ree too), **Café Del Sol** (no phone) for great Italian and fish and chips (amongst many other goodies), and **Dirty Nelly's** (no phone) down near the pier, a great place for pub grub and a pint of Irish beer.

NIGHTLIFE

Most of the action is right on Mae Had beach, where you'll find stacks of stylish retro bars and dance spots where international DJs spin their best sounds, and amazing fire jugglers perform amidst stunning sand sculptures. **Whitening** is a popular beachside bar perfect for cocktails and soothing sounds. For a more upscale drinking venue, **Dragon Bar** has an unusually upscale vibe for Ban Mae Had.

Most big bars here also have dance floors; one of the best is at **Pure Beach Lounge,** which has frequent parties and is a great place to sprawl on beanbags or chill out watching the sunset.

DIVING

Known as one of the best diving areas in Thailand, Koh Tao is a great place to get a very affordable start with the sport or to advance on your levels. Responsible divers should check out the **Koh Tao Dive Operators' Club (DOC),** which imposes a uniform code of conduct and safety standards on its members (listed on **http://kohtao online.com/ktdoc.htm**) and is therefore a good way of finding the more eco-friendly and reliable dive operators. Here are some to consider:

- **Big Blue Diving, Koh Tao** in Ban Mae Had (© 07745-6415; www.bigbluediving. com).
- **Easy Divers** in Ban Mae Had (at the catamaran jetty; © 07745-6010; www.thai dive.com).
- **Big Bubble** at the south end of the island (© 07745-6669; www.bigbubble.info).

SIDE TRIPS FROM KOH TAO

Koh Nang Yuan consists of three small islands joined by a sandbar just off the northwest tip of Koh Tao. Because it's famed for its wonderful snorkeling, numerous companies offer day trips here. Look into unique dive-and-stay packages at **Nang Yuan Resort** (© 07745-6088; www.nangyuan.com), uniquely set over the three islands, with rooms starting as low as 1,500B (US$29/£23) to plush family suites around 14,000B (US$400/£215).

---

7 The Far South & on to Malaysia

From Surat Thani south, Thailand slowly gives way to Malay culture, and Buddhism—predominant in the central and northern parts of the country—is replaced by Islam. Nakhon Si Thammarat is an ancient Buddhist city of note but often ignored by visitors from overseas. In the far south, Had Yai is a major transport hub and a destination popular with Malay and Singaporean sex tourists, where HIV rates are known to be extremely high; in 2000, a *Time* magazine report called it a boom town "built on the sex trade." It's mostly a stopover for onward travel to or from Malaysia.

Note: The far south of Thailand has seen years of violence by separatist insurgents. Their attacks are becomingly increasingly widespread and untargeted but are aimed at any institution with government or Buddhist links. Few travelers pass Nakhon Si Thammarat except those going on to Malaysia, or Singapore via Had Yai. Stay abreast of events before traveling here.

NAKHON SI THAMMARAT

Nakhon Si Thammarat is one of the south's oldest cities, though it has a rather unappealing "new" town in addition to its more charming older quarters. It has long been a religious capital and stages some dazzling festivals. **Wat Phra Mahathat,** the town's 1,000-year old main temple, houses some of the Buddha's relics in its large *chedi* brought from Sri Lanka, from where it is believed Theravada Buddhism came to Thailand; it's therefore an important place of pilgrimage for Thai Buddhists. This region is also the locus for traditional Thai shadow plays. **Ban Nang Thalung Suchart Subsin** (Mr. Subsin's House of Shadow Plays), at 110/18 Sri Thammasok, Soi 3 (© 07534-6394), makes for an interesting introduction to this art form.

Budget carrier **Nok Air** (© 1318; www.nokair.com) connects Nakhon Si Thammarat with Bangkok from Don Meuang, and Suvarnabhumi International airports, respectively, and **PB Air** (© 02261-0271; www.pbair.com) sometimes flies seasonally.

All north–south trains make a stop at the main train station (© **07535-6364**), and affordable minivans (which are the best way to travel in the south) can be arranged from any tour company. Southeast of the city, the **Twin Lotus Hotel,** 97/8 Phattanakan Rd. (no phone), is a high-rise block, providing comfortable rooms starting at 1,000B (US$28/£15).

HAD YAI

Known to travelers as the gateway to Malaysia and one of the bigger cities in Thailand, Had Yai is today a hotbed of political unrest. For some time now, it has been plagued with bouts of violence, with regular pipe bombs, fatal attacks, and frequent murders of Buddhist monks, rubber workers, and school children. The situation is now extremely unstable. Its busy Night Market was once a highlight but these days, I recommend asking around if it's safe to visit. Still, the unspoiled beaches at nearby **Songkhla** (45-min. away) are a great escape from the urban sprawl of Had Yai. Famous for its seafood and the attractive island of Koh Yo, floating in the inland sea, this little isle is a cotton-weaving center with a folklore museum and nice hikes.

Had Yai International Airport, 9km (6 miles) from downtown Had Yai, welcomes flights from Malaysia and Singapore frequently throughout the week via Silk Air, Malaysia Airlines, and some budget airlines, and there are domestic connections to Bangkok and Phuket. Check chapter 2 for airline info.

Minibuses still make trips to the border at Pedang Besar and connect from other parts of the region, and long-distance buses connect with the **Bangkok Southern Bus Terminal** (© **02435-1199**). Five trains depart daily from **Bangkok's Hua Lampong Station** (© **02223-7010** or 1690) to Had Yai Junction with connections on to Malaysia. The once daily Singapore–Bangkok Express also stops at HadYai.

There are dozens of low- and midpriced hotels located near the railway station, most with air-conditioned rooms, and several tourist class hotels with the usual amenities. The best on offer (if you like characterful old charm) is the **Regency Hotel,** 23 Prachathipat Rd. (© **07423-4400**), with rooms from 1,000B (US$28/£15) and **J&B Hotel,** 99 Jootee-Ausom Rd., Had Yai (© **07423-4300**), with rooms from 300B (US$9/£4). The popular backpacker haunt, **Cathay Guest House,** 93/1 Niphat Uthit 2 Rd. (© **07424-3815**), could do with a lick of paint, but it has dorms from only 100B (US$2.85/£1.55) and reasonable singles from 200B (US$5.70/£3.10).

Southern Peninsula: The West Coast & Islands

The island of **Phuket,** linked by a causeway to peninsular Thailand, was one of Thailand's first tourist developments. Today, it's a perennially popular mass tourism magnet. In the dry season (Nov–Mar), this coast is a great place to island-hop, either by the new Destination Air's amphibious aircraft service or by ferry.

With its increasing wealth and popularity come less savory influences, however: Mafia activity and unscrupulous developers keen to earn a fast buck from the pristine environment are common, especially as resort centers like **Patong** in Phuket continue to rebuild after damage caused by a tsunami in December of 2004.

The province of **Krabi** has been a bit more eco-savvy than bolder, brassier Phuket and has long banned beach activities like jet skis and parasailing, making it popular with crowds looking for nature, not nightlife. The province encompasses all the land east of **Phang Nga Bay,** including **Koh Phi Phi** and **Koh Lanta.** Close to Krabi town, **Ao Nang Beach** and **Railay** offer backdrops of dramatic limestone cliffs, powder soft beaches, and high-end resorts. **Koh Phi Phi** is still a popular venue for snorkeling and dive trips despite the tsunami damage; however, the island's National Park designation (theoretically, meant to preserve its outstanding beauty) has been shamefully ignored. **Koh Lanta Yai,** better known as **Koh Lanta,** lies southeast of

Krabi Town. Once home solely to Muslim fishing villages, it now boasts the whole gamut of resorts from budget to super-luxe.

Right at the southernmost tip of Phuket is the idyllic isle of **Koh Racha** (sometimes called Koh Raja or Raya) with its jade-green seas. Northwards is **Phang Nga** province and, on its west coast, **Khao Lak,** the gateway to popular dive spots around the **Similan** and **Surin Islands.** This coastline was worst hit by the tsunami in 2004 but volunteer groups such as **ETC** (see "Side Trips from Phuket: Khao Lak and Offshore Islands") are doing much to alleviate the pain and reskill the unemployed. To the south, **Trang Province**'s white sand beaches, caves, and waterfalls make it one of Thailand's best kept secrets.

During high season (Nov–Apr), bookings for all West coast resorts should be made well in advance; expect hefty surcharges across the Christmas/New Year weeks. This season is great for all watersports. Many hotels offer discounts in the off-season when heavy rains bring very strong winds and rough seas (the latter being blamed for fatal air crashes that occurred in Phuket in 2007). Swimming becomes dangerous then, with heavy surf and a strong undertow. Islands in the eastern Gulf of Thailand (**Koh Samui, Koh Pha Ngan,** and **Koh Tao**) are more sheltered, and off-season discounts and fewer crowds make this region most appealing at off-season.

1 Phuket

About 867km (539 miles) SW from Bangkok

The name "Phuket" is derived from the Malay word "Bukit" (meaning hill); true to the name, lush, green hills dominate much of the island's interior. There are still some rubber plantations and relics of the island's tin mining operations remaining. Most folks head south for the beaches; Phuket's are some of the best in Thailand. The best way to see the island is by taking an (albeit utterly hair-raising) drive around the cliff roads, a totally touristy "elephant safari" into the jungle, or opt for an unforgettable sea kayak tour with John Gray, whose guided trips visit incredible offshore caves and limestone *hongs*.

In dry season, Phuket is at its best: you'll get long sandy beaches, warm water, and excellent snorkeling and scuba diving. It also boasts some of the best seafood in Thailand. Sure, its prices are more than a tad overblown, but for well-heeled fun-seekers who want to be at the heart of the action, Phuket is a fabulous choice.

Phuket does, however, have a downside: Tracts of hideous overdevelopment have spawned unsightly concrete bunkers patronized by budget tour groups from Asia, Russia, and Europe. Areas like Patong, with its seedy commercial strip and sleazy nightlife, can be a bit much for families or single women travelers in search of tranquillity, but with the arrival of a swish shopping mall, JungCeylon, and the new adjoining Millennium Phuket Resort, plus upmarket diners such as Brit super chef Keith Floyd's Brasserie and the classy venue Indochine, things are at last, looking up.

If escape at no cost is what you need, Phuket has heaps of elegant resorts designed for tropical solitude; a good number, such as the Banyan Tree, offer private villas and pools. Evason Phuket even offers a honeymoon villa on its own island, Koh Bon. Expect superlative facilities with levels of service beyond those in Europe. But with prices here way above those even in Bangkok, it's not ideal for those on a tight budget. If you need to keep costs down, consider the Eastern Gulf islands or lesser known atolls in Phang Nga Bay, or go south to more reasonable Trang.

Even after 4 years, the impact of the 2004 tsunami, which struck a devastating blow to the resorts along Thailand's west coast, including Phuket, and across the now up and coming region of Khao Lak, cannot be glossed over. Today, most resorts are back to full capacity; many in fact used the disaster as an opportunity to renovate and upgrade. Khao Lak is fast becoming the "next" Phuket, whereas Phi Phi is still struggling to go upmarket. A One-Two-GO air crash in September 2007 was equally tragic; at the same time, it has resulted in authorities reviewing and improving weather alerts at the airport. While some may feel put off about visiting this region, tourism is still the mainstay of the economy. Without support from travelers, Thais in this region simply have no chance to get back on their feet.

ARRIVING

BY PLANE   Thai Airways (© **02545-3690** domestic reservations in Bangkok; www.thaiair.com) flies daily from both **Bangkok's Don Mueang Airport** and **Suvarnabhumi International Airport** (trip time: 1 hr. 20 min.). Thai Airways' office in Phuket is at 78 Ranong Rd. (© **07621-1195** in Thailand, or 07621-2499 international).

Bangkok Airways (© **02265-5555** in Bangkok or 07724-5601 on Koh Samui; www.bangkokair.com) connects Phuket with Koh Samui at least two times daily. The

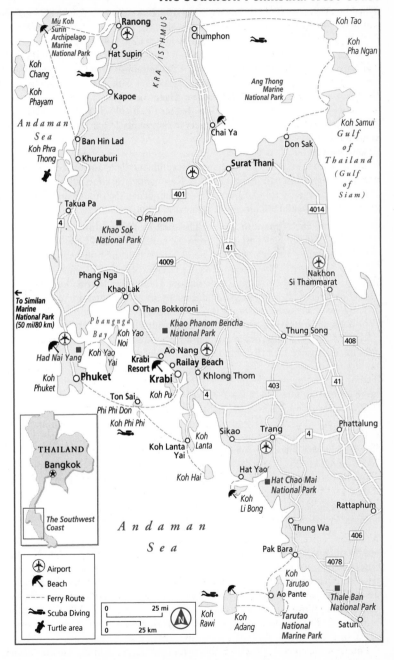

The Southern Peninsula: West Coast

Mu Koh Surin Archipelago Marine National Park

Ranong

Hat Supin

Chumphon

Koh Tao

Koh Pha Ngan

Koh Chang

Koh Phayam

Kapoe

Ang Thong Marine National Park

Andaman Sea

Koh Phra Thong

Ban Hin Lad

Khuraburi

Chai Ya

Don Sak

Gulf of Thailand (Gulf of Siam)

Koh Samui

Surat Thani

Takua Pa

Phanom

4

Khao Sok National Park

401

4014

Phang Nga

Khao Lak

Than Bokkoroni

4009

41

Nakhon Si Thammarat

To Similan Marine National Park (50 mi/80 km)

Phangnga Bay

Koh Yao Noi

Koh Yao Yai

Khao Phanom Bencha National Park

Ao Nang

Railay Beach

Thung Song

408

Had Nai Yang

Krabi Resort

Krabi

Khlong Thom

Koh Phuket

Phuket

Ton Sai

Koh Pu

4

403

41

Phi Phi Don

Koh Phi Phi

Sikao

Trang

Phattalung

THAILAND

Bangkok

Koh Lanta Yai

Koh Lanta

Koh Hai

Hat Yao

4

The Southwest Coast

Andaman Sea

Hat Chao Mai National Park

Rattaphum

Koh Li Bong

Thung Wa

406

Pak Bara

4078

Airport

Beach

Ferry Route

Scuba Diving

Turtle area

Koh Tarutao

Ao Pante

Thale Ban National Park

0   25 mi

0   25 km

N

Koh Rawi

Koh Adang

Tarutao National Marine Park

Satun

Bangkok Airways office in Phuket is at 158/2–3 Yaowarat Rd., Phuket Town (© 07622-5033, or 07632-7114 at Phuket Airport).

Budget airlines flying here include **Air Asia** (© 02515-9999; www.airasia.com), **Nok Air** (© 1318; www.nokair.com), and **One-Two-GO Airlines** (© 1126 in Bangkok, or 1141 in other provinces; www.fly12go.com); they all fly daily between Bangkok and Phuket. Connecting with Singapore is **Silk Air** (© 07630-4018 in Phuket; www.silkair.com). Budget carriers **Tiger Airways** (© 02351-8333; www. tigerairways.com) and Qantas subsidiary **Jetstar** (© 02267-5125; www.jetstar.com) also have regular connections from Phuket to Singapore; Jetstar flies directly to Australia, too.

Destination Air (© 07632-8637-39; www.destinationair.com) is a new air service based at Phuket Airport, running small, amphibious light aircraft between island resorts such as Krabi (trip time: 12 min.), Koh Lanta (trip time: 28 min.) and Koh Phi Phi (trip time: 16 min.). Operated by foreign pilots, their routes are growing fast and more routes and local offices are planned in 2008.

Getting from the Airport to Town   The modern **Phuket International Airport** (© 07732-7230, information) is located in the north of the island, about a 45-minute drive from Patong Beach in off-peak hours, or an hour in rush hour (8–9am and 4–7pm). There are banks, money-changing facilities, car rental agents (see "Getting Around," below), and a post office at the airport. The **Phuket Tourist Business Association** booth there can help you make hotel arrangements if you need accommodations.

For a fee, many resorts will pick you up at the airport; check if this is included in your booking. A new **airport bus** connecting with Phuket Town bus terminal costs 52B (US$1.50/80p). Just outside the terminal to the right is a new (and long overdue) meter taxi stand. You'll need to check the estimated price with the driver—based on how far you are going, plan on spending 500B to 800B (US$14–US$23/£7–£12). There is a ready supply at the right on exiting the terminal. To book a meter taxi, allow up to 2 hours for a response; call © 07625-0333.

The airport limousine counter, operated by **Tour Royale** (© 07634-1214), offers many options for getting to your hotel from the airport. A prepaid **car** from the airport can also be arranged at the limousine counter; you'll pay between 400B (US$11/ £6.15) to Phuket Town and 700B (US$20/£11) to Kata Beach. Alternatively, you can take a **minibus,** which operates every hour, on the hour, from 9am to 11pm daily. Stopping between Patong, Kata, Karon, and Phuket Town, they charge from 250B (US$7.15/£3.85), depending on how far you're going. Paying 300B (US$8.60/£4.60) gets you as far south as Kata Beach (*Note:* This van *may* stop at a small travel agency en route in an attempt to sell rooms.)

BY BUS   Three super-cooled air-conditioned VIP buses leave daily from **Bangkok's Southern Bus Terminal** (© 02434-7192) and cost from 750B (US$21/£12). These buses feature fewer seats, more room, a usually deafening all-night action movie, hostesses, and snacks. Numerous regular air-conditioned buses go each day and cost as little as 275B (US$7.85/£4.25). Standard buses make frequent connections to Surat Thani and nearby towns on the mainland (to Surat is 6 hrs. and 105B/US$3/£1.60).

The intercity bus terminal is at the **City Park Complex** on Phang Nga Road (© 07621-1480), east of Phuket Town just opposite the Royal Phuket City Hotel. For information on how to get from here to the beaches, see "Getting Around," below.

BY MINIVAN   Minivans to and from Surat Thani, Krabi, Nakhon Si Thammarat, Ranong, and other southern cities leave on regular schedules throughout the day. In

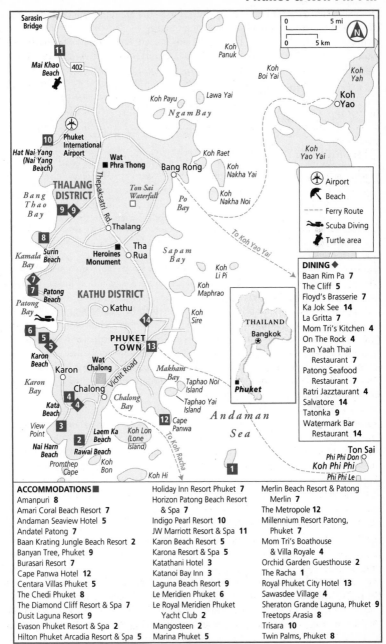

Sarasin Bridge

11 Mai Khao Beach

402

10 Phuket International Airport

Hat Nai Yang (Nai Yang Beach)

Bang Thao Bay

THALANG DISTRICT

Wat Phra Thong

Bang Rong

Ton Sai Waterfall

Thalang

Thepkasattri Rd

9 **9**

8 Surin Beach

Kamala Bay

Heroines Monument

Tha Rua

7
7 Patong Beach

Patong Bay

KATHU DISTRICT

Kathu

6

5
5 Karon Beach

Karon

Wat Chalong

PHUKET TOWN **13**

14

Karon Bay

Chalong

Vichit Road

4
4 Kata Beach

View Point

3

2 Laem Ka Beach

Nai Harn Beach

Rawai Beach

Promthep Cape

Koh Bon

Koh Hi

Koh Lon (Lone Island)

12 Cape Panwa

Makham Bay

Taphao Noi Island

Taphao Yai Island

Chalong Bay

Andaman Sea

Koh Payu

Ngam Bay

Lawa Yai

Koh Panuk

Koh Boi Yai

Koh Yah

Koh Yao

Koh Raet

Koh Nakha Yai

Koh Nakha Noi

Po Bay

Sapam Bay

Koh Li Pi

Koh Maphrao

Koh Sire

Koh Yao Yai

To Koh Yao Yai

THAILAND

Bangkok

Phuket

To Koh Racha

Ton Sai
Phi Phi Don
Koh Phi Phi
Phi Phi Le

1

0 — 5 mi
0 — 5 km

✈ Airport
☂ Beach
--- Ferry Route
🤿 Scuba Diving
🐢 Turtle area

each city, minivan operators work with the hotels and arrange free pickup, so it is best to book through your hotel front desk or a travel agent. Tickets to destinations in the south, to places like Surat Thani or Had Yai, go for between 200B and 500B (US$5.71–US$14.30/£3.10–£7.70). *Note:* Operators of minivan companies rarely speak English.

VISITOR INFORMATION

The **Tourism Authority of Thailand (TAT)** has an office in Phuket Town at 191 Klang Rd. (© **07621-2213**), but traditionally, hotel concierge or tour desks offer more up-to-date information. There are lots of free maps on offer (all are full of advertisements); for driving around the island, pick up the very detailed *Map of Phuket* (Periplus Editions) at bookstores. Restaurants and hotel lobbies are good places to pick up any of a number of free local publications: *Phuket Food-Shopping-Entertainment* is packed with dining suggestions and ads for many of the island's activities; *What's on South* has some useful information on Phuket, Koh Phi Phi, and Krabi; and there a few fun local magazines for sale. Also look out for the useful *Art & Culture South* and *Old Phuket Treasure Map.*

ISLAND LAYOUT

If you arrive by car or coach, you'll cross into Phuket from the mainland at the northern tip of the island via the **Sarasin Bridge** along Route 402. Phuket Town, the island's historic and commercial center, is in the southeast of the island at the terminus of Route 402; local buses connect at **Phuket Town Bus Station** on Phang Nga Road. Phuket's picturesque stretches of sand dot the western coast from Nai Harn, on the southern tip, to Mai Khao, about 48km (30 miles) north, via Kata Noi, Kata, Karon, Patong, Kamala, Surin, Bang Tao, and a number of smaller beaches north along this corridor. A busy coastal road links the popular tour towns in the south, but stops north of Patong, requiring a short detour from the main highway. The four corners of Phuket are linked with just a few busy main arterial roads. Many visitors rent vehicles to tour the island's smaller byways or make the trip to jungle parks like **Khao Phra Thaew Royal Wildlife & Forest Reserve** in the northeast of the isle, famed for diverse flora and fauna. The western beaches have all the services visitors might need, but everything comes with resort prices—and don't expect to find any real Thai feel here. For a taste of Thai life, affordable services, and authentic restaurants, explore Phuket Town (especially if this is your only urban destination down south).

THE BEACHES   There's a beach for everyone in Phuket, from private stretches belonging to exclusive hideaways to sandy bays reached only by long-tail. There's even camping spots close to places like pristine Mai Khao beach. Each beach is distinct, and selecting the appropriate area makes all the difference.

Nai Harn, the southernmost bay on the west coast, is home to only one major beachfront resort with a host of smaller family-friendly resorts and bungalows back from the coast. Laid-back and quiet in the monsoon season, Nai Harn attracts surfers and other water sports enthusiasts. The sand is fine and the water deep. As a public beach, with a few local eateries, it makes for a great day trip if you're staying at a more populated beach and want to run away for the day (a good long motorbike/car ride south of Kata/Karon).

Rawai Beach and **Chalong Beach** are two well-known, eastern-facing beaches both hosting a few resorts such as the luxurious Evason Phuket and some outdoor seafood or barbecue restaurants. **Cape Panwa,** between Chalong and Phuket Town, also has scenic hidden beaches with a range of hotels and restaurants.

North of Nai Harn are the more popular developed beaches: **Kata, Kata Noi,** and **Karon Beaches.** Though they are getting developed, they're not quite reaching the levels of over-the-top Patong. Along these beaches you'll find resorts large and small. In general this is the least expensive area on Phuket, with still a few hold-out budget places that haven't been bulldozed and made high-end yet. Sandy beaches are long and picturesque, and the water is deep, with some nice wave breaks. This beach area has more restaurants than the remote bays and some shopping, nightlife, and travel agent options as well. But you won't find rowdy crowds here and, even with all the development, the area manages to maintain a laid-back character.

North of the Kata and Karon bays, you'll pass through **Relax Bay,** a small cove with a few resorts, before rolling down the mountain to **Patong Beach,** the most famous (perhaps infamous) strip on the island. Patong's draw is its seamy Patpong-styled nightlife, busy shops and restaurants, and brash in-your-face beat. Not surprisingly, commercial sex workers flock here to service lovelorn foreign customers. Accommodations run the gamut from five-star resorts to budget motels. Love it or hate it, the town has the most diverse selection of dining facilities and highest concentration of tour and dive operators, watersports, shopping, and nightlife. Most visitors end up spending a few nights on this strip. The drawbacks are all too visible—endless parades of pushy touts pounce on you at every step. While some adults may find the nightlife titillating, families with kids may want to avoid some of the lurid displays of obscenity on offer. If you love to be in the center of it all, stay in Patong; if you want some peace, stay away.

Still north of Patong, **Kamala Bay, Surin Beach,** and **Bang Tao Beach** have more secluded resorts on lovely beaches for those who want the convenience of nearby Patong, but cherish the serenity of a quiet resort.

About two-thirds of the way to the northern tip of the island, **Bang Tao Beach** is home to the **Laguna Resort Complex,** a partnership of five world-class resorts sharing excellent facilities and a fabulous beach. While this area is rather far from both Patong Beach and Phuket Town, the many dining and activity options make it quite self-sufficient for those with the means.

Far north of the main resort areas, **Nai Yang National Park** has limited facilities and may not appeal to most, but for real beach lovers, it is a dream come true. There is a coral reef just 1,400m (4,592 ft.) off shore, and if you are looking to get back to nature, Nai Yang beach is your best bet.

Mai Khao is the northernmost beach in Phuket and is famed as being prime habitat for sea turtles. It is designated National Parkland, but with all the development in the area, few sea turtles are returning here to lay eggs. Since 1996, an Italian-run marine charity has been working with (paying) volunteers and school kids to reverse this (see **www.naucrates.org** for info). For the time being, this steep, desolate beach hosts just one luxury resort: the JW Marriott, Phuket, which was carefully built to respect the ecology. More developments, with no interest in eco-ethics, are sadly encroaching on this supposedly "protected" stretch of coast, though.

GETTING AROUND

Public transportation on Phuket is a problem that never seems to get solved. If you've spent any time in other parts of the country, you'll know that the covered pickup trucks that cruise the streets picking up and dropping off passengers are called *songtaews,* while the noisy motorized three-wheel vehicular demons are known as tuk-tuks. Not on Phuket: here, locals call communal pickup trucks "tuk-tuks," while *songtaews* are the giant colorful buses that ply the main roads (also called "baht buses").

Here's the problem: *Songtaews* are only permitted to travel from a beach to Phuket Town (not from beach to beach). Tuk-tuk drivers have exclusive rights to transport people between beaches and so the "service" is run as a racket—pay the fare they demand, or walk. At night, tuk-tuk drivers are known to charge solo passengers up to a thousand baht to go from Karon to Patong beach, but they are the only game in town. Budget travelers on limited funds must bear this in mind to avoid getting stranded late at night.

BY SONGTAEW   The local bus terminal is in front of the Central Market on Ranong Road in Phuket Town. Fares to the most popular beaches range from 20B to 30B (60¢–85¢/30p–45p). *Songtaews* leave when full, usually every 30 minutes, and they run from 7am to 6pm between Phuket Town and the main beaches on the west coast.

BY TUK-TUK   Within Phuket Town, tuk-tuks cost about 50B to 100B (US$1.40–US$2.85/75p–£1.55) for in-town trips: they're a good way to get to the bus station or to Phuket Town's restaurants.

In the busy west-coast beaches, tuk-tuks and small Daihatsu mini-trucks roll around town honking at any tourist on foot, especially in Patong. It is the only way to travel between beaches. Bargain hard and beware that these guys will try to eke every baht out of you. Expect to pay about 500B (US$14/£7.70) from town to the airport, 400B (US$11/£6.15) from town to Patong Beach, and 200B (US$5.70/£3.10) from Patong Beach to Karon Beach. It costs more late at night, and unless you can bargain ruthlessly, you'll have to pay through the nose, usually double the normal day rates (but remember that you're choosing from tens of drivers, so walking away, or to the next vehicle, when the price isn't right, is an effective tactic). In early 2007, the beach and main roads began using one-way traffic, and transport prices have been rising further due to the longer distance.

BY MOTORCYCLE TAXI   Motorcycle taxi drivers, identifiable by colored vests, make short trips within Phuket Town or along Patong Beach for fees as steep as 100B (US$2.85/£1.55). Don't let them talk you into anything but short in-town rides, unless you're looking for a death defying F1-style race along the switchback highways between beaches.

BY CAR   You should be extremely cautious when driving yourself around Phuket. Roads between the main beaches in the west and connecting with Phuket Town across the center of the island are dangerously steep and winding, with more than a few hairpin turns and lots of unpredictable traffic. As in other parts of the kingdom, drivers pass aggressively, even on blind curves, and self-driving visitors should be defensive and alert at all times.

Avis (© 07635-1243) has a counter at Phuket Airport. Plan on spending up to 1,800B (US$51/£28) per day for a Suzuki Caribbean 4WD sport vehicle. **Budget** (© 07620-5396) is a bit cheaper and has an airport location, as well as counters at a number of hotels (JW Marriott, Evason Resort, and Club Andaman Beach Resort in Patong). **Hertz** also has a counter at the airport (© 07632-8545). All international renters offer sedans and have sound insurance coverage available, which is highly recommended.

Inexpensive (but notoriously unsafe) Suzuki Caribbeans can be rented from almost all travel agents and from hotels at the beach areas. Prices start at 800B (US$23/£12) per day. Independent agents hang around under umbrellas along Patong Beach and offer great bargains if you negotiate, but don't count on them having an insurance policy.

BY MOTORCYCLE   Also along the Patong strip, the same car-rental guys will offer cheap bike rental. A 100cc Honda scooter goes for 200B (US$5.70/£3.10) per day, while a 400cc Honda Shadow chopper will set you back at least 600B (US$17/£9.25) per day. Significant discounts can be negotiated if you plan to rent for a longer time. Wear your helmet, as police enforce fines of 500B (US$14/£7.70) for going without, and practice caution while driving. For the best big bikes, try **Nickys Handlebar** (41 Rat-U-Thit 200 Rd., Patong; ✆ **07634-5199;** www.nickyshandlebar.com).

FAST FACTS: Phuket

Banks   Banks are located in Phuket Town, with many larger branches on Ranong and Rasada roads. There are bank branches of major Thai banks at Chalong, Nai Harn, Kata, Karon and Patong beaches. **Money changers** are located at the airport, major shopping areas on each beach, and at most resorts. Banks offer the best rates. **ATMs** are now found all over Phuket.

Bookstores   There are lots of book shops to be found at the mega-malls of Central Festival Phuket Town, and JungCeylon Centre, Patong. Also look for **The Books** in Patong at 198/2 Rat-U-Thit Rd. (✆ **07634-2980**).

Hospitals   There are three major private hospitals, all with English-speaking staff: **Bangkok Phuket Hospital,** at 2/1 Hongyok-Uthit Rd. (off Yaowarat Rd. in Phuket Town; ✆ **07625-4421**), has high-quality facilities and has a clinic in Laguna Canal Village, Laguna Phuket (✆ **07632-5442**). **Phuket International** (✆ **07624-9400**) is located next to Big C Shopping Mall, outside Phuket Town. **Mission Hospital** also offers good medical services and is located on Thepkasattri Road, Phuket Town (✆ **07621-2386**).

Internet   Internet service is fairly easy to find on the island. Good connections can be found at small cafes and tour agencies at most beaches. In Patong, the best Internet cafes are farther away from the beach. Along Rat-U-Thit Road in the center of Patong (a 5-min. walk east, away from the beach), you'll find 1B per minute (US$1.71/90p per hour) service.

Police   The emergency number for the **Tourist Police** is ✆ **1155** or 1699; for **Emergency Police,** dial ✆ **191;** for **Marine Police,** dial ✆ **07621-1883**.

Post Office   The General Post Office in Phuket Town (✆ **07621-1020**) is at the corner of Thalang and Montri roads.

SPECIAL EVENTS

If you are on Phuket around October/November, don't miss the **Vegetarian Festival.** The name is misleading—it is not about Animal Rights or being health conscious, but a Thai-Chinese tradition on Phuket (and now celebrated widely throughout southern Thailand) that corresponds with the Buddhist Lent. For 9 days, not only do devotees refrain from meat consumption, but many also submit to violent public acts of self-mutilation through piercing their bodies with long skewers or swords, and often walking over hot coals. The festival began as an act of penance to the spirits to help early inhabitants ward off malaria, but these days, the rituals are more for young men to prove themselves and for gaining merit and good luck. Early morning processions follow through the streets of Phuket Town and major temples around the island, with onlookers clad in white for the occasion. During this time you can also feast on terrific vegetarian buffets at just about any restaurant in Thailand. See **www.phuket vegetarian.com** for info.

THINGS TO DO & SEE

If Phuket is your only destination in Thailand, you'll certainly want to get to some of the Muslim fishing villages, small rural temples, and Phuket Town. Outdoor activities top the list of things to do, and there's something for everyone (see "Exploring Phuket," later).

Thalang National Museum, in the east just off Highway 402 at the Heroines' Monument (© **07631-1426;** daily 9am–4pm; 30B/86¢/45p), exhibits Phuket's indigenous cultures, the history of Thai settlements on Phuket, and crafts from the southern Thai regions as well as a 9th century statue of the Hindu deity Vishnu—evidence of early Indian merchants visiting the burgeoning kingdom.

There are a few Buddhist temples on the island that are quite notable: The most unique is **Wat Phra Thong,** located along Highway 402 in Thalang just south of the airport. Years ago, a boy fell ill and dropped dead after tying his buffalo to a post sticking out of the ground. It was later discovered that the post was actually the top of a huge Buddha image that was buried under the earth. Numerous attempts to dig out the post failed—during one attempt in 1785, workers were chased off by hornets. Everyone took all this failure to mean that the Buddha image wanted to just stay put, so they covered the "post" with a plaster image of The Buddha's head and shoulders and built a temple around it.

The most famous temple among Thai visitors here is **Wat Chalong.** Chalong was the first resort on Phuket, back when the Thais first started coming to the island for vacations. Nowadays, the discovery of better beaches on the west side of the island has driven most tourists away from this area, but the temple still remains the center of Buddhist worship. The temple is on the Chaofa West Road, about 8km (5 miles) south of Phuket Town.

Sea Gypsies, or Chao Ley, are considered the indigenous people of Phuket. This minority group used to shift around the region living off subsistence fishing, but commercial fishing interests and shoreline encroachment increasingly threaten their livelihoods. Related to the Malaysian Orang Laut people and the southern Thai Sakai tribes, Phuket and Phang Nga's Sea Gypsies form a few small settlements on Phuket island: one on Koh Siray (aka Koh Sire), east of Phuket Town, and another at Rawai Beach just south of Chalong Bay. The villages are simple, seashore shacks, with vendors selling souvenir shells. It's quite educational to visit these people and their disappearing culture; sadly, however, thanks to too many tourist hand-outs, be prepared also for pestering, dollar-hungry children.

2 Where to Stay

The hotels and resorts below are divided by beach area to simplify your choices on the island. Phuket is thick with development, so the list below is but a small selection, according to each beach. Nowadays, hotels do not always publish rack rates—instead the rates are governed by occupancy. In Phuket, the high-season peaks from December 15 to January 15 when rates are at their most expensive. If the rate here is marked "from," it means no rack rate is available, and the price has been based on Internet rates. In low-season, rates can drop 30% to 50%.

NAI HARN BEACH

Far to the south, Nai Harn Beach is a good escape, with a range of accommodations on offer. Adjacent beaches on the eastern side of the island, **Rawai** and **Chalong,** are also home to a few good, high-end resorts: **Evason Phuket Resort and Spa** (100 Vised Rd.; ℂ **07638-1010;** fax 07638-1018; www.sixsenses.com) is a luxury, family-friendly enclave and popular day-spa destination; and **Mangosteen** (99/4 Moo 7, Soi Mangosteen; ℂ **07628-9399;** fax 07628-9389; www.mangosteen-phuket.com) is a newer high-end choice. Both have rooms starting at around 6,000B (US$171/£92).

From Chalong Bay, there's a hulking daily ferry service to the idyllic islet of **Koh Racha** (aka Koh Raya), a delightful island getaway with a perfect white sand beach. It's hugely popular with day-trippers in the dry season. Sybarites in search of seclusion can also splash out at their own pool villa at **The Racha,** (ℂ **07635-5455;** fax 07635-5637; www.theracha.com), a magnificent contemporary-styled luxury hotel that cascades down the hill to the cerulean sea. (The hotel offers speedboat transfers to its guests, subject to the weather.) You'll need deep pockets for their premium Lighthouse suite, which costs 65,000B (US$1,857/£977), but if you're fast, you can get superior villa rates online for 8,500B (US$243/£128).

EXPENSIVE
Le Royal Meridien Phuket Yacht Club 🏵🏵🏵   Perched above the northern edge of Nai Harn Beach, the Yacht Club is one of the earliest luxury accommodations in Phuket, yet it still rivals nearly anything on the island for setting and comfort. Staff members in pith helmets greet guests with heel-clicking salutes. The pagoda-style foyer overlooks terraced gardens overflowing with pink and white bougainvillea. Common areas have terra-cotta tiles and open views. Interiors are spacious and decorated with cheerful fabrics and wicker furniture; bathrooms are huge, many with sunken tubs. All rooms have large balconies for viewing the beach and Promthep Cape.

23/3 Viset Rd., Nai Harn Beach, Phuket 83130 (above Nai Harn Beach, 18km/11 miles south of Phuket). ℂ 800/225-5843 or 07638-0200. Fax 07638-0280. www.lemeridien.com. 110 units. 4,550B–9,800B (US$130–US$280/£70–£151) double (varies with view); from 7,525B–13,650B (US$215–US$390/£116–£210) suite. AE, DC, MC, V. **Amenities:** 3 restaurants; lounge; outdoor pool; 2 outdoor lighted tennis courts; fitness center; spa; extensive watersports equipment; tour desk; car-rental desk; airport transfer; business center; salon; 24-hr. room service; babysitting; same-day laundry service/dry cleaning; nonsmoking rooms; Internet. *In room:* A/C, satellite TV, minibar, fridge, coffee-making facilities, hair dryer, safe.

MODERATE
Just up the coast road from Le Meridien are quaint seaside, forest bungalows at **Baan Krating Jungle Beach Resort** (11/3 Viset Rd.; ℂ/fax **07638-1108;** www.baan krating.com/phuket). There are few services to speak of, but it is a good getaway. Rooms start at 3,990B (US$114/£61).

INEXPENSIVE
Orchid Garden Guest House (49/9 Soi Ruam Nana Chat, Rawai ℂ **07638-8191**) is a lush oasis of poolside garden bungalows just 2km/1 mile from Nai Harn Beach. Good value basic accommodations start at 500B (US$14/£7.35).

KATA BEACH

One of Phuket's best tourist beaches, Kata is a wide strip of soft sand and rolling surf. Rent an umbrella, get a massage, or grab a kayak or surfboard and hit the waves (there's good surf May–Oct). Unfortunately, the best beachfront real estate is taken up by the sprawling **Phuket Club Mediterranée** (© **07633-0455**), an all-inclusive, club-style resort (www.clubmed.com), but the beach is open to all. After dark, Kata comes alive in the bars and music cafés along the beach roads.

EXPENSIVE

Katathani Hotel 𝒜𝒜𝒜   The Katathani is the best option on the cul-de-sac of lovely Kata Noi Beach, a haven of quiet luxury. Rooms are contemporary, but cozy— all with large balconies and cozy indoor sitting areas. Wide, well-groomed lawns surround sizable pools and lead to the graceful curve of the pristine cove. There is a nightly poolside buffet. The Katathani's best feature is that it is right on the beach and all rooms have good sea views.

3/24 Patak Rd., Kata Noi Beach, Phuket 83100 (north end of Kata Noi Beach). © 07633-0124. Fax 07633-0426. www.katathani.com. 530 units. 4,550B–14,350B (US$130–US$410/£70–£221) junior suite; from 6,300B–36,225B (US$180–US$1,035/£97–£557) suite. AE, DC, MC, V. **Amenities:** 5 restaurants; lounge and library; 5 outdoor pools; golf course nearby; 2 outdoor lighted tennis courts; fitness center; aromatherapy spa; watersports equipment/scuba diving; game room; tour desk; car-rental desk; airport transfer; salon; 24-hr. room service; babysitting; same-day laundry service/dry cleaning. In room: A/C, satellite TV, minibar, coffee-making facilities, hair dryer, safe.

Mom Tri's Boathouse (aka "The Boathouse") and Villa Royale 𝒜𝒜𝒜   At the quieter south end of Kata Beach, this small inn has been a long-time favorite with many returning visitors. More inn than resort, there's a real home-style feeling here. Comfortable, attractive rooms all face the sea, each with a terrace overlooking a courtyard pool and beach beyond; they're not particularly luxurious, but they are clean and adequate. For a very special stay, there's **Villa Royale,** a collection of extravagant suites. These huge rooms are perched over a steep cliff with stunning views of the sea and are sumptuously decorated in a unique mix of local materials: dark teak, mosaics of bamboo and coconut, black tile with stone inlay, and elegant textiles. The Boathouse Wine and Grill, the first-floor restaurant, is an old favorite for visiting connoisseurs (see "Where to Dine," later in this chapter). **Mom Tri's Kitchen,** the hotel's other restaurant, offers some of the best dining on the island (see "Where to Dine"). They offer fun cooking classes, too.

The Boathouse: 182 Koktanod Rd., Kata Beach, Phuket 83100. © 07633-0015. Fax 07633-0561. www.boathouse phuket.com. 36 units. 4,000B–10,000B (US$114–US$286/£62–£154) double; from 9,000B–17,000B (US$257– US$486/£138–£262) suite. **Villa Royale:** 12 Kata Noi Rd., Kata Noi Beach, Phuket 83100. © 076330-0157. www.villaroyalephuket.com. 26 units. From 6,500B–25,000B (US$186–US$714/£100–£385) suite. AE, DC, MC, V for both. **Amenities:** 3 restaurants; lounge and library; outdoor pool; golf course nearby; fitness center; spa; airport transfer; limited room service (7am–10:30pm); babysitting; same-day laundry service/dry cleaning. In room: A/C, satellite TV, minibar, fridge, coffee-making facilities, hair dryer, safe.

MODERATE

Sawasdee Village 𝒜𝒜 (Finds)   Just a short walk from Kata Beach, you'll pass a small portico of stone with some Khmer statuary; walk in and you'll find a little Eden among the less pricey resorts of Kata. Before reaching the rooms at the lush central courtyard, you'll walk past the hotel's restaurant, spa, and pretty garden. The garden surrounds a small pool with ornate fountains bordered with fine masonry and overflowing with greenery. Rooms are midsize and stylish, with canopy beds. Bathrooms are shower-only and not too small. There are elegant Thai touches throughout, such as *salas* for relaxing and sliding doors that connect each room to the courtyard.

68/69 Patak Rd., Kata Beach, Phuket 83100 (down a small road north of the sprawling Club Med), © 07633-0979. Fax 07633-0905. www.phuketsawasdee.com. 46 units. 3,600B–10,400B (US$103–US$297/£55–£160) double. MC, V. **Amenities:** Restaurant; bar; small outdoor pool; spa; tour desk; laundry service; dry cleaning; free Wi-Fi. *In room:* A/C, minibar, fridge, no phone.

INEXPENSIVE

Katanoi Bay Inn   The Katanoi offers basic, motel-style rooms adjacent to the Kata Thani Hotel. Most rooms have balconies and firm beds. There is little in the way of facilities, but quiet Kata Noi Beach is just across the road for great snorkeling and watersports.

4/16 Moo 2 Patak Rd., Kata Noi Beach, Phuket 83100 (Kata Noi is south of Kata Beach). ©/fax 07633-3308. www.phuket.com/katanoibayinn. 28 units. 1,200B (US$34/£18) double. MC, V. **Amenities:** Restaurant; tour desk; car-rental desk; same-day laundry service/dry cleaning; Internet cafe. *In room:* Fridge, no phone.

KARON BEACH

Karon Beach is a popular, long, stretch of beach lined with upper and midrange hotels and resorts. You'll find heaps of tailors, gift shops, bars, small restaurants and cafes, Internet service, local markets, and mini-marts on the north end of the beach.

EXPENSIVE

Andaman Seaview Hotel ★★ *(Finds)*   A real Karon Beach gem, Andaman Seaview's bright and airy public spaces are decorated in (Sino-Portuguese–inspired) hues of pale blue and white, flanked by ponds and a large central courtyard with a garden and meandering pool. Rooms overlook the pool area and are large and nicely appointed—they're better than most in this category. The hotel is charming in a way that is less about luxury, and more about the warm welcome and tidy appearance of the place. As a result, it pulls in a friendly crowd. The restaurant is a typical hotel coffee shop, but the poolside seats make for a great dining experience. In fact, I recommend taking as much advantage of the nearby beach as possible, including hitting up the waterside small spa.

1 Karon Rd., Soi 4., Phuket 83100 (along the main strip at Karon Beach). © 07639-8111. Fax 07639-8177. www.andamanphuket.com. 161 units. 6,200B (US$177/£95) superior double; 9,900B (US$283/£152) deluxe double. AE, MC, V. **Amenities:** Restaurant; bar (poolside); 2 outdoor pools; small fitness center; spa; tailor; 24-hr. room service; same-day laundry/dry cleaning service; Wi-Fi. *In room:* A/C, satellite TV, minibar, fridge, coffee-making facilities, safe.

Centara Villas Phuket ★★ *(Kids)*   Formerly known as Central Karon Village Resort, the newly reborn Centara Villas is one of the best in the area. Set on its hillside perch on the north end of Karon Beach—along the crest of a hill between Karon and Relax Bay—the resort is a hillside hideaway of free-standing, luxury bungalows in tropical garden surrounds, overlooking the majestic crashing surf. The guest room decor is tasteful; bathrooms are done up in slick, polished concrete with skylights. The Cliff Restaurant is tops (see "Where to Dine" later for more info), and this self-contained gem has a friendly staff who can handle any eventuality, including a Hertz rental car office and tour desk. The outdoor waterfall pool overlooks the sea and is a good little escape, and their outdoor spa *salas* are a great place to learn the word *Sabai*. Thai cooking classes are on offer as well.

701 Patak Rd., Tambon Karon, Phuket 83100. © 07628-6300. Fax 07628-6315. www.centralhotelsresorts.com. 72 units. From 6,000B (US$171/£62) suite. AE, MC, V. **Amenities:** 2 restaurants; bar; 2 outdoor pools; tour desk; car-rental desk; limited room service; massage; babysitting; laundry service. *In room:* A/C, satellite TV, minibar, fridge, coffee-making facilities, hair dryer, safe.

Hilton Phuket Arcadia Resort & Spa 𝔊𝔊𝔊   Set in 75 acres of lawns and lush tropical gardens, the Hilton Phuket Arcadia is a modern, full-facility resort. Many of the stylish guest rooms overlook Karon Beach. Ocean-view rooms are set in three wings. Upgraded rooms are luxurious, with cool Thai touches and great Thai contemporary furnishings throughout. The hotel sports a large spa village with 15 purpose-built spa villas connected by raised wooden platforms in a mellow, wooded glen at the heart of the resort. The in-house dining choices are great (go for the Thai restaurant), and everything about the place is classy, with snappy service that doesn't leave out a genuine Thai smile of welcome. There are no rack rates, but the below rates are a good overall guide.

78/2 Patak Rd., Karon Beach, Phuket 83100 (middle of Karon Beach Rd.). ℂ 07639-6433. Fax 07639-6136. www. hilton.com. 685 units. From 3,200B–12,800B (US$91–US$366/£49–£197) double. AE, DC, MC, V. **Amenities:** 6 restaurants; lounge bar w/live band; 3 pools; scuba diving lessons; golf course nearby and putting green on site; outdoor lighted tennis courts; fitness center; spa; gameroom; tour desk; airport transfer; salon; 24-hr. room service; babysitting; same-day laundry service/dry cleaning; Wi-Fi. *In room:* A/C, satellite TV; minibar, coffee-making facilities, safe.

MODERATE

Karon Beach Resort 𝔊𝔊   This is the only Karon Beach property with direct beach access (from all others you'll have to walk across the road). Its beachside location, coupled with the classy decor, makes it a good, cozy choice. Rooms are midsize, with darkwood entrances, clean tile floors, and some Thai touches in the decor, but are most noteworthy for their orientation to the sea: Balconies are stacked in receding, semi-circular tiers and all look onto the pool below (first floor with direct pool access) or to the beach and sea beyond. High season rates rise markedly.

51 Karon Rd., Tambon Daron, Phuket 83100 (the south end of Karon Beach, just as the road bends up to cross to Kata). ℂ 07633-0006. Fax 07633-0217. www.katagroup.com. 81 units. 7,200B (US$205/£106) double; from 12,000B (US$342/£162) suite. AE, MC, V. **Amenities:** 2 restaurants; 2 outdoor pools; tour desk; car-rental desk; airport transfer; massage; laundry service; Internet center. *In room:* A/C, satellite TV, minibar, fridge, safe (charge of 50B/US$1.25/73p).

Marina Phuket 𝔊𝔊   These simple cottages tucked in the jungle above a scenic promontory between Kata and Karon beaches are quite comfortable, and offer four room types. They are the best choice of the many midrange choices nearby. Rates vary according to the view, but all have a jungle bungalow charm, connected by hilly walkways and boardwalks past the lush hillside greenery (keep your eyes peeled for wildlife). It is a hike down to the rocky shore and the swimming isn't great, but they have a good seaside restaurant, On the Rock (see "Where to Dine," later), and their in-house **Marina Divers** (ℂ 07638-1625) is a PADI International Diving School, which conducts classes, rents equipment, and leads good multiday expeditions. Heavy discounts apply during low season.

47 Karon Rd., Karon Beach, Phuket 83100 (on bluff at south end of Karon Beach Rd.). ℂ 07633-0625. Fax 07633-0516. www.marinaphuket.com. 92 units. 4,900B–9,800B (US$140–US$280/£72–£144) double; from 20,650B (US$590/£390) grand villa. MC, V. **Amenities:** 2 restaurants; pool; dive center; limited room service; same-day laundry service; free Internet. *In room:* A/C, satellite TV, minibar, safe.

INEXPENSIVE

Karona Resort and Spa 𝔊   Tucked in a little side street where Karon and Kata beaches meet, the Karona Resort is a low-luxe find, with simple rooms surrounding a tiered central pool, all just a short walk from Karon Beach and the busy Kata strip. Deluxe rooms, in a block overlooking the pool, are worth the upgrade—you'll get a few more amenities, such as a safe. They also have good, affordable spa treatments, and the place is quite stylish and the service good for the price. Long-stay discounts apply.

6 Karon Soi 2, Karon Beach, Phuket 83100. ✆ **07628-6406**. Fax 07628-6411. www.karonaresort.com. 92 units. From 1,200B–1,800B (US$34–US$51/£19–£28) superior double; 2,800B–5,000B (US$80–US$143/£43–£77) suite. MC, V. **Amenities:** Restaurant; bar; outdoor pool; spa; tour desk; car-rental desk; limited room service; massage; laundry service. In room: A/C, satellite TV, minibar, fridge.

RELAX BAY

Le Meridien Phuket ★★★ *Kids*   Tucked away on secluded Relax Bay, the Le Meridien features a lovely 549m (600-yd.) beach, with trained lifeguards, and 16 hectares (40 acres) of tropical greenery—making it one of the largest resorts on the island. After being hit hard by the 2004 tsunami, the resort has been renovated in grand style. The advantages of this large resort remain its numerous facilities—two big swimming pools, watersports, four tennis courts, putting green and practice range, and a great fitness center; but its popularity makes it very busy. The resort caters to families, and there are lots of activities and a good day-care center that kids seem to love. The large building complex combines Western and traditional Thai architecture, and one of the advantages to its U-shape layout is that it ensures that 80% of the rooms face the ocean, with the lowest category getting a garden view. The modern furnishings in cheerful rooms are of rattan and teak, each with a balcony and wooden deckchairs. The seven restaurants on hand mean you'll have all kinds of dining choices.

29 Soi Karon Noi, Relax Bay, Phuket 83100. ✆ **800/225-5843** or 07637-0100. Fax 07634-0479. www.lemeridien. com. 470 units. From 7,000B–25,375B (US$200–US$725/£108–£390) garden superior–royal suite. AE, DC, MC, V. **Amenities:** 7 restaurants; 3 bars w/games and live shows; 2 large outdoor pools; spa; golf driving range and on-site pro; minigolf; outdoor lighted tennis courts; squash courts; fitness center; watersports equipment and dive center; bike rental; kids' club; gameroom; tour desk; car-rental desk; airport transfer; business center; shopping arcade; salon; 24-hr. room service; babysitting; same-day laundry service/dry cleaning; nonsmoking rooms. In room: A/C, satellite TV, minibar, fridge, coffee-making facilities, hair dryer, safe.

PATONG

Once the popular haunt of the U.S. Navy's 9th Fleet, Patong built its nightlife on cheap sex and even cheaper beer. Today, it's Phuket's main tourist center, with plenty of cheap shopping, dining, clubbing—and prostitution. The main strip can be unpleasant for those not used to catcalling touts who incessantly hassle passers-by, accompanied by the constant beeping of tuk-tuks attempting to take tourists for a ride (quite literally). Though one of the hardest hit of Phuket's towns in the 2004 tsunami, the damage here was fairly limited (in international media reports, Patong was often confused with Khao Lak—3 hours drive farther north—which was almost completely wiped out). With a few exceptions, mid- and high-range hotels on this busy strip were up and running soon after the tsunami and prices are still rocketing. The town did lose some of its nicest budget options (such as Duangjit Villas and Seagull Guest House), however.

These days, sprawling Patong is a heap of what appears to be hastily built—or where the tsunami hit, hastily re-built—three-story concrete bunkers. Though some new landscaping has greatly improved a few parts of town—especially along the beach— once you move into the backstreets, many are disappointed to find a tawdry mess of touts and tatty beer halls, interspersed with the odd smart resort or posh diner. It's not all bad: Patong has heaps of great eateries and some good accommodations options. With the opening of the swish new JungCeylon shopping mall and the glamorous five-star Millennium Resort next door, there's a feeling that Patong is attempting to move away from its sad and sordid past. Hopefully the arrival of more upscale bars and restaurants will speed up this process.

EXPENSIVE

Amari Coral Beach Resort ★★★
The Amari Coral Beach stands on the rocks high above the southern end of busy Patong, well away from the congested beach strip, but close enough to dip into the mayhem. This seafront resort, from the very grand terraced lobby, guest rooms, and fine pool, is oriented to the incredible views of the majestic bay below. The rooms have ocean tones, cozy balconies, and all the comforts of home. There is live music nightly and the hotel's Italian restaurant, La Gritta (see "Where to Dine," later), is a great lazy option. Don't miss The Jetty for sunset cocktails and evening BBQ. Overall, this is an affordable and atmospheric choice.

2 Meun Ngern Rd., Phuket 83150 (south and uphill of Patong Beach). ✆ 07634-0106. Fax 07634-0115. www.amari. com. 200 units. From 2,275B–5,075B (US$65–US$145/£35–£78) double; from 8,540B (US$244/£131) suite. AE, DC, MC, V. **Amenities:** 3 restaurants; lounge; bar; 2 outdoor pools; outdoor lighted tennis court; fitness center; spa; dive center; game room; tour desk; car-rental desk; airport transfer; salon; 24-hr. room service; massage; babysitting; same-day laundry service/dry cleaning. *In room:* A/C, satellite TV, minibar, safe.

The Diamond Cliff Resort & Spa ★★★
The Diamond Cliff is a gleaming hilltop resort, with rooms commanding great ocean views. The grounds are attractively landscaped and common areas are luxurious. An irregular shuttle service covers the distance down the hill and into town—or it's a long (and hot) stroll to central Patong. You may want to get wheels. The selection of facilities is ample and the place is in tiptop shape. Check their website for significant discounts when booking directly.

284 Prabaramee Rd., Patong, Phuket 83150 (far south end, on the road to Kamala Beach). ✆ 07634-0501. Fax 07634-0507. www.diamondcliff.com. 330 units. 7,600B–14,000B (US$217–US$400/£117–£215) double; from 45,000B–65,000B (US$1,286–US$1,857/£692–£1,000) villas. AE, DC, MC, V. **Amenities:** 8 restaurants; lounge; outdoor pool; minigolf; outdoor lighted tennis courts; fitness center; spa; dive center; game room; tour desk; car-rental desk; airport transfer; salon; 24-hr. room service; babysitting; same-day laundry service/dry cleaning. *In room:* A/C, satellite TV, minibar, safe.

Holiday Inn Resort Phuket ★★ (Kids)
What distinguishes this place from the others on the busy front is that it's well equipped for families and has some creative cost-saving services. The central pool areas have elaborate fountains and a fun meandering pool suited to kids of all ages, and there are kids' programs and a kids' club; plus there's a babysitting service when parents want some time off. There are lots of family activities and excursions to choose from. Family Suites with separate "kids' rooms" come with jungle- or pirate-theme decor, TV with video and PlayStation, stocked toy boxes, and some with bunk beds. The hotel also has a self-service launderette, so you don't have to pay hotel laundry prices. Also unique is the hotel's minibar scheme—rooms have just a bare fridge, but guests can pick out supplies from a small convenience store in the lobby and have them delivered for not much more than standard minibar prices.

52 Thaweewong Rd., Patong Beach, Phuket 83150 (Patong Beach strip). ✆ 800/HOLIDAY or 07634-0608. Fax 07634-0435. www.holiday.phuket.com. 369 units. From 4,400B–13,500B (US$126–US$385/£68–£208) double/suite; 4,900B–15,000B (US$140–US$428/£75–£231) studio/villa. AE, DC, MC, V. **Amenities:** 3 restaurants; lounge; 4 outdoor pools; fitness center; kid's club; tour desk; car-rental desk; airport transfer; business center; 24-hr. room service; babysitting; same-day laundry service/dry cleaning and self-service launderette. *In room:* A/C, satellite TV, choose-your-own minibar items, fridge, coffee-making facilities, hair dryer, safe.

Merlin Beach Resort and Patong Merlin ★★★
The Merlin company owns two massive compounds in Phuket, with one in central Patong right on the sea front, and the other, more choice property, 3km (2 miles) south on scenic Merlin Beach. Both

are popular with Australian tourists and feature particularly attractive common areas, spacious open-plan lobbies with oversize rattan furniture, and rooms with balconies and views of the pool or seaside. Both facilities also offer stunning lagoon-style swimming pools, each with a pool bar, and some rooms even have private "swim-up" access. There are nicely manicured gardens throughout. The all-inclusive digs mean guests have access to facilities ranging from a fine fitness club, watersports, game room, gym, sauna, and snooker. The Merlin Beach resort, with its private beach access, is the better of the two, with newer rooms just a hitch higher in standard. That resort is somewhat remote from the action of Patong (it lies on a small horseshoe of sand in an isolated bay—the beach is all coral, though not for swimming), but for some that's its greatest asset.

Patong Merlin: 44 Thaweewong Rd., Patong Beach, Phuket 83150 (on Patong strip near south end of town). (C) **07634-0037.** Fax 07634-0394. www.merlinphuket.com. 386 units. From 5,500B (US$157/£85) double; from 12,000B (US$343/£185) suite. AE, DC, MC, V. **Amenities:** 3 restaurants; lounge; 3 pools; outdoor lighted tennis courts; fitness center; watersports equipment; game room; tour desk; airport transfer; 24-hr. room service; massage; babysitting; same-day laundry service/dry cleaning. *In room:* A/C, satellite TV, minibar, fridge.

Merlin Beach Resort: 99 Muen-Ngoen Rd., Tri-Trang Beach, Patong, Phuket 83150 (3km/2 miles south and west of Patong). (C) **07629-4300.** Fax 07629-4310. www.merlinphuket.com/merlinbeach. 414 units. From 6,500B (US$186/£100) deluxe double; from 20,000B (US$571/£308) suite. AE, DC, MC, V. **Amenities:** 4 restaurants; bar and lounge; 2 outdoor pools; tennis; small fitness center; spa w/massage, Jacuzzi, sauna, steam; tour desk; car-rental desk; business center w/Internet; shopping arcade; limited room service; babysitting; same-day laundry/dry-cleaning service; nonsmoking rooms. *In room:* A/C, satellite TV, minibar, fridge, coffee-making facilities, safe.

Millennium Resort Patong, Phuket ★★★   Partially opened in late November 2007, this low-rise, ultra-contemporary hotel is the first truly international five-star chain to set up a resort on the Patong strip. And what a change it makes. Two completely separate wings (named "Beachside" or "Lakeside") fan out from a beautiful atrium, linked by a grand staircase to a good-size ballroom. Upstairs on the rooftop area is the pool and spa level, facing the lush mountains. Clean, modern lines and slick designer touches such as the "glass cube" bathrooms, and muted, earthy tones in each guest room bring a touch of smart, urbane comfort to the town, yet the tropical landscaping reminds guests that they're just a short walk to the sea. Catering to more upscale leisure and business travelers, the Millennium sets a new benchmark for Patong. Since it's annexed to the JungCeylon mall, there are dozens of eating options close by, in addition to the stylish restaurants and bars within the resort.

199, Rat-U-Thit, 200 Pee Rd., Patong, Phuket 83150 (within JungCeylon shopping mall). (C) **07636-6100.** Fax 07636-6101. www.millenniumhotels.com. 421 units. From 4,500B–9,100B (US$128–US$260/£69–£140) lakeside rooms. Check the website for the latest news and special deals.

MODERATE

Burasari Resort ★★   Welcoming staff make the Burasari a great choice if you prefer it chic and petite; just don't expect a sea view. This teeny-weeny resort-styled hotel has been squeezed into the middle of a *soi* just off the main drag, and styled as a contemporary hanging-garden resort. The stylish rooms set amid a narrow courtyard of waterfalls, pools, and greenery are delightful, fusing a delightful blend of contemporary, and rustic Thai design—however, they are rather small. At ground level, some have sleek open balconies dropping right into the pool, but these afford little privacy. The overall result is refreshing in essence, but rather claustrophobic, compared to the other sprawling resorts in Patong. For these rates and convenient location, just a stroll to the beach and madness of the main street, though, it's worth sacrificing on size.

There's also stellar dining, courtesy of a new restaurant branded by the 1980s Brit TV chef, Keith Floyd (see "Where to Dine").

18/110 Ruamjai Rd., Patong, Phuket 83150; ℂ 07629-2929. Fax 07629-2930. www.burasari.com. 186 units. From 2,500B–3,200B (US$71–US$91/£38–£49) double/suite. AE, DC, MC, V. **Amenities:** 2 restaurants; 2 bars; lobby lounge; 2 outdoor pools; fitness room; spa; tour desk; airport transfer; business center; 24-hr. room service; babysitting; same-day laundry service/dry cleaning; nonsmoking rooms. In room: A/C, satellite TV, DVD, minibar, fridge, hair dryer, safe.

Horizon Patong Beach Resort & Spa ✸

This midrange hotel in the middle of busy Patong provides a compact little oasis with cozy, affordable rooms and friendly, efficient service. The grounds feature two pools, and most rooms are right at the pool's edge. Plain tile rooms are clean, with hard beds and simple tile baths (shower only). The place attracts lots of individual European travelers, and the vibe is fun—without being too wild.

Thaweewong Rd., Soi Kep Sap, Patong Beach, Phuket 83150. ℂ 07629-2526. Fax 07629-2535. www.horizonbeach. com. 127 units. From 2,300B–2,800B (US$66–US$80/£35–£43) double. From 3,100B (US$88/£48) suites. MC, V. **Amenities:** 2 restaurants; 2 bars; 2 outdoor pools; tour desk; car-rental desk; limited room service; massage; babysitting; laundry service. In room: A/C, satellite TV, minibar, fridge, safe.

INEXPENSIVE

Andatel Patong (41/9 Rat-U-Thit 200 Pee Rd.; ℂ 07629-0480) is one good central option with rooms around 1,000B to 3,000B (US$28–US$86/£15–£46), but better budget accommodations are found along Kata and Karon beaches in the southern end of the island.

In Patong, the best budget hotels and cheaper bungalows used to be situated just off the beach near Thaweewong Road, before they were wiped out in the tsunami in 2004. What's left are generally run-down places catering to cheap Chinese or Russian tour groups, or those patrons who frequent the hostess bars. Your best bet is to walk to the end of the busy main Thaweewong Road (toward the Amari) and hunt around the quieter end of the beach, where many of the smaller tsunami-hit hotels are still rebuilding. Alas, the prices of places like the 1980s **Absolute Sea Pearl Beach Resort** (ℂ 07634-1910; www.seapearl-beach.com) are now midrange—affordable in off-season, but hardly budget-oriented year round.

THE NORTHWEST COAST

SURIN BEACH

Also known as Pansea Beach, this area has coconut plantations, steep slopes leading down to the beach, and small, private coves dominated by some of the most exclusive hotels on the island.

VERY EXPENSIVE/EXPENSIVE

Amanpuri ✸✸✸   Amanpuri has long been billed as the address of note for international celebrities; however, by today's standards of luxury and style, some may find it falling short considering the high prices it demands. The teak-filled rooms are certainly masterfully designed in a traditional Thai style, with teak and tile floors, sliding doors, and well-chosen antiques. But they are a tad small in the light of the oversized villas now on offer and can be musty in the rainy season; some may also find the ubiquitous concrete decor too stark. In addition, their location, scattered across extremely steep slopes, makes it a bit of a trek from the pool and difficult to negotiate in rain (when the steamy climb up steep steps to the hillside rooms can become hard work); there are golf carts to help. These things apart, the Aman style is still omnipresent: The spacious villas are sumptuously decorated and their private pools are all extremely elegant;

private *salas* are perfect for romantic dining or secluded sunbathing. The Aman Spa offers six large spa suites, a grand herbal steam bath, and sauna. A third restaurant opened in December 2007, on the beach.

Surin Beach Rd., Chuerng Talay, Thalang, Phuket 83110 (north end of cove). ✆ **800/477-9180** or 07632-4333. Fax 07632-4100. www.amanresorts.com. 53 units. 21,000B (US$600/£323) garden view pavilion; from 34,000B (US$970/£523) sea-view pavilion; from 73,500B (US$2,100/£1,131) 2-bedroom villa. AE, DC, MC, V. **Amenities:** 3 restaurants; pool; golf course nearby; outdoor lighted tennis courts; squash courts; fitness center; spa; watersports equipment; private yacht; library; airport transfer; limited room service; babysitting; same-day laundry service/dry cleaning; Wi-Fi and broadband. *In room:* A/C, minibar, fridge, CD/DVD player.

The Chedi Phuket 🌸🌸🌸 Like its august sister resort and immediate neighbor (Amanpuri), the Chedi commands an excellent view of the bay and has its own private stretch of sand. It's perhaps a more kid-friendly option than Amanpuri, plus the site enjoys shady wooden walkways under the trees. From the exotic lobby, with columns and a lily pond, to sleek private bungalows, it is one of the most handsome properties on the island. True, the quality comes with a big price tag, but this romantic getaway has all the details down pat. Each room is a thatched mini-suite with a lovely private sun deck and top amenities. The black-tile swimming pool is large and luxurious. The fine service here caters to the likes of honeymooners and celebrities, and everyone is treated like a VIP. While it may not be as outwardly impressive as its ritzy neighbor, The Chedi is quiet, comfortably informal, and unpretentious, with fine dining options.

118, Moo 3, Surin Beach Rd., Chuerng Talay, Thalang, Phuket 83110 (next to the Amanpuri). ✆ **07632-4017.** Fax 07632-4252. www.ghmhotels.com. 108 units. From 9,555B (US$273/£147) hillside cottage; from 12,845B (US$367/£198) superior cottage; from 16,905B (US$483/£260) deluxe cottage; from 23,170B–30,100B (US$662–US$860/£356–£463) beach cottage. AE, DC, MC, V. **Amenities:** 3 restaurants; bar; outdoor pool; 2 outdoor lighted tennis courts; volleyball and badminton; spa; watersports equipment; kids' club; game room; tour desk; car-rental desk; airport transfer; 24-hr. room service; massage; babysitting; same-day laundry service/dry cleaning. *In room:* A/C, satellite TV, minibar, coffee-making facilities, safe.

Treetops Arasia 🌸🌸🌸 Fancy hillside suites give guests at this ultra-contemporary resort the impression of being suspended high above the cliffs, but there are snappy golf carts to take you to your rooms, and once there, you won't want to leave. Accommodations come in just two types: villas or suites, many with private plunge pools; plus their dining is tops. It all makes for a good little honeymoon hideaway.

125 Moo 3 Srisoonthon Rd., Cherngtalay, Thalang, Phuket 83110. ✆ **07627-1271.** Fax 07627-1270. www.treetops-arasia.com. 48 units. From 4,500B–32,500B (US$128–US$928/£69–£500) room/suite. AE, MC, V. **Amenities:** Restaurant; bar; outdoor pool; health club; spa; tour desk; car-rental desk; 24-hr. room service; massage; babysitting; laundry service. *In room:* A/C, satellite TV, minibar, fridge, coffee-making facilities, hair dryer, safe.

Twin Palms, Phuket 🌸🌸🌸 The brainchild of a Swedish entrepreneur, this gorgeous Thai contemporary resort is not as flashy as its neighbors, but nonetheless has sublime charm and a timeless, yet cutting-edge style. A stunning Thai-inspired open-rafter lobby with glassy stone floors makes way to a vast tropical Water Garden, the centerpiece of the property. Guest have use of an excellent spa and highly acclaimed restaurant, Oriental Spoon (sister to Kuppa in Bangkok), as well as an extensive wine room, but the big attraction to wannabe jetsetters must be the additional 21 residences (all with private pools) that will open by early 2008. Less pricey are the airy Lagoon rooms and suites, some of which have terraces that go straight into the water. The room decor uses numerous Thai references, such as sleek dark wood floors and local art and crafts (including rugs made by the Mae Fah Luang crafts charity). Ultra peak season starts December 19 to January 10, after which, rates fall slightly until March.

106/46 Moo 3, Surin Beach Rd., Chuerng Talay, Thalang, Phuket 83110 (opposite the golf course). © 07631-6500. Fax 07631-6599. www.twinpalms-phuket.com. 97 units. From 8,200B (US$234/£126) deluxe palm room; from 10,000B (US$286/£154) deluxe lagoon room; from 17,500B (US$500/£269) 1-bedroom lagoon junior suite; from 37,600B (US$1,074/£578) 2-bed penthouse residence. AE, DC, MC, V. **Amenities:** 2 restaurants; bar; wine room; outdoor pool; beach club; watersports equipment; tour desk; DVD library; 24-hr. room service; massage; babysitting; same-day laundry service/dry cleaning; Internet. *In room:* A/C, satellite TV, minibar, coffee-making facilities, safe.

BANG THAO BAY (THE LAGUNA RESORT COMPLEX)

Twenty minutes south of the airport and just as far north of Patong Beach on the western shore of Phuket, this isolated area is Phuket's high-end, "integrated resort" of five properties that share the island's most top-rated facilities. Among them you'll find world-class health spas, countless restaurants, and the island's best golf course. The grounds are impressively landscaped, and the hotel properties are scattered among the winding lagoons, all navigable by boat. The best thing about staying here is that you can dine at any of the fine hotel restaurants, connecting by boat or free shuttle, and be charged on one simple bill at whatever resort you choose. The three below are the best, but also consider the original **Laguna Beach Resort** (© **07632-4352;** www. lagunabeach-resort.com), with a similar high standard of rooms and services (popular with groups). In the high season, expect standard double rooms (with two breakfasts) to cost 13,770B (US$393/£207); for the lowest category of suite (with breakfast) you'll pay 32,290B (US$923/£460).

VERY EXPENSIVE

Banyan Tree Phuket ✸✸✸   Banyan Tree is possibly Phuket's most famous hideaway for honeymooners, sports stars, and high society. Private villas with walled courtyards, many with private pools or Jacuzzis, are spacious and grand, and lavishly styled in teakwood with outdoor bathtubs. The main pool is truly impressive—a free-form lagoon, landscaped with greenery and rock formations—with a flowing water canal. A small village in itself, the spa provides a wide range of beauty and health treatments in luxurious rooms—you can request a private massage in your room or in outdoor pavilions. The resort can arrange barbecues at your villa, or you can dine at the Tamarind Restaurant, which serves delicious, light, and authentic health food. There's even an international golf course on-site and private tour office. The Banyan Tree garners many international awards, especially for its Green Initiative and eco-friendly stance. In high season, peak surcharges apply.

33 Moo 4, Srisoonthon Rd., Cherngtalay District, Amphur Talang, Phuket 83110 (north end of beach). © **800/525-4800** or 07632-4374. Fax 07632-4375. www.phuket.com/banyantree. 121 units. From 15,750B-45,500B (US$450–US$1,300/£242–£700) villas. AE, DC, MC, V. **Amenities:** 6 restaurants; lounge; outdoor pool; golf course; 3 outdoor lit tennis courts; fitness center; spa; watersports equipment; tour desk; car-rental desk; airport transfer; 24-hr. room service; in-room massage; babysitting; same-day laundry service/dry cleaning. *In room:* A/C, satellite TV, minibar, fridge, coffee-making facilities, safe.

Dusit Laguna Resort ✸✸✸ *Kids*   The Dusit hotel group has some fine properties in Thailand, and the Dusit Laguna is no exception. Opt for a deluxe room with a balcony and ocean view and you'll pay not much more than a standard. Suites are large and luxurious. The hotel offers four excellent restaurants; of note is their quaint Italian restaurant, La Trattoria, serving authentic Italian cuisine in a chic, but laid-back pavilion decorated in cool whites and blues. The well-landscaped gardens have an especially delightful waterfall and an excellent pool. The grounds open onto a wide, white sand beach flanked by two lagoons. Facilities for families are excellent, with a whole gamut of entertainment including computer games.

390 Srisoonthon Rd., Cherngtalay District, Phuket 83110 (south end of beach). © 07632-4320. Fax 07632-4174. www.dusit.com. 226 units. From 4,305B–8,260B (US$123–US$236/£66–£127) double; from 13,545B (US$387/£208) suite. AE, DC, MC, V. **Amenities:** 4 restaurants; lounge; outdoor pool; pitch and putt on premises and golf course nearby; outdoor lighted tennis courts; fitness center; spa; watersports equipment; bike rental; tour desk; car-rental desk; airport transfer; business center; shopping arcade; salon; 24-hr. room service; babysitting; same-day laundry service/dry cleaning; nonsmoking rooms. *In room:* A/C, satellite TV, minibar, fridge, coffee-making facilities, safe.

Sheraton Grande Laguna Phuket ✦✦ This is a sprawling, luxury campus of two- and three-story pavilions. Rooms are quite large with tiled floors, cozy sitting areas, and large balconies; some bathrooms have sunken tubs. The hotel design carefully traces the natural lines, coves, and jetties of its surrounding lagoon, and the area is quiet and private. A fair-size pool meanders through the resort and there are good amenities for kids of all ages, from a kids' club (called VIK or Very Important Kids) to beach games and sailboat rental at the lagoon. With its professionalism and an enormous range of outlets, plus casual eateries and cafes (including a good bakery), the Sheraton is a fine, familiar choice.

10 Moo 4, Srisoonthorn Rd., Cherng Talay, Talang, Phuket 83110. © 07632-4101. Fax 07632-4108. www.laguna phuket.com/hotels/sheraton. 335 units. From 5,775B–7,525B (US$165–US$215/£89–£116) double; from 9,100B–14,700B (US$260–US$420/£140–£226) villa. AE, DC, MC, V. **Amenities:** 6 restaurants; bar and lounge; freeform outdoor pool; golf course nearby; 2 outdoor lighted tennis courts; fitness center; spa; watersports equipment/rentals; bike rental; kids' club; tour desk; car-rental desk; airport transfer; business center w/Internet; shopping arcade; 24-hr. room service; babysitting; same-day laundry service/dry cleaning; nonsmoking rooms. *In room:* A/C, satellite TV, minibar, fridge, coffee-making facilities, hair dryer, safe.

NAI YANG BEACH & NAI THON

Nai Yang National Park is a long stretch of shoreline peeking out from underneath a dense forest of palms, casuarinas trees, and various shrubs. There are 115 species of birds and a coral reef offshore. It's good for leaving the crowds behind, but be warned that it is isolated and, short of Indigo Pearl Resort (formerly Pearl Village; see below) and a few bungalow resorts nearby, the park offers little in the way of luxury.

Nai Yang is known for its annual release of hatchling sea turtles into the Andaman Sea. Mature sea turtles weigh from 100 to 1,500 pounds and swim the waters around Phuket, and though the law is supposed to protect them from fishermen and poachers, who collect their eggs from beaches, their numbers are dwindling. If not for the efforts of international volunteer groups such as **Naucrates** (www.naucrates.org) who have spent years working out of a small conservation center at Koh Phra Thong near Kuraburi, these creatures would probably be extinct in this region. Annual releases take place on April 13, during the Songkran holiday. You'll have to pay 400B (US$11/£6.15) to enter the park, and there is a small information kiosk and restaurant at the park headquarters. Tent accommodations are available for 600B (US$17/£9.25) and sleep up to five guests. For more information, contact **Sirinath Park Campground,** 89/1 Moo 1, Talang, Phuket 83110 (© **07632-8226;** www.dnp.go.th/parkreserve).

Nai Thon is just south of Nai Yang (closer to Laguna) and is home to one deluxe resort: Trisara.

NAI THON
Very Expensive

Trisara ✦✦ Well away from the fray, Trisara is a small boutique property some 15 minutes from the airport. The resort affords a high level of comfort in a clutch of private, contemporary pool villas right at the seaside. There's a high price tag attached to its luxury villas, which are priced according to proximity to the sea. It's definitely not as classy as The Chedi, nor as celebrity-friendly as The Banyan Tree, but it would like to think it outdoes both; at times, you'll rub up against a distinct attitude here. Still, its private spaces are picturesquely flamboyant, with pools overlooking the blue water below—it should appeal to those who don't mind the isolation.

60/1 Moo 6, Srisoonthon Rd., Cherngtalay, Talang, Phuket 83110. ⓒ 07631-0100. Fax 07631-0300. www.trisara. com. 42 units. 27,300B–57,750B (US$780–US$1,650/£420–£888) pool villa; from 67,900B (US$1,940/£1,045) multibedroom villa. AE, V, MC. **Amenities:** Restaurant; bar; all units have private outdoor pool; seaside public pool; tennis courts; diving; health club; spa; detox program; watersports equipment/rentals; bike rentals; library; tour desk; car-rental desk; shopping arcade; salon; 24-hr. room service; babysitting; laundry service; dry cleaning; Internet. *In room:* A/C, satellite TV, fax, minibar, fridge, coffee-making facilities, hair dryer, iron, safe.

NAI YANG
Moderate

Indigo Pearl Resort 🕷🕷🕷   One of the earliest resorts on Phuket, the Pearl Village was destroyed in the 2004 tsunami and, after extensive restoration, was reborn as Indigo Pearl Resort. Its reincarnation was the work of landscape designer and Bangkok-resident, Bill Bensley, and a team of local artisans. The new resort is a creative masterpiece. On the periphery of the National Park, the hotel is isolated from the ravages of over-development characterizing the rest of touristy Phuket. The facilities are excellent, especially for families—with rooms ranging from pavilions and villas to exquisitely furnished suites. The one drawback is that you're out in the sticks here but, for rest and recreation, the resort is perfectly self-contained and close to nature. The resort was the winner of the 2007 *Condé Naste Traveller* "Best New Resort" award.

Nai Yang Beach and National Park, Phuket 83104 (5 min. south of the airport). ⓒ 07632-7006. Fax 07632-7015. www.indigo-pearl.com. 243 units. From 3,000B (US$86/£46) double; 4,500B (US$128/£69) villa; from 20,500B (US$586/£315) suite. AE, DC, MC, V. **Amenities:** 6 restaurants; bar; lounge; pool; outdoor lit tennis courts; fitness center; watersports and dive center; bike rental; international golf course nearby; kid's club; game room; tour desk; car-rental desk; airport transfer; room service; babysitting; same-day laundry service/dry cleaning; Thai cooking classes; Internet. *In room:* A/C, satellite TV, minibar, fridge, coffee-making facilities, hair dryer, safe.

MAI KHAO BEACH & THE FAR NORTH OF PHUKET

Mai Khao is a wide sweep of beach on the northeastern shore close to the airport. It is Phuket's longest beach and is the site where sea turtles lay their eggs during December and January. The eggs are coveted by Thai and Chinese people, who eat them for the supposed life-sustaining power, but large-scale efforts are underway to assist these glorious animals and protect their potential hatchlings.

VERY EXPENSIVE

JW Marriott Phuket Resort and Spa 🕷🕷🕷   The clean lines of the sprawling JW Marriott could make a haiku poet out of anyone. Along the endless stretch of sand and roaring surf that makes up desolate Mai Khao Beach, this resort is a stylish (and eco-friendly) masterpiece. Anyone arriving at night will be awed by the flaming torches lining the steep drive. The airy lobby faces an enormous, black reflecting pool that sparkles with torchlight. The rooms are pretty average, except for a small meditation and reading corner with Thai cushions, in an alcove by the window. Higher rooms offer glorious views onto the sumptuous gardens and sea. If you have the cash, stay in one of the expansive suites. There is little by way of entertainment outside of the hotel, but the huge beach, pools, numerous restaurants and shops, and an ochre-walled, Moroccan-inspired spa keep guests happy. Due to the strong rip tides, sea swimming is not recommended, but there are sail boats. It is a 30-minute drive to the nearest tourist town, but the resort facilities are complete and few guests will find the need to leave, unless it's to take a bike ride to the next village or a kayak ride with nearby eco-outfit, John Gray. Service at the JW Marriott is impeccable and the dining exemplary.

231 Moo 3, Mai Khao, Talang, Phuket 83110. © 07633-8000. Fax 07634-8348. www.marriott.com. 265 units. From 5,200B (US$148/£80) double; from 12,000B (US$343/£185) suite. AE, DC, MC, V. **Amenities:** 7 restaurants; 3 bars; 2 outdoor pools; 2 tennis courts; fitness center; extensive spa; watersports equipment; kids' club; teen activity center w/computers; tour desk; bike rental; car-rental desk; airport transfer; business center; shopping arcade; salon; 24-hr. room service; babysitting; same-day laundry/dry cleaning; nonsmoking rooms; Thai cooking school; executive level rooms w/private check-in; high-speed Internet. *In room:* A/C, satellite TV, minibar, fridge, coffee-making facilities, hair dryer, safe.

PHUKET TOWN

Most just pass through the island's commercial hub, but Old Phuket culture abounds in the many Sino-Portuguese homes and unusual architecture. It's well worth a look, especially if Phuket Island is your only destination (see "Where to Dine," below, for dining options here).

MODERATE

Cape Panwa Hotel ★★   Just 10 minutes outside Phuket Town, set on a former beachfront coconut plantation, Cape Panwa Hotel is one of Phuket's best kept secrets. Just a short drive from the old town culture, the cape is a haven of tranquillity. European-run, but with fabulous Thai staff, the hotel is popular with families and honeymooners who come for the relaxed charm and island ambience. All rooms, villas, and suites face the Andaman Sea and are set in lush tropical gardens. Dinner, or sunset cocktails at Panwa House—a grand Sino-Portuguese mansion—is a highlight after a day spent combing Old Town streets or relaxing on the beach.

27, Moo 8, Sakdijej Rd., Cape Panwa, Phuket 83000. © 07639-1123. Fax 07639-1177. www.capepanwa.com. 246 units. From 2,900B (US$83/£45) double; from 5,500B (US$157/£85) suite; from 9,600B (US$274/£148) villa. AE, DC, MC, V. **Amenities:** 4 restaurants; bar; lounge; 2 outdoor pools; tennis court; fitness center; salon; tour desk; airport transfer; business center; sailing and canoeing; limited room service; babysitting; same-day laundry service/dry cleaning; nonsmoking rooms; Thai cooking classes. *In room:* A/C, satellite TV, DVD player, minibar, fridge, hair dryer, safe.

The Metropole   Just around the corner from the Royal Phuket City Hotel, the Metropole is a fine business hotel. Public spaces are all spit-and-polish (though not especially grand), and the rooms are large and fully appointed (if bland), with good black-and-white tile bathrooms. Service is passable, on a good day.

1 Soi Surin, Montri Rd., Phuket Town 83000. © 07621-5050. Fax 07621-5990. www.metropolephuket.com. 248 units. 3,200B–3,800B (US$91–US$108/£49–£58) double; from 6,000B (US$171/£92) suite. AE, MC, V. **Amenities:** 2 restaurants; lounge; bar; pool; small fitness center; tour desk; business center; salon; 24-hr. room service; laundry service; dry cleaning; Internet. *In room:* A/C, satellite TV, minibar, fridge, safe.

Royal Phuket City Hotel ★★   For a small town like Phuket, this hotel is surprisingly cosmopolitan. A true city hotel, Royal Phuket's facilities include one of the finest fitness centers going, a full-service spa with massage, large outdoor swimming pool, and a very professional executive business center. Above the cavernous marble lobby, guest rooms are smart, done up in contemporary hues and style. Views of the busy little town below pale in comparison to the beachfront just a short ride away. The Red Onion Restaurant serves international cuisine, the street-side Café 154 offers great coffee and cakes, and the Atrium Lounge cocktail bar is one of the smartest in town.

154 Phang Nga Rd., Amphur Muang, Phuket 83000 (located to the east of Phuket Town, across from the intercity bus terminal). ✆ **07623-3333.** Fax 07623-3335. www.royalphuketcity.com. 251 units. From 2,000B–3,200B (US$57–US$91/£31–£49) double; from 6,000B (US$171/£92) suite (discounts available). AE, DC, MC, V. **Amenities:** 2 restaurants; lounge; bar; outdoor pool; golf course nearby; fitness center; spa; tour desk; airport transfer; business center; 24-hr. room service; babysitting; same-day laundry service/dry cleaning; nonsmoking rooms; Wi-Fi. *In room:* A/C, satellite TV, minibar, fridge, hair dryer, safe.

3 Where to Dine

From tip-to-toe, north to south, it takes about an hour to drive all of Phuket, but the availability of hired tuk-tuks, hotel transport, or even self-drive vehicles means that for dining and nightlife, you can choose from any of the many options on the island. The beach areas in the west are chockablock with small eateries or smart hotel restaurants. In the throbbing Patong strip, culinary options stretch from fast food outlets clustered around the beach to snazzy designer diners and Asian chains.

KATA & KARON

The busy road between Kata and Karon (as well as the many side streets) are crammed with small cafes and restaurants serving affordable Thai and Western food. Stop by **Euro Deli** (58/60 Karon Rd.; ✆ **07628-6265**) for a good sandwich or a coffee. Also note the outdoor beer bars and travelers cafes on the far southern end of Kata Beach, just behind Club Med; these places rock late and are good spots to grab a quick bite, local style. On the north end of Karon, stop by **Karon Café** (526/17 Soi Islandia Park Resort, off of Patak Rd.; ✆ **07639-64217;** www.karoncafe.com) for good, casual Western dining (like great Aussie steaks). For a more expensive treat, **Joe's South** (Kata Gardens on Kata Noi Rd., ✆ **07628-5385**) is a fabulous new fine dining spot in a great setting.

EXPENSIVE

Mom Tri's Kitchen ★★★ *Finds* THAI/INTERNATIONAL So legendary is the Thai and Western cuisine at The Boathouse that the management arranges cooking lessons from its chef. The Boathouse also has an excellent selection of international wines—420 labels. Mom Tri's is a veritable island institution, and its popularity has spawned a new outlet, along with a luxury resort, just up the hill from the original. **Mom Tri's Kitchen at Villa Royale** is the latest upscale venture from the folks at The Boathouse and serves excellent fine cuisine from its luxury perch.

The Boathouse Inn, 114 Patak Rd., Kata Beach. ✆ **07633-0557.** Reservations recommended during peak season. Main courses 280B–850B (US$8–US$24/£4.30–£14); seafood is sold at market price. AE, DC, MC, V. Daily 7am–10:30pm.

MODERATE/INEXPENSIVE

The Cliff ★ INTERNATIONAL High above Karon on the rise heading toward Patong, The Cliff is part of the newly renamed Centara Villas group (formerly Central Hotels Resorts, which explains its Web address). Serving delicious contemporary Thai and Mediterranean dishes from atop their hilltop perch, the restaurant offers a great escape from town. Try the thinly sliced tuna for an appetizer. They also have good grill items, from Aussie tenderloin to roast lamb, and a long list of excellent Thai curries, all artfully presented.

701 Patak Rd., Tambon Karon. ✆ **07639-8111.** www.centralhotelsresorts.com. Main courses 180B–650B (US$5–US$19/£2.75–£10). AE, MC, V. Daily 6–11pm.

On the Rock ★★ THAI/SEAFOOD Part of the Marina Phuket (see "Where to Stay," earlier in this chapter), this little unassuming restaurant serves excellent Thai cuisine on a scenic deck high above the south end of Karon Beach. Try the Seafood Basket, a medley of grilled and fried local seafood. The staff is friendly and the restaurant is a great choice for a candlelit evening.

47 Karon Rd., Karon Beach (on bluff at south end of Karon Beach Rd.). ✆ **07633-0625**. Fax 07633-0516. www.marina phuket.com. Main courses 120B–580B (US$3.40–US$17/£1.85–£8.90). AE, MC, V. Daily 8am–11pm.

Ratri Jazztaurant ✿✿ THAI   Perched high at the top of a precipitous hill slope, Ratri is worth the 1km (hideously steep) climb for their classic Thai dishes, most of which pack an explosively spicy punch. There's a cacophonous live jazz band that plays late into the night. The music is great, but if you are looking forward to some dinnertime conversation, it makes that hard (you should go before sunset, in that case). There's a full wine cellar and cigar bar (so nonsmokers beware). The somewhat surly service is the only drawback.

Patak Rd., Kata Hill (behind Big One convenience store). ✆ **07633-3538**. www.ratrijazztaurant.com. Main courses 210B–500B (US$6–US$14/£3.25–£7.70). MC, V. Daily 5pm–late; live band 8:30pm–late.

PATONG

With the arrival of the new **JungCeylon** (www.jungceylon.com) shopping mall, dining options in Patong have not just broadened, but smartened up radically. In addition to the usual low-cost Western food and drink chains (**Subway, Starbucks**) there are now some smarter places such as the Singaporean restaurant chain, **Indochine,** all packed into this gargantuan air-conditioned mall.

Most of the small seafront *sois* offer pricey Thai and Italian food—in often expat-run places. If you have a hankering for seafood, head to the end of the beach drag (Thaweewong Rd.). What was once just a collection of wooden shacks 10 years ago is now a long strip of chic diners. Though this road is plagued with touts, armed with menus and imploring tourists to choose their restaurant, this end of it is slightly less intense, so stand your ground. Pick a menu that you like the look of, and order from a wide selection of fresh seafood that is displayed on ice at the front.

One of the best fine dining choices around here is at the newly opened **Floyd's Brasserie** (see below) at the boutique Burasari hotel on Ruanjai Road (aka Soi Holiday Inn). One popular little breakfast place is **Sabai-Sabai** (100/3 Thaweewong Rd.; ✆ **07634-0222**); the name means "relaxed" and it is indeed so, just a laid-back storefront in a small *soi* off busy Patong Beach Road. Or try the little restaurant **Orchid** (78/304 Thaweewong Rd., Soi Perm Pong; ✆ **07634-0462**) on the next *soi* south for good, affordable Thai and European dishes.

Scruffy Murphy's (Soi Bangla; ✆ **07629-2590**) is a popular Irish pub (see "Phuket After Dark," later) that also serves good pub grub and fry-ups (great hangover chow). Also look for little **Zen** (✆ **07629-3053**), a popular Thai sushi chain with a busy outlet on the main beach road in Patong. You'll find lots of international fast food chains, overpriced coffee, and, of course, the obligatory 7-Eleven here, too.

EXPENSIVE

Baan Rim Pa ✿✿ THAI   In a beautiful Thai-style teak house, Baan Rim Pa has dining in a romantic indoor setting or with gorgeous views of the bay from outdoor terraces. Among high-end travelers, the Thai cuisine restaurant is one of the most popular stops on the island, so be sure to reserve your table early. The owner of Baan Rim Pa has opened up a few other restaurants next door on the cliffside, including **Joe's Downstairs** for cool cocktails and tapas (✆ **07634-4254**), and the Italian restaurant **Da Maurizio Bar and Ristorante** (✆ **07634-4079**).

223 Kalim Beach Rd. (on the cliffs just north of Patong Beach). ℂ **07634-0789**. www.baanrimpa.com. Reservations necessary. Main courses 250B–1,200B (US$7–US$34/£3.85–£18). AE, DC, MC, V. Daily noon–2:30pm and 6–10pm.

MODERATE

Floyd's Brasserie ✦ THAI   Two decades ago, Keith Floyd was a household name in Britain, and one of the first TV chefs to find celebrity (not just for his cooking, but for his famously frequent inebriety). Floyd's Brasserie is his first restaurant in Asia, tucked into a pocket-size space at the Burasari Resort. The brunch and evening supper menus all carry Floyd's innovative style, and Sunday's loaded buffets are served with free-flowing smoothies, Bellinis, sangria, and wine.

18/110 Ruamjai Rd. (aka Soi Holiday Inn). Patong, ℂ **07629-2929**. Fax 07629-2930. www.burasari.com. Main courses 195B–450B (US$5.60–US$13/£3–£6.90). AE, V, MC. Daily 11am–10pm.

La Gritta ✦ ITALIAN   Throughout 2006-2007, the Amari chain has consistently upgraded its properties, including renovating and reinvigorating their dining facilities. La Gritta is notable not just for its food but its stunning views of Patong Beach, which unfurl in a long silver strip off into the distance. It's well away from the fray, yet only a 15-minute walk northwards to the end of the main beachfront road up on the headland. The walk will let you work up an appetite for the restaurant's extensive menu and excellent wine list. The colorful *antipasto misto* makes a great shared appetizer, while main dishes include plenty of seafood like sea bass, prawns, or scallops—though there are imported steaks, veal, and salmon, too. For dessert, don't miss the pink peppercorn ice cream or the chocolate Amaretti custard.

At the Amari Coral Beach Resort & Spa; 2 Meun-ngern Rd., (beyond Patong Beach). ℂ **07634-0106**. Main courses 170B–520B (US$4.15–US$13/£2.60–£8). AE, MC, V. Daily 11am–10pm.

INEXPENSIVE

Pan Yaah Thai Restaurant THAI   Here is a good escape from busy Patong and some real Thai home cooking. The restaurant is a wooden deck overlooking the bay some 2km north of central Patong. The menu is classic Thai, with some one-dish meals like fried rice or noodles, but best enjoyed with friends sharing a number of courses, such as spicy *tom yam* soup with prawns, stir-fried dishes, and whole fish cooked to order. Prices are low and service is friendly and laid back.

249 Prabaramee Rd., Patong, (2km north of Patong along the coast). ℂ **07634-4473**. Main courses 90B–150B (US$3–US$4.30/£1.40–£2.30). MC, V. Daily 11am–11pm.

Patong Seafood Restaurant SEAFOOD   Take an evening stroll along the lively strip next to the beach and you'll find dozens of open-air seafood restaurants displaying their catch of the day on ice out front, accompanied by a pushy tout. This one is pretty typical of the lot, but has a long-established reputation. Like all its neighbors along here, it offers a selection of local fish such as groper *(garoupa)*, lobster, squid, prawn, shellfish, and sometimes crab. Service is on the ball, and they're always popular—so head here early to avoid the crowds.

98/2 Thaweewong Rd., Patong Beach. ℂ **07634-0247**. Reservations not accepted. Main courses 80B–700B (US$1.95–US$20/£1.25–£11); seafood at market prices. AE, DC, MC, V. Daily 7am–11pm.

BANG TAO BAY (THE LAGUNA RESORT COMPLEX)

The many hotel restaurants of the five-star properties in the Laguna Complex could fill a small guidebook of their own. You can't go too wrong in any of the hotels, with **The Banyan Tree, Phuket** (p. 242) topping the lot for sheer style and enormous variety (try the pan-Asian delicacies at **Saffron**, or delicious Mediterranean fare at **Watercourt**).

One restaurant just outside the complex is worth mentioning; it's where all the hotel managers eat when they get out of work.

Tatonka ★★ INTERNATIONAL   Billed as "Globetrotter Cuisine," dining at Tatonka is indeed a foray into the realm of nomadic gastronomy. The young owner is himself a well-traveled chef (check out his resume written on the bathroom wall). Dishes here reflect those travels, a creative fusion of Mediterranean and Pacific-Rim cuisine. Ask the waiter for a recommendation and enjoy.

382/19 Moo 1, Srisoonthon Rd., Cherngtalay (at the entrance of the Laguna Resort in Bang Tao Bay). ℂ/fax 07632-4349. Main courses 150B–420B (US$4.30–US$12/£2.30–£6.45). MC, V. Daily 6pm–last order.

CHALONG BAY & RAWAI

A good bet for fresh seafood is in the far south of the island at Chalong Bay's **Kan Eang Seafood** (9/3 Chaofa Rd., Chalong Bay; ℂ 07638-1323). You'll find whole fish or Phuket lobster (a giant clawless langoustine) just fresh from the ocean. If you've rented a car, a ride down this way makes for a fun day out. The **Drunken Monkey** (21/6 Moo 4, Viset Rd., Rawai; ℂ 0810-878742) is a great gay-friendly eatery for home-cooked meals and Sunday roast; Londoners Martyn and Ian are wonderful hosts. **Nikita's Café Bar** (no phone) on the Rawai seafront is a cool seaside hangout for coffee and sundowners. Down Nai Harn Beach way, look out for **Los Amigos Cantina** (next to Nai Harn Lake; no phone) for excellent Mexican. The **Breakfast Hut** (no phone) on the same road serves tasty Western food.

PHUKET TOWN

Though quite a long ride from the West coast beach areas, a night out in Phuket Town is worth it for some fine meals and a taste of local culture. One place to visit is the slickly styled **Siam Indigo Exotique Bar and Restaurant** (8 Phang Nga Rd.; ℂ 07625-6697), which has fabulous steaks, cocktails, and tapas. Happy hours are on Friday and Saturday from 6 to 8pm.

Ka Jok See ★★ (Finds) THAI   A truly special find, Ka Jok See is a smart and intimate European-styled venue set in an old Sino-Portuguese house. This classy Thai restaurant run by Khun Lek has been here for years and hides mysteriously behind a façade dripping with ivy. Patronized by well-heeled local professionals, it's so well known there is no sign (look for the small Kanasutra Indian restaurant next door). Though its name means stained glass, the decor opts for ceilings of huge wooden beams, giant plants, and candlelight instead of painted glass. A great selection of music sets the stage for a romantic evening, one that's well worth a venture from the beach.

26 Takua Pa Rd., Phuket Town (a short walk from central Rasada Rd.). ℂ 07621-7903. Reservations recommended. Main courses 150B–380B (US$4.30–US$11/£2.30–£5.85). No credit cards. Tues–Sun 6pm–midnight (kitchen closes around 11pm).

Salvatore ★ ITALIAN   This is the real thing: huge salads, pasta, and great pizza in a large air-conditioned dining room at the town center. The wine list is excellent, and if you're lucky, Salvatore himself may drop in on your table. Commendable pasta, lasagna, steaks, and a range of daily specials are all made with loving care, plus, many of the wines are imported. Don't miss the Limoncello Truffle, which melts in your mouth and goes well with a stiff black coffee.

15 Rasada Rd., Tambol Taladyai (central Phuket Town). ℂ/fax 07622-5958. Main courses 140B–650B (US$4–US$19/£2.15–£10). AE, MC, V. Daily 11:30am–3pm and 6–11pm.

Watermark Bar Restaurant 🦀 THAI/INTERNATIONAL   Not to be confused with The Banyan Tree's restaurant of the same name, the Watermark is an expat hang-out serving a good choice of mostly fusion seafood dishes overlooking the lagoon, just north of Phuket Town. Try the seared *ahi* tuna appetizer, with a pasta or grilled main course, or some of the deliciously spicy contemporary-styled Thai dishes.

Phuket Boat Lagoon, 22/1 Moo 2 Thepkasattri Rd., Koh Kaew (10 min. north of Phuket Town, 30 min. from the west coast beaches). ✆ 07623-9730. www.watermarkphuket.com. Main courses 175B–700B (US$5–US$20/£2.70–£11). MC, V. Daily 11am–10pm.

4 Exploring Phuket

You can spend a lot of time on Phuket and still not do everything. Thanks to years of resort growth, there are a host of activities here, appealing mostly to those who like a bit of action. The beachfront areas are full of tour operators, each vying for your business and offering similar trips (or copycat tours). Listed below are the most reputable firms, but still, ask lots of questions before signing up for anything so there are no surprises.

BEACHFRONT WATERSPORTS

A 10-minute **parasailing ride** is 800B (US$23/£12) at most beaches. You'll also find **Hobie Cats** for around 600B (US$17/£9.25) per hour, as well as **windsurf boards** for 200B (US$6/£3.10) per hour. On Patong, there are no specific offices to organize these activities, just small operators with hand-painted signs usually hanging around under umbrellas—bargain furiously.

Jet skis are technically illegal, but alas, as you'll hear all the length of Patong, there are still plenty of people willing to spend their money on screaming up and down the beach on a gasoline-belching scooter. (Most of the noisier watersports activities are concentrated along Patong Beach.) Accidents are now so common between swimmers, or divers and jet skis (some resulting in amputations or death) that areas are now being cordoned off from these (wholly un-ecological) aquatic toys. Play safe.

You'll find small **sailboats and kayaks** for rent along all of the beaches. Kata is a good place to rent a kayak and play in the waves for 200B (US$6/£3.10) per hour, but ask about the strong rip tides along this dangerous coast.

DAY-CRUISING & YACHTING

The turquoise waters of the Andaman Sea near Phuket are every city dweller's dream. Every December, Phuket hosts the increasingly popular **King's Cup Regatta,** in which almost 100 international racing yachts compete. For more information, check out www.kingscup.com.

For a different view of gorgeous Phang Nga Bay, book a trip aboard one of Asian Oasis' three luxury Chinese junks, the *June Bahtra 1, 2,* and *3.* Full-day trips include lunch and hotel transfers. Passage on an all-day cruise in stunning Phang Nga Bay, to the likes of the (now totally ruined) "James Bond" Island, starts from 2,900B (US$83/£44) per person, depending on the number in a group (alcoholic beverages not included). Book through their website, www.asian-oasis.com.

There are more and more options for chartering yachts in Phuket. Contact **Thai Marine Leisure** for details (c/o Phuket Boat Lagoon, 20/2 Thepkasattri Rd., Tambon Koh Kaew, Phuket 83200; ✆ 07623-9111; www.thaimarine.com) or **Sunsail Asia Pacific** (Phuket Boat Lagoon, 20/5 Moo 2, Thepkasattri Rd., Phuket 83200; ✆ 07623-9057; www.sunsail.com).

Many of the high-end resorts, such as the **Amanpuri** (© **07632-4333;** www.aman resorts.com), have their own fleets of pleasure boats for in-house guests, or can make arrangements.

FISHING

Blue Water Anglers are deep-sea fishing experts with well-equipped boats. They'll take you out for marlin, sailfish, swordfish, and tuna, and also have special night-fishing programs; but be warned that if you're new to the sport, it ain't cheap—the trip will set you back thousands of baht. Stop by at 35/7 Sakadidet Rd., Phuket Town, or call © **07639-1287.** Or look up www.bluewater-anglers.com.

GOLF

There are some superb golf courses on Phuket attracting enthusiasts from around the globe. Golf package tour companies offer some great discounts on greens fees; try **Phuket Golf** (www.phuket-golf.com) or alternatively, give **Phuket Golf vacation** (www.phuketgolfcourse.com) a go. Below is a selection of some of the best courses on the island.

- **The Blue Canyon Country Club,** 165 Moo 1, Thepkasattri Rd., near the airport (© **07632-7440;** fax 07632-7449; www.bluecanyonclub.com), is a par-72 championship course with natural hazards, trees, and guarded greens (greens fees: from 3,800B/US$108/£58).
- **Laguna Phuket Golf Club,** 34 Moo 4, Srisoonthon Rd., at the Laguna Resort Complex on Bang Tao Bay (© **07627-0991;** fax 07632-4351), is a par-71 championship course with many water features (greens fees: 3,400B/US$97/£52; guests of Laguna resorts receive a discount).
- **Mission Hills Golf Resort & Spa,** 195 Moo 4 Phla Khlok (© **07631-0888;** fax 07631-0899; www.missionhillsphuket.com), is the island's newest international course. It's designed by Jack Nicklaus and offers ocean views over 18 holes and a 9-hole bay-view, night course (greens fees: 3,800B/US$108/£58).
- An older course, the **Phuket Country Club,** 80/1 Vichitsongkram Rd., west of Phuket Town (© **07632-1038;** fax 07632-1721; www.phuketcountryclub. com), has beautiful greens and fairways, plus a giant lake (greens fees: 3,000B/ US$86/£46).

HORSEBACK RIDING

A romantic and charming way to see Phuket's jungles and beaches is on horseback. The **Phuket Laguna Riding Club,** 394 Moo 1, Bangtao Beach (© **07632-4199**), welcomes riders of all ages and experience levels, and can provide instruction for beginners and children. Prices start at 500B (US$12/£7.70) per hour.

SEA KAYAKING

Phang Nga Bay National Park, a ½-hour drive north of Phuket, hosts great day trips by sea kayak. The scenery is stunning, with limestone karst towers rising from the bay of more than 120 islands. These craggy rock formations were the backdrop for the James Bond classic *The Man with the Golden Gun.* Sadly, due to unfettered commercialism, they are completely overrun with teeming tour groups dropping litter and packing the narrow paths. Sea kayaks are a perfect way to avoid these crowds and explore the many breathtaking caves and chambers that hide beneath the jagged cliffs. All tours include the hour-plus ride to and from Phang Nga, the cruise to the island area, paddle-guide, kayak, and lunch. **John Gray Sea Canoe** ⍟ (124 Soi 1 Yaowarat

Rd., Phuket Town 83000; © **07625-4505;** http://phuketdir.com/johngrayseacanoe/index.com) is the most respected, low-impact, eco-tour operator and a pioneer of sea kayaking in the region. The company is much imitated, but is by far the best choice for day trips through island caves to hidden interior lagoons (called *hongs*). The standard day trip runs 3,500B (US$100/£54) per adult (1,750B/US$50/£27 per child), with two persons sharing an inflated boat. A guide will paddle you dexterously in and out of the caves—which is frustrating if you actually like paddling—but the caves are stunning, and there's free time for paddling on your own later. Multiday and more adventurous "self-guided" tours are also offered.

The folks at **Paddle-Asia** (9/71 Rasdanusorn Rd., Tambon Rasada, Phuket 83000; © **07624-0952;** fax 07621-6145; www.paddleasia.com) make Phuket their home and do trips throughout the region, with a focus more on custom adventure travel, not day junkets. They have great options for anyone from beginner to expert, and on any trip you'll paddle real decked kayaks, not inflatables. A highlight is their trip to **Khao Sok National Park** (see "Day Trips from Surat Thani" in chapter 8), a 3-day adventure in which you may even spot amazing jungle wildlife. Due to recent tragedies in this park in rainy season, Thai authorities are considering closing it during storms, so stay abreast of the weather, especially in monsoon season. In Phuket, Paddle Asia can arrange offshore trips to outlying islands, kayak-surfing on Kata Beach, or custommade adventures ranging as far as Laos.

SCUBA DIVING

Since it's world renowned for its access to nearby **Surin** and **Similan Islands,** scuba diving is a huge draw to the island of Phuket. Thailand is one of the most affordable places to get into this hugely rewarding sport, yet it is not without its risks—safety is paramount when choosing your operator. When you are selecting a company, always check that it is certified with PADI. Many of the storefront operations are just consolidators for other companies (meaning you get less quality care and pay a fee to a middle man), so ask if they have their own boats and make sure you'll be diving with the folks you meet behind the counter. Also check about the ratio of divers to instructor or dive master; anything more than five-to-one is not acceptable, and it should be more like two-to-one for beginner courses.

Below are a few of the best choices in Phuket. All these companies can arrange day trips to the nearby coral wall and wrecks, as well as overnight or long-term excursions to the Similan Islands (also PADI courses, Dive Master courses, or 1-day introductory lessons and Open Water certification). Multiday Open Water courses can begin at around 9,800B (US$280/£151).

- **Fantasea Divers** is a highly reputable firm on Phuket appealing to serious divers. Their main office is at 43/20 Moo 5, Viset Road, in Chalong Bay, (© **07628-1388;** fax 07628-2389; www.fantasea.net). Dive packages include live-aboard trips to the Burmese coast and 4-day PADI certification courses, in addition to full-day dives around Phuket. Longer cruises go farther afield to Malaysia or even into India's Andaman and Nicobar region and they have some exciting new Golf and Dive packages. All these trips are very heavily booked; do plan well in advance.
- The folks at **Scuba Cat** ⑀ (94 Thaweewong Rd., Patong; © **07629-3120;** www.scubacat.com) have got one of the best things going in Patong. With some 10 years of experience, a large expatriate, friendly staff, and their own fleet of boats, Scuba Cat is very much a professional outfit, offering the full range of trips

for anyone from beginner to expert (and at competitive prices). You can't miss the small practice pool in front of their beachside Patong office.

- **Sea Bees Diving** (1/3 Moo 9, Viset Rd., Chalong Bay; ✆/fax **07638-1765;** www. sea-bees.com) is another good outfit offering day trips.
- **Sunrise Diving** (49 Thaweewong Rd., Patong; ✆ **07629-2052;** www.sunrise diving.net) provides competitive services; they also have their own boats.

SNORKELING

In the smaller bays around the island, such as Nai Harn Beach or Relax Bay, you'll come across some lovely **snorkeling** right along the shore. For the best coral just off the shoreline, trek up to **Had Nai Yang National Park** for its long reef in clear shallow waters. Nearby Raya Island is popular, and many venture farther to the **Similan Islands** or **Koh Phi Phi.** The best times to snorkel are from November to April before the monsoon comes and makes the sea too choppy. Almost every tour operator and hotel can book day trips by boat that include hotel transfers, lunch, and gear for about 1,500B (US$43/£23) per person.

TREKKING & OTHER ACTIVITIES

To experience the wild side of Phuket's interior, try a **rainforest trek** through the Khao Phra Thaew Wildlife & Forest Reserve in northeast Phuket; it's still relatively rich with tropical trees and wildlife. The park trails were recently upgraded and the reserve also houses the **Gibbon Rehabilitation Project** (see "Back to Nature" below for info).

Then there's **elephant trekking,** a perennial favorite for children and adults. Elephants are not indigenous to Phuket, so what you get here is more-or-less a pony ride, but arguments over captive elephant-tour programs aside, the elephants are possibly better cared for here and the tour cost goes toward their enormous feed bill. **Siam Safari Nature Tours** (45 Chaofa Rd., Chalong; ✆ **07628-0116;** www.siamsafari. com) coordinates daily treks on elephants, Land Rovers, and river rafts. Their "three-in-one, half day eco-adventure" includes 4 hours on an elephant trek through jungles to rubber estates, followed by a road tour to see local wildlife, and then a light river-rafting journey to Chalong Bay. A full day tour is the "three-in-one" plus a trek on foot through Khao Phra Thaew National Park and a Thai lunch. **Siam Adventures** (60/4 Rat-U-Thit Rd., Patong Beach; ✆ **07634-1799**) arranges similar adventures.

River Rovers (✆ **07628-0420;** www.riverrovers.com) is a great way to see old Phuket and nature at its finest; this cruise takes in the fishing villages of Koh Sire on a journey through the southeasterly islands, with a fabulous fresh seafood lunch at a floating restaurant and the chance to do a bit of exploring by kayak.

BACK TO NATURE

Had Nai Yang National Park, 90 sq. km (35 sq. miles) of protected land in the northwest corner of the island, offers a peaceful retreat from the rest of the island's tourism madness. There are two fantastic reasons to make the journey out to the park. The first is for Phuket's largest coral reef in shallow water, only 1,400m (460 ft.) from the shore. The second is for the rare chance of spotting the endangered leatherback turtles that once came to nest every year between November and February. The Park headquarters is a very short hop from Phuket Airport off Highway 402.

At bars, restaurants, and guesthouses around Thailand, caged or drugged **lar gibbon** offer a dubious form of entertainment to tourists, many of whom are completely ignorant of the abuse these endangered creatures endure. These fragile primates are poached as pets when young, caged until they mature—and become aggressive. At this point they are sold to a bar, dressed in children's clothes, and fed amphetamines to stay awake at night (when they are normally asleep). Imprisoned by their owners by day, by night, they are fed a diet of cigarettes and whisky—all in the name of "entertaining" the tourists. Many develop psychological problems and become extremely menacing, and a simple bite can bring dire consequences. **The Gibbon Rehabilitation Project,** off Highway 4027 at the Bang Pae waterfall in the northeastern corner of the island (© **07626-0492;** www.gibbonproject.org), cares for mistreated gibbons. Volunteer guides offer tours of the facility, open daily from 10am to 4pm. Admission is free, but donations are expected (ask for a receipt).

The newly renovated **Phuket Aquarium** (© **07638-1226;** www.pmbc.go.th) at the **Phuket Marine Biological Center** seeks to educate the public about local marine life and nature preservation. Most of the signs throughout are in Thai but it is still worth a trip. It's open daily 8:30am to 4pm, and admission is 50B (US$1.40/75p).

Phuket Butterfly Garden & Insect World, Soi Phaniang, Samkong, Phuket Town (© **07621-0861,** www.phuketbutterfly.com) breeds hundreds of gorgeous butterflies in a large, enclosed garden. There are plenty of chances for photos. It's open daily from 9am to 5pm; adult admission is 300B (US$9/£4.60), and children 9 and under pay 150B (US$4.30/£2.30).

You'd never think seashells were fascinating until you visit the **Phuket Shell Museum** (12/2 Moo 2, Viset Rd., Rawai Beach, just south of Chalong Bay; © **07638-1266;** admission 200B/US$6/£3.10, free for kids). Billed as "the largest shell museum in the world," it's actually not the quantity that amazes, but the quality. As always, the gift shop sells a range of tempting high-quality shell products; however, these days, any eco-savvy traveler will be well aware that the retail shell industry is depriving a sea creature of a home, and that countries like Australia actively prohibit their import. The museum is open daily from 8am to 7pm.

SPAS 🐵🐵🐵

If you've come to Phuket to escape and relax, there's no better way to accomplish your goal than to visit one of Phuket's spas. Even the smallest resort now offers full spa services (of varying quality), and you can find good, affordable massages along any beach and in storefronts in the main tourist areas.

For luxury treatments, the most famous and exclusive facility here is **The Spa at The Banyan Tree, Phuket** 🐵🐵🐵. In its secluded garden pavilions, you'll be treated regally; you may choose from many types of massage, body and facial treatments, or health and beauty programs. To make reservations, call © **07632-4374** or visit www. lagunaphuket.com/spa. Expect to pay for the luxury, from 7,000B (US$200/£108) for special treatments, and more for packages.

Another high-end resort in the farthest southeast part of the island, **Evason Phuket** makes for a great day-spa experience. Its **Six Senses Spa** is at 100 Vised Rd., Rawai Beach, Phuket 83130 (© **07638-1010;** fax 07638-1018; www.sixsenses.com) and it's as renowned, both in standards and price, to the five-star places on the island.

Hilton Phuket Arcadia Resort and Spa (Karon Beach; © **07639-6433; www. phuket.com/arcadia**) is now home to one of the finest spas on the island, a Thai village complex of individual spa suites connected by a meandering boardwalk; it's a great choice for luxury treatments.

Mom Tri's Spa Royale at Mom Tri's Villa Royale, Kata Noi Beach (12 Kata Noi Rd.; © 07633-3568; www.villaroyalephuket.com) is home to a chic spa area at their luxury hilltop resort, with well-trained staff.

Patong Medical Spa (behind Patong Hospital, 222 Rat-U-Thit 200 Pee Rd.; © 07634-1938; www.baantamachartthaispa.com) is a more affordable day spa with trained Thai practitioners offering uniquely Thai treatments such as herbal steam, foot reflexology, or the soothing, hot herbal poultice, called *prakob* in Thai. A 1-hour Thai massage begins at 700B (US$20/£11).

SHOPPING

Patong Beach is the center of handicraft and souvenir shopping in Phuket, and its main streets and small *sois* are teeming with storefront tailors, leather shops, jewelers, and ready-to-wear clothing boutiques. Vendors line the sidewalks, selling everything from bras to batik clothing, arts and crafts, northern hill-tribe silver, and of course the usual fake brands and dodgy CDs—their importation is now illegal in many countries. Vendors everywhere in Patong have the nasty habit of hassling passers-by; don't respond to any greeting, and you may get away tout-free. Most prices are inflated compared to Bangkok or other tourist markets in Thailand, but some hard bargaining can get you the right price. Many items, such as northern handicrafts, are best if purchased closer to the source, but if this is your only stop in Thailand, everything is cheap compared to the West—you might as well stock up.

To avoid rip-off merchants, take a stroll to the new **JungCeylon** (on Rat-U-Thit Rd.; © 02663-7593; www.jungceylon.com), a mega-mall devoted to shopping and entertainment, whose entire basement (curiously called "That's Siam") is filled with a great range of local handicrafts from all over Thailand. JungCeylon also hosts some of the popular teenager label boutiques, sport shops, fast food, and fashions, as well as popular Asian brands. It's a much more relaxed and hassle-free shopping experience than most here.

The island's other malls consist of the humongous **Central Festival** (© 07629-1111), about 10km (6 miles) inland from Patong and 3km (2 miles) inland from Phuket Town on Chalermprakiet Road. **Big C** (no phone), a midrange mall, is next door; nearby **Tesco Lotus** (no phone) is unlike the British supermarket in everything but name; it sells mostly Thai-oriented consumer and food items.

Visit **Phuket Town** for local arts, a few whacky boutiques and some reputable antiques stores, as well as **Robinson** department store (no phone) and **Ocean Mall** market. For good quality shopping suggestions and a great walking map of the Old Town, see www.ArtandCultureAsia.com. The *Art & Culture South* guide, available around town, offers pointers on where to buy antiques and original art, from the **Artists' Village** at Nai Harn to the galleries of Surin Beach and beyond.

One of the best tailors in the area is **Peach,** in Patong (9/8 Prachanukhro Rd., © 07634-5614; www.tailorsofthailand.com).

PHUKET AFTER DARK

Patong is the center of nightlife on the island, though it serves up the same old sordid stuff as Patpong in Bangkok; you'll find plenty of bars, nightclubs, karaoke lounges, snooker halls, and dance shows with pretty sleazy entertainment. While some wide-eyed teenagers or washed-up barflies may find it titillating to trawl the hundreds of hostess bars, many people, especially couples with families, may find these venues a complete turnoff. Lit up like a seedy Las Vegas in miniature, the Patong bar areas are filled with (often underage) working girls and boys in pursuit of wealthy foreign men. Since the Vietnam War, prostitutes (some of which are transsexuals) have plied Patong's girlie bars. See p. 34 in chapter 2 for info on the risks associated with going with any commercial sex worker (CSW) during your visit.

Many hotels realize their guests may not want to barge their way through smoke-filled go-go bars, so they duly put on nightly **Thai dance shows** which, if done well, can be mesmerizing; check with the resorts listed earlier for info.

For those who don't head for the bars (which are open pretty much all night), Patong's endless markets and restaurants usually stay open till 11pm around the main beach towns, especially Patong.

BARS & CLUBS

Scruffy Murphy's (℗ 07629-2590), 50m from the beach down Bangla Road in Patong, is an obligatory Irish pub with mostly young Aussie or Brit tourists revving up to make a night of it, and a good place to catch a game on the big screen. Set to open imminently, is a branch of the Singapore late-night dining and live music venue **Indochine,** located at the heart of the swish JungCeylon mall (on Rat-U-Thit Rd.); this gigantic mall will soon offer stacks more new pubs, dining, and entertainment options. **Paradise** complex, in Soi Paradise (off Rat-U-Thit Rd.; no phone), is a gay-friendly zone of funky bars, clubs, and cafes. The classy **Seduction Disco** (off Soi Bangla; no phone) usually has fabulous DJs and dancing, whatever your persuasion.

Joe Kool's at Ramada Resort, Karon Beach (568 Patak Rd.; ℗ 07639-6666; www. joekoolsphuket.com) is a family-friendly diner and entertainment venue with live music on weekends. Near the center of the island, on the road between Kata Beach and Phuket Town, is **The Green Man** (82/15 Moo 4, Patak Rd., Chalong; ℗ 07628-1445; www.the-green-man.net), a half-timbered English pub, filled with local expats. There's live music nightly, and it's open until 1am.

Phuket Town also offers a few worthy music clubs, check out **Jammin'** for live bands (78/28 Bangkok Rd.; ℗ 07622-0189; www.jamminphuket.com) and **Phukana Wine & Music** (6 Mealuan Rd.; ℗ 07623-4496), an intimate club with an excellent live dance band. In the southern beaches, try **Sirocco Wine Bar & Dance** (28/46 Moo 1 Bzenter Mall, Nai Harn Beach Rd., Rawai; ℗ 081970-2028) for some funky tunes; it's open 6pm to late.

LIVE ENTERTAINMENT

It's kitschy, it's exhilarating, and, heck, it's *so* lifelike: **Dino Park Mini Golf** ✦ (℗ 07633-0625; www.dinopark.com) is a great night out for bored teenagers or unruly whippersnappers who will love the Jurassic Park background of giant, roaring mechanical dinosaurs and (very lifelike) erupting volcanoes. Not only is it a good place to let them loose, but adults can even enjoy some grown-up time in the outdoor Flintstone-inspired bar and restaurant while the kids hit the links. Find the course in the heart of Kata Beach, adjoining the popular Marina Phuket Hotel (see "Where to Stay," earlier).

The island's premiere theme attraction, **Phuket Fantasea** (℗ 07638-5111 for reservations; www.phuket-fantasea.com), is as touristy and kitschy as the huge bill-boards and glossy brochures around town make it seem. The show—set in a theme park filled with glitzy shops—is at Kamala Beach, north of Patong, on the coastal road. After a huge buffet in the palatial Golden Kinaree Restaurant, visitors proceed to the Palace of the Elephants for the show. As one might expect, the prices are inflated; the souvenirs, an exercise in *haute* tackiness; and the supper so-so (you can at least save your stomach by buying a show-only ticket). That said, the spectacle itself is enormously entertaining. You can buy a ticket (including transport) in most any hotel lobby or travel agency, so check for deals. The park opens at 5:30pm, the buffet begins at 6:30pm, and the show starts at 9pm. Tickets for the show are 1,000B (US$28/£15) for adults and 750B (US$21/£12) for children, while dinner and trans-fer fees usually add at least 500B (US$14/£7.70) for adults.

On the south end of Patong, crowds of tourists pack the long-established transsex-ual extravaganza **Simon Cabaret,** 100/6-8 Moo 4, Patong-Karon Road (© 07634-2011; www.phuket-simoncabaret.com). There are two evening shows nightly, at 7:30 and 9pm. This glitzy entertainment features scantily-clad beauties (yes, they really are all male, or male transsexuals) who lip-sync their way through popular Asian and Western pop songs. If you enjoy theatrical high camp, it can be a lot of fun and its burlesque humor draws busloads (especially Asian grannies). The dance numbers have pretty impressive sets and costumes and the numbers are interspersed with light comic acts. The cost is around 600B (US$17/£9.25), but it's worth asking at your hotel to see if the staff can get better rates.

Sphinx is a slick show nearer the heart of Patong (120 Rat-U-Thit Rd.; © 07634-1500; www.sphinxthai.com). It's similar to Simon Cabaret (see above), but it includes female dancers as well as transsexuals. The dinner is the best dinner-show meal on the island. Cocktails and set menus vary widely in price and inclusions, but tour opera-tors usually offer packages from 500B (US$14/£7.70) for drinks only, to 1,400B (US$40/£22), which includes a Western set meal with cocktails. Performances can run up to three times nightly, except Sundays. Ask about shuttle options if you don't have transport.

5 Side Trips from Phuket: Khao Lak and Offshore Islands

KHAO LAK

There are lots of adventure tour operators and travel agents on Phuket, all offering a variety of day and overnight trips. Phang Nga Bay is popular for adventure travel; see the "Day Trips from Surat Thani" in chapter 8 for information about great trips to **Khao Sok National Park.**

Just over an hour from the northernmost tip of Phuket, the province of **Phang Nga,** which includes **Khao Lak** on its western flanks, was the area hardest hit by the 2004 tsunami. Now almost entirely rebuilt, today it's a burgeoning eco-tourism des-tination with some magnificent resorts, some new, and some wholly rebuilt. Popular with the Euro and Scandinavian crowds, it attracts nature lovers and provides some great bird-spotting opportunities, waterfalls, lush national parks, and pristine dive spots around the **Similan Islands National Marine Park** and **Koh Surin National Park.** (The best diving is from Dec to May.)

Comprising nine islands, the **Similan Islands** are rated in the top ten best dive sites in the world for the stunning arrays of unspoiled corals, sea fans, sponges, and other marine life. Numerous local dive operators offer short (approx. 3 hrs.) or long trips to these regions from Thap Lamu Pier, just south of Khao Lak. For bungalow or camp-ing accommodations, contact Similan National Park (local office © 07641-1913). A similar style of basic accommodations is also available in **Koh Surin National Park,** (© 07649-1378), which comprises five islands with some of the best shallow water corals. Whale sharks are known to frequent these waters, which, in the past, were once the exclusive domain of Phuket's indigenous people, the Sea Gypsies.

Boats leave from Khuraburi Pier, north of Khao Lak, with a journey time of 4 hours to the islands. From here, fans of marine life can take a day trip to isolated **Koh Phra Thong** to visit the island's conservation center. Manned (only in dry season) by an international team of experts and volunteers, it surveys and protects rare turtles and the region's disappearing, yet ecologically vital, mangroves. See www.naucrates.org for info.

Another stellar outfit, the **Ecotourism Training Center (ETC),** is a nonprofit organization set up by dynamic American, Reid Ridgway, to provide long-term career training to tsunami-affected youth. Established in 2005, the Khao Lak program trains local Thais in sustainable community tourism and diving skills to PADI dive master and instructor level. It now offers trips to interested divers and visitors. For more information, see www.etcth.org.

Other local attractions include miles of peaceful white sand beaches, elephant trekking, temple tours, white water rafting, and jungle treks. Visit **Dior Travel** (4/118 Moo 7, Khao Lak; © **07644-3248**) for offbeat tour suggestions.

WHERE TO STAY

Many visitors who are tired of Phuket's high prices and full-on party vibe head up here for long or short breaks. Those with the cash can hunker down in some truly sublime oases, such as the award-winning **The Sarojin** ✹✹✹ (60 Moo 2, Kukkak, Takuapa, Phang Nga; © **07642-7900-4;** fax 07642-7906; www.sarojin.com); its lowest rates start at 12,000B (US$243/£180). There's also the totally rebuilt **Le Meridien Khao Lak Beach & Spa Resort** north of Khao Lak town (9/9 Moo 1, Kukkak, Takuapa, Phang Nga 82190; © **07642-7500;** www.lemeridien.com), and **Merlin Khao Lak,** south of Khao Lak town (7/7 Moo 2, Petchkasem Rd., Khao Lak Beach, Lamkan, Taimuang, Phang Nga 82210; © **07642-8300;** fax 07644-3200; www.merlin phuket.com). All are pitched at the very high end (so don't think about spending less than 9,000B/US$257/£135 per night, even in low season), and rival the best of Phuket's cushiest hotels and spas.

Midrange hotels come in all shapes and sizes. Try the peaceful area of Cape Pakarang, which is home to the **Best Western Palm Galleria Resort** (27/102 Moo 2 Kuk Kak, Khao Lak, Phang Nga 82190; © **07642-7000;** www.khaolakpalmgalleria. com) or **Apsaras Beach Resort & Spa** (45 Moo 2, Kuk Kak, Khao Lak, Phang Nga 82190; © **07658-4444;** www.apsarasresort.com). Or closer to town, check out **Ramada Resort Khao Lak** (59 Moo 5 Bang Niang, Khao Lak, Phang Nga 82190; © **07642-7777;** www.ramadakhaolak.com).

On the budget end, there are beachside jungle bungalows at **Similana Resort** (4/7 Moo 1 Kuk Kak, Khao Lak, Phang Nga 82190; © **07642-0166;** www.khaolak-tropicana.com), with rooms starting at 1,700B (US$48/£26).

WHERE TO DINE

In addition to the many hotel restaurants on hand, there are countless dining venues in town. Among the best, try **Joe's Steak House** (56 Moo 5 Bang Niang, Khao Lak; © **0878-936833**), which is open for dinner only—reservations are highly recommended. For Thai food, **Jai Restaurant** (Main Rd.; no phone) is excellent and just two doors down from Khao Lak's most happening late-night live music bar, **Happy Snapper** (Main Rd, 5/2 Moo 7, Khao Lak; © **07648-5500;** www.happysnapperbar. com). **O'Connor's Irish Pub** (no phone) is a few steps away. The German owner offers Thai cooking classes and serves great Guinness with his home-cooked European meals.

YAO ISLANDS

Midway to Krabi and 1 hour's boat ride from Phuket's Bang Rong Pier (north of Boat Lagoon, turn east at the Heroines' Monument), the twin islands of **Koh Yao Yai** and **Koh Yao Noi** are where nature lovers head to enjoy some scenery and relax. Described as "Phi Phi 20 years back," Phang Nga Bay's two largest islands are not at all touristy and great for cruising by motorbike (available for rent on both islands at 200B/US$6/£3.10 per day). The nearest things to civilization here are the 7-Eleven store and ATM on Koh Yao Noi. (*Note:* If you're running out of cash on Yao Yai, you'll need to head here.)

More active travelers can go kayaking, bird-watching, or head off to explore nearby uninhabited islands by long-tail. In addition, there's fishing, jungle walks, or the exhaustive sport of hammock-swinging: It all makes for a perfect island escape.

Ferries to both islands leave Bang Rong Pier at 9am, 11am, 12:30pm, 2:30pm, and 5pm; local ferries also depart daily from Koh Sire Pier in Phuket Town. Call ahead to your accommodations to arrange transport from the pier.

WHERE TO STAY

There are 10 to 12 bungalow resorts on **Koh Yao Noi** that are open all year. Prices vary from 700B to 12,000B (US$20–US$343/£11–£185) a night. For budget bungalow resorts, try **Sabai Corner** (✆ 07659-7497; www.sabaicornerbungalows.com), which has fairly standard rooms from 1,000B (US$28/£15). A midrange favorite is **Koh Yao Island Resort** (✆ 07659-7474; www.koyao.com), with rooms from 4,000B (US$114/£62). For luxury bungalows, prices at **Koh Yao Pavilions** (✆ 07659-7441; www.koyaobay.com) start at a fairly reasonable 5,500B (US$157/£85).

On **Koh Yao Yai**, the **Yao Yai Island Resort** (✆ 08947-19110; www.yaoyairesort.com) has bungalows from 1,200B (US$34/£18) and the similarly priced **Heimat Gardens Guesthouse** (✆ 08579-47428; www.heimatgardens.com) is equally close to the beach and offers friendly service.

RACHA ISLANDS AND PHANG NGA BAY

The islands collectively known as **Koh Racha** (also spelt Raja, or Raya) are yet another popular side trip from southern Phuket, either for day excursions or longer escapes. Speedboats (trip time: 20 min.) or long-tails (trip time: 1–2 hrs.) can be hired from Chalong Pier or Rawai beachfront for the journey in clement weather. Accommodations on the main **Koh Racha (Yai)** range from simple bungalows from 800B (US$23/£11.75) to five-star glamour at **The Racha** ★★ (✆ **07635-5455** or 07628-0811; www.theracha.com) on the unforgettably beautiful white sands of Batok Bay. Prices for villas start from 8,500B to 65,000B (US$243–US$1,857/£130–£1,000).

Phang Nga Bay, with its arching karst limestone spires, made famous in the James Bond film *The Man with the Golden Gun,* is a very popular day trip by boat—some might say *too* popular, with hordes of tour groups massing on its tiny beaches. A more peaceful trip around the bay by sea kayak is possibly a better bet. **Koh Phi Phi** is another oversold day trip for snorkeling, or more commonly an overnight stay from Phuket. See p. 266 in this chapter for information.

6 Krabi (Ao Nang, Railay & Khlong Muang Beaches)

814km (505 miles) S of Bangkok; 165km (109 miles) E of Phuket; 42km (26 miles) E of Koh Phi Phi; 276km (171 miles) N of Satun; 211km (131 miles) SW of Surat Thani

For many tourists, Krabi has become a popular, more eco-friendly alternative to the heavily commercialized Phuket and backpacker boomtown of Koh Phi Phi. For others, it's an easy stop along the way. Flights connecting with Krabi's international airport mean tourists can in fact bypass Bangkok and arrive directly from other parts of Asia, or arrange an air or road transfer from Phuket International airport. Destination Air, a new amphibious light plane service based in Phuket, also services this popular resort region. Ferries and minivans from other destinations connect via *songtaew* and boats to the nearby tourist strip of Ao Nang and farther-flung beaches. Railay, with its famed soft sands, and limestone cliffs with ample abseiling opportunities, is accessed by boat (from either Krabi Town to the northeast, or from Ao Nang Beach to the west). Khlong Muang Beach, only recently developed, lies just north of Ao Nang by road.

The best time to visit the Krabi area is November through April, with January and February the ideal months. The rainy season runs May through October when the crowds disperse and the wet weather and choppy seas drive away all but the hardiest.

ESSENTIALS
GETTING THERE

There are daily bus and minibus connections between Krabi-Phuket and Krabi-Surat Thani, for the east coast islands (Samui, Koh Pha Ngan). A ferry also leaves daily connecting Phuket (dep. 8am) and Ao Nang (dep. 3pm); check ahead for weather reports. Tickets are available from the **Ao Nang Tourist Office** (© 07563-7730) or Phuket Pier in Phuket Town (© 07623-2040); the trip takes 2 hours and costs 350B (US$10/£5.40).

By Plane   **Tiger Airways** (© 02351-8333 in Bangkok; www.tigerairways.com) has direct flights from Singapore. **Thai AirAsia** (© 02515-9999; www.airasia.com) and **One-Two-GO Airlines** (© 1126 in Bangkok or 1141; www.fly12go.com) fly from Suvarnabhumi International Airport. **Nok Air** (© 1318; www.nokair.com) and **Thai Airways** (© 02545-3690; www.thaiair.com) fly from both Bangkok's former airport, Don Mueang, and Suvarnabhumi International Airport. Do check which venue you are flying from or to, and allow 90 to 100 minutes *minimum* travel times between the two Bangkok airports, in case of traffic.

From Krabi airport, you can catch a minivan to town for 100B (US$3/£1.55), more for farther beaches. Taxis start at 300B (US$9/£4.60).

By Boat   Thrice-daily trips leave from Koh Phi Phi to Krabi (trip time: 2 hr.; 300B/US$8.60/£4.60). There are two daily boats from Koh Lanta to Krabi in the high season (trip time: 2½ hr.; 250B/US$7.10/£3.85). See www.krabi.com for more details.

By Bus   Two air-conditioned VIP 24-seater buses leave daily from **Bangkok's Southern Bus Terminal** (© 02435-1199; trip time: 12 hr.; 800B/US$23/£12) to Krabi Town. Frequently scheduled air-conditioned minibuses leave daily from Surat Thani to Krabi (trip time: 2¾ hr.; 250B/US$7.10/£3.85). Three air-conditioned minibuses leave daily from Phuket Town to Krabi (trip time: 3½ hr.; 300B/US$9/£4.60).

VISITOR INFORMATION

Most services in Krabi town are on Utarakit Road, paralleling the waterfront (to the right as you alight the ferry). Here you'll find the **TAT Office** (© **07562-2163**) and a number of **banks** with ATM service. The **post office** and **police station** (© **07563-7208**) are located south on Utarakit Road, to the left as you leave the pier. There are also banks in Ao Nang, near the Phra Nang Inn, but nothing at Railay.

Check the small shops around town for a copy of the local free map of the resort area, town, and surrounding islands.

GETTING AROUND

Krabi Town is the commercial hub in the area, but few bother to stay. There is frequent *songtaew* (pickup truck) service between Krabi Town and Ao Nang Beach; just flag down a white pickup (the trip takes 30 min. and costs 20B/57¢/30p).

Railay Beach and the resorts on the surrounding beaches are cut off by a ridge of cliffs from the mainland and are therefore accessed by boat. From the pier in Krabi Town, you'll pay anything from 100B (US$3/£1.55; trip time: 45 min.). From the beach at Ao Nang (at the small pavilion across from the Phra Nang Inn), the trip takes just 20 minutes and costs 80B (US$2.30/£1.25).

Khlong Muang beach is some 25km (16 miles) northwest of Krabi Town. Expect to pay at least 300B (US$8.60/£4.60) for a taxi.

The limestone formations around the coastline here are not only gorgeous visually, but are also great spots to explore by small boat. Some, such as the famous **Koh Hong,** are almost entirely enclosed—with brilliant blue lagoons at their heart. Boats slip inside them at low tide via almost invisible, narrow chasms; visit **www.krabi.com** for info on boat tours.

If you're checking in at any resort, ask about transportation arrangements (which are often included) and prevailing weather conditions.

WHAT TO SEE & DO

Krabi has a number of sites, but most head straight for the beaches to relax. Popular activities are day boat trips, snorkeling, and rock climbing at Railay East.

Just north and east of Krabi Town, though, you will find **Wat Tham Sua (The Tiger Temple),** a stunning hilltop pilgrimage point. A punishing 30- to 40-minute climb brings you to the rocky pinnacle where a Buddhist statuary overlooks the surrounding area stretching from Krabi Town to the cliffs near Railay. There is a large monastery and temple compound built into the rock at the bottom of the mountain where you may chance upon a monk in silent meditation or chat with one of the friendly temple stewards (most are eager to practice English). The abbot speaks English and welcomes foreign students of meditation. If you decide to climb the steep temple mountain, go either in the early morning or late afternoon to beat the heat. The view from above is worth it (plus, think of all the good karma you can accrue). *Note:* Be careful of the many monkeys here. Ignore them at all cost, and don't hold anything tempting in your hands or it will be taken.

The beaches and stunning cliffs of **Railay Beach** are certainly worth a day trip even if you don't stay there (see "Where to Stay," below). Divided into Railay East and West, the former offers the best rock climbing cliffs, situated next to mudflats. The West has the sort of soft powdery sands that attract beach bunnies; though long-tails dock right here and the resulting noise of the motors can ruin the peacefulness of the gorgeous cerulean sea. At **Ao Nang,** long-tail boat drivers try to drum up groups of passengers at a small pavilion just across from the Phra Nang Inn for the 80B (US$2.30/£1.25) ride (20 min). From the docks in Krabi Town, it costs 100B (US$3/£1.55) and takes 40 minutes. (The trip is offered dawn till dusk only.)

The craggy limestone cliffs of Railay make it one of the best-known **rock climbing** spots in the region. It is certainly not for the fainthearted; nevertheless, the whole cliff area is well organized (with mapped routes) and safety bolts drilled into the rock. There are a number of companies offering full and half-day courses, as well as rental equipment for experienced climbers. There are also many routes suitable for beginners. Climbing schools set up "top rope" climbing for safety, whereby climbers are attached by a rope through a fixed pulley at the top, and to a guide on the other end, holding you fast. The schools all offer similar rates and have offices scattered around Railay Beach, with posters and pamphlets everywhere. Try **King Climbers** (© 07563-7125; www.railay.com) or **Cliffs Man** (© 07562-1768; www.cliffsman.com). Half-day courses start at about 1,000B (US$29/£15), full-day courses are from 1,800B (US$51/£28), and 3-day courses run from 6,000B (US$171/£92).

Nearby Railay's beach is **Phra Nang Beach,** a secluded section of sand that is either a short 50B (US$1.40/75p) boat trip from Railay proper, or a cliffside walk east, past Rayavadee Resort and south along a shaded cliffside path (watch out for monkeys). From here, you can swim or kayak around the craggy hunk of rock just a few meters away offshore, or explore the **Tham Phra Nang Nok,** or Princess Cave, a small cavern at the base of a tall cliff, filled with huge phallic sculptures, where legend has it, donors attain fertility. The cliffs are stunning and the sunsets spectacular.

Along the path to **Phra Nang Beach,** you'll find signs pointing up to a small cleft in the rocks. After a short hike up a steep escarpment before an often treacherously muddy downward climb (use the old ropes there to guide you), you'll arrive at a shallow, saltwater lagoon. How it got up here is anyone's guess.

Full-day boat trips and **snorkeling** to **Koh Poda** 🏝 can be arranged from any beachfront tour agent or hotel near Krabi, which will take you to a few small coral sites as well as any number of secluded coves and islets (or *hongs*), starting at 800B (US$23/£12) for a half-day or 1,500B (US$43/£23) for a full day. During the monsoon season, boats leave from Nam Mao Beach (near Krabi Town) only and are subject to cancellation in rough weather. Or you can rent snorkel gear from any of the tour operators along Ao Nang or Railay for about 50B (US$1.45/75p) per day.

Day **kayak tours** to outlying islands, or the mangroves near **Ao Luk,** are becoming popular for visitors to Ao Nang. Contact **Sea, Land and Trek Co.** (21/1 Moo 2, Ao Nang; © 07563-7364; www.sealandandtrek.com) or **Sea Kayak Krabi** (40 Maharach Soi 2, Krabi; © 07563-0270; www.seakayak-krabi.com) to set up a trip. Rates begin at 1,500B (US$43/£23).

There are some dive operators in Krabi, but you'll have to travel farther to reach the better sites. Most people prefer to book from Koh Phi Phi (p. 269) or Phuket (p. 252).

WHERE TO STAY
KRABI TOWN

Few travelers stay in Krabi Town, but if you're stuck or are too tired to leave, the best hotel in town is **Krabi City Seaview Hotel** (77/1 Longkha Rd.; © 07562-2885), with basic air-conditioned rooms starting at 800B (US$23/£12).

RAILAY BEACH
Very Expensive
Rayavadee ✦✦✦   Rayavadee offers unique two-story rondavels (circular pavilions), most of which are large and luxurious. These come with every modern convenience and some, set in enclosed gardens, can be very private. Ground floor sitting rooms have a central, double-size hanging lounger with cushions. Upper story bedrooms are all silk and teak, and private bathrooms have big Jacuzzi tubs and luxury products. Some gardens feature hammocks or (unheated) whirlpools. The resort grounds lie at the base of towering cliffs on the island's most choice piece of property, a triangle of land where each point accesses the island's beaches: Phra Nang, Nam Mao, and Railay. Their main dining outlet is of high quality, while their seaside Thai restaurant, Raitalay, provides a more romantic and relaxed atmosphere outdoors. The resort feels very much like a peaceful village, with paths meandering among private lotus ponds and meticulous landscaping. The price is high, but the location, luxury, and exclusivity warrants it.

214 Moo 2, Tambol Ao Nang, Amphur Muang, Krabi 81000 (30 min. northwest of Krabi Town by long-tail boat or 70 min. from Phuket on the resort's own launch). ✆ 07562-0740. Fax 07562-0630. www.rayavadee.com. 100 units. 20,000B–35,000B (US$571–US$1,000/£208–£538) deluxe pavilion; from 26,000B (US$743/£400) hydro-pool pavilion; from 32,000B (US$914/£492) family pavilion; from 62,000B (US$1,771/£954) specialty villas. AE, DC, MC, V. **Amenities:** 2 restaurants; lounge and library; outdoor pool w/children's pool; outdoor lighted tennis courts; air-conditioned squash court; fitness center; spa; watersports equipment and scuba center; 24-hr. room service; same-day laundry service. *In room:* A/C, satellite TV, minibar, fridge, safe.

Moderate
Sand Sea Resort   Just down the beach from Rayavadee, along Railay Beach, the compact Sand Sea is a good little bungalow resort, a few feet from the busy beachfront. Flowering bushes surround its lawns, and simple rattan-walled bungalows line the garden paths. Most rooms have air-conditioning and offer the comfort you'd expect from a basic hotel room (including screened windows to stop the many mosquitoes). There's a small pool, a small but well stocked supermarket, a (somewhat unreliable) Internet station, and a good restaurant right on the busy beach. You can step right out front and join a game of soccer, rent a kayak, or go snorkeling by the offshore cliffs. Overall, this is a good, simple choice, though it's horribly hard to book in high season.

39 Moo 2, Railay Beach, Ao Nang, Krabi 81000 (on Railay Beach, long-tails from Ao Nang pull up on shore out front). ✆ 07562-2574. Fax 07562-2608. www.krabisandsea.com. 68 units. 1,350B–1,950B (US$38–US$56/£21–£30) double with fan; 2,100B–4,750B (US$60–US$135/£32–£73) double with A/C. MC, V. **Amenities:** Restaurant; pool; kayak rental; tour desk; mini-mart; massage; laundry service; Internet. *In room:* A/C in some, TV, minibar, fridge, no phone.

Inexpensive
Diamond Cave Bungalows & Resort   Located on the eastern side of the peninsula, Diamond Cave is a clean, cozy, bungalow resort set in shady gardens—it's a nice place to escape the vagaries of life and enjoy some nearby climbing. Since Diamond Cave is at the far end of Railay Beach East, it's far from the good sandy beaches, but close to lots of budget dining and bars.

36 Moo 1, Ao Nang Krabi 81000 (north end of Railay East Beach). ✆ 07562-2589. Fax 07562-2590. www.diamond cave-railay.com. 32 units. From 1,300B (US$37/£20) double. MC, V. **Amenities:** Restaurant; bar; pool; tour desk; mini-mart; laundry service. *In room:* A/C in some, no phone.

AO NANG BEACH
Moderate
Golden Beach Resort   Comparable in service to the nearby Phra Nang Inn (see below), the Golden Beach's deluxe rooms are a slightly higher standard. The

free-standing, pagoda suites make masterful use of curved lines inside and out, and feature luxurious canopy beds and indoor/outdoor bathrooms. Standard rooms are cozy. The pool is large and inviting, and the resort is just a short hop down a cul-de-sac and away from busy, central Ao Nang.

254 Moo 2, Ao Nan, Krabi 81000 (the eastern end of Ao Nang, behind the boat pavilion for trips to Railay). ℂ 07563-7870. Fax 07563-7875. www.goldenbeach-resort.com. 66 units. From 2,250B (US$64/£35) double; from 3,000B (US$86/£46) suite. AE, MC, V. **Amenities:** Restaurant; bar; large outdoor pool; tour desk; car-rental desk; limited room service; massage (poolside); laundry service. *In room:* A/C, satellite TV, minibar, fridge.

Krabi Resort   The popular Krabi Resort is the only property in Ao Nang with direct beach access. It is a compound of two hotel blocks and an array of free-standing beachside bungalows. Tidy grounds surround a fine swimming pool, but other resort amenities are unused and aging. More private sea-view bungalows are the best choice: they're large and clean with parquet floors, high ceilings, rattan furnishings, and lots of little Thai touches. The resort is just north of the main shopping and restaurant area at Ao Nang, but a lovely beach walk. Ask about their overnight trips to rustic bungalows on nearby Poda Island.

53–57 Patthana Rd., Ao Nang Beach, Krabi 81000 (overlooking beach at Ao Nang). ℂ 07563-7051. www.krabi resort.com. 75 units. 2,400B–7,150B (US$68–US$204/£37–£110) bungalow priced according to view; 4,750B–11,250B (US$136–US$321/£73–£173) suite. MC, V. **Amenities:** Restaurant; lounge; pool; outdoor lighted tennis courts; fitness center; watersports equipment; bike rental; tour desk; limited room service; massage; same-day laundry service. *In room:* A/C, satellite TV, minibar, fridge, safe.

Phra Nang Inn   The exterior of the eccentric Phra Nang Inn looks like a rustic woodland lodge set amid straggly gardens. Inside, the rooms are furnished in a unique mix of Chinese tiles, concrete furnishings built into the walls, seashell and stucco mosaics, and a twisted wood canopy bed hung with strands of shells. The hotel's two wings are on either side of the busiest intersection in Ao Nang and the helpful staff can help arrange tours and onward boat travel (from right across the street).

119 Ao Nang Beach (P.O. Box 25), Krabi 81000 (overlooking beach at Ao Nang-Railay boat dock). ℂ 07563-7130. Fax 07563-7134. www.phrananginn.com. 88 units. 2,300B–4,000B (US$66–US$114/£35–£62) double; from 4,000B (US$114/£62) suite. MC, V. **Amenities:** 2 restaurants; 2 bars; small pool; spa w/massage; sauna; tour desk; 24-hr. room service; laundry service. *In room:* A/C, satellite TV w/in-house movies, dataport, minibar, fridge, safe.

Inexpensive

Ao Nang has lots of budget guesthouses to choose from. The friendly folks at **Ao Nang Orchid Bungalows** (141 Moo 2, Ao Nang; ℂ 07563-7697) have clean, newly renovated, and air-conditioned garden bungalows starting at 800B (US$23/£12), just 100m from the beach. Also try **Ao Nang Village Bungalows** (49/3 Moo 2, Ao Nang Village; ℂ 07563-7544), with garden view rooms from 600B (US$17/£9.25).

KHLONG MUANG BEACH

Following the coast north of the busy Ao Nang strip, you'll come to quiet Khlong Muang with a long stretch of quiet beach and a few excellent resorts from which to choose.

Expensive

Nakamanda   A collection of luxurious private villas sprinkled among indigo pools and pavilions, surrounded by high stone walls, this slickly designed resort sits on the far northern end of Krabi (just past the Sheraton; see below). The name means the "sacred sea dragon," and this stylish outcrop does look otherworldly. Public spaces are delightfully spartan; the eclectic decor tends to mix Angkorian antiquities with a cool contemporary style; and everything is set amid meticulously kept gardens. Villas are aligned for optimal privacy, and inside everything is sumptuous bleached wood and granite. Rooms range from a basic villa to over-the-top private pool villas with huge terraces and sea views. The spa is inviting; the seaside pool, an oasis; and the resort restaurant, excellent.

Khlong Muang Beach, Tambon Nongtalay, Krabi 81000. ℘ 07562-8200. Fax 07564-4389. www.nakamanda.com. 39 units. From 9,200B (US$263/£142) sala villa; 18,000B (US$514/£277) Jacuzzi villa; 40,000B (US$1,143/£615) pool villa. AE, DC, MC, V. **Amenities:** Restaurant; 2 bars; outdoor pool; health club; spa; watersports rentals; library; tour desk; car-rental desk; limited room service; laundry service; Internet. *In room:* A/C, satellite TV, fridge, minibar, coffee-making facilities, hair dryer, safe.

Sheraton Krabi Beach Resort ★★★
A large circular drive and luxurious modern lobby pavilion ushers you into this expansive resort. Rooms are set in large blocks, a U-shaped configuration connected by boardwalks above mangrove flats that flood with the daily tide. Moderate-size rooms come with fine tile and dark wood furnishings, a fusion of simple lines, and more flamboyant Art Deco decor. Services range from fine dining choices in the main building, to more laid-back fare taken by the large, luxurious beachside pool. Also on hand are plenty of fitness facilities, which offer a great variety of programs (from kickboxing to meditation) after which, a treat at the spa will dispel all aches or stress.

155 Moo 2, Baan Khlong Muang Beach, Nong Talay, Krabi 81000. (15km/9 miles north of Ao Nang, 26km/16 miles from Krabi Town). ℘ 07562-8000. Fax 07562-8028. www.sheraton.com. 246 units. From 4,550B (US$130/£70) double; 12,250B (US$350/£188) suite. AE, DC, MC, V. **Amenities:** 3 restaurants; 3 bars; outdoor pool; tennis court; fitness center; spa; sailboat and kayak rental; bike rental; kids' club; library w/games, tour desk; car-rental desk; shopping arcade; 24-hr. room service; babysitting; laundry service; nonsmoking rooms; meeting facilities; Wi-Fi. *In room:* A/C, satellite TV, dataport, minibar, fridge, coffee-making facilities, hair dryer, safe.

Sofitel Phokeethra Krabi ★★★ (Kids)
The latest luxury resort to grace this pretty coastline has the full complement of extensively manicured lawns, and a gigantic sculpted pool, surrounded by newly planted coconut groves. Boasting an opulent mix of Thai and colonial architecture, this awesome new property features a palatial lobby and magnificent views. The vast rooms are classically furnished, with polished teak floors, broad balconies, and a warm butterscotch and cream decor. Since it caters not just to upscale tourists but also to large conference groups and wedding parties, expect high standards of service and dining—including a Lancôme spa, a wide range of business facilities, as well as a children's playground for the hotel's junior guests.

Khlong Muang Beach, Tambon Nongtalay, Krabi 81000. ℘ 07562-7800. Fax 07564-4389. www.sofitel.com. 276 units. From 7,000B (US$200/£108) superior ocean view; 10,000B–44,000B (US$286–US$1,257/£154–£677) suite. AE, DC, MC, V. **Amenities:** 3 restaurants; 5 bars; outdoor pool; fitness center; spa; watersports rentals; tour desk; 24-hr room service; laundry service; Wi-Fi. *In room:* A/C, satellite TV, fridge, minibar, coffee-making facilities, hair dryer, safe.

Moderate
In addition to the hotel reviewed below, also try the family run, eco-friendly **Krabi Sands Resort & Seafood Restaurant** (118 Moo 3 Khlong Muang; ℘ 07560-0027; www.yourkrabi.com/krabi-sands-resort) with bungalows from 2,200B (US$63/£34).

Andaman Holiday Resort ★★
Set between the Sheraton and Nakamanda, the Andaman Holiday is a cozy, Thai-style alternative at a fraction of the price (and a fraction of the luxury). Rooms are large and clean, ranging from hotel-style rooms to small cottages to large family suites—which are more rustic lodge than resort. There is a good central pool and a large garden area near the sea. The beach is a wide, open

stretch of sand and often deserted. Hotel services are limited but adequate (it's a long ride to any alternative).

98 Moo 3, Khlong Muang Beach, Tambon Nongtalay, Krabi 81000 (16km/10 miles north of Ao Nang, 27km/17 miles from Krabi Town). © 07562-8300. Fax 07564-4320. www.andamanholiday.com. 116 units. 2,500B–6,000B (US$71–US$171/£38–£92) double; from 3,800B (US$108/£58) villa. AE, DC, MC, V. **Amenities:** 3 restaurants; bar; 2 outdoor pools; small fitness center (open-air); tour desk (scuba trips); car-rental desk; shopping arcade; salon; massage; laundry service. In room: A/C, satellite TV, minibar, fridge, coffee-making facilities.

WHERE TO DINE

Apart from the good dining choices at the many resorts listed above, here are a few more recommendations around the region: In the north end of Krabi Town, the **Night Market** (no phone) just off Utarakit riverside road on Maharaj Soi 10 has good local specials like deep fried oysters and noodles. Also try **Hong Ming** (no phone) for vegetarian food (you'll find great desserts and fresh fruit here, too). In Ao Nang, the beachside tourist street is already turning into a mini-Patong, with heaps of neon-lit shops and storefront eateries: Try **Ao Nang Cuisine** (no phone) for good Thai fare, **Navrang Mahal** (no phone) for Indian, or **Irish Rover** (no phone) for continental cuisine. On Railay, all the beachside bars and bungalows serve good Thai and continental nosh.

7 Koh Phi Phi

814km (505 miles) S of Bangkok, then 42km (26 miles) W of Krabi; 160km (99 miles) SW of Phuket

Phi Phi is in fact two islands: **Phi Phi Ley** and **Phi Phi Don.** The latter is the main barbell-shaped island whose central isthmus (the barbell handle) was hit badly by the tsunami. Koh Phi Phi is a popular choice for day trips, snorkeling, and scuba junkets from Krabi. Crowds of noisy tourists also descend upon **Maya Bay,** on Phi Phi Ley, where filmmakers shot the Hollywood film *The Beach*, with Leonardo DiCaprio. Thai students and environmentalists have long protested the amounts of rubbish left by these tour groups. (*Note:* Day-trippers should dispose of trash after arriving back onto the mainland, not while they are here.)

Small beachfront outfits rent snorkel gear and conduct long-tail boat tours to quiet coves with great views of coral reefs and sea life for as little as 800B (US$23/£12) for an all-day trip (packing your own lunch). You can rent kayaks and do a little exploring on your own, hike to one of the island viewpoints, or just enjoy the sea and sand on busy **Tongsai Bay.**

All visitors arrive at the busy ferry port in Phi Phi Don's **Loh Dalam Bay,** and the sandy beaches at Tonsai (just opposite) are good for sunbathing but packed liked sardine cans in high season.

Phi Phi Ley is famed for its coveted **swallow nests** and the courageous pole-climbing daredevils who collect them (the saliva-coated nests fetch a hefty price as the main ingredient in a much-favored Chinese soup). This smaller island is protected as a park, but can be visited as part of most day trips.

Before the 2004 tsunami, many of the settlements and hotels on Koh Phi Phi, and the thin isthmus of Tonsai Bay, had been built illegally by squatters on land belonging to the once pristine Marine National Park. These facilities were—almost literally, wiped off the map by the tragic disaster. With the help of many international volunteers who cleared the land of refuse, the crowds have returned to the island, but so has the unplanned chaos of pre-tsunami days. Beaches are once again crammed with hotels, low-end guesthouses and end-of-the-road backpackers.

In the aftermath of the tsunami, the government had hinted at earmarking Phi Phi Don as a luxury destination (indeed Phi Phi already supported a number of high-end resorts on more far-flung stretches of beach), but amid the unregulated rush to make as much money as possible from this once sublime location, the plan failed. In terms of wholesale environmental degradation we are, sadly, right back to square one.

GETTING THERE

The easiest but costliest method to get here is to take a flight from Phuket on **Destination Air** (© **07632-8637-9;** fax 07632-8598, www.destinationair.com) whose fleet of amphibious Cessnas fly regularly in high season to resort islands like Phi Phi. The journey takes just under half an hour. These run from both Phuket and Krabi. Boats from the pier in central Krabi Town run three times daily (10am, 2:30pm, and 4pm or more in high season) and cost from 300B (US$8.60/£4.60).

From Phuket, there are a number of ferry services leaving from the Ratchada (Rasada) Pier near Phuket Town, at 8:30am and 1:30pm, with rates as low as 450B (US$13/£6.95) for the 2-hour trip. Be sure to check out where the lifejackets are stashed as several Phi Phi ferries sank during 2007, fortunately with no serious injuries.

WHERE TO STAY

Since Koh Phi Phi is very crowded these days, it's difficult to find good, budget accommodations at a reasonable price. It's best to book in advance. Most cheaper bungalows are along the beach and hills to the right of the ferry pier in the little backpacker neighborhood. In addition to the hotels below, options include **Phi Phi Hotel** and **Phi Phi Banyan Villa** (near the ferry dock; © **07561-1233;** www.phiphi-hotel. com), good choices on the main beach, with rooms from 1,700B (US$48/£26). On Loh Dalam bay, the luxury resort **Phi Phi Island Cabana** (no phone; www.phiphi-cabana.com) has recently reopened after major rebuilding. Rooms start from 7,000B (US$200/£108) for a double.

EXPENSIVE

Holiday Inn Phi Phi   Holiday Inn is part of further expansion of resort development on the more distant shores of Koh Phi Phi (you can only get here by boat, just past Phi Phi Island Village). Luxury bungalows cluster along a thin stretch of beach and the resort provides high standards of amenities throughout.

Laem Thong Beach, Koh Phi Phi, Krabi. Phuket Office: 100/435 Moo 5 Chalermprakiet Rama 9 Rd., T. Rassada, Phuket 83000. © **07562-7300.** www.holiday-inn.com. 77 units. 4,000B–6,000B (US$114–US$171/£62–£92). AE, DC, V, MC. **Amenities:** 2 restaurants; bar; outdoor pool; health club; spa; Jacuzzi; watersports rentals; tour desk; limited room service; laundry service; high-speed Internet; Wi-Fi. *In room:* A/C, satellite TV, DVD and CD player, fridge, minibar, coffee/tea-making facilities.

Phi Phi Island Village Beach Resort & Spa ✸✸✸   Accessible only by a 30-minute boat ride (regular shuttles are available from the ferry pier), this is a top choice among the islands' more far-flung resorts. Deluxe bungalows offer private balconies and unusual open-plan bathrooms (shower only); with such unrivalled ocean views, it's not surprising this place proves a popular choice for families, couples, and honeymooners. A luxury spa, two large pools, fine dining options, as well as an in-house tour program service and scuba school complete the picture. There's obviously a need to be self-contained with this location; apart from a few nearby jungle walks, it's all about relaxing. The beachfront at high tide is lovely and sunset is inspiring.

Phuket Office: 89 Satoon Rd., Phuket 83000. (Hotel located on Loh Ba Khao Bay, at the NE end of the island, 30 min. by long-tail boat). ⓒ 07621-5014. Fax 07621-4918. www.ppisland.com. 100 units. 4,700B–7,500B (US$134–US$215/£72–£115) double; from 11,300B (US$323/£174) villa. AE, MC, V. **Amenities:** 3 restaurants; 3 bars; 2 outdoor pools; spa; scuba school; watersports rentals; tour desk; courtesy boat transport to main beach area; babysitting, laundry service; Internet. *In room:* A/C, satellite TV, minibar, fridge, no phone.

WHERE TO DINE & DRINK

Phi Phi Don is packed with eateries. In downtown central Tonsai, look out for **Mama's Restaurant, Phi Phi Bakery, McPluto Burger, Ton Sai Seafood, Little Britain Café, Hibachi, Cosmic Pizza**—you may even find some Thai food. You'll also find a few little halal food stands and vendors with wheeled carts making Southern-style sweet *roti* (pancake) with banana.

Once a Muslim village, Phi Phi now parties into the night at places like the **Reggae Bar** (with a Thai boxing ring), **Hippies Bar** (with a nightly fire show), **Apache,** and **Carlito's;** there's even an Irish pub and a sports bar. Don't miss the laid-back, beachfront **Sunflower Bar** on Loh Dalam Bay.

ACTIVITIES

Kayaks can be rented on the beach for leisurely paddling for around 100B (US$3/£1.50). **Snorkeling** trips around the island are popular and can be arranged with any hotel or with any of the many beachfront travel agencies for as little as 500B (US$14/£7.60) per day.

Scuba diving is quite popular here, too, and **Aquanauts Scuba** (ⓒ 07421-2640; www.aquanauts-scuba.com), among other full-service, professional outfits, offers anything from day trips to multiday adventures, as well as all the requisite PADI course instruction. Alternatively, try **Visa Diving** (ⓒ 07560-1157; www.visadiving.com) on the main strip just east of the ferry pier. Check the websites for prices.

Cat's Climbing Shop, at Tonsai Bay (www.catsclimbingshop.com), runs rock climbing trips around the gnarled cliffs of the two Phi Phi islands; check the website for prices.

8 Koh Lanta

About 70km (43 miles) SE of Krabi

The two islands of Koh Lanta Yai (Big Lanta Island) and Koh Lanta Noi (Small Lanta island) are a few hours' road and boat trip from Krabi airport. In a few years, Koh Lanta Yai has already become a bohemian alternative to heady Samui, or pricey Phuket. However, the island is big enough such that during the high season (Nov–Mar) small pockets of seclusion can be found—especially in the far south and over on the east coast where Muslim fishing villagers carry on with their traditional economy, ignoring the rolling cement trucks and bangs of construction on the upper west coast where most resorts are located. Despite the island's growing popularity, the endless white sand beaches are far from crowded. A great mix of international visitors ensures an excellent nightlife, with a good array of funky bars and small dance clubs. During March, when the crowds have left, regional locals head to historic Lanta Old Town for the annual Laanta Lanta Festival—a celebration of street art, performance, cultural shows, music, dance, fun, and games.

GETTING THERE

Minivans from Krabi Town, Trang, and Phuket make connections to Koh Lanta Yai via two vehicular ferries: one from the mainland to Koh Lanta Noi and across the island by car before another ferry to Koh Lanta Yai. Most transport stops in the small town of Saladan near the ferry pier on the northern tip of Lanta Yai. From Saladan, catch a pickup truck ride to the resort of your choice (whether you book with them or not, it is part of the minivan fee). Contact **Kanokwan Tour** (Lanta office: ℭ **07568-4419,** or Krabi office: 07563-0192) or **Lanta Transport Co.** (ℭ **07568-4482**) to make budget transportation arrangements.

Destination Air's (ℭ **07632-8637-9;** www.destinationair.com) amphibious Cessnas can fly you from Phuket to your destination on Koh Lanta in a matter of minutes; check availability and pricing well in advance.

WHERE TO STAY
EXPENSIVE

Layana 👍👍 A small boutique resort, with an excellent spa, Layana offers contemporary accommodations close to the ocean and a grand pool uniquely calibrated to the same salinity as human tears. Each room has an open, airy feel with lush decor of hard woods, silks, and local art. It's a tad less pricey than the competitors, but if you don't need the glamour, it's still a good bet.

272 Moo 3 Saladan, Phra-Ae Beach, Koh Lanta, Krabi 81150. ℭ **07560-7100.** Fax 07560-7199. www.layanaresort.com. 50 units. From 6,120B (US\$175/£94) double; 10,000B (US\$286/£154) suite. AE, MC, V. **Amenities:** 2 restaurants; 2 bars; outdoor pool; health club; spa; watersports rentals; bike rentals; library; tour desk; car-rental desk; limited room service; laundry service; Internet. *In room:* A/C, satellite TV, fridge, minibar, coffee-making facilities, safe.

Pimalai Resort and Spa 👍👍👍 Located in the far southwest of the island close to the National Park, Pimalai was the first luxury resort on the island. Designed by a young, eco-sensitive Thai architect, it continues to win awards in hospitality excellence and environmental awareness. A fine marriage of comfort and proximity to nature, these stylish villas sprawl down rolling hills and lush gardens right onto the pristine beach; some have pools and small luxuries such as CD and DVD players. Shady walkways have been built around the trees and the infinity pool is delicious; there's excellent dining in a large open air *sala* (pavilion) or down on the beach in a funky thatched bar and eatery hewn from logs. Guests have the diversion of a well-stocked library and gym, and resort staffers are happy to share their knowledge of the local area or arrange day trips. The design throughout—from the simple thatched treatment *salas* and trickling waterfall in the spa, to the many small touches of Thai arts—reminds you that you are indeed in Thailand. The rates below are for low season only.

99 Moo 5, Ba Kan Tiang Beach, Lanta Yai Island, Krabi 81150 (on the far SE coast of Lanta Yai). ℭ **07560-7999.** Fax 07560-7998. www.pimalai.com. 118 units. Low season from 4,800B (US\$137/£74) double; from 10,800B (US\$308/£166) suite; from 13,800B (US\$394/£212) beach villa; from 15,800B (US\$451/£243) pool villa. AE, DC, MC, V. **Amenities:** 3 restaurants; bar; pool; spa; watersports rentals; bike rental; dive center; library; tour desk; car-rental desk; airport transfer; business center; 24-hr. room service; same-day laundry service; Internet. *In room:* A/C, satellite TV, fridge, minibar, safe.

MODERATE/INEXPENSIVE

Costa Lanta 👍👍 Lauded for its unique architectural design, the Costa Lanta boasts sleek rooms, which beautifully balance Western minimalism and Thai rustic decor, ocean-side decks, and long pools. The resort has also garnered positive reviews for its innovative back-to-nature approach, and for its reputation for offering some of the island's best cuisine and cocktails. In the interest of environmental preservation, the resort is built back from the beach under the natural tree line and caters to Thai yuppies as much as foreign tourists.

212 Moo 1, Saladan, Koh Lanta Yai, Krabi 81150. ✆ 02662-3550. Fax 02260-9067. www.costalanta.com. From 3,025B–10,780B (US$86–US$308/£47–£166) double. MC, V. **Amenities:** Restaurant; bar; outdoor pool; watersports rentals; car-rental desk; massage; laundry service. *In room:* A/C, CD player, fridge, minibar.

Mango House 🐱 This unique guesthouse is on the east coast, in an area that was once a hub of Chinese mercantile trade. The studio and two-bedroom villas here are historic Thai fisherman's homes built on stilts over the sea adjacent to a sea gypsy village. The recently renovated solid post and beam structures feature modern touches of Chinese decor with spectacular views from private seafront patios. Downstairs, there's the first-rate **Mango Bistro** for eats. This is Old Town living at its finest.

Mango House, Ban Saladan, Lanta Old Town, Koh Lanta Yai, Krabi 81150. ✆ 07569-7181 or 086948-6836 (mobile). From 500B–3,900B (US$14–US$111/£7.70–£60) double (varies with location and size). MC, V. **Amenities:** Bistro; bar; satellite TV; library; tour desk; Wi-Fi. *In room:* Fridge, minibar.

Moonlight Bay Resort 🐱🐱 Long popular in the far south of Lanta, Moonlight Bay is situated by a small river facing the sea. Recently renovated, the cottages are more contemporary chic than rustic these days, but the vibe is laid back and for many, the isolation blissful. Don't miss the new Aroma spa.

69 Moo 8, Khlongtob, Koh Lanta Yai, Krabi 81150. ✆ 07566-2590. Fax 07566-2594. www.moonlight-resort.com. 30 units. 1,500B–7,900B (US$43–US$226/£23–£122) double (varies with location and size). AE, V. **Amenities:** Restaurant; bar; small outdoor pool; Jacuzzi; tour desk; car-rental desk; massage; laundry service. *In room:* A/C, satellite TV, fridge, minibar.

WHERE TO DINE & DRINK

Cool places to chill on Koh Lanta include **Red Snapper** at Long Beach (176 Moo 2, Phra Ae Beach; ✆ **07885-6965;** www.redsnapper-lanta.com); **Mango Bistro** (see above) at Lanta Old Town; **Time for Lime Cooking School** at Khlong Dao Beach (✆ **07568-4590;** www.timeforlime.net); and, with funky tunes by international DJs, the groovy **Club IBARK** at Khlong Nin Beach (www.ibarkkrabi.com).

9 Trang

About 129km (80 miles) SE of Krabi

Trang Province, south of Krabi, is where it's at if you're looking for a real Thai-style beach holiday in the south. Popular with Thai tourists, the large province is spectacularly placed, with plenty of unspoiled national parks and 46 islands. Most tourists head first for **Ha Pak Mieng Beach** and then to outlying islands by ferry. Day-tours for snorkelers are affordable and the scenery is much like nearby Krabi, but cheaper and without as many tourists.

Trang province is also great for light adventure activities such as sea kayaking and diving. **Had Chao Mai National Park,** which consists of several islands—**Koh Kradan,** known for its coral reefs; **Koh Mook** (Muk), famous for the Emerald Cave, and accessible only by water; **Koh Waen** and **Koh Chueak,** which offer excellent deep sea diving and also a chance to spot the rare dugong (a dolphin-like creature). For mainland nature visits, visit wildlife sanctuaries such as **Namtok Khao Chong** and **Khlong Lamchan Park,** which boast waterfalls, trails, and caves. The **Southern Thailand Botanical Garden** (Thung Khai) on the Trang-Palian Road (Hwy. 404) offers stunning nature trails through lowland jungle and tropical gardens. For keen adventurers, there are some pretty remote islands such as **Tarutao Marine National Park,** which lies close to the Malaysian border, in Satun province. This region is great for kayaking and pristine diving. For more adventure tour info, see **www.paddleasia.com**.

GETTING THERE

By Air   One daily flight from Bangkok is serviced by **Nok Air** (© 02900-9955; www.nokair.com).

By Train   Trang city is connected by **train** with Bangkok on the main north–south line. Two daily departures make the 16-hour trek. Ask for details at **Bangkok's Hua Lampong Station** (© 1690).

By Bus   There are frequent buses from Bangkok's Southern Bus terminal (© 02434-7192) and minibus connection from Krabi and Surat Thani. When you arrive in Trang, connect by minibus with Ha Pak Mieng for 200B (US$5.70/£3.10); it's a 30-minute ride.

Ferry boats to the outlying islands leave regularly all day from the pier on the north end of the beach. It costs around 1,000B (US$29/£15) for an all-day tour by boat (including lunch), and they can drop you off at any number of islands (Koh Ngai, Koh Mook, or Koh Kradung). Try **Chao Mai Tour** (© 07521-4742), just one among many at the port, or contact any of the hotels below and they can help with arrangements.

WHERE TO STAY

Near the Amari is **Pakmeng Resort** (60/1 Moo 4, Tambol Maifad, Trang; © 07527-4112; www.pakmengresort.com), rustic but cozy and quiet in a mangrove plantation near the sea wall. Rooms range from 900B to 1,200B (US$26–US$34/£14–£18). **Southern Thailand Botanical Gardens** (© 07521-8435) also has basic accommodations available for around 200B (US$6/£3).

Amari Trang Beach Resort   Trang's foremost luxury beach resort weaves an inspiring spell that echoes the resort's gently flowing waters and dancing light. With fine dining, a great spa facility, and neat contemporary Thai room design, this is the kind of place that is now attracting escapees from overpriced Phuket and Phi Phi. The hotel hosts a "day resort" on a private beach at nearby Koh Kradung, which works like a Beach Club for those who love to get away from the crowds, but still like a modicum of luxury at hand. Check the Internet for special rates.

Changlang Beach, Trang 92150. © 07520-5888. Fax 07520-5899. www.amari.com. 138 units. From 1,470B (US$42/ £23) double; from 6,545B (US$187/£101) suite. AE, MC, V. **Amenities:** 3 restaurants; 2 bars; outdoor pool; spa; fitness center; kayak and bicycle rental; tour desk; limited room service; same-day laundry service. *In room:* A/C, satellite TV, fridge, minibar, safe.

WHERE TO STAY ON THE ISLANDS

Choose an island and head to the ferries that leave from Pak Mieng Pier. Go for **Charlie Beach Resort** on **Koh Mook** (© 07521-7671 or 07520-3281; www.kohmook. com), which is basic and affordable with rooms starting at 1,000B (US$29/£15). On **Koh Ngai,** try the quaint **CoCo Cottages** (© 07522-4387; www.coco-cottage.com), an environmentally friendly cluster run by a cheerful Thai family; beach cottages range from 1,000B to 4,500B (US$29–US$129/£15–£69).

10

Central Thailand

Going north from Bangkok, travelers who trace the route of the Chao Phraya River will feel as if they are traveling back in time. Starting with the ruins of Ayutthaya, as you go north you will discover a series of former capitals: first Ayutthaya, then Lopburi. Farther north, the nation's most famous architectural wonder, Sukhothai, is traditionally considered the seat of the first Thai kingdom, from 1238. Beyond Sukhothai, to the north, is the land once called Lanna, or the Land of Ten Thousand Rice Fields. This distinct ancient kingdom meandered between Chiang Mai and Chiang Rai (chapters 12–14), and brought totally different customs and architecture.

Central Thailand is also the country's "Great Rice Bowl," known for its agricultural abundance. Winding rivers cut through a mosaic of rice fields, and smaller villages and towns provide a window into the heart of Thailand's rural culture. If you have the time, the most atmospheric way to travel from Bangkok to Ayutthaya is by boat. It's also a short ride by train, and many make the hop to Lopburi before going on to Phitsanulok, the commercial and transportation hub of the Central Plains. Farther west, bordering Myanmar (Burma), the town of Mae Sot is surrounded by refugee camps, which for years have been offering humanitarian aid to the Burmese. Travelers can also choose to continue north to Chiang Mai by road or rail from Phitsanulok.

1 Ayutthaya ★ ★

76km (47 miles) N of Bangkok

Ayutthaya is one of Thailand's travel highlights. Many travelers take the day tour from Bangkok, which allows about 3 hours at the sites (the majority of these lie inside the Historical Park), but for folks with an interest in archaeological ruins, Ayutthaya justifies an overnight or more.

From its establishment in 1350 by King U Thong (Ramathibodi I) until its fall to the Burmese in 1767, Ayutthaya was Thailand's capital, home to 33 kings and numerous dynasties. At its zenith and until the mid-18th century, Ayutthaya was a majestic city with three palaces and 400 temples on an island threaded by canals. The former capital rivaled European cities in splendor and was a source of marvel for foreigners.

Then, in 1767, after a 15-month siege, the town was destroyed by the Burmese. Today there is little left but ruins and rows of headless Buddhas where once an empire thrived. The temple compounds are still awe-inspiring even in disrepair, and a visit here is memorable and a good starting point for those drawn to the relics of history.

The architecture of Ayutthaya is a fascinating mix of styles. Tall, ornate spires called *prangs* point to ancient Khmer (Cambodian) influence (best seen in Bangkok at Wat

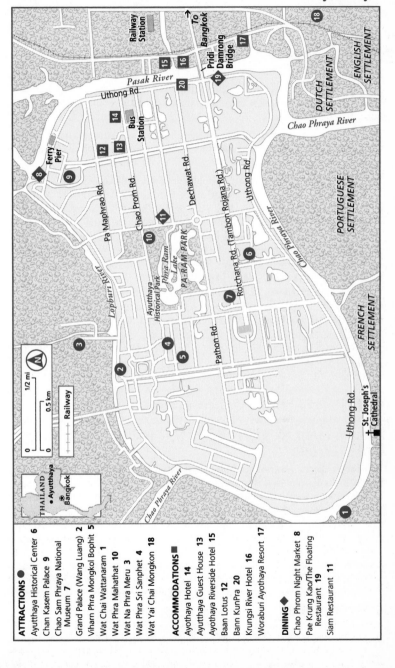

Ayutthaya

ATTRACTIONS ●
Ayutthaya Historical Center **6**
Chan Kasem Palace **9**
Chao Sam Phraya National
  Museum **7**
Grand Palace (Wang Luang) **2**
Viharn Phra Mongkol Bophit **5**
Wat Chai Wattanaram **1**
Wat Phra Mahathat **10**
Wat Na Phra Meru **3**
Wat Phra Sri Sanphet **4**
Wat Yai Chai Mongkon **18**

ACCOMMODATIONS ■
Ayothaya Hotel **14**
Ayutthaya Guest House **13**
Ayothaya Riverside Hotel **15**
Baan Lotus **12**
Bann KunPra **20**
Krungsi River Hotel **16**
Woraburi Ayothaya Resort **17**

DINING ◆
Chao Phrom Night Market **8**
Pae Krung Kao/The Floating
  Restaurant **19**
Siam Restaurant **11**

Arun). These bear a resemblance to the architecture of Angkor Wat in Cambodia. The pointed *stupas* are ascribed to the Sukhothai style.

ESSENTIALS

GETTING THERE

By Train   Trains depart 17 times daily from Bangkok's **Hua Lampong Railway Station** (© 1690) from 5:20am to 11:20pm (trip time: 1½ hr.; 20B/71¢/30p third class). Look for second class trains with A/C from 40B (US$1.15/60p), which is a promotional fare.

By Bus   Buses leave every 15 minutes from Bangkok's **Northern Bus Terminal** on Kampaengphet 2 Rd., Mo Chit (© 02936-2841), from 4:30am to 7:30pm (trip time: 1½ hr.). Rates run from 50B (US$1.40/75p) for second class.

By Boat   All-day river cruises are a popular option to and from Ayutthaya and there are a number of companies making the connection. **Grand Pearl Cruises** (© 02861-0255) runs a huge floating diner-cum-dance club; it can be booked through most hotels. Departure points are at River City pier (off Charoen Krung [New] Rd.) daily at approximately 7:30am. Day trips involve a morning air-conditioned coach ride to the ancient city and then returning by boat, where a buffet lunch is served. On Fridays the order is reversed, with travel by boat in the morning and a return by coach (trip time: all day; 1,800B/US$51/£28).

The most luxurious way to travel upriver is aboard the *Manohra Song,* a renovated teak rice barge, or its newer and even more exclusive sister, the *Manohra Dream.* For reservations, call the **Bangkok Marriott Resort and Spa** (© 02476-0021; www. manohracruises.com). Three-day, 2-night trips on the *Song* leave the hotel pier every Monday and Thursday, while trips on the *Dream* can be arranged to leave any time. The *Song* has four staterooms with en suite bathrooms, while the *Dream* has two large rooms with A/C, full showers, and king-size beds. Each ship's crew serves cocktails, snacks, and Thai meals in its covered lounge. The trip includes a stop at Wat Bang Na temple, among others. Inclusive of meals, tours, and transfers (but not alcohol), the *Song* runs at a steep 40,250B (US$1,150/£619) plus service and tax for two, while the *Dream* costs a hefty 199,500B (US$5,700/£3,069) per couple.

ORIENTATION

Ayutthaya's old city is surrounded by a canal fed by three rivers—Chao Phraya, Lopburi, and Pasak—and thus is often referred to as the "island." The main ferry pier is located on the east side of the island, just opposite the train station. The Bangkok bus makes its last stop at the station adjacent to the Siam Commercial Bank Building, off Chao Prom Road in downtown. Buses from Phitsanulok stop 10km (6 miles) north of town; you'll need to take a 70B (US$2/£1.10) motorcycle taxi into the center.

VISITOR INFORMATION

There is a **Tourism Authority of Thailand (TAT)** office at Si Sanphet Road opposite the National Museum (© 03532-2730-1). Stop by for maps and other information.

GETTING AROUND

A tuk-tuk from the train station into town will cost about 40B (US$1.15/60p), but about 50m (150 ft.) from the station is a small river ferry that will take you to the central island for a few baht, from 5:30am to 9pm daily. From there you can take a tuk-tuk to your hotel. There are also a few *samlors* (bicycle taxis), which are a unique and environmentally friendly way to get around. Or you can take a noisier but faster long-tail boat to see the city for about 700B (US$20/£11) per hour for up to 10 people (look for the small independent operators on the northeast end of the island, near the night market). There is regular minibus service between Ayutthaya and the pretty 19th-century palaces at Bang Pa-In, departing from Chao Prom Market on the road of the same name (trip time: 50 min.; 20B/57¢/30p).

FAST FACTS

Bank of Ayudhya (which uses yet another spelling of the city's name) has a branch on U Thong Road next to the ferry pier across the river from the train station, and there are plenty of ATMs in the city. The main **post office** is also on U Thong Road in the northeast corner of town (but any hotel or guesthouse can help with posting mail). A number of shops on Naresuan Rd. Soi 1 offer **Internet** service for 30B (85¢/45p) per hour.

WHAT TO SEE & DO

The bulk of the historical sites here are concentrated on the "island," with ancient ruins interspersed with the modern buildings that have risen around them. The Ayutthaya Historical Park lies in the center of the island, but the sites below are just a few of many, and a guide can be helpful (contact any hotel front desk to arrange one).

Most temples sell tickets until 5:30pm and close at 6pm. Though you can't go inside them after that time, several of the exteriors are dramatically lit at night, and worth seeing on their own.

MUSEUMS

Ayutthaya Historical Study Center ★★ As a resource for students, scholars, and the public, the center presents displays of the ancient city, including models of the palace and the port area and reconstructions of ships and architectural elements, as well as a fine selection of historical objects.

Rotchana Rd. ✆ 03524-5124. Admission 100B (US$2.85/£1.55), students 50B (US$1.40/75p). Mon–Fri 9am–4:30pm; Sat–Sun 9am–5pm.

Chan Kasem Palace ★ Housing the **Chantharakasem National Museum,** the impressive Chan Kasem Palace was built in 1577 by King Maha Thamaraja (the 17th Ayutthaya monarch) for his son, who became King Naresuan. It was destroyed, but was later restored by King Mongkut (Rama IV), who stayed there whenever he visited Ayutthaya. On display are gold artifacts, jewelry, carvings, Buddha images, and domestic and religious objects from the 13th through 17th centuries.

Northeast part of the island. Admission 30B (85¢/45p). Wed–Sun 9am–4pm.

Chao Sam Phraya National Museum ★★ This museum, one of Thailand's largest, boasts a comprehensive collection of antique bronze Buddha images, carved panels, religious objects, and other local artifacts. It's close to the Ayutthaya Historical center (see above) and across from the TAT office.

Rotchana Rd. (1½ blocks west of the center near the junction of Si Sanphet Rd.). ✆ 03524-1587. Admission 30B (85¢/45p). Wed–Sun 9am–4pm.

THE TEMPLES & RUINS

Grand Palace Sometimes called Wang Luang, this palace lies in ruins, having been completely destroyed by the Burmese in the late 1700s. Located in the northwestern section of the city, the foundations of the three main buildings can still be made out, and the size of the compound is impressive.

Si Sanpet Rd., in the northwest part of the city, near Wat Phra Si Sanphet. Admission by joint ticket, 250B (US$7/£4). Daily 8am–6pm.

Viharn Phra Mongkon Bophit ✦   Home to Thailand's largest seated bronze Buddha, this cozy sanctuary was reconstructed in the 1950s. The area was originally designated for royal creation ceremonies, and the *viharn* was later constructed to house the Buddha image.

West of Wat Phra Mahathat and near Wat Si Sanphet. Free admission. Daily 8am–6pm.

Wat Chai Wattanaram   A long bike ride from the other main temple sites, in the southwest of the city, this *wat* is an excellently preserved example of Khmer architecture in the Ayutthaya period. You can climb to the steep steps of the central *prang* for beautiful views. Its intact structure offers visitors a good sense of what a working temple might have looked like some 300 years ago.

Opposite bank of the Chao Phraya River, southwest of town. Admission 30B (85¢/45p). Daily 8am–6pm.

Wat Na Phra Meru   Located on the Lopburi side of the river, Wat Na Phra Meru survived Ayutthaya's destruction in 1767 because it was used as a base for the invading Burmese army. It's worth visiting to see the black-stone Buddha dating from the Mon (Devaravati) period, as well as the central sanctuary, with the principal 6-foot-tall Buddha and stunning vaulted ceilings supported by ornate columns. A Burmese king died here when his cannon backfired whilst attempting an attack.

Across the Lopburi River, north of the Grand Palace area. Admission 20B (57¢/30p). Daily 8am–5pm.

Wat Phra Mahathat ✦✦   The most striking of all of the temples in Ayutthaya, Wat Phra Mahathat was built in the heart of the city in 1384 during the reign of King Rachatirat. It is typical of Ayutthaya ruins, with large crumbling stupas surrounded by low laterite walls and rows of headless Buddhas. One Buddha head remains a draw for merit-makers and photographers, however—it's embedded in the gnarled trunk of the old tree that has grown to surround it.

Opposite Wat Phra Mahathat stands **Wat Ratburana,** built in 1424 and splendidly restored—the towering monuments (both rounded Khmer-style *prangs* and Sukhothai-style pointed *chedis*) have even retained some of their original stucco. In the two crypts, excavators found bronze Buddha images and votive tablets, as well as golden objects and jewelry, many of which are displayed in the Chao Sam Phraya Museum. There are also murals, as well as a frieze of heavenly beings and some Chinese scenes. Both *wats* remain damaged despite restoration.

Along Chee Kun Rd., near the intersection with Naresuan. Admission for each 30B (85¢/45p). Daily 8am–6pm.

Wat Phra Si Sanphet   Built in the 14th century for private royal use, Si Sanphet lies just south of the raised Grand Palace area. The buildings were renovated in the 16th and 17th centuries. The 17m (55 ft.) bronze standing Buddha was originally cast and covered in gold. In 1767, the Burmese tried to melt the gold, causing a fire that destroyed the image and the temple; this one is a replica. Nearby are three, 15th-century, Sri Lankan–style *chedis,* enshrining the ashes of three Ayutthayan kings.

Just south of the Grand Palace ruin in the northwest end of the island. Admission 30B (85¢/45p). Daily 9am–4pm.

Wat Yai Chai Mongkhon   Visible for miles around, the gold *chedi* of Wat Yai is a long walk (or a short 20B/57¢/30p tuk-tuk ride) southeast of ancient Ayutthaya (across the river and out of town). King U Thong founded the temple in 1357, and the white reclining Buddha near the entrance was built by King Naresuan. The massive pagoda celebrates the defeat of the Burmese at Suphanburi in 1592 and King Naresuan's defeat of the crown prince of Burma in an elephant joust.

East of the city, across the Pridi Damrong Bridge and south on Dusit Rd. Admission 20B (57¢/30p). Daily 8am–6pm.

WHERE TO STAY
EXPENSIVE
Woraburi Ayothaya Convention Resort   Overlooking the Pasak River, this new hotel offers some of the best facilities in town. It's especially well-suited for large groups. Riverboat dining cruises, complete with floating karaoke fun, are available for up to 100 guests.

89 Watkluay Rd., Ayutthaya 13000. ℂ **03524-9600-49**. Fax 03524-9625. www.woraburi.com. 172 units. 1,600B–2,500B (US$45–US$72/£25–£38) double; 3,500B (US$100/£54) suite. MC, V. **Amenities:** Restaurant; coffee shop; fitness center; riverside pavilion; river tours; business center; laundry service. *In room:* A/C, satellite TV, minibar, fridge.

MODERATE
Ayothaya Hotel   The Ayothaya Hotel (same city, different spelling) is a basic low-end business standard in the center of town near the popular backpacker street, Naresuan Road. Facilities are limited, but the location is convenient for temple touring. Be sure to check rooms first, as they can be musty and quite basic out back.

12 Moo Tessabarn Soi 2, Ayutthaya 13000 (just west of the Chao Phrom pier, across from the market). ℂ **03523-2855**. Fax 03525-1018. www.ayothayahotel.com. 101 units. 1,200B–1,500B (US$34–US$43/£18–£23) double; 3,500B (US$100/£54) suite. AE, DC, MC, V. **Amenities:** Restaurant; small pool; massage; laundry service; Internet center. *In room:* A/C, TV, minibar, fridge.

Ayothaya Riverside Hotel   Just across from the train station, this is a Thai business class hotel worth the upgrade from the town's small guesthouses—though not particularly special. Their riverside restaurant is a pleasant spot for a drink, and many of their large, clean rooms overlook the river. Five units are available for longer stays.

91/1 Moo 10 Wat Pako Rd., Ayutthaya 13000 (across from the train station). ℂ **03523-8737**. Fax 03424-4139. www.ayothayariverside.com. 102 units. 1,200B (US$34/£18) superior double; 1,600B (US$46/£25) deluxe double. **Amenities:** 2 restaurants (one floating at riverside); tour desk and bike rentals; laundry service. *In room:* A/C, satellite TV, fridge.

Krungsri River Hotel ⍟   This hotel is within walking distance of the train station and provides one of the better standards of comfort in town. Rooms have large bathrooms and some look over the river; the hotel also offers a coffee shop and a small pool. Prices in baht listed below look odd because the hotel explicitly adds 25% for foreigners. You'll need to take the shuttle to the main sights on the island.

7/2 Rotchana Rd., Ayutthaya 13000 (northeast side of Pridi Damrong Bridge). ℂ **03524-4333**. Fax 03524-3777. www.krungsririver.com. 212 units. From 1,766B (US$51/£27) double; from 4,333B (US$124/£66) suite. AE, DC, MC, V. **Amenities:** 3 restaurants; beer garden and pub; pool; fitness center w/sauna; game room; bowling alley; tour desk; small business center w/Internet; salon; 24-hr. room service; babysitting; same-day laundry service/dry cleaning; non-smoking rooms. *In room:* A/C, satellite TV, minibar, fridge, safe.

INEXPENSIVE
All along Naresuan you'll find good budget accommodations, and the street gets busy in the high season (Nov–Feb). In addition to Ayutthaya Guesthouse, try the lively

Tony's Place (12/18 Naresuan Soi 1; ✆ **03525-2578**), with wireless Internet, or **P.U. Guest House** (20/1 Moo 4, off Naresuan; ✆ **03525-1213**), which has some units with A/C, TV, and minibar.

Ayutthaya Guesthouse On busy Naresuan Road, this guesthouse has been expanded by its owners (Mr. Hong and family), and it now occupies three large buildings. The place is still popular with travelers who don't mind the functional but not fancy furnishings, but some of the shared bathrooms are a hike from the rooms.

12/34 Naresuan Soi 1, Ayutthaya 13000. ✆ 03523-2868. 20 units. From 200B (US$6/£3) double with fan and shared bath; from 450B (US$13/£7) double with A/C and bath. No credit cards. **Amenities:** Restaurant; bike rental; tour information; laundry service. In room: No phone.

Baan Lotus This lovely restored teak house lies a bit outside the town's main cluster of budget options, but you'll be glad you took the short walk to get there. The welcoming staff makes it a nice place to unwind, as does the large garden and pond, but it's a bit noisy. They also offer tours at night, when the ruins are romantically lit.

20 Pa Maphrao Rd., Ayutthaya 13000. ✆ 03525-1988. 20 units. 250B (US$7.15/£3.85) single with shared bathroom; 400B (US$11/£6.15) double with private bathroom; 600B (US$17/£9.25) double A/C with private bath. No credit cards. **Amenities:** Tours; laundry service. In room: A/C in some, no phone.

Bann KunPra Bann KunPra is a beautiful riverside teak house converted into comfortable if very basic guest quarters. These traditional fan-only rooms are small with high ceilings and, set around a small common area, exude a rustic charm. Their open-air candlelit restaurant overlooks the river. *Note:* Ask for a room at the back where it's quieter and there's a river view.

48 Moo 3 U Thong Rd., Ayutthaya 13000. ✆ 03524-1978. www.bannkunpra.com. 15 units. 250B (US$7.15/£3.85) dorm with shared bath; 300B–600B (US$8.60–US$17.15/£4.60–£9.25) double with shared bath. No credit cards. **Amenities:** Riverside restaurant; tour information. In room: No phone.

WHERE TO DINE

Particularly if this is your first stop outside of Bangkok, don't miss the **Chantharakasem Night Market** along the river in the northeast of town, with fresh produce and a wide selection of Thai/Muslim dishes. More central is the **Chao Phrom Night Market** near the pier. Many of the guesthouses along **Naresuan** serve decent Thai fare geared to foreigners, and now Naresuan hosts a few **open-air restaurants** right on the street, a great place to meet, greet, eat and party late.

Pae Krung Kao/The Floating Restaurant THAI/CHINESE On low floating pallets at riverside, this restaurant allows diners to have great views of passing boats and river life. The satisfying Thai/Chinese stir-fry and curries are further complemented by a tranquil Chinese garden, a strumming balladeer, and candlelight at water's edge.

4 Moo 2, U Thong Rd. (west bank of Pasak River, north of Pridi Damrong Bridge). ✆ 03525-1807. Main courses 60B–200B (US$1.50–US$4.90/90p–£3.10). MC, V. Daily 5–10pm.

Siam Restaurant THAI Just across from the large temple of Wat Phra Mahathat, Siam Restaurant is a good spot to fill up on Thai dishes like fried rice and noodles, while taking a break from temple touring. Alternatively, enjoy a cool drink here after a temple sunset.

11/3 Pratuchai Rd. (across from Wat Phra Mahathat). ✆ 03521-1070. Main courses 70B–250B (US$2–US$7/£1.10–£3.85). MC, V. Daily 10am–10pm.

SIDE TRIPS FROM AYUTTHAYA
BANG PA-IN

Only 61km (38 miles) north of Bangkok, this delightful royal palace is usually combined with Ayutthaya in most 1-day tours and is accessible by minivan. Much of the palace isn't open to the public so, if pressed for time, stick to Ayutthaya.

The 17th-century temple and palace at Bang Pa-In were originally built by Ayutthaya's King Prasat Thong, later abandoned when the capital moved in the late 1700s, and then rebuilt again by King Chulalongkorn in the late 1800s.

The architecture is Thai with strong European influences. In the center of the small lake, **Phra Thinang Aisawan Thippa-At,** is an excellent example of classic Thai style. Behind it, in Versailles style, are the former **king's apartments,** which today serve as a hall for state ceremonies. The **Phra Thinang Wehat Chamrun,** also noteworthy, is a Chinese-style building (open to the public) where court members generally lived during the rainy and cool seasons. Also worth visiting is the **Phra Thinang Withun Thatsuna,** an observatory on a small island that affords a fine view of the countryside.

2 Lopburi

77km (48 miles) N of Ayutthaya; 153km (95 miles) N of Bangkok; 224km (139 miles) S of Phitsanulok

Lopburi is as famous for its 14th to 17th century temple ruins, as much as for its sometimes very aggressive troupes of monkeys that call them home. The town hosted kings and emissaries from around the world some 400 years ago, and archaeological evidence suggests a highly developed Buddhist society was here as early as the 11th century. These days, Lopburi is a popular day trip from Ayutthaya or a good stopover on the way north.

ESSENTIALS
GETTING THERE

Lopburi is along Highway 1 just past Saraburi (connect with Lopburi via Hwy. 3196 to Rte. 311). The fastest way to go straight there from Bangkok is by minivan from Victory Monument (accessible by BTS) for 100B (US$2.85/£1.55). Vans leave from in front of Rachavithee Hospital. Regular buses connect to Lopburi via Ayutthaya from Bangkok's **Northern Bus Terminal** (② 02936-2841) for the same price. Numerous trains make daily connection with Lopburi via Ayutthaya from Bangkok's **Hua Lampong Railway Station** (② 1690), from 138B (US$3.95/£2.10) upwards.

INFORMATION & ORIENTATION

The **TAT Office** is located in a teak house built in the 1930s just a short walk from the train station (follow the signs) on Rop Wat Phra That Road (② 03642-2768). They have a useful map and can point you to sites within walking distance.

WHAT TO DO & SEE

Do Lopburi in a clockwise circle. From the train station, stop in to **Wat Phra Si Ratana Mahathat** just out front. Built in 1257, Mahathat is a stunning ruin much like the temples of Ayutthaya (entrance 30B/85¢/45p; daily 7am–5pm). On a small side street just north of the temple, is the TAT office.

Directly west of the TAT, the large complex of **King Narai's Palace** was built in 1666 and combines a large museum of Lopburi antiquities with the *wats* and palace of the king. When nearby Ayutthaya was little more than a marsh, King Narai hosted emissaries from around the world (note the many Islamic-style doorways). The museum now houses displays of Thai rural life and traditions from weaving and agriculture to shadow puppetry (admission 30B/85¢/45p; daily 8am–5pm).

Exiting Narai's palace, head north through the town's small streets and market areas to **Wat Sao Thong Thong,** which houses a large golden Buddha and fine Khmer and Ayutthaya period statues. Farther north brings you to **Ban Vichayen,** the manicured ruins of the fine housing built for visiting dignitaries (admission 30B/85¢/45p; Wed–Sun 7am–5pm).

Going east along Vichayen Road toward the town center, the three connected towers at **Phra Prang Sam Yot** are a stunning example of the Khmer influence in what is known as "Lopburi style." This is the site where you'll find the town's famous *macaques* (monkeys) most hours of the day (admission 30B/85¢/45p; Wed–Sun; 7am–5pm). Be careful around these mischievous apes: They have been known to get aggressive and can be very dangerous. You can take pictures, but don't carry any food.

Reaching Prang Sam Yot brings you full-circle back to the train tracks just north of the station. If you're in Lopburi in late spring, ask about the occasional *macaque* **banquets,** where a formal table is set for the little beasts who tear it to bits—they've no manners at all. Most days they are fed at a temple just east of Sam Yot, called **San Phra Khan** (across the train tracks). Groups of the mischievous animals trapeze along the high wires and swoop down on shop owners armed with sticks, who keep a close eye on outdoor merchandise. It's a different kind of rush hour altogether.

WHERE TO STAY & DINE

Few stay in little Lopburi, instead making it a day trip from Ayutthaya or a brief stopover on the way to points north. If you do choose to stay here, try the **Lopburi Inn** (28/9 Naraimaharat Rd.; ✆ **03641-2300**) with rooms from 600B (US$17/£9.25) with A/C, TV, and breakfast.

There are lots of small open-air restaurants in and around town. One of the best options is the friendly, air-conditioned **Taisawan Vietnamese Food** (11/8 Sorasak Rd.; ✆ **03641-1881**), just southeast of the main entrance to King Narai's Palace. Signature Vietnamese dishes such as *bun hoi,* noodles and pork, or shrimp kebabs start at just 60B (US$1.45/90p).

3 Phitsanulok

377km (234 miles) N of Bangkok; 93km (58 miles) SE of Sukhothai

Phitsanulok is a bustling agricultural, transportation, and military center, with a population of over 100,000, nestled on the banks of the Nan River. It is the crossroads of Thailand, located in the center of the country and roughly equidistant from Chiang Mai and Bangkok. Like most transportation hubs, it's hectic, noisy, and just a stopover for most people on their way to the more charming Sukhothai.

Outside of town, the terrain is flat and the rice paddies endless—they turn a vivid green in the late spring. In winter, white-flowering tobacco and pink-flowering soybeans are planted in rotation. Rice barges, houseboats, and long-tail boats ply the Nan and Song Kwai rivers, which eventually connect to the Chao Phraya River and feed into the Gulf of Thailand.

For 25 years, Phitsanulok served as the capital and is the birthplace of King Naresuan (the Great), the Ayutthayan king who, on elephant-back, defended Thailand from the Burmese army during the 16th century. Other Ayutthayan kings used Phitsanulok as a staging ground for battles with the Burmese.

The Central Plains

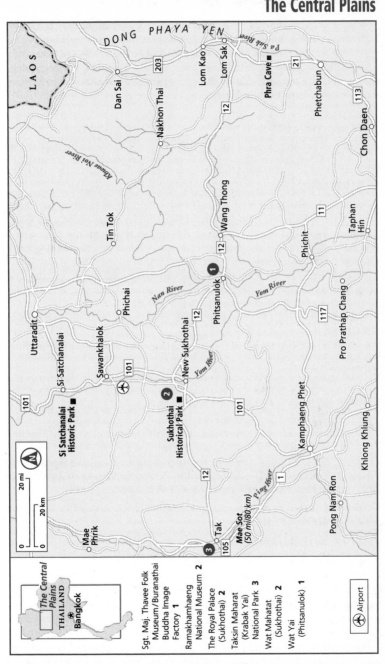

The Central Plains
THAILAND
Bangkok

Sgt. Maj. Thavee Folk
Museum/Buranathai
Buddha Image
Factory **1**

Ramakhamhaeng
National Museum **2**

The Royal Palace
(Sukhothai) **2**

Taksin Maharat
(Krabak Yai)
National Park **3**

Wat Mahatat
(Sukhothai) **2**

Wat Yai
(Phitsanulok) **1**

✈ Airport

When a tragic fire burned most of the city in 1959, one of the only buildings to survive was Wat Yai, famed for its unique statue of Buddha; the temple is now a holy pilgrimage site. For travelers, Wat Yai is worth a visit on the way west to Sukhothai or farther to the Burmese border. Phitsanulok is also famous for the Bangkaew dog, a notoriously fierce and faithful breed that's prized globally, and is thought to have originated from the Bang Rakham District.

ESSENTIALS
GETTING THERE
By Plane   Thai Airways (© **1566;** www.thaiair.com) has two flights daily to Phitsanulok from Bangkok, leaving at 6:05am and 8:40pm (flying time: 56 min.). The Thai Airways office in Phitsanulok is at 209/26–28 Boromtrailokanart Rd. (© **05528-0060**). Taxis cost 50B (US$1.40/75p) into town from the airport.

By Train   About 10 trains per day travel between Phitsanulok and Bangkok. The trip time is about 7 hours and costs 369B (US$11/£5.70) for an air-conditioned second-class seat. "Rapid" trains can take up to 9 hours, so it is worth the expense to go "sprinter" or "express" class—the difference being that express has sleeping berths. There are eight daily connections between Phitsanulok and Chiang Mai (7 hrs.; 440B/US$13/£6.75). For information and reservations, call Bangkok's **Hua Lampong Railway Station** (© **1690**), **Chiang Mai Railway Station** (© **05324-5363**), or the **Phitsanulok Railway Station** (© **05525-8005**).

In front of the station in Phitsanulok, throngs of *samlors* (pedicabs) and motorcycle taxis wait to take you to your hotel. The station is right in town, so expect to pay just 50B (US$1.45/75p) to get where you need to go. The bidding will start at around 100B (US$2.85/£1.55); smile and get ready to haggle.

By Bus   Standard air-conditioned buses leave daily every hour for the trip to Phitsanulok from Bangkok from 7am to midnight (trip time: 7 hr.; 277B/US$8/£4.25). The V.I.P. bus leaves at midnight and is about the same price; the wide seats recline enough to get a decent sleep, and the overnight trip is a time saver. Buses depart from Chiang Mai in similar numbers. Frequent non-A/C buses connect with Sukhothai. The intercity bus terminal in Phitsanulok is 2km (1¼ miles) east of town on Highway 12 (about 50B/US$1.40/75p by tuk-tuk or taxi). Contact **Bangkok's Northern Bus Terminal** (© **02936-2841**), the **Arcade Bus Station in Chiang Mai** (© **05324-2664**), or the **Phitsanulok Bus Terminal** (© **05521-2090**).

By Minivan   Travel to Sukhothai or on to Mae Sot can be arranged with **Win Tour** (© **05326-0295**).

VISITOR INFORMATION
The **TAT office** (© **05525-2742**) has maps and basic information, but is inconveniently located on Boromtrailokanart Road, 2 blocks south of the central clock tower down a small side street. Most hotels offer free city maps.

ORIENTATION
The town is fairly compact, with the majority of services and sights for tourists concentrated along or near the east bank of the Nan River. Naresuan Road extends from the railway station and crosses the river from the east over the town's main bridge. Wat Yai is north of the bridge and just a hitch north of busy Highway 12. The main market, featuring souvenirs in the day and food stalls at night, is just south of the bridge

on riverside Phutta Bucha Road. One landmark is the clock tower at the southern end of the commercial district, Boromtrailokanart Road.

GETTING AROUND

By Tuk-Tuk & Songtaew   Tuk-tuks (called taxis here) stop near the bus and train stations. Negotiate for an in-town fare, usually about 40B (US$1/60p). *Songtaews* (covered pickup trucks) follow regular routes outside of town.

By Bus   There's a well-organized city bus system with a main terminal south of the train station on A-Kathotsarot Road. Trips are about 10B (30¢/15p), but you would do just as well to hire tuk-tuks or taxis.

There are frequent (every half-hour 6am–6pm) buses from the intercity bus terminal east of town to **New Sukhothai** (trip time: 1 hr.; 42B/US$1.20/65p).

By Hired Minivan   Any hotel in Phitsanulok can arrange minivan tours in the area and to Sukhothai. Expect to pay 2,000B (US$57/£31) with a driver, plus fuel.

By Tram   The **Phitsanulok Tour Tramway** offers a 45-minute sightseeing tour, departing from Wat Yai from 9am to 3pm and returning to the temple.

By Rental Car   Budget (© 05530-1020) and Avis (© 05524-2060) have offices at the airport.

SPECIAL EVENTS

The **Buddha Chinarat Festival** is held annually on the sixth day of the waxing moon in the third lunar month (usually late Jan or early Feb). Then, Phitsanulok's Wat Yai is packed with well-wishers, dancers, monks and abbots, children, and tourists, all converging on the temple grounds for a 6-day celebration.

FAST FACTS

Bangkok Bank has an after-hours (until 8pm) exchange service at 35 Naresuan Rd. The **General Post Office** is on Phuttha Bucha Road, along the river 2 blocks north of Naresuan Road. The **Overseas Call Office** is on the second floor of the post office and offers **Internet,** at about 20B (57¢/30p) per hour.

WHERE TO STAY
MODERATE

Amarin Lagoon Hotel ⚐   If you've got your own wheels, the most attractive resort hotel in the area is the Amarin, near the railway station. The location is a slight drawback, but rooms are spacious, attractive, and quiet. There is a huge pool and spa and the hotel offers good business facilities such as Wi-Fi; plus, it's only 40 minutes from a golf course.

52/299 Moo 6, Praongkhao Rd., Phitsanulok 65000. © **05522-0999.** Fax 05522-0944. www.amarinlagoon hotel.com. 301 units. 1,200B–2,000B (US$34–US$57/£18–£31) double. AE, MC, V. **Amenities:** Restaurant; lounge; pool; fitness center; car-rental desk; 24-hr. business center; room service; same-day laundry service; Wi-Fi. *In room:* A/C, satellite TV, minibar, fridge.

Pailyn Hotel   Though it's an acceptable choice for in-town lodging, this is more or less a business hotel that services the occasional large tour group. The bright marble lobby gives the place some panache, and rooms are clean, fairly quiet for the location, with rattan decor. Rooms are priced according to size; upper standards are slightly smarter. Bathrooms are standard, with no frills.

38 Borom Trailokanart Rd., Phitsanulok 65000. © **05525-2411.** Fax 05525-8185. www.pailynhotel.com. 247 units. 1,150B (US$33/£18) single; 1,250B (US$36/£19) double; 2,600B (US$75/£40) suite. AE, MC, V. **Amenities:** 2 restaurants;

bar and disco; sauna; tour desk; car-rental desk; limited room service; massage; babysitting; same-day laundry service/dry cleaning. *In room:* A/C, satellite TV, minibar, fridge.

Phitsanulok Thani Hotel 🏛 The Phitsanulok Thani is clean and comfortable: an international business hotel standard convenient to the airport. Rooms are spacious and clean but bland. Bathrooms are neat but small. Suites are just larger versions of standard rooms. It is a popular stop for big tour groups, and though it is located a bit out of the center of town, shuttle service is provided and it is a short tuk-tuk ride from anywhere. Helpful staff can make any travel arrangements.

39 Sanambin Rd., Phitsanulok 65000 (4km/2½ miles southeast of clock tower, about 1km [⅔ mile] from airport). 📞 05521-1065. Fax 05521-1071. www.phitsanulok.com. 110 units. 800B–1,200B (US$23–US$35/£12–£18) double; 2,000B–4,000B (US$57–US$115/£31–£62) suite. AE, DC, MC, V. **Amenities:** Restaurant; lounge and karaoke pub; pool; airport transfer; business center; limited room service; massage; babysitting; same-day laundry service/dry cleaning; executive-level rooms. *In room:* A/C, satellite TV, minibar, fridge, coffee-making facilities, safe.

Topland Hotel and Convention Center 🏛🏛 Adjoining the town's largest shopping center and just a stone's throw from Wat Yai, this is one of the most comfortable, well-run hotels in Phitsanulok and has the best location. Service is snappy, though the lobby can be a pretty busy place at check-out time. Deluxe rooms are tidy, and bathrooms are large, with marble counters and wood trim.

68/33 Akathodsarod St., Phitsanulok 65000. 📞 05524-7800. Fax 05524-7815. www.toplandhotel.com. 253 units 1,200B (US$34/£18) superior double; 2,400B (US$69/£37) business suite. Rates include breakfast. AE, MC, V. **Amenities:** Restaurant; 2 bars; pool; fitness center; spa; tour desk; airport transfer; shopping arcade; salon; 24-hr. room service; laundry service; dry cleaning. *In room:* A/C, satellite TV, minibar, fridge, hair dryer, safe.

INEXPENSIVE

The bright, clean rooms at **Lithai Guest House** (73 Phayalithai Rd.; 📞 05521-9626) are a welcome addition to the city's accommodations options; the price (240B–350B/US$6.85–US$10/£3.70–£5.40 single; 460B/US$13/£7.10 double) includes breakfast. South of town, near the airport and the Phitsanulok Thani Hotel (see above), the **Phitsanulok Youth Hostel** (38 Sanambin Rd.; 📞 05524-2060) has basic rooms starting from 120B (US$3.45/£1.85) for a dorm room and 300B (US$8.60/£4.60) for a double.

WHERE TO DINE

No fine dining options exist in Phitsanulok; lots of small eateries are in and around the train station. Be sure to try the local specialty, *khaew tak,* sun-dried banana baked with honey; packages are sold everywhere and cost just 30B (86¢/45p). At the **Night Bazaar** you can enjoy "flying vegetables"—morning-glory greens sautéed, tossed high in the air, and adeptly caught in the chef's pan.

Pae Pha Thai Floating Restaurant THAI The best of many similar places along the riverbank just opposite the main tour attraction, Wat Yai, Pae Pha Thai is a friendly, casual eatery with no pretense. Indulge in the kind of spread you might find in a Thai home—*tod man plaa* (deep fried fish cakes), *phad kaprow* (chicken with basil and chili), *tom yum* soup, and a whole fish encrusted with garlic and lemon. All dishes seem to be made all the better by being served at water's edge.

Phutta Bucha Rd. (on Nan River across from Wat Yai). 📞 05524-2743. Main courses 80B–160B (US$2.30–US$4.60/£1.25–£2.45). MC, V. Daily 10am–11pm.

PHITSANULOK AFTER DARK

You won't find much in the way of nightlife in Phitsanulok, but for a beverage or a late snack set to noisy Thai Pop music, stop by **The Tree House** (✆ 05521-2587), a small bar with an adjoining garden across from the Phitsanulok Thani Hotel.

WHAT TO SEE & DO

Most use Phitsanulok as a jumping-off point for Sukhothai, but there are a few sights in the town proper—with Wat Yai being the foremost among them (see below).

The Sgt. Maj. Thavee Folk Museum ✿   This small campus of low-slung pavilions houses a private collection of antique items from Thai rural life. Farming and trapping equipment, household items, and old photographs of the city are lovingly displayed by the sergeant major, with descriptions in English. Just across the road is the **Buranathai Buddha Image Factory,** where you can see the carving and casting of large Buddhas, most of which are copies of the Chinarat Buddha image from Wat Yai.

26/43 Wisut Kasat Rd. ✆ **05525-8715.** Admission 20B (57¢/30p) for Thai children, 50B (US$1.50/75p) Thai adults; 200B (US$5.70/£3.10) for foreigners. Tues–Sun 8:30am–4:30pm.

Wat Chulamanee   The oldest temple in the area and the site of the original city, Wat Chulamanee is still an active monastery. The temple was restored in the 1950s and is admired for its fine laterite *prang* and elaborate stucco. It's best to have your own transport if you want to visit, or you may find yourself stranded due to limited public transportation.

7km south of the Nakon Sawan Hwy. on Boromtrailokanart Rd. Suggested donation 20B (50¢/30p). Daily 6am–7pm.

Wat Yai ✿✿   This temple's full name is **Wat Phra Si Ratana Mahathat,** and it's one of the most highly important temples in the country. The Phra Buddha Chinarat statue is a bronze image cast in 1357 under the Sukhothai king Mahatmmaracha; its most distinctive feature is its flamelike halo *(mandorla),* which symbolizes spiritual radiance. Only the Emerald Buddha in Bangkok is more highly revered by the Thai people.

The *viharn* housing the Buddha is a prized example of traditional Thai architecture, with three eaves, overlapping one another to emphasize the nave, and graceful black and gold columns. The mother-of-pearl inlaid doors leading into the chapel were added in 1576 as a gift from King Borommakot of Ayutthaya. Inside you'll discover an Italian marble floor, two painted *thammas* (pulpits), and murals illustrating the life of Buddha. Other than the main *bot*, the *wat's* most distinctive architectural feature is the Khmer-style *prang*, rebuilt by King Boromtrailokanart. It houses the relic from which the *wat* takes its name; *mahathat* means "great relic." The small museum houses a collection of Sukhothai- and Ayutthaya-era Buddhas.

The *wat* is always packed with worshippers paying their respects and making offerings. Conservative dress is obligatory—this means clothing that covers the shoulders, elbows, and knees; you'll also need to remove shoes before entering the *wat.*

1 block north of the Hwy. 12 bridge and just a short walk east of the river. Suggested donation of 50B (US$1.40/75p). Wat daily 6am–6pm (during the Buddha Chinarat Festival 6am–midnight); museum daily Wed–Sun 9am–4pm.

4 Sukhothai & Si Satchanalai Historical Parks

Sukhothai: 58km (36 miles) E of Phitsanulok; Si Satchanalai: 56km (35 miles) N of Sukhothai

The emergence of Sukhothai ("Dawn of Happiness" in Pali) in 1238 is considered the birth of the first Thai kingdom. Under King Ramkhamhaeng the Great, Sukhothai's influence covered a larger area than that of present-day Thailand. The ruins here are more intact and less encroached upon than those in Ayutthaya, making this the country's most gratifying historical site.

The **Sukhothai Historical Park,** the main attraction, is situated 12km (7½ miles) west of the town of Sukhothai, also known as **New Sukhothai.** There are a few little guesthouses outside of the park gates, but New Sukhothai offers more in the way of comfort and services, though not surprisingly, it lacks any of Old Sukhothai's historic grandeur.

Si Satchanalai, north of New Sukhothai, is another legacy of the Sukhothai kingdom. Visitors often enjoy these ruins the most, and they are certainly worth the 1-day detour.

ESSENTIALS
GETTING THERE
By Plane   From Bangkok, **Bangkok Airways** (© 02265-5678; www.bangkokair. com) operates two flights per week connecting the capital, Sukhothai, and Chiang Mai, through their private airport 27km (17 miles) from Sukhothai. Contact them in Chiang Mai (© 05328-1519), or at the Sukhothai airport (© 05564-7224). Bangkok Airways can arrange transfers to New Sukhothai by minivan for 90B (US$2.60/ £1.40).

By Train   The nearest rail station is in Phitsanulok (p. 282). From there you can **connect by local air-conditioned bus,** leaving hourly for New Sukhothai (1 hr.; 40B/US$1.15/60p) from the intercity terminal on Highway 12.

By Bus   Three daily first class, nonstop, air-conditioned buses leave from Bangkok (10am–10:30pm; trip time: 7½ hrs.; 328B/US$9.40/£5.05), departing from the **Northern Bus Terminal** (© 02576-5599). There are also more arduous second-class buses, but avoid them unless you're desperate. From Chiang Mai, **Win Tour** (© 05326-0295) operates air-conditioned service to Sukhothai hourly from 6:30am to 5:30pm (5hrs.; 218B/US$6.25/£3.35).

VISITOR INFORMATION
Sukhothai has no **TAT** office; the closest one is in Phitsanulok (© 05525-2742). There's a tourist police point (© 1155) opposite the Ramkhamhaeng National Museum. The main police station is at the junction of Singhawat and Si Intharathit roads. The **Sukhothai Hospital** (© 05561-0280) is at 2/1 Jarot Withithong Rd. The **Post Office** is down near the river on Nikhon Kasem Road.

ORIENTATION
Sukhothai Historical Park (or *meuang kao,* "old city") lies 12km (7½ miles) east of **New Sukhothai.** Built along the banks of the Yom River, New Sukhothai offers the bulk of the best accommodations options. The selection is growing—whether you're looking for laid-back cool or decked-out comfort, you're likely to find your desired niche. **Si Satchanalai Historic Park,** also along the Yom River, is 56km (35 miles) north of New Sukhothai.

SPECIAL EVENTS
The **Loy Krathong** festival here is an exceptional spectacle. This 3-day festival is held on the full moon of the 12th lunar month (usually Nov). Crowds gather at rivers, *klongs,* lakes, and temple fountains to drop small banana leaf floats or *krathong,* bearing candles, incense, a flower, and a coin. As the *krathong* glides downstream, it symbolizes

a letting go of the previous year's sins and unhappiness. Sukhothai celebrates with fireworks, traditional dancing, and a music and light show.

WHERE TO STAY
EXPENSIVE/MODERATE

Ananda Museum Gallery Hotel ⍟   Located to the east of New Sukhothai town (on the opposite side from the temples), Ananda is well designed, with pretty decor and lots of Thai elements, giving it more character than the rest of the area hotels. Artisan handicrafts and antiques are on display in the gallery.

10 Moo 4, Bantum Muang, Sukhothai 64000. ⓒ 05562-2428. Fax 05562-1885. www.anandasukhothai.com. 32 units. 2,500B–3,100B (US$71–US$89/£38–£48) double. MC, V. **Amenities:** 2 restaurants; bar and coffee lounge (in the gallery); spa; tour desk; limited room service; laundry service. *In room:* A/C, TV, fridge, minibar.

Lotus Village ⍟   This place has a spa, boutique, and an abundance of style. Garden paths connect the raised Thai-style bungalows, housing large, sturdy air-conditioned rooms with polished teak. The helpful owners, a Franco-Thai couple, can arrange a tour with a certified guide; plus, it's only a short walk from New Sukhothai's market and town center.

170 Ratchathanee Rd., Sukhothai 64000. ⓒ 05562-1484. Fax 05562-1463. www.lotus-village.com. 28 units. 600B (US$17/£9.25) double with fan; 800B (US$23/£12) A/C bungalow; 900B–1,100B (US$26–US$32/£14–£17) double with A/C. MC, V accepted on purchases over 2,000B (US$57/£31). **Amenities:** Restaurant; lounge; spa; tour desk; carrental desk; laundry service. *In room:* Fridge and minibar in deluxe only, no phone.

Pailyn Sukhothai Hotel ⍟   Pailyn's biggest advantage is its location, about halfway between the town and temples. The four-story structure is bright, modern, and comfortable, with a granite lobby, carpeted rooms, and a small pool and sun deck. Higher rates bring minibars, fridges, and TVs. The suites are enormous, but their bathrooms are a shade on the small side.

10/2 Moo 1, Jarot Withithong Rd., Sukhothai 64210. ⓒ 05561-3310. Fax 05561-3317. www.pailynhotel.com. 238 units. 950B–1,400B (US$23–US$34/£15–£22) double; from 2,600B (US$63/£40) suite. MC, V. **Amenities:** 2 restaurants; disco; pool; fitness center; sauna; tour desk; limited room service; massage; laundry service. *In room:* A/C, satellite TV, no phone.

Ruean Thai Hotel ⍟   Stay once at this charming establishment and it's likely you'll keep coming back. Rooms surround a pool, and the Thai-style design employs lots of wood and pretty antiques. Bathrooms are very spacious and there's a garden in which to kick back. (Watch out for the resident rabbits.) Ask if they can offer useful extras like complimentary breakfast and transfer to the bus station.

181/20 Jarot Withithong Rd., Sukhothai 64000. ⓒ 05561-2444. www.rueanthaihotel.com. 28 units. 1,200B–3,200B (US$34–US$91/£18–£49) double. MC, V. **Amenities:** Restaurant; pool; tour desk; sports rentals; massage; laundry service; Wi-Fi. *In room:* A/C, satellite TV, minibar, fridge.

Tharaburi Resort ⍟⍟⍟   After being remodeled from a simple backpacker pad to a high-class haven, this resort now boasts rooms covering a huge range of prices. Luxurious double rooms and suites are fitted with Jacuzzis, flat-screen TVs, and spacious balconies. The original guesthouse, Baan Thai, has been renovated and, if booked in advance, can accommodate a large family with its seven rooms and four bathrooms. Individual rooms in the house are also available.

11/3 Srisomboon Rd., Sukhothai 64000. ⓒ 05569-7132. Fax 05569-7131. www.tharaburiresort.com. 20 units. 900B–1,500B (US$26–US$43/£14–£23) double with A/C and shared bath; 4,500B (US$128/£69) double with Jacuzzi and DVD; 4,500B (US$128/£69) family suite with 2 bedrooms, 1 bath; 5,000B (US$143/£77) suite; 6,500B–7,500B

(US$185–US$214/£100–£115) house (incl. 7 bedrooms, 4 baths). MC, V. **Amenities:** Restaurant; pool; tour desk; limited room service; massage; laundry service; cooking course; Wi-Fi. *In room:* A/C, TV, fridge, minibar.

INEXPENSIVE

Ban Thai Guesthouse   Ban Thai is the best budget choice in New Sukhothai, and even if you don't stay here, you'll want to drop in, have a fruit shake, and peruse maps and their helpful advice book. If you have the cash, splash out on the newer bungalows with air-conditioning and private bathrooms. Great mountain biking tours are on offer daily.

38 Pravet Nakhon Rd., Sukhothai 64000. © **05561-0163.** 8 units. 150B (US$4.30/£2.30) with fan and shared bath; 250B (US$7/£3.85) bungalow with fan; 500B (US$14/£7.70) bungalow with A/C. No credit cards. **Amenities:** Restaurant; sports rentals; tour desk; laundry service. *In room:* A/C in some, no phone.

WHERE TO DINE

Eating in Sukhothai is all about sampling the city's famous dish, *kway tiaw,* or **Sukhothai noodles**—a mouth-watering plate of rice noodles with crispy pork, garlic, green beans, cilantro, chili, and peanuts in a broth seasoned with soy sauce. For the best, try **Baan Kru Iew** on Vichien Chamnong Road; **Kwaytiaw Thai Sukhothai,** on Jarot Withithong Road, close to the Ruean Thai Hotel (see above); or **Ta Bui,** on the left-hand side of the highway on the way to the historical park. New Sukhothai's **night food stalls** (close to the bus stop for the Historical Park) are also good for casual grazing.

Dream Café ✵ THAI/INTERNATIONAL   This is a cozy place bathed in warm, soft light. With its oddball collection of ceramics, memorabilia, and old jewelry, it looks more like an antiques store than a restaurant. In addition to Thai dishes, including many family recipes, Dream also serves excellent European and Chinese cuisine. Try the Sukhothai Fondue, a "cook-it-yourself" hot-pot of meat, veggies, and noodles. Save room for an ice-cream sundae for dessert.

86/1 Singhawat Rd. (center of new city). © **05561-2081.** Main courses 80B–200B (US$2.30–US$5.70/£1.25–£3.10). V. Daily 10am–10pm.

EXPLORING SUKHOTHAI ✵✵✵

In 1978, UNESCO named Sukhothai a World Heritage Site, and the Thai government, with international assistance, completed the preservation of these magnificent monuments and consolidated them with an excellent museum into one large park.

Every Saturday night at 10pm, a **"walking street"** outside the historical park comes alive with food, handicrafts, and cultural shows. It's a recent addition to Sukhothai nightlife and worth checking out. Also, from 7 to 8pm on Friday, Saturday, and Sunday, there is a **light and sound show** at the park, weather permitting.

GETTING TO THE SITE   You can reach the Sukhothai Historical Park by public bus, three-wheeled motorcycle taxi (a *samlor*), or private car. On Jarot Withithong Road, west of the traffic circle, you can catch an open-air public bus to the park entrance for 15B (43¢/25p). The *samlors* that cruise around New Sukhothai can be hired to whiz you out to the monuments on a 3-hour tour around the park for about 400B (US$11/£6.15). Bikes can be rented either from a stall next to the bus stop on the main Route 101, or from the Information Center; prices start at 20B (57¢/30p).

TOURING THE SITE   The best way to explore the ruins is by bicycle (see "Getting to the Site," above for info on rentals). Maps are available at the museum or at the bicycle rental shops near the entrance. The park is open daily 8:30am to 5pm; admission is 40B (US$1.15/60p) to the central area within the park walls, with additional charges of 30B (85¢/45p) for each of the four zones outside the walls of the park. Save money with a 150B (US$4.30/£2.30) **combination ticket** for admission to the Ramkhamhaeng National Museum, all areas of the Historical Park, Si Satchanalai National Park, and Sawankhaworanayok National Museum. Be sure to bring water and go early in the morning to beat the tour buses. Or, consider coming back in the evening with picnic provisions when it's cooler and the sun is going down.

SEEING THE HIGHLIGHTS

RAMAKHAMHAENG NATIONAL MUSEUM This museum, located in the center of the old city near the park entrance, houses a detailed model of the area, and an admirable display of Sukhothai and Si Satchanalai archaeological finds. Before exploring the temple sites, stop here for maps and information. It's open every day from 9am to 4pm; admission is 30B (78¢/45p). Call © **05569-7367** for info.

WAT PHRA MAHATHAT 🐸🐸 The most extraordinary monument in the park, this temple is dominated by a 14th-century lotus bud tower and encircled by a moat. Surrounding its unique Sukhothai-style *chedi* are several smaller towers of Sri Lankan and Khmer influence, and a grouping of Buddhist disciples in the adoration pose. An imposing cast-bronze seated Buddha used to be placed in front of the reliquary (this image, Phra Si Sakaya Muni, was removed in the 18th century to Bangkok's Wat Suthat). Be sure to examine the lowest platform (south side of Wat Phra Mahathat) and its excellent stucco sculpture, the crypt murals, and two elegant Sri Lankan–style *stupas* at the southeast corner of the site. Some of the best architectural ornamentation in Sukhothai is found on the upper, eastern-facing levels of the pediments in the main reliquary tower. Dancing figures, Queen Maya giving birth to Prince Siddhartha, and scenes from Buddha's life are among the best-preserved details.

WAT SI SAWAI Southwest of the palace, you'll come to this 12th-century Hindu shrine later converted to a Buddhist temple. The architecture is distinctly Khmer, with three Lopburi-style *prangs* commanding center stage.

OTHER MONUMENTS IN THE PARK Circling north, just west of Wat Phra Mahathat, is **Wat Traphang Tong,** set on its own pond. Though little remains other than an attractive *chedi,* the vistas of the surrounding monuments are among the most superb in the park. North of Wat Phra Mahathat is **Wat Chana Songkram,** where there's a Sri Lankan–style *stupa* of note. Nearby is **Wat Sa Si,** also on a small island.

Outside the old city walls, **Wat Phra Phai Luang,** lies 150m (500 ft.) beyond the northern gate. Originally a Hindu shrine, it housed a *lingam,* a phallic sculpture representing Shiva. To the northwest, **Wat Si Chum** holds one of the more astonishing and beautiful monuments in Sukhothai: a majestic seated Buddha 15m (50-ft.) tall, in the Subduing Evil pose.

A few kilometers west of the old city walls, the ruins of **Wat Saphan Hin** sit atop a hill that's visible for miles. It is worth the steep, 5-minute climb to visit the Phra Attaros Buddha, his right hand raised in the Dispelling Fear pose, and towering above the *wat*'s laterite remains.

LUNCH AT THE HISTORICAL PARK There are a number of small store-front eateries in and among the bike rental shops and souvenir stands at the gate of the park (just across from Ramkhamhaeng Museum).

EXPLORING SI SATCHANALAI 𝓰

Many people enjoy the secluded ruins at Si Satchanalai even more than those at Sukhothai, so try to make this day trip if you have the time. There is an **information center** at the park, and bicycles (20B/57¢/30p), tents (80B/US$2.30/£1.25), and sleeping bags (20B/57¢/30p) for rent if you'd like to camp near the park entrance. It's open daily from 8:30am to 5pm. Admission is 40B (US$1.15/60p) unless you have a **combination ticket.**

A LOOK AT THE PAST   Si Satchanalai's riverside site was crucial to the development of its famous ceramics industry. More than 1,000 kilns operated along the river, producing highly prized pots that carried a greenish-gray glaze known as celadon. These were eventually exported throughout Asia. Academics believe that ceramic manufacture began more than 1,000 years ago at Ban Ko Noi (there's a small site museum 6km/3¾ miles north of Satchanalai) and ceramic shards are today sold as souvenirs.

GETTING TO THE SITE   Si Satchanalai is north of New Sukhothai on Route 101. Buses from Sukhothai depart every half-hour from the bus stop on Jarot Withithong Road for 38B (US$1.10/60p). Just ask the driver to let you off at "meuang kao" (old city). There are two stops; the second is closer to the park entrance, across the river. The last bus returns at 4:30pm. A taxi, private car, or guided tour can also be arranged through your hotel or guesthouse.

In addition, a daily "Sprinter" express (train 3) runs daily at 10:50am (7hrs.; 482B/US$14/£7.40) from Bangkok to Sawankhalok, 20km (12½ miles) south of Si Satchanalai park, stopping at Phitsanulok on the way. The train returns to Bangkok at 7:40pm. It is second-class, with air-conditioning but no sleepers, and fare includes dinner and breakfast. For information, call Bangkok's **Hua Lampong Railway Station** (© 1690) or the **Phitsanulok Railway Station** (© 05525-8005).

SEEING THE HIGHLIGHTS

WAT CHANG LOM   The discovery of presumed relics of Lord Buddha at this site during the reign of King Ramakhamhaeng prompted the construction of the temple, an event described in stone inscriptions found at Sukhothai. Thirty-nine elephant buttresses surround a central *stupa*—it's unusual to find so many elephant forms intact. From the base of the *stupas* you can admire the 19 Buddhas installed in niches above the terrace.

WAT CHEDI CHET THAEW   Opposite Wat Chang Lom to the south, within sandstone walls, this *wat* is distinguished by a series of lotus bud towers and rows of *chedis* resembling those at Sukhothai's Wat Phra Mahathat and thought to contain the remains of the royal family.

OTHER MONUMENTS IN THE PARK   You can see most of the monuments within the ancient city walls in an hour. Nothing compares to **Wat Phra Si Ratana Mahathat,** located 1km (⅗-mile) southeast of the big bridge and directly adjacent to the footbridge connecting to the main road. The exterior carving and sculpture are superb, particularly the walking Buddha done in relief.

5 Tak Province: Mae Sot & The Myanmar (Burma) Border

Tak: 138km (86 miles) W of Phitsanulok. Mae Sot: 80km (50 miles) W of Tak

Tak Province doesn't get a lot of tourists, possibly because it's considered the hottest province in the kingdom, but it's certainly not lacking in natural beauty. It is home to

Bhumibol Dam, the country's largest, and is covered in lush forests once used as hideouts by Thai Communists. Rugged Umphang boasts some of the best trekking and whitewater rafting in the kingdom, and its wildlife sanctuary rewards the patient nature lover. Mae Sot, which sits a few kilometers from the border with Myanmar (Burma), displays all the hallmarks of a small border town, and for decades has played host to refugee camps for Myanmar's fleeing hordes, many of whom are from the persecuted Karen tribe. Since the political unrest in Myanmar in late September 2007, many more ethnic Burmese have fled across this border. In terms of tourism, the province is likely to stay relatively undeveloped, though.

ESSENTIALS
GETTING THERE
By Plane   There's an airport in Tak, but currently no flights serve the province.

By Bus   From Bangkok's **Northern Bus Terminal** (℃ 02576-5599), one first-class, air-conditioned bus leaves for **Tak** city's bus terminal (℃ 05551-1057) daily at 10pm. The trip takes 6½ hours and rates are 313B/US$9/£4.80. There are also three second-class trips per day, but travel on those buses can be slow and uncomfortable.

From **Bangkok to Mae Sot**'s bus terminal (℃ 05556-3435), a VIP bus runs four times daily, from 9:30pm to 10:40pm (8 hrs.; 610B/US$17/£9.40). First-class buses leave three times daily from 9am to 10:20pm (8 hrs.; 394B/US$11/£6.05).

There are also second-class connections from **Phitsanulok's Bus Terminal** (℃ 05521-2090) to Tak (8 departures daily; trip time 3 hrs.; 90B/US$2.60/£1.40) and hourly to Mae Sot from 7am to 3pm (5 hrs.; 153B/US$4.40/£2.35).

Privately operated minivans connect Tak and Mae Sot, leaving when they're full (about every half-hour), for about 60B (US$1.70/90p) per person. Trip time is 1½ hours. There are good buses operated by the **Green Bus Line** (℃ 01141-8000) from Mae Sot to Tak and on to Lampang and Chiang Mai (departs 6am and 8am from Mae Sot; 7 hrs. to Chiang Mai; 315B/US$9/£4.85).

From the bus terminals in Tak and Mae Sot, motorcycle taxis, *samlors,* and *songtaews* wait to take you to any hotel for about 40B (US$1.15/60p).

VISITOR INFORMATION
Tak has a **TAT** office near the bus terminal, at 193 Taksin Road (℃ 05551-3584).

SPECIAL EVENTS
Every year from December 28 to January 3, the **Taksin Maharachanuson Fair** is held in Tak to honor King Taksin the Great. The streets around his shrine (on Taksin Rd. at the north side of town) fill with food vendors, dancers, musicians, and monks. The shrine is decorated with floral wreaths and gold fabric to welcome pilgrims.

FAST FACTS
In Tak, there are a handful of **ATMs** along Mahat Thai Bamrung Road, and where it meets Thetsaban 1 Road, there's a **police station.** In Mae Sot, banks with ATMs are located on the main thoroughfare, on Prasat Withee Road. The **post office** in Mae Sot is on Intharakhiri Road diagonally opposite the main police station. There are a number of **Internet** cafes along Intharakhiri Road in the center of Mae Sot, the largest being inside the Southeast Express Tours office.

WHERE TO STAY

TAK

Suansin Lanna Garden Resort   This new establishment offers excellent value in a city that previously had very few accommodations options. Rooms (doubles and triples) are decorated simply in yellows and creams, with pretty, dark wood furniture, and have TVs and air-conditioning. Plus, the place is clean as a whistle. You can dine outside on the restaurant's delightful, shady terrace.

8 Moo 8, Paholyothin Rd., Tak 63000. © 05551-7777. www.suansin.com. 76 units. 250B (US$7.15/£3.85) double with fan; 350B (US$10/£5.40) double with A/C. No credit cards. **Amenities:** Restaurant; laundry service. *In room:* A/C, satellite TV, fridge.

Viang Tak 2 ✪   This unremarkable Ping River low-rise offers good service and a surprisingly wide range of amenities, including a pool and Internet cafe. The location isn't bad at all, just a 5-minute tuk-tuk ride from the bus terminal at 236 Jompol Rd. Check to see if breakfast is included. Its older sibling, the original Viang Tak, is sadly past its prime; only use it as a last option.

236 Jompol Rd., Tak 63000. © 05551-2507. www.viangtakhotel.com. 144 units. 600B–2,100B (US$17–US$60/£9.25–£32) double. AE, MC, V. **Amenities:** Restaurant; 2 lounges; pool; convention hall; massage; snooker; laundry service. *In room:* A/C, satellite TV, fridge.

MAE SOT
Moderate

Centara Mae Sot Hill Resort ✪   This contemporary four-story hotel is built in two long wings fanning out from a classy open atrium lobby. This is the highest standard in town and makes for a comfortable base from which to explore the area. The staff is helpful and can arrange tours and onward travel. All rooms have modern amenities and views of the mist-shrouded, wooded hills. Check if the rate you are offered can include breakfast.

100 Asia Rd., Mae Sot, Tak 63110. © 05553-2601. Fax 05553-2600. www.centralhotelsresorts.com. 115 units. 1,600B (US$45/£25) standard; 1,800B (US$51/£28) deluxe; 2,500B (US$71/£38) suite. MC, V. **Amenities:** 2 restaurants; lounge; 2 pools; 2 outdoor tennis courts; disco; limited room service; laundry service; nonsmoking rooms. *In room:* A/C, satellite TV, minibar, fridge.

First Hotel *(Finds* ✪   First Hotel's dull concrete exterior belies an interior that's like a wood-carved wedding cake, with intricate representations of flora and fauna. Standard rooms have large carved headboards and furnishings, as well as tidy marble baths. It all adds up to a memorable place to stay, right in the town center.

444 Intharakiri Rd., Mae Sot, Tak 63110. © 05553-1233. Fax 05553-1340. 35 units. 270B (US$7.70/£4.15) double with fan; 450B (US$13/£6.90) double with A/C. No credit cards. **Amenities:** Laundry service. *In room:* A/C, TV, no phone.

Inexpensive

Mae Sot has quite a number of small, affordable guesthouses lining the main street. **DK Hotel** (298/2 Intharakiri Rd. near the police station; © 05553-1378) is a local business hotel with fan rooms starting at 250B (US$7.15/£3.85) and 400B (US$11/£6.15) with air-conditioning. **Ban Thai** (740 Intharakiri Rd.; © 05553-1590) also offers rooms from 250B (US$7.15/£3.85).

DINING IN MAE SOT

Khaomao-Khaofang Restaurant ✪ THAI   This little oasis along the Burmese border verges on the surreal, but the food is delicious. Ponds overgrown with lush vegetation surround an enormous central thatched pavilion. Be sure to go to the bathroom, even if you don't have to; these water closets are large grottos with flushable fixtures at odd heights and stalactites hanging from the ceiling. The menu surveys the whole country, with an emphasis on curries and authentic spice. Portions are small, so order up a few dishes, and ask about the daily specials.

382 Moo 9, Maepa, Maesod (head for the Myanmar border, turn north just before the checkpoint, and follow the hwy. 2km/1¼ mile). © 05553-2483. Fax 05553-3607. Main courses 60B–180B (US$1.70–US$5.15/90p–£2.75). AE, MC, V. Daily 10am–10pm.

Krua Canadian INTERNATIONAL   This restaurant's name is Thai for "Canadian kitchen," and that's just how it feels—as if you've been invited into the home of Canadian Dave and his wife, Chulee. From this simple, central storefront, they serve hearty breakfasts, local coffee, and a unique tofu burger that is messy and delicious. Drop in for a drink and for some advice on local happenings.

3 Si Panich Rd. Mae Sot. © 05553-4659. Main course 50B–150B (US$1.40–US$4.30/75p–£2.30). No credit cards. Daily 7am–10pm.

EXPLORING THE AREA

Mae Sot is perched on the Myanmar border and the area is always buzzing with trade. The town has a surplus of Burmese woven cotton blankets, lacquerware, jewelry, bronze statues, cotton sarongs, and wicker ware. Business is conducted in Thai baht, U.S. dollars, or Myanmar kyat.

There is a dark side to the border, though: Trade means not just the movement of produce and crafts, but drugs, precious stones, and women (or children) for prostitution. There's something disquieting about the many European luxury cars parked in front of two-story brick homes lining this village's main street—they hint at the substantial illegal profiteering. Be careful about buying gems unless you know what you're doing; you can find yourself walking away with a handful of plastic and a dent in your wallet. The border also sees a heavy flow of refugees, especially since the anti-government uprisings in September 2007, and there are a number of camps in the surrounding hills. Cynthia Maung, a tireless Karen doctor, runs **Mae Tao clinic** and refugee camp on the outskirts of Mae Sot, helping to treat the thousands who cross this border in search of help. The camp is not open to visitors, but there are ways to get involved. Contact them at P.O. Box 67, Mae Sot, Tak 63110 (© **05553-3644**).

The border between Mae Sot (at the town of Rim Moei) and Myawaddy, Myanmar, is open daily 8am to 4:30pm, and—when relations are good—you can cross the bridge on foot or by car with a 1-day visa on arrival for 410B (US$11/£6.30). Many visitors cross for a day just for a glimpse of Burmese culture. Remember that any official fees you pay to the Myanmar government only add to their coffers, though.

Highland Farm and Gibbon Sanctuary (© **09958-0821**; www.highland-farm. org), along Route 1090 on the way south to Umpang, is often included in day trips of the area. Gibbons, which are small apes, can be gentle, playful creatures, and for that very reason are prized as pets. This facility provides a refuge for gibbons that have been abandoned or abused. You can tour the site; they also have volunteer and homestay programs (900B/US$25/£14 per night; see website for details).

Along the Asia Highway, 25km (15½ miles) east of Tak, is the **Taksin Maharat National Park,** known as the home of *Krabak Yai,* Thailand's largest tree. A hike brings you to this colossal tree beside a stream—it takes 16 people's stretched arms to wrap around the conifer. Accommodations are available at the park (© **05551-1429**).

Park admission is 200B (US$5.70/£3.10) for adults and 100B (US$2.85/£1.55) for children.

Trekking and rafting in this remote area is gaining popularity, but it may not remain unspoiled for long. At the moment, however, Mae Sot is still far behind its northern neighbors when it comes to organized trips. One quality agency is **Mae Sot Conservation Tours,** 415 Intarakeeree Rd. (©/fax **05553-2818**). They offer 3-day, 2-night trips that visit the Mae Klong River and Tee Lo Su waterfall, including elephant trekking. You'll overnight in jungle tents or in a Karen village. The price of the tour is 3,000B (US$86/£46).

11

Exploring Northern Thailand

Northern Thailand is home to the majority of Thailand's more than 700,000 tribal peoples, many of whom emigrated from Laos, southwestern China, Myanmar (Burma), and Tibet, and retain their traditional costumes, religion, art, and way of life. Opportunities to visit these distinctive ethnic enclaves and to enjoy the region's scenic beauty make the rural north one of the country's most popular destinations.

Hill-tribes traditionally practiced slash-and-burn agriculture: burning forests to clear land; planting poppies as a cash crop; and then setting up new bamboo and thatch villages whenever their farmland's soil became depleted. This unsustainable practice has now changed.

Visitors should practice cultural awareness and encourage only positive methods of sustainable tourism (i.e., trek with local guides and avoid littering or damaging the natural environment).

Both self-guided trips and scheduled tours—by car or motorbike—are great ways to get around the area. Hill-tribe tours and trekking are also very popular activities and bring visitors into intimate contact with the hospitable minority groups of the north. Many use Chiang Mai as a hub for forays into the surrounding hills. With its cooler climes and pleasant towns, it is a great region to get adventurous and explore.

1 The Land & Its People

THE REGION IN BRIEF

Northern Thailand is composed of 15 provinces and borders Myanmar (Burma) to the northwest and Laos to the northeast. This verdant, mountainous terrain, which includes Thailand's largest mountain, 2563m (8,408-ft.) Doi Inthanon, supports nomadic farming, teak logging at high altitudes, and systematic agriculture in the valleys. The hill-tribes' traditional poppy crops have largely been replaced with rice, tobacco, soybeans, corn, and sugarcane. Northeast of Chiang Mai, lowland farmers also cultivate seasonal fruits such as strawberries, longan *(lamyai),* mandarin oranges, mango, and melon. The lush fields and winding rivers make sightseeing—particularly in the spring—a visual treat. Lumber (especially teak), textiles, mining, handicrafts, and tourism-related industries also contribute to the growing northern economy.

A LOOK AT THE REGION'S PAST

In the late 13th century, King Mengrai united several Tai tribes that had migrated from southern China and built the first capital of the Lanna kingdom in Chiang Rai. Mengrai, whose rule was characterized by strategic alliances, was threatened by Mongol emperor Kublai Khan and his incursion into Myanmar (Burma). He quickly forged ties with the powerful kingdom of Sukhothai in the south. The Lanna king vanquished the vestiges of the Mon Empire in Lamphun and, in 1296, moved his new capital south to what is now Chiang Mai. There is a monument to King Mengrai, around the corner from Chiang Mai's Wat Phan Tao, where he is said to have been struck by lightning and killed in 1317.

For the next century, Chiang Mai prospered and the Lanna kingdom grew, absorbing most of what now comprises the Northern provinces. In cahoots, Chiang Mai and Sukhothai were able to resist significant attacks from Khmer and Mon neighbors. After the Lanna dynasty absorbed Sukhothai, forces from Ayutthaya tried repeatedly to take Chiang Mai, but the city refused to yield. Instead, Chiang Mai grew in strength and prospered until the late 16th century, when it eventually fell to the Burmese in 1557.

After 2 centuries of relentless warfare, the Burmese captured Chiang Mai in 1558, and for the next 2 centuries the Lanna kingdom was a Burmese vassal—Burmese culture is still in evidence today, especially with regard to clothing and cuisine. After Lampang's Lord or "Chao" Kavila recaptured Chiang Mai from the Burmese in 1775, the city was so weakened that Kavila moved its surviving citizens to nearby Lampang. For 2 decades, Chiang Mai was akin to a ghost town. Though the city was still nominally under the control of local princes, their power continued to decline, and in 1939 Chiang Mai was formally incorporated into the modern Thai nation.

A PORTRAIT OF THE HILL-TRIBE PEOPLE

The north is a tapestry of the divergent customs and cultures of the many tribes that migrated from China or Tibet to Myanmar (Burma), Laos, and Vietnam and ultimately settled in Thailand's Northern provinces such as Chiang Rai, Chiang Mai, Mae Hong Son, Phayao, and Nan. The six main tribes are the Karen, Akha (also known as the Kaw), Lahu (Mussur), Lisu (Lisaw), Hmong (Meo), and Mien (Yao), each with subgroups that are linked by history, lineage, language, costume, social organization, and religion.

Hill-tribes in northern Thailand are sub-divided into Sino-Tibetan speakers (Hmong, Mien) and Tibeto-Burman speakers (Lahu, Akha, Lisu, and Karen), though most now speak some Thai.

In addition, tribes are divided geographically into lowland, or valley dwellers, who grow cyclical crops such as rice or corn, and high-altitude dwellers, who traditionally grew opium poppies. The so-called indigenous tribes who have occupied the same areas for hundreds of years are those that tend to inhabit the lower valleys in organized villages of split-log huts. The nomadic groups generally live above 1,000m (3,250 ft.) in easy-to-assemble bamboo and thatch housing, ready to resettle when required.

Highland minorities believe in spirits, and it is the role of the village shaman, or spiritual leader, to understand harbingers and prescribe appeasing rites.

KAREN An estimated 350,000 Karen make up the largest tribal group in Thailand, accounting for more than half of all tribal people in the country. In nearby Myanmar (Burma), it is estimated that there are more than four million people of Karen descent (who are practicing Buddhist and Christians). For years, the Burmese government has been suppressing Karen independence fighters who want an autonomous homeland. Many Burmese Karen have sought refuge in Thailand, ranging from Chiang Rai to as far south as Kanchanaburi. Practicing either Buddhism or an amalgamation of Christianity absorbed from missionaries and ancient animism, Karen can be easily identified by their method of greeting one another: an exaggerated, hearty handshake.

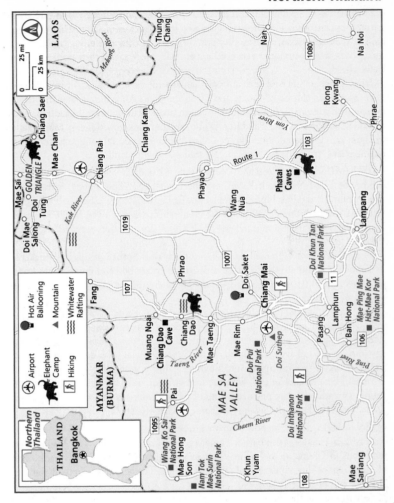

The Karen are among the most assimilated of Thailand's hill-tribes, making it difficult to identify them by any outward appearance. However, the most traditional tribespeople wear silver armbands and don a beaded sash and headband, while unmarried women wear all white.

HMONG (MEO)   The Hmong are a nomadic tribe scattered throughout Southeast Asia and China. About 150,000 Hmong live in Thailand, with the greatest number residing in Chiang Mai, Chiang Rai, Nan, Phetchabun, and Phrae provinces; there are approximately four million Hmong living in China. Within Thailand, there are several subgroups; the Hmong Daw (White Hmong) and the Hmong Njua (Blue Hmong) are the main divisions. The Hmong Gua Mba (Armband Hmong) is a subdivision of the Hmong Daw.

Hmong live in the highlands, cultivating corn, rice, and soybeans, which are grown as subsistence crops. Their wealth is displayed in a vast array of silver jewelry. Women are easily recognized by the way they pile their hair into an enormous bun on top of their heads. The Hmong are also excellent animal breeders, and their ponies are especially prized.

Hmong are pantheistic and rely on shamans to perform spiritual rites. Hmong place particular emphasis on the use of doors: doors for entering and exiting the human world, doors to houses, doors to let in good fortune and to block bad spirits, and doors to the afterlife. The Hmong also worship their ancestors—a reverberation of their Chinese past. Since they're skilled entrepreneurs, Hmong are increasingly moving down from the highlands to ply trades in the lowlands.

LAHU (MUSSUR)   The Lahu people (pop. 82,000) are composed of two main bands: the Lahu Na (Black Lahu) and the Lahu Shi (Yellow Lahu), with a much smaller number of Lahu Hpu (White Lahu), La Ba, and Abele. Most Lahu villages are situated above 1,000m (3,250 ft.) in the mountains around Chiang Mai, Chiang Rai, Mae Hong Son, Tak, and Kamphaeng Phet, where "dry soil" rice, corn, and other cash crops are grown.

The *lingua franca* in the hills is Thai, but many of the other groups can speak a little Lahu. The Lahu are skilled musicians, and their bamboo and gourd flutes feature prominently in their compositions—flutes are often used by young men to woo the woman of their choice.

Originally animists, the Lahu adopted the worship of a deity called G'ui sha (possibly Tibetan in origin), borrowed the practice of merit-making from Buddhism (Indian or Chinese), and ultimately incorporated Christian (British/Burmese) theology into their belief system. G'ui sha is the Supreme Being who created the universe and rules over all spirits. Spirits inhabit animate and inanimate objects, making them capable of benevolence or evil, with the soul functioning as the spiritual force within people. In addition, they practice a kind of Lahu voodoo, as well as following a messianic tradition. The Lahu warmly welcome foreign visitors.

MIEN (YAO)   There are now estimated to be 42,000 Mien living in Thailand, concentrated in Chiang Rai, Phayao, Lampang, and Nan provinces. The Mien are still numerous in China, as well as in Vietnam, Myanmar (Burma), and Laos. Like the Hmong, tens of thousands of Mien fled to northern Thailand from Vietnam and Laos after the end of the Vietnam War.

Even more than the Hmong, the Mien (the name is thought to come from the Chinese word for "barbarian") are closely connected to their origins in southern China. They incorporated an ancient version of southern Chinese into their own writing and oral language, and many Mien legends, history books, and religious tracts are recorded in this rarely understood script. The Mien people also assimilated ancestor worship and a form of Taoism into their theology, in addition to celebrating their New Year on the same date as the Chinese, using the same lunar calculations.

Mien farmers practice slash-and-burn agriculture but do not rely on opium poppies, choosing instead to cultivate rice (grown in soil, not paddy fields) and maize. The women produce rather elaborate and elegant embroidery, which often adorns their clothing. Their silver work is intricate and highly prized, even by other tribes, particularly the Hmong. Much of Mien religious art appears to be strongly influenced by Chinese design, particularly Taoist (Daoist) motifs, clearly distinguishing it from other tribes' work.

LISU (LISAW)   The Lisu represent less than 5% of all hill-tribe people. They arrived in Chiang Rai province in the 1920s, migrating from nearby Myanmar (Burma), and in time some intermarried with the Lahu and ethnic Chinese. The Lisu occupy high ground and, traditionally, grew opium poppies as well as other subsistence crops. Their traditional clothing is vibrant, with brightly colored tunics punctuated by hundreds of silver beads and trinkets.

The Lisu live well-structured lives; everything from birth to courtship to marriage to death is ruled by an orthodox tradition, with much borrowed from the Chinese.

AKHA (KAW)   Of all the tradition-bound tribes, the Akha, accounting for only 10% of all hill-tribe people living in Thailand, have probably maintained the most profound connection with their past. At great events in one's life, the full name (often more than 50 generations of titles) of an Akha is proclaimed, with each name symbolic of a lineage dating back more than 1,000 years. All aspects of life are governed by the Akha Way: an all-encompassing system of myth, ritual, plant cultivation, courtship and marriage, birth, death, dress, and healing.

The first Akha migrated from Myanmar (Burma) to Thailand in the beginning of the 20th century, originally settling in the highlands above the Kok River in Chiang Rai province. Today, they are increasingly migrating to the lower altitudes within China and Indochina in search of more arable land. They are "shifting" cultivators, depending on subsistence crops planted in rotation and raising domestic animals for their livelihood.

The clothing of the Akha is regarded as one of the most attractive of all the hill-tribes. Simple black jackets with skillful embroidery are the everyday attire for both men and women. Akha shoulder bags—woven with exceptional skill—are adorned with silver coins and all sorts of baubles and beads.

2 When to Go

THE CLIMATE   Northern Thailand has three distinct seasons. The **hot season** (Mar–May) is dry, with temperatures up to 97°F (36°C). Many Thais vacation in this region to get away from scorching temperatures elsewhere. The **rainy season** (June–Oct) is cooler, with the heaviest daily rainfall in September (predictably heavy daily afternoon downpours). While trekking and outdoor activities are still possible, rainy and mud should be taken into consideration. The **cool season** (Nov–Feb) is brisk, with daytime temperatures as low as 59°F (21°C) in Chiang Mai town, and 41°F (5°C) in the hills. Bring a sweater and some warm socks. November to May is the best time for trekking, with February, March, and April (when southern Thailand gets extremely hot) usually the most crowded months. In October and November, after the rainfall, the forests are lush, rivers swell, and waterfalls are more splendid than usual.

FESTIVALS   Northern Thailand celebrates many unique festivals—even the nation-wide ones—in different ways than the rest of the country. Many Thais travel to participate in these festivals and advance booking in hotels is a must.

NORTHERN THAILAND CALENDAR OF EVENTS

Many of these annual events are based on the lunar calendar. Contact the **Tourism Authority of Thailand** (TAT; ✆ 02694-1222; www.tourismthailand.org) in Bangkok for exact dates.

January

Umbrella Festival, Bo Sang. Held in a village of umbrella craftspeople and painters about 9km (5.5 miles) east of Chiang Mai, the Umbrella Festival features handicraft competitions, an elephant show, and a local parade. Third weekend of January.

February

Flower Festival, Chiang Mai. Celebrates the city's undisputed accolade as the "Rose of the North" with a parade, concerts, flower displays, and competitions. A food fair and a beauty contest take place at the Buak Hat Park, on the first weekend in February.

King Mengrai Festival, Chiang Rai. Known for its special hill-tribe cultural displays and a fine handicrafts market (early Feb).

Sakura Blooms Flower Fair, Doi Mae Salong. Sakura (Japanese cherry trees) were imported to this hilly village 50 years ago by fleeing members of China's Nationalist, or Kuomintang, party (KMT). Their abundant blossoms bring numerous sightseers. Early to mid-February.

March

Poy Sang Long. A traditional Shan ceremony honoring Buddhist novices—widely celebrated in the northwestern town of Mae Hong Son. Late March or early April.

April

Songkran (Water) Festival. Thai New Year is celebrated at home and in more formal ceremonies at *wats*. Presents and merit-making acts are offered and water is "splashed" over Buddha figures, monks, elders, and tourists to celebrate the beginning of the harvest and ensure good fortune. Those who don't want a good soaking should avoid the streets. The festival is celebrated in all Northern provinces and throughout the country, but Chiang Mai's celebration is notorious for being the longest (up to 10 days) and the rowdiest. The first day is always April 13.

May

Visakha Bucha. Honors the birth, enlightenment, and death of the Lord Buddha on the first full moon day in May. Celebrated nationwide, it is a particularly dramatic event in Chiang Mai, where residents walk up Mount (Doi) Suthep in homage.

Harvest Festival, Kho Loi Park, Chiang Rai. This festival honors the harvest of litchis (lychees), a small, fragrant fruit encased in bumpy red skin. There is a parade, litchi competition and display, a beauty contest to find Miss Chiang Rai Litchi Nut, and lots of great food. Mid-May.

Mango Fair, Chiang Mai. This fair honors mangoes, the favorite local crop. Second weekend in May.

August

Longan (lamyai) Fair, Lamphun. Celebrates another of the town's favorite fruits and one of Thailand's largest foreign-exchange earners. There is even a Miss Longan competition. First or second weekend of August.

October

Lanna Boat Races. In mid- to late October, Nan Province holds 2 days of boat racing, with wildly decorated, long, low-slung crafts zipping down the Nan River. The Lanna Boat Races are run 7 days after the "Rains' Retreat," marking the beginning of the dry season.

November

Loy Krathong. Occurs nationwide on the full moon, on the 12th lunar month. Small *krathongs* (banana-leaf floats bearing candles incense and garlands) are sent downriver to carry away the previous year's sins. In Chiang Mai, the waterborne offerings are floated on the Ping River. In the city, enormous 1m-tall paper lanterns *(khom)* are released in the night sky; and there's a parade of women in traditional costumes. Late October to mid-November.

December
Day of Roses, Chiang Mai. Exhibitions and cultural performances are held in Buak Hat Park. First weekend in December.

3 Getting There & Getting Around

GETTING THERE

Before the 1920s, when the railway's Northern Line to Chiang Mai was completed, one traveled throughout this area either by long-tail boat or elephant. So when your train ride gets boring or the flight is crowded, remember that the original trip here took more than 2 weeks.

BY PLANE   Thai Airways, Bangkok Airways, and new budget carriers One-Two-GO, Nok Air, and Air Asia all fly from Bangkok to Chiang Mai, Chiang Rai, Mae Hong Son, Nan and Phrae. SGA Airways' excellent light aircraft service links Pai and Chiang Rai with Chiang Mai. There are also flights between many of these destinations and to, or from, Phitsanulok (in central Thailand). Bangkok Airways connects Bangkok and Chiang Mai with a stop in Sukhothai in the central plains. See destination chapters for details.

BY TRAIN   Express and rapid trains leave Bangkok daily for Chiang Mai, the northern terminus. Sleeper cars are available on certain trains and are highly recommended for the 13-hour overnight trip (reserve as early as possible). See destination chapters for details.

BY BUS   There are dozens of daily and nightly air-conditioned VIP buses to Chiang Mai and other northern cities, as well as a cheaper, less comfortable, bus from Bangkok's Northern Bus Terminal. See destination chapters for details.

GETTING AROUND

BY TAXI   In late 2004, a dozen or so new taxis finally arrived in Chiang Mai heralding what was hoped to be the advent of metered fares. But, because of the simple laws of demand, they simply set up their own work hours and rules. Often drivers refuse to use the meter except for very short hops, easily charging up to 100 times Bangkok rates. They are hard to find on weekdays and even harder to hire on Sundays—when taxi drivers take their families out. If you can find one, negotiate hard and ask for the driver's namecard and mobile phone number. Many drivers are ex-army or police and therefore do not take kindly to accusations of racketeering; it's often foolish (and pointless) to take them to task.

BY PUBLIC BUS   There's a frequent, inexpensive bus service between Chiang Mai and other northern cities. You'll also find *songtaews* (shared pickup trucks) fitted with long bench seats (also known locally as *seelor*) along the streets of Chiang Mai as well as all the major roads throughout the north. They have no fixed schedule, stopping points, or price; just flag them down and ask how much they are.

Tips on Jungle Trekking

You won't have any problems finding a trek—there are many companies, from small storefronts to hotel concierges that offer treks out of Chiang Mai, Chiang Rai, Mae Hong Son, and Pai—what presents some difficulty is finding the right mix of experienced and knowledgeable guides, an intelligent itinerary, a compatible group, and appropriate timing, all at a reasonable price. Be sure to ask for specifics before departure, because once you're out on the trail there will no longer be any room for debate. Consider the criteria below for any tour.

THE GUIDE If there's one single element of a trek that will make or break the experience, it is the guide. Few guides are native to these jungles—although some have quite a few years of experience and most can speak the relevant phrases of a few hill-tribe languages (though their command of English is perhaps most important). All guides are required to attend a special 1-month course at Chiang Mai University and must be licensed by the Tourism Authority. Hill-tribe guides are familiar with the best trails, are well informed about the area and people, and are usually pretty interesting characters. Try to meet your prospective guide and ask lots of questions before signing on.

THE ITINERARY Several well-known Chiang Mai agencies offer regularly scheduled routes. Any company can arrange custom tours for a higher fee. Be sure to get specifics about daily schedules. Most treks involve transport to and from the start and end-point of the trek. How long does it take and what are the conditions? Expect 3 to 6 hours of unhurried walking each day. Gauge your fitness level and adjust to that or adjust the itinerary. When is lunch/dinner each day? What is lunch/dinner? What are the sleeping arrangements? Nearly all trekking itineraries list the various hill-tribe villages visited; try to read as much as you can and decide for yourself which you'd most like to see.

THE GROUP You can end up making lifelong friends on trekking trips and, conversely, spend uncomfortably long days and nights in the company of folks with whom you wouldn't want to share a cab ride, much less days in the jungle. If you're planning a long, arduous trip, try to meet your fellow travelers before committing; you might find that their stamina, assumptions, interests, and/or personalities are not compatible with yours. Look for an agency that limits the number of people to about ten per trek. Having at least four in the group minimizes personality clashes and adds conviviality.

THE SEASON See "When to Go" earlier in this chapter.

WHAT TO BRING Most trekkers come to Thailand on vacation, totally unprepared for a serious trek, but trekkers should pack differently. Most routes require good sneakers or walking shoes. A wool sweater for evenings and some outerwear to sleep in will come in handy (many trekking companies only provide blankets). It's best to wear long trousers because of dense underbrush, leeches, and mosquitoes. A flashlight, supply of tissues or toilet paper, mosquito repellent, and a basic first-aid kit with blister remedies is also recommended.

Some groups bring gifts for remote villages. Ask your guide for specifics, because he may know the needs of the villagers in the places you'll be visiting. It sounds heartless, but charitable trusts in the Third World ask that visitors do not give away the likes of pens and sweets, as this reinforces unsustainable habits that result in begging and harassment of foreigners.

PRICE   Even the most expensive treks cost less than 1 night at a hotel and three restaurant meals. Some negotiation may be in order, especially if you are traveling with a larger group of people. Expect to pay between 1,500B–4,500B (US$43–US$129/£23–£69) per person per night, depending on the itinerary. Typically, food, transport and equipment (backpack, water bottle, and so on) are included in the fee. *Caution:* Be sure to get specifics about what is included. Once on the trail, there are no negotiations, and many a trekker comes down from the hills tired, angry, and feeling "taken," because of some minor misunderstanding. "You get what you pay for," of course, but be sure that you know what you'll get *before* you pay.

SAFETY   Never set out on your own on a trek. Despite the best efforts of local authorities, it is impossible to police the jungle and there are still some occurrences of banditry on village trails. Do not bring any valuables with you on your trek. You can make arrangements with your hotel or guesthouse in town, or even the trekking company you go with, to stow things safely.

A NOTE ON DRUGS   This region (which is close to the famed Golden Triangle and smuggler trails from nearby Myanmar) is still notorious for the availability of drugs, especially opium. Despite government crackdowns and programs to move hill-tribe economies to reliance on more sustainable farming of alternative produce, you may be offered opium, or even invited to the village opium den. If the dangers of taking illegal and addictive drugs in a rural village aren't obvious, consider the financial and cultural impact of supporting local drug economies and encouraging poor models of cultural exchange. Don't forget the corruption factor either. Narcotic use is illegal and the Thai government imposes a ruthless, zero-tolerance policy on drug use. Trek guides, many of whom are addicted to opium, are tested, and tour operators run the risk of being shut down if found promoting drug use on their treks. Drug dealers or addicts are often executed. Foreigners, if they're lucky, merely go to prison for life.

BY CAR   Renting your own car offers you freedom and the chance to see some beautiful countryside at your own pace; main roads are well-paved with frequent petrol stations. It must be stressed, however, that upcountry driving regulations do not really exist, and in some seasons—especially at festivals—drunk driving, passing on blind bends, or overtaking in the lane reserved solely for uphill drivers is especially common. Both **Budget Car Rental** and **Avis** have branches in Chiang Mai and Chiang Rai, and rent out a selection of vehicles. While these larger rental companies have better insurance policies, they will cost more. Patronizing local companies in Chiang Mai and Chiang Rai will save you money, but cost you dearly if you end up in an accident or hospitalized (remember Thais usually don't carry any insurance). If you're driving out to mountain destinations, select the best-maintained car on the lot (older cars are only for in-town driving). Refer to the "Getting Around" section in chapters 12 and 13 for specific office locations and rates. Consider hiring a car and driver from a smaller private company for 1,200B (US$34/£18) per day, depending on the distance traveled and fuel usage.

BY MOTORCYCLE   Motorcycle touring in northern Thailand is another option and best considered only in dry season, over the winter. Chiang Mai can be used as a hub for the region. Inexperienced riders should stick to day trips, and all should arm themselves with up-to-date information about the weather. Hot, precipitous roads doused in monsoon showers make for an early (and easy) death. Stay left, expect the unexpected (such as head on traffic, putrid exhaust fumes from farmers' trucks, and total abandonment of road rules), and keep to 40 to 50kpm to be safe. Carry a map to be sure you don't stray into Myanmar (Burma). No one in his or her right mind would dream of riding without full medical insurance, so do make an investment. Bear in mind some of Chiang Mai's hospitals are notoriously ill-equipped, obliging serious accident victims to be evacuated by air to Bangkok.

4 Tours & Trekking in the Far North

The face of rural life has changed in the far north; a partial result of the tourist influx, but mainly due to the growing industrialization and economies of Thailand as a whole. Northern hill-tribe peoples have been exposed to the outside world and are being asked by Thai officials to stop slash-and-burn agricultural techniques and participate in the Thai economy by growing crops other than opium. Within the bounds of these influences, minorities struggle to maintain their cultural identities, livelihoods, and centuries-old ways of life.

Many travelers are drawn to the hill-tribe villages in search of a "primitive" culture, unspoiled by modernization—and tour and trekking operators in the region are quick to exploit this. Companies advertise treks as nontourist, authentic, or eco-tours in an effort to set them apart from tacky tourist operations or staged cultural experiences. Do not be misled: There are no villages here that are untouched by foreign curiosity. In the worst cases, they have become nothing more than human zoos with fees paid to individuals for photographs and zero long-term sustainability. This shouldn't discourage anyone from joining a trek or tour; just be aware and avoid any bogus claims. It is also advisable to leave any preconceptions of "primitive" people to 19th-century anthropological journals; rather come to learn how these cultures on the margin of society grapple with complex economic and social pressures to maintain their unique identities. Awareness of one's impact as tourists is also important: practice cultural sensitivity. With this as a mission, visitors can have an experience that is quite authentic, and, refreshingly, that has little to do with preconceptions and expectations.

TOUR OPTIONS

There are two kinds of hill-tribe operators in northern Thailand: tribal village tours and jungle treks.

Tribal village tours take large and small groups to visit villages that are close to major cities and towns. If you join one of these groups, you'll travel by van or coach to see up to three villages—each inhabited by a different tribe—and you'll spend about an hour in each one. These villages have had decades of exposure to foreigners, and because roads connect them to Chiang Mai, have many modern conveniences. Some overnight trips will put you up in small hotels or hostels that have been built especially for foreigners. Many trips include elephant trekking, visits to roadside craft vendors, and staged cultural performances of costume parades with music and dance. These short trips are great for a closer view of these cultures without undertaking a three-day hill trek.

Jungle treks are more rugged trips with smaller groups of about 4 to 10 people trudging off to get up-close-and-personal with tribal people. Treks last anywhere from 3 days and 2 nights, to full-on 2-week itineraries. Every trek starts with a bumpy road journey before groups head for the hills on foot accompanied by a local guide, and some tours have bamboo rafting and elephant trekking thrown in for variety.

The guides keep a controlled pace and even those who aren't particularly fit won't have a problem keeping up. Most guides have some knowledge of a few tribal languages and will serve as your go-between. Good guides will be familiar with the villages they'll take you to, will rehearse you in etiquette and protocol, and will negotiate the terms of your "invitation" with the local village leaders. Your guides will also feed you "jungle food"—usually simple meals of rice and fish. If you're a vegetarian, it is a good idea to discuss this with your guide well in advance. Sometimes villagers will entertain guests with music and dance. All guests are invited to sleep in a separate area of the headman's house, which is usually the largest in the compound, but accommodations are very basic (straw mats and blankets). It is unwise to try to go trekking on your own, and in fact, it is important to have a guide who can navigate local customs. Look for recommended trekking companies listed in each section in this book. Below are some important pointers:

12

Chiang Mai

From 1296, under King Mengrai, Chiang Mai (meaning *New City*) was the cultural and religious center of the northern Tai. The city was overtaken and occupied by the Burmese in 1558 until Lord "Chao" Kavila retook the city in 1775, driving the Burmese forces back to near the present border. Burmese influence on religion, architecture, language, cuisine, and culture, however, remained strong. Local feudal lords (sometimes referred to as princes) carrying the title *chao,* remained in nominal control of the city in the late-18th and early 19th centuries, but under continued pressure from King Chulalongkorn (Rama V), the Lanna kingdom was brought under the control of the central government in Bangkok. In 1933, the city was formally and fully integrated into the kingdom of Thailand, becoming the administrative center of the north.

These days, Chiang Mai is booming, with an estimated population of 250,000 (in a province of some 1.6 million) and growing; with those numbers come the attendant "big city" problems of suburban sprawl, noxious pollution, rush-hour traffic, and water shortages, as well as serious flooding (from June to Aug).

It would be difficult to find a city that reflects more of the country's diverse cultural heritage and modern aspirations than Chiang Mai. Its heart is its Old City, an area surrounded by vestiges of walls and moats originally constructed for defense. It lies in the shadow of an increasingly expanding city, encircled by gargantuan concrete highways, lined by giant hoardings and superstores. Massive modern tour buses crowd Burmese-style *wats* ablaze with saffron robes and chanting ancient mantras. Increasingly, old shophouses are giving way to multistory shopping malls and boutique and big name resorts, while towering condominiums fill the skyline. Vendors dressed in hill-tribe costumes sell souvenirs in the busy market next to fast food outlets. Narrow streets lined with ornately carved teak houses lie in the shadow of contemporary skyscrapers.

Because of its temperate climate, many Thais choose Chiang Mai as a retreat during March, April, and May, when the rest of the country is wilting under the heat. In the cooler months, Chiang Mai is an excellent base for exploring the north.

1 Orientation

ARRIVING

BY PLANE When planning your trip, keep in mind that Chiang Mai has international links with major cities throughout the region. **Lao Airlines** (© 05322-3401; www.laoairlines.com) connects Chiang Mai to Vientiane and Luang Prabang in Laos four times each week. **Air Mandalay** (© 05381-8049; www.airmandalay.com) has limited flights to Yangon and Mandalay, in Myanmar (Burma). **Silk Air** (© 05390-4985; www.silkair.com), the regional arm of Singapore Airlines, connects Singapore with direct service three times a week. Budget option **Tiger Airways** (© 02351-8333; **www.tigerairways.com**) connects Chiang Mai to Singapore four times a week. **Thai Airways** has direct services from Kunming in Yunnan, Southern China. For international reservations in Chiang Mai, call © **05392-0999.**

Domestically, **Thai Airways** (240 Phra Pokklao Rd.; © **05392-0999;** www.thai air.com) flies from Bangkok to Chiang Mai nine times daily (trip time: 1 hr. 10 min.). There's a direct flight from Chiang Mai to Phuket daily (note the return sector is *not* direct). The daily 35-minute hop is also the fastest way to get out to Mae Hong Son. **Bangkok Airways** has an office at the airport in Chiang Mai (© **05328-1519,** or 02229-3434 in Bangkok; www.bangkokair.com) and flies at least twice daily from Bangkok.

For rock-bottom prices, check with new budget carriers such as **Air Asia** (© 05392-2170; www.airasia.com); they fly from Bangkok to Chiang Mai for as little as 800B (US$22/£12). **Nok Air** (© 05392-2183 or © 1318; www.nokair.com) offers similar deals (book well in advance via the Internet, or via ticketing agents listed on their sites), while **SGA** (© 02664-6099; www.sga.co.th) works in tandem with Nok Air to provide connections to Chiang Rai and Pai from Chiang Mai. **One-Two-GO** (© 05392-2159; www.fly12go.com) also has regular flights.

Chiang Mai International Airport (© 05327-0224; about 30 minutes from Old Town) has several banks for changing money, a post and overseas call office, and an information booth. Taxis from the airport are a flat 100B (US$2.85/£1.55) to town, a bit more for places outside of Chiang Mai proper. Buy a ticket from the taxi booth in the arrival hall, and then proceed to the taxi queue with your ticket.

BY TRAIN   Of the seven daily trains from Bangkok to Chiang Mai, the 8:30am Sprinter (11 hrs.; 611B/US$17.45/£9.40, second-class air-conditioned seat) is the quickest, but you sacrifice a whole day to travel and spend the entire trip in a seat. The other trains take between 13 and 15 hours, but for overnight trips, second-class sleeper berths are a good choice (881B/US$25/£14 upper berth, air-conditioned; 791B/US$23/£12 lower berth, air-conditioned). Private sleeper cabins are also available, but at 1,353B (US$39/£21), the cost is the same as flying.

Purchase tickets at Bangkok's **Hua Lampong Railway Station** (© 02223-7010 or 1690) up to 90 days in advance. For local train information in Chiang Mai, call © **05324-5363;** for advance booking, call © **05324-2094.** Reservations cannot be made over the phone, but you can call and check to see if space is available.

BY BUS   Buses from Bangkok to Chiang Mai are many and varied: from rattle-trap, non-air-con numbers to fully reclining VIP buses. The trip takes about 10 hours. From **Bangkok's Northern Bus Terminal** close to the Mo Chit BTS (© 02936-2841), six daily, 24-seater VIP buses provide the most comfort, with larger seats that recline (755B/US$22/£12). There is also a frequent service between Chiang Mai and Mae Hong Son, Phitsanulok, and Chiang Rai.

Most buses arrive at the **Arcade Bus Station** (© 05324-2664) on Kaeo Nawarat Road, 3km (2 miles) northeast of the Thapae Gate; a few arrive at the Chang Puak station (© 05321-1586), north of the Chang Puak Gate on Chotana Road. Expect to pay 60B to 150B (US$1.70–US$4.30/95p–£2.30) for a tuk-tuk, and just 30B (85¢/45p) for a red pickup, *songtaew,* to the town center and your hotel.

VISITOR INFORMATION

The **TAT** office is at 105/1 Chiang Mai-Lamphun Rd., 400m (1,312 ft.) south of the Nawarat Bridge on the east side of the Ping River (© **05324-8604**). There are a couple of free magazines available at hotels and businesses—*Guidelines Chiang Mai, Welcome to Chiang Mai and Chiang Rai,* and *What's on Chiang Mai*—which contain maps and useful information. You can also find any of a number of detailed maps distributed free, chock-full of adverts for local shopping, dining, and events.

CITY LAYOUT

The heart of Chiang Mai is the **Old City,** completely surrounded by a moat (restored in the 19th century) and scattered remains of the massive wall, laid out in a square aligned on the cardinal directions. Several of the original gates have been restored and serve as handy reference points, particularly **Thapae Gate** to the east. The most important temples are within the walls of the Old City.

All major streets radiate from the Old City. The main business and shopping area is the 1km (⅔-mile) stretch between the east side of the Old City and the **Ping River.** Here you will find the **Night Bazaar,** many shops, trekking agents, hotels, guesthouses, and restaurants—and some of the most picturesque backstreets in the area.

To the west of town and visible from anywhere in the city is the imposing wall of Doi Suthep Mountain, where, at its crest, you'll find the most regal of all Chiang Mai Buddhist compounds, Wat Phra That Doi Suthep, standing stalwart as if to give its blessing to the city below. The road leading to the temple takes you past a big mall, a strip of modern hotels, the zoo, and the university.

The superhighway circles the outskirts of the city and is connected by traffic-choked arteries emanating from the city center. If driving or riding a motorbike in Chiang Mai, the many one-way streets in and around town are confounding. The moat that surrounds the city has concentric circles of traffic: The outer ring runs clockwise, and the inner ring counterclockwise, with U-turn bridges between. The streets in and around the Night Bazaar are all one-way as well. This means that even if you know where you're going, you'll have to pull your share of U-turns.

GETTING AROUND

BY BUS There are five routes in and around the city, each charging a fixed 10B (30¢/15p) fare. Services start at 6am, finish close to 10pm, and run approximately every 15 minutes. From Chang Puak Bus Station, there is frequent, inexpensive bus service to the nearby craft villages of Sankampaeng and Bo Sang, and to Lamphun.

BY SONGTAEW *Songtaews* (red pickup trucks) cover all routes. Fitted with two long bench seats, they are also known locally as *seelor* (four-wheels). They follow no specific route and have no fixed stopping points. Hail one going in your general direction and tell the driver your destination. If it fits in with the destinations of other passengers, you'll get a ride to your door for only 15B to 30B (43¢–86¢/20p–45p). Some drivers will ask exorbitant fees as if they are a taxi (especially when they're empty); let these guys just drive on. If you can deal with a bit of uncertainty along the confusing twist of roads, a *songtaew* is a great way to explore the city.

Songtaews can also take you up to the top of Doi Suthep Mountain for 40B (US$1.15/60p) and only 30B (85¢/45p) for the easier downhill return trip.

BY TUK-TUK The ubiquitous tuk-tuk (motorized three-wheeler) is the next best option to the *songtaew* for getting around Chiang Mai. Fares are negotiable—and you will have to bargain hard to get a good rate—but expect to pay at least 40B (US$1.15/ 60p) for any ride.

When talking prices, it is good to write it down on a scrap of paper, so there is no argument when you get there and the driver asks for 200B (US$5.70/£3.10) instead of the 20B (60¢/30p) you agreed on.

BY CAR   **Avis** has an office conveniently located at the airport (© **05320-1798;** www.avisthailand.com). Avis self-drive rental rates for Chiang Mai are the same as they are elsewhere in Thailand, from 2,500B and up (US$71/£38) for a compact sedan. **Budget** has an office at the airport and offers comparable rates and services; contact them at © **05320-2871** (www.budget.co.th). Both companies offer comprehensive insurance and provide good maps—even a mini guidebook.

There are dozens of **local car-rental companies** with sedans for 1,200B to 1,800B (US$34–US$51/£18–£28) per day, and Suzuki Caribbeans (oft-derided as a death trap) for as low as 1,000B (US$28/£15) per day. Most travel agents will arrange a car and driver for about 1,600B (US$45/£25) per day. **North Wheels,** 70/4-8 Chaiyaphum Rd. (© **05374-0585**), is tops in this category and does pickup or drop-off service to the airport or your hotel.

BY MOTORCYCLE   Many guesthouses along the Ping River and shops around Chaiyaphum Road (north of Thapae Gate in the Old City) rent 100cc to 150cc motorcycles for about 200B (US$5.70/£3.10) per day (discounts for longer durations). Larger 250cc Hondas (as well as others) with good suspension are commonly available and are the best choice for any trips up-country because of their added power and large fuel tanks; they rent for about 700B (US$20/£11). Try **Mr. Mechanic** (4 Soi 5, Moon Muang Rd.; © **05321-4708**), one of many near Thapae. Helmets are mandatory—even if locals tend to ignore this law, they may be able to wriggle out of arrest, but as a foreigner, you won't be let off lightly. Expect to leave your passport as security (don't leave any credit cards). Traffic congestion and confusing one-way streets make riding within the city dangerous, so if you are tempted, employ defensive driving techniques and take it slow.

BY BICYCLE   Cycling in the city is fun and practical, especially for getting around to the temples within the Old City. Avoid rush hour and take great care on the busy roads outside of the ancient walls. Bikes are available at any of the many guesthouses in or around the old city and go for about 30B (85¢/45p) per day.

FAST FACTS: Chiang Mai

Airport See "Arriving," above.

ATMs For ATMs and money changers, go to Chang Klan and Charoen Prathet roads, around the Night Bazaar, for the most convenient major bank branches.

Bookstores **Backstreet Books** (© **05387-4143**) and **Gecko Books** (© **05387-4066**) are neighbors on Chang Moi Kao, a side street north of eastern Thapae Road just before it meets the city wall. Both have a good selection of new and used books, and do exchanges at the usual rate (two for one, depending on the condition).

Car Rentals See "Getting Around: By Car," above.

Climate See "When to Go" in chapter 11, "Exploring Northern Thailand."

Consulates There are many representative offices in Chiang Mai. Contacts are as follows: **American Consulate General,** 387 Wichayanond Rd. (© **05325-2629**), **Canadian Honorary Consul,** 151 Super Highway Rd. (© **05385-0147**), **Australian Honorary Consul,** 165 Sirimungklajarn Rd. (© **05349-2480**), and **British Consul,** 198 Bumrungraj Rd. (© **05326-3015**).

Dentist/Doctor The American Consulate (see "Consulates," above) will supply you with a list of English-speaking dentists and doctors. There are also medical clinics; but do bear in mind, for reliable results from any tests, or for serious illness, you must seek professional and advanced care in Bangkok.

Emergencies Dial © **1155** to reach the Tourist Police in case of emergency.

Holidays See "When to Go" in chapter 2, "Planning Your Trip to Thailand," and the "Northern Thailand Calendar of Events" in chapter 11, "Exploring Northern Thailand."

Hospitals In Chiang Mai, standards of hospital care have fallen both medically and ethically. If you—or especially your child—fall seriously sick, it is essential that you head immediately to a more reliable and modern hospital in Bangkok, where physicians will offer better and more up-to-date diagnoses. Otherwise, try the private **McCormick** hospital on Kaeo Nawarat Road (© **05324-1311**), out toward the Arcade Bus Terminal. Neither The Ram nor Lanna hospital is recommended.

Internet In the Old City, there are numerous small, inexpensive cafes with service sometimes costing only 20B (57¢/30p) per hour. Just outside the city and featuring the speediest service in town for just 1B per minute (about 3¢/1p per minute) is **NET Generation** at 404/4 Thapae Rd. (© **05323-3919**). In the Night Bazaar area, try **Click and Drink Internet Café** opposite the Royal Princess Hotel at 147 Chang Klan Rd. (© **05327-5333**). Just across from the entrance to Gad Suan Kaew/Central Department Store in the northwest corner of the Old City, **Buddy Internet** is at 12 Huaykaew Rd. (© **05340-4550**) and is open 8am to midnight. **Buddy 2** is at 56 Chaiyaphum Rd. (© **05387-4121**), and **Buddy 3** is in the Sompetch Gold Palace on Chaiyaphum Road (© **05323-2970**).

Pharmacies There are dozens of pharmacies throughout the city; most are open daily 7am to midnight. Bring along any prescriptions that you need filled.

Police For police assistance, call the **Tourist Police** at © **1155,** or see them at the TAT office.

Post Office The most convenient branch is at 186/1 on Chang Klan Road (© **05327-3657**). The General Post Office is on Charoen Muang (© **05324-1070**), near the train station. The Overseas Call Office, open 24 hours, is upstairs from the GPO and offers phone, fax, and telex services. There is a 24-hour branch at the airport (© **05327-7382**). **UPS** has an office in the basement of the Night Bazaar (Chang Klan Rd.; © **05382-0222**; daily 7am–10pm), making it easy to send your finds back home.

2 Accommodations

City accommodations listed below are separated as follows: outside of town; east of town near the Ping River/Night Bazaar area; within the Old City walls; or outside of town on the road to Doi Suthep (near the university).

OUTSIDE CHIANG MAI

VERY EXPENSIVE

Mandarin Oriental Dhara Dhevi ★★★   A good 30 minutes east of Chiang Mai proper on Sankampaeng Road, this super-luxe resort is designed like an enclosed Lanna city, complete with a small moat, grand city gate, and delightfully lush gardens and flowering trees. Burmese-style horse-drawn carts or modern golf carts bring guests to a palatial lobby. The resort comprises immaculate suites and a bevy of rustic, free-standing villas, all sumptuously decorated. Standard perks in the villas include a sauna, piano, sun deck, and Jacuzzi. Around a working rice paddy lie delightful pool villas with outdoor pavilions, and even hill-tribe–style stilt cottages next to a working vegetable patch. All units have large balconies, but the rice barns offer two stories of teak-lined luxury. Colonial suites are nearer the main lobby and have Persian rugs, pretty fretwork, high ceilings, and delightful pastel hues. At times the style of some of the more over-the-top suites may teeter on kitsch, but it somehow seems to work well with the contrasting rustic ambience. The all-teak Dhevi Spa is a masterful recreation of an extant wooden palace in Myanmar (Burma). The resort offers daily courses in Lanna culture as well as yoga courses. Upmarket boutiques and a first-class cafe are discreetly hidden at the entrance. Two pools, a gym, a brick amphitheater, huge library, and a bevy of delightful dining options make the resort completely self-contained. The gorgeous little *viharn* by the lawn is totally authentic, as are a few of the older buildings that were transplanted from the countryside. None of this architecture is whimsy; every building has elements borrowed from extant Lanna structures dating back 300 years.

51/4 Chiang Mai–Sankampaeng Rd., Moo 1, Chiang Mai 50000 (On the road to Sankampaeng, 25-min. from downtown). ✆ **05388-8888.** Fax 05388-8999. www.mandarinoriental.com. 123 units. 11,165B (US$319/£172) villa; 19,250B (US$550/£296) colonial suite, 30,765B (US$879/£473) grand deluxe colonial suite; 70,000B (US$2,000/£1,077) resident suite. AE, DC, MC, V. **Amenities:** 4 restaurants; 3 bars; 2 pools; tennis courts; health club; spa; bike rentals; kids' club; cultural programs; tour desk; airport transfer; business center; 2 shopping arcades; salon; 24-hr. room service; babysitting; laundry service; dry cleaning; free Wi-Fi. *In room:* A/C, satellite TV, minibar, fridge, kitchenette, coffeemaker, hair dryer, iron, safe, piano, sauna, massage table, Jacuzzi.

NEAR THE PING RIVER

VERY EXPENSIVE

The Chedi ★★★   On what was once the site of the venerable old British Consulate, The Chedi is a luxurious oasis facing some beautiful river scenery along the Ping River, just south of the Night Bazaar area. Mixing an eclectic mix of architecture by the inimitable Kerry Hill, along with pretty lawns and a central riverside location, the hotel has finally brought luxury downtown. As expected from the GHM group, The Chedi offers nothing but the highest standards, with a superb exterior of minimalist wooden slats giving way to a crisp interior of large reflecting pools and polished concrete paths leading to a gem of a colonial mansion: In sum, it's all a delightful mix of modern and colonial. Rooms are up to crisp business hotel standard, and all offer a private courtyard entrance. Chedi Club Suites are enormous and come with lots of extras. The glassy pool pops right out of a fashion shoot, and spa treatments are on tap. Dining options include exquisite Northern Thai specialties, a selection of unusual Pacific Rim dishes, and a sublime afternoon tea.

123 Charoen Prathet Rd., Chang Klan Rd., Chiang Mai 50100. © 05325-3333. Fax 05325-3352. www.ghmhotels. com. 84 units. 10,780B (US$308/£166) deluxe double; 16,170B (US$462/£249) suite. AE, MC, V. **Amenities:** Restaurant; 3 bars; outdoor pool; health club; spa; tour desk; car-rental desk; airport transfer; business center; salon; 24-hr. room service; babysitting; laundry service/dry cleaning. *In room:* A/C, satellite TV, fax, dataport, minibar, fridge, coffeemaker, hair dryer, iron, safe.

EXPENSIVE

Holiday Inn Chiang Mai ★★

Just a short ride out of town, and a popular business and meeting address, the Holiday Inn (formerly Sheraton) is a good, familiar choice. From the enormous pillars, chandeliers, frescoes, and filigree of the grand lobby, to their international standard of guest rooms and service—everything is tiptop. What the Holiday Inn lacks in "local" touches it more than makes up for with comfortable familiarity. Complimentary shuttles to the Night Bazaar and airport help offset the out-of-the-way locale. Rooms, particularly deluxe rooms, are vast but not particularly luxurious. Services are extensive, including Wi-Fi on executive floors.

318/1 Chiang Mai–Lamphun Rd., Chiang Mai 50000 (south of city center, across Mengrai Bridge on east bank of river). © 05327-5300. Fax 05327-5299. www.ichotelsgroup.com. 526 units. 2,500B (US$71/£38) double; 3,500B (US$100/£54) executive deluxe; from 6,500B (US$186/£100) suite. AE, DC, MC, V. **Amenities:** 3 restaurants; lounge; outdoor pool; golf course nearby; fitness center; sauna; tour desk; car-rental desk; airport transfer; business center; 24-hr. room service; massage; babysitting; same-day laundry service/dry cleaning; nonsmoking rooms; executive floor. *In room:* A/C, satellite TV, minibar, fridge, hair dryer.

The Imperial Mae Ping Hotel ★★

This imposing, crescent-shaped tower hotel is one of the city's most popular choices for its good location—just a short stroll from the Night Bazaar, yet far enough away to get a good night's sleep. The unusual two-story lobby interprets Thai architectural elements in bold white-and-gold accents. Large, bright guest rooms are modern and feature traditional blond teak furnishings and contemporary Thai elements like sculpted lamp bases, reproductions of temple murals, and Thai weavings. Deluxe rooms have better-than-average amenities for just a small jump up in price. Be sure to ask for a room with a mountain view. There's a popular beer garden in the hotel's large courtyard area, and the pool is a good escape after city shopping. Overall, this is a good midrange downtown choice.

153 Sri Dornchai Rd., Chiang Mai 50100 (corner of Kampaengdin Rd., 2 blocks southwest of Night Bazaar). © 05328-3900. Fax 05327-0181. www.imperialmaeping.com. 371 units. 4,500B–5,500B (US$128–US$157/£69–£85) double; from 8,000B (US$228/£123) suite. AE, DC, MC, V. **Amenities:** 3 restaurants; lounge and beer garden; outdoor pool; fitness center; tour desk; airport transfer; business center; salon; 24-hr. room service; massage; babysitting; same-day laundry service/dry cleaning; nonsmoking rooms; executive floor. *In room:* A/C, satellite TV, minibar, fridge.

Royal Princess Hotel ★★

Having recently undergone major renovations, this northern cousin of Bangkok's Dusit Thani is now a slightly better choice than other center city hotels. Guest rooms are done in a mix of cool pastels set against panels, or whole walls, of saturated primary colors, featuring poetry in elegant Thai calligraphy. Upper-floor deluxe rooms have an interesting Japanese theme. The downtown location means easy access to shopping and nightlife; all guest rooms have a good vantage on the glittering lights of the city. You're right in the heart of it here, so be warned that stepping out of the hotel means that touts and tuk-tuk drivers will be waiting to pounce.

112 Chang Klan Rd., Chiang Mai 50100 (located just south of the Night Bazaar). © 05328-1033. Fax 05328-1044. www.royalprincess.com. 198 units. 2,800B–3,500B (US$80–US$100/£43–£54) double; from 8,000B (US$228/£123)

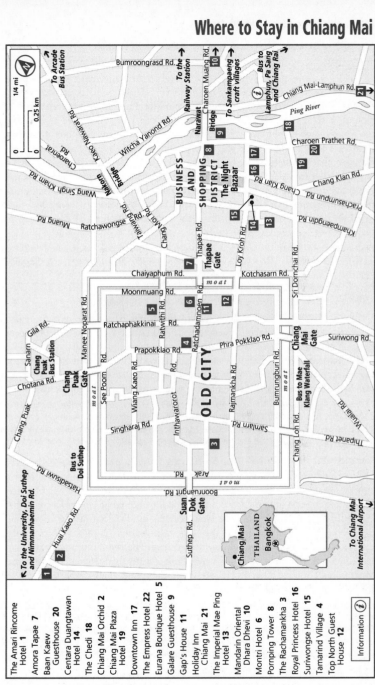

Where to Stay in Chiang Mai

The Amari Rincome Hotel **1**
Amora Tapae **7**
Baan Kaew Guesthouse **20**
Centara Duangtawan Hotel **14**
The Chedi **18**
Chiang Mai Orchid **2**
Chiang Mai Plaza Hotel **19**
Downtown Inn **17**
The Empress Hotel **22**
Eurana Boutique Hotel **5**
Gap's House **11**
Holiday Inn Chiang Mai **21**
The Imperial Mae Ping Hotel **13**
Mandarin Oriental Dhara Dhevi **10**
Montri Hotel **6**
Pornping Tower **8**
The Rachamankha **3**
Royal Princess Hotel **16**
Suriwongse Hotel **15**
Tamarind Village **4**
Top North Guest House **12**

Information ⓘ

313

suite. AE, DC, MC, V. **Amenities:** 3 restaurants; lobby lounge and pub; small outdoor pool; tour desk; airport transfer; 24-hr. room service; massage; babysitting; same-day laundry service/dry cleaning. *In room:* A/C, satellite TV, minibar, fridge, hair dryer, safe.

MODERATE

Amora Tapae ⚐ For years, there was a moratorium on high-rise building in and around the Old City. Then someone slipped in this 12-story eyesore on the edge of the historic, two-story Old City. The chain-hotel style rooms have no distinguishing features, other than their good size and cleanliness. Having said that, from rooms on its upper floors, Amora Tapae offers great vistas of the Old City and the mountains beyond, and there is a small pool. The place attracts lots of luxury lager louts for its proximity to the beer bars near Thapae gate, and a festive air prevails (that means late-night hall hooting), so bring those earplugs. If you are visiting Chiang Mai during *Songkran* (the Apr water festival), this is the perfect location for all the aquatic mayhem that takes place next to the moat.

22 Chaiyapoom Rd., Chiang Mai 50300 (north of Thapae Gate and just across the moat from the Old City). ✆ 05325-1531. Fax 05325-1721. 204 units. 1,800B–2,400B (US$44–US$59/£28–£37) double; from 4,000B (US$98/£62) suite. AE, MC, V. **Amenities:** Restaurant; lounge; beer garden; outdoor pool; tour desk; limited room service; babysitting; same-day laundry service/dry cleaning; nonsmoking rooms. *In room:* A/C, satellite TV, minibar, fridge, coffeemaker, safe.

Centara Duangtawan Hotel Close to the Night Bazaar, the recently renamed Centara Duangtawan Hotel (formerly the Central Duangtawan Hotel) is the cream of the crop of midrange chains with many properties throughout Thailand. More a business hotel than anything, and far more popular with Thai travelers than Westerners, the hotel is still a fair choice with large, somewhat bland, but comfortable rooms. A number feature great views of the mountain (especially from the top floors).

132 Loy Kroh Rd., Chiang Mai 50100. ✆ 05390-5000. Fax 05327-5429. www.centralhotelsresorts.com. 500 units. 3,700B–4,300B (US$105–US$123/£57–£69) double; 5,700B (US$163/£88) deluxe. MC, V. **Amenities:** 2 restaurants; 2 bars; outdoor pool; fitness center; Jacuzzi; sauna; tour desk; car-rental desk; business center; shopping arcade; salon; limited room service; massage; laundry service/dry cleaning. *In room:* A/C, satellite TV, minibar, fridge, safe.

Chiang Mai Plaza Hotel The Plaza's two 12-story towers, completed in 1986, form a bland, modern Western hotel, but guest rooms are large, plush, and offer city and mountain views. The lobby is so spacious that the decorative furniture seems almost lost in acres of brilliantly polished granite, and recent renovations give it that extra-glitzy touch. The Plaza is also well located—in town, but just far enough away, toward the Ping River, to be out of the congestion. It is very popular with group tours, but the place is so big you won't know they're there. The swimming pool is surrounded by Lanna-style pavilions, and their newly built spa area is a catacomb in deep umber tones, dim lights, and Thai decoration, where the gamut of affordable but high-quality health and beauty treatments is on offer.

92 Sri Dornchai Rd., Chiang Mai 50100 (between Chang Klan and Charoen Prathet rds., midway between Old City and river). ✆ 05390-3161. Fax 05327-9457. www.cnxplaza.com. 475 units. 2,500B–3,000B (US$71–US$86/£38–£46) double; from 12,000B (US$343/£185) suite. AE, DC, MC, V. **Amenities:** Restaurant; lounge; outdoor pool; fitness center; spa w/massage and sauna; tour desk; car-rental desk; business center; limited room service; babysitting; same-day laundry service/dry cleaning; nonsmoking rooms. *In room:* A/C, satellite TV, minibar, fridge, hair dryer.

The Empress Hotel ⚐ This 17-story tower, opened in 1990, is south of the main business and tourist area, which makes it especially quiet. The hotel has all the standard amenities, and even when swarming with tourist groups, doesn't seem overrun. The impressive public spaces are filled with glass, granite, and chrome, with integrated

Thai touches and flairs. Large rooms with picture windows are done in a tasteful, modern interpretation of Asian decor of rose and peach tones. Bathrooms are small but decked-out in marble and offer good complimentary amenities. Ask to be on the mountain side, since there are nice views from upper floors there.

199/42 Chang Klan Rd., Chiang Mai 50100 (a 15-min. walk south of Night Bazaar, 2 blocks from river). © 05327-0240. Fax 05327-2467. www.empresshotels.com. 375 units. 3,000B–4,000B (US$86–US$114/£46–£62) double; from 8,400B (US$240/£129) suite. AE, DC, MC, V. **Amenities:** 3 restaurants; lobby lounge and disco; pool; fitness center w/sauna; massage; tour desk; business center; shopping arcade; salon; 24-hr. room service; babysitting; same-day laundry service/dry cleaning; executive floor. *In room:* A/C, satellite TV, minibar, fridge, hair dryer.

Pornping Tower ☆ Right in the heart of the busy shopping and nightlife area near the Night Bazaar, this 16-story hotel bustles with evening activity. Public spaces are full of polished marble, glass, and mirrors; rooms use cool colors and have a contemporary style. There's an excellent pool with an inviting sun deck, good in-house dining, and attentive service. If you fancy subjecting yourself to some seriously dubious nightlife, the Bubble Disco is famously as low as it goes in this town.

46–48 Charoen Prathet Rd., Chiang Mai 50100 (corner of Loy Kroh Rd., 1 block from river). © 05327-0099. Fax 05327-0119. www.pornpinghotelchiangmai.com. 325 units. 2,100B–3,150B (US$60–US$90/£32–£48) double; from 7,000B (US$200/£108) suite. AE, DC, MC, V. **Amenities:** 3 restaurants; popular disco, lounge and karaoke; outdoor pool; tour desk; 24-hr. room service; babysitting; same-day laundry service/dry cleaning. *In room:* A/C, satellite TV, minibar, fridge.

Suriwongse Hotel ☆ For the shopper or party animal looking to be close to the Night Bazaar area, this hotel is tops, but everyone knows it, and Suriwongse has been around a while, so it is looking a little worse for the wear. The unique hardwood paneling in the lobby lends warmth to the place, and spacious, teak-trimmed rooms have clean carpets, large, firm beds, and are done in cool off-whites and pastels (if you can ignore the red bordello drapes). This is one of Chiang Mai's better values, but not luxurious. Higher-priced rooms have similar amenities but offer a balcony and better views. The town's McDonald's and Starbucks franchises are both within a stone's throw (if throwing stones is your thing).

110 Chang Klan Rd., Chiang Mai 50100 (corner of Loy Kroh Rd., just southwest of Night Bazaar, half-way between Old City and river). © 05327-0051. Fax 05327-0063. www.suriwongsehotels.com. 190 units. 2,200B–3,500B (US$63–US$100/£34–£54) double; from 4,800B (US$137/£74) suite (seasonal rates available). AE, DC, MC, V. **Amenities:** 2 restaurants; lounge; pool; tour desk; business center; limited room service; massage; babysitting; same-day laundry service/dry cleaning; nonsmoking rooms. *In room:* A/C, satellite TV, minibar, fridge.

INEXPENSIVE

Baan Kaew Guesthouse ☆ This motel-style guesthouse, an enclosed compound in a quiet neighborhood just a short walk south of the Night Bazaar, has a well-tended garden and a manicured lawn. Rooms are very simple but spotless, with new floor coverings (guests are asked to remove shoes before entering) and tiled bathrooms with hot-water showers. Breakfast is served in a shaded pavilion. You're close to the market, but the place is quiet.

142 Charoen Prathet Rd., Chiang Mai 50100 (south of Loy Kroh Rd. opposite Wat Chaimongkol; enter gate, turn left, and find guesthouse well back from street). © 05327-1606. Fax 05327-3436. www.baankaew-guesthouse.com. 20 units. 800B (US$23/£12) double. No credit cards. **Amenities:** Restaurant (breakfast only); tour desk; laundry service. *In room:* A/C.

Downtown Inn ☆ A more affordable version of the Empress Hotel (under the same management), diminutive Downtown Inn is a good, simple budget choice close to the action of the Night Bazaar area. Rooms are plain with hard mattresses and offer showers only. It has a cozy coffee shop, and a simple breakfast is included. The courtyard swimming pool is tiny, but good for cooling off. Discounts are available sporadically.

172/1-11 Loy-Kroh Rd., Anusarn Night Market, Chiang Mai 50100. © **05327-0662.** Fax 05327-2406. www.empress hotels.com. 74 units. 1,900B–2,600B (US$54–US$74/£29–£40); from 6,500B (US$186/£100) suite. MC, V. **Amenities:** Restaurant; outdoor pool; massage; laundry service. *In room:* A/C, TV, fridge.

Galare Guest House This Thai-style, three-story, brick-and-wood motel has broad covered verandas overlooking a pleasant garden and courtyard. Rooms are small but have air-conditioning and king-size beds. Even with linoleum floors, it is very comfortable. The restaurant serves breakfast, lunch, and dinner on a covered deck overlooking the river. An in-house trekking agency organizes trips to hill-tribe villages, as well as local tours of Chiang Mai; ask about discounts in the off-season.

7 Charoen Prathet Rd., Soi 2, Chiang Mai 50100 (on river south of Thapae Rd.). © **05381-8887.** Fax 05327-9088. www.galare.com. 35 units. 950B–1,150B (US$27–US$39/£15–£18) double. MC, V. **Amenities:** Restaurant; tour desk; car-rental desk; laundry service; computer w/Internet access. *In room:* A/C, TV, fridge, no phone.

IN THE OLD CITY
EXPENSIVE
The Rachamankha ★★★ *Moments* This immaculate hotel is by far the best abode within the city walls—it's a great escape from the city gridlock and pollution. Just behind Wat Phra Singh, the unique, boutique property is superbly designed in a courtyard-style. Service is professional, and rooms are luxurious, with terra-cotta tile floors, high ceilings, and stylish contemporary built-ins; plenty of stunning Lanna antiques are scattered around the long, cool verandas. Deluxe rooms are just larger versions of superior ones. Bathrooms are bright and large. An indigo pool lies in the peaceful courtyard, and onsite is an excellent and fully stocked library. Hotel dining is either in a gravel courtyard or the long, peaceful antiques-filled hall; upstairs is a spectacular boutique.

6 Rachamankha 9 (on the western edge of the Old City), Phra Singh Rd., Chiang Mai 50200. © **05390-4111.** Fax 05390-4114. www.rachamankha.com. 23 units. 5,775B (US$165/£89) superior double; 6,875B (US$196/£106) deluxe double; 15,700B (US$448/£242) suite. AE, MC, V. **Amenities:** Restaurant; bar; outdoor pool; tour desk; limited room service; massage; laundry service/dry cleaning. *In room:* A/C, satellite TV, minibar, fridge, coffeemaker, hair dryer, safe.

MODERATE
Tamarind Village ★★ After passing down a long, shaded lane lined with new-growth bamboo, and following meandering walkways among the gobo buildings of this stylish little hideaway in the heart of the Old City, it'll be hard to believe that you're in Chiang Mai (though you can still hear the traffic). Rooms at the Tamarind are marvels of polished concrete burnished to an almost shining glow, complemented by straw mats and chic contemporary Thai furnishings, all making for a pleasing minimalist feel. Bathrooms are spacious, with large double doors connecting with the guest rooms, topped off with vaulted ceilings. There's an almost Mediterranean feel to the whole complex—with all of the arched, covered terra-cotta walks joining buildings in a village-style layout. Short of the fine pool and a dandy restaurant, amenities are sparse, but the staff members are helpful and the atmosphere quite unique.

50/1 Rachadamnoen Rd., Sri Phum, Chiang Mai 50200 (a short walk from the center of the Old City from Thapae Gate). © **05341-8896.** Fax 05341-8900. www.tamarindvillage.com. 45 units. 6,000B (US$171/£92) double; 8,000B (US$228/£123) deluxe. MC, V. **Amenities:** Restaurant; bar; outdoor pool; tour desk; same-day laundry/dry cleaning. *In room:* A/C, satellite TV, minibar, fridge, hair dryer.

INEXPENSIVE

Eurana Boutique Hotel   This cozy little courtyard hotel recently underwent some major renovations. In the heart of the busy backpacker area near the city center (just inside the moat), the Eurana offers a serious degree of luxury. Though the cheapest rooms are on the small size, splurge out and you'll enjoy delightful contemporary digs with fun, colorful decor and even a glimpse of the (tiny) gardens. It's also convenient for many services (restaurants, cooking schools, and massage parlors) in the Old City.

7/1 Moon Muang Rd. Soi 7, Chiang Mai 50200. ℭ 05321-4522. Fax 05322-3042. www.euranaboutiquehotel.com. 72 units. 1,500B–3,500B (US$43–US$100/£23–£54). MC, V. **Amenities:** Restaurant; outdoor pool; spa; tour services; laundry service. *In room:* A/C, TV, fridge.

Gap's House   Gap's House is tucked down a quiet lane just inside the city wall at Thapae. Long popular among budget travelers, the hotel boasts a calm atmosphere, with a leafy central garden area surrounding a large, teak Lanna pavilion. Rooms are in free-standing teak houses and feature woven rattan beds and small tiled bathrooms. Time is taking a toll on the room facilities: The rustic charm borders are just plain tatty and management is rather indifferent. It's still a cheap, atmospheric choice in the town center, though. (Just avoid the budget singles in the separate cement building.)

3 Soi 4, Ratchadamnoen Rd., Chiang Mai 50000 (1 block west of Thapae Gate on left). ℭ/fax 05327-8140. www. gaps-house.com. 19 units. 450B–650B (US$13–US$18/£6.95–£10) double. MC, V. **Amenities:** Restaurant; laundry service; cooking classes. *In room:* A/C, no phone.

Montri Hotel ✯   The earliest address of note for foreigners in Chiang Mai, the Montri is still a convenient, inexpensive location just inside the Old City—and across from Thapae Gate—however, it doesn't offer much in the way of charm. Dark parquet floors are standard throughout, and bathrooms are shower-in-room style. Newly renovated rooms with built-in cabinets try to be attractive, but merely pass as comfortable. Their main advantage is that they are a good value. *Note:* Ask for a room at the rear; you'll get more peace and quiet, and from the higher floors you can see the outline of Doi Suthep.

2–6 Rachadamnoen Rd., Chiang Mai 50100 (just northwest across from Thapae Gate). ℭ 05321-1069. Fax 05321-7416. 75 units. 750B (US$21/£12) double. MC, V. **Amenities:** Restaurant; tour desk; small business center; laundry service; nonsmoking rooms. *In room:* A/C, satellite TV, fridge, minibar.

Top North Guest House   South of Thapae and down one of the Old City's narrow lanes, laid-back Top North is comfortable and affordable. Its small central pool is unique in this category and is a popular hangout for backpackers going upscale. There are many room categories. All have high ceilings, and the top rooms (500B/US$14/£7.70) are large and clean with tile floors and large bathrooms with bathtubs. Time is not kind to budget hotels, though, and some of the room furnishings here look like they've seen better days—ask to check rooms out before signing on. Rooms on the lower echelon vary in price and amenities (with or without air-conditioning or TV), but all have hot-water showers. Top North has a good tour operation, an Internet cafe on the premises, and shows DVDs in the bar in the evenings. Their sister property, **Top North Hotel** (ℭ 05327-9623), is an old standby just south of the Thapae Gate within the Old City and offers a slightly higher class of rooms. It seems to attract a rougher lot, though; stay there only if Top North Guest House is booked up.

15 Moon Muang Rd., Soi 2, Chiang Mai 50100. ℭ 05327-8684. Fax 05327-8485. www.topnorthgroup.com. 90 units. 500B (US$14/£7.70) double with A/C; 300B (US$8.60/£4.60) double with fan. MC, V. **Amenities:** Restaurant; outdoor pool; bike and motorcycle rental desk; tour desk; laundry service; Internet center. *In room:* A/C (in some), TV, no phone.

WEST SIDE/UNIVERSITY AREA

EXPENSIVE

The Amari Rincome Hotel ★★ *Value* This tranquil hotel complex is a favorite because of its unpretentious atmosphere and friendly service. The public spaces are lively, and around the gigantic pool, the gardens—which contain a huge aviary—are impressive. The best (and quieter) rooms offer pool views and come with west-facing balconies on which to enjoy a cool breakfast and sunset. There is a certain amount of (daytime) noise from low-flying planes, so light sleepers will do well to use earplugs. Most guest rooms are decorated in pastel hues, and the bathrooms are functional, with small tubs and fixed hair dryers. Dining at their **La Gritta** restaurant is good, and the hotel is located near the best upscale shopping in town. The staff's professionalism is evident from the moment the minibus meets you at the airport. They can help with any eventuality (tours, transport, and so on).

1 Nimmanhaemin Rd., off Huay Kaeo Rd., Chiang Mai 50200 (near Superhighway, northwest of Old City). ℂ 05322-1130. Fax 05322-1915. www.amari.com. 158 units. 2,900B (US$83/£45) double; from 6,200B (US$177/£95) suite. AE, DC, MC, V. **Amenities:** 3 restaurants; lounge; 2 outdoor pools; outdoor lit tennis court; tour desk; airport transfer; business center; shopping arcade; salon; 24-hr. room service; massage; babysitting; same-day laundry service/dry cleaning; nonsmoking rooms; executive floor. *In room:* A/C, satellite TV, minibar, fridge, hair dryer.

Chiang Mai Orchid ★ The Orchid has attractive facilities, friendly service and is just next to the town's most popular hangout, Gad Suan Kaew Shopping Complex. Spacious, quiet rooms are large, familiar, and pleasantly decorated with local wood-carvings. The lobby and other public spaces are furnished with clusters of chic, low-slung rattan couches and chairs and are decorated with flowers. They cover all the bases in amenities, from dining to car rental—plus there's a knowledgeable tour desk.

23 Huai Kaeo Rd., Chiang Mai 50200 (northwest of Old City, next door to Gad San Kaew/Central Shopping Complex). ℂ 05322-2099. Fax 05322-1625. www.chiangmaiorchid.com. 267 units. 1,800B–2,700B (US$51–US$77/£28–£42) double; from 5,800B (US$166/£89) suite. AE, DC, MC, V. **Amenities:** 3 restaurants; lounge and pub; outdoor pool; fitness center; sauna; children's playground; tour desk; car-rental desk; limited room service; massage; babysitting; same-day laundry service. *In room:* A/C, satellite TV, dataport, minibar, fridge.

INEXPENSIVE

Yes, The Village People are here in Chiang Mai: The rooms at **YMCA International Hotel** (11 Sermsuk Rd., Mengrairasmi; ℂ **05322-1819**) have attracted missionaries and budget travelers for years. The place is a bit run-down these days, but rooms start at just 600B/US$17/£9.25 for a basic double. In off-season, you may find the Montri Hotel (see above) to be a more economical and better-located option.

3 Dining

Northern-style Thai cooking is influenced by the nearby Burmese, Yunnanese, and Lao cuisines. Many northern Thai dishes are not served with steamed rice, but *khao niaow* (glutinous or sticky rice), which can be cooked as an accompaniment to a savory dish or used in dessert. Sticky rice is sometimes served simply in a knotted banana leaf or in a small cylindrical basket with a lid. Chiang Mai specialties include *sai ua* (Chiang Mai sausage), *khao sawy* (a spicy, yellow, Burmese-style curry with pickles and both fried and boiled noodles), as well as many other slightly sweet meat and fish curries. You may be relieved to know that chili peppers are used less than in other Thai regional cuisines.

The formal northern meal is called *khan toke* and refers to the (recently invented) practice of sharing a variety of main courses, with guests seated around *khan toke* (low,

Where to Dine in Chiang Mai

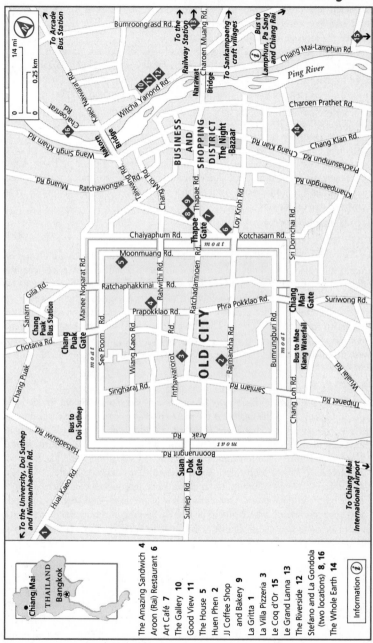

The Amazing Sandwich **4**
Aroon (Rai) Restaurant **6**
Art Café **7**
The Gallery **10**
Good View **11**
The House **5**
Huen Phen **2**
JJ Coffee Shop
  and Bakery **9**
La Gritta **1**
La Villa Pizzeria **3**
Le Coq d'Or **15**
Le Grand Lanna **13**
The Riverside **12**
Stefano and La Gondola
  (two locations) **8, 16**
The Whole Earth **14**

ⓘ Information

lacquered teak tables); eating is done using the hands. Most of the restaurants that serve *khan toke* combine a dance performance with the meal. The best such places are covered in "Chiang Mai After Dark," later.

Chiang Mai is also blessed with good street food and markets. **Anusarn Market** on the corner of Sri Dornchai and Chang Klan roads near the Night Bazaar is a good place for authentic local food. Also try **Somphet Market** on the northeast corner of the old city; it's a good place to pick up snacks like fried bananas or sticky-rice desserts in the daytime or have a good cheap meal in the evening, at which point the area bustles with locals and young backpackers.

Chiang Mai folks take their *khao sawy*—Burmese curry and noodles—pretty seriously. The best is to be had in **Fa Ham,** an area about 1km (⅔ mile) north of central Nawarat Bridge on Charoenrat Road along the east bank of the Ping River. A number of open-air places serve the delicacy for just 25B (71¢/35p), along with tasty skewers of chicken and pork satay. Count on this place always being packed, since it's well known to tuk-tuk drivers.

NEAR THE PING RIVER
EXPENSIVE
Le Coq d'Or ✿✿✿ FRENCH   In a colonial house setting, Le Coq d'Or has been around for years and is known for its nice atmosphere and good service. The menu offers imported beef, lamb, and local fish prepared in French and Continental styles. Try the *chateaubriand,* or the poached Norwegian salmon as a lighter choice. For starters, the foie gras is popular, as is the unique salmon tartare served with toast and a sour cream and horseradish sauce. They have a long wine list to complement your meal.

11 Soi 2 Koh Klang Rd. (5-min. drive south of the Sheraton, following the river). ✆ **05328-2024.** Reservations recommended for weekend dinner. Main courses 400B–1,800B (US$11–US$51/£6.15–£28). AE, DC, MC, V. Daily noon–2pm and 6–10pm.

MODERATE
The Gallery ✿ THAI   Built in 1892 and one of the oldest original wooden structures in Chiang Mai, The Gallery is the most charming of the riverside restaurants on the eastern bank of the Ping River. However, the rumor mill suggests its lease is now expired, so its time may be limited. It has been on the backpacker and tourist route for so long (even Hillary Clinton came here) that it can sometimes seem like it caters to foreigners only. Try the local fish or *hor mok curry.* The proximity to the river is agreeable, but apply plenty of mosquito repellent, since mosquitoes come here to eat too. Candlelight, soft Thai music, and a great view of the river—plus the city's twinkling lights beyond—top off what's sure to be a lovely evening of dining. Let's hope it stays.

25–29 Charoenrat Rd. (east side of river, north of Nawarat Bridge). ✆ **05324-8601.** Main courses 120B–340B (US$3.40–US$9.70/£1.85–£5.25). AE, MC, V. Daily noon–1am.

Good View ✿ THAI/INTERNATIONAL   This place packs in raucous crowds of young rock music fans from early evening until late, but once the live band revs up, forget any conversation. Thais tend to come here to eat, drink, and over-drink before they party, so it is always busy and, yes, very noisy. The food is fair and unimaginative, offering the usual tourist menu; it's probably best to stick with the Thai dishes. The picture menu makes it easy and the staff is friendly. Come early, around 6pm, to enjoy a good, quiet meal overlooking the river at sunset, and then—if your eardrums can take it—stick around for the band and party on.

13 Charoenrat Rd. (east side of river, north of Nawarat Bridge). ✆ 05324-1866. Main courses 100B–350B (US$2.80–US$10/£1.55–£5.40). MC, V. Daily 5pm–1:30am.

The House ✮✮✮ PACIFIC RIM/MODERN ASIAN   This wonderful supper-only bistro was established by a resident Dane who immediately upped the culinary standards in Chiang Mai. Set in an old 1960s edifice that's been lovingly restored, the main dining room has large windows with gorgeous drapes, silk cushions, and candlelit tables; upstairs there are two rooms which are even cozier. An internationally trained Thai chef works his magic on a constantly evolving menu of regionally influenced classical dishes, a medley of grilled items and imported steaks, and lamb and seafood when available—there are fabulous desserts to boot. Outside is a Moorish souk-styled lounge bar with lights in the trees, and a separate tapas bar for snacks. This refined dining spot, with its romantic nooks and funky furnishings, caters to the discerning traveler. If it's over your budget, check out the new low-priced bistro next door.

199 Moon Muang Rd. (just north of Thapae gate on the inside edge of the city moat). ✆ 05341-9011. Main courses 400B–700B (US$11–US$20/£6.15–£11). MC, V. Daily kitchen 6–10:30pm; bar 6pm–1am.

Le Grand Lanna ✮✮✮ *Finds* THAI   Since the opening of the luxury Mandarin Oriental Dhara Dhevi, which took over this long-established, traditional eatery, nothing much has changed but the prices. Modeled on a Lanna nobleman's home, it's entirely built of old teak and is on raised stilts. Located a 20- to 30-minute ride east of town, it's a good stop before, or after, a trip to the craft workshops at Sankampaeng. The restaurant provides icy cool air-conditioned rooms inside, or terrace seating outside, with cooling mist-spraying fans and umbrellas. You'll be surrounded by Lanna art and a beautiful tropical garden with birds and butterflies. Evening meals are candlelit, with flaming torches and the dulcet tones of traditional music accompanying your choice of food. For starters, try pomelo salad (if needed, ask to reduce the spiciness) as a main course; then try the superb *khao sawy* or *gaeng hang lan mop*, a dry, fiery red curry that will knock your socks off and which is best mollified by a sweet mango chutney. Also don't pass up their signature *sai ua,* or Chiang Mai spicy sausage. Follow up with great homemade ice-cream made of local litchi (lychee) or taro (yam). If you're short of time or money, come for a drink, at least.

51/4 Chiang Mai-Sankampaeng Rd. (4km/2½ miles east on Charoen Muang). ✆ 05388-8888. Main courses 400B–1,200B (US$11–US$34/£6.15–£18). AE, MC, V. Daily 11:30am–2.30pm; 6:30–10:30pm.

The Riverside ✮✮ THAI/INTERNATIONAL   Casual and cool is what Riverside is all about. It is a tavern with riverside terrace views—make sure you get there before the dinner rush, so you get your pick of tables. There's live music, from blues to soft rock, great Thai and Western food (including burgers), and a full bar. Even if you just stop by for a beer, it is a jovial place that always has a jolly crowd of travelers, locals, and expatriates. Riverside also operates a dining cruise at 8pm (boards at 7:15pm) for just 90B (US$2.60/£1.40) per person (drinks and dining a la carte). Call ahead.

9–11 Charoenrat Rd. (east side of river, north of Nawarat Bridge). ✆ 05324-3239. Main courses 90B–330B (US$2.60–US$9.45/£1.40–£5.10). AE, MC, V. Daily 10am–1am.

Stefano and La Gondola ✮✮ ITALIAN   Stefano is in the heart of town in a colorful alley off Thapae Road, and La Gondola overlooks the Ping River. Under the same management, both take you on a pleasant culinary journey from Lanna to Italy. The eateries are equally lively and popular, offering an extensive catalogue of Northern Italian cuisine, from steaks to excellent pastas. Portions are big, the wine list is deep, and there are good daily set menus and specials. La Gondola boasts a collection of glass aviaries with balcony seating and is certainly the more romantic choice of the two. Stefano has its own more raucous allure, with brash decor and a younger clientele, mostly backpackers who dust off the credit cards for a bit of a splurge after long journeys.

Stefano: 2/1-2 Chang Moi Kao Rd. (just to the east of Thapae Gate). © 05387-4189. La Gondola: Rimping Condo, 201/6 Charoenrat Rd. (on the east side of Mae Ping River and north of town near Nakhon Ping Bridge). © 05324-7776. Main courses 90B–300B (US$2.60–$8.60/£1.40–£4.60). AE, MC, V. Stefano: Daily 11:30am–10:30pm; La Gondola: 11am–11pm, except Mon 4–11pm.

The Whole Earth ★(Value) VEGETARIAN/INDIAN   Featuring Asian foods, mostly Indian and Thai, prepared with light, fresh ingredients in healthy and creative ways, this 30-year-old Chiang Mai institution is a real find. The restaurant is set in a traditional Lanna Thai pavilion and has an indoor air-conditioned nonsmoking section, and a long open-air veranda with views of the gardens. The menu is extensive, and everything on it is good. Try the spicy house vegetarian curry with tofu wrapped in seaweed and finish with a fresh mango lassi.

88 Sridonchai Rd., A. Muang. © 05328-2463. Main courses 200B–350B (US$5.70–$10/£3.10–£5.40). MC, V. Daily 11am–10pm.

AROUND THE OLD CITY
INEXPENSIVE
The Amazing Sandwich CONTINENTAL   The recipe is simple here: Create your own "amazing" sandwich for eat-in or take-away. The palette for your masterwork is a list of ingredients and you simply tick the appropriate boxes to your heart's delight. Even if you are more interested in local food, this is a great place to get a packed lunch for a self-guided day trip. As popular among expat locals as travelers, The Amazing Sandwich now has two locations in Chiang Mai.

252/3 Phra Pokklao Rd. (near the Thai Airways office). © 05321-8846. 20/2 Huay Kaew Rd. (across from Central Kad Suan Kaew). www.amazingsandwich.com. Main courses 65B–150B (US$1.85–US$4.30/£1–£2.30). No credit cards. No. 1: Mon–Sat 10am–7pm; Sun 11am–5pm. No. 2: Mon–Sat 8:30am–8pm; Sun 8:30am–4pm.

Aroon (Rai) Restaurant ★★ NORTHERN THAI   For authentic northern food, adventurous eaters should try this nondescript garden restaurant. Their *khao sawy*, filled with egg noodles and crisp-fried chicken bits and sprinkled with dried fried noodles, is spicy and coconut-sweet at the same time. Chiang Mai sausages are served sliced over steamed rice; puffed-up fried pork rinds are the traditional, cholesterol-lover's accompaniment. Dishes are all made to order in an open kitchen, so you can point to things that interest you, including the myriad fried insects and frogs, for which this place is famous. You can even get prepackaged spices and recipes for make-it-yourself dishes back home.

45 Kotchasarn Rd. (2 blocks south of Thapae Gate, outside Old City). © 05327-6947. Main courses 40B–80B (US$1.15–US$2.30/60p–£1.25). No credit cards. Daily 9am–10pm.

Art Café INTERNATIONAL   This cheery corner cafe has black-and-white tile floors and cozy booths with picture windows overlooking the busy terminus of Thapae Road. That makes it a good spot for people-watching, resting from city touring, or to pick up free maps and city guides and meet other travelers. The menu is ambitious and offers good, familiar fare, from steaks and delicious thin-crust pizzas to Mexican dishes, meatloaf, cake, and coffee.

291 Thapae Rd. (just opposite Thapae Gate). © 05320-6365. Main courses 90B–320B (US$2.60–US$9.15/£1.40–£4.95). MC, V. Daily 8am–11pm.

Huen Phen THAI   Just a short walk south and west of Wat Phra Singh, Huen Phen is a good, authentic place to take a break and eat when temple touring. They have an English menu, but peek in the open kitchen and you'll see an extensive range of local dishes. Of course, there's *khao sawy,* Chiang Mai's famed Burmese curry with noodle, but try the specialty: *khanom jeen nam ngua,* a beef stew in a hearty broth. One small dining room has air-conditioning. You can't beat the prices here.

112 Rachamankha Rd. © 05381-4548. Main courses 20B–60B (57¢–US$1.70/30p–95p). Cash only. Daily 8:30am–3pm and 5–10pm.

JJ Coffee Shop and Bakery ✿ INTERNATIONAL   A Thai-style diner, JJ's is like an American Denny's and is in fact a local chain with three locations. Each air-conditioned restaurant has spotless tables and booths and big windows facing the street. The extensive menu includes excellent sandwiches and burgers, good fries, and all other things familiar; the waiters have personality and can even be a bit caustic, a comfortable familiarity for the true diner aficionado. Breakfasts are tops and reasonably priced, with tasty baked goods. The Thapae Road branch has a sandwich and salad bar in the evenings. There's a second branch at the Rimping Superstore across the river at 129 Lamphun Road.

388 Thapae Rd., Chiang Mai. © 05323-4007. Main courses 40B–220B (US$1–US$5.40/60p–£3.40). V. Daily 6am–8pm.

La Villa Pizzeria ITALIAN   La Villa is a friendly Italian-run operation. Light snacks like imported *prosciutto* and sardines are a treat, and main courses include *fegato alla veneziana* (beef liver fried with onions and butter) and tasty pastas. The wood-fired thin-crust pizzas, with authentic tomato sauce and vegetable or meat toppings, are light and delicious.

Pensione La Villa, 130 Ratchapakinai Rd. (north of Rachamankha Rd.). © 05327-1914. Main courses 100B–250B (US$2.85–US$7.15/£1.55–£3.85). No credit cards. Daily 11am–11pm.

WESTSIDE/HUAI KAEO ROAD

La Gritta ✿ ITALIAN   Come for their lunch buffets or order from an extensive menu of a la carte entrees ranging from *osso buco* to homemade pasta. La Gritta is in an elegant Thai-style pavilion adjoining the Amari Hotel located to the west of town. The dining room is done up in rich, carved teak, and candlelight conspires with a sultry live jazz band to make for a delightful evening. Authentic Italian dishes include fresh pasta cooked to order at a pasta station. A great wine list compliments any entree.

Amari Rincome Hotel, 1 Nimmanhaemin Rd. © 05322-1130. Main courses 250B–650B (US$7.15–US$19/£3.85–£10); buffet lunch 375B (US$11/£5.75). AE, MC, V. Daily 11:30am–2pm and 6:30–10pm.

SNACKS & CAFES

Kalare Food & Shopping Center, 89/2 Chang Klan Rd., on the corner of Soi 6, behind the bazaar (© 05327-2067; call for hours), is where you'll find a small food court next to the nightly Thai culture show (buy coupons at a booth and then pick what you want from vendors).

   Bake and Bite (6/1 Kotchasarn Rd. Soi 1; © 05328-5185; Mon–Sat 7am–6pm and Sun 7am–3pm) is on a small side street to the south of Thapae Gate and has tasty baked goods, fine bread, and good coffee.

The Kafe (127-129 Moon Muang Rd.; © **05321-2717;** call for hours) is just north of Thapae Gate and it's a good traveler's crossroads where you can pick up handy information, have a great meal of Thai or basic Western food, and throw back a few cold ones.

Mike's Original (© **086269-9145,** mobile; daily 8am–3am) serves hotdogs, burgers, and fries in an open-air 1950s American hotdog stand. Just north of Thapae Road (and the Amora Hotel) on the east edge of the Old City, it's a popular stop for post-drinking eats before the hangover hits.

All along Nimmanheimin Road new, trendy eateries and coffee shops are springing up next to little juice bars and ice-cream parlors; take a stroll and pick your place.

4 Exploring Cultural Chiang Mai

THE WATS

Chiang Mai has more than 700 temples, the largest concentration outside of Bangkok, and unique little sites are around every corner. In one very full day you can hit the highlights in Old Chiang Mai if you travel by tuk-tuk.

Wat Chedi Luang ✷✷✷   Because this temple is near the Thapae Gate, most visitors begin their sightseeing here, where there are two *wats* of interest. This complex, which briefly housed the Emerald Buddha (now at Bangkok's Wat Phra Kaew), dates from 1411 when the original *chedi* was built by King Saen Muang Ma. The already-massive edifice was expanded to 84m (280 ft.) in height in the mid-1400s, only to be ruined by a severe earthquake in 1545, just 11 years before Chiang Mai fell to the Burmese. (It was never rebuilt.) Buddhas still grace its exterior, and it is not unusual to spot a saffron-robed monk bowing to them as he circles the *chedi.*

Wat Phan Tao, also on the grounds, has a wooden *viharn* (assembly hall) and *bot* (central shrine in a Buddhist temple), a reclining Buddha, and fine carving on the eaves and door. After leaving the temple, walk around to the monks' quarters on the side, taking in the traditional teak northern architecture and delightful landscaping.

Propokklao Rd. south of Ratchadamnoen Rd. Suggested donation 20B (57¢/30p). Daily 6am–5pm.

Wat Chiang Man   Thought to be Chiang Mai's oldest *wat,* this was built during the 14th century by King Mengrai, the founder of Chiang Mai, on the spot where he first camped. Like many of the *wats* in Chiang Mai, this complex reflects many architectural styles. Some of the structures are pure Lanna. Others show influences from as far away as Sri Lanka; notice the typical row of elephant supports. Wat Chiang Man is most famous for its two Buddhas: Phra Sae Tang Khamani (a miniature crystal image also known as the **White Emerald Buddha**) and the marble **Phra Sila Buddha.** Unfortunately, the *viharn* that safeguards these religious sculptures is almost always closed.

Ratchapakinai Rd. south of the Si Phum Rd. moat. Suggested donation 20B (57¢/30p). Daily 6am–5pm.

Wat Jed Yod ✷✷   Also called Wat Maha Photharam, Wat Jed Yod ("Temple of the Seven Spires") is one of the central city's most elegant sites. The *chedi* was built during the reign of King Tilokkarat in the late 15th century (his remains are in one of the smaller *chedis*), and in 1477 the World Sangkayana convened here to revise the doctrines of the Buddha.

The unusual design of the main rectangular *chedi* with seven peaks was copied from the Maha Bodhi Temple in Bodhgaya, India, where the Buddha first achieved

Chiang Mai Attractions

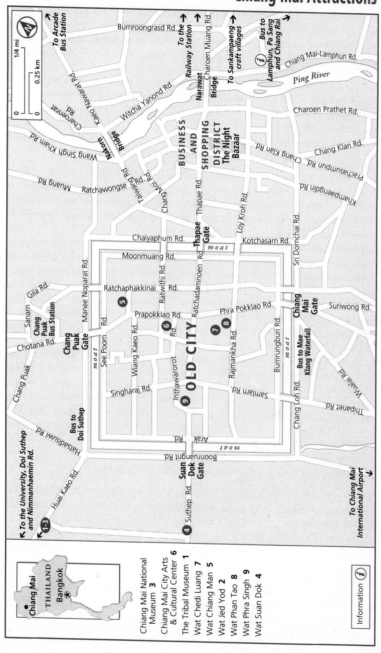

To Arcade Bus Station
1/4 mi
0.25 km

Bumroongrasd Rd.
To the Railway Station
Charoen Muang Rd.
Bus to Lamphun, Pa Sang and Chiang Rai
Chiang Mai-Lamphun Rd.
Ping River

Witcha Yanond Rd.
Narawat Bridge
To Sankampaeng craft villages
Charoen Prathet Rd.

Kaeo Nawarat Rd.
Charoenrat Rd.

BUSINESS AND SHOPPING DISTRICT
The Night Bazaar
Chang Klan Rd.

Nakorn Bridge
Wang Singh Kham Rd.
Muang Rd.
Ratchawongse Rd.
Thapae Rd.
Prachasumpun Rd.
Khampaengdin Rd.

Taiwang Rd.
Chang Moi Rd.
Loy Kroh Rd.

Chaiyaphum Rd.
Thapae Gate
moat
Kotchasarn Rd.

Moonmuang Rd.
Sri Domchai Rd.

Ratchaphakkinai Rd.
Ratwithi Rd.
Ratchadamnoen Rd.
Manee Noparat Rd.
⑤
Phra Pokklao Rd.
Chiang Mai Gate
Suriwong Rd.

Gila Rd.
Sanarn
Prapokklao Rd.
⑥
⑦ ⑧

Chang Puak Bus Station
Chang Puak Gate
See Poom Rd.
Wiang Kaeo Rd.
OLD CITY
Rajmankha Rd.
Bus to Mae Klang Waterfall
Bumrungburi Rd.

Chotana Rd.
moat
Inthawarorot Rd.
⑨
Samlarn Rd.
Chang Loh Rd.
Wualai Rd.

Chang Puak
Singharaj Rd.
Thipanet Rd.

Huai Kaeo Rd.
Hatsadisawi Rd.
Bus to Doi Suthep
Arak Rd.
Suan Dok Gate
Boonruangrit Rd.
moat

To the University, Doi Suthep and Nimmanhaemin Rd.
⑬
Suthep Rd.
④
To Chiang Mai International Airport

THAILAND
Bangkok
Chiang Mai

Information ⓘ

enlightenment. The temple also has architectural elements reflecting Burmese and early Chinese influences supposed to date back to the Yuan and Ming dynasties. The extraordinary proportions, the angelic, levitating *devata* figures carved into the base of the *chedi,* and the juxtaposition of the other buildings make Wat Jed Yod a masterpiece.

The Lanna-style Buddha hidden in the center was sculpted in the mid-15th century; a door inside the niche containing the Buddha leads to the roof on which rests the **Phra Kaen Chan (Sandalwood Buddha).** There is a nice vista from up top, but unfortunately, dinosaur-aged tradition prevails and only men are allowed to ascend the stairs.

Superhighway near the Chiang Mai National Museum (north of the intersection of Nimmanhaemin and Huai Kaeo rds., about 1km/⅗ mile on the left). Suggested donation 20B (57¢/30p). Daily 6am–5pm.

Wat Phra Singh ★★★ This compound was built during the zenith of Chiang Mai's power and is one of the more venerated shrines in the city. It is still the site of many important religious ceremonies, particularly during the Songkran Festival. More than 700 monks study here and you will probably find them especially friendly with tourists.

King Phayu, of Mengrai lineage, built the *chedis* (stupas) in 1345, principally to house the cremated remains of King Kamfu, his father. As you enter the grounds, head to the right toward the 14th-century library. Notice the graceful carving and the characteristic roofline with four separate elevations. The sculptural *devata* (Buddhist spirits) figures, in both dancing and meditative poses, are thought to have been made during King Muang Kaeo's reign in the early 16th century. They decorate a stone base designed to keep the fragile *saa* (mulberry bark) manuscripts elevated from flooding and vermin.

On the other side of the temple complex is the 200-year-old **Lai Kham (Gilded Hall) Viharn,** housing the venerated image of the Phra Singh or **Lion Buddha,** brought to the site by King Muang Ma in 1400. The original Buddha's head was stolen in 1922, but the reproduction in its place doesn't diminish the homage paid to this figure during Songkran. Inside are frescoes illustrating the stories of Sang Thong (the Golden Prince of the Conchshell), and Suwannahong. These images convey a great deal about the religious, civil, and military life of 19th-century Chiang Mai during King Mahotraprathet's reign.

Samlarn and Ratchadamnoen rds. Suggested donation 20B (57¢/30p). Daily 6am–5pm.

Wat Suan Dok This complex is special less for its architecture (the buildings, though monumental, are undistinguished) than for its contemplative spirit and pleasant surroundings.

The temple was built amid the pleasure gardens of the 14th century Lanna Thai monarch, King Ku Na. Unlike most of Chiang Mai's other *wats* (more tourist sights than working temples and schools), Wat Suan Dok houses quite a few monks who seem to have isolated themselves from the distractions of the outside world.

Among the main attractions in the complex are the *bot,* with a very impressive **Chiang Saen Buddha** (one of the largest bronzes in the north) dating from 1504 and some garish murals. Also of interest is the *chedi,* built to hold a relic of the Buddha, and a royal cemetery with some splendid shrines. There is an informal "monk chat" here each week (see the box, below).

Suthep Rd. (from the Old City, take the Suan Dok Gate and continue 1.6km/1 mile west). Suggested donation 20B (57¢/30p). Daily 6am–5pm.

Monk Chat

What do you say to these tonsured men in orange robes one sees piously padding barefoot around Thailand? The answer is: "Hello. How are you?" Monks, especially seniors, deserve a special level of respect, of course, but are quite human, and the best way to find out is to stop by Mahachulalongkorn University (adjoining Wat Suan Dok, see above, east of town on Suthep Rd.). Every Monday, Wednesday, and Friday, from 5 to 7pm, they welcome foreign visitors for "monk chat," a classroom venue of small, informal discussion groups where visitors and monks come to connect, share culture, and learn about Buddhism from novices eager to explain and, of course, practice their English. It is a mostly informal discussion about one's own country or sports (young novices are nuts about David Beckham and English Premier League football), but the more senior monks can give you some insights into Buddhist practice and monastic life. They also meet for meditation groups and retreats. Call ℂ **05327-8967,** e-mail thaimonkchat@yahoo.com, or visit www.monkchat.net for info.

MUSEUMS

Chiang Mai City Arts and Cultural Center   In the building adjacent to the Three Kings Monument in the heart of the Old City, this museum houses a permanent exhibit that walks visitors through a tour of pre-history to the present. Another section houses short-term local exhibits of all types. This is a popular choice (it gets crowded with school trips) for those looking for some historical insights.

Phra Pokklao Rd.. ℂ **05321-7793.** Admission 90B (US$2.60/£1.40). Tues–Sun 8:30am–5pm.

Chiang Mai National Museum   While its collection of historical treasures is not nearly as extensive as that of Bangkok's National Museum, this quick stop does provide something of a historical overview—and the highlights—of the region and the city. The Lanna kingdom, Tai people, and hill-tribes are highlighted in simple displays with English explanations.

Just off the superhighway northwest of the Old City near Wat Jed Yod. ℂ **05322-1308.** Admission 30B (85¢/40p). Wed–Sun 9am–4pm.

The Chiang Mai Zoo *Kids*   One of Chiang Mai's most popular attractions for locals is the pair of pandas, **Thewan** and **Thewee,** the stars of Chiang Mai's extensive zoo. It's nothing by international standards, but a good day out with kids who may be wilting from temple overdose.

100 Huai Kaeo Rd. (west of town on the road to Doi Suthep). ℂ **05322-1179.** Admission 100B (US$2.85/£1.55) adults, 50B (US$1.45/£75) children. Daily 8am–6pm.

The Tribal Museum   Formerly part of Chiang Mai University's Tribal Research Institute, this small exhibit showcases the cultures and daily lives of the hill-tribe people of Thailand's north. It is recommended as a good introductory course for those who plan to visit many northern villages.

In Ratchamankhla Park on Chotana Rd. ℂ **05322-1933.** Free admission. Mon–Fri 9am–4pm.

CULTURAL PURSUITS
THAI COOKING SCHOOL

If you love Thai food and fancy yourself a chef, consider taking a cooking class in Chiang Mai. The priciest cookery classes are offered at top resorts like the **Mandarin Oriental Dhara Dhevi** (covered earlier), but very reasonable courses abound in town as well, such as those offered at **Chiang Mai Cookery School** ★, the oldest establishment of its kind in Chiang Mai. They have 5-day courses, each teaching basic Thai cooking skills, but daily menus feature up to seven new dishes—over a week you can learn a lot. You'll have hands-on training and a lot of fun. Classes start at 10am, last until 4pm, and cost 990B (US$28/£15) for the day. Contact them at their main office at 1–3 Moon Muang Rd., opposite the Thapae Gate (✆ **05320-6388;** www.thaicookeryschool.com).

Another school to try is **Kao Hom** (✆ **05386-2967;** www.kaohom.com), established by two sisters. It is open daily except Mondays. Group classes are held from 10:30am to 2:30pm and cost 2,500B (US$71/£38) per person; private lessons run 4:30 to 7:30pm and cost a bit more—3,500B (US$100/£53).

MASSAGE SCHOOL

The **Thai massage schools** in Bangkok and Phuket teach the southern style of Thai massage, which places pressure on muscles to make them tender and relaxed. Northern-style Thai massage is something closer to yoga, where your muscles are stretched and elongated to enhance flexibility and relaxation. There are a number of schools in Chiang Mai, and many are no more than small storefronts where, for very little, you'll get individual instruction of varying quality. It is best to go with a more established school: **International Training Massage,** or **ITM,** has popular courses (conducted in English) for anyone from first-timers to experts. Each five-day course is 3,500B (US$100/£54). Contact them at 17/7 Morakot Rd., Hah Yaek Santitham (✆ **05321-8632;** fax 05322-4197).

MEDITATION

The **Northern Insight Meditation Center** at Wat Rampoeng (Kan Klongchon-prathan Rd.) is a well-respected center for learning Vipassana meditation. "Are you ready?" is all they'll ask you upon arrival, because the daily schedule means rising early and many hours spent in concentration. The monks, nuns, and lay volunteers who run the center invite only men and women who bring a certain resolve or at least a willingness to stay for 10 days (though the 26-day course is highly recommended). Volumes have been written about the practice of Vipassana, but the main idea is to develop mindfulness and observe one's body, mind, and emotions—to eventually gain "insight" and to see things as they are, without delusion. Come prepared to "peel the onion" of the ego. Participants are assigned very sparse private rooms, are asked to wear white, loose-fitting clothes (available at the temple store), and basic meals are served at 6 and 10:30am only (there isn't an evening meal). Rules are drawn from the monastic precept and are thus rigid. There is no charge for the course, but you will be asked to make a contribution to the temple of whatever amount you see fit. Retreats are ongoing, but they try to consolidate first-timer's start dates for orientation purposes. Call ahead (3 weeks in advance is preferred) at ✆ **05327-8620.** The temple also welcomes day visitors, and it might be a good idea for those considering a course to have a look. Located on a rural road south and west of town (past the airport), the temple is best reached by tuk-tuk, *songtaew,* or rented motorbike. (Wat Rampoeng, Tambol Suthep, Chiang Mai; ✆ **05327-8620;** www.watrampoeng.com.)

5 Chiang Mai Activities

TOURS, TREKS & OUTDOOR ADVENTURE

There are so many tour groups in Chiang Mai that specialize in trekking that it can seem impossible to choose one. Below are some of the better options—and most reputable operators—for each type of trip. Most of the smaller companies have offices along Thapae Road, in guesthouses, and all along the major tourist routes in the city, and they are always happy to talk about what's on offer. Many adventure tours mix mountain biking or motorcycling with tribal village tours. See "Tours & Trekking in the Far North" in chapter 11 for more information on the hill-tribes themselves, descriptions of what to expect on tours, how to select a good operator, and how to prepare for your trip.

For **jungle trekking,** there are a number of small outfits arranging trips from Chiang Mai, but **Contact Travel** (www.activethailand.com) is in a category all its own. Combining treks and village stays with multisport adventures by Jeep, bicycle, and kayak, the folks at Contact can cater a tour to any needs and price range. They also offer more traditional itineraries with elephant treks, visits to caves, and relaxing bamboo raft river trips, and their English-speaking guides are the best in the area. Treks from Chiang Mai stop at Lisu, Lahu, and Karen villages. A 2-day/1-night trip is 4,600B (US$131/£71) per person if you join their regular tour, or 5,600B (US$160/£86) per person for a private group trip. A 3-day/2-night trip, which takes you to a greater variety of villages, is 5,500B (US$157/£85) per person if you join their regular tour or 6,850B (US$196/£105) per person for a private group. For an additional 1,500B (US$43/£23) per person you can hire a porter to wrestle your bags along. Their office in Chiang Mai is at 420/3 Chang Klan Rd. (© 05327-7178; fax 05327-9505).

Small operators that cater to the low-end backpacker market offer trips for as little as 1,500B (US$43/£23) per day. This usually means being in a large group, with care and feeding at a lower standard, but that's budget-trekking—and there is a kind of fun in commiseration over post-trek beers. You might try the following companies:

Top North Tours (41 Moon Muang Rd., Chiang Mai; © 05320-8788) offers a range of short tours featuring trekking, bamboo rafting, and elephant riding. They're a reliable budget choice, but that means big groups and basic services. **Queen Bee Travel Service** (5 Moon Muang Rd., Chiang Mai; © 05327-5525; www.queen-bee. com) has a whole range of budget trekking services and cultural tours.

BOAT TRIPS

Within the city, a **long-tail boat trip** along the Mae Ping River is a fun diversion. Head for the boat landing of **Mae Ping River Cruise Co.** (133 Charoen Prathet Rd.; © 05327-4822; www.maepingrivercruise.com) at **Wat Chaimongkol** on Charoen Prathet Rd., opposite Alliance Française). A tour lasts about 2 hours and costs 500B (US$14/£7.70) with fruit and drinks included. Starting in the city center, you'll get great views of old teak riverside mansions, behind which rises the tall skyline of this developing burg. While on the outskirts of town, you'll see villages that offer scenes of more suburban and rural living.

ELEPHANT ENCOUNTERS ★

One of Thailand's greatest treasures, the domesticated Asian elephant has worked alongside men since the early history of Siam, and these gentle giants are an important symbol of the kingdom. Elephant training culture is strongest in parts of Isan (the northeast) and the far north. In and around Chiang Mai alone, there are a grand total of 14 elephant camps that try to cash in on the popularity of these gentle giants. Not all elephant camps are pleasant: at shoddier camps, creatures are drugged to keep them placid, and conditions are grim. Choose your elephant camp wisely. Resort-run ele-camps such as those at Anantara and **Four Seasons' Tented Camp,** both north of Chiang Rai in the Golden Triangle, are among the most humane. By far the best way to interact with the animals is a visit to the **Thai Elephant Conservation Center** in Lampang (see the Lampang section in "Side Trips from Chiang Mai," later in this chapter). In and around the immediate Chiang Mai area, though, you have your pick of day trips. Just north of town in the Mae Rim Valley you'll find a number of camps offering packaged programs (all similar) that are fun, especially for kids. Most day-tours include a few hours of hill trekking on elephant back with groups of three or four in a *howdah* (elephant seat), which is followed by ox-cart rides to so-called "prim-itive" tourist villages and even bamboo rafting back to camp. **Maetamann Elephant Camp** (535 Rimtai, Mae Rim, Chiang Mai 50180; © 05329-7060) is one recom-mended camp to try. They charge a hefty 1,500B (US$43/£23) per person, but this ticket includes the show, bamboo rafting, elephant ride, and a simple meal.

MOUNTAIN BIKING
Out in the fresh air in the hills outside of town you can get a slower, closer look at nature, sights, and people. Many small trekking companies and travel agents offer day trips, but I recommend the folks at **Contact Travel** (420/3 Chang Klan Rd; © 05327-7178) for their 1-day excursions just north of town or for multi-day adventures in the region. Day trips start at 1,800B (US$51/£28).

OTHER ACTIVITIES
Chiang Mai has a few noteworthy venues for adventure and extreme sports. This is the only place in Thailand where commercial **Hot-Air Ballooning** ✯✯✯ has been approved. **Earth, Wind and Fire** (158/60 Moo 6 Cheungdoi, Doi Saket; © 05329-2224; www.balloon.wind-and-fire.com) is a highly reputable and certified outfit with professional pilots operating pre-dawn rides between November and March—depend-ing on the weather. Prices are available on request.

Chiang Mai has succumbed to the **bungee jumping** craze; addicts can head north to the Mae Rim area to try this sport out. First-timers pay 1,500B (US$43/£23), but thereafter it's 1,000B (US$29/£15). For details, call © 05329-8442.

Rock climbers can practice on a challenging man-made rock wall at **The Peak** (28/2 Chang Klan Rd.; © 05382-0776-8), near the Night Bazaar. Single climbs cost 200B (US$5.70/£3.10), and hourly rates are available. They also arrange trips for climbing the real rocks in the surrounding hills.

Ultra-light aircraft flights have come to Chiang Mai as well. A small but very organized operation, **Chiang Mai Sky Adventures,** flies from a private airstrip north of the city in Doi Saket. A 15-minute flight, more or less a piggy-back ride on the pilot's shoulders, costs just 1,700B (US$49/£26) and takes you on a great loop out over a large dam and reservoir and past a spectacular hilltop temple. They also do flight instruction and certification. Call Mr. Chaimongkol at © 05386-8460 or visit www.skyadventures.info for info.

HITTING THE LINKS

For Thais and Western retirees, golf is a favored hobby in Chiang Mai, especially in the cooler months. All courses below are open to the public and offer equipment rental. Call ahead to reserve a tee-time.

- **Chiang Mai Green Valley Country Club,** located in Mae Rim, 20 minutes north of town on Rte. 107, 183/2 Chotana Rd. (℃ **05329-8249;** fax 05327-9386), is in excellent condition with flat greens and fairways that slope toward the Ping River (greens fees: weekdays 1,200B–1,800B/US$29–US$51/£18–£28; weekends 2,000B–2,400B/US$49–US$69/£31–£37).

- **Chiang Mai–Lamphun Golf Club,** Baan Thi Road, 10km (6 miles) east of Sankampaeng (℃ **05324-8397;** fax 05324-8937), located in a valley to the east, is a fine 18-hole course (greens fees: weekdays 1,400B–1,600B/US$34–US$46/£22–£25; weekends 1,800B–2,000B/US$44–US$57/£28–£31).

- **Lanna Golf Club,** on Chotana Road, 2km (1¼ miles) north of the Old City (℃ **05322-1911;** fax 05322-1743), is a challenging, wooded 27 holes, and a local favorite with great views of Doi Suthep Mountain (greens fees: weekdays 600B–1,000B/US$15–US$29/£9.25–£15; weekends 800B–1,200B/US$20–US$34/£12–£18).

SPAS & MASSAGE

The spa industry is taking off all over Thailand and Chiang Mai is no exception. There are a few fine, full-service spas in and around town, and treatments come with a price but are worth it. Many hotels offer massage and beauty treatments, but some new "spa" areas are no more than converted guest rooms with subdued lighting and overpriced services. You can pay a fraction of the cost for the same treatment at one of the many small storefront massage parlors in and around any tourist area of the city. *Note:* The offer of an oil massage in a back room often covers for soliciting for sexual services.

Some of the most luxurious spas can be found in luxury resorts near Chiang Mai:

The Dhevi Spa ⚜⚜⚜ at the **Mandarin Oriental Dhara Dhevi** (51/4 Chiang Mai–Sankampaeng Rd., 5 km [3 miles] east of town; ℃ **05388-8888; www.mandarin oriental.com**) is an enormous complex built of teak to mimic a Burmese palace. The treatments and spa environment are extensive, with the unusual addition of a starlit sauna or *rasoul,* and therapies which reflect local Lanna culture.

Oasis Spa ⚜ offers a good standard of service at its four locations in town: at 102 Sirimangkalajarn Rd., 4 Samlan Rd., 22 Chaiyaphum Rd., and 200 Moo 7, Chiang Mai–Doi Saket Rd. For reservations, call ℃ **05381-5000** or visit www.chiangmaioasis.com. A luxury campus of private spa villas, Oasis Spa offers a long roster of treatments and provides free pickup and drop-off from hotels in Chiang Mai.

Baan Sabai (on 17/7 Charoen Prathet Rd.; ℃ **05328-5204;** or 216 Moo 9, San Pee Sua; ℃ **05385-4775**) is the bridge between the expensive services of a five-star spa and the affordable street-side places. You get the best of both worlds here: a stylish facility and escape for a few hours at affordable rates. You can visit either their convenient in-town hideaway (near the Night Bazaar), or the more spacious "Village" location just northeast of town.

Let's Relax, located in Chiang Mai Pavilion (on the second floor above McDonald's, 145/27 Chang Klan Rd.; ℃ **05381-8498**) and its sister, **Rarin Jinda,** located opposite the Riverside Restaurant (14 Charoenrat Rd.; ℃ **05324-7000**) have affordable massages and are perfect for a quick rest and recharge when wading through the Night Bazaar area.

6 Shopping

If you plan to shop in Thailand, save your money for Chiang Mai. Quality craft pieces and handmade, traditional items still sell for very little, and large outlets for fine antiques and high-end goods abound in and around the city. Many shoppers pick up an affordable new piece of luggage to tote their finds home and, if you find that huge standing Buddha or oversized Thai divan you've been searching for, all shops can arrange shipping—or look for the **UPS** office in the basement of the Night Bazaar (Chang Klan Rd.; © **05382-0222;** Mon–Fri 7am–10pm).

WHAT TO BUY

Thailand has a rich tradition of handicrafts, developed over centuries of combining local materials, indigenous technology, and skills from Chinese and Indian merchants. Drawing on such ancient technologies and the abundance of hardwoods, precious metals and stones, raw materials (for fabrics and dyes), and bamboo and clay, modern craftsmen have refined traditional techniques and now cater their wares to the modern market. Below is a breakdown of what you might find:

Tribal weaving and craftwork is for sale everywhere in the Lanna capital and you can come away with some unique finds. Check out the highly innovative **Sop Moei Arts** at 9 Charoenrat Rd. (www.sopmoeiarts.com), whose homegrown crafts and ceramics help sustain Pwe Karen hill-tribes, or the well-known **Mae Fah Luang** shops (a branch is at Chiang Mai airport), which is part of a different charity assisting hill-tribe communities and abused women.

Of late, **hill-tribe embroidery crafts** have been modified into more modern items; you'll find anything from chic shoulder bags and backpacks to pleated mini skirts and appliqué shirts. The hill-tribes' **hand-woven textiles** are rich in texture and natural tones, and dyed with natural plants dyes. Cool, ready-made cotton clothing can also be found anywhere for a song.

Some of the city's best **art galleries** and **crafts stores** are all clustered around Charoenrat Road. Pop into **La Luna** (© **05330-6678**) for contemporary **Asian art, ceramics, art photography,** and **furniture,** while a few minutes' walk away are **Vila Cini** (© **05324-6246**) and **Oriental Style** (no phone); both have racks of stunning **silk** collections and tasteful **souvenirs,** with some truly outstanding **hand-loomed silk furnishings.**

Fine **silver** works are synonymous with Chiang Mai. Early smiths are believed to have emigrated from Myanmar (Burma) with the coming of Kublai Khan, and skills have been passed from generation to generation. While silver is not a local resource, early raw materials were acquired from coins brought by traders. Traditional bowls feature intricate raised (*repoussé*) floral designs—the deeper the imprint, the higher quality the silver (some up to 80%). Some hill-tribe groups are known for their fine **silver jewelry**—necklaces, bangles, and earrings—in unusual traditional ethnic designs or more ordinary Western styles. For all hill-tribe handicrafts, the best place to shop is at the Night Bazaar.

Jewelry items are crafted in delicate filigree designs in styles copied by many Western manufacturers. Modern jewelry can be found at boutiques along Nimmanhaemin Road or at La Luna (see above). Many families set up shop along Wua Lai Road, and there are a number of (albeit touristy) outlets on Sankampaeng Road.

The early royals commissioned carvers to produce wood furnishings for use in palaces, thrones, temple doors and adornments, carriages, pavilions, *howdahs* (seats for riding elephants), and royal barges. The excellent quality of hardwoods in Thailand's forests allowed these items to be adorned with grand and intricate wood carvings. The skills survived, and talented craftspeople still produce furniture, boxes, and all varieties of gift items imaginable. **Wood carving** today is perhaps more influenced by foreign preferences, and most pieces are mass-produced.

Lacquer skills came from China with early migrants. Sap is applied in layers to wooden, clay, or bamboo items and can be carved, colored, and sometimes inlayed with mother-of-pearl for a very elegant finished product. Today it is acknowledged as a traditional Chiang Mai craft, having been perfected over centuries by the Tai Khoen people who live in communities outside the city. **Lacquerware** vases, boxes, bangles, and traditional items are lightweight gifts, practical for carrying home. Larger tiered boxes and furnishings can be shipped.

Celadon pottery is elegantly simple in tones of the palest gray-greens. The distinctive color of the glaze comes from a mixture of local clay and wood ash. Chiang Mai has some of the largest and best celadon factories in the country. The best places to purchase celadon are at the beautiful Lanna-style compound of Baan Celadon (www.baanceladon.com), 10km (6 miles) out of town, or at the large factory outlets.

Authentic antiques, except for furniture, are virtually extinct in the tourist areas of Chiang Mai. Most furniture is from China. Some shops may offer certificates of authenticity, but as anywhere, the rule is "buyer beware." If you do get your hands on the genuine article, you may have a problem getting it home (see "Customs," in chapter 2's "Fast Facts: Thailand").

MARKETS

For many, the **Night Bazaar** is the city's premier attraction, and hours spent wandering amid the cacophony of hawkers, noisy haggling, and all manner of traditional goods and electronic gadgets are part and parcel of the city's charms—but for those who know Bangkok or Phuket's night markets, there will be little variety in goods sold.

Located on north-to-south running Chang Klan Road between Thapae and Loy Kroh roads, the market starts around 6pm each night and slows down at about 11pm. The actual Night Bazaar is a modern, antiseptic, three-story building, but the indoor and outdoor market extends south to Sri Dornchai Road and far beyond. Many shops and stalls remain open throughout the day and evening too, especially along Chang Klan Road.

The stalls have grandiose names, like Harrods (with the familiar logo), and most carry poor counterfeit copies of international brand-name clothing, watches, and luggage. Follow the old adage: You only get what you pay for. If it falls to bits in a week, count yourself lucky. Despite many countries cracking down on them, illegally pirated DVDs—usually of very shoddy quality—are widespread, together with so-called "antiques," such as opium pipes or opium weights. You name it; nothing here will be real—or last much longer than the homeward journey.

Inside the Night Bazaar there are mass-manufactured Chinese goods like low-cost fashions and souvenirs. More interesting are the tribal bric-a-brac stalls or items sold by wandering vendors dressed in hill-tribe get-up. The top floor has booths selling locally produced handicrafts, fake antiques, and decorative arts.

The **Anusarn Night Market** down Charoen Prathet Road, south of Suriwongse Road, carries more hill-tribe goods in authentic traditional styles.

The **Warowot Market** on Chang Moi and Wichayanon roads opens every morning at 7am and stays open until 4pm. This central indoor market is the city's largest.

Produce, colorful fruits, spices, and food products jam the ground floor. On the second floor, things are calmer, with dozens of vendors selling cheap cotton sportswear, Thai-made shoes, and some hill-tribe handicrafts and garments: It's fun and inexpensive.

SHOPPING IN THE CITY CENTER & OLD TOWN

Small shops and boutiques line the areas around the market and Old Town, luring visitors from the many nearby hotels, but many local designer boutiques have moved out to Nimmanhaemin Road (see below). **Ginger** (199 Moon Muang Rd. Soi 7; ⓒ 05341-9014) is a Thai-Danish affair selling gorgeous contemporary day wear (large European sizes are sadly limited), fun accessories, and fabulous twinkly costume jewelry. **Nova Collection** (201 Thapae Rd.; ⓒ 05327-3058) carries a unique line of decorative jewelry in contemporary styles with Asian influences. They make custom pieces and even offer courses in metalwork and jewelry making. **Princess Jewelry** (147/8 Chang Klan Rd., near the Night Bazaar; ⓒ 05327-3648) offers customized and ready-made jewelry, and good personalized service. **Mengrai Kilns** (79/2 Arak Rd., Soi Samlarn 6; ⓒ 05327-2063), is in the southwest corner of the old city and specializes in fine celadon and decorative items. There are lots of silk dealers and tailors in and around town of varying quality. Try **City Silk** (336 Thapae Rd., 1 block east of the gate; ⓒ 05323-4388) among the many for its good selection and affordable tailoring. Though its retail arm closed in October 2007, **Living Space** (no phone; www.livingspace.com), the city's most famous purveyor of sleek gifts, home furnishings, celadon, lacquerware and decorative items, is still thriving, but is hoping to focus more on wholesale orders—see its website for updates.

WEST SIDE OF THE OLD CITY

All along the *sois* of **Nimmanhaemin Road**, across from the Amari Rincome Hotel, are new boutiques selling crafts and designer wear. These make for good one-stop shopping if your time is short. Soi 1, next to the hotel, is especially good for textiles, homeware, and candles. Look for **Gong Dee Gallery** (ⓒ 05322-5032), which has an extensive collection of gifts and original artwork. **Design One** (ⓒ 05322-5833) produces lovely teak furnishings. **Tawan Decor** (ⓒ 05389-4941) features a host of unique knickknacks and furnishings, and **Wit's Collection** (ⓒ 05321-7544) is a truly sublime, all-white boutique featuring a treasure trove of fantastic contemporary furniture, ceramics, and homeware.

WULAI ROAD

Chiang Mai's silver industry is located just south of Chiang Mai Gate. **Siam Silverware** (5 Wua Lai Rd., Soi 3; ⓒ 05327-9013) tops the list of many offering fine crafted jewelry and silverwork.

SANKAMPAENG ROAD

Shopaholics will be thrilled by the many outlets along the Chiang Mai–Sankampaeng Road (Rte. 1006). Hop in a taxi (or find a *songtaew* plying this busy road) due east of town; after several kilometers, you'll reach the many shops, showrooms, and factories extending along a 9km (5½ miles) strip here. Talk to any concierge or travel agent about a full- or half-day shopping tour. *Important:* Do not arrange a day of shopping with a tuk-tuk or taxi driver, as they will collect a commission and drive up the price of your purchases.

The many shops along Sankampaeng feature anything from lacquerware to ready-made clothes, and from silver to celadon pottery. Among the many, try: **Laitong**

Lacquerware (140/1–2 Moo 3, Chiang Mai-Sankampaeng Rd.; ℂ **05333-8237**), which carries a host of fine lacquer gifts (among other items). Some of the smaller items, like jewelry boxes, can be quite lightweight, so you won't have to lug tons home with you. *Saa* (mulberry bark) paper cards with pressed flowers, stationery, notebooks, and gifts are not only top quality, but they're perfect for light travelers. **Mesa U&P Company**'s selection is quite good. Head for 78–78/3 Moo 10, Sankampaeng Road (ℂ **05333-1141**).

For larger housewares and objets d'art, **Pa Ker Yaw Basket & Textile,** 136/1 Moo 2, Sankampaeng Road (ℂ **05333-8512**), deals in fabulous baskets of all shapes and sizes, featuring weaving techniques from hill-tribes in Thailand, Myanmar (Burma), Laos, and Vietnam. For a large selection of lettuce-green celadon in traditional Thai designs, **Baan Celadon** has a lovely rustic compound at 7 Moo 3, Chiang Mai–Sankampaeng Road (ℂ **05333-8288**). Smooth and lustrous vases, jars, bowls, and decorative objects spring to life from the local hardwoods sold here; you'd almost think these turned-wood products were porcelain. Nearby **Aroon Colorware,** 67 Moo 4, Baan Sankaokaepgang (ℂ **05388-1605**), turns out some great modern gifts that make use of Thai materials—the coconut wood items are especially nice.

Jolie Femme Thai Silk, 8/3 Sankampaeng Rd. (ℂ **05311-6777**) weaves traditional silks in rich colors and they style much of their stock into modern ready-to-wear creations. There's also the rather outmoded **Shinawatra Thai Silk,** 145/1–2 Sankampaeng Rd. (ℂ **05322-1076**). But for truly exquisite woven silk, head to **Vila Cini's** ✦✦ branch at Mandarin Oriental Dhara Dhevi (on Sankampaeng Rd.); a bigger selection is available at the Charoenraj Road shop. Though focusing less on fashions and more on silk furnishings, this homegrown silk merchant outdoes even Jim Thompson's (p. 143) for creativity and sumptuously stylish designs, all following traditional Lanna hues and inspiration.

VILLAGES

Many of the handicrafts you'll find in town—and out at Sankampaeng Road—are the fine work of local villagers around Chiang Mai. They welcome visitors to their villages to see their traditional craft techniques that have been handed down through generations. Purchase these items directly from the source, and you might save.

East of Chiang Mai, **Sri-pun-krua** (near the railway station) specializes in bamboo products and lacquerware. Near Sankampaeng Road, the village of **Tohn Pao** (about 8km/5 miles outside the city) produces *saa* paper products; **Bor Sarng** (10km/6 miles outside the city) is a nationally renowned center for painted paper umbrellas and fans; and **Baan Tohn** (13km/21 miles outside the city) makes fine wood carvings, in addition to umbrellas. Just to the south, **Pa-bong** (about 6km/3¾ miles down Superhighway 11) manufactures furnishings and household items from bamboo.

South of the city, **Muang Goong** (along Hwy. 108) is a center for clay pottery; **Roi-Jaan** (about 8km/5 miles along the same highway) weaves cottons, dying them in natural colors extracted from natural products; while **Tha-wai** (14km/8½ miles south) employs families that craft carved wood antique reproductions.

7 Chiang Mai After Dark

Pick up a copy of *Welcome to Chiang Mai & Chiang Rai* magazine at your hotel for listings of special events in town during your stay. But most folks will spend at least one evening at the Night Bazaar (see above). For an impromptu bar scene, you can duck into one of the back alleys behind the Night Bazaar mall that are lined with tiny bars—there local singer-guitarists play modern tunes.

If you get tired and hungry during bar hopping at the Night Bazaar, you'll want to stop at **Kalare Food & Shopping Center,** 89/2 Chang Klan Rd., on the corner of Soi 6, behind the bazaar (✆ 05327-2067). Free nightly traditional Thai folk dance and musical performances grace an informal beer garden, where shoppers can stop for a drink or pick up inexpensive Chinese, Thai, and Indian food from the stalls there.

For a more studied **cultural performance,** the **Old Chiang Mai Cultural Center,** 185/3 Wua Lai Rd. (✆ 05320-2993), stages a good show at 7pm every night for 320B (US$9.15/£4.90), which includes dinner. Live music accompanies female dancers in lavish costumes who perform traditional dances. In between sets, men dance with knives and swords. A *khan toke* dinner is served, and despite the crowds, the wait staff is attentive. Yes, it is touristy—busloads find their way here—but it is a good time. Call ahead and they'll plan transportation from your hotel.

Most **discos and lounges,** located in major hotels, feature live music, whether it is a quiet piano bar or a rock pub featuring a band. **Good View** (13 Charoenrat Rd.; ✆ 05324-1866) and **The Riverside** (9/11 Charoenrat Rd.; ✆ 05324-3239) are both popular restaurants along the Ping River (see "Dining," earlier in this chapter) and feature live music after 8pm and on into the evening. Directly east of the Night Bazaar and in the large compound of the old Diamond Riverside Hotel, **River Bar** (33/11 Charoen Prathet Rd.; ✆ 05320-6169) has live music nightly and is always full. The Amari Hotel's **La Gritta** (see "Dining," earlier in this chapter; 1 Nimmanhaemin Rd.; ✆ 05322-1130) has a good jazz band every Saturday night. The small streets in and around Thapae and Loy Kroh roads constitute the town's red-light district with many "hostess clubs" or street-side bars doubling up as brothels or pickup joints.

The **Bubble Disco** in Pornping Tower (see "Accommodations," earlier in this chapter; 46 Charoen Prathet Rd.; ✆ 05327-0099), and **Crystal Cave Disco** at Empress Hotel, Chang Klan Road (✆ 05327-0240), are two rather dodgy night spots which seem to attract a fair supply of hookers and take turns getting shut down.

8 Side Trips from Chiang Mai

Day trips tend to promote Wat Phra That Doi Suthep, Chiang Mai's famed mountain and temple; however, don't miss the charming allure of nearby Lampang or Lamphun, both sleepy rural towns with old teak homes and some very lovely Lanna temples—you can pop into the Elephant Training Camp in Lampang en route.

WAT PHRA THAT DOI SUTHEP ✿

The jewel of Chiang Mai, Wat Phra That Doi Suthep glistens in the sun on the slopes of the mountain, known as Doi Suthep. One of four royal *wats* in the north, at 1,000m (3,250 ft.), it occupies an extraordinary site with a cool refreshing climate, expansive views over the city and the mountain's idyllic forests, waterfalls, and flowers.

In the 14th century, during the installation of a relic of the Buddha in Wat Suan Dok (in the Old City), the holy object split in two, with one part equaling the original size. A new *wat* was needed to honor the miracle. King Ku Na placed the new relic on a sacred white elephant and let it wander freely through the hills. The elephant climbed to the top of Doi Suthep, trumpeted three times, made three counterclockwise circles, and knelt down, choosing the site for Wat Phra That Doi Suthep.

The original *chedi* was built to a height of 8m (26½ ft.). Subsequent kings contributed to it, first by doubling the size and then by adding layers of gold and other ornamentation to the exterior. The gilded-copper decorative umbrellas around the central *chedi* and the murals showing scenes from the Buddha's life are especially attractive.

Other structures were raised to bring greater honor to the Buddha and various patrons. The most remarkable is the steep 290-step *naga* (sacred riverine snake) staircase, added in 1557, leading up to the *wat*—one of the most dramatic approaches to a temple in all of Thailand. To shorten the 5-hour climb, the winding road was constructed in 1935 by thousands of volunteers under the direction of a local monk.

Visitors with exposed legs are offered a sarong at the entrance. Most Thai visitors come to make an offering—usually flowers, candles, incense, and small squares of gold leaf that are applied to a favored Buddha or to the exterior of a *chedi*—and to be blessed. Believers kneel down and touch their foreheads to the ground three times in worship. Some shake prayer sticks to learn their fortune.

Wat Phra That Doi Suthep is open daily 7am to 5pm; come early or late to avoid the crowds. To get here, take the minibus from Chang Puak (White Elephant) Gate on the north side of the Old City. The fare is 40B (US$1.15/60p) going up and 30B (86¢/45p) for the descent. The ride can get cool, so bring a sweater or jacket. The bus stops at the base of the *naga* staircase. If you'd rather not climb the 290 steps, a special part of the experience, there's a motorized gondola to the top for 40B (US$1.15/60p). You can simplify matters by booking a half-day trip though any tour agency for 600B (US$17/£9.25), including a stop at Phuping Palace.

Phuping Palace (Doi Bua Ha) is the summer residence of Thailand's royal family, which is 4km (2½ miles) beyond Doi Suthep, 22km (14 miles) west of the Old City off Route 1004. When the royal family isn't present, visitors are allowed to enter and stroll through its beautiful gardens. When it is open (check with the TAT), the hours are Friday to Sunday 8:30am to 4:30pm, and admission is free. You really have to dress conservatively for this one; military guards at the gate act like the fashion police. The Doi Suthep minibus continues to the Phuping Palace from Wat Phra That Doi Suthep (see above).

LAMPHUN 🐘🐘

The oldest continuously inhabited city in Thailand, just 26km (16 miles) south of Chiang Mai, Lamphun was founded in A.D. 663 by the Mon Queen Chammadevi as the capital of Nakhon Hariphunchai. Throughout its long history, the Hariphunchai Kingdom, an offspring of the Mon Empire, was fought over and often conquered; yet it remained one of the powers of the north until King Mengrai established his capital in neighboring Chiang Mai.

The best way to get there is by car, taking the old highway Route 106 south to town. The Superhighway no. 11 runs parallel and east of it, but you'll miss the tall *yang* (rubber) trees, which shade the old highway until Sarapi, and the bushy yellow-flowered *khilik* (cassia) trees. Buses to Lamphun and Pasang leave from the **Chang Puak Bus Station** (© 05321-1586); the 45-minute ride costs 12B (34¢/16p).

The town is legendary for its beautiful women. There are some historical *wats,* including excellent Dvaravati-style *chedis,* and a fine museum. Longan *(lumyai),* a native fruit that resembles clusters of fuzzy brown grapes—which peel easily to yield luscious, crisp white flesh—are popular here. The trees can be recognized by their narrow, crooked trunks and large, droopy oval leaves. On the second weekend in August, Lamphun goes wild with its **Longan Festival,** with a parade of floats decorated only in longans and a beauty contest to select that year's Miss Longan. Lamphun and

Pasang (to the south) are also popular with shoppers for their excellent cotton and silk weaving.

The highlight of Lamphun is **Wat Phra That Hariphunchai** 𝄐𝄐, one of the most striking temples in all of Thailand. (Wat Phra That Doi Suthep was modeled after it.) The central *chedi*, in Chiang Saen–style and said to house a hair of the Buddha, is more than 45m (150 ft.) high and dates from the 9th century, when it was built over a royal structure. The nine-tiered umbrella at the top contains 6,498.75 grams of gold, and the *chedi's* exterior is of bronze. Also of interest in the temple complex are an immense bronze gong (reputedly the largest in the world), and several *viharn* (rebuilt in the 19th and 20th centuries) containing Buddha images. According to legend, the Buddha visited a hill about 16km (10 miles) southeast of town, where he left his footprints; the site is marked by Wat Phra Phuttabat Tak Pha. During the full-moon day in May, there's a ritual bathing ceremony for the Phra That.

The **Hariphunchai National Museum,** Amphur Muang (② 05351-1186), is across the street from Wat Phra That Hariphunchai's back entrance. It is worth a visit to see the many bronze and stucco religious works from the *wat.* The museum also contains a fine collection of Dvaravati- and Lanna-style votive and architectural objects. It's open Wednesday to Sunday 9am to 4pm; admission is 30B (86¢/45p).

Wat Chamadevi (Wat Kukut) 𝄐 is probably one of the most unique temple complexes in the country, located less than 1km (⅔ mile) northwest of the city center. The highlights here are the superb examples of late Dvaravati-style (pyramid) *chedis,* known as Suwan Chang Kot and Ratana, built in the 8th and 10th centuries, respectively, and thought to be modeled on those in Sri Lanka's ancient capital Polonnaruwa. The central one is remarkable for the 60 standing Buddhas that adorn its four corners. The original temple was built by Khmer artisans for King Mahantayot around A.D. 755. The relics of his mother, Queen Chamadevi, are housed inside, but the gold-covered pagoda was stolen, earning this site its nickname Kukut (topless).

LAMPANG 𝄐

The sprawling town of Lampang (originally called Khelang Nakhon) was once famous for its exclusive reliance on the horse and carriage for transportation, even after the "horseless carriage" came into fashion. These often florally adorned buggies can still be rented near the center of town next to the City Hall or arranged through any hotel for about 300B (US$8.60/£4.60) per hour (200B/US$5.70/£3.10 with *hard* bargaining); it's an enchanting mode of transport and a pleasant (and more eco-friendly) way to travel.

Lampang is graced with some of the finest Burmese temples in Thailand and supports the celebrated Thai Elephant Conservation Center (see below). Because of the region's fine kilns, there are dozens of ceramics factories producing new and reproduction "antique" pottery. For visitor information, contact the **Lampang District Tourist Center,** Boonyawat Road, near the central clock tower (② 05421-8823). The easiest way to reach Lampang is by car, taking the old highway Route 106 south to Lamphun, and then Superhighway No. 11 southeast for another 64km (40 miles). Buses to Lampang leave throughout the day from **Chiang Mai's Arcade Bus Terminal** (② 05324-2664). The 2½-hour trip costs 60B (US$1.45/90p).

For a lunch break or an overnight sojourn, the **Wienglakor Hotel** (138/35 Phaholyothin Rd.; ② 05422-4470) is the best choice in town. Rooms start at 1,450B (US$41/£22) and are comfortable and clean with all the right amenities, and a nice pool and good dining choices are located in and around the formal lobby. **Tipchang Hotel** (54/22 Tarkraonoi Rd.; ② 05422-6501; fax 05422-5362) comes a close second.

Lampang's *wats* are best toured by car or taxi. **Wat Phra Kaew Don Tao** is 1km (0.6 miles) to the northeast of the town center on the other side of the Wang River. For 32 years, this highly revered 18th-century Burmese temple housed the Emerald Buddha that's now in Bangkok's Wat Phra Kaew. Legend has it that one day the prince of Chiang Mai decided to move the Emerald Buddha from Chiang Rai to Chiang Mai. His attendants traveled there with a royal elephant to transport the sacred icon. But when the elephant got to this spot, it refused to go on to Chiang Mai with its burden, and so a *wat* was built here to house the image. There's an impressive carved wooden chapel and Buddha: a 49m-high (162-ft.) pagoda houses a strand of the Buddha's hair. Poke around in the small Laan Thai Museum to the left of the entrance; it contains some fine woodwork and an old *phra viharn* (Spirit House).

Wat Phra That Lampang Luang ✤ is on Tambon Lampang Luang in Koh Kha, 18km (11 miles) southwest of the center of Lampang. This impressive complex is considered one of the finest examples of northern Thai architecture. If you mount the main steps toward the older temples, you'll see a site map, a distinguished *viharn* (inspired by Wat Phra That Hariphunchai in Lamphun), and behind it to the west, a *chedi* with a fine seated Buddha. Go back to the parking area and cross through the lawn filled with contemporary, painted-plaster Chinese gods. Past the old Bodhi tree—whose stems are supported by dozens of bamboo poles and ribbons—you'll see signs for the Emerald Buddha House. The small Phra Kaew Don Tao image wears a gold necklace and stands on a gold base; it's locked behind two separate sets of gates and is difficult to see.

The **Thai Elephant Conservation Center** ✤✤✤ (on the Lampang–Ngao Hwy.; ℭ **05422-9042;** www.thailandelephant.org) is 37km (23 miles) west of Lampang. It is not a tourist site per se and nothing like the pony-ride atmosphere of most elephant camps; instead, the focus at the Thai Elephant Conservation Center is on the animals. Visitors here are not spectators, but participants in a hands-on seminar with these complex and intelligent creatures. Be ready to get dirty and up close with these jumbos. The elephants are not chained but roam free over the grounds and sleep in the jungle each night, coming to the central area at prescribed times for feeding and training sessions (watch out, the animals come running to get treats like sugar-cane and bananas). One-day courses show participants the basics of being a *mahout*, or elephant handler: first how to climb onto its back and, straddling the neck, to speak the extensive "language" of the elephants (a dialect of the Karen people) and command movement. There is no comparison (nor going back) to sitting in the usual bucket on elephant-back at the average elephant camp. Knowledgeable Thai *mahouts* and a hearty group of expats share their passion for elephants with visitors, and their enthusiasm is infectious. They offer multi-day treks (trekkers are assigned their own pachyderm for the journey) and homestay programs of varying lengths. Many of the elephants are sent here to be rehabilitated after abuse in captivity, and there is an on-site veterinary hospital for elephants with debilitating injuries (many are victims of land mines from neighboring Laos). Program costs begin at 1,500B (US$43/£23) for one-day programs and go up to 5,000B (US$143/£76) for deluxe multi-day treks. It is pricey for Thailand, but more than worth it. Call ahead for info and reservations. Day visitors are welcome and, if the timing is right, you may be able to hop on for a quick 100B (US$2.85/£1.55) ride with the help of a *mahout*.

DOI INTHANON NATIONAL PARK

Thailand's tallest mountain, **Doi Inthanon**—2,563m (8,408 ft.)—is 55km (34 miles) southwest of Chiang Mai. It crowns a 482 sq. km (186 sq. miles) national park filled with impressive waterfalls and wild orchids. Doi Inthanon Road climbs 48km (30 miles) to the summit. Along the way is the 30m-high (100-ft.) **Mae Klang Falls,** a popular picnic spot with food stands. Nearby **Pakan Na Falls** is less crowded because it requires a bit of climbing along a path to reach. At the top of the mountain, there's a fine view and two more falls, **Wachirathan** and **Siriphum,** both worth exploring. At the end of the park road, you are at the highest point in Thailand. There is a small visitor's center and a short trail into a thick wooded area of mossy overhanging trees; called the Michael Trail after one of the park's early naturalist researchers, the trail makes for a short but picturesque walk.

Admission to **Doi Inthanon National Park** is 200B (US$5.70/£3.10). It's open daily from sunrise to sunset. Camping is allowed in the park, but you must check with the TAT or the national park office to obtain permits and schedule information.

The area is a popular day trip destination for residents of Chiang Mai. Day trips organized by Chiang Mai tour companies will cost around 1,800B (US$51/£28), including lunch and a few other stops for sightseeing. You can always use your own rented car, too—just know that the terrain is rather hilly; take Route 108 south through San Pa Tong, and continue south following signs to the national park. You can take a 13km (8-mile) side trip to Lamphun on Route 1015.

MAE SA VALLEY

The lovely Mae Sa Valley area, more developed than Doi Inthanon National Park, is about 20km (12 miles) northwest of Chiang Mai. A rash of condo construction and the sprouting of roadside billboards all indicate that Mae Sa Valley is being developed as a rural tourist resort, but it still has an unhurried feel. Current attractions include an elephant show (including rides), a snake show, bungee jumping, and a nature park, as well as orchid nurseries. Most of these attractions are packaged by Chiang Mai tour operators as a half-day trip costing 1,000B (US$29/£15).

CHIANG DAO

The town of Chiang Dao, 72km (45 miles) north of Chiang Mai, and its environs offer several small resort hotels and a few fun activities, but if you don't have a car, the easiest way to sightsee is by joining a day trip organized by Chiang Mai operators, which costs about 1,500B (US$43/£23) per person (half-day trips are also offered). The **Elephant Training Center Chiang Dao,** close to the 56km marker from Chiang Mai, is rather touristy and not as good as that in Lampang (p. 339), but it's still a nice treat for kids. The adventure begins as you cross a rope bridge and walk through a forest to the camp. After the elephants bathe in the river (showering themselves and their *mahouts*), they demonstrate log hauling and log rolling. After the show, you can climb into a *howdah* and take a safari across the Ping River to a Lisu village.

Sixteen kilometers (10 miles) north of the Elephant Training Center is the **Chiang Dao Cave (Wat Tham Chiang Dao),** one of the area's more fascinating sites. Two caverns are illuminated by electric lights, and you can see a number of Buddha statues, including a 4m-long (13-ft.) reclining one. The row of five seated Buddhas in the first cavern is particularly impressive. The cave and two connected caverns extend over 10km (6 miles) into the mountain, but you'll have to hire a local guide with a lantern to explore the unlighted areas. It is open daily from 8:30am to 4:30pm, and a stop here can be included with any itinerary that brings you to the elephant camp.

13

Touring the Northern Hills

North of Chiang Mai and its satellite cities, travelers enter a stunning mountainous region replete with opportunities for adventure. Rugged landscape, proximity to Myanmar (Burma) and Laos, and the diverse ethnic hill-tribe groups living here distinguish northern Thailand from the rest of the country.

Connected by highways that undulate through forested mountains, descend into picturesque valleys, and pass through quaint farming villages, the country's northern points are best explored overland, in a rented vehicle (with a driver, if possible). There are lookout viewpoints along the way, and plenty of places to stop and eat, refuel, relax, and stay. Travelers can choose from a number of routes: from Chiang Mai to Chiang Rai; north from Chiang Rai to the Myanmar/Laos/ Thai border at the Golden Triangle; or the rugged area northwest of Chiang Mai known as the Mae Hong Son Loop. Any trip in the region means mountain scenery and the opportunity to visit with unique ethnic groups; trekking by foot, Jeep, elephant back, or boat through the forested hill-tribe homelands is very popular.

1 The Mae Hong Son Loop

The "Loop" through the rugged hills northwest of Chiang Mai is gaining popularity among seasoned travelers who like to escape cities and head out to the well-loved tourist destinations of Pai and Mae Hong Son. This circuit continues to out-of-the way Mae Sariang before returning to Chiang Mai. For all but the ultra-intrepid, going by tour or a hired car with driver is recommended—but a self-guided tour means freedom to take side trips and explore at one's own pace. Give yourself at least 4 days to do it, preferably more, staying 1 night at least in each town. The road, especially on the northernmost points, is serpentine and precipitous, and calls for good driving skills. Traffic is normally not too heavy, but drivers must be on the alert for everything from water buffalo to slow-moving, smoke-belching trucks and buses.

MAPS & INFORMATION

The most useful resource for a self-guided tour by car or motorbike is a map entitled *Mae Hong Son, The Loop* (published by the adventurous souls at The Golden Triangle Rider and priced at 175B/US$5/£2.70; www.gt-rider.com). The GT-Rider map gives exact details of even the smallest dirt track as well as useful site-maps of each town. You can pick it up in any bookstore in Thailand. The TAT offices in Chiang Mai (p. 308) or Mae Hong Son (p. 348) are also good resources for maps and advice on side trips.

GETTING AROUND

By Air   Regular flights by **Nok Air** (© **02900-9955;** www.nokair.com) link Mae Hong Son and Chiang Mai daily, or there's a Cessna service out of Chiang Mai, operated by **SGA** (© **02664-6099;** www.sga.co.th) serving Pai and Chiang Rai.

By Car This is certainly the best option for doing the "loop" or even just touring the hills around Pai and Mae Hong Son. See "Getting Around" in the Chiang Mai section of chapter 12. Travel agents and hotels can arrange a car with driver for about 1,500B (US$43/£23) per day, while budget rental agencies (see chapter 12) can go as low as 1,000B (US$28/£15).

By Motorcycle Though an increasingly popular option, this mode of transport is recommended only for experienced riders. Motorcycle travel around the Mae Hong Son Loop means less traffic than your average Thai highway, but the same warnings apply as anywhere: Wear a helmet, be defensive, and remember that there's not much between you and the road. A variety of good rental bikes is available in Chiang Mai. See the "Getting Around" section in "Chiang Mai," chapter 12, for info.

By Minivan A number of travel agents in Chiang Mai (see p. 309) arrange group tours here by minivan.

By Bus Regular public buses ply the winding tracks between all towns on the loop (Chiang Mai, Pai, Mae Hong Son, and Mae Sariang), but bus travelers are limited in their exploration of the countryside.

2 Pai ⓡ

831km (515 miles) NW of Bangkok; 135km (84 miles) NW of Chiang Mai

Halfway between Chiang Mai and Mae Hong Son, the mountain road makes a winding descent into a large green valley carpeted with rice paddies and fruit groves. Mountains rise on all sides, and on warm afternoons, butterflies flit along the streets. Here you'll find a village called Pai, named after the river that runs through the valley. Pai is a speck of a place with main roads (all four of them) littered with homegrown guesthouses, laid-back restaurants and bars, local trekking companies, and small souvenir shops.

The Pai River itself is one of the main attractions here. Outfitters organize rafting adventures on some pretty raucous rapids from July to January. Trekking is also popular, with 2- and 3-day treks to Karen, Lahu, and Lisu villages. The adventurous can find a local map for self-guided hikes to nearby waterfalls and caves, but quite a few wayfarers just lounge in town living simply and enjoying the nightlife. In Pai it seems every day is a lazy Sunday. Many local business owners are foreigners, or bohemian Thais, who come here for a slower pace than bustling Bangkok or Chiang Mai.

Note: Pai was hit with devastating flash floods in September 2005. Flash flooding flattened the central market, and the overflowing Pai River claimed a few riverside bungalows. Over 20—mostly ethnic hill-tribe people—were lost.

ESSENTIALS
GETTING THERE

By Air The only air link to Pai is from Chiang Mai on **SGA** (ⓒ **02664-6099;** www. sga.co.th), who fly light aircraft here; check the Web for current prices and schedules.

By Bus Five public buses a day leave for Pai from Chiang Mai (trip time: 3–4 hr.; 80B/US$2.30/£1.25). Six buses daily connect Pai and Mae Hong Son (trip time: 3 hr.; 74B/US$2.10/£1.15). The area's numerous but more expensive minivan services make better sense on such gut-wrenchingly winding roads; see below for info. The **Chiang Mai Arcade Bus Terminal** is off Kaew Nawarat Road, northeast of the old city across the Ping River (ⓒ **05324-2664**). The **bus terminal** in **Mae Hong Son** is

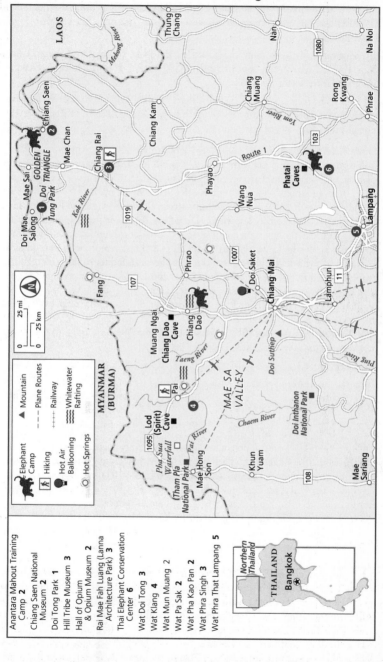

LAOS

Mekong River

Thung Chang

Nan

Na Noi

1080

Chiang Saen **2**

GOLDEN TRIANGLE

Mae Chan

Chiang Muang

Rong Kwang

Phrae

Mae Sai

Doi Mae Salong

1 Doi Tung Park

Chiang Rai

3

Chiang Kam

Yom River

103

Kok River

Route 1

Phatai Caves **6**

1019

Phayao

Wang Nua

Lampang

Fang

107

1007

Phrao

Doi Saket

Chiang Mai

5

Lamphun

11

Muang Ngai

Chiang Dao Cave

Chiang Dao

Taeng River

Doi Suthep

Ping River

MYANMAR (BURMA)

Pai

4

MAE SA VALLEY

Doi Inthanon National Park

Lod (Spirit) Cave

Pai River

Chaem River

1095

Pha Sua Waterfall

Mae Hong Son

Khun Yuam

Mae Sariang

108

Tham Pla National Park

0   25 mi

0   25 km

KEY:
- 🐘 Elephant Camp
- 🥾 Hiking
- 💡 Hot Air Ballooning
- ○ Hot Springs
- ▲ Mountain
- --- Plane Routes
- +++ Railway
- ≋ Whitewater Rafting

THAILAND

Northern Thailand

Bangkok

on Khunlumprapas Road (the main street), 2 blocks north of the main intersection. All buses drop off and pick up at this "bus terminal" (it's more like a vacant lot than a terminal).

By Minivan Frequent minivans (called *rot too*) make connections between Chiang Mai, Pai, and Mae Hong Son for 180B (US$5.15/£2.75) for each leg. Contact any storefront travel agent for details.

By Car The scenic route is long, with steep winding roads that make for some very pretty rural scenery: Take Route 107 north from Chiang Mai, and then Route 1095 northwest to Pai.

ORIENTATION & GETTING AROUND

You won't find a formal tourist information booth in Pai, but restaurateurs, bungalow owners, and fellow travelers are usually happy to share their knowledge and experience. Most guesthouses and restaurants offer photocopied maps of town and the surrounding areas. Tiny Pai consists of four streets: Route 1095, or the Pai–Mae Hong Son Highway (colloquially known as Khetkelang Rd.) runs parallel to Rangsiyanon Road—which is the main commercial street. Chaisongkhram and Ratchadamnoen roads run perpendicular, and many guesthouses and restaurants are in or around this central grid (with many more guesthouses in the surrounding countryside). You can walk the town in 5 minutes. Mountain bikes and motorcycles are available at guesthouses or shops along the main streets for about 50B (US$1.45/75p) and 200B (US$4.90/£3.10), respectively. **Rent a motorcycle,** the best choice to go exploring the hills around Pai, at **Aya Service** (22/1 Moo 3, Chaisongkhram Rd.; ✆ 05369-9940); 100cc scooters start at just 80B (US$2.26/£1.25) for 24 hours, and 250cc motocross numbers go for as low as 500B (US$14/£7.60).

FAST FACTS

There is one **ATM** in Pai, at the Krung Thai Bank on Rangsiyanon Road, which offers money-changing services. There are Internet cafes along central Chaisongkhram Road.

TREKKING & ADVENTURE

Small trekking companies, operated by locals, are at every guesthouse and all along the main streets. It is hard to choose from the many, but **Duang Trekking** (at Duang Guesthouse across from the bus terminal; ✆ 05369-9101) has a good reputation. Also look for **Outdoor Explorer** (15 Chaisongkhram Rd., ✆ 05369-9815; www. outdoorexplorer.info), which has a strong eco-tour and educational focus. Group treks go for 3 days and 2 nights to Lisu, Karen, Tai Yai and Lahu villages in the hills around Pai for 1,500B (US$43/£23) per person (some trips include bamboo rafting). Trekking offices can tailor any trek or provide private guides according to need.

The **Pai River** is really the most exciting attraction going. Overnight **rafting** trips take you through some exciting rapids as well as more scenic lazy spots, through canyons walled with prehistoric fossilized lime and shell, as well as a **wildlife sanctuary.** A pioneer of the rafting business here, long-time resident Guy Gorias runs **Thai Adventure Rafting** ✫✫ (Rangsiyanon Rd. in the town center; ✆ 05369-9111; www.activethailand.com). There are regular trips from June to January. Three-day adventures begin and end in Pai, at a cost of 8,400B (US$240/£129) per person. There are many imitators in town, but Thai Adventure is the best outfitter by far, with high safety standards and quality equipment and a good base-camp on a hill above town in Pai (ask about affordable rooms for rent). They can also make the necessary arrangements for pickup and drop-off in Mae Hong Son.

You can also go on **elephant treks** out of Pai, from where there are a number of hourly, all-day, and multiday programs to choose from. There are also a number of elephant camps on the ridge overlooking town; the best is **Thom's Pai Elephant Camp** (5/3 Moo 4, Rangsiyanon Rd.; © **05369-9286**).

THINGS TO SEE & DO

There's little in the way of tour sites in Pai (most people simply come to put their feet up), but it is a great place to stroll along country lanes or even rent a motorbike and buzz around the countryside. There are a few small temples: **Wat Klang** is next to the bus station and has several small pagodas surrounding a central *stupa,* and **Wat Hodana** and **Wat Nam Hu** are west of Route 1095—Nam Hu is known for its Chiang Saen-era Buddha, whose hollow head is filled with holy water. There's a **waterfall** about 7km(4⅓ miles) west of town past the two *wats,* and a **hot spring** about 7km (4⅓ miles) to the southeast, past the Pai High School.

Tiny Pai boasts quite a few traditional massage places. The best option is **Mr. Jan's Herbal Sauna and Massage** (no phone), where you'll get a Burmese-style massage. Ask around for directions to Mr. Jan's—it's on the narrow Soi Wanchaloem, off Chaisongkhram Road.

WHERE TO STAY

There are now a handful of posh resorts outside of town; in Pai, you'll find mostly guesthouses. You have your choice of some pretty rough little dives starting at 100B (US$2.85/£1.55), but I've listed the few comfortable options for people on any budget. Many midrange places are on the outskirts in Ban Mae Yen, Ban Mae Hi, and Ban Juang.

MODERATE

Belle Villa Resort 🎿🎿 *(Finds*   A swish, out-of-town resort consisting of pretty bungalows, built along a quiet, rural stretch of the Pai River, the Belle Villa has no rival anywhere along the Mae Hong Son Loop. Large, clean bungalow rooms boast contemporary conveniences like digital safes and cable TV without sacrificing the rustic charm of thatched roof and bamboo walls. The yellow polished concrete bathrooms are resplendent affairs. Spacious shower areas are surrounded by small rock gardens and have windows with views to the river. The restaurant is a cozy, open affair overlooking a small pool and the riverside beyond. You'll be swatting 'skeeters like anywhere in Pai, but the peace, quiet, scenery, and friendly service of this burgeoning little idyll are matchless.

113 Moo 6, Huay Poo-WiangNua Rd., Tumbol WiangTai, Amphur Pai, Mae Hong Son 58130 (down a small *soi* off the Mae Hong Son Road, 2km/1¼ miles north of Pai). © 05369-8226. Fax 05369-8228. www.bellevillaresort.com. 26 units. 2,472B (US$71/£38) double/low season; 3,600B (US$103/£55) double/high-season. MC, V. **Amenities:** Restaurant; outdoor pool; tour desk; shuttle service; laundry service. *In room:* A/C, satellite TV, DVD player, minibar, fridge, coffeemaker, hairdryer, safe.

Pai River Corner 🎿🎿   Having lost its budget riverside bungalows to flash floods in 2005, Pai River Corner has been left with only its finest rooms set in two-story, four-unit villas right in the center of town. Interiors are lavish, decorated in a modern Thai style with lots of color and local flair. Even more unique are their two oversize suite rooms, one with an indoor Jacuzzi the size of a duck pond. The property boasts a cozy riverside perch for drinks and dining and the location is the best in town.

94 Moo 3, Viengtai, Pai, Mae Hong Son 58130. (C) **05369-9049.** Fax 05369-9049. www.pairivercorner.com. 9 units. 3,000B (US$86/£45) standard double; 4,000B–6,000B (US$114–US$171/£58–£88) suite. **Amenities:** Restaurant; bar; tour desk; car and motorbike rental desk; laundry service. *In room:* A/C.

Rim Pai Cottages   Though billed as cottages, this property comprises an unassuming cluster of bungalows. You'll find little in the way of luxury, but lots of character in rooms that range from tiny, airless sheds to spacious rustic pavilions on stilts with small balconies and riverside views. There are also only a few choice amenities: a welcoming restaurant pavilion and a helpful tour desk. It's set apart from the rougher budget accommodations by virtue of its airy campus and good location—it occupies some of the best real estate in the center of Pai Town proper.

99 Moo 3, Viengtai, Pai, Mae Hong Son 58130 (right in town at riverside). (C) **05369-9133.** Fax 05369-9234. www. rimpaicottage.com. 37 units. 600B–1,500B (US$17–US$43/£9.25–£23) fan bungalow; 1,600B–3,500B (US$46–US$100/£25–£54) A/C bungalow/villa. MC, V. **Amenities:** Restaurant; tour desk; car and motorbike rentals; massage; laundry service. *In room:* No phone.

INEXPENSIVE

Cheap and cheerful little **Charlie's House** is in the middle of town (9 Rangsiyanon Rd., (C) **05369-9039**), with basic rooms with a fan from 100B (US$2.85/£1.55) or A/C units from 400B (US$11/£6.15).

Thapai Spa Camping   Perched on the banks of the river just a 10-minute drive outside of town, this rustic resort was built to take advantage of the small hot springs nearby. Boiling water is piped in and mixed with cool water in various pools (in the actual springs you could boil an egg). Bathing areas with adjoining showers are scattered about the garden. Rooms vary: Some are motel-style and plain; others feature fine rock masonry and have large, open-concept bathrooms with mineral water showers. This is a popular getaway for large Thai groups and families: A raucous, communal atmosphere pervades.

Chiang Mai reservation office: 58/1 Patanachangpuak Rd., Chiang Mai (located 6km/3¾ miles from Pai on the way toward Chiang Mai; look for the sign at the turnoff along Rte. 1095). (C) **05321-8583.** Fax 05321-9610. www.thapai spa.com. 38 units. 1,500B–3,000B (US$43–US$86/£23–£46) double. No credit cards. **Amenities:** Restaurant; mineral water pool and spa; herbal sauna; bike rental; tour desk; massage; laundry service. *In room:* A/C, no phone.

WHERE TO DINE

Little Pai plays host to a bevy of expatriate restaurants and bars as well as a whole range of street-side dining. The most popular spots in town are the retro **Charnos Bar** and **Be-bop,** a bar, restaurant, and live music hangout on the southern tip of town (a 15-minute walk down Khet Klang opposite the Tourist Police). There's an excellent house band and a young party crowd keeps the place hopping late into the night (about 1am). Live music starts at 9:30pm.

Below are the other best restaurants in town.

Baan Benjarong ✦ THAI   As you overlook mountain rice paddies from this friendly and casual open-air restaurant, you can choose from a poster-size menu of delicious Thai dishes. Any of the many hearty stir-fries and spicy soups will do the trick. But I most recommend the savory curry made with crabs dipped in a sweet and sour sauce and the *tam long krop:* a unique dish of crispy, deep-fried gourd. This is a great place to fill up cheaply after trekking.

179 Moo 8 (adjacent to Be-bop Bar). (C) **05369-8010.** Main courses 70B–150B (US$2–US$4.30/£1.10–£2.30). Cash only. Daily 11am–10pm.

Baan Pai THAI   Right in the center of town, Baan Pai is a fine choice for authentic Thai food in an open-air Thai house, and it's a good place for people-watching. A first-rate English-language menu offers up all manner of Thai dishes, from spicy vermicelli salads to creamy soups and fiery curries. Everything is good.

7 Moo Rangsiyanon Rd. (around the corner from the bus station). (📞) 05369-9912. Main courses 80B–200B (US$2.30–US$5.70/£1.25–£3.10). Cash only. Daily 8am–11pm.

BETWEEN PAI & MAE HONG SON

Either as a day trip from Pai or as a stop on the way to Mae Hong Son, the best little detour going is the *lod,* or **Spirit Cave,** off Route 1095 (about 30km/18½ miles northwest of Pai on Route 1095 in the town of Soppong, and then about 8km, or 5 miles, north of the highway). This large, awe-inspiring cave filled with colorful stalagmites, stalactites, and small caverns will keep you exploring for hours. The cavern was discovered in the 1960s jam-packed with **antique pottery** dating from the Ban Chiang culture. There are three caves. The first chamber is a magnificent grotto and the second contains a prehistoric cave painting of a deer (which unfortunately has been largely blurred from curious fingers). The third cavern contains **prehistoric coffins** shaped like canoes. A guide to all three caves costs 100B (US$2.85/£1.55), with lantern rental included. Be sure to take the canoe ride to the third cave (the ferryman will hit you up for an extra 100B/US$2.85/£1.55) where, especially in the late afternoon and evening, you can see clouds of bats and swallows vying for space in the cave's high craggy ceiling (the boat ride is fun, too). Pay again to get back by boat or you can follow the clear jungle path a few clicks back to the parking lot. Bring your own flashlight for self-exploration as well.

There are lots of little guesthouses along the road near the entrance to the Spirit Caves in Soppong; the best is the friendly **Little Eden Guesthouse** (295 Moo 1, T. Soppong, (📞) 05361-7054; www.littleeden-guesthouse.com). They have basic bungalows around a postage-stamp pool, as well as an authentic rustic suite overlooking the river (450B–1,500B/US$13–US$43/£6.95–£23).

As the road curves south heading into Mae Hong Son, **Tham Pla Park** (17km/10½ miles north of Mae Hong Son on Rte. 1095) is a small landscaped park leading up to the entrance of Tham Pla, or Fish Cave. It is a small grotto crowded with carp (legend says there are 10,000 of them) that mysteriously prefer the cave to the nearby streams. You can buy fish food in the parking lot (10B/29¢/14p per packet), but the fish don't eat it. Have a look—it is meant to be good luck (also a good leg stretch after the long drive). The grotto, once unsuccessfully explored by Thai Navy divers, is said to be several meters deep and to extend for miles.

Ten kilometers (6 miles) away in the Tham Pla Park interior is the huge **Pha Sua Waterfall,** which tumbles over limestone cliffs in seven cataracts. The water is at its most powerful after the rainy season in August and September. The Meo hill-tribe village of Mae Sou Yaa is beyond the park on a road suitable for Jeeps, just a few kilometers from the Burmese border.

3 Mae Hong Son

924km (573 miles) NW of Bangkok; 355km (220 miles) NW of Chiang Mai via Pai; 274km (170 miles) NW of Chiang Mai via Mae Sariang

Not far from the Burmese border, Mae Hong Son, the provincial capital of Mae Hong Son province, is the urban center of this large patch of scenic woodlands, waterways, and unique hill-tribe villages. The town's surrounding hills, famed for their eerie morning mist, burst into color each October and November when *tung buatong* (wild sunflowers) come into bloom. The hot season (Mar–Apr) has temperatures as high as 104°F (40°C), and the rainy season is longer (May–Oct), with several brief showers daily.

The mountains around Mae Hong Son are scarred by slash-and-burn agriculture and evidence of logged teak forests from departed hill-tribe settlements. Roads, airfields, and public works projects have since opened up the scenic province as poppy fields gave way to terraced rice paddies and garlic crops. At the same time, the surge in tourism brought foreigners trekking into villages where automobiles were still unknown. Although the busy town of Mae Hong Son continues to grow and develop, its picturesque valley setting and lovely Burmese-style *wats* are still the star attractions here.

ESSENTIALS

GETTING THERE

By Plane   Two daily Thai Airways flights connect Mae Hong Son to major routes via Chiang Mai (flight time: 45 min.). During the July to August and November to December peak seasons, book in advance as flights fill up early, and in low-season check to see if the flights are actually running (flights cancel often due to fog). **Thai Airways** in Chiang Mai is at 240 Prapokklao Rd. (© **05392-0999** for domestic reservations in Chiang Mai; www.thaiair.com), and in Mae Hong Son at 71 Singhanat Bamrung Rd. (© **05361-1297**). **Nok Air** (© **05392-2183** or © 1318; www.nokair.com) runs a daily flight from Chiang Mai as well.

The **Mae Hong Son Airport** is in the northeast section of town, about 20 minutes from the town center. Tuk-tuks and *songtaews* are always waiting for passengers outside the airport.

By Bus   Seven non-air-conditioned buses connect with Pai or beyond to the **Chiang Mai Arcade Bus Terminal** (trip time: 4 hrs.; 74B/US$2.10/£1.15; © **05324-2664**). Bus service to Mae Sariang to the south leaves in the morning (trip time: 8 hr.; 140B/US$4/£2.15). The bus terminal in Mae Hong Son is on Khunlumprapas Road (the main street), 2 blocks north of the main intersection and a short walk from most hotels in the town center.

By Car   The 6-hour journey to Mae Hong Son from Chiang Mai is a pleasant mountain drive with spectacular views and some fun attractions (see "Between Pai & Mae Hong Son," above). The road is winding but paved and safe, with places to stop for gas, food, and toilets, as well as scenic pull-offs. Take Route 107 north from Chiang Mai to Route 1095 northwest through Pai. For car rental info, see chapter 12, "Chiang Mai."

VISITOR INFORMATION

The **TAT** office (© **05361-2982**), Khunlumprapas Road, opposite the post office, has helpful staff. The **Tourist Police** office (© **05361-1812** or 1155), Singhanat Bamrung Road, is open daily 8:30am to 5pm.

ORIENTATION

Mae Hong Son is small and easy to navigate. Khunlumprapas Road, part of the Pai–Mae Sariang highway (Rte. 108), is the town's main street and home to travel agents, most hotels listed below, and restaurants. **Jong Kham Lake** is just east of the main street, and **Wat Phra That Doi Kong Mu** overlooks town from the west.

GETTING AROUND

You can walk to most places in town, but there are a few tuk-tuks parked outside the market for longer trips. At some guesthouses, you'll find bicycle rental for 50B (US$1.45/75p) or 100cc motorbikes for rent at 200B (US$5.70/£3.10) per day.

FAST FACTS

There are major **banks** with ATMs and currency-exchanges along Khunlumprapas and Singhanat Bamrung roads. In addition, several banks are open for each flight arrival at the airport. The **Sri Sangawan Hospital** is east of town on Singhanat Bamrung Road (© **05361-1378**). The **post office** is opposite the King Singhanat Rajah statue. There are a few **Internet cafes** along Khunlumprapas near the Baiyoke Chalet, most with good DSL for 40B (US$1.15/60p) per hour. The **Tourist Police** are at © **05361-1812.**

WHAT TO SEE & DO

Wat Jong Klang and **Wat Jong Kham** are reflected in the serene waters of Jong Kham Lake, in the heart of town. Their striking white *chedis* and dark teak *viharn* tell of Burmese influence. Wat Jong Klang was constructed from 1867 to 1871 as an offering to Burmese monks who made the long journey here for the funeral of Wat Jong Kham's abbot. Inside are a series of folk-style glass paintings depicting the Buddha's life and a small collection of dusty Burmese wood carvings and dolls. The older Wat Jong Kham (ca. 1827) was built by King Singhanat Rajah and his queen, and is distinguished by gold-leaf columns supporting its *viharn*. Don't miss the colorful Burmese-style donation boxes; they're like musical arcade games with spinning discs and cups to drop your change in, only the end result is not "game over" but "make merit."

   Wat Phra That Doi Kong Mu (also known as Wat Plai Doi) dominates the western hillside above the town, particularly at night when the strings of lights rimming its two Mon pagodas are silhouetted against the dark forest. The oldest part (ca. 1860) of this compound was constructed by King Singhanat Rajah, and a 15-minute climb up its new *naga* (snake) staircase rewards one with grand views of the mist-shrouded valley, blooming pink cassia trees, and Jong Kham Lake below. Each April, the national **Poy Sang Long Festival** honoring Prince Siddhartha's decision to become a monk is celebrated here by a parade of novice monks. Below Wat Phra That Doi Kong Mu, there's a 12m-long (40-ft.) **Reclining Buddha** in Wat Phra Non.

   For short **1-day hill-tribe treks** in the region, **Rose Garden Tours** (86/4 Khunlumprapas Rd. in the center of town; ©/fax **05361-1577**) offers many options including stops at local Lahu, Shan and Karen villages, and adventure activities like elephant trekking and bamboo rafting.

   There are two **Padaung villages** populated by the famed **"long-neck Karen" people** close to Mae Hong Son. Rose Garden Tours (see above) includes village visits in its all-day tours or can arrange special half-day trips. **Huay Sua Tao** village is closest to town and easily reached by car or minivan (entrance is 250B/US$7.15/£3.85), and Nam Phiang Din Village is accessible by boat for 750B (US$21/£12).

WHERE TO STAY

The early '90s brought large-scale development to Mae Hong Son, so today there are a few high-end hotel options downtown and a few rustic resorts in the surrounding hills.

EXPENSIVE

Imperial Tara Mae Hong Son 🏆🏆   The Tara is the top choice for the upscale traveler in Mae Hong Son. Though it's some 2km (1¼ miles) out of town, the hotel's style, service, many amenities, and upkeep set it far above the rest. Guest rooms overlook a teak forest, garden, and stream. All furnishings are in blond wood and wicker on "bowling-alley" shined floors. Most rooms have spacious balconies, and suites are large and luxurious. The serpentine free-form pool is surrounded by a wooden deck and the open-air restaurant has views of the grounds and garden. The staff is very professional and can help with any eventuality, from day-tours to flat tires.

149 Moo 8, Tambon Pang Moo, Mae Hong Son 58000 (2km/1¼ miles south of town). ⓒ 05368-4444. Fax 05368-4440. www.imperialhotels.com. 104 units. 2,520B (US$72/£39) double; from 3,675B (US$105/£57) suite. AE, DC, MC, V. **Amenities:** Restaurant; 2 bars; lounge; outdoor pool; fitness center; sauna; tour desk; limited room service; massage; laundry service. *In room:* A/C, satellite TV, minibar, fridge, hair dryer, safe.

MODERATE

Baiyoke Chalet   With an ideal location on the main street—and in walking distance of everything in town—this hotel offers simple, midsize rooms with high ceilings, hardwood floors, and clean guesthouse-style baths. Rooms overlooking the back are quieter; the place is often overrun by adventure groups—a young and rowdy crowd sometimes. The hotel bar and restaurant, **Chalet,** looks over the main street in town, hosts live bands, and is where it's at for locals in Mae Hong Son.

90 Khunlumprapas, Jong Kham, Amphur Muang, Mae Hong Son 58000 (midtown across from post office). ⓒ 05361-1536. Fax 05361-1533. 40 units. 1,050B–1,650B (US$30–US$47/£16–£25) double. AE, MC, V. **Amenities:** Restaurant; tour desk; laundry service. *In room:* A/C, satellite TV, minibar, fridge.

Fern Resort 🏆 *Finds*   Out in the sticks some 8km (5 miles) south of town and just next to the Mae Surin National Park, the Fern Resort rests in a quiet valley along a rushing stream and promises comfort and harmony with nature. Tai Yai (Shan)-style bungalows have simple but comfortable local-style furnishings like *tong tueng* leaf roofs, glass windows, and doors; bathrooms offer slate-tiled showers with hot water. They have good trail maps of the immediate area and the resort's friendly troupe of dogs will accompany you on a self-guided tour (borrow a walking stick and just follow the pups). Experienced human guides are also available for more extensive treks. Fern's restaurant offers local Thai and international cuisine, or you can ride the shuttle to town (thrice daily) to dine at their in-town restaurant (see "Where to Dine," below).

64 Bann Hua Num Mae Saket, T. Pha Bong, Mae Hong Son 58000 (8km/5 miles south of town). ⓒ 05368-6110. Fax 05368-6111. www.fernresort.info. 30 units. 2,000B–2,500B (US$57–US$71/£31–£38) bungalow. MC, V. **Amenities:** Restaurant; bike rental; tour desk; laundry service. *In room:* A/C, no phone.

Golden Pai & Suite Resort   Here's one for folks who are traveling with their own car—the Golden Pai is 5km (3 miles) north of town (toward Pai) and not accessible by public transport. Suite rooms (the best value) are large and cozy, with spacious balconies overlooking a small central pool. Mid- and low-end rooms are basic bungalows. They have a good riverside restaurant offering some spa treatments and mud baths, as well as local adventure tours. The very friendly staff ensures that this place stays popular with groups of visiting Thais.

285 Moo 1, Ban Pangmoo, Mae Hong Son 58000. ⓒ 05361-2265. Fax 05362-0417. www.goldenpai.com. 70 units. 1,400B–2,500B (US$40–US$71/£22–£28) MC, V. **Amenities:** Restaurant; bar; outdoor pool; tour desk; laundry service. *In room:* A/C, TV, minibar, fridge.

Mae Hong Son Mountain Inn   You can't miss the dynamic angular spire of the oversized Thai Yai–style peaked roofs marking the entrance to this compound. The place has lots of charm and is in a good location just south of the town center. Comfortable guest rooms are arranged in two stories around lush central gardens. The hotel is a bit light on amenities, and you won't find many English speakers on staff, but they're helpful as all get-up. Spring for a deluxe room with parquet floors (instead of old carpeting), more local accents, and a bit more panache. Deluxe bathrooms are large and done up using terra-cotta tiles and granite.

112/2 Khunlumprapas Rd., T. Jong Kham, Mae Hong Son 58000 (on the southern end of the main drag). ℭ 05361-1802. Fax 05361-2284. www.mhsmountaininn.com. 69 units. 1,500B–1,800B (US$43–US$51/£23–£28) double; from 4,300B (US$123/£66) suite; seasonal rates and discounts always available. AE, MC, V. **Amenities:** Restaurant; tour desk; car-rental desk; massage; laundry service. In room: A/C, satellite TV, minibar, fridge.

INEXPENSIVE

Piya Guest House   This is the best budget choice on beautiful Jong Kham Lake, easily the nicest part of town—and a short walk to the two lakeside temples. Piya is a one-story wooden house with a garden courtyard. Basic rooms have private baths, hot-water showers, and air-conditioning, but aren't particularly nice (be sure to check first because many are musty). Piya also runs a trekking service and rents out bikes and motorbikes at reasonable prices.

1/1 Khunlumprapas, Soi 3, Jong Kham, Mae Hong Son (east side of Jong Kham Lake). ℭ 05361-1260. 14 units. 600B (US$17/£9.25) bungalow. No credit cards. **Amenities:** Restaurant; bike rental; tour desk; laundry service. In room: A/C, no phone.

WHERE TO DINE

The local **Night Market** on central Khunlumprapas is the busiest venue in town for budget travelers. There you can sample noodle soups, crisp-fried beef, dried squid, roast sausage, fish balls, and other snacks sold by vendors for very little. It's open early until late daily.

Also look for a little Italian storefront pizza joint, **La Tasca** (88/4 Khunlumprapas Rd., ℭ **05361-1344;** daily 9am–10pm; 120B–200B/US$3.45–US$5.70/£1.85–£3.10; cash only), in the town center. It's a great place for a real coffee and to watch the world go by.

Fern Restaurant and Bar   THAI/CHINESE/INTERNATIONAL   The biggest and best restaurant in town serves an especially wide variety of food for this part of the country—all of it well prepared and pleasantly served. The bar at the entrance has an inviting quality, and behind it an open-air deck stretches back toward an entertainment area with live music and a karaoke bar. If you come in the early evening, head for the far back to get a view of the mountain-top temple, Wat Phra That Doi Kong Mu, in the evening glow.

87 Khunlumprapas Rd. (1½ blocks south of traffic light, on left). ℭ **05361-1374.** Main courses 70B–250B (US$2–US$7.15/£1.10–£3.85). AE, MC, V. Daily 10am–10pm.

Kai-Mook   THAI/CHINESE   This is a tin-roofed pavilion with more style than most: Overhead lights are shaded by straw farmer's hats and Formica tables are interspersed between bamboo columns. The Thai and Chinese menu includes Kai-mook salad (a tasty blend of crispy fried squid, cashews, sausage, and onions), and a large selection of light and fresh stir-fried dishes.

23 Udom Chaonitesh Rd. (1 block south of traffic light, turn left). ℭ **05361-2092.** Main courses 50B–150B (US$1.45–US$4.30/75p–£2.30). No credit cards. Daily 9:30am–2pm and 5:30–9pm.

4 Mae Sariang: Completing the Mae Hong Son Loop

180km (112 miles) W of Chiang Mai; 130km (81 miles) S of Mae Hong Son

The tiny town of Mae Sariang proper boasts no grand museums or shiny hilltop temples; it is just a cozy river-town along the border with Myanmar and the best halfway stopover on the long southern link between Mae Hong Son and Chiang Mai. Driving in the area, along Route 108, takes you past pastoral villages, scenic rolling hills, and a few enticing side trips to small local temples and waterfalls. Mae Sariang offers only basic accommodations.

GETTING THERE

By Car　Navigation is a cinch. Just follow Route 108 between Mae Hong Son, Mae Sariang, and Chiang Mai. Carry a good road map for following side roads, and put aside a day for travel time.

By Bus　Standard and air-conditioned buses connect Mae Hong Son, Mae Sariang, and **Chiang Mai Arcade Bus Terminal** (© 05324-2664) along the southern leg of Route 108. Seven daily non-air-conditioned buses depart Chiang Mai for the 8- to 9-hour journey and cost 145B (US$4.15/£2.25) to Mae Hong Son and just 78B (US$2.25/£1.20) to stop in Mae Sariang (4 hr.). Two air-conditioned buses make the same trip and depart Chiang Mai at 11am and 9pm (261B/US$7.45/£4 to Mae Hong Son; 140B/US$4/£2.15 to Mae Sariang).

WHAT TO SEE

The road is good and the scenery is lush on the long stretch of Route 108 west of Chiang Mai. Don't forget to stop and smell the fertilizer or take side trips wherever possible. Roadside dining and service facilities are limited, but adequate.

Sixty-three kilometers south of Mae Hong Son, in the village of **Khun Yuam,** you'll come to a junction with a road that no longer exists: a ghost trail remembered as "The Road of Japanese Skeletons," the path of retreat for Japanese soldiers fleeing what was Burma (now Myanmar) at the end of WWII. The road lives only in the memory of those who met the starved and dying troops, an estimated 20,000 of whom lie in mass graves in the surrounding area. The **Japanese War Museum** (just south of the junction of Rte. 108 and Rte. 163) commemorates this sorry chapter in history and is worth a visit. The museum features rusting tanks and weaponry, photos, personal effects, and written accounts (in Japanese, English, and Thai) of soldiers' struggles and the kindness of the locals.

Mae Sariang has a few outfits offering day treks and rafting (stop in any of the riverside cafes or hotels), but most people just spend a night here before making their way to Chiang Mai.

Between Mae Sariang and Chiang Mai, you'll pass near **Doi Inthanon National Park** and the city of **Lamphun.** For details of these, see "Side Trips from Chiang Mai," in chapter 12.

WHERE TO STAY & DINE

There are lots of budget accommodations along the Mae Yuam River in the town center. The best choice is new **Riverhouse Resort** (6/1 Moo 2, Mae Sariang, © 05368-3066; fax 05368-3067; www.riverhousehotels.com), a small resort of cozy wooden pavilions overlooking the Mae Yuam. Rooms start at 1,200B/US$34/£18. Riverhouse is also the best bet for dining in their riverside *sala,* but a short stroll through town will take you past any number of local greasy spoons where the adventurous can find one-dish noodle or rice meals for next to nothing.

5 Chiang Rai

780km (484 miles) NE of Bangkok; 180km (112 miles) NE of Chiang Mai

Chiang Rai is Thailand's northernmost province. The Mekong River makes its borders with Laos to the east and Myanmar to the west. The smaller yet scenic Mae Kok River, which supports many hill-tribe villages along its banks, flows right through the provincial capital of the same name.

Chiang Rai City lies some 565m (1,885 ft.) above sea level in a wide fertile valley, and its cool refreshing climate, tree-lined riverbanks, and popular but more subdued Night Market lure travelers weary of traffic congestion and pollution in Chiang Mai. Chiang Rai also has some good accommodations choices, and many travelers use the city as a base for trekking and trips to Chiang Saen and the Golden Triangle.

Note: Some trips include a stop at the Mae Rim valley on their way north to Chiang Rai (30 min. north of the city on Rte. 107). Mae Rim is an area popular for elephant trekking, rafting, and bungee-jumping. See "Chiang Mai Activities," in chapter 12.

Just over 100km north of Chiang Mai on the way to Chiang Rai, look for little **Suanthip Vana Resort** (49 Chiang Mai–Chiang Rai Rd., Tambon Takok; ℂ 05372-4226; www.suanthipresort.com), a semi-luxe property with cool honeymoon bungalows that overlook a river valley.

ESSENTIALS
GETTING THERE
By Plane   **Thai Airways** (ℂ 02356-1111 in Bangkok; www.thaiair.com) has two daily flights from Don Mueang, Bangkok, and one daily from Suvarnabhumi International Airport in Bangkok to Chiang Rai (flying time: 85 min.). Thailand's many budget carriers, **Air Asia** (ℂ 05392-2170; www.airasia.com), **Nok Air** (ℂ 05392-2183 or ℂ 1318; www.nokair.com), and **One-Two-GO** (ℂ 05392-2159; www.fly12 go.com) all make regular connections.

Chiang Rai International Airport (ℂ 05379-3048) is about 10km (6 miles) north of town. There is a bank exchange open daily 9am to 5pm and a gift shop. Taxis hover outside and charge 150B (US$4.30/£2.30) to town and more to other towns in the province.

By Bus   Three air-conditioned VIP 24-seat buses leave daily from Bangkok's **Northern Bus Terminal** (ℂ 02936-2852) to Chiang Rai (trip time: 11 hr.; 900B/US$26/ £14). Buses leave hourly between 6am and 5:30pm from **Chiang Mai's Arcade Bus Terminal** (ℂ 05324-2664; trip time: 3½ hr.; 77B/US$2.20/£1.20 non-air-conditioned; 139B/US$4/£2.15 air-conditioned). Chiang Rai's **Khon Song Bus Terminal** (ℂ 05371-1369) couldn't be more conveniently located—on Phrasopsook Road off Phaholyothin Road near the Night Market just in the center of town. Tuk-tuks and *samlors* are easy to catch here for trips around town for 30B to 60B (86¢–US$1.70/ 45p–90p).

By Car   The fast, not particularly scenic, route from Bangkok is Highway 1 North, direct to Chiang Rai. A slow, attractive approach on blacktop mountain roads is Route 107 north from Chiang Mai to Fang, and then Route 109 east to Highway 1.

VISITOR INFORMATION

The **TAT** (© **05374-4674**) is located at 448/16 Singhakai Rd., near Wat Phra Singh on the north side of town, and the Tourist Police are next door. The monthly guide *Welcome to Chiang Mai and Chiang Rai* is distributed free by most hotels and has a good, reliable map of the town.

ORIENTATION

Chiang Rai is a small city, with most services grouped around the main north–south street, Phaholyothin Road. There are three noteworthy landmarks: the small clock tower in the city's center; the statue of King Mengrai (the city's founder) at the north-east corner of the city on the superhighway to Mae Chan; and the Mae Kok River at the north edge of town. Singhakai Road is the main artery on the north side of town, parallel to the river. The bus station is on Prasopsuk Road, 1 block east of Pha-holyothin Road, near the Wiang Inn Hotel. The Night Market is on Phaholyothin Road near the bus station.

GETTING AROUND

By *Samlor* or Tuk-Tuk   You'll probably find walking to be the best way to get around town. However, there are *samlors* (pedicabs) parked outside the Night Market and on the banks of the Mae Kok River; they charge 20B to 30B (57¢–86¢/30p–45p) for in-town trips. During the day, there are tuk-tuks, which charge 30B to 60B (86¢–US$1.70/45p–90p) for in-town trips.

By Bus   Chiang Rai's frequent local buses are the easiest and cheapest way to get to nearby cities. All leave from the bus station (© **05371-1369**) on Prasopsuk Road near the Wiang Inn Hotel.

By Motorcycle   Motorcycling is another good way to get out of town. **Soon Motor-cycle,** 197/2 Trirat Rd. (© **05371-4068**), charges 200B (US$5.70/£3.10) for a 100cc motorbike.

By Car   Budget has a branch at the Golden Triangle Inn (see "Where to Stay," below), 590 Phaholyothin Rd. (© **05374-0442**), offering the standard rate beginning at 2,000B (US$57/£31) for a Suzuki Caribbean.

FAST FACTS

Several **bank** exchanges are located on Phaholyothin Road in the center of town and are open daily from 8:30am to 10pm. The **post office** is 2 blocks north of the Clock Tower on Utarakit Road. There are a few **Internet cafes** along the main drag, Pha-holyothin Road, with service for as little as 30B (86¢/45p) per hour.

THINGS TO SEE & DO

Wat Phra Kaew, on Trirat Road on the northwest side of town, is the best known of the northern *wats* because it once housed the Emerald Buddha now at Bangkok's royal Wat Phra Kaew. Near its Lanna-style chapel is the *chedi,* which (according to legend) was struck by lightning in 1436 to reveal the precious green jasper Buddha. There is now a green jade replica of the image on display.

   Wat Phra Singh is 2 blocks east of Wat Phra Kaew. The restored *wat* is thought to date from the 15th century. Inside is a replica of the Phra Singh Buddha, a highly revered Theravada Buddhist image; the original was removed to Chiang Mai's Wat Phra Singh.

The Burmese-style **Wat Doi Tong** (Phra That Chomtong) sits atop a hill above the northwest side of town, up a steep staircase off Kaisornrasit Road, and offers an overview of the town and a panorama of the Mae Kok valley. It is said that King Mengrai himself chose the site for his new Lanna capital from this very hill. The circle of columns at the top of the hill surrounds the city's new *lak muang* (city pillar), built to commemorate the 725th anniversary of the city and King Bhumibol's 60th birthday. It is often criticized for its failure to represent local style. (You can see the old wooden *lak muang* in the *viharn* of the *wat*.)

The **Population and Community Development Association (PDA)**, 620/1 Thanalai Rd., east of Wisetwang Road (© **05371-9167**), is a NGO responsible for some of the most effective tribal development projects in the region. The popular Cabbages & Condoms restaurants, with branches here and in Bangkok (and now a resort in Pattaya), carry their important message of safe sex and family planning. On the top floor of this office is a small **Hill-tribe Museum** (no phone) that's heavy on shopping and light on museum exhibits, but the admission goes to a good cause. It's open daily 9am to 7pm, and admission is 50B (US$1.45/75p).

The **Mae Kok River** is one of the most scenic attractions in Chiang Rai. You can hire a long-tail boat to ferry you up and down the river. You'll have the option to stop at the Buddha cave (a temple within a cavern), an elephant camp (for trekking), a hot spring, and a riverside Lahu village. Trips range from 500B to 1,000B (US$14–US$29/£7.70–£15), depending on the stops you make. The ferry pier is beyond the bridge across from the Dusit Island Resort. Contact **Maesalong Tours,** 882–4 Phaholyothin Rd. (© **05371-2515;** fax 05371-1011), or ask at your hotel.

TREKKING & HILL-TRIBE TOURS

Most of the **hill-tribe villages** within close range of Chiang Rai have long ago been set up for routine visits by group tours (not recommended). If your time is too limited for a trek, in-town travel agencies offer day trips to the countryside and areas less-traveled. Guided tours with transport are priced on a two-person minimum and greater discounts are available for groups of three or more.

The best operation in Chiang Rai is **Golden Triangle Tours** ⚑, 590 Phaholyothin Rd. (© **05371-3918;** fax 05371-3963; www.goldenchiangrai.com). They are professional, experienced, and offer an array of tours and cater to personal interests. For hill-tribe treks, choose anything from a day trip to a week of adventure. **Day trips** to surrounding villages begin at 2,300B (US$66/£35) and can include light trekking to villages as well as elephant trekking for groups of two or three people (private tours cost a bit more). **Longer treks** range in price from 6,500B to 7,800B (US$186–US$223/£100–£120) for anything from multi-day trips in the Golden Triangle to 3- to 5-day sojourns among Akha, Hmong, Yao, Karen, and Lahu tribes. Exciting 4×4 treks along the **opium trail** follow new routes cut by government agencies to hurry local produce to market and thus replace community reliance on cultivating opium poppies.

WHERE TO STAY

This city of 40,000 has an impressive 2,000 hotel rooms, but group tours fill them up in high season. With the exception of the resorts across the river, most hotels are within walking distance of the sights and shopping.

EXPENSIVE

Dusit Island Resort Hotel 𝔊𝔊 One of Chiang Rai's best resorts occupies a large delta island in the Mae Kok River. The resort offers international comfort at the expense of local flavor and hominess. The dramatic lobby is a soaring space of teak, marble, and glass, as grand as any in Thailand, with panoramic views of the Mae Kok. Rooms are luxuriously appointed in pastel cottons and teak trim. The Dusit Island has manicured grounds, a pool, and numerous facilities, making the resort quite self-contained. The hotel's most formal dining room is Peak on the 10th floor, with sweeping views and a grand terrace overlooking the Mae Kok; the food is pricey but good. Chinatown is a more casual Cantonese restaurant serving a great dim sum lunch. In the evening, stop by the Music Room bar for live entertainment.

1129 Kraisorasit Rd., Chiang Rai 57000 (over bridge at northwest corner of town). ⓒ 05371-5777. Fax 05371-5801. www.dusit.com. 271 units. 3,873B–4,202B (US$110–US$120/£60–£65) superior/deluxe double; from 6,427B (US$184/£99) suite. AE, DC, MC, V. **Amenities:** 3 restaurants; lounge; pub; outdoor pool; lit tennis courts; fitness center; Jacuzzi; sauna; steam; game room; tour desk; car-rental desk; airport transfer; 24-hr. room service; massage; babysitting; same-day laundry service/dry cleaning; nonsmoking rooms; executive floor. *In room:* A/C, satellite TV, minibar, fridge, safe.

The Legend Chiang Rai 𝔊 The Legend is a unique and attractive rural boutique resort. Rooms are private sanctuaries with smooth-finish concrete and stucco walls; the end result is a crisp, modern look, with many natural touches. Some rooms overlook the river, others line a narrow garden pond, and all have great indoor and outdoor sitting areas, which allow for a constant connection with your surroundings. There are a few different configurations, including huge private pool villas and family suites, but all include large outdoor shower areas, some with a Jacuzzi bath, and large, luxuriant canopy beds. One highlight is the small infinity edge pool at the center of the resort. They have a great spa with outdoor *salas* and indoor treatment rooms, and the resort runs a number of day trips and activities. It may not have the reputation, or all the facilities, of the nearby Dusit, but it has endless charm.

124/15 Kohloy Rd., Chiang Rai 57000. ⓒ 05391-0400. Fax 05371-9650. www.thelegend-chiangrai.com. 76 units. 3,900B–6,700B (US$111–US$191/£60–£103) studio; 4,800B–7,500B (US$137–US$214/£74–£115) deluxe; 500B–10,900B (US$214–US$311/£115–£168) river view villa. MC, V. **Amenities:** Restaurant; bar; outdoor pool; spa; tour desk; limited room service; babysitting; laundry service; dry cleaning. *In room:* A/C, satellite TV, minibar, fridge, coffeemaker, safe.

The River House 𝔊𝔊 The River House is a luxurious campus just across the river from town (near Rimkok Resort; see below). Set around a large pool flanked by laughing elephant sculptures, the resort has a full-service spa and dining area. Rooms are all a very high standard, similar almost to a stylish city hotel, with elegant built-in wooden cabinetry and fine furnishings. Second floor rooms flank a large veranda overlooking farmer's fields at riverside—they're a great place to watch the dragonflies at dusk. River House caters mostly to high-end Thai travelers and an increasing number of European and North Americans. They have regular evening shuttles to town, and the front desk staff is very friendly and helpful.

482 Moo 4, Tambon Rim Kok, Chiang Rai 57000. ⓒ 05375-0829. Fax 05375-0822. www.riverhouse-chiangrai.com. 36 units. 6,300B (US$180/£97) deluxe in high season; 8,900B (US$254/£137) suite in high season. **Amenities:** Restaurant; bar; outdoor pool; health club; tour desk; limited room service; massage; laundry service; dry cleaning. *In room:* A/C, satellite TV, minibar, fridge, safe.

MODERATE

Rimkok Resort Hotel *&* Everything is done on a large scale at the Rimkok. Public spaces are capped with high-peaked Thai roofs and are grand, featuring Thai decor and artwork. Lushly planted lawns surround the large central pool. Guest rooms are airy, with high ceilings/balconies and some Thai touches—the end result is an overall bland but comfortable setup. Though the resort is rather distant from town, it's thoroughly self-contained enough that you may not need to venture out. The Rimkok Resort offers shuttle service to town (to visit the market). Since it's popular with group tours, the place sometimes gets overrun. Discounts are frequently available.

6 Moo 4, Tathorn Rd., Chiang Rai 57000 (on Kok River, about 6km/3¾ miles north of town center). © 05371-6445. Fax 05371-5859. www.rimkokresort.com. 256 units. 1,950B (US$56/£30) double; from 7,000B (US$200/£108) suite. AE, DC, MC, V. **Amenities:** 3 restaurants; bar and lounge; large outdoor pool; Jacuzzi; tour desk; airport transfer; business center; shopping arcade; salon; limited room service; babysitting; same-day laundry service. *In room:* A/C, satellite TV, minibar, fridge.

Wangcome Hotel The Wangcome is located just a stone's throw from the Night Market. Rooms are small but comfortable, detailed with Lanna Thai touches like their fine-carved teak headboards. Central rooms face an outdoor swimming pool. There's a lively coffee shop and a moody cocktail lounge, a popular rendezvous spot after the Night Market closes.

869/90 Penawibhata Rd., Chiang Rai Trade Center, Chiang Rai 57000 (west off Phaholyothin Rd.). © 05371-1800. Fax 05371-2973. www.wangcome.com. 234 units. 800B (US$51/£12) double; from 4,000B (US$114/£62) suite. AE, DC, MC, V. **Amenities:** Restaurant; lounge; small pool; tour desk; airport transfer; business center; massage; laundry service. *In room:* A/C, satellite TV, minibar, fridge.

Wiang Inn *&* Wiang Inn has a convenient location (just around the corner from the bus station and opposite the Night Market), and with recent renovations is a just a notch better than the Wangcome Hotel (see above). Large rooms are trimmed in dark teak, with pale teak furniture and Thai artwork—including Lanna murals over the beds and ceramic vase table lamps. It is very well maintained, despite the steady stream of group tours, which makes an early booking advisable.

893 Phaholyothin Rd., Chiang Rai 57000 (center of town, south of bus station). © 05371-1533. Fax 05371-1877. www.wianginn.com. 256 units. 1,800B–2,200B (US$51–US$63/£28–£34) double; from 5,000B (US$143/£77) suite. AE, DC, MC, V. **Amenities:** 2 restaurants; bar and karaoke lounge; outdoor pool; tour desk; limited room service; massage; babysitting; laundry service/dry cleaning. *In room:* A/C, satellite TV, minibar, fridge.

INEXPENSIVE

The Golden Triangle Inn *&& Finds* A charming little hotel that offers comfort and lots of style and character, Golden Triangle is set in its own quiet little garden patch—once inside you'd never believe bustling Chiang Rai is just beyond the front entrance. Large rooms have terra-cotta tile floors, traditional-style furniture, and reproductions of Lanna artifacts and paintings. The owners and management are very down to earth and extremely helpful; they are the local operators of Budget Car Rental and their in-house travel agency, **Golden Triangle Tours,** is the best choice in town for arranging travel in the area. Their restaurant is excellent (see "Where to Dine," below), too.

590 Phaholyothin Rd., Chiang Rai 57000 (2 blocks north of bus station). © 05371-3918. Fax 05371-3963. www.goldenchiangrai.com. 30 units. 900B (US$26/£14) double. MC, V. **Amenities:** Restaurant; tour desk; car-rental desk; laundry service. *In room:* A/C, no phone.

WHERE TO DINE

The Night Market is the best for budget eats here, but beyond that there are a few good restaurants from which to choose. Be sure to sample the town's delicacies, like the *kaeng hang lay* or Burmese-style pork curry, the litchis (lychees) which ripen in June and July, and the sweet *nanglai* (pineapple) wine.

Cabbages & Condoms ✿ THAI   Sister restaurant to Cabbages & Condoms in Bangkok, this northern branch was opened by the Population & Community Development Association to promote their humanitarian work in the region. The extensive Thai menu is excellent and features local catfish cooked as you like. They play host to lots of events and live bands and it is a popular stop for tour groups, which also come for the exhibit upstairs (see "Things to See & Do," above).

620/25 Thanalai Rd. ✆ 05371-9167. Main courses 70B–200B (US$2–US$5.70/£1.10–£3.10). MC, V. Daily 10am–11pm.

Golden Triangle Café ✿ THAI   At the entrance to the Golden Triangle Inn (see "Where to Stay," above), one of the best accommodations choices in town is also where you can find the best Thai meal. Everything is delicious, but perhaps the best reason to eat here is for the menu, which carefully explains the various dishes that make up a standard Thai meal, describing the ingredients and preparation of each. They have the obligatory sandwiches and burgers, but go for regional treats, especially the curry sweetened with local litchis (when in season). After studying the menu, you can order what you like in any restaurant—in Thai, too!

Golden Triangle Inn, 590 Phaholyothin Rd. ✆ 05371-3918. Entrees 80B–250B (US$2.30–US$7.15/£1.25–£3.85). MC, V. Daily 8am–10:30pm.

The Night Market/Food Stalls ✿ THAI   Every night after 7pm, the cavernous, tin-roofed Municipal Market at the town center comes alive with dozens of chrome-plated food stalls that serve steamed, grilled, and fried Thai treats. It is where locals meet, greet, and eat, and really the heart of the town (a busy mercantile market as well), so don't miss a wander here even if you're not into street-eats. For standard dining in the market, try **Rattanakosin,** a little market-side edifice done up in contemporary Thai style and serving good local cuisine (mostly for tour groups). Just outside the main entrance to the market on the main drag is **Aye's Restaurant** (869/170 Phaholyothin Rd.; ✆ 05375-2534) serving some familiar, if not all that exciting, European fare. Also try **Da Vinci** (879/4-5 Phaholyothin Rd.; ✆ 05375-2535), an Italian restaurant with good fresh salads, thin crust pizzas, and pasta.

SHOPPING

The recent influx of tourists has made Chiang Rai a magnet for hill-tribe clothing and crafts. You'll find many boutiques in the Night Market near the bus terminal off Phaholyothin Road, as well as some fine shops scattered around the city.

CHIANG RAI AFTER DARK

The main activity is wandering the **Night Market,** which is really just a more toned-down version of the raucous Night Bazaar in Chiang Mai. Like its big-city model, you can find a few bars and clubs (a bit seedy but fun). In Chiang Rai there are the standard "beer bar" storefronts with names like **Patpong Bar, Lobo,** and **Butterfly** lining the road just a short walk west of the market along Punyodyana Road, behind the Wangcome Hotel. There are also a few quiet pubs.

CHIANG RAI TO MAE SAI

This is a popular "visa run" route, where you can cross the border to Myanmar and re-enter Thailand for another 30 days (as long as you have not been in Thailand for 60 consecutive days previously; you'll have to pay 250B [US$7.15/£3.85]). Most visitors coming from the north of Chiang Rai zip through the little border town of Mae Sai on their way to the Golden Triangle and Chiang Saen, but the town is worth a stop. It is the northernmost point in Thailand. Just to the right of the border gate to Myanmar (the end of the highway) you'll find a busy market area with rows of tacky souvenirs—and silver jewelry brought from Myanmar. There is also a busy hotel used mostly by Thai tourists, called the **Wang Thong Hotel** (299 Phaholyothin Rd.; © **05373-3388;** from 1,000B/US$29/£15 double). Its rooms look out over Burmese temples, and their lunchtime buffet is pretty basic but edible.

6 Chiang Saen ★ & the Golden Triangle

935km (580 miles) NE of Bangkok; 239km (148 miles) NE of Chiang Mai

The small village of Chiang Saen, the gateway to the Golden Triangle area, has a sleepy, rural charm, as if the waters of the Mekong carry a palpable calm from nearby Myanmar and Laos. The road from Chiang Rai (59km/37 miles) follows the small Mae Nam Chan River past coconut groves and lush rice paddies. Poinsettias and gladiola decorate thatched Lanna Thai houses with peaked rooflines that extend into Xs like buffalo horns.

Little Chiang Saen, the birthplace of expansionary King Mengrai, was abandoned for the new Lanna capitals of Chiang Rai, then Chiang Mai, in the 13th century. With the Mekong River and the Laos border hemming in its growth, modern developers went elsewhere. Today, the slow rural pace, decaying regal *wats,* crumbling fort walls, and overgrown moat contribute to its appeal.

Once upon a time, the Golden Triangle was the center point of many illicit activities. The name was given to the area where Thailand, Laos, and Myanmar come together—a proximity that facilitated overland drug transportation of opium and heroin in its first steps toward international markets. Thai authorities have mounted a concerted effort to stop the drug traffic here and, while some illegal activity goes unchecked, the area is hardly dangerous. Rather, Ban Sob Ruak, the Thai town at the junction, is a long and disappointing row of souvenir stalls. Still, if you stand at the crook of the river, you can look to the right to see Laos and to the left to see Myanmar (Burma). When the river is low, a large sandbar appears that is apparently unclaimed by any authority.

A common route here is to leave from Chiang Rai by car (or motorbike) and travel directly north to the Burmese border town of **Mae Sai,** a great stop for gem and souvenir shopping. Then follow the Mekong River going east along the border, making a stop at **The Hall of Opium,** and the town of **Ban Sob Ruak,** before catching the museum and many temples of Chiang Saen. If overnighting in the area, the best stops are in the Golden Triangle proper (west of Chiang Saen).

ESSENTIALS
GETTING THERE

By Bus   Buses from **Chiang Rai's Khon Song Bus Terminal** leave every 15 minutes from 6am to 6pm (trip time: 1½ hr.; 25B/71¢/35p). The bus drops you on Chiang Saen's main street. The museum and temples are within walking distance. Public *songtaews,* or pickups, make frequent trips between Chiang Saen and the Golden Triangle for about 25B (71¢/35p).

By Car Take the superhighway Route 110 north from Chiang Rai to Mae Chan, and then Route 1016 northeast to Chiang Saen.

ORIENTATION

Route 1016 is the village's main street, also called Phaholyothin Road, which terminates at the Mekong River. Along the river road there are a few guesthouses, eateries, and souvenir, clothing, and food stalls.

The Golden Triangle and the town of Ban Sob Ruak are just 8km (5 miles) west of the town of Chiang Saen, and the choicest accommodations (the Anantara and the Imperial) are just a few clicks west from there. Mae Sai is some 30km (19 miles) west of the Golden Triangle.

GETTING AROUND

On Foot There's so little traffic it is a pleasure to walk around here; all of the in-town sights are within a 15-minute walk of each other.

By Bicycle & Motorcycle It's a great bike ride (45 min.) from Chiang Saen to the prime nearby attraction, the Golden Triangle. The roads are well paved and pretty flat. **Chiang Saen House Rent Motor,** on the river road just east of the main street intersection, has good one-speed bicycles for 50B (US$1.45/75p) per day, and 100cc motorcycles (no insurance, no helmets) for 200B (US$5.70/£3.10) per day.

By Samlor Motorized pedicabs hover by the bus stop in town to take you to the Golden Triangle for 60B (US$1.70/90p) one-way. Round-trip fares with waiting time are negotiable to about 250B (US$7.15/£3.85) for about 2 hours.

By Songtao Songtaos (truck taxis) can be found on the main street across from the market; rides cost only 25B (71¢/40p) to the Golden Triangle.

By Long-tail Boat Long-tail boat captains down by the river offer Golden Triangle tours for as little as 800B (US$23/£12) per boat (seating eight) per half-hour. Many people enjoy the half-hour cruise, take a walk around the village of Ban Sob Ruak after they've seen the Golden Triangle, and then continue on by bus.

FAST FACTS

There is a **Siam Commercial Bank** in the center of Phaholyothin Road, Route 1016, the main street, close to the **bus stop, post, and telegram office** (no overseas service and few local telephones), the police station, the many temples, and the Chiang Saen National Museum. There is a **currency exchange** booth at the Golden Triangle.

WHAT TO SEE & DO

Allow half a day to see all of Chiang Saen's historical sights before exploring the Golden Triangle. To help with orientation, make the museum your first stop. There is a good map about local historical sites on the second floor.

The **Chiang Saen National Museum** (702 Phaholyothin Rd.; ℂ **05377-7102**) houses a small but very fine collection of this region's historic and ethnographic products. The ground floor's main room has a collection of large bronze and stone Buddha images dating from the 15th- to 17th-century Lanna kingdom. Pottery from Sukhothai-era kiln sites is displayed downstairs and on the balcony.

The handicrafts and cultural items of local hill-tribes on display here are fascinating, particularly the display of Nam Bat, an ingenious fishing tool. Burmese-style lacquer ware, Buddha images, and wood carvings scattered through the museum reinforce the similarities seen between Chiang Saen and its spiritual counterpart, Pagan (in Myanmar). Allow an hour to go through the museum carefully. It's open Wednesday to Sunday 9am to 4pm, but is closed holidays; admission is 30B (86¢/45p).

Wat Pa Sak, the best preserved *wat* here, is set in a landscaped historical park that contains a large, square-based *stupa* and six smaller *chedis* and temples. The park preserves what's left of the compound's 1,000 teak trees. The *wat* is said to have been constructed in 1295 by King Saen Phu to house relics of the Buddha, though some historians believe its ornate combination of Sukhothai and Pagan styles dates it later. The historical park is about 201m (660 ft.) west of the Chiang Saen Gate (at the entrance to the village). It is open daily 8am to 6pm; admission is 30B (86¢/45p).

The area's second oldest *wat* is still an active Buddhist monastery. Rising from a cluster of wooden dorms, **Wat Chedi Luang** (or Jadeeloung) has a huge brick *chedi* that dominates the main street. The *wat* complex was established in 1331 under the reign of King Saen Phu and was rebuilt in 1515 by King Muang Kaeo. The old brick foundations, now supporting a very large, plaster seated Buddha flanked by smaller ones, are all that remain. Small bronze and stucco Buddhas excavated from the site are now in the museum. It is open daily from 8am to 6pm. Admission is free.

There are several other *wats* of note in and around the town. **Wat Mung Muang** is the 15th-century square-based *stupa* seen next to the post office. Above the bell-shaped *chedi* are four small *stupas.* Across the street, you can see the bell-shaped *chedi* from **Wat Phra Bouj.** It's rumored to have been built by the prince of Chiang Saen in 1346, though historians believe it is of the same period as Mung Muang. As you leave Chiang Saen on the river road, going northwest to the Golden Triangle, you'll pass **Wat Pha Kao Pan,** with some sculpted Buddha images tucked in niches and on its *stupa,* and then the unrestored ***viharn*** mound of **Wat Sangakaeo Don Tan.** Both are thought to date from the 16th century.

THE GOLDEN TRIANGLE

The infamous Golden Triangle (12km/7½ miles northwest of Chiang Saen) is the point where Thailand, Myanmar, and Laos meet at the confluence of the broad, slow and silted Mekong and Mae Ruak rivers. They create Thailand's northern border, separating it from overgrown jungle patches of Myanmar to the west and forested, hilly Laos to the east. The area's appeal as a vantage point over forbidden territories is quickly diminishing as there is now a legal crossing into Laos from nearby Chiang Khong.

Nonetheless, a "look" at the home of ethnic hill-tribes and their legendary opium trade is still interesting, and there are some good sites to see. In fact, the appeal of this geopolitical phenomenon has created an entire village—Ban Sob Ruak—of thatch souvenir stalls, cheap river-view soda and noodle shops, and large, fancy hotels. The most interesting of these is:

The Hall of Opium ✿✿✿ Sponsored by the late Princess Mother as part of a larger effort to educate and find alternatives for hill-tribe peoples of the north, the museum complex covers some 16 hectares (40 acres) of garden overlooking the Mekong. You enter the museum and follow a long corridor through a mountain. In the dark, all you can see are a few murals that portray the pain and anguish of addiction, and then emerge in a grand atrium with a large glowing golden triangle (the irony is a bit much). From there it is a multimedia romp of films and light-up displays that tell of the growth of the poppy, its vital importance in British and international trade with

Onward to Laos

Many make Chiang Rai or Chiang Saen their last port of call in the land of Thai and head overland to rugged but inviting Laos. It is possible to travel downriver 70km (43 miles) to Chiang Khong, a small border town (buses and local *songtaews* also make the connection from either Chiang Rai or Chiang Saen). Most travelers head right across the border, but if you are stuck in Chiang Khong, try **Bamboo Guesthouse** (✆ 05379-1621; www. thai-bamboo.eu), with basic rooms from 150B (US$4.30/£2.30); or **Reuan Thai Sophaphan** (✆ 05379-1023), on the river with simple rooms, some with A/C, from 350B to 600B (US$10–US$17/£5.40–£9.25). You'll need to arrange a visa to enter Laos, which is best done in Bangkok or Chiang Mai at any travel agent. Once over the border, the slow boat to Luang Prabang is rugged but memorable (pick up *Frommer's Southeast Asia* or check out www.frommers.com for information on travel in Laos).

China, the many conflicts over opium, the drug's influx into Thailand, and useful information about recent efforts to suppress international smuggling and address rampant addiction throughout the region. Media-savvy exhibits are in both Thai and English. The "Hall of Excuses" at the end highlights (or lowlights?) many of the world's most well-known addicts, and the museum ends in the "Hall of Reflections," where guests are invited to ruminate on their experience. And it *is* an experience (taking about 1½ hr. to go through). There's nothing like it anywhere else in Thailand.

10km/6 miles NW of Chiang Saen. ✆ 0578-4444. www.goldentrianglepark.com. Entrance fee 300B (US$8.60/£4.60). Tues–Sun 10am–3:30pm.

Opium Museum   The hand-painted description and battered old display cases here pale in comparison to the multi-media extravaganza that is the Hall of Opium (see above), but here you can find much of the same info about cultivation, distribution, and opium's place in global trade. There's lots of paraphernalia and a certain battered charm to the place (plus there's a good little souvenir shop and toilet stop for on the way to Chiang Saen).

212 House of Opium, Chiang Saen (just opposite the golden Buddha at the very heart of the Golden Triangle). ✆ 05378-4060. Entrance fee 50B (US$1.40/75p). Daily 7am–9pm.

WHERE TO STAY

There are a few guesthouses in Chiang Saen and two fine resort hotels in the Golden Triangle area. The area is very scenic and relaxing.

EXPENSIVE

Anantara Resort and Spa Golden Triangle ★★★ *Finds*   The superbly swish Anantara is a triumph of upscale, local design. Every detail reminds you that you're in the scenic hill-tribe region; and the resort's elegance and style depend on locally produced weavings, carved teak panels, and expansive views of the juncture of the Ruak and Mekong rivers. The balconied rooms have splendid views and are so spacious and private, you will feel like you're in your own bungalow. Tiled foyers lead to large bathrooms, and bedrooms are furnished in teak and traditional fabrics. The hotel supports a small elephant camp and their busy tour desk can arrange any number of trips to far-flung corners of the region (or just across the road to the Hall of Opium). Rooms are a luxurious city hotel standard, many with windows connecting large bathrooms with the main room area. This is the top choice in the far north hills.

229 Moo 1, Chiang Saen 57150, Chiang Rai (above river, 12km/7½ miles northwest of Chiang Saen). ℂ 800/225-5843 in the U.S., or 05378-4084. Fax 05378-4090. www.anantara.com. 90 units. 8,925B (US$255/£137) double; 14,175B (US$405/£218) suite. AE, DC, MC, V. **Amenities:** 3 restaurants; lounge and bar; outdoor pool; outdoor lit tennis courts; fitness center; spa; bike rental; tour desk; car-rental desk; airport transfer; business center; shopping arcade; salon; limited room service; babysitting; same-day laundry service. *In room:* A/C, satellite TV w/in-house movies, minibar, fridge, coffee/tea-making facilities, hair dryer, safe.

MODERATE

The Imperial Golden Triangle Resort ✿   This five-story hotel block stands in the western corner of the tiny souvenir village of Ban Sob Ruak. Modern, spacious guest rooms with pastel and rattan decor have large balconies, and the more expensive rooms overlook the Golden Triangle. It is a fine, comfortable choice if you're passing through, but pales in comparison to the nearby Anantara (see above).

222 Golden Triangle, Chiang Saen, Chiang Rai (in Ban Sob Ruak, 11km/7 miles northwest of Chiang Saen). ℂ 05378-4001. Fax 05378-4006. www.imperialhotels.com. 73 units. 2,520B–2,940B (US$72–US$84/£39–£45) double; from 5,880B (US$168/£90) suite. AE, MC, V. **Amenities:** Restaurant; lounge; pool; tour desk; laundry service. *In room:* A/C, satellite TV, minibar, fridge.

INEXPENSIVE

Chiang Saen River Hill Hotel   This is the best choice for in-town, budget accommodations in Chiang Saen. The River Hill is about 1km (⅔ mile) east of the main drag. They have bicycle rentals for guests, and it is an easy peddle to the center of town. Guest rooms are concrete block rooms with simple tile floors but are dressed in northern finery, with wood carving details and funky little Lanna-style seating arrangements (floor cushions around low *khan toke* tables under regal umbrellas). The large and colorful coffee shop (in shades of blue and aqua with little star lights from the ceiling) is open for breakfast, lunch, and dinner, with good selections and a relaxed and refreshing atmosphere.

714 Moo 3, Sukhapibansai 2 Rd., Tambon Viang, Chiang Saen, Chiang Rai (5-min. *samlor* ride from bus stop). ℂ 05365-0826. Fax 05365-0830. 60 units. 1,062B (US$30/£16) double. No credit cards. **Amenities:** Restaurant; bike rental; laundry service. *In room:* A/C, TV, no phone.

14

Exploring Isan:
Thailand's Frontier

The 19 provinces of northeastern Thailand are collectively called Isan (*e-sahn*) and account for roughly one-third of the country's land mass, and a quarter of the population. Bordered by Laos to the north (along the Mekong) and by Cambodia to the southeast, the region suffers from a stagnant rural economy. Life is hard on the scorched plains of Isan, but the friendly people of this region welcome travelers warmly—you'll experience something along the lines of America's southern hospitality. There are a few tourist attractions, mostly off the beaten track, including some important archaeological sites (mostly dating from the Khmer period), lovely river towns, finely made crafts, and fiery food. The areas in the far north and along the Mekong are particularly worth the trip.

The weather is especially hot in Isan but follows a pattern much like the rest of Thailand: It's coolest from November to February; hot and dry from March to May; and rainy from June to October.

Windswept and infertile in parts, but verdant along the Mekong, the region is attracting more international tourists who come for the trekking options, but also because Isan is a good jumping-off point for trips to Laos.

Indeed, much about Isan, from the weather to the local dialect and culture, resembles Laos and is quite distinct from mainstream Thai culture. As a result, many joke about *Prathet Isan,* or "the Nation of Isan," for its unique language, culture, and stubbornly snail pace. As the poorest region of Thailand, with little opportunity for its young populace, Isan is experiencing an ever-increasing drain on people as young folks move to the area's larger cities. A few learned phrases of the Isan dialect will endear you to a large part of the Bangkok cab driver population, for example. You are sure to meet kind folks from Isan in every region of Thailand, and the fact that you know the name of their town, much less have been there, will be a source of wonder.

1 Information & Tours

A few **PB Air** (✆ **02261-0220;** www.pbair.com) flights are available to these parts, as well as regular bus and train connections throughout Isan. In more remote parts, buses are slow and won't stop near sights, so try to arrange a tour, or go by your own rented vehicle with a driver. The latter is a relatively affordable proposition; expect to pay about 1,600B (US$46/£25) per day, plus fuel. Contact **North by Northeast Tours** in Nakhon Phanom (746/1 Sunthornvichit Rd., Nakhon Phanom 48000; ✆ **04251-3572;** fax 04251-3573; www.north-by-north-east.com), a small, expat-owned tour company; they can arrange a private itinerary covering the region.

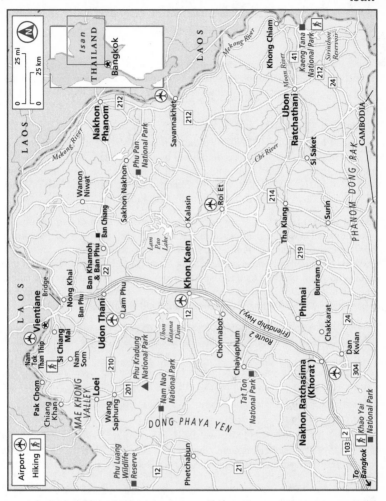

There are **Tourist Authority of Thailand (TAT)** offices in many tour centers through the region (though few are conveniently located). Check out www.tourism thailand.org, or call ☎ **1672** for assistance.

2 Nakhon Ratchasima (Khorat)

259km (161 miles) NE of Bangkok; 150km (94 miles) W of Buriram; 305km (189 miles) S of Udon Thani

Nakhon Ratchasima, popularly known as Khorat, isn't a wildly interesting city, but it is close to Bangkok and makes a good base for excursions to beautiful **Khao Yai National Park** (see "Side Trips from Bangkok" in chapter 6) and the temples at **Phimai** and other nearby Khmer sites. It is a rapidly developing industrial city and is called the "Gateway to Isan" because all train lines, bus routes, roads, and communications pass through it. There are some comfortable accommodations in Khorat and a few temples and city monuments worth seeing.

GETTING THERE

The airport in Khorat is no longer operational, but there are numerous daily trains from Bangkok's **Hua Lampong Station** (© **1690**), and frequent bus connections from Bangkok's Northern Bus Terminal, **Mo Chit** (© **02936-2852**). It's about a 3-hour journey by train or bus.

WHAT TO SEE & DO

A trip to **Phimai,** 60km (37 miles) northeast of town, is worth it if you are interested in Khmer archaeology. Phimai is dominated by the Prasat Hin Phimai temple complex and there is a large museum as well. In Khorat, the most interesting temple houses an image of Narayana, a sacred Hindu deity, at **Wat Phra Narai Maharat** along Prajak Road, where you'll also find the **City Pillar.**

WHERE TO STAY

The best hotel in town is the **Royal Princess Khorat** (1137 Suranarai Rd., northeast of town near the stadium; © **04425-6629**), with fair amenities and rooms starting from 2,000B (US$57/£31). A close second is **Sima Thani** (2112 Mittraphap Rd., next to the TAT office, west of town; © **04421-3100;** www.simathani.com), with rooms starting at 2,000B (US$57/£28). **Chomsurang Hotel** (2701/1-2 Mahatthai Rd. near the Night Market; © **04425-7088**) has basic rooms from 850B (US$24/£13).

3 Khon Kaen

449km (278 miles) NE of Bangkok; 190km (118 miles) N of Nakhon Ratchasima; 115km (71 miles) S of Udon Thani

For most travelers, Khon Kaen is just a stopover en route to Udon and Nong Khai. The town is along Route 2, connects by rail with Bangkok and Nong Khai, and has a large commercial airport.

GETTING THERE

Thai Airways (© **02356-1111;** www.thaiairways.com) and budget carrier **Air Asia** (© **02515-9999;** www.airasia.com) connect with Bangkok. There are also two third-class trains running daily from Bangkok via Khorat (see above), and bus services abound.

WHERE TO STAY

You'll find many accommodations options in Khon Kaen, since it's a busy regional convention center. The top choice is the **Hotel Sofitel Raja Orchid** (9/9 Prachasumran Rd.; © **04332-2155;** www.sofitel.com) with stylish rooms from 2,500B (US$71/£38). Or try the **Charoen Thani Princess** (Srichan and Na-Muang rds.; © **04322-0400;** www.dusit.com), a popular meeting and convention address with doubles from 1,225B (US$35/£19). Budget **Khon Kaen Hotel** (43/2 Phimpasut Rd.; © **04333-2222**) has small but cheap rooms from 650B (US$19/£10).

4 Udon Thani & Ban Chiang

564km (350 miles) NE of Bangkok; 305km (189 miles) N of Nakhon Ratchasima

"No sweat, man," was once a common vocabulary amongst tuk-tuk drivers. The use of 1960s slang reminds tourists that Udon Thani (or Udon) was home to a large contingent of U.S. armed forces during the Vietnam War and memories still linger. Today you might see a few retired U.S. servicemen around, and each year the area welcomes a contingent of the U.S. military for joint training with Thai forces (mostly the Air Force).

Udon is not very interesting, but it is a good jumping-off point to small towns like Loei to the west. **Ban Chiang** is a well-known archaeological site east of Udon.

GETTING THERE

Thai Airways (© 02280-0060; www.thaiair.com) has daily flights, as do budget carriers **Nok Air** (© 02325-5555; www.nokair.com) and **Air Asia** (© 02515-9999; www.airasia.com). Numerous trains (best as an overnight in a second-class sleeper) connect from Bangkok's **Hua Lampong Station** (© 1690) daily via Khorat and Khon Kaen; and there are bus connections from Udon to anywhere in the region. *Note:* **Budget Car Rental** has an office at the airport (© 04224-6805). It is a good idea to fly to Udon and rent a car here to explore the Mekong Valley to the north (see the following sections).

WHERE TO STAY

The hub of this town is the **Charoensri Shopping Complex,** around which you'll find many services. The best way to get around is by *samlor* (pedal powered taxis that are, oddly, called "skylabs"), or tuk-tuks.

Charoensri Grand Royal Hotel (277/1 Prachak Rd., west of the railway station and adjacent to the mall; © 04234-3555; www.charoensrigrand.com) is the best choice in town, with cozy rooms that are centrally located, from 1,500B (US$43/£23). **Charoen Hotel** (549 Phosi Rd., near the train station; © 04224-8155; www.udonthani.com/charoen) has basic rooms from 1,000B (US$29/£15), and older **Udorn Hotel** (81–89 Makkang Rd.; © 04224-8160) has budget rooms from 500B (US$14/£7.70).

EXPLORING THE AREA

BAN CHIANG NATIONAL MUSEUM ✛   The tiny hamlet of Ban Chiang, approximately 50km (31 miles) east of Udon on the Sakon Nakhon highway, boasts a history of more than 5,600 years and as such, the area was declared a UNESCO World Heritage Site in 1992. It was—quite literally—stumbled upon in 1974 and since then, has been excavated by an international team. The findings at Ban Chiang prove the existence of a distinct and very sophisticated Bronze Age culture in Southeast Asia, long before any earlier findings. The museum was funded by the Kennedy Foundation and houses a fine collection of early statuary as well as pottery and ritual implements. The site is open Wednesday to Sunday from 8am to 5pm; admission is 30B (86¢/45p). Ban Chiang is close to the main highway between Udon and Nakhon Phanom. It's best visited by private vehicle, but you can also ask local buses to stop at the Ban Chiang junction and take a tuk-tuk to the site. Along the main road to the site, look for the many villages producing replica Ban Chiang ceramic ware.

5 The Mekong Valley Loop

This loop takes you from **Udon** to the west and the little town of **Loei,** then along the Mekong, the natural Thai–Laos border, through **Nong Khai,** and on to **Nakhon Phanom.** With a side trip to **That Phanom** (and a possible stop at Ban Chiang) you return to Udon, from where you can fly back to Bangkok. You could also amend the route to follow the Mekong all the way south from Nakhon Phanom to **Ubon Ratchathani.** This is adventurous off-the-track travel, and it's not a bad idea to hire a guide (see "Information & Tours" at the beginning of this chapter) or a car and driver.

6 Loei

520km (322 miles) NE of Bangkok; 344km (213 miles) N of Nakhon Ratchasima

Cool and usually rainy because of its higher elevation (the town is reputedly the coldest spot in the kingdom), little Loei is a lazy riverside town worth an overnight stop, but this route is more about the beautiful road journey, not the destination. Dan Sai 80km (50 miles) southwest of Loei hosts the annual **Pi Tha Khon Festival,** a Thai-style Mardi Gras in which young men dress as spirits and go crazy in the streets. "The devil made me do it!" is the excuse for all kinds of outlandish behavior; it's lots of fun. Outside of Loei town is **Phu Kradung National Park,** and one of Thailand's most dramatic sights: a bell-shaped tabletop mountain of 1,200m (4,000 ft.). The park is 82km (51 miles) south of Loei and well worth the trip.

GETTING THERE

There is neither a train line nor airport in Loei. Regular buses from Udon putter along the only road—or the most direct route from Khon Kaen.

WHERE TO STAY

Loei Palace Hotel (167/4 Charoenrat Rd., ✆ **04281-5668;** www.amari.com) is by far the best choice in town; it's a huge courtyard hotel with lots of amenities, including a pool and affordable rooms (from 1,200B/US$34/£19). **King's Hotel** (11/9-12 Chumsai Rd., at town center; ✆ **04281-1701**) is a basic, affordable choice with rooms from 400B (US$11/£6.15).

7 Along the Mekong from Loei to Nong Khai

One of the most scenic areas in Thailand—and delightfully secluded—the northwestern perimeter of Isan runs along the wide Mekong River, which forms the border with Laos. The terrain is relatively flat, the road is only lightly trafficked and in a good state of repair, and you can stop at a number of villages.

The loop begins in Loei and ends in Nong Khai. Directly north of Loei you'll reach the riverside town of **Chiang Khan,** where you'll find a few riverside guesthouses, a *wat* worth visiting, and a few expatriates who've discovered the real simple life. You can take a short day trip by long-tail boat for just 400B (US$11/£6.15) for 1 hour (contact any riverside guesthouse).

From Chiang Khan, Route 212 follows the Mekong east to **Pak Chom** and **Si Chiang Mai** before arriving in Nong Khai. Buses and *songtaew* make all of these connections, but it is a hassle, so it's best to have your own transport. The route passes lush banana plantations, terraced fruit farms, and wonderful river views. Cotton and tomato fields fan out along the verdant flood plains of the Mekong basin. Farther inland are lovely waterfalls like **Nam Tok Than Thip** (between Pak Chom and Si Chiang Mai), which are fun for hiking and ideal for picnics.

Don't miss the unique gold tower of the **Prasutham Chedi,** just west of Si Chiang Mai along the main road, and **Wat Hin Mak Peng,** which is some 30km (19 miles) west of Si Chiang Mai and a glorious temple site overlooking the Mekong.

Si Chiang Mai is opposite Vientiane, the Laos capital, and is but 58km (36 miles) due west of Nong Khai. The town is just a quiet Thai backwater. Walks along the long concrete pier or relaxing and watching Laos and Thai long-tail boats load and unload or chugging up- and down-river is about all that's going on here. In the evenings, join in a game of badminton or a circle of people juggling a *takraw* (a small bamboo ball).

There are lots of little open-air eateries at the riverside and a few small guesthouses along the quay at town center: Try **Maneerat Resort** (74 Rimkong Rd., along the eastern end of the quay; © **04245-1311**), with basic but clean air-conditioned rooms starting at 500B (US$14/£7.70) and a friendly and helpful staff.

8 Nong Khai

615km (381 miles) NE of Bangkok; 51km (32 miles) N of Udon Thani

The little border town of Nong Khai is nothing special but its sprawling riverside market **Tha Sadet** is full of interesting goods from Laos and China, and the place has a palpable calm with some good, laid-back riverside guesthouses. Nong Khai is a popular jumping-off point for travel to Laos.

GETTING THERE

The nearest airport is in Udon Thani (p. 367), but Nong Khai is the terminus of the Northeast train line from Bangkok and is an enjoyable, if rocky, overnight journey. Regular buses connect with points throughout the region.

WHAT TO SEE & DO

Tha Sadet, or the **Indochina Market,** located at the heart of town at riverside, is the main attraction in Nong Khai and it is certainly worth a wander. Also check out **Sala Kaew Ku Sculpture Park** (about 4km/3 miles east of town on Rte. 212), where you'll find recently cast concrete Buddhas, Hindu deities, and other fantastic statues of enormous proportions in an attractive garden setting—all the brainchild of the eccentric Mr. Luang Phu Boonlua Surirat. He studied with an Indian guru in Vietnam and later taught in Laos, and his mummified body can be viewed on a tour of the main temple building (he also built a similar sculpture garden just across the river near Vientiane, Laos). Entry is 10B (29¢/14p), and the site is open daily from 8:30am to 6pm.

Good day trips from Nong Khai include a day (or overnight) across the border to **Vientiane** (visas are available at the border), or head out to **Phu Phrabat Historical Park,** some 70km/43 miles southwest of Nong Khai; the site is a unique grouping of natural sandstone towers that were fashioned into rudimentary cave dwellings.

Goodness Gracious! Great Balls of . . . Fire?

In late October when the moon is full, heralding the end of the Buddhist Lent, a ghostly phenomenon occurs that is, as yet, unexplained. From the waters of the Mekong rise glowing balls of red fire that ascend high into the night sky. This mystical event attracts thousands from all over Thailand. The explanation? Some say it is the rising *Naga*, or river dragon, coming to greet Lord Buddha. On the other hand, scientists claim it is instead bubbles of gas originating from rotting organic matter in the river bed being released into the air. Whether believer or nonbeliever, superstitious Thais love to flock to the venue and hotels are usually full this time of year. *Note:* There is little or no public transport available on these nights, so rent a bike in advance.

WHERE TO STAY & DINE

Budget accommodations line the small streets all over town. **Mutmee Guesthouse** (111/4 Kaeworawut Rd.; ℂ **04246-0717;** www.mutmee.net) is foreign-run, and a comfortable budget choice (from 150B/US$4.30/£2.30). It's also a great place to get good local info (and great food) and they can try to help with transport options on Naga Fireball nights. The best hotel in Nong Khai is the **Nong Khai Grand Hotel** (589 Moo 5, Nong Khai-Poanpisai Rd., just south of town; ℂ **04242-0033;** www.nongkhaigrand.com), with comfortable air-conditioned rooms from 1,250B (US$36/£19).

For good local dining, try **Daeng Namnuang** (on a small side street just off the central market; ℂ **04241-1961**), serving a popular do-it-yourself Vietnamese pork spring roll. Alternatively, stop by **Udomros** (ℂ **04242-1084**), which serves real Thai food in the heart of the market area overlooking the Mekong.

9 Nakhon Phanom

740km (459 miles) NE of Bangkok; 252km (156 miles) E of Udon Thani; 481km (298 miles) NE of Nakhon Ratchasima

Travelers rarely make it out to these parts of Thailand; apart from a few good riverside hotels catering to Westerners, the place is pretty quiet. That's the allure. Walk riverside streets and look for the old Vietnamese clock tower—a gift from grateful Vietnamese Catholic refugees escaping Ho Chi Minh's Communists in North Vietnam. South of town is **That Phanom,** an important pilgrimage site for Thai Buddhists; from there, pass through Sakon Nakhon to return to Udon Thani (with a possible side trip to Ban Chiang) completing the loop. Many travelers follow the Mekong south from Nakhon Phanom all the way to Ubon Ratchathani, where they can catch a train back to Bangkok. Each year, Nakhon Phanom hosts the famed "Lai Rua Fai" or Fire Boat Festival, where barges float downstream, twinkling with small candles in the night (also dragon boat races by day), all to celebrate the end of the rains in late October.

GETTING THERE

PB Air (ℂ **02261-0220;** www.pbair.com) has daily flights to Bangkok; otherwise, you'll arrive by road from Sakon Nakhon, or via the Mekong from Nong Khai.

WHAT TO DO & SEE

Contact **North by Northeast Tours** in Nakhon Phanom (746/1 Sunthornvichit Rd., Nakhon Phanom 48000; ℂ **04251-3572;** www.north-by-north-east.com) for good local tours to weaving and silversmith villages in the area. The city's *wats* were all built relatively early on, and the exterior bas-reliefs, attributed to the Laotian Lan Xang kingdom, are said to date back some 300 years. An hour to the south, **That Phanom** is a temple built around a tall 9th-century *stupa* that collapsed in 1975. It's an important pilgrimage site for Thai Buddhists and makes for a pleasant trip.

WHERE TO STAY

The Mae Nam Kong Grand View Hotel (527 Soonthornvijitra Rd.; ℂ **04251-3564;** www.mgvhotel.com) has tidy rooms stacked right over the Mekong starting at 1,500B (US$43/£23).

10 Southeast Isan

Branching off on the eastern spur of the rail-line at Khorat as you head north and east of Bangkok, you trace the edge of the Cambodian border on your way to Laos. First reach **Buriram,** a town with a few notable hilltop Khmer ruins, and then **Surin,** an area famous for raising elephants, before reaching **Ubon Ratchathani.** There are few jaw-dropping sites—and few Western tourists—in this city.

11 Surin

457km (283 miles) NE of Bangkok; 227km (141 miles) W of Ubon Ratchathani

Surin is elephant country and is justly famed for it is annual roundup, a nearly 200-year tradition; the city is also a good base for exploring far-flung Khmer ruins.

GETTING THERE

Three daily express trains and numerous lower-class trains connect from Bangkok via the spur line from Khorat (about 8½ hr.), and there are numerous buses; see p. 73 in chapter 4, "Introducing Bangkok," for details.

WHAT TO DO & SEE

If you haven't come with your own guide, the best way to visit the sporadically scattered sites around Surin is to book a tour with friendly Mr. Pirom at the **Pirom Guest House** (© 04451-5140). Mr. Pirom has been in the business for years and guiding is just an extension of his passion for the ancient history and culture of this rural region. The most popular tours are to the many secluded Khmer temples in the area, and he combines such visits with stops at elephant-training villages, Khmer cultural sites, handicraft villages, and even trips to the weekend market at the Cambodian border. Expect to pay from 1,000B (US$29/£15) per person.

WHERE TO STAY

Thong Tarin Hotel (60 Sirirat Rd., just east of the bus station and town center; © 04451-4281; www.thongtarinhotel.com) is the best in town, with tidy rooms from 900B (US$26/£14); nearby **Petchkasem Hotel** (104 Chitbumrung Rd. in the town center; © 04451-1274) is a basic business hotel (from just 600B/US$17/£9.25). **Pirom Guesthouse** (242 Krungsrinai Rd., 2 blocks west of the market; © 04451-5140) is a very rustic but authentic guesthouse (rooms start at 180B/US$5.15/£2.75)—you will feel as though you're a special guest of Mr. and Mrs. Pirom when you stay here.

OUTSIDE OF SURIN

Buriram is about half-way between Surin and Khorat, and easily reached overland or by **PB Air**'s (© 02261-0220-6; www.pbair.com) four weekly flights from the capital. It's home to **Prasat Hin Phanom Rung,** a stunning Khmer ruin dominated by **Phanom Rung (Great Mountain),** which was deserted in the late 13th century, rediscovered in 1935, and restored in the 1970s. Another popular side trip from Surin is **Prasat Khao Phra Viharn,** a striking Khmer site.

Appendix A:
Thailand in Depth

"Thailand in Depth" introduces you to Thailand's history, its people, cultural traditions, and cuisine.

1 The Thai People

Most of Thailand's 64 million people live in the countryside or in rural villages where they earn a living in agriculture, predominantly rice farming. But because of its growing wealth and opportunities, rural youth populations are—like everywhere—migrating to the city. Most estimates put Bangkok's population well past the 10 million mark as a result of this rural influx. The population in the capital is divided between wealthy Thais, often of Chinese ancestry, who are educated and hold formidable positions, and mostly uneducated workers who came from the rural hinterland (termed "upcountry" by Thais). These migrants speak Thai dialects and many inhabit the city's numerous slums. Hierarchy, or class, is an important distinction to Thais, who, like many of the region's nations, inherited a loose version of India's caste system. When a Thai meets someone, he or she can instantly size that person up and, depending on that individual's social status, will treat the person accordingly. Interestingly, as a foreigner, you are automatically awarded a position of stature, regardless of your social standing back home, just as long you don't flout Thai etiquette.

So, who exactly are the Thai people? It's hard to say. There really are no historically "ethnic" Thais. Today's Thais (about 75% of the population) emerged from waves of various immigrants going back around 10 centuries. "A Look at the Past," below, explains these waves in greater detail, but by and large the main bloodline is infused with indigenous people from the Bronze Age, southern Chinese tribes, Mons from Myanmar (Burma), Khmers from Cambodia, Malays, Arabs, and Europeans, plus more recent immigrants from China, Laos, Cambodia, and Myanmar. Central Thailand is a true melting pot; however, southern Thais have a closer ancestral affinity with Malays, while Thais in the north are more closely related to the Chinese hill-tribes and Burmese. In the northeast province of Isan, Laotian influence prevails. The remaining 25% are divided between Chinese (14%) and Indians, Malays, Karens, Khmer, and Mons (11%).

The Thai people are generally warm and welcoming. Locals delight in any foreigner who takes an interest in their heritage, learns a little bit of the language, eats Thai food, and follows Thai customs. Above all, the Thai people have an incredible sense of humor—a lighthearted spirit and a hearty chuckle go a long way toward making friends.

ETIQUETTE Thai customs can be a bit confusing; foreigners are not expected to know and follow local etiquette to the letter, but good manners and appropriate dress will earn you instant respect. A few small gestures and a general awareness will help foster a spirit of good will. First-time visitors are sure to make a few laughable mistakes; read below carefully in order to avoid the more offensive faux pas.

Thais greet each other with a graceful bow called a *wai*. Hands are pressed together; the higher they are held, the greater the respect. Younger people are always expected to *wai* an elder first, who will almost always return the gesture. Foreigners are more or less exempt from this custom. In hotels, doormen, bellhops, and waitresses will frequently *wai* to you. Don't feel compelled to return the greeting; a simple smile of acknowledgment is all that's necessary. In situations where a *wai* is appropriate, like when meeting a person of obvious status, a friend's mother or father, or a monk, don't fret about the position of your hands. To keep them level to your chest is perfectly acceptable. Two exceptions—never *wai* a child, and never expect a monk to *wai* back (they are exempted from the custom).

One of the most important points of Thai etiquette to remember is that Thais expect a certain level of equanimity, calm, and light-heartedness in any personal dealings. If you are prone to temper, aggravation, and frustration, Thailand can be a challenge. Displays of anger and confrontational behavior, especially from foreign visitors, get you nowhere. Thais don't just think such outbursts are rude but believe them to be an indication of a lesser-developed human being. Getting angry and upset is in essence "losing face" by acting shamefully in front of others, and Thai people will walk away or giggle, to spare revealing their embarrassment. Travelers who throw fits often find themselves ignored or abandoned by the very people who could help.

So what do you do if you encounter a frustrating situation? The Thai philosophy advocates *chai yen,* meaning, "Take it easy. Chill." If it's a situation you can't control, like a traffic jam or a delayed flight—*chai yen.* If you find yourself at loggerheads with the front desk, arguing with a taxi driver, or in any other truly frustrating situation, keep calm, try a little humor, and find a non-confrontational, compromising solution that will save face for all involved.

The Thais hold two things sacred: their religion and their royal family. In temples and royal palaces, strict dress code is enforced. Wear long pants or skirts, with a neat shirt, and tops with shoulder-covering sleeves. Remove shoes and hats before entering temple buildings if it is the custom (that's always indicated at entry), and give worshippers their space. Be mindful of your feet—sit with your legs curled beside you, never in front, or pointing at the Buddha image. While photographing images is sometimes allowed, do not climb on any image or pose near it in a way that can be seen as showing disrespect. Women should be especially cautious around monks, who are not allowed to touch members of the opposite sex. If a woman needs to hand something to a monk, she should either hand it to a man to give to the monk, or place the item in front of him. *Important:* Never, ever, say anything critical or improper about the royal family, past or present, not even in jest. Never deface images of royalty (on coins, stamps, or posters); this will result in a hefty prison sentence. In movie theaters, everyone is expected to stand for the national anthem, which is played before every screening.

Young Thai society may seem very liberal, but it is in fact remarkably conservative and sartorially prudish. You will notice that educated Thais always cover their shoulders and wear knee- or ankle-length hemlines. Men tend to wear a mix of casual-smart gear with collared shirts and would never be unkempt. In the city, it is considered extremely improper to dress in cut-off shorts, skimpy tops, singlets, or postage-stamp miniskirts. This may look good for a night's clubbing but is regarded by locals as unacceptable attire—unless you are working in a go-go bar, or want to give that impression. On beaches, European women sometimes sunbathe topless; this is never accepted by locals, many of whom are Muslim. Foreign men who choose to go bare-chested are regarded with equal distaste, and moreover, distrust.

Thais avoid public displays of affection. While straight members of the same gender often hold hands, or walk arm in arm (this includes men), you'll rarely see a Thai man and woman acting this way. Thai women who date foreign men flaunt these rules openly, but as a rule of thumb, Thais frown upon lovers who touch, hug, or kiss in public.

Buddhists believe the feet are the lowliest part of the body, so using the foot to point or touch an object in Thailand is unbelievably insulting. Do not point your feet at a person or a Buddha image, or use your foot to tap a runaway coin (it bears the king's image).

In contrast, the head is considered the most sacred part of the body. Don't touch a Thai on the head or tousle a child's hair, but rather offer a friendly pat on the back. Even barbers have to ask permission to touch a customer's crown.

2 A Look at the Past

THE EARLY PEOPLE Archaeologists believe that Thailand was a major thoroughfare for *homo erectus* en route from Africa to China and other parts of Asia. Stone tools, dating back some 700,000 years have been excavated around Lampang in northern Thailand. Cave paintings, found throughout the country, are believed to originate as early as 2000 B.C.; these show people dancing and hunting, as well as domesticated and wild animals in grass-like settings that appear to be rice paddies. There are also images of different forms of marine life, dolphins (in the south), and catfish (in the north). Human remains have been excavated at many sites, the most famous of which, Ban Chiang, in the northeastern province of Udon Thani, contained copper and bronze items originally believed to date back to 4000 B.C., and said to be the earliest examples of the Bronze Age in Thailand. This suggests that this particular Bronze Age settlement developed independently of the few other world centers at this time. More accurate radiocarbon testing, however, has put Thailand's Bronze Age at about 2500 to 2000 B.C., which was in fact later than that of the Middle East and roughly at the same time as China's.

Modern civilization did not arrive in Thailand until about 1,000 years ago.

There is archaeological evidence that points to areas in both central and southern China as a cultural heartland for the descendants of many of the peoples of Southeast Asia. These people began to appear in northern Southeast Asia in the first millennium A.D. and continued to migrate south, east, and west in waves over the following 8 centuries, settling primarily in what is now Vietnam, Laos, Thailand, and Myanmar (Burma). Known as the *Tai*, they dispersed over a vast area of space and shared a similar culture and language. Their descendants are the core bloodline of the Thai people of today: the Shan of northern Myanmar, the Tai people of northern Laos, the Lu of Yunnan province in southern China, as well as groups in Vietnam, on the Chinese island of Hainan, and others in northeastern India. The total number of Tai people today is estimated at 70 million.

The early Tais lived in nuclear families with a dozen or two households forming an independently ruled *muang*, or village. They lived in raised houses in the lowlands, making a living from subsistence agriculture. In times of threat, either to economic stability or from outside aggression, many *muang* would combine forces. The organization was usually led by the strongest village or family. What developed were loosely structured feudal states where both lord and villager benefited—the lord from manpower and the villager from stability. The Tais expanded as ruling fathers sent sons out into the world to conquer or colonize neighboring areas, establishing new *muang* in increasingly broad regions.

THE DVARAVATI (MON) PERIOD

From the 6th century, Southeast Asia underwent a gradual period of Indianization. Merchants and missionaries from India introduced Brahmanism and Buddhism to the region, as well as Indian political and social values—and art and architectural preferences. Many Tai groups adopted Buddhism, combining its doctrine with their own animistic beliefs. But the true significance of India's impact can be seen in the rise of two of the greatest Southeast Asian civilizations—the Mon and Khmer.

Little information exists about the **Mon civilization.** No one knows where these people came from, how far they reached, or where their capital was located. What we do know is that around the 6th century A.D., the Mon were responsible for establishing Buddhism in central Thailand. Ancient Mon settlements lined the fringes of Thailand's central plains area, presumably stretching as far as Myanmar (Burma), Chiang Mai, and Nakhorn Ratchasima (also called Khorat), and into Cambodia and northern Laos.

THE SRIVIJAYA EMPIRE

In the southern peninsula, the **Srivijaya Empire,** based in Java, Indonesia, began to play an important role in cultural affairs. Before the 9th century A.D., southern port cities had drawn traders from all over the region and beyond. However, the Srivijayas, who had assimilated their own unique brand of Buddhism from India, would leave a lasting impression on these cities, linking them with other parts of Southeast Asia by importing Buddhist

and Buddhist art. While the empire never actually conquered the area, its cultural influence is still evident in Nakhon Si Thammarat and from the southern art of this period. Some historians argue that Chaiya, near Surat Thani, could have been the capital of the empire for a time, but the claim is largely disputed. Srivijaya power, ground down by endless warring with southern India, headed into decline and disappeared from Thailand by the 13th century.

THE KHMERS By the early 9th century A.D., the **Khmer Empire** had risen to power in Cambodia, spreading into surrounding areas. Indravaraman (877–89) saw the kingdom reach Nakhorn Ratchasima (Khorat) in northeastern Thailand. **Suryavarman I** (1002–50) extended the kingdom to the Chao Phraya River valley and north to Lamphun, driving out the Mons. **Suryavarman II (1113–50)** pushed the kingdom even farther, forcing the Mons still deeper into Myanmar (Burma) until his death in 1150.

With each conquering reign, magnificent Khmer temples honoring Hindu deities were constructed in outposts, thus expanding the Cambodian presence in the empire. Brahmanism, having been brought to Cambodia with traders from southern India, influenced not only Khmer religion and temple design (with the distinct corncob shaped *prang,* or tower), but also government administration and social order. Conquering or forcing villages into their control, the Khmers placed their own leaders in important centers and supplied them with Khmer administrative officers. The empire was extremely hierarchical, with the king exerting supreme power and ruling from his capital.

The populations of these outposts were largely Tai, and while the Khmers had the authority, Tais were assimilated as laborers, slaves, and temple workers. Temple murals in Angkor show quite clearly the Khmer attitude toward what they called

Syam. The mural shows a stiff orderly regiment of Khmer soldiers following Tais who were unkempt and fierce.

Angkor, Cambodia's great ancient temple city, was built during the reign of Suryavarman II. It is believed the temples of Phimai and Phanom Rung in Isan province predated the Khmers' capital temple complex, thus influencing its style. By this time, however, the Khmer empire was already in decline. The last great Khmer ruler, **Jayavarman VII** (1181–1219), extended the empire to its farthest limits—north to Vientiane in Laos, west to Myanmar (Burma), and down to the Malay peninsula. It was he who finally shifted Khmer ideology away from Hindu-based religion toward Buddhism, which eventually led to temples constructed in Khmer style. His newfound Buddhism inspired him to build extensive highways (portions of which are still evident today), plus more than 100 resthouses for travelers, and hospitals in the outer provinces. Jayavarman VII's death in 1220 marks Thailand's final break from Khmer rule. The last known Khmer settlement is at the sight of Wat Kamphaeng Laeng in Phetchaburi.

THE LANNA KINGDOM: THE NORTHERN TAIS

By A.D. 1000, the last of the Tai immigrants had traveled south from China to settle in northern Thailand. Several powerful centers of Tai power—Chiang Saen in northern Thailand, Xishuangbanna in southern China, and Luang Prabang in Laos—were linked by a common heritage and the rule of extended families. In the region, *muang* grew stronger and better organized, but internal conflict remained a problem. In 1239, a leader was born in Chiang Saen who would conquer and unite the northern Tai villages and create a great kingdom. Born to the king of Chiang Saen and a southern Chinese princess, **Mengrai** ascended the throne in 1259 and established the first capital of the Lanna

kingdom at Chiang Rai in 1263. He then conquered and assimilated what remained of Mon and Khmer settlements in northern Thailand, and in 1296 shifted his base of power to Chiang Mai, which translates to "The New City."

The Lanna empire would strengthen and ebb over five periods; at its height, it extended into Burma (now Myanmar), Luang Prabang in Laos, and Yunnan province in China. Lanna society mixed animist beliefs with Mon Buddhism. Retaining Mon connections with what is today Sri Lanka, the Lanna era saw the rise of a scholarly Buddhism with strict adherence to orthodox doctrines. Lanna kings were advised by a combination of monks and astrologers and ruled over a well-organized government bureaucracy. Developments were made in transportation and irrigation, medicine, law, and the arts through religious sculpture, sacred texts, and poetry. By and large, the people were only mildly taxed and were allowed a great deal of autonomy.

It was the expansionist Mongols under Kublai Khan who began to threaten Lanna with forays into the region. Mengrai succeeded in keeping these marauders at bay by allying his kingdom with Shan leaders in Myanmar (Burma) and two separate Tai kingdoms to the south; one of these was Sukhothai, which in time would rise to a position of dominance.

SUKHOTHAI: THE DAWN OF SIAMESE CIVILIZATION

While Mengrai was busy building Lanna, a small southern kingdom was simultaneously growing in power. After the demise of first the Dvaravarti civilization, and later the Khmers, the Tai people who had migrated south to the Chao Phraya River valley found themselves in small disorganized vassal states. A tiny kingdom based in Sukhothai would dwell in obscurity until the rise of founding father King Indraditya's second son, Ram. Single-handedly defeating an invasion from neighboring

Mae Sot on the Burmese border, Ram proved a powerful force, winning the respect of his people. Upon his coronation in 1279, **Ram Khamhaeng,** or "Ram the Bold," set the scene for what is recognized as the first truly Siamese civilization.

In response to the Khmers' authoritarian approach, Ram Khamhaeng established himself as an accessible king. It is told he had a bell outside his palace for any subject to ring in the event of a grievance. The king himself would come to hear the dispute and would make a just ruling on the spot. He was seen as a fatherly and fair ruler who allowed his subjects immense freedoms. His kingdom expanded rapidly, it seems; through voluntary subjugation, it reached as far west as Pegu in Myanmar (Burma), north to the Laotian cities of Luang Prabang and Vientiane, and south beyond Nakhon Si Thammarat to include portions of present-day Malaysia.

After centuries of divergent influences from external powers, we see for the first time an emerging culture that is uniquely Siamese. The people of the central plains had a mixed heritage made up of Tai, Mon, Khmer, and indigenous people, with Indian and Chinese elements woven into their cultural tapestry. Ram Khamhaeng was a devout Buddhist, adopting the orthodox and scholarly Theravada Buddhism from missionaries hailing from Nakhon Si Thammarat and Sri Lanka. A patron of the arts, the king commissioned many great Buddha images. While few sculptures from his reign remain today, those that do survive display a cultivated creativity. For the first time, physical features of the Buddha are Siamese in manner. Images have graceful, sinuous limbs and robes, insinuating a radiant and flowing motion. Ram Khamhaeng initiated the many splendid architectural achievements of Sukhothai and nearby Si Satchanalai.

He is also credited with developing the modern Thai written language, derived from Khmer and Mon examples of an archaic South Indian script. Upon Ram Khamhaeng's death in 1298, he was succeeded by kings who would devote their attentions to religion rather than affairs of state. During the 14th century, Sukhothai's brilliant spark faded almost as quickly at it had ignited.

AYUTTHAYA: SIAM ENTERS THE GLOBAL SCENE In the decades that followed, the nation faltered with no figurehead, until the arrival of U Thong—the son of a wealthy Chinese merchant family. He was also distantly related to the royals of Chiang Saen. Crowning himself **Ramathibodi,** he set up a capital at Ayutthaya, on the banks of the Lopburi River. From there he set out to conquer what was left of the Khmer outposts, eventually engulfing the remains of Sukhothai. The new kingdom incorporated the strengths of its population—Tai military manpower and labor, Khmer bureaucratic sensibilities, and Chinese commercial talents—to create a strong empire. Ayutthaya differed greatly from its predecessor. Following Khmer models, the king rose above his subjects atop a huge pyramid-shaped administration. He was surrounded by a divine order of Buddhist monks and Brahman sanctities. During the early period of development, Ayutthaya rulers created strictly defined laws, caste systems, and labor units. Foreign traders from China, Japan, and Arabia were required to sell the first pick of their wares to the king for favorable prices. Leading trade this way, the kingdom was buttressed by great riches. Along the river, a huge fortified city was built with temples that equaled those in Sukhothai. This was the Kingdom of Siam that the first Europeans, the Portuguese, encountered in 1511.

But peace and prosperity would be disrupted with the coming Burmese invasion that would take Chiang Mai (part of the Lanna kingdom) in 1557, and finally Ayutthaya in 1569. The Lanna kingdom that King Mengrai and his successors built was never to regain its former glory. Fortunately, Ayutthaya had a better fate with the rise of one of the greatest leaders in Thai history. **Prince Naresuan,** born in 1555, was the son of the puppet Tai King—placed in Ayutthaya by the Burmese. Although Naresuan was a direct descendent of Sukhothai leaders, it was his early battle accomplishments that distinguished him as a ruler. Having spent many years in Burmese captivity, he returned to Ayutthaya to raise armies to challenge the Burmese. His small militias proved inadequate, but in a historic battle scene, Naresuan, atop an elephant, challenged the Burmese crown prince and defeated him with a single blow.

With the Tais back in control, Ayutthaya continued through the following 2 centuries in grand style. Foreign traders—Portuguese, Dutch, Arab, Chinese, Japanese, and English—not only set up companies and missionaries, but also were even encouraged to rise to some of the highest positions of power within the administration. Despite numerous internal conflicts over succession and struggles between foreign powers for court influence, the kingdom managed to proceed steadily. While its Southeast Asian neighbors were falling under colonial rule, the court of Siam was extremely successful in retaining its own sovereignty. It has the distinction of being the only Southeast Asian nation never to have been colonized—a point of great pride for Thais today.

The final demise of Ayutthaya would be brought about by two more Burmese invasions. The first, in 1760, was led by **King Alaunghpaya,** who would fail, retreating after he was shot by one of his own cannons. But 6 years later, two Burmese contingents, one from the north and one from the south, would besiege the city. The Burmese raped, pillaged and plundered the kingdom—capturing fortunes and laborers for return to Burma. The Thai people still hold a bitter grudge against the Burmese for these atrocities.

THE RISE OF BANGKOK: THE CHAKRI DYNASTY

The Siamese did not hesitate to build another capital. Taksin, a provincial governor of Tak in the central plains, rose to power on military excellence and charisma. Over time he was able to successfully propagate the false notion that he was in fact divinely appointed as ruler. Rather than build upon the ashes of Ayutthaya, Taksin moved the capital to Thonburi Si Mahasamut, an already well-established settlement on the western bank of the Chao Phraya River, now part of present-day Bangkok. Within 3 years he'd reunited the land from the previous kingdom, but his rule would not last. Legend tells that Taksin suffered from paranoia and his claims to divinity offended many, including the monastic order. His own wife, children, and monks were purported to have been murdered on his orders. Regional powers acted fast. He was swiftly kidnapped, placed in a velvet sack and beaten to death with a sandalwood club—so no royal blood touched the soil. He was then buried secretly in his own capital. These same regional powers turned to the brothers Chakri and Surasi, great army generals *(phaya)* who had recaptured the north from Burma to lead the land. In 1782, **Phaya Chakri** ascended the throne as **King Ramathibodi,** the first king of Thailand, founder of today's Chakri dynasty.

The Thai capital was relocated by the new king across the Chao Phraya River to the settlement of Bangkok where he built the Royal Palace, royal homes, administrative buildings and great temples. The city teemed with canals as the river played a central role in trade and commerce. Siam was now a true melting pot of cultures, no longer limited to the Tai, Mon, and Khmer descendants of former powers, but now including Arab, Indian, European, and powerful Southern Chinese clans. Ramathibodi's first priorities involved reorganizing the Buddhist monkhood under an orthodox Theravada Buddhist doctrine and reestablishing the state ceremonies used during the Ayutthaya period with less emphasis on Brahman and animistic rituals. He revised all laws so they were based upon the notion of justice. He also wrote the *Ramakien,* based upon the Indian Ramayana, which has become a beloved Thai tale and a subject for many Thai classical arts, such as dance and shadow theater.

Despite military threats from all directions, the kingdom continued to grow through a succession of kings from the new royal bloodline. Ramathibodi, later known as Rama I, and his two successors expanded the kingdom to the borders of present-day Thailand and beyond. Foreign relations in the modern sense were developed during this early era with formal ties to European powers.

King Mongkut (1851–68) had a unique upbringing. During his monkhood, a tradition all Thai men are expected to follow even today, he developed an avid curiosity, which, throughout his reign, lead to enormous innovation, dynamism, and appreciation for the West. With his son, **King Chulalongkorn** (1868–1910), he led Siam into the 20th century as an independent nation, by establishing an effective civil service, formalizing global relations, and introducing industrialization. He united the royal line under the title *Rama* and assigned the title Rama I to the dynasty's first king. Mongkut thus became Rama IV, and his son, Rama V. It was King Mongkut who employed Anna Leonowens

as an English tutor for his children. Her account of court life is still considered grossly inaccurate and offensive by Thais; indeed anyone found with copies of the book, or the movies—all of which are banned—can be tried for lèse-majesté.

The reign of **King Prajadhipok,** Rama VII (1925–35), saw the growth of the urban middle class, and the increasing discontent of a powerful elite. By the beginning of his reign, economic failings and bureaucratic bickering weakened the position of the monarchy, which was severely affected by the Great Depression. To the credit of the king, there had been a call to instate a constitutional monarchy, but in 1932 a group of midlevel officials went ahead and instigated a coup d'état. Prajadhipok eventually abdicated in 1935.

THAILAND IN THE 20TH & 21ST CENTURIES   Democracy had a shaky hold on Siam. Its original constitution, written in 1932, was more a tool for leaders to manipulate than a political blueprint. Over the following decades, government leadership changed hands fast and frequently. The army has always had an imposing influence; most likely the result of its ties to the common people as well as its strong unity. In 1939, the nation adopted the name "Thailand"—land of the free.

During World War II, democracy was stalled in the face of the Japanese invasion in 1941. Thailand speedily submitted, choosing collaboration over conflict, even going so far as to declare war against the Allied powers. But at the war's end, no punitive measures were taken against Thailand, thanks to the Free Thai Movement organized by Ambassador Seni Pramoj in Washington, D.C., who had placed the declaration of war in his desk drawer rather than delivering it.

Thailand avoided direct involvement in the Vietnam War but assisted the Americans by providing runways for their

B-52s and storage for the toxic defoliant, Agent Orange. In turn it benefited enormously from U.S. military-built infrastructure. The United States pumped billions into the Thai economy, bringing riches to many but further impoverishing the rural poor, who were hit hard by the resulting inflation. Communism became an increasingly attractive political philosophy to the poor as well as to liberal-minded students and intellectuals. A full-scale insurrection seemed imminent, and this naturally fueled further political repression by the military rulers.

In June 1973, thousands of Thai students demonstrated in the streets, demanding a new constitution and a return to democratic principles. Tensions grew until October when armed forces attacked a demonstration at Thammasat University in Bangkok, killing 69 students and wounding 800, paralyzing the capital with terror.

The constitution was restored and a new government was elected. Many students, however, were not yet satisfied and continued to complain that the financial elite were still in control and resisting change. In 1976, student protests again broke out, and there was a replay of the grisly scene of 3 years before at Thammasat University. The army seized control in an effort to impose order, and another brief experiment with democracy was at an end. Thanin Kraivichien was installed as prime minister of a new right-wing government, which suspended freedom of speech and of the press, further polarizing Thai society.

In 1980, Prem Tinsulanonda became prime minister, and during the following 8 years he managed to bring remarkable political and economic stability to Thailand. The Thai economy grew steadily through the 1980s, fueled by Japanese investment and the departure of Chinese funds from Hong Kong.

Things changed dramatically in July 1997 when Thailand became the first victim of the **Asian Economic Crisis.** Virtually overnight, the Baht lost 20% of its value, followed by similar downturns in money markets throughout other major Asian nations. A legacy of suspicious government activity is linked to industry, massive overseas borrowing, inflated property markets, and lax bank lending practices. In November of 1997, **Chuan Leekpai** was elected to power to lead the country out of crisis, but 3 years later, Thais were still unsatisfied.

In January 2001, the Thai people elected populist candidate **Thaksin Shinawatra.** A self-made telecom tycoon, ex-police officer, and member of one of the nation's wealthiest families, Thaksin came into office promising economic restructuring and an end to widespread corruption and cronyism. Thaksin's popularity grew from aggressive reforms that brought the country out of debt. In November 2003, Thailand paid back its $12 billion loan to the International Monetary Fund, money borrowed during the 1997 currency crisis. The popular prime minister also waged a "War on Poverty and Dark Influence," cracking down on mafia activity and bribery; however, his tactics were often heavy handed and wholly ignored human rights. Most glaringly, he is held responsible for the on-the-spot killing of suspected drug-traffickers (estimates claim that as many as 3,000 people were shot dead with no legal process during his reign). Similarly, Thaksin's aggressive response to Muslim unrest in the far south came under international criticism.

In September 2006, the Royal Thai army, backed by the King, staged a bloodless coup d'état. Thaksin, who was preparing to address the United Nations in New York, was ousted overnight. During 2007, under the military junta, democratic reforms were stalled, press freedoms curbed, and Thaksin's own Thai Rak Thai party banned from politics for 5 years. Meanwhile, the tycoon and his family have been charged *in absentia* for fraud.

Thailand's elections held on December 23, 2007, passed without much disturbance, but the surprising outcome gave the People's Party—a staunch supporter of former Prime Minister Thaksin—a strong lead. However, without a clear majority, the party has been forced into an uneasy coalition with five other parties. Whatever transpires, it is clear the nation faces continuing political uncertainty.

Just weeks after the elections took place, the sister of Thailand's much loved King, HRH Princess Galyani, passed away. Distraught Thais publicly displayed their grief in huge numbers; the kingdom immediately declared a period of mourning. Black bunting draped portraits of the late princess and all flags were lowered to half mast throughout the country.

Throughout this, **HM King Bhumibol Adulyadej** has played an active role in stabilizing the nation. The King has been the nation's figurehead since 1946 and now, in his eightieth year, is the world's longest living monarch. A compassionate man, he commands enormous loyalty from the Thai people by promoting cultural traditions and supporting rural reforms, especially among the poor.

3 The Buddha in Thailand

Thai culture cannot be fully appreciated without some understanding of Buddhism, which is practiced by 90% of the population. The Buddha was a great Indian sage who lived in the 6th century B.C. He was born Siddhartha Gautama, a prince who was carefully sheltered from the outside world. When he ventured beyond the palace walls, he encountered an old man, a sick man, a corpse, and a wandering monk. He concluded that a never-ending cycle of suffering and relief exists everywhere. Sensing that the pleasures of the physical world were impermanent and the cause of pain, he shed his noble life and went into the forest to live as a solitary ascetic. Nearing starvation, however, he soon realized this was not the path to happiness, so he turned instead to the "Middle Way," a more moderate practice of meditation, compassion, and understanding. One night, while mediating under a Bodhi (fig) tree after being tormented by Mara, the god of death, Siddhartha Gautama became enlightened: With his mind free of delusion, he gained insight into the nature of the universe and viewed the world without defilement, craving, or attachment but as unified and complete. He explained his newfound ideology, The Dhamma, to his first five disciples at Deer Park in India in a sermon now known as "The Discourse on Setting into Motion the Wheel of the Law."

After the death of Buddha, two schools were formed. The oldest, **Theravada** (Doctrine of the Elders), is sometimes referred to, less accurately, as **Hinayana** (the Lesser Vehicle). This school of thought prevails in Sri Lanka, Myanmar (Burma), Thailand, and Cambodia. It focuses on the enlightenment of the individual with emphasis on the monastic community and the monks who achieve Nirvana in this lifetime. The other methodology, **Mahayana** (the Greater Vehicle), is practiced in China, Korea, and Japan, and subscribes to a notion of all of mankind attaining enlightenment at the same time.

The basic document of Thai, or Theravada, Buddhism is the Pali canon, which was documented in writing for the first time in the 1st century A.D. The doctrine is essentially an ethical and psychological system in which no deity plays a role in the mystical search for the intuitive realization of the *oneness* of the universe. While it is a religion without a god, Theravada traditions follow a certain hierarchy based on age among monks and practitioners. The practice requires individuals to find truth for themselves through an inward-looking practice cultivated by meditation and self-examination. Although interpretation varies, the Buddha's final words are said to be "strive on with diligence."

If there is no deity to worship, then what, you might ask, are people doing in temples prostrating themselves before images or statues of the Buddha? Making offerings of flowers or fruit and lighting incense are displays of respect. Worshippers bow three times before the image: once for the Buddha himself, once for the *sangha* (the order of monks), and once for the *dhamma* (truth). Orthodox Theravada traditions tend to mingle with local animism and superstition, meaning that practitioners often appeal to the Buddha as well as to Buddhist images in an effort to "make merit," or *boon*. That said, Buddhist images and prostrations at the temple are also a way to honor Buddhist teachers and those who pass on the tradition, to show respect for the Buddha's meditative repose and equanimity, and to offer reverence for relics (many sites, particularly *stupas,* house important artifacts).

Buddhism has one aim only: to abolish suffering. Buddhist practice offers a path to rid oneself of the causes of suffering, which are desire, malice, and delusion. Practitioners eliminate craving and ill will by exercising self-restraint and showing kindness to all sentient beings. Monks and members of the Buddhist Sangha, or community, are revered as those most diligently working toward enlightenment and the attainment of wisdom.

Other aspects of the philosophy include the law of *karma,* whereby every action has an effect and the energy of past action, good or evil, continues forever and is "reborn." (Some argue, though, that the Buddha took transmigration quite literally.) As a consequence, *tam bun* (merit making)—basically performing any act of

kindness no matter how small—is taken very seriously.

Merit can be gained by entering the monkhood, which most Thai males do for a few days or months to assist with the construction of a monastery or *stupa.* But these days it can equally be gained by transferring Frequent Flyer points to a charity.

When monks in Thailand go from house to house each dawn, they are not begging, but are giving the people an opportunity to make merit; similarly the people selling caged birds, which people purchase and then free, are allowing people to gain merit by freeing the birds. When making merit, it is the motive that is important—the intention in the mind at the time of action—which determines the karmic outcome, not the action itself. Buddhism calls for self-reliance; the individual embarks alone on the **Noble Eightfold Path to Nirvana** with the aim "to cease to do evil, learn to do good, cleanse your own heart."

Theravada Buddhism does not seek converts, nor does it ask practitioners to believe in any truths but those they learn themselves through experience and meditation. Opportunities to study Buddhism or practice meditation in Thailand are abundant. There are a number of programs designed particularly for foreigners, since practicing is in fact the best way to understand the heart of Buddhism. See p. 48 in chapter 2 for some suggestions.

Most Chinese and Vietnamese living in Thailand follow Mahayana Buddhism, and numerous temples and monasteries in the country support this tradition as well. Other religions and philosophies are also followed in Thailand, including Islam, Christianity, Hinduism, and Sikhism. Sunni Islam is followed by more than two million Thais, mostly in the south. Most are of Malay origin and are descendants of the Muslim traders and missionaries who spread their teachings in the southern peninsula in the early 13th century. There are approximately 2,000 mosques in Thailand.

Christianity was first introduced in the 16th century by generations of Jesuit, Dominican, and Franciscan missionaries from Europe and later Protestant missionaries from America. In fact, Bangkok has some superb churches, many of which are along the river. Even after centuries of evangelism, there are only a quarter of a million Christians living in the country. Yet Thais have accepted much that has come from Christian missionaries, particularly ideas on education, health, and science.

4 The Language

The Thai language is derived principally from Mon, Khmer, Chinese, Pali, Sanskrit, and, increasingly, English. Since there are no verb conjugations, verb tense indicators are easily learned, or you can even stick with the present tense. The writing system is derived from Mon and Khmer—which in turn is from a southern Indian model—and is composed of 44 consonants (with only 21 distinct sounds) and 32 vowels (with 48 simple and diphthong variables). It reads from left to right, often without breaks between words—thus making some very long words! Casual visitors can get along by simply picking up simple greetings or a few polite phrases to show respect to their hosts.

Unfortunately, there is no universal transliteration system, so you will see the usual Thai greeting written as *sawatdee, sawaddi, sawasdee, sawusdi,* and so on. Do not be afraid of getting lost in the different spellings. Derivations of most city names are close enough for anyone to figure out. The model most often used is more similar to French than English: *th* usually represents our t (as in Thailand); *t* represents our d; *ph* represents our p; *p* sounds more like our b; *kh* represents our k; *k* sounds like g; *r* often sounds like *l,* and *l* can become an *n.* This is because Thai pronunciation is lackadaisical. Taxi drivers, in particular, often do not come from Bangkok and speak with regional accents or use dialect. Sometimes *r* is used merely to lengthen a vowel sound (Udon is often written *Udorn*), and *l* or *r* at the end of a word is pronounced more like *n.* The word

Oriental is universally pronounced *Orienten* and Ubon is often written *Ubol.* There is no *v* sound in Thai, and when you see it written, as in *Sukhumvit,* it should actually sound like our *w.* There is also an *ng,* which sounds like letters in our word sing, used as an initial consonant and difficult for English speakers to hear and pronounce though the distinction can be important: *noo* means rat or kid (informal for child), but *ngoo* means snake.

Central Thai is the official written and spoken language of the country, and most Thais understand it, but there are three other major dialects: Northeastern Thai, spoken in Isan, and closely related to Lao; Northern Thai, spoken in the northwest, from Tak Province to the Burmese border; and Southern Thai, spoken from Chumphon Province south to the Malaysian border. Each of these dialects also has several variations. The hill-tribes in the North have their own distinct languages, closely related to Burmese or Tibetan.

Just as in English, there are various degrees of formality, and words that are acceptable in certain contexts are impolite in others. The most common word for eat is *khin* (also written *gin*), *khin khao* means "eat rice" (but is used to indicate or inquire about eating a meal in general); *thaan* is more polite, while *raprathaan* is reserved for royalty.

For some helpful Thai phrases and vocabulary, see appendix B, "A Little Bit of Thai to Help You Get By."

5 Thai Architecture 101

The Sukhothai period (13th–14th centuries) is regarded as a period of notable achievement in Thai culture, with big advancements made in art and architecture. One of the lasting legacies of the Sukhothai period is its sculpture, characterized by the graceful aquiline-nosed Buddha either sitting in meditation or, more strikingly, seemingly flowing contemplatively. These Buddha figures are considered to be some of the most beautiful representations ever produced of this genre. The city of Sukhothai itself is said to be an expansion of the decorative style typified by Khmer works. With the inclusion of Chinese wood building techniques, polychromatic schemes, and elegant lines from Japanese-influenced carvings, the *wat*, or temple—with its murals, Buddha sculptures, and spacious design—is defined as the first "pure" Thai Buddhist style. During this period came the mainstays of Thai wat architecture: the *phra chedi* (stupa), *bot, viharn, phra prang, mondop,* and *prasat.*

The dome-shaped *phra chedi*—usually called simply *chedi* and better known in the West as *stupa*—is the most highly regarded edifice here. It originally was used to enshrine relics of the Buddha, but later included holy men and kings. A stupa consists of a dome or tumulus, constructed atop a round base (drum), and enveloped by a cubical chair, representing the seated Buddha, over which is the *chatra* (umbrella) in one or several (usually nine) tiers. There are many different types of stupas in existence in Thailand: The tallest, oldest, and most sacred is the golden chedi of **Nakhon Pathom.**

The *bot* (*ubosoth* or *uposatha*) is where the *bhikku* (monks) meditate and also where all ceremonies are performed. It consists of either one large nave or a nave with lateral aisles built on a rectangular design where the Buddha image is enshrined. At the end of each ridge of the roof are graceful finials, called *chofa* (meaning "sky tassel"), which are reminiscent of animal horns but are thought to represent celestial geese or the **Garuda** (a mythological animal ridden by the god Shiva). The triangular gables are adorned with gilded wooden ornamentation and glass mosaics.

The *viharn* (*vihaan* or *vihara*) is a replica of the *bot* (the central shrine in a Buddhist temple) and is used to keep Buddha images. The *phra prang,* which originated with the corner tower of the Khmer temple, is a new form of Thai stupa, elliptical in shape and also housing images of the Buddha. The *mondop* may be made of wood or brick. On a square pillared base, the pyramidal roof is formed by a series of receding stories, enriched with the same decoration, and tapering off to a pinnacle. It may be used to enshrine holy objects as at Saraburi, where it enshrines the footprint of the Lord Buddha, or it may serve as a library for religious ceremonial objects, as it does at Wat Phra Kaew in Bangkok.

The *prasat* (castle) is a direct stylistic descendant of the Khmer temple, with its round-topped spire and Greek-cross layout. At the center is a square sanctuary with a domed *sikhara* and four porch-like antechambers that project from the main building, giving the whole temple a multileveled contour. The *prasat* serves either as the royal throne hall or as a shrine for venerated objects such as the *prasat* of Wat Phra Kaew in Bangkok, which enshrines the statues of the kings of the present dynasty.

Less recognized architectural structures include the *ho trai* (library) which houses palm-leaf books; the *sala,* an open pavilion used for resting; and the *ho rakhang,* the Thai belfry.

The Ayutthaya and Bangkok periods further cultivated the Sukhothai style by refining materials and design. The Ayutthaya period saw a Khmer revival when Ayutthayan kings built a number of neo-Khmer style temples and edifices. The art and architecture evident in early Bangkok allude to the dominant styles of the former capital. After the destruction of Ayutthaya in the 18th century, the new leaders moved to Bangkok. They first established a palace in what is today the Thonburi district, only to move across the Chao Phraya River to its current location, where they constructed replicas of some of Ayutthaya's most distinctive buildings. This meant incorporating Khmer with Chinese, northern Thai, and Western elements to create contemporary wats, palaces, sculptures, and murals (as seen by Wat Arun in Bangkok).

Over time, Thailand's architectural and artistic development has become increasingly diluted, somewhat compromisingly, by the West. During the latter days of the Ayutthaya period, Jesuit missionaries and French merchants brought with them distinctly baroque fashions. Although Thailand was initially reluctant to foster relations with the West, these European influences eventually became evident in architecture. Neoclassical devices were increasingly apparent, notably in the Marble Wat in Bangkok, which was started by King Chulalongkorn in 1900 and designed by his half-brother, Prince Naris. This style can also be seen in the splendid riverside façade of Siam Commercial Bank (1908) near the River City shopping complex. Thanks to a number of Italian engineers, Art Deco became an important style in Bangkok and is seen today at the arched Hua Lampong Rail Station, the Governor's House, and along Ratchadamnoen Avenue. In fact, the style is so ubiquitous that many writers use the term Thai Deco to describe certain buildings.

Today's Bangkok is almost indistinguishable from other Third World Asian capitals; a mix of Thai classical, modernist, neo-Greco, Bauhaus, and Chinese shophouse styles all meld into a unique, urban mishmash. Sadly, vernacular styles such as old Thai wooden houses are rapidly being cleared and the *klongs* (canals) filled to give way to high-rise offices and apartments. Happily, efforts are now being made by a new generation of educated Thais to bring architectural integrity to the city. One notable example is the plan for a new ultra-contemporary structure, which will be an annex to the existing Central Department Store, near Chidlom. The gallant aim is for this (as yet unrevealed) building to, at last, give Bangkok an iconic modern landmark.

6 Thailand's Exotic Bill of Fare: From Tiger Prawns to Pad Thai

Food is one of the true joys of Thailand. If you are not familiar with Thai cooking, imagine the best of Asian food ingredients combined with the sophistication of fragrant spices, sweet coconut or citrus, and topped off with ripe red and green chilies. You can find all styles of Thai (and international) cooking in Bangkok, from southern fiery curries to smooth northern cuisine. Basic ingredients range from shellfish, fresh fruits, vegetables—asparagus, bean sprouts, morning glory, baby eggplant, bamboo shoots, and countless types of mushrooms—and spices, including lemongrass, mint, chili, garlic, and coriander (cilantro). Thai cooking also incorporates coconut milk, curry paste, peanuts, and a large variety of noodles and rice.

Among the popular dishes you'll find are: *tom yam goong,* a Thai hot-and-sour shrimp soup; *satay,* charcoal-broiled chicken, beef, or pork strips skewered on a bamboo stick and dipped in a peanut-coconut sauce; spring rolls (similar to egg rolls but thinner and usually containing only vegetables); *larb,* a spicy chicken or ground-beef salad with mint-and-lime flavoring; spicy salads, made with a breadth of ingredients, but most have a dressing made with onion, chili pepper, lime juice, and fish sauce; *pad thai,* rice noodles usually served with large shrimp, eggs, peanuts, fresh bean sprouts, lime, and a delicious sauce; *khao sawy,* a northern-style Burmese soup with light yellow curry and layers of crispy and soft noodles; a wide range of explosive curries; and spicy *tod man pla,* fried fish cakes with a sweet honey sauce.

Seafood is a great treat in Thailand and is served at a fraction of the cost one would pay elsewhere. In the south, Phuket lobster (a giant langoustine) has no pincers and a firm trunk, and is generally different from the cold water variety you'll get in Maine or Brittany.

A word of caution: Thais enjoy incredibly spicy food, much hotter than is tolerated in even the most piquant Western cuisine. Protect your palate by saying *"Mai khin phet,"* meaning "I do not take it spicy." Also note that most Thai and Chinese food, particularly in the cheaper restaurants and food stalls, is cooked with a lot of **MSG** (known locally as *phong churot*), and it's almost impossible to avoid. If you don't want MSG, say *"mai sai phong churot."* However, if dining in restaurants where foreign clientele are regulars, the kitchen will have usually made allowances for this.

Traditionally, Thai menus don't offer fancy desserts. The most you'll find are coconut milk–based sweets or a variety of fruit-flavored custards, but the local fruit is luscious enough for a perfect dessert. Familiar fruits are pineapple (served with salt to heighten the sweet flavor), mangoes, bananas, guava, papaya, coconut, and watermelon. Less familiar options are

durian (in season during June and July, this Thai favorite is an acquired taste, as it smells like old socks); **mangosteen** (a purplish, hard-skinned fruit with delicate, whitish-pink bits that melt in the mouth but stain your hands and clothes, and is available Apr to Sept); and **jackfruit** (large and yellow-brown with a thick, thorny skin that envelops tangy-flavored flesh and is available year-round). The pink **lychee** or the smaller tan-skinned **longan** have very sweet white flesh and are available July to October. Other unusual fruits include **tamarind** (a sour, pulpy seed in a pod that you can eat fresh or candied); **rambutan** (small, red, and hairy with transparent sweet flesh clustered around a woody seed, available May to July); and **pomelo** (similar to a sweet and thirst-quenching grapefruit, available Oct to Dec). Some of these fruits are served as salads; pomelo and raw green papaya salads, for example, are excellent.

Thai families usually have an early breakfast of *khao tom,* a rice soup (made from leftovers) to which chicken, seafood, or meat may be added. Typically, it's served with a barely cooked egg floating on top and a variety of pickled vegetables, relishes, and spicy condiments to add flavor.

Thais take eating very seriously and also love to snack nonstop. Business lunches consist of several dishes, but most casual diners have a one-course rice, noodle, or curry dish. If dining for two, order two hot dishes and perhaps a cold salad (mostly of the "not spicy" variety). Meals are almost always accompanied by rice or noodles. Most restaurants throughout the country offer lunch from 11am to 1pm; in Bangkok, street eateries, markets, and food stalls are packed during this busy time.

Thais usually stop at one of the country's many street-side food stalls for a large bowl of noodle soup (served with meat, fish, or poultry), or dine at a department store food court where they can buy snacks from many different vendors and have a seat in air-conditioning. *A note on etiquette:* You won't see Thais walking down the street munching. Take a seat while you eat.

Dinner is the main meal and consists of a soup *(gaeng jued)*; a curried dish *(gaeng ped)*; a steamed, fried, stir-fried, or grilled dish *(nueng, thod, paad,* or *yaang)*; a side dish of salad or condiments *(krueang kiang)*; steamed rice *(khao)*; and some fruit *(polamai)*. Thais always share a variety of dishes (typically balanced as sweet, salty, sour, bitter, and spicy), helping themselves to a bit at a time (so as not to appear greedy). Dishes are brought to the table as they're cooked, and eaten in no particular order, family style.

7 Drinks

In Thailand men enjoy a strong drink; the majority of well-educated women and many practicing Buddhists abstain from alcohol. Liquor, beer, and soft drinks are widely available—except during certain hours in the afternoon—at 7-Eleven stores and TOPS supermarkets. Bars serve liquor at all hours, except on Buddhist holidays, but they must now close at 1am after a clampdown on licensing imposed by the ex-prime minister Thaksin. Thailand brews several beers; the best known is **Singha. Kloster** (German) and **Carlsberg** (Danish), as well as imported **Heineken,** are also widely available. **Beer Chiang** is a popular malt-liquor that really packs a wallop and costs little. Despite high costs, wine is becoming a favorite among the country's new middle class; local Thai and regional vintages are increasing in quality, too.

Mekong and **Sang Thip** are two of the more popular local "whiskeys," even though they're actually rum (fermented from sugarcane). Thais will either buy a bottle or bring one to a restaurant where they can buy ice and mixers—usually Coke or soda water. Beware that some of the cheaper varieties are reputedly laced with some nasty chemicals.

Carbonated drinks such as **soda, Fanta, Coke,** and **Pepsi** are sold everywhere. Fruit shake vendors make fruit smoothies on the street, but diabetics should know that even fresh carrot or watermelon juice is heavily sweetened with thick syrup; insist on no syrup and be sure to watch the beverage being made. *Gek huey* (**chrysanthemum juice)** is another popular treat.

Water is served at most meals although you may have to ask for ice *(nam kheng)*. Be sure the ice cubes have holes in their center; this indicates they have been made from a purified water source. Many shops sell affordable **bottled** or **filtered water.** Do not purchase the inexpensive water in light-blue plastic bottles (sold on the street) as it contains no sodium or minerals and will not remedy dehydration. If you suffer from the heat, stock up on **electrolyte drinks** such as **Gatorade,** or inexpensive rehydration powders, sold in sachets. Both items are available from 7-Eleven stores.

Appendix B:
A Little Bit of Thai
to Help You Get By

Thai is a tonal language, with low, mid, high, rising, or falling tones. There are five tonal markings:

low tone: `
falling tone: ^
middle tone (no marking)
rising tone: ˇ
high tone: ´

Most importantly, Thai also differentiates between the language used by a male or a female. Thus, males use **Pôm** for I, and females use **Deè-chân**. The suffix **khrap** is an affirmation used by men only, and **kha** is used similarly for women. It can be used as a lazy reply, like "Uh-huh."

1 Basic Phrases & Vocabulary

English	Thai Pronunciation	Phonetic Pronunciation
Hello (male)	Sa-wat-dii-khrap	sah-wah-dee-kup
Hello (female)	Sa-wat-dii-kha	sah-wah-dee-kah
How are you?	Sabai-dii mai?	sah-bye-dee-my
I am fine	Sabai-dii	sah-bye-dee
Do you speak English?	Phuut phaa-saa angrit dai mai?	poot pa-sah ang-krit dye-my?
I do not understand	mâi khâo jai	my-cow-jy
Excuse me/Sorry	Khaw thoht (-khrap, -kha)	cor-tort (-kup, -kah)
Thank you	Khòp khun (-khrap, -kha)	cop-koon (-kup, -kah)
No; I do not want . . .	Mai âo . . .	my ow . . .
Yes; I want . . .	Chai, ao . . .	chai, ow . . .
Stop here!	Yut tii nii!	jortinnee
Where is the (public) toilet?	Hawng nam yùu thii nâi?	hong-nam yutin-nye
I need to see a doctor	Pôm/Deè-chân tawngkaan	pom/dee-charn mâw tong-garn mor
Call the police!	Riâk tam-rùat nawy!	Reeyuk tamru-at noy!

English	Thai Pronunciation	Phonetic Pronunciation
Never mind/no problem	Mâi pen rai	my pen rye
Do you have . . .	Mii . . . mai?	mee . . . my?

2 Getting Around

English	Thai Pronunciation	Phonetic Pronunciation
I want to go to . . .	yak ja pai . . .	yark jar by . . .
Where is the . . .	yuu thii nai . . .	yutin-nye . . .
taxi	thaek-sii	dek-see
bus station	sa thaânee khon song	sartarnee kornsong
train station	sa thaânee rót fai	sartarnee rot fye
airport	sa nâam bin	sanam-bin
boat jetty	thâ reua	taa-ru-er
hotel	rohng ra-em	rorngrem or lornglem
hospital	rohng pha yaa baan	rorn-pye-aban
How much . . . ?	Thâo rai?	Tao-rye?
What time (does it depart)?	(jà àwk) kii mohng?	Jar-ork-kee-mung?

3 In a Restaurant

English	Thai Pronunciation	Phonetic Pronunciation
coffee	kaa-fae	gar-fay
tea (hot)	châa-rawn	char-rawn
bottled water	nam khuât	nam kwat
water	nam	nam
ice	nam khaeng	nam-keng
beer	bia	bee-ya
noodles	kway tiaw	kway-tee-ow
rice	khâo	cow
fried rice	khao phat	cow pat
chicken	kài	guy
beef	neúa	nuhr
pork	muu	moo
fish	plaa	blar
shrimp	kung	goong
mango with sticky rice	khao niaw mamuang	cow-neeow mar-mwang
Thai desserts (general)	khanom	knom
I am a vegetarian	kin ahaan mangsawirat	gin aharn mangsaweerat
I don't like it spicy	Mâi chawp phèt	my chorp pet

English	Thai Pronunciation	Phonetic Pronunciation
I like it spicy	chawp phèt	chorp pet
Delicious!	Ah-ròy!	Ah-roy
Check/bill please	Khaw chek-bin	gor chek-bin

4 Shopping

English	Thai Pronunciation	Phonetic Pronunciation
It's too expensive	Phaeng koen pai	peng kurn-pye
I don't like this one	Mai chawp anii	my chorp a-nee
Do you have a (smaller/larger) size?	Mii sai (lék /yài) nii mâi?	mee sai (lek/yai) nee my?
Do you have a black one?	Mii sii tham mai?	mee see dam my?

5 Numbers

English	Thai Pronunciation	Phonetic Pronunciation
0	suun	soon
1	neung	nung
2	sawng	song
3	saam	sam
4	sii	see
5	haa	hah
6	hok	hork
7	jed	jet
8	paet	bet
9	kao	gao
10	sip	sip
11	sip-et	sip-ett
12	sip-sawng	sip-song
100	neung rawy	nung-roy
1,000	neung phan	nung-pan
10,000	neung muen	nung mwuen

To conjugate numbers like 30, 40, and so on, you simply say three-ten, or four-ten. For example, 30 is *saam-sip*. There are exceptions:

- Numbers like 11, 21, 31, and so on, use the suffix *et*, not *neung*, so 11 is *sip-et*.
- Number 20 is *yee-sip* or simply *yip*, not *song-sip*.

Therefore, 21 is *yee-sip*-et or *yip-et*, not *song-sip neung*, as one might logically surmise!

Index

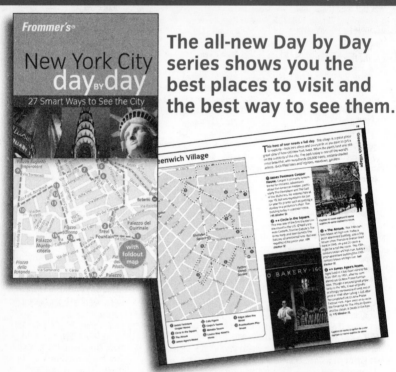

FROMMER'S® COMPLETE TRAVEL GUIDES

FROMMER'S® DAY BY DAY GUIDES

PAULINE FROMMER'S GUIDES: SEE MORE. SPEND LESS.

FROMMER'S® PORTABLE GUIDES

Acapulco, Ixtapa & Zihuatanejo
Amsterdam
Aruba, Bonaire & Curacao
Australia's Great Barrier Reef
Bahamas
Big Island of Hawaii
Boston
California Wine Country
Cancún
Cayman Islands
Charleston
Chicago
Dominican Republic

Florence
Las Vegas
Las Vegas for Non-Gamblers
London
Maui
Nantucket & Martha's Vineyard
New Orleans
New York City
Paris
Portland
Puerto Rico
Puerto Vallarta, Manzanillo &
    Guadalajara

Rio de Janeiro
San Diego
San Francisco
Savannah
St. Martin, Sint Maarten, Anguilla &
    St. Bart's
Turks & Caicos
Vancouver
Venice
Virgin Islands
Washington, D.C.
Whistler

FROMMER'S® CRUISE GUIDES

Alaska Cruises & Ports of Call

Cruises & Ports of Call

European Cruises & Ports of Call

FROMMER'S® NATIONAL PARK GUIDES

Algonquin Provincial Park
Banff & Jasper
Grand Canyon

National Parks of the American West
Rocky Mountain
Yellowstone & Grand Teton

Yosemite and Sequoia & Kings
    Canyon
Zion & Bryce Canyon

FROMMER'S® WITH KIDS GUIDES

Chicago
Hawaii
Las Vegas
London

National Parks
New York City
San Francisco

Toronto
Walt Disney World® & Orlando
Washington, D.C.

FROMMER'S® PHRASEFINDER DICTIONARY GUIDES

Chinese
French

German
Italian

Japanese
Spanish

SUZY GERSHMAN'S BORN TO SHOP GUIDES

France
Hong Kong, Shanghai & Beijing
Italy

London
New York
Paris

San Francisco
Where to Buy the Best of Everything.

FROMMER'S® BEST-LOVED DRIVING TOURS

Britain
California
France
Germany

Ireland
Italy
New England
Northern Italy

Scotland
Spain
Tuscany & Umbria

THE UNOFFICIAL GUIDES®

Adventure Travel in Alaska
Beyond Disney
California with Kids
Central Italy
Chicago
Cruises
Disneyland®
England
Hawaii

Ireland
Las Vegas
London
Maui
Mexico's Best Beach Resorts
Mini Mickey
New Orleans
New York City
Paris

San Francisco
South Florida including Miami &
    the Keys
Walt Disney World®
Walt Disney World® for
    Grown-ups
Walt Disney World® with Kids
Washington, D.C.

SPECIAL-INTEREST TITLES

Athens Past & Present
Best Places to Raise Your Family
Cities Ranked & Rated
500 Places to Take Your Kids Before They Grow Up
Frommer's Best Day Trips from London
Frommer's Best RV & Tent Campgrounds in the U.S.A.

Frommer's Exploring America by RV
Frommer's NYC Free & Dirt Cheap
Frommer's Road Atlas Europe
Frommer's Road Atlas Ireland
Retirement Places Rated

— I don't speak sign language.

A hotel can close for all kinds of reasons.
Our Guarantee ensures that if your hotel's undergoing construction, we'll let you know in advance. In fact, we cover your entire travel experience. See www.travelocity.com/guarantee for details.

There's a parking lot where my ocean view should be.

 À la place de la vue sur l'océan, me voilà avec une vue sur un parking.

 Anstatt Meerblick habe ich Sicht auf einen Parkplatz.

 Al posto della vista sull'oceano c'è un parcheggio.

 No tengo vista al mar porque hay un parque de estacionamiento.

 Há um parque de estacionamento onde deveria estar a minha vista do oceano.

 Ett parkeringsområde har byggts på den plats där min utsikt över oceanen borde vara.

 Er ligt een parkeerterrein waar mijn zee-uitzicht zou moeten zijn.

 هنالك موقف للسيارات مكان ما وجب ان يكون المنظر الخلاب المطل على المحيط .

 眼前に広がる紺碧の海・・・じゃない。窓の外は駐車場！

 停车场的位置应该是我的海景所在。

— I'm fluent in pig latin.

Hotel mishaps aren't bound by geography.
Neither is our Guarantee. It covers your entire travel experience, including the price. So if you don't get the ocean view you booked, we'll work with our travel partners to make it right, right away. See www.travelocity.com/guarantee for details.

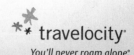
You'll never roam alone.